Intercultural Communication: A Reader

Sixth Edition

LARRY A. SAMOVAR
San Diego State University

RICHARD E. PORTER
California State University, Long Beach

Wadsworth Publishing Company
Belmont, California
A Division of Wadsworth, Inc.

Communication Editor: Peggy Randall
Editorial Assistant: Sharon Yablon
Production Editor: Karen Garrison
Managing Designer: Donna Davis
Print Buyer: Karen Hunt
Permissions Editor: Peggy Meehan
Copy Editor: Rene Lynch
Compositor: TypeLink, Inc.
Cover: Donna Davis
Cover Photograph: "Stones along St. Mary
Lake, Glacier National Park, Montana"
© Charles Gurche. All rights reserved.

Printed in the United States of America   19
  2 3 4 5 6 7 8 9 10—95 94 93 92 91

Library of Congress Cataloging in Publication Data

Intercultural communication: a reader / [edited by]
    Larry A. Samovar, Richard E. Porter.—6th ed.
        p. cm.
        Includes bibliographical references and index.
        ISBN 0-534-14772-0
        1. Intercultural communication.   I. Samovar,
Larry A.   II. Porter, Richard E.
HM258.I52   1991
303.48'2—dc20   90-44310

Contents

Chapter 3   Co-Cultures: Living in Two Cultures   113

Chapter 4   Cultural Contexts: The Influence of the Setting   168

Chapter 8   Ethical Considerations: Prospects for the Future   392

Preface

We approached the occasion of this sixth edition of our book with excitement, but also with prudence. As a starting point, we wanted to be cautious enough to preserve the basic framework and philosophy that has sustained us through five previous editions. It would have been imprudent to have abandoned an orientation to intercultural communication that has found wide acceptance for nearly two decades. The field and the authors, however, have continued to evolve; we knew, therefore, that some reshaping was necessary. This latest edition grants us the opportunity to combine two complementary positions. First, it reflects our continued belief that the basic core of the field should not be changed simply for the sake of being novel. This type of change would rob the book of those concepts that have been infused into all the other editions. Second, we believe that as our intercultural contacts change both in number and intensity, there is a need to present essays that mirror that change. We have always perceived each new edition as an opportunity to examine the changes in the field and to stake out new territory—territory that now must take into account the complexities of communicating in the 1990s.

As the field of intercultural communication has grown, we have attempted in each new edition to grow with the field and to fuse the old with the new. In 1972, the first edition contained thirty-four articles and essays. The fifth edition contained forty; now there are forty-five articles in our collection of readings. Some of these have appeared in all previous editions. In this sixth edition, we have nineteen new essays, eleven of which were prepared especially for this volume.

APPROACH

The basic motivation driving this book has remained the same since both authors became interested in the topic of intercultural communication some twenty-five years ago. It is our sincere belief that the ability to communicate effectively with people from diverse cultures and co-cultures benefits each of us as individuals and has the potential to benefit the other 5.5 billion people with whom we share this planet. We have intentionally selected materials that will assist you in understanding those intercultural communication principles that are instrumental to the achievement of success when interacting with people from diverse cultures.

Fundamental to our approach is the conviction that communication is a social activity; it is something people do with and to each other. While the activity might begin in our heads, we manifest it in our behaviors—be they verbal or nonverbal. In both explicit and implicit ways, the information and the advice contained in this book is usable; the ideas presented can be translated into action.

USE

As in the past, we intend this anthology for the general reader. We have, consequently, selected materials that are broadly based, comprehensive, and suitable for both undergraduate and graduate students. Although the level of difficulty varies from article to article, we have not gone beyond the level found in most textbooks aimed at college and university students.

Intercultural Communication: A Reader is designed to meet three specific needs. First, this book is designed to serve as a *basic anthology* for courses concerned with the issues associated with human interaction. This need comes from a canon that maintains that successful intercultural communication is a matter of the highest importance if humankind and society are to survive. Events during the last twenty years have created a world that sees us linked together in a multitude of ways. From pollution to economics to health care, what happens to one culture has the potential to happen to all cultures. Our intention is to make this book theoretical and practical so that the issues associated with intercultural communication can be both understood and acted upon.

Second, the book may be used as a *supplementary text* in existing service and basic communication skills courses and interpersonal communication courses. The rationale is a simple one: Understanding other cultures is indispensable in this age of cross-cultural contact. It matters very little if that contact is face to face or on the public platform.

Third, the book provides *resource material* for courses in communication theory, small group communication, organizational and business communication, and mass communication, as well as for courses in anthropology, sociology, social psychology, social welfare, business, and international relations. The long list of possible uses underscores the increased level of intercultural interaction that is characteristic of what is often called the global village.

ORGANIZATION

The book is organized into four closely related parts. In Part One, "Intercultural Communication: An Introduction," our purpose is twofold. We hope to acquaint you with the basic concepts of intercultural communication while at the same time arousing your interest in the topic. Hence, the essays in this part are both theoretical and philosophical. The selections explain what intercultural communication is and why it is important.

Part Two, "Socio-cultural Backgrounds: What We Bring to Intercultural Communication," has three chapters that all have the same goal: They seek to examine the influence of socio-cultural forces on human interaction. Chapter Two deals with how these forces direct the communication patterns of people from international cultures. To make this point, we have selected cultures from Asia, India, black Africa, the Arab world, and Latin America. While many cultures have been left out, you will still be able to appreciate the link between culture and behavior.

Chapter Three moves us from the international arena to co-cultures that operate within the United States. Here again, space constraints have limited the total number of co-cultures we can scrutinize. Yet we believe that in reading about groups such as blacks, the aged, disabled, gays, women, the deaf, and Hispanics, you will get an image of the cultural diversity found in groups that most of you come in contact with on a regular basis. Many of these co-cultures, and others, are so very important to the study of intercultural communication that we will return to them in later chapters.

Chapter Four continues with the theme of how culture modifies interaction. This time, however, the interaction is examined in a specific context, with the assumption that there are culturally diverse rules that influence how members of a culture behave in certain settings. To clarify this important issue, we have selected seven settings where cultures often follow rules that differ from those found in North America: business, groups, negotiations, counseling, education, health care, and the courtroom.

In Part Three, "Intercultural Interaction: Taking Part in Intercultural Communication," our analysis focuses on the verbal and nonverbal symbols used in intercultural communication. In Chapter Five, we offer essays that will introduce you to some of the difficulties you might encounter when your intercultural partner employs a different language system. We will look at how these verbal idiosyncrasies and distinctions influence problem solving, speaking, perception, translation, interpreting, and understanding.

Chapter Six, which is also concerned with symbols, explains some of the ways in which cultural diversity in nonverbal messages can influence the entire transaction. Differences in movement, facial expressions, eye contact, silence, space, time, and the like are detailed so that you have a better appreciation of how culture and communication work in tandem.

Part Four, "Intercultural Communication: Seeking Improvement," has two chapters that are concerned with improving intercultural communication. The readings offered in Chapter Seven are intended to provide you with knowledge and practical recommendations for improving intercultural communication.

The eighth and final chapter probes the ethical dimensions of intercultural communication, centering on essays that deal with moral issues and the future directions and challenges of intercultural communication. This chapter asks you not to conclude your study of intercultural communication with the reading of a single book or the completion of one course. We believe that the study of intercultural communication should be a lifetime endeavor. Each time we want to share an idea or feeling with someone from another culture, we face a new and exhilarating learning experience. We urge everyone to seek out as many of these experiences as possible, to follow the philosopher who once wrote, "Tomorrow, when I know more, I recall that piece of knowledge and use it better."

ASSISTANCE

As in the past, a number of people have helped us rethink and reshape this project. We are especially thankful for the energy and friendship provided by Susan Hellweg, Summer Smith, and Lisa Skow. We also want to express appreciation to our editors, Kristine Clerkin and Peggy Randall, and, of course, to Rebecca Hayden, who had enough courage and insight twenty years ago to decide that intercultural communication should and would become a viable discipline. All three of these editors were stern enough to keep us in check while at the same time allowing us the flexibility to move in new directions.

In a culture that values change, this collection would not have survived for nearly twenty years if we had not been fortunate enough to have so many scholars willing to contribute original essays to each of the editions. Here in the sixth edition we want to acknowledge the work of Felipe Korzenny, June Ock Yum, Nemi C. Jain, Lisa Skow, Edith A. Folb, Carl W. Carmichael, Dawn O. Braithwaite, Kathy Jankowski, Judy C. Pearson, Randall E. Majors, Susan A. Hellweg, Janis W. Anderson, Robert Powell, Kim Witte, Wayne A. Beach, Devorah A. Lieberman, Robert Shuter, Shirley N. Weber, Peter Andersen, LaRay M. Barna, Brian H. Spitzberg, Young Yun Kim, and David W. Kale. We thank all of you for letting us expose your work to thousands of other people who share your commitment to intercultural matters.

Finally we express our gratitude to the countless users of prior editions who have allowed us to "talk to them" about intercultural communication. It may have been a rather intangible connection, but we have greatly appreciated it.

Larry A. Samovar
Richard E. Porter

PART ONE

Intercultural Communication: An Introduction

Precision of communication is important, more important than ever, in our era of hair-trigger balances, when a false or misunderstood word may create as much disaster as a sudden thoughtless act.

—James Thurber

Intercultural communication, as we might rightly suspect, is not new. There has been intercultural communication as long as people from different cultures have been encountering one another. What is new, however, is the systematic study of exactly what happens when intercultural contacts and interaction take place—when the communication process involves culturally diverse people.

Perhaps the initial impetus for the study of intercultural communication was the knowledge that technology has produced the means of our own self-destruction. Historically, intercultural communication, more often than not, has employed a rhetoric of force rather than reason. With the forces of change sweeping the world, however, perhaps we are now seeking forms of communication other than traditional force. The reason for this new study is also pragmatic. Our mobility, increased contact among cultures, a widening world marketplace, and the emergence of multicultural organizations and work forces require that we develop communication skills and abilities appropriate to a multicultural society, which is like life in a global village.

Traditionally, intercultural communication took place among only an extremely small proportion of the world populace. Ministers of state and government, certain merchants, and a few tourists were primarily the travelers who visited foreign lands. Until rather recently, we Americans had little contact with other cultures, even within our own country, as members of nonwhite races were segregated. Only in recent years have the laws changed to foster integrated schools, work forces, and, to some extent, neighborhoods. In addition, those who made up the vast white middle America remained at home, rarely leaving their own county. This situation, of course, has changed markedly; we are now a mobile society among ever-increasing mobile societies around the world.

This increased contact with other cultures and domestic co-cultures makes it imperative for us to make a concerted effort to understand and to get along with people who may be vastly different from ourselves. The ability, through increased awareness and understanding, to coexist peacefully with people who do not necessarily share our background, views, beliefs, values, customs, habits, or life styles not only can benefit us in our own neighborhoods but can also be a decisive factor in forestalling international conflict.

As we begin our inquiry, there is a need to specify the nature of intercultural communication and to recognize that various viewpoints of it are somewhat different. From what we have already said, you should suspect that there is a variety of ways in which the topic of intercultural communication can be explored. There are perspectives that look at intercultural communication from a mass media point of view. Scholars who follow this approach are concerned with such issues as international broadcasting, worldwide freedom of expression, Western domination of information, and the use of modern electronic technologies for instantaneous worldwide transmission of information. Other groups investigate international communication, with the emphasis on communication between nations and between governments. It is the communication of diplomacy and propaganda. Still others are interested in communication inherent in international business, which includes such diverse concerns as negotiations and communication within multicultural organizations. Our concern is with the more personal aspects of communication— what happens when people from different cultures interact face-to-face. Hence, we identify our approach as one that examines the interpersonal dimensions of intercultural communication as it occurs in a variety of contexts. For this reason, we have selected articles for this collection because

they focus on those variables of both culture and communication that come into play *during the communication encounter*—during the time that participants from different cultures are trying to share ideas, information, and feelings.

Inquiry into the nature of intercultural communication has raised many questions, but it has produced few theories and far fewer answers. Most of the inquiry has been associated with fields other than communication: primarily anthropology, international relations, social psychology, and socio- and psycholinguistics. Although the direction of research has been diverse, the knowledge has not been coordinated. Much that has emerged has been more a reaction to current socio-racial-ethnic concerns than an attempt to define and to explain intercultural communication, but it is quite clear that knowledge of intercultural communication can aid in solving communication problems before they arise. School counselors who understand some of the reasons why the poor perceive school as they do might be better able to treat young truants. Those who know that native Americans and Hispanics use eye contact in ways that differ from other Americans may be able to avert misunderstanding. And, perhaps, those who realize that some people treat illness as a curse may be better able to deliver necessary health care. Thus the message of this book is that many problems can be avoided by understanding the components of intercultural communication.

1

Approaches:
Understanding
Intercultural
Communication

We begin the exploration of intercultural communication with a series of diverse articles that (1) introduce the philosophy that underlies our concept of intercultural communication, (2) provide a general orientation and overview of intercultural communication, (3) theorize about the analysis of intercultural transactions, (4) provide insight into cultural differences, and (5) demonstrate the relationships between culture and perception. Our purpose at this point is to give you a sufficient introduction to the many diverse dimensions of intercultural communication that you will be able to approach the remainder of this volume with an appropriate frame of reference to make your further inquiry interesting, informative, and useful.

We begin with "Basic Principles of Intercultural Communication" to present in rather broad terms what intercultural communication involves and to introduce some of the specific topics and issues associated with its study. We start by defining and explaining the role of human communication. We then turn our attention to the specific areas of culture and communication and show how they interrelate to form the field of intercultural communication. By examining the major variables that affect it, we better understand how it operates. By knowing at the outset of the book what the study of intercultural communication entails, you should have a greater appreciation for the selections that follow.

Dean C. Barnlund in "Communication in a Global Village" traces communication and transportation developments that have led to the apparent shrinking of the contemporary world and the emergence of the global community. He points out the ramifications of the global village in terms of the forms and kinds of interactions that necessarily accompany such a new community of people. Barnlund considers problems of meaning associated with cultural differences, interpersonal encounters, intercultural encounters, and the role of the "collective unconscious" in intercultural interactions.

Next, Michael Argyle provides us with a different overview of intercultural communication in "Intercultural Communication." He begins with the basic assumption that "many people have to communicate and work with members of other cultures." Because the differences that exist between these cultures have an impact on interpersonal interaction, Argyle believes that particular communication problems will arise. These problems can serve as an outline for the study of intercultural communication because they point out which areas of human interaction must be examined and understood before successful intercultural communication can occur. Argyle places these areas of difficulty into six categories: (1) language, including forms of polite usage; (2) nonverbal communication; (3) rules of social behavior, which include bribing and gift giving; (4) social relationships that govern family and work relationships; (5) motivation, which includes cultural concerns with achievement and face saving; and (6) concepts and ideology involving ideas derived from religion and politics.

The importance of culture in human interaction is underscored by Edward T. Hall in his selection "Context and Meaning." The grand connection between culture and human communicative behaviors is revealed when Hall demonstrates how culture provides a highly selective screen between people and their outside worlds. This cultural filter effectively designates what people attend to as well as what they choose to ignore. The link between culture and behavior is futher illustrated through Hall's discussion of high- and low-context communication, in which he shows how people from different cultural backgrounds learn to concentrate on the unique aspects of their environments.

The final article in this chapter summarizes for us where our exploration of intercultural communication has led us. Felipe Korzenny in his article "Relevance and Application of Intercultural Communication Theory and Research" provides us with three major insights. First, Korzenny demonstrates the relationships between culture and communication. Second, he addresses the role of intercultural theory and research on the practice of intercultural communication and outlines four barriers to successful intercultural communication. Third, he emphasizes the importance of intercultural communication, stressing nine advantages derived from its study: advantages ranging from remediation of self-imposed cultural filters to the prevention of war.

Basic Principles of Intercultural Communication

RICHARD E. PORTER
LARRY A. SAMOVAR

During the past thirty years, a number of events have led to many changes in worldwide and local interaction patterns. First, changes in transportation technology made the world "shrink" by providing means for people to be almost anywhere within a few hours flying time. (The suborbital aircraft now being designed will cause greater shrinkage. Travel time between China and the United States, for example, will be measured in minutes rather than in hours.) This increase in travel technology was soon followed by changes in communication technology, which made it possible for people to have instantaneous vocal, pictorial, and textual communication anywhere in the world without the need for traveling. Indeed, with a few hundred dollars worth of equipment in the form of a portable facsimile machine and a cellular telephone, it is possible to have instant oral and print communication almost anywhere in the world while driving the freeways in the United States.

These changes have wrought many effects; two, however, stand out as being significant for our purposes. The first is that new communication technology has created an almost free flow of news and information throughout the world and has become so important in the everyday activity of conducting commerce and government that it cannot be set aside. Because of this, it is also impossible to keep communication capabilities out of the hands of the people. Government attempts to censor the free flow of ideas, opinions, and information have been thwarted. In China, for instance, during the Tiananmen Square demonstrations of mid-1989, the Chinese government attempted to ban foreign correspondents from reporting on observed incidents by cutting their access to telephone and television broadcast facilities. American television viewers, however, were shown many incidents of reporters using their cellular telephones to call the United States via the handy communications satellite in stationary orbit over Asia. By the time the government reacted to this technology, the story and information had long since been disseminated to the world. In other parts of the world, similar incidents have occurred; for example, the widespread and multiple changes currently taking place in Eastern Europe are due in part to the availability of news and information.

Communication technology has also broken down our isolation. One hundred years ago it was virtually impossible for the average citizen to have an informed awareness of what was happening in the world. People had to wait for reports to arrive by mail or appear in newspapers, where the news could be up to several months old. Today is quite different. With existing communication technology, we can sit in our living rooms and watch events anywhere on earth, or, indeed, in orbit around the earth, as these events are actually happening. Only a scant few years ago we had to wait hours, days, and even weeks to see who won gold medals in the Olympic Games. Today, we can watch these events as they occur.

This new communication technology has a considerable impact upon us. When we received news and information days and weeks after an event, it was difficult to develop a feeling about or a caring for what was happening thousands of miles away. But, consider the differences in the impact upon us when we read in the newspaper that the South African police had put down a disturbance in a black township three weeks ago and when we sit today in the living room and watch while a police officer actually clubs someone with a baton. The ability to deny the cruelty of that act is reduced virtually to zero.

The second change has brought us to the brink of a McLuanesque global village. While transportation and communication technology have figuratively shrunk the world, immigration patterns have physically shifted segments of the world population. People from Vietnam, Cambodia, Laos, Cuba, Haiti, Columbia, Nicaragua, El Salvador, and Ecuador, among others, have entered the United States and become our neighbors. As these people try to adjust their lives to this culture, we will have ·many opportunities for intercultural contacts in our daily lives. Contacts with cultures that previously appeared unfamiliar, alien, and at times mysterious are now a normal part of our day-to-day routine. All of this means that we are no longer isolated from one another in time and space.

While this global phenomenon involving transportation, communication, and migration was taking place, there was also a kind of cultural revolution within our own boundaries. Domestic events made us focus our attention upon new and often demanding co-cultures. Asians, blacks, Hispanics, women, homosexuals, the poor, the disabled, the drug culture, the homeless, and countless other groups became highly visible and vocal as they cried out for recognition and their place in our new global village.

This attention to co-cultures made us realize that although intercultural contact is inevitable, it is often not successful. Frequently, the communicative behavior of the co-cultures disturbed many of us. Their behavior seemed strange, at times even bizarre, and it frequently failed to meet our normal expectations. We discovered, in short, that intercultural communication is difficult. Even after the natural barrier of a foreign language is overcome, we can still fail to understand and to be understood.

These interaction failures, both in the international arena and on the domestic scene, give rise to a major premise: *The difficulty with being thrust into a global village is that we do not yet know how to live like villagers; there are too many of us who do not want to live with "them."* Ours is a culture where racism and ethnocentrism still run deep below the surface. Although there has been a lessening of overt racial violence since the 1960s, the enduring racist/ethnocentric belief system has not been appreciably affected. In many respects, racism and ethnocentrism have become institutionalized and are practiced unconsciously. The result is a structured domination of people of color by the white Anglo power structure. Until this deep-seated antagonism can be eliminated, we will not be able to assume our place in a global village community.

Our inability to yet behave as villagers in the global village is cause for major concern because not only have we not learned to respect and accept one another, we have not learned to communicate with one another effectively, to understand one another, because our cultures are different. Thus, even if we have the strongest desire to communicate, we are faced with the difficulties imposed upon us by cultural diversity and the impact that diversity has on the communication process.

The difficulties cultural diversity poses for effective communication have given rise to the marriage of culture and communication and to the recognition of intercultural communication as a field of study. Inherent in this fusion is the idea that intercultural communication entails the investigation of culture and the difficulties of communicating across cultural boundaries.

To help us understand what is involved in intercultural communication, we will begin with a fundamental definition: *Intercultural communication occurs whenever a message produced in one culture must be processed in another culture.* The rest of this article will deal with intercultural communication and point out the relationships between communication, culture, and intercultural communication.

COMMUNICATION

To understand intercultural interaction, we must first understand human communication. Understanding human communication means knowing something about what happens when people interact, why it happens, the effects of what happens, and finally what we can do to influence and maximize the results of that event.

Understanding and Defining Communication

We begin with a basic assumption that communication is a form of human behavior that is derived from a need to interact with other human beings. Almost everyone desires social contact with other people, and this need is met through the act of communication, which unites otherwise isolated individuals. Our behaviors become messages to which other people may respond. When we talk, we are obviously behaving, but when we wave, smile, frown, walk, shake our heads, or gesture, we also are behaving. These behaviors frequently become messages; they communicate something to someone else.

Before behaviors can become messages, however, they must meet two requirements: First, they must be observed by someone, and second, they must elicit a response. In other words, any behavior that elicits a response is a message. If we examine this last statement, we can see several implications.

The first implication is that the word *any* tells us that both verbal and nonverbal behaviors may function as messages. Verbal messages consist of spoken or written words (speaking and writing are word-producing behaviors) while nonverbal messages consist of the entire remaining behavioral repertory.

Second, behavior may be either conscious or unconscious. We frequently do things without conscious awareness of them. This is especially true of nonverbal behavior, habits such as fingernail biting, toe tapping, leg jiggling, head shaking, staring, and smiling. Even such things as slouching in a chair, chewing gum, or adjusting glasses are frequently unconscious behaviors. Since a message consists of behaviors to which people may respond, we must thus acknowledge the possibility of producing messages unknowingly.

A third implication of the behavior-message linkage is that we frequently behave unintentionally, in some cases uncontrollably. For instance, if we are embarrassed we may blush or speak with vocal disfluencies; we do not intend to blush or to stammer, but we do so anyway. Again, these unintentional behaviors can become messages if someone sees them and responds to them.

This concept of conscious-unconscious, intentional-unintentional behavior relationships gives us a basis to formulate a definition of communication. *Communication may be defined as that which happens whenever someone responds to the behavior or the residue of the behavior of another person.* When someone observes our behavior or its residue and attributes meaning to it, communication has taken place regardless of whether our behavior was conscious or unconscious, intentional or unintentional. If we think about this for a moment, we must realize that it is impossible for us not to behave. Being necessitates behavior. If behavior has communication potential, then it is also impossible for us not to communicate. In other words, we cannot not communicate.

The notion of behavior residue just mentioned in our definition refers to those things that remain as a record of our actions. For instance, this article that you are reading is a behavior residue—it resulted from certain behaviors. As the authors we had to engage in a number of behaviors; we had to research, think, and use our word processors. Another example of behavior residue might be the odor of cigar smoke lingering in an elevator after the cigar smoker has departed. Smoking the cigar was the behavior; the odor is the residue. The response you have to that smell is a reflection of your past experiences and attitudes toward cigars, smoking, smoking in public elevators, and, perhaps, people who smoke cigars.

Our approach to communication has focused on the behavior of one individual causing or provoking a response from another by the attribution of meaning to behavior. Attribution means that we draw upon our past experiences and give meaning to the behavior that we observe. We might imagine that somewhere in each of our brains is a meaning reservoir in which are stored all of the experience-derived meanings we possess. These various meanings have developed throughout our lifetimes as a result of our culture acting upon us as well as the result of our individual experiences within that culture. Meaning is relative to each of us because each of us is a unique human being with a unique background and a unique set of experiences. When we encounter a behavior in our environment, each of us dips into our individual, unique meaning reservoirs and selects the meaning we believe is most likely to be the most appropriate for the behavior encountered and the social context in which it occurred. For instance, if someone walks up to us and says: "If you've got a few minutes, let's go to the student union and get a cup of coffee," we observe this behavior and respond to it by giving it meaning. The meaning we give it is drawn from our experience with language and word meaning and also from our experience with this person and the social context. Our responses could vary significantly depending upon the circumstances. If the person is a friend, we may interpret the behavior as an invitation to sit and chat for a few minutes. On the other hand, if the behavior comes from someone with whom we have had differences, the response may be one of attributing conciliatory good will to the message and an invitation to try and settle past differences. Yet another example could be a situation in which the person is someone you have seen in a class but do not know. Then your ability to respond is lessened because you may not be able to guess fully the other person's intention. Perhaps this is someone who wants to talk about the class; perhaps it is someone who only wants social company until the next class; or perhaps, if gender differences are involved, it may be someone attempting to "put the make" on you. Your response to the observed behavior is dependent upon knowledge, experience, and social context.

Usually this works quite well, but at other times it fails and we misinterpret a message; we attribute the wrong meaning to the behavior we have observed. This may be brought about by inappropriate behavior where someone does or says something they did not intend. Or it could be brought about by the experiential backgrounds of people being sufficiently different that behavior is misinterpreted.

The Ingredients of Communication

In this section we will examine the ingredients of communication; that is, we will look at the various components that fit together to form what we call communication. Since our purpose in studying intercultural communication is to develop communication skills to apply with conscious intent, our working definition of communication must specify intentional communication. *Communication is defined, therefore, as a dynamic transactional behavior-affecting process in which people behave intentionally in order to induce or elicit a particular response from another person.* Communication is complete only when the intended behavior is observed by the intended receiver and that person responds to and is affected by the behavior. These transactions must include all conscious or unconscious, intentional or unintentional, verbal, nonverbal, and contextual stimuli that act as cues about the quality and credibility of the message. The cues must be clear to both the behavioral source of the transaction and the processor of that behavior.

This definition allows us to identify eight specific ingredients of communication within the framework of intentional communication. First is a *behavior source*. This is a person who has both a need and a desire to communicate. This need may range from a social desire to be recognized as an individual to the desire to share information with others or to influence the attitudes and behaviors of one or more others. The source's wish to communicate indicates a desire to share his or her internal state of being with another human being. Communication, then, is really concerned with the sharing of internal states with varying degrees of intention to influence the information, attitudes, and behaviors of others.

Internal states of being cannot be shared directly; we must rely on symbolic representations of our internal states. This brings us to the second ingredient, *encoding*. Encoding is an internal activity in which verbal and nonverbal behaviors are selected and arranged to create a message in accordance with the contextual rules that govern the interaction and according to the rules of grammar and syntax applicable to the language being used.

The result of encoding is expressive behavior that serves as a *message*, the third ingredient, to represent the internal state that is to be shared. A message is a set of verbal and/or nonverbal symbols that represent a person's particular state of being at a particular moment in time and space. Although encoding is an internal act that produces a message, a message is external to the source; it is the behavior or behavior residue that must pass between a source and a responder.

Messages must have a means by which they move from source to responder, so the fourth communication ingredient is the *channel*, which provides a connection between a source and a responder. A channel is the physical means by which the message moves between people.

The fifth ingredient is the *responder*. Responders are people who observe behavior or its residue and, as a consequence, become linked to the message source. Responders may be those intended by the source to receive the message or they may be others who, by whatever circumstance, observe the behavior once it has entered a channel. Responders have problems with messages, not unlike the problems sources have with internal states of being. Messages usually impinge on people in the form of light or sound energy, although they may be in forms that stimulate any of the senses. Whatever the form of sensory stimulation, people must convert these energies into meaningful experiences.

Converting external energies into a meaningful experience is called *decoding*, which is the sixth ingredient of communication. Decoding is akin to a source's act of encoding, because it also is an internal activity. Through this internal processing of a message, meaning is attributed to a source's behaviors that represent his or her internal state of being.

The seventh ingredient we need to consider is *response*, what a person decides to do about a message. Response may vary from as little as a decision to do nothing to an immediate overt physical act of violent proportions. If communication has been somewhat successful, the response of the message recipient will resemble to some degree that desired by the source who created the response-eliciting behavior.

The final ingredient of communication we will consider is *feedback*—information available to a source that permits him or her to make qualitative judgments about communication effectiveness. Through the interpretation of feedback, one may adjust and adapt his or her behavior to an ongoing situation. Although feedback and response are not the same thing, they are clearly related. Response is what a person decides to do about a message, and feedback is information about the effectiveness of communication. They are related because a message recipient's behavior is the normal source of feedback.

These eight ingredients of communication make up only a partial list of the factors that function during a communication event. In addition to these elements, when we conceive of communication as a process there are several other characteristics that help us understand how communication actually works.

First, communication is *dynamic*: It is an ongoing, ever-changing activity. As participants in communication, we constantly are affected by each other's messages and, as a consequence, we undergo continual change. Each of us in our daily lives meets and interacts with people who exert some influence over us. Each time we are influenced we are changed in some way, which means that as we go through life we do so as continually changing dynamic individuals.

A second characteristic of communication is that it is *interactive*. Communication must take place between people. This implies two or more people who bring to a communication event their own unique backgrounds and experiences that serve as a backdrop for communicative interaction. Interaction also implies a reciprocal situation in which each party attempts to influence the other—that is, each party simultaneously creates messages designed to elicit specific responses from the other.

Third, communication is *irreversible*. Once we have said something and someone has received and decoded the message, we cannot retrieve it. This circumstance sometimes results in what is called "putting your foot in your mouth." The source may send other messages in attempts to modify the effect, but it cannot be eliminated. This is frequently a problem when we unconsciously or unintentionally send a message to someone. We may affect them adversely and not even know it; then during future interactions we may wonder why that person is reacting to us in what we perceive to be an unusual manner.

Fourth, communication takes place in both a *physical* and *social context*, which establishes the rules that govern the interaction. When we interact with someone, it is not in isolation but within specific physical surroundings and under a set of specific social dynamics. Physical surroundings include specific physical objects such as furniture, window coverings, floor coverings, lighting, noise levels, acoustics, vegetation, presence or absence of physical clutter, as well as competing messages. Many aspects of the physical environment can and do affect communication: The comfort or discomfort of a chair, the color of the walls, or the total atmosphere of a room are but a few. Also affecting communication is the symbolic meaning of the physical surroundings—a kind of nonverbal communication. Social context defines the social relationships that exist between people as well as the rules that govern the interaction. In our culture here in the United States, we tend to be somewhat cavalier toward social hierarchies and pay much less attention to them than do people in other cultures. Nevertheless, such differences as teacher-student, employer-employee, parent-child, admiral-seaman, senator-citizen, physician-patient, and judge-attorney establish rules that specify expected behavior and thus affect the communication process.

Quite frequently, physical surroundings help define the social context. The employer may sit behind a desk while the employee stands before the desk to receive an admonition. Or, in the courtroom, the judge sits elevated facing the courtroom, jurors, and attorneys, indicating the social superiority of the judge relative to the other officers of the court. The attorneys sit side by side, indicating a social equality between accuser and accused until such time as the jury of peers renders a verdict. No matter what the social context, it will have some effect on communi-

cation. The form of language used, the respect or lack of respect shown one another, the time of day, personal moods, who speaks to whom and in what order, and the degree of nervousness or confidence people express are but a few of the ways in which the social context can affect communication.

At this point, we should see clearly that human communication does not take place in a social vacuum. Rather, communication is an intricate matrix of interacting social acts that occur in a complex social environment that reflects the way people live and how they come to interact with and get along in their world. This social environment is culture, and if we are to truly understand communication, we must also understand culture.

CULTURE

In all respects, everything so far said about communication applies to intercultural communication. The functions and relationships between the components of communication obviously apply, but what especially characterizes intercultural communication is that sources and responders come from different cultures. This alone is sufficient to identify a unique form of communicative interaction that must take into account the role and function of culture in the communication process. In this section, intercultural communication will first be defined and then discussed through the perspective of a model and then its various forms will be shown.

Intercultural Communication Model

Intercultural communication occurs whenever a message is produced by a member of one culture for consumption by a member of another culture, a message that must be understood. This circumstance can be problematic because, as we have already seen, culture forges and shapes the individual communicator. Culture is largely responsible for the construction of our individual social realities and for our individual repertoires of communicative behaviors and meanings. The communication repertories people possess can vary significantly

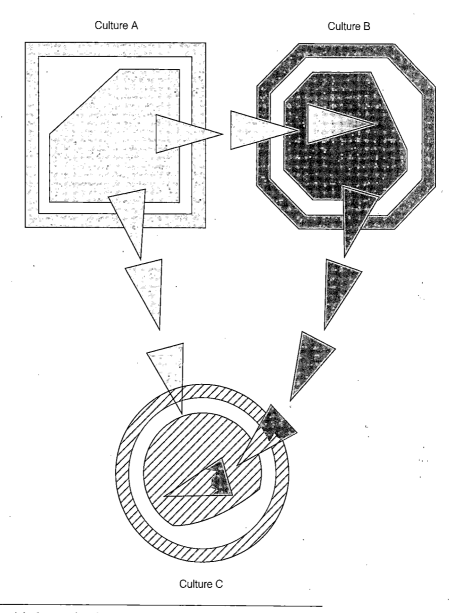

Culture A

Culture B

Culture C

Figure 1 Model of Intercultural Communication

from culture to culture, which can lead to all sorts of difficulties. Through the study and understanding of intercultural communication, however, these difficulties at the least can be reduced and at best nearly eliminated.

Cultural influence on individuals and the problems inherent in the production and interpretation of messages between cultures are illustrated in Figure 1. Here, three cultures are represented by three distinct geometric shapes. Cultures A and B are purposefully similar to one another and are represented by a square and an irregular octagon that resembles a square. Culture C is intended to be quite different from Cultures A and B. It is represented both by its circular shape and its physical distance from Cultures A and B. Within each represented culture is another form similar to the shape of the influencing parent culture. This form represents a person who has been molded by his or her culture. The shape of the person, however, is somewhat different from that of the parent culture. This difference suggests two things: First, there are other influences besides culture that affect and help mold the individual, and, second, although culture is the dominant shaping force on an individual, people vary to some extent from each other within any culture.

Message production, transmission, and interpretation across cultures is illustrated by the series of arrows connecting them. When a message leaves the culture in which it was encoded, it carries the content intended by its producer. This is represented by the arrows leaving a culture having the same pattern as that within the message producer. When a message reaches the culture where it is to be interpreted, it undergoes a transformation because the culture in which the message is decoded influences the message interpretation and hence its meaning. The content of the original message changes during the interpretation phase of intercultural communication because the culturally different repertoires of social reality, communicative behaviors, and meanings possessed by the interpreter do not coincide with those possessed by the message producer.

The degree of influence culture has on intercultural communication is a function of the dissimilarity between the cultures. This also is indicated in the model by the degree of pattern change that occurs in the message arrows. The change that occurs between Cultures A and B is much less than the change between Cultures A and C and between Cultures B and C. This is because there is greater similarity between Cultures A and B. Hence, the repertoires of social reality, communicative behaviors, and meanings are similar and the interpretation effort produces results more nearly like the content intended in the original message. Since Culture C is represented as being quite different from Cultures A and B, the interpreted message is also vastly different and more nearly represents the pattern of Culture C.

The model suggests that there can be wide variation in cultural differences during intercultural communication, due in part to circumstances or forms. Intercultural communication occurs in a wide variety of situations that range from interactions between people for whom cultural differences are extreme to interactions between people who are members of the same dominant culture and whose differences are reflected in the values and perceptions of subcultures, subgroups, or racial groups. If we imagine differences varying along a minimum-maximum dimension (see Figure 2), the degree of difference between two cultural groups depends on their relative social uniqueness. Although this scale is unrefined, it allows us to examine intercultural communication acts and gain insight into the effect cultural differences have on communication. In order to see how this dimensional scale helps us understand intercultural communication, we can look at some examples of cultural differences positioned along the scale.

The first example represents a case of maximum differences—those found between Asian and Western cultures. This may be typified as an interaction between two farmers, one who works on a communal farm on the outskirts of Beijing in China and the other who operates a large mechanized and automated wheat, corn, and dairy farm in Michigan. In this situation, we would expect to find the greatest number of cultural factors subject to variation. Physical appearance, religion, philosophy, economic systems, social attitudes, language, heritage, basic conceptualizations of self and the universe, and degree of technological development are cultural factors that differ sharply. We must recognize, however, that these two farmers also share the commonality of farming, with its rural life style and love of land. In some respects, they may be more closely related than they are to members of their own cultures who

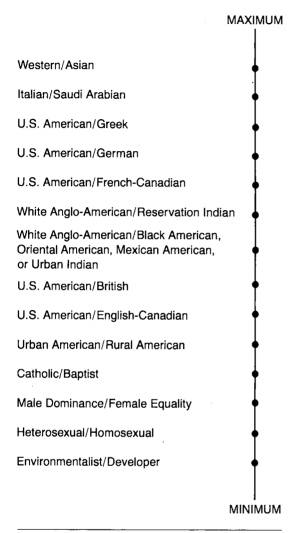

MAXIMUM

Western/Asian

Italian/Saudi Arabian

U.S. American/Greek

U.S. American/German

U.S. American/French-Canadian

White Anglo-American/Reservation Indian

White Anglo-American/Black American,
Oriental American, Mexican American,
or Urban Indian

U.S. American/British

U.S. American/English-Canadian

Urban American/Rural American

Catholic/Baptist

Male Dominance/Female Equality

Heterosexual/Homosexual

Environmentalist/Developer

MINIMUM

Figure 2 Arrangement of Compared Cultures, Subcultures, and Subgroups Along a Scale of Minimum to Maximum Socio-cultural Differences

tics are similar, and the English language is derived in part from German and its ancestor languages. The roots of both German and American philosophy are found in ancient Greece, and most Americans and Germans share some form of the Christian religion. Yet there are some significant differences. Germans have political and economic systems that differ somewhat from those found in the United States. German society tends toward formality while in the United States we tend toward informality. Germans have memories of local warfare and the destruction of their cities and economy, of having been a defeated nation on more than one occasion. The United States has never lost a war on its own territory.

Examples near the minimal end of the dimension can be characterized in two ways. First are variations found between members of separate but similar cultures—for instance, between U.S. Americans and English Canadians. The differences are less than those found between American and German cultures, between American and Greek cultures, between American and British cultures, or even between American and French-Canadian cultures, but greater than generally found within a single culture. Second, minimal differences also may be seen in the variation between subcultures, subgroups, or racial groups within the same dominant culture. Socio-cultural differences may be found between members of the Catholic church and the Baptist church, between ecologists and advocates of further development of Alaskan oil resources, between middle-class Americans and the urban poor, between mainstream Americans and the gay/lesbian community, between the able and the disabled, or between male dominance advocates and female equality advocates.

In both of these categorizations, members of each cultural group have much more in common than in the examples found in the middle or at the maximum end of the scale. They probably speak the same language, share the same general religion, attend the same schools, and live in the same neighborhoods. Yet, these groups to some extent are culturally different; they do not fully share the same

live in large urban settings. In other words, across some cultural dimensions, the Michigan farmer may have more in common with the Chinese farmer than with a Wall Street securities broker.

An example nearer the center of the scale is the difference between American culture and German culture. Less variation is found: Physical characteris-

experiences, nor do they share the same perceptions. They see their worlds differently.

CULTURE AND COMMUNICATION

The link between culture and communication is crucial to understanding intercultural communication because it is through the influence of culture that people learn to communicate. A Korean, an Egyptian, or an American learns to communicate like other Koreans, Egyptians, or Americans. Their behavior conveys meaning because it is learned and shared; it is cultural. People view their world through categories, concepts, and labels that are products of their culture.

Cultural similarity in perception makes the sharing of meaning possible. The ways in which we communicate, the circumstances of our communication, the language and language style we use, and our nonverbal behaviors are primarily all a response to and a function of our culture. And, as cultures differ from one another, the communication practices and behaviors of individuals reared in those cultures will also be different.

Culture is an all-encompassing form or pattern for living. It is complex, abstract, and pervasive. Numerous aspects of culture help to determine communicative behavior. These socio-cultural elements are diverse and cover a wide range of human social activity. For the sake of simplicity and to put some limitation on our discussion, we will examine a few of the socio-cultural elements associated with *perception, verbal processes*, and *nonverbal processes*.

These socio-cultural elements are the constituent parts of intercultural communication. When we combine them, as we do when we communicate, they are like the components of a stereo system—each one relates to and needs the other in order to function properly. In our discussion, the elements will be separated in order to identify and discuss them, but in actuality they do not exist in isolation nor do they function alone. They form a complex matrix of interacting elements that operate together to constitute the complex phenomenon called intercultural communication.

Perception

In its simplest sense, *perception is the internal process by which we select, evaluate, and organize stimuli from the external environment*. In other words, perception is the conversion of the physical energies of our environment into meaningful experience. A number of corollary issues arising out of this definition help explain the relationship between perception and culture. It is believed generally that people behave as they do because of the ways in which they perceive the world, and that these behaviors are learned as part of their cultural experience. Whether in judging beauty or describing snow, we respond to stimuli as we do primarily because our culture has taught us to do so. We tend to notice, reflect on, and respond to those elements in our environment that are important to us. In the United States we might respond principally to a thing's size and cost, while to the Japanese color might be the important criterion.

Social Perception. Social perception is the process by which we construct our unique social realities by attributing meaning to the social objects and events we encounter in our environments. It is an extremely important aspect of communication. Culture conditions and structures our perceptual processes so that we develop culturally inspired perceptual sets. These sets not only help determine which external stimuli reach our awareness, but more important, they significantly influence the social aspect of perception—the social construction of reality—by the attribution of meaning to these stimuli. The difficulties in communication caused by this perceptual variability can best be lowered by knowing about and understanding the cultural factors that are subject to variation, coupled with an honest and sincere desire to communicate successfully across cultural boundaries.

Our contention is that intercultural communication can best be understood as cultural diversity in the perception of social objects and events. A central tenet of this position is that minor communication problems are often exaggerated by perceptual diversity. To understand others' worlds and actions, we must try to understand their perceptual frames of reference, we must learn to understand how they perceive the world. In the ideal intercultural encounter, we would hope for many overlapping experiences and a commonality of perceptions. Cultural diversity, however, tends to introduce us to dissimilar experiences and, hence, to varied and frequently strange and unfamiliar perceptions of the external world.

There are three major socio-cultural elements that have a direct and major influence on the meanings we develop for our perceptions. These elements are our *belief/value/attitude systems*, our *world view*, and our *social organization*. When these three elements influence our perceptions and the meanings we develop for them, they are affecting our individual, subjective aspects of meanings. We all may see the same social entity and agree upon what it is in objective terms, but what the object or event means to us individually may differ considerably. Both an American and a Chinese might agree in an objective sense that a particular object is a young dog, but they might disagree completely in their interpretation of the dog. The American might see it as a cute, fuzzy, loving, protective pet. The Chinese, on the other hand, might see the dog as something especially fit for the Sunday barbecue. You see, it is an American's cultural background that interprets the dog as a pet, and it is the Chinese cultural background that regards dog meat as a delicacy.

Belief/Value/Attitude Systems. Beliefs, in a general sense, can be viewed as individually held subjective probabilities that some object or event possesses certain characteristics. A belief involves a link between the belief object and the characteristics that distinguish it. The degree to which we believe that an event or an object possesses certain characteristics reflects the level of our subjective probability and, consequently, the depth or intensity of our belief. That is, the more certain we are in a belief, the greater is the intensity of that belief.

Culture plays an important role in belief formation. Whether we accept the *New York Times*, the Bible, the entrails of a goat, tea leaves, the visions induced by peyote, or the changes specified in the Taoist *I Ching* as sources of knowledge and belief depends on our cultural backgrounds and experiences. In matters of intercultural communication, there are no rights or wrongs as far as beliefs are concerned. If someone believes that the voices in the wind can guide one's behavior along the proper path, we cannot throw up our hands and declare the belief wrong (even if we believe it to be wrong); we must be able to recognize and to deal with that belief if we wish to obtain satisfactory and successful communication.

Values are the valuative aspect of our belief/value/attitude systems. Valuative dimensions include qualities such as usefulness, goodness, aesthetics, need satisfaction, and pleasure. Although each of us has a unique set of values, there are also values called *cultural values* that tend to permeate a culture. Cultural values are a set of organized rules for making choices, reducing uncertainty, and reducing conflicts within a given society. They are usually derived from the larger philosophical issues inherent in a culture. These values are generally normative in that they inform a member of a culture what is good and bad, right and wrong, true and false, positive and negative, and so on. Cultural values define what is worth dying for, what is worth protecting, what frightens people, what are considered to be proper subjects for study or ridicule, and what types of events lead individuals to group solidarity. Cultural values also specify which behaviors are important and which should be avoided within a culture.

Values express themselves within a culture as rules that prescribe the behaviors that members of the culture are expected to perform. These are called *normative values*. Thus, Catholics are supposed to attend Mass, motorists are supposed to stop at stop signs, and workers in our culture are supposed to arrive at work at the designated time. Most people follow normative behaviors; a few do not. Failure to do so may be met with either informal or codified sanctions. The Catholic who avoids Mass may receive a visit from a priest, the driver who runs a stop sign may receive a fine, and the employee who is tardy too frequently may be discharged.

Normative values also extend into everyday communicative behavior by specifying how people are to behave in specific communication contexts. This extension acts as a guide to individual and group behavior that minimizes or prevents harm to individual sensitivities within cultures.

Beliefs and values contribute to the development and content of *attitudes*. An attitude may be defined formally as *a learned tendency to respond in a consistent manner with respect to a given object of orientation*. This means that we tend to avoid those things we dislike and to embrace those things we like. Attitudes are learned within a cultural context. Whatever cultural environment surrounds us helps shape and form our attitudes, our readiness to respond, and ultimately our behavior.

World View. This cultural element, though somewhat abstract, is one of the most important ones found in the perceptual aspects of intercultural communication. World view deals with a culture's orientation toward such philosophical issues as God, humanity, nature, the universe, and others that are concerned with the concept of being. In short, our world view helps us locate our place and rank in the universe. Because world view is so complex, it is often difficult to isolate during an intercultural interaction. In this examination, we seek to understand its substance and its elusiveness.

World view issues are timeless and represent the most fundamental basis of a culture. A Catholic has a different world view than a Moslem, Hindu, Jew, Taoist, or atheist. The way in which native Americans view the individual's place in nature differs sharply from the Euro-American's view. Native Americans see themselves as one with nature; they perceive a balanced relationship between humankind and the environment, a partnership of equality and respect. Euro-Americans, on the other hand, see a human-centered world in which humans are supreme and are apart from nature. They may treat the universe as theirs—a place to carry out their desires and wishes through the power of science and technology.

World view influences a culture at very profound levels. Its effects are often quite subtle and not revealed in such obvious and often superficial ways as dress, gestures, and vocabulary. We can think of a world view as analogous to a pebble tossed into a pond. Just as the pebble causes ripples that spread and reverberate over the entire surface of the pond, world view likewise spreads itself over a culture and permeates every facet of it. World view influences beliefs, values, attitudes, uses of time, and many other aspects of culture. In its subtle way, it is a powerful influence in intercultural communication because as a member of a culture, each communicator's world view is so deeply imbedded in the psyche that it is taken for granted, and each communicator tends to assume automatically that everyone else views the world as he or she does.

Social Organization. The manner in which a culture organizes itself and its institutions also affects how members of the culture perceive the world and how they communicate. It might be helpful to look briefly at two of the dominant social units found in a culture.

The *family*, although it is the smallest social organization in a culture, is one of the most influential. The family sets the stage for a child's development during the formative periods of life, presents the child with a wide range of cultural influences that affect almost everything from a child's first attitudes to the selection of toys, and guides the child's acquisition of language and the amount of emphasis on it. Skills from vocabulary building to dialects are the purview of the family. The family also offers and withholds approval, support, rewards, and punishments, which have a marked effect on the values children develop and the goals they pursue. If, for example, children learn by observation and communication that silence is paramount in their culture, as do Japanese children, they will reflect that aspect of culture in their behavior and bring it to intercultural settings.

The *school* is another social organization that is important. By definition and history schools are endowed with a major portion of the responsibility for passing on and maintaining a culture. They are a community's basic link with its past as well as its taskmaster for the future. Schools maintain culture by relating to new members what has happened, what is important, and what one as a member of the culture must know. Schools may teach geography or wood carving, mathematics or nature lore; they may stress revolution based on peace or predicated on violence, or they may relate a particular culturally accepted version of history. But whatever is taught in a school is determined by the culture in which that school exists.

Verbal Processes

Verbal processes include not only how we talk to each other but also the internal activities of thinking and meaning development for the words we use. These processes (*verbal language* and *patterns of thought*) are vitally related to perception and the attachment and expression of meaning.

Verbal Language. Any discussion of language in intercultural settings must include an investigation of language issues in general before dealing with specific problems of foreign language, language translation, and the argot and vernacular of co-cultures. Here, in our introduction to the various dimensions of culture, we will look at verbal language as it relates to our understanding of culture.

In the most basic sense, language is an organized, generally agreed-on, learned symbol system used to represent human experiences within a geographic or cultural community. Each culture places its own individual imprint on word symbols. Objects, events, experiences, and feelings have a particular label or name solely because a community of people has arbitrarily decided to so name them. Thus, because language is an inexact system of symbolically representing reality, the meanings for words are subject to a wide variety of interpretations. Language is the primary vehicle by which a culture transmits its beliefs, values, norms, and world view. Language gives people a means of interacting with other members of their culture and a means of thinking. Language thus serves both as a mechanism for communication and as a guide to social reality. Language influences perceptions, transmits meaning, and helps mold patterns of thought.

Patterns of Thought. The mental processes, forms of reasoning, and approaches to problem solution prevalent in a community make up another major component of culture. Unless they have had experiences with people from other cultures who follow different patterns of thought, most people assume everyone thinks and solves problems in much the same way. We must be aware, however, that there are cultural differences in aspects of thinking and knowing. This diversity can be clarified and related to intercultural communication by making a general comparison between Western and Eastern patterns of thought. In most Western thought there is an assumption of a direct relationship between mental concepts and the concrete world of reality. This orientation places great stock in logical considerations and rationality. There is a belief that truth is out there somewhere and that it can be discovered by following correct logical sequences—one need only turn over the right rocks in the right order and it will be there. The Eastern view, best illustrated by Taoist thought, holds that problems are solved quite differently. To begin with, people are not granted instant rationality, truth is not found by active searching and the application of Aristotelian modes of reasoning. On the contrary, one must wait, and if truth is to be known, it will make itself apparent. The major difference in these two views is in the area of activity: To the Western mind, human activity is paramount and ultimately will lead to the discovery of truth; in the Taoist tradition, truth is the active agent, and if it is to be known, it will be through the activity of truth making itself apparent.

A culture's thought patterns affect the way individuals in that culture communicate, which in turn affects the way each person responds to individuals from another culture. We cannot expect everyone to employ the same patterns of thinking, but understanding that many patterns exist and learning to accommodate them will facilitate our intercultural communication.

Nonverbal Processes

Verbal processes are the primary means for the exchange of thoughts and ideas, but closely related nonverbal processes often can overshadow them. Most authorities agree that the following topics comprise the realm of nonverbal processes: gestures, facial expressions, eye contact and gaze, posture and movement, touching, dress, objects and artifacts, silence, space, time, and paralanguage. As we turn to the nonverbal processes relevant to intercultural communication, we will consider three aspects: *nonverbal behavior* that functions as a silent form of language, the *concept of time*, and the *use and organization of space*.

Nonverbal Behavior. It would be foolish for us to try to examine all of the elements that constitute nonverbal behavior because of the tremendous range of activity that constitutes this form of human activity. An example or two will enable us to visualize how nonverbal issues fit into the overall scheme of intercultural understanding. For example, touch as a form of communication can demonstrate how nonverbal communication is a product of culture. German women as well as men shake hands at the outset of every social encounter; in the United States, women are less likely to shake hands. Vietnamese· men do not shake hands with women or elders unless the woman or the elder offers the hand first. In Thailand, people do not touch in public, and to touch someone on the head is a major social transgression. You can imagine the problems that could arise if one did not understand some of the differences.

Another illustrative example is eye contact. In the United States we are encouraged to maintain good eye contact when we communicate. In Japan and other Asian countries, however, eye contact often is not important, and among native Americans, children are taught that eye contact with an adult is a sign of disrespect.

The eyes can also be used to express feelings. For instance, widening the eyes may note surprise for an Anglo, but the feelings denoted by eye widening are culturally diverse. Widened eyes may also indicate anger by a Chinese, a request for help or assistance by a Hispanic, the issuance of a challenge by a French person, and a rhetorical or persuasive effect by a black.

As a component of culture, nonverbal expression has much in common with language: Both are coding systems that we learn and pass on as part of the cultural experience. Just as we learn that the word "stop" can mean to halt or cease, we also learn that an arm held up in the air with the palm facing another person frequently means the same thing. Because most nonverbal communication is culturally based, what it symbolizes often is a case of what a culture has transmitted to its members. The nonverbal symbol for suicide, for example, varies among cultures. In the United States it is usually a finger pointed at the temple or drawn across the throat. In Japan, it is a hand thrust onto the stomach, and in New Guinea it is a hand placed on the neck. Both nonverbal symbols and the responses they generate are part of cultural experience—what is passed from generation to generation. Every symbol takes on significance because of one's past experience with it. Even such simple acts as waving the hand can produce culturally diverse responses: In the United States, we tend to wave goodbye by placing the hand out with the palm down and moving the hand up and down; in India and in parts of Africa and South America, this is a beckoning gesture. We should also be aware that what may be a polite or friendly gesture in one culture may be an impolite and obscene gesture in another. Culture influences and directs those experiences, and is, therefore, a major contributor to how we send, receive, and respond to nonverbal symbols.

The Concept of Time. A culture's concept of time is its philosophy toward the past, present, and future and the importance or lack of importance it places on time. Most Western cultures think of time in lineal-spatial terms; we are time bound and well aware of the past, present, and future. In contrast, the Hopi Indians pay very little attention to time. They believe that each object—whether a person, plant, or animal—has its own time system.

Even within the dominant mainstream of American culture, we find groups that have learned to perceive time in ways that appear strange to many outsiders. Hispanics frequently refer to Mexican or Latino time when their timing differs from the predominant Anglo concept, and blacks often use what is referred to as BPT (black people's time) or hang-loose time—maintaining that priority belongs to what is happening at that instant.

Use of Space. The way in which people use space as a part of interpersonal communication is called _proxemics_. It involves not only the distance between people engaged in conversation but also their physical orientation. We are all most likely to have some familiarity with the fact that Arabs and Latins tend to interact physically closer together than do North American Anglos. What is important is to realize that people of different cultures have different ways in which they relate to one another spatially. Therefore, when talking to someone from another culture, we must expect what in our culture would be a violation of our personal space and be prepared to continue our interaction without reacting adversely. We may experience feelings that are difficult to handle; we may believe that the other person is overbearing, boorish, or even making unacceptable sexual advances when indeed the other person's movements are only manifestations of his or her cultural learning about how to use space.

Physical orientation is also culturally influenced, and it helps to define social relationships. North Americans prefer to sit where they are face to face or at right angles to one another. We seldom seek side-by-side arrangements. Chinese, on the other hand, often prefer a side-by-side arrangement and may feel uncomfortable when placed in a face-to-face situation.

We also tend to define social hierarchies through our nonverbal use of space. Sitting behind a desk while speaking with someone who is standing is usually a sign of a superior-subordinate relationship, with the socially superior person seated. Misunderstandings can easily occur in intercultural settings when two people, each acting according to the dictates of his or her culture, violate each other's expectations. If we were to remain seated when expected to rise, for example, we could easily violate a cultural norm and insult our host or guest unknowingly.

Room furnishings and size can also be an indication of social status. In corporate America, status within the corporation is often measured by desk size, office size, whether one has carpet on the office floor, and whether the carpet is wall to wall or merely a rug.

How we organize space also is a function of our culture. Our homes, for instance, preserve nonverbally our cultural beliefs and values. South American house designs are extremely private, with only one door opening onto the street and everything else behind walls. North Americans are used to large unwalled front yards with windows looking into the house, allowing passersby to see what goes on inside. In South America, a North American is liable to feel excluded and wonder about what goes on behind all those closed doors.

COMMUNICATION CONTEXT

Any communicative interaction takes place within some social and physical context. When people are communicating within their culture, they are usually aware of the context and it does little to hinder the communication. When people are engaged in intercultural communication, however, the context in which that communication takes place can have a strong impact. Unless both parties to intercultural communication are aware of how their culture affects the contextual element of communication, they can be in for some surprising communication difficulty.

Context and Communication

We begin with the assumption that communicative behavior is governed by rules—principles or regulations that govern conduct and procedure. In communication, rules act as a system of expected behavior patterns that organize interaction between individuals. Communication rules are both culturally and contextually bound. Although the social setting and situation may determine the type of rules that are appropriate, the culture determines the rules. In Iraq, for instance, a contextual rule prohibits females from having unfamiliar males visit them at home; in the United States, however, it is not considered socially inappropriate for unknown males to visit females at home. Rules dictate behavior by establishing appropriate responses to stimuli for a particular communication context.

Communication rules include both verbal and nonverbal components—the rules determine not only what should be said but how it should be said. Nonverbal rules apply to proper gestures, facial expressions, eye contact, proxemics, vocal tone, and body movements.

Unless one is prepared to function in the contextual environment of another culture, he or she may be in for an unpleasant experience. The intercultural situation can be one of high stress, both physically and mentally. The effects of this stress are called culture shock. In order to avoid culture shock, it is necessary to have a full understanding of communication context and how it varies culturally. We must remember that cultural contexts are neither right nor wrong, better or worse; they are just different.

Having determined that cultures develop rules that govern human interaction in specific contexts, we need now to gain some insight into the general concept of context. Anthropologist Edward T. Hall has written extensively about context.[1] Although he categorizes cultures as being either high-context or low-context, context really is a cultural dimension that ranges from high to low. An example of various cultures placed along that dimension can be seen in Figure 3.

In high-context cultures most of the information is either in the physical context or is internalized in the people who are a part of the interaction. Very little information is actually coded in the verbal message. In low-context cultures, however, most of the information is contained in the verbal message and very little is embedded in the context or within the participants. In high-context cultures such as those of Japan, Korea, and Taiwan, people tend to be more aware of their surroundings and their environment and do not rely on verbal communication as their main information source. The Korean language contains a word *nunchi* that literally means being able to communicate through your eyes. In

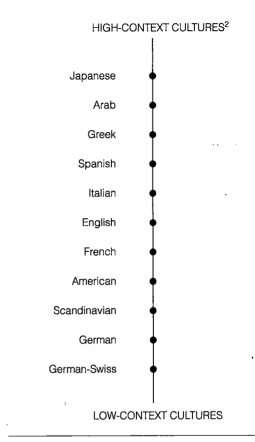

Figure 3 is headed "HIGH-CONTEXT CULTURES[2]" with the following cultures listed from top to bottom: Japanese, Arab, Greek, Spanish, Italian, English, French, American, Scandinavian, German, German-Swiss, and at the bottom "LOW-CONTEXT CULTURES".

Figure 3 High- and Low-Context Cultures

high-context cultures, so much information is available in the environment that it is unnecessary to state verbally that which is obvious. Oral statements of affection, for instance, are very rare—when the context says "I love you," it is not necessary to state it orally.

There are four major differences in how high- and low-context cultures affect the setting. First, verbal messages are extremely important in low-context cultures. It is in the verbal message that the information to be shared is coded; it is not readily available from the environment because people in low-context cultures do not tend to learn how to receive information from the environment through perception. Second, low-context people who rely primarily on verbal messages for information are perceived as less attractive and less credible by people in high-context cultures. Third, people in high-context cultures are more adept at reading nonverbal behavior and reading the environment. And, fourth, people in high-context cultures have an expectation that others are also able to understand the unarticulated communication; hence, they do not speak as much as people from low-context cultures.

SUMMARY

In many respects the relationship between culture and communication is reciprocal—each affects and influences the other. What we talk about; how we talk about it; what we see, attend to, or ignore; how we think; and what we think about are influenced by our culture. In turn, what we talk about, how we talk about it, and what we see help shape, define, and perpetuate our culture. Culture cannot exist without communication; one cannot change without causing change in the other.

We have suggested that the chief problem associated with intercultural communication is error in social perception brought about by cultural diversity that affects the perceptual process. The attribution of meaning to messages is in many respects influenced by the culture of the person responding to the message behavior. When the message being interpreted is encoded in another culture, the cultural influences and experiences that produced that message may have been entirely different from the cultural influences and experiences that are being drawn on to interpret and respond to the message. Consequently, unintended errors in meaning may arise because people with entirely different backgrounds are unable to understand one another accurately.

We have discussed several socio-cultural variables that are major sources of communication difficulty. Although they were discussed in isolation, we cannot allow ourselves to conclude that they are unrelated—they are all related in a matrix of cultural complexities. For successful intercultural communication, we must be aware of these cultural factors affecting communication in both our own culture and in the culture of the other party. We need to understand not only cultural differences, which will help us determine sources of potential problems, but also cultural similarities, which will help us become closer to one another.

The approach we have taken is also based on a fundamental assumption: The parties to intercultural communication must have an honest and sincere desire to communicate and to seek mutual understanding. This assumption requires favorable attitudes about intercultural communication and an elimination of superior-inferior relationships based on membership in particular cultures, races, religions, or ethnic groups. Unless this basic assumption has been satisfied, our theory of cultural diversity in social perception will not produce improvement in intercultural communication.

At the beginning of this article we mentioned how changes in transportation and communication technology had brought us to the brink of the global village. We also suggested that we, as a people, do not yet know how to live as global villagers. We want to return to this point as we finish here and leave you with some thoughts about it.

The prevailing direction in the United States today seems to be toward a pluralistic, multicultural society. An underlying assumption of this position, one that is seldom expressed or perhaps often realized, is that this requires that we as a society be accepting of the views, values, and behaviors of other cultures. This means that we must be willing to "live and let live." We do not seem able or willing to do this, however, nor are we sure that it is proper to do so in all circumstances. But if we are to get along with one another, we must develop this toleration for others' culturally diverse customs and behaviors—a task that will be difficult.

Even within the dominant mainstream culture, we are unable to accept diversity; for example, we find ourselves deeply divided over such issues as right to life versus freedom of choice. When we must cope with the diversity of customs, values, views, and behaviors inherent in a multicultural society, we will find ourselves in much greater states of frustration and peril. As an example, the CNN News Network carried a story on March 2, 1990 about fundamentalist Christians in a town who were demanding the removal of a statue of Buddha from in front of an Oriental restaurant because "it was the idol of a false God; it's in the New Testament." Also, several months ago the newspapers carried a story about a judge who dismissed wife-beating charges against an Asian man because this form of behavior was appropriate and acceptable in the man's culture. The action by the judge was immediately assailed by the feminist movement. This is not the arena to argue the rightness or the wrongness of the judge's decision, but this is the place to make you aware of the problems that we must face as we move toward a pluralistic, multicultural society. We hope that your thinking about this issue now will prepare you for your life in the global village.

NOTES

1. Hall, E. T. (1976). *Beyond Culture.* Garden City, N.Y.: Doubleday.

2. Copeland, L., and L. Griggs. (1985). *Going International: How to Make Friends and Deal Effectively in the Global Marketplace.* New York: Random House.

Communication in a Global Village

DEAN C. BARNLUND

Nearing Autumn's close.
My neighbor—
How does he live, I wonder?

—Bashō

These lines, written by one of the most cherished of *haiku* poets, express a timeless and universal curiosity in one's fellow man. When they were written, nearly three hundred years ago, the word "neighbor" referred to people very much like one's self—similar in dress, in diet, in custom, in language—who happened to live next door. Today relatively few people are surrounded by neighbors who are cultural replicas of themselves. Tomorrow we can expect to spend most of our lives in the company of neighbors who will speak in a different tongue, seek different values, move at a different pace, and interact according to a different script. Within no longer than a decade or two the probability of spending part of one's life in a foreign culture will exceed the probability a hundred years ago of ever leaving the town in which one was born. As our world is transformed our neighbors increasingly will be people whose life styles contrast sharply with our own.

The technological feasibility of such a global village is no longer in doubt. Only the precise date of its attainment is uncertain. The means already exist: in telecommunication systems linking the world by

From Dean C. Barnlund, *Public and Private Self in Japan and the United States* (Tokyo: Simul Press, Inc., 1975), pp. 3–24. Reprinted by permission of the publisher. Professor Barnlund teaches at San Francisco State University. Footnotes deleted.

satellite, in aircraft capable of moving people faster than the speed of sound, in computers which can disgorge facts more rapidly than men can formulate their questions. The methods for bringing people closer physically and electronically are clearly at hand. What is in doubt is whether the erosion of cultural boundaries through technology will bring the realization of a dream or a nightmare. Will a global village be a mere collection or a true community of men? Will its residents be neighbors capable of respecting and utilizing their differences, or clusters of strangers living in ghettos and united only in their antipathies for others?

Can we generate the new cultural attitudes required by our technological virtuosity? History is not very reassuring here. It has taken centuries to learn how to live harmoniously in the family, the tribe, the city state, and the nation. Each new stretching of human sensitivity and loyalty has taken generations to become firmly assimilated in the human psyche. And now we are forced into a quantum leap from the mutual suspicion and hostility that have marked the past relations between peoples into a world in which mutual respect and comprehension are requisite.

Even events of recent decades provide little basis for optimism. Increasing physical proximity has brought no millennium in human relations. If anything, it has appeared to intensify the divisions among people rather than to create a broader intimacy. Every new reduction in physical distance has made us more painfully aware of the psychic distance that divides people and has increased alarm over real or imagined differences. If today people occasionally choke on what seem to be indigestible differences between rich and poor, male and female, specialist and nonspecialist within cultures, what will happen tomorrow when people must assimilate and cope with still greater contrasts in life styles? Wider access to more people will be a doubtful victory if human beings find they have nothing to say to one another or cannot stand to listen to each other.

Time and space have long cushioned intercultural encounters, confining them to touristic ex-

changes. But this insulation is rapidly wearing thin. In the world of tomorrow we can expect to live—not merely vacation—in societies which seek different values and abide by different codes. There we will be surrounded by foreigners for long periods of time, working with others in the closest possible relationships. If people currently show little tolerance or talent for encounters with alien cultures, how can they learn to deal with constant and inescapable coexistence?

The temptation is to retreat to some pious hope or talismanic formula to carry us into the new age. "Meanwhile," as Edwin Reischauer reminds us, "we fail to do what we ourselves must do if 'one world' is ever to be achieved, and that is to develop the education, the skills and the attitudes that men must have if they are to build and maintain such a world. The time is short, and the needs are great. The task faces all men. But it is on the shoulders of people living in the strong countries of the world, such as Japan and the United States, that this burden falls with special weight and urgency."

Anyone who has truly struggled to comprehend another person—even those closest and most like himself—will appreciate the immensity of the challenge of intercultural communication. A greater exchange of people between nations, needed as that may be, carries with it no guarantee of increased cultural empathy; experience in other lands often does little but aggravate existing prejudices. Studying guidebooks or memorizing polite phrases similarly fails to explain differences in cultural perspectives. Programs of cultural enrichment, while they contribute to curiosity about other ways of life, do not cultivate the skills to function effectively in the cultures studied. Even concentrated exposure to a foreign language, valuable as it is, provides access to only one of the many codes that regulate daily affairs; human understanding is by no means guaranteed because conversants share the same dictionary. (Within the United States, where people inhabit a common territory and possess a common language, mutuality of meaning among Mexican-Americans, White Americans, Black-Americans, Indian-Americans—to say nothing of old and young, poor and rich, pro-establishment and anti-establishment cultures—is a sporadic and unreliable occurrence.) Useful as all these measures are for enlarging appreciation of diverse cultures, they fall short of what is needed for a global village to survive.

What seems most critical is to find ways of gaining entrance into the assumptive world of another culture, to identify the norms that govern face-to-face relations, and to equip people to function within a social system that is foreign but no longer incomprehensible. Without this kind of insight people are condemned to remain outsiders no matter how long they live in another country. Its institutions and its customs will be interpreted inevitably from the premises and through the medium of their own culture. Whether they notice something or overlook it, respect or ridicule it, express or conceal their reaction will be dictated by the logic of their own rather than the alien culture.

There are, of course, shelves and shelves of books on the cultures of the world. They cover the history, religion, political thought, music, sculpture, and industry of many nations. And they make fascinating and provocative reading. But only in the vaguest way do they suggest what it is that really distinguishes the behavior of a Samoan, a Congolese, a Japanese, or an American. Rarely do the descriptions of a political structure or religious faith explain precisely when and why certain topics are avoided or why specific gestures carry such radically different meanings according to the context in which they appear.

When former President Nixon and former Premier Sato met to discuss a growing problem concerning trade in textiles between Japan and the United States, Premier Sato announced that since they were on such good terms with each other the deliberations would be "three parts talk and seven parts 'haragei.'" Translated literally, "haragei" means to communicate through the belly, that is to feel out intuitively rather than verbally state the precise position of each person.

Subscribing to this strategy—one that governs many interpersonal exchanges in his culture—Premier Sato conveyed without verbal elaboration his comprehension of the plight of American textile firms threatened by accelerating exports of Japanese fabrics to the United States. President Nixon—similarly abiding by norms that govern interaction within his culture—took this comprehension of the American position to mean that new export quotas would be forthcoming shortly.

During the next few weeks both were shocked at the consequences of their meeting: Nixon was infuriated to learn that the new policies he expected were not forthcoming, and Sato was upset to find that he had unwittingly triggered a new wave of hostility toward his country. If prominent officials, surrounded by foreign advisers, can commit such grievous communicative blunders, the plight of the ordinary citizen may be suggested. Such intercultural collisions, forced upon the public consciousness by the grave consequences they carry and the extensive publicity they receive, only hint at the wider and more frequent confusions and hostilities that disrupt the negotiations of lesser officials, business executives, professionals and even visitors in foreign countries.

Every culture expresses its purpose and conducts its affairs through the medium of communication. Cultures exist primarily to create and preserve common systems of symbols by which their members can assign and exchange meanings. Unhappily, the distinctive rules that govern these symbol systems are far from obvious. About some of these codes, such as language, we have extensive knowledge. About others, such as gestures and facial codes, we have only rudimentary knowledge. On many others—rules governing topical appropriateness, customs regulating physical contact, time and space codes, strategies for the management of conflict—we have almost no systematic knowledge. To crash another culture with only the vaguest notion of its underlying dynamics reflects not only a provincial naïvete but a dangerous form of cultural arrogance.

It is differences in meaning, far more than mere differences in vocabulary, that isolate cultures, and that cause them to regard each other as strange or even barbaric. It is not too surprising that many cultures refer to themselves as "The People," relegating all other human beings to a subhuman form of life.

To the person who drinks blood, the eating of meat is repulsive. Someone who conveys respect by standing is upset by someone who conveys it by sitting down; both may regard kneeling as absurd. Burying the dead may prompt tears in one society, smiles in another, and dancing in a third. If spitting on the street makes sense to some, it will appear bizarre that others carry their spit in their pocket; neither may quite appreciate someone who spits to express gratitude. The bullfight that constitutes an almost religious ritual for some seems a cruel and inhumane way of destroying a defenseless animal to others. Although staring is acceptable social behavior in some cultures, in others it is a thoughtless invasion of privacy. Privacy, itself, is without universal meaning.

Note that none of these acts involves an insurmountable linguistic challenge. The words that describe these acts—eating, spitting, showing respect, fighting, burying, and staring—are quite translatable into most languages. The issue is more conceptual than linguistic; each society places events in its own cultural frame and it is these frames that bestow the unique meaning and differentiated response they produce.

As we move or are driven toward a global village and increasingly frequent cultural contact, we need more than simply greater factual knowledge of each other. We need, more specifically, to identify what might be called the "rulebooks of meaning" that distinguish one culture from another. For to grasp the way in which other cultures perceive the world, and the assumptions and values that are the foundation of these perceptions, is to gain access to the experience of other human beings. Access to the world view and the communicative style of other cultures may not only enlarge our own way of experiencing the world but enable us to maintain constructive relationships with societies that operate according to a different logic than our own.

SOURCES OF MEANING

To survive, psychologically as well as physically, human beings must inhabit a world that is relatively free of ambiguity and is reasonably predictable. Some sort of structure must be placed upon the endless profusion of incoming signals. The infant, born into a world of flashing, hissing, moving images, soon learns to adapt by resolving this chaos into toys and tables, dogs and parents. Even adults who have had their vision or hearing restored through surgery describe the world as a frightening and sometimes unbearable experience; only after days of effort are they able to transform blurs and noises into meaningful and therefore manageable experiences.

It is commonplace to talk as if the world "has" meaning, to ask what "is" the meaning of a phrase, a gesture, a painting, a contract. Yet when thought about, it is clear that events are devoid of meaning until someone assigns it to them. There is no appropriate response to a bow or a handshake, a shout or a whisper, until it is interpreted. A drop of water and the color red have no meaning, they simply exist. The aim of human perception is to make the world intelligible so that it can be managed successfully; the attribution of meaning is a prerequisite to and preparation for action.

People are never passive receivers, merely absorbing events of obvious significance, but are active in assigning meaning to sensation. What any event acquires in the way of meaning appears to reflect a transaction between what is there to be seen or heard, and what the interpreter brings to it in the way of past experience and prevailing motive. Thus the attribution of meanings is always a creative process by which the raw data of sensation are transformed to fit the aims of the observer.

The diversity of reactions that can be triggered by a single experience—meeting a stranger, negotiating a contract, attending a textile conference—is immense. Each observer is forced to see it through his own eyes, interpret it in the light of his own values, fit it to the requirements of his own circumstances. As a consequence, every object and message is seen by every observer from a somewhat different perspective. Each person will note some features and neglect others. Each will accept some relations among the facts and deny others. Each will arrive at some conclusion, tentative or certain, as the sounds and forms resolve into a "temple" or "barn," a "compliment" or "insult."

Provide a group of people with a set of photographs, even quite simple and ordinary photographs, and note how diverse are the meanings they provoke. Afterward they will recall and forget different pictures, they will also assign quite distinctive meanings to those they do remember. Some will recall the mood of a picture, others the actions; some the appearance and others the attitudes of persons portrayed. Often the observers cannot agree upon even the most "objective" details—the number of people, the precise location and identity of simple objects. A difference in frame of mind—fatigue, hunger, excitement, anger—will change dramatically what they report they have "seen."

It should not be surprising that people raised in different families, exposed to different events, praised and punished for different reasons, should come to view the world so differently. As George Kelly has noted, people see the world through templates which force them to construe events in unique ways. These patterns or grids which we fit over the realities of the world are cut from our own experience and values, and they predispose us to certain interpretations. Industrialist and farmer do not see the "same" land; husband and wife do not plan for the "same" child; doctor and patient do not discuss the "same" disease; borrower and creditor do not negotiate the "same" mortgage; daughter and daughter-in-law do not react to the "same" mother.

The world each person creates for himself is a distinctive world, not the same world others occupy. Each fashions from every incident whatever meanings fit his own private biases. These biases, taken together, constitute what has been called the "assumptive world of the individual." The world each person gets inside his head is the only world he knows. And it is this symbolic world, not the real world, that he talks about, argues about, laughs about, fights about.

Interpersonal Encounters

Every communication, interpersonal or intercultural, is a transaction between these private worlds. As people talk they search for symbols that will enable them to share their experience and converge upon a common meaning. This process, often long and sometimes painful, makes it possible finally to reconcile apparent or real differences between them. Various words are used to describe this moment. When it involves an integration of facts or ideas, it is usually called an "agreement"; when it involves sharing a mood or feeling, it is referred to as "empathy" or "rapport." But "understanding" is a broad enough term to cover both possibilities; in either case it identifies the achievement of a common meaning.

If understanding is a measure of communicative success, a simple formula—which might be called the *Interpersonal Equation*—may clarify the major factors that contribute to its achievement.

Interpersonal Understanding = f (Similarity of Perceptual Orientations, Similarity of Belief Systems, Similarity of Communicative Styles)

That is, "Interpersonal Understanding" is a function of or dependent upon the degree of "Similarity of Perceptual Orientations," "Similarity of Systems of Belief," and "Similarity of Communicative Styles." Each of these terms requires some elaboration.

"Similarity in Perceptual Orientations" refers to a person's prevailing approach to reality and the degree of flexibility he manifests in organizing it. Some people can scan the world broadly, searching for diversity of experience, preferring the novel and unpredictable. They may be drawn to new foods, new music, new ways of thinking. Others seem to scan the world more narrowly, searching to confirm past experience, preferring the known and predictable. They secure satisfaction from old friends, traditional art forms, familiar life styles. The former have a high tolerance for novelty; the latter a low tolerance for novelty.

It is a balance between these tendencies, of course, that characterizes most people. Within the same person attraction to the unfamiliar and the familiar coexist. Which prevails at any given moment is at least partly a matter of circumstance: when secure, people may widen their perceptual field, accommodate new ideas or actions; when they feel insecure they may narrow their perceptual field to protect existing assumptions from the threat of new beliefs or life styles. The balance may be struck in still other ways: some people like to live in a stable physical setting with everything in its proper place, but welcome new emotional or intellectual challenges; others enjoy living in a chaotic and disordered environment but would rather avoid exposing themselves to novel or challenging ideas.

People differ also in the degree to which their perceptions are flexible or rigid. Some react with curiosity and delight to unpredictable and uncategorizable events. Others are disturbed or uncomfortable in the presence of the confusing and complex. There are people who show a high degree of tolerance for ambiguity; others manifest a low tolerance for ambiguity. When confronted with the complications and confusions that surround many daily events, the former tend to avoid immediate closure and delay judgment while the latter seek immediate closure and evaluation. Those with little tolerance for ambiguity tend to respond categorically, that is, by reference to the class names for things (businessmen, radicals, hippies, foreigners) rather than to their unique and differentiating features.

It would be reasonable to expect that individuals who approach reality similarly might understand each other easily, and laboratory research confirms this conclusion: people with similar perceptual styles attract one another, understand each other better, work more efficiently together and with greater satisfaction than those whose perceptual orientations differ.

"Similarity in Systems of Belief" refers not to the way people view the world, but to the conclusions they draw from their experience. Everyone develops a variety of opinions toward divorce, poverty, religion, television, sex, and social customs. When belief and disbelief systems coincide, people are likely to understand and appreciate each other better. Research done by Donn Byrne and replicated by the author demonstrates how powerfully human beings are drawn to those who hold the same beliefs and how sharply they are repelled by those who do not.

Subjects in these experiments were given questionnaires requesting their opinions on twenty-six topics. After completing the forms, each was asked to rank the thirteen most important and least important topics. Later each person was given four forms, ostensibly filled out by people in another group but actually filled out to show varying degrees of agreement with their own answers, and invited to choose among them with regard to their attractiveness as associates. The results were clear: people most preferred to talk with those whose attitudes duplicated their own exactly, next chose those who agreed with them on all important issues, next chose those with similar views on unimportant issues, and finally and reluctantly chose those who disagreed with them completely. It appears that most people most of the time find satisfying relationships easiest to achieve with someone who shares their own hierarchy of beliefs. This, of course, converts many human encounters into rituals of ratification, each person looking to the other only to obtain endorsement and applause for his own beliefs. It is, however, what is often meant by "interpersonal understanding."

Does the same principle hold true for "Similarity of Communicative Styles"? To a large extent, yes. But not completely. By "communicative style" is meant the topics people prefer to discuss, their favorite forms of interaction—ritual, repartee, argument, self-disclosure—and the depth of involvement they demand of each other. It includes the extent to which communicants rely upon the same channels—vocal, verbal, physical—for conveying information, and the extent to which they are tuned to the same level of meaning, that is, to the factual or emotional content of messages. The use of a common vocabulary and even preference for similar metaphors may help people to understand each other.

But some complementarity in conversational style may also help. Talkative people may prefer quiet partners, the more aggressive may enjoy the less aggressive, those who seek affection may be drawn to the more affection-giving, simply because both can find the greatest mutual satisfaction when interpersonal styles mesh. Even this sort of complementarity, however, may reflect a case of similarity in definitions of each other's conversational role.

This hypothesis, too, has drawn the interest of communicologists. One investigator found that people paired to work on common tasks were much more effective if their communicative styles were similar than if they were dissimilar. Another social scientist found that teachers tended to give higher grades on tests to students whose verbal styles matched their own than to students who gave equally valid answers but did not phrase them as their instructors might. To establish common meanings seems to require that conversants share a common vocabulary and compatible ways of expressing ideas and feelings.

It must be emphasized that perceptual orientations, systems of belief, and communicative styles do not exist or operate independently. They overlap and affect each other. They combine in complex ways to determine behavior. What a person says is influenced by what he believes and what he believes, in turn, by what he sees. His perceptions and beliefs are themselves partly a product of his manner of communicating with others. The terms that compose the Interpersonal Equation constitute not three isolated but three interdependent variables. They provide three perspectives to use in the analysis of communicative acts.

The Interpersonal Equation suggests there is an underlying narcissistic bias in human societies that draws similar people together. Each seeks to find in the other a reflection of himself, someone who views the world as he does, who interprets it as he does, and who expresses himself in a similar way. It is not surprising, then, that artists should be drawn to artists, radicals to radicals, Jews to Jews—or Japanese to Japanese and Americans to Americans.

The opposite seems equally true: people tend to avoid those who challenge their assumptions, who dismiss their beliefs, and who communicate in strange and unintelligible ways. When one reviews history, whether he examines crises within or between cultures, he finds people have consistently shielded themselves, segregated themselves, even fortified themselves, against wide differences in modes of perception or expression (in many cases, indeed, have persecuted and conquered the infidel

and afterwards substituted their own cultural ways for the offending ones). Intercultural defensiveness appears to be only a counterpart of interpersonal defensiveness in the face of uncomprehended or incomprehensible differences.

INTERCULTURAL ENCOUNTERS

Every culture attempts to create a "universe of discourse" for its members, a way in which people can interpret their experience and convey it to one another. Without a common system of codifying sensations, life would be absurd and all efforts to share meanings doomed to failure. This universe of discourse—one of the most precious of all cultural legacies—is transmitted to each generation in part consciously and in part unconsciously. Parents and teachers give explicit instruction in it by praising or criticizing certain ways of dressing, of thinking, of gesturing, of responding to the acts of others. But the most significant aspect of any cultural code may be conveyed implicitly, not by rule or lesson but through modelling behavior. The child is surrounded by others who, through the mere consistency of their actions as males and females, mothers and fathers, salesclerks and policemen, display what is appropriate behavior. Thus the grammar of any culture is sent and received largely unconsciously, making one's own cultural assumptions and biases difficult to recognize. They seem so obviously right that they require no explanation.

In *The Open and Closed Mind*, Milton Rokeach poses the problem of cultural understanding in its simplest form, but one that can readily demonstrate the complications of communication between cultures. It is called the "Denny Doodlebug Problem." Readers are given all the rules that govern his culture: Denny is an animal that always faces North, and can move only by jumping; he can jump large distances or small distances, but can change direction only after jumping four times in any direction; he can jump North, South, East or West, but not diagonally. Upon concluding a jump his master places some food three feet directly West of him. Surveying the situation, Denny concludes he must jump four times to reach the food. No more or less. And he is right. All the reader has to do is explain the circumstances that make his conclusion correct.

The large majority of people who attempt this problem fail to solve it, despite the fact that they are given all the rules that control behavior in this culture. If there is difficulty in getting inside the simplistic world of Denny Doodlebug—where the cultural code has already been broken and handed to us—imagine the complexity of comprehending behavior in societies where codes have not yet been deciphered. And where even those who obey these codes are only vaguely aware and can rarely describe the underlying sources of their own actions.

If two people, both of whom spring from a single culture, must often shout to be heard across the void that separates their private worlds, one can begin to appreciate the distance to be overcome when people of different cultural identities attempt to talk. Even with the most patient dedication to seeking a common terminology, it is surprising that people of alien cultures are able to hear each other at all. And the peoples of Japan and the United States would appear to constitute a particularly dramatic test of the ability to cross an intercultural divide. Consider the disparity between them.

Here is Japan, a tiny isolated nation with a minimum of resources, buffeted by periodic disasters, overcrowded with people, isolated by physical fact and cultural choice, nurtured in Shinto and Buddhist religions, permeated by a deep respect for nature, nonmaterialist in philosophy, intuitive in thought, hierarchical in social structure. Eschewing the explicit, the monumental, the bold and boisterous, it expresses its sensuality in the form of impeccable gardens, simple rural temples, asymmetrical flower arrangements, a theater unparalleled for containment of feeling, an art and literature remarkable for their delicacy, and crafts noted for their honest and earthy character. Its people, among the most homogeneous of men, are modest and apologetic in manner, communicate in an ambiguous and evocative language, are engrossed in interpersonal rituals and prefer inner serenity to influencing others. They occupy unpretentious buildings of wood and paper and live in cities laid out as casually as farm villages. Suddenly from these rice paddies emerges an industrial giant, surpassing rival nations with decades of industrial experience, greater resources, and a larger reserve of technicians. Its labor, working longer, harder and more frantically than any in the world, builds the earth's largest city, constructs some of its ugliest buildings, promotes the most garish and insistent advertising anywhere, and pollutes its air and water beyond the imagination.

And here is the United States, an immense country, sparsely settled, richly endowed, tied through waves of immigrants to the heritage of Europe, yet forced to subdue nature and find fresh solutions to the problems of survival. Steeped in the Judeo-Christian tradition, schooled in European abstract and analytic thought, it is materialist and experimental in outlook, philosophically pragmatic, politically equalitarian, economically competitive, its raw individualism sometimes tempered by a humanitarian concern for others. Its cities are studies in geometry along whose avenues rise shafts of steel and glass subdivided into separate cubicles for separate activities and separate people. Its popular arts are characterized by the hugeness of Cinemascope, the spontaneity of jazz, the earthy loudness of rock; in its fine arts the experimental, striking, and monumental often stifle the more subtle revelation. The people, a smorgasbord of races, religions, dialects, and nationalities, are turned expressively outward, impatient with rituals and rules, casual and flippant, gifted in logic and argument, approachable and direct yet given to flamboyant and exaggerated assertion. They are curious about one another, open and helpful, yet display a missionary zeal for changing one another. Suddenly this nation whose power and confidence have placed it in a dominant position in the world intellectually and politically, whose style of life has permeated the planet, finds itself uncertain of its direction, doubts its own premises and values, questions its motives and materialism, and engages in an orgy of self criticism.

It is when people nurtured in such different psychological worlds meet that differences in cultural perspectives and communicative codes may sabotage efforts to understand one another. Repeated collisions between a foreigner and the members of a contrasting culture often produce what is called "culture shock." It is a feeling of helplessness, even of terror or anger, that accompanies working in an alien society. One feels trapped in an absurd and indecipherable nightmare.

It is as if some hostile leprechaun had gotten into the works and as a cosmic caper rewired the connections that hold society together. Not only do the actions of others no longer make sense, but it is impossible even to express one's own intentions clearly. "Yes" comes out meaning "No." A wave of the hand means "come," or it may mean "go." Formality may be regarded as childish, or as a devious form of flattery. Statements of fact may be heard as statements of conceit. Arriving early, or arriving late, embarrasses or impresses. "Suggestions" may be treated as "ultimatums," or precisely the opposite. Failure to stand at the proper moment, or failure to sit, may be insulting. The compliment intended to express gratitude instead conveys a sense of distance. A smile signifies disappointment rather than pleasure.

If the crises that follow such intercultural encounters are sufficiently dramatic or the communicants unusually sensitive, they may recognize the source of their trouble. If there is patience and constructive intention the confusion can sometimes be clarified. But more often the foreigner, without knowing it, leaves behind him a trail of frustration, mistrust, and even hatred *of which he is totally unaware*. Neither he nor his associates recognize that their difficulty springs from sources deep within the rhetoric of their own societies. Each sees himself as acting in ways that are thoroughly sensible, honest and considerate. And—given the rules governing his own universe of discourse—each is. Unfortunately, there are few cultural universals, and the degree of overlap in communicative codes is always less than perfect. Experience can be transmitted with fidelity only when the unique properties of

each code are recognized and respected, or where the motivation and means exist to bring them into some sort of alignment.

THE COLLECTIVE UNCONSCIOUS

Among the greatest insights of this modern age are two that bear a curious affinity to each other. The first, evolving from the efforts of psychologists, particularly Sigmund Freud, revealed the existence of an "individual unconscious." The acts of human beings were found to spring from motives of which they were often vaguely or completely unaware. Their unique perceptions of events arose not from the facts outside their skins but from unrecognized assumptions inside them. When, through intensive analysis, they obtained some insight into these assumptions, they became free to develop other ways of seeing and acting which contributed to their greater flexibility in coping with reality.

The second of these generative ideas, flowing from the work of anthropologists, particularly Margaret Mead and Ruth Benedict, postulated a parallel idea in the existence of a "cultural unconscious." Students of primitive cultures began to see that there was nothing divine or absolute about cultural norms. Every society had its own way of viewing the universe, and each developed from its premises a coherent set of rules of behavior. Each tended to be blindly committed to its own style of life and regarded all others as evil. The fortunate person who was able to master the art of living in foreign cultures often learned that his own mode of life was only one among many. With this insight he became free to choose from among cultural values those that seemed to best fit his peculiar circumstances.

Cultural norms so completely surround people, so permeate thought and action, that few ever recognize the assumptions on which their lives and their sanity rest. As one observer put it, if birds were suddenly endowed with scientific curiosity they might examine many things, but the sky itself would be overlooked as a suitable subject; if fish were to become curious about the world, it would never occur to them to begin by investigating water. For birds and fish would take the sky and sea for granted, unaware of their profound influence because they comprise the medium for every act. Human beings, in a similar way, occupy a symbolic universe governed by codes that are unconsciously acquired and automatically employed. So much so that they rarely notice that the ways they interpret and talk about events are distinctively different from the ways people conduct their affairs in other cultures.

As long as people remain blind to the sources of their meanings, they are imprisoned within them. These cultural frames of reference are no less confining simply because they cannot be seen or touched. Whether it is an individual neurosis that keeps an individual out of contact with his neighbors, or a collective neurosis that separates neighbors of different cultures, both are forms of blindness that limit what can be experienced and what can be learned from others.

It would seem that everywhere people would desire to break out of the boundaries of their own experiential worlds. Their ability to react sensitively to a wider spectrum of events and peoples requires an overcoming of such cultural parochialism. But, in fact, few attain this broader vision. Some, of course, have little opportunity for wider cultural experience, though this condition should change as the movement of people accelerates. Others do not try to widen their experience because they prefer the old and familiar, seek from their affairs only further confirmation of the correctness of their own values. Still others recoil from such experiences because they feel it dangerous to probe too deeply into the personal or cultural unconscious. Exposure may reveal how tenuous and arbitrary many cultural norms are; such exposure might force people to acquire new bases for interpreting events. And even for the many who do seek actively to enlarge the variety of human beings with whom they are capable of communicating there are still difficulties.

Cultural myopia persists not merely because of inertia and habit, but chiefly because it is so difficult to overcome. One acquires a personality and a cul-

ture in childhood, long before he is capable of comprehending either of them. To survive, each person masters the perceptual orientations, cognitive biases, and communicative habits of his own culture. But once mastered, objective assessment of these same processes is awkward since the same mechanisms that are being evaluated must be used in making the evaluations. Once a child learns Japanese or English or Navaho, the categories and grammar of each language predispose him to perceive and think in certain ways, and discourage him from doing so in other ways. When he attempts to discover why he sees or thinks as he does, he uses the same techniques he is trying to identify. Once one becomes an Indian, an Ibo, or a Frenchman—or even a priest or scientist—it is difficult to extricate oneself from that mooring long enough to find out what one truly is or wants.

Fortunately, there may be a way around this paradox. Or promise of a way around it. It is to expose the culturally distinctive ways various peoples construe events and seek to identify the conventions that connect what is seen with what is thought with what is said. Once this cultural grammar is assimilated and the rules that govern the exchange of meanings are known, they can be shared and learned by those who choose to work and live in alien cultures.

When people within a culture face an insurmountable problem they turn to friends, neighbors, associates, for help. To them they explain their predicament, often in distinctive personal ways. Through talking it out, however, there often emerge new ways of looking at the problem, fresh incentive to attack it, and alternative solutions to it. This sort of interpersonal exploration is often successful within a culture for people share at least the same communicative style even if they do not agree completely in their perceptions or beliefs.

When people communicate between cultures, where communicative rules as well as the substance of experience differs, the problems multiply. But so, too, do the number of interpretations and alternatives. If it is true that the more people differ the harder it is for them to understand each other, it is equally true that the more they differ the more they have to teach and learn from each other. To do so, of course, there must be mutual respect and sufficient curiosity to overcome the frustrations that occur as they flounder from one misunderstanding to another. Yet the task of coming to grips with differences in communicative styles—between or within cultures—is prerequisite to all other types of mutuality.

Intercultural Communication

MICHAEL ARGYLE

INTRODUCTION

Many people have to communicate and work with members of other cultures, and social skills training is now being given to some of these who are about to work abroad. Intercultural communication is necessary for several kinds of people:

1. Tourists are probably the largest category, though they stay for the shortest periods and need to master only a few simple situations—meals, travel, shopping, taxis, etc. To a large extent they are shielded from the local culture by the international hotel culture.

2. Business, governmental, and university visitors, on short-business trips, have to cope with a wider range of problems, but are often accommodated in hotels or somewhere similar, and looked after by other expatriates. They, too, are somewhat shielded from the local culture; they rarely learn the language and are given a great deal of help.

3. Businessmen, or others on longer visits of up to five years, students who stay from one to three years, and members of the Peace Corps and Voluntary Service Overseas who stay for two years. This is much more demanding, involving living in a house or apartment, coping with many aspects of the local culture and learning at least some of the language.

From Stephen Bochner (ed.), *Cultures in Contact: Studies in Cross-Cultural Interaction* (Oxford: Permagon Press, 1982), pp. 61–79. Reprinted by permission of the publisher and the author. Mr. Argyle is a reader in Social Psychology in the Department of Experimental Psychology at Oxford University.

4. Immigration may take place as a deliberate move, or as a gradual process while a visit becomes extended. This requires mastery of the new culture, as well as changes of attitude and self-image.

5. Those who stay at home may meet visitors from abroad, and may need to work effectively with them. They may also have to deal with refugees, those from other racial groups and other social classes. However, these contacts are usually limited to meals and work settings.

A number of category schemes have been produced to describe the main modes of response of visitors to different cultures. The principal alternatives are: (1) detached observers, who avoid involvement; (2) reluctant and cautious participants in the local culture; (3) enthusiastic participants, some of whom come to reject their original culture; and (4) settlers (Brein and David 1971).

How can intercultural effectiveness be assessed? An important minimal criterion is whether an individual manages to complete the planned tour or whether he packs up and returns home early. For some British firms as many as 60 percent of those posted to Africa or the Middle East fail to complete their tours, at great costs to the firms. For those who succeed in staying the course there are several possible indices of success:

1. Subjective ratings of comfort and satisfaction with life in the other culture (e.g., Gudykunst, Hammer, and Wiseman 1977).

2. Ratings by members of the host culture of the acceptability or competence of the visitor (e.g., Collett 1971).

3. Ratings by the field supervisor of an individual's effectiveness at the job, as has been used in Peace Corps studies. The effectiveness of salesmen could be measured objectively, and this applies to a number of other occupational roles.

4. Performance in role-played intercultural group tasks, as used by Chemers et al. (1966).

Hammer, Gudykunst, and Wiseman (1978) analyzed ratings by returned visitors to other cultures and found that they recognized three dimensions of intercultural competence (ICC): (a) ability to deal with psychological stress, (b) ability to communicate effectively, and (c) ability to establish interpersonal relations.

Competent performance as a visitor to another culture, or in dealing with members of another culture, can be regarded as a social skill, analogous to the skills of teaching, interviewing, and the rest. ICC is different in that a wide range of situations and types of performance are involved, together with a variety of goals. Intercultural skills may include some quite new skills, where quite different situations or rules are involved, such as bargaining, or special formal occasions. It may be necessary to perform familiar skills in a modified style, e.g., a more authoritarian kind of supervision, or more intimate social relationships. There are often a number of themes or modes of interaction in a culture, which are common to a wide range of situations. I suggest that these themes can be the most useful focus of training for ICC. In the next section we shall examine the main themes of this kind.

There is a special phenomenon here which has no clear equivalent among other social skills, i.e., "culture shock." Oberg (1960) used this term to refer to the state of acute anxiety produced by unfamiliar social norms and social signals. Others have extended the notion to include the fatigue of constant adaptation, the sense of loss of familiar food, companions, etc., rejection of the host population or rejection by it, confusion of values or identity, discomfort at violation of values, and a feeling of incompetence at dealing with the environment (Taft 1977).

Some degree of culture shock is common among those living abroad for the first time, especially in a very different culture, and it may last six months or longer. Those going abroad for a limited period, like a year, show a U-shaped pattern of discomfort: in the first stage they are elated, enjoy the sights, and are well looked after. In the second stage they have to cope with domestic life, and things get more difficult; they keep to the company of expatriates and are in some degree of culture shock. In the third phase they have learned to cope better and are looking forward to returning home. There may be problems when they do return home, and many people experience problems of re-entry, due for example to a loss of status, or a less exciting life (Brein and David 1971).

Another special problem for ICC is how far a visitor should accommodate to local styles of behavior. It is the general experience of Europeans and Americans in Africa and Third World countries generally, that they are *not* expected to wear local clothes or engage in exotic greetings. There seems to be a definite "role of the visitor" to which one is expected to conform. Rather greater accommodation to local ways is expected of those who stay for longer periods, and this may include mastering the language. In the United States, on the other hand, much greater conformity is expected, probably as a result of the long history of assimilating immigrants. Where total conformity is not required, it is still expected that visitors shall show a positive attitude towards the local culture, that one should not complain or criticize, like the so-called "whingeing Pom" in Australia. There may be a temptation to keep to hotels, clubs, and cantonment, but this will lead to isolation from the local community. Bochner, McLeod, and Linn (1977) found that foreign students usually had friends both from their home country and the local one—the latter were needed to help them cope with the culture.

In this article I shall examine some of the areas of difference between cultures, which can give rise to communication problems. Any successful form of social skills training (SST) for ICC should take account of these differences. Then I shall discuss the main forms of training which have been developed for this purpose.

CULTURAL DIFFERENCES IN SOCIAL INTERACTION

Language

This is one of the most important differences between many cultures, and one of the greatest barriers. The person who has learned a language quite well can still make serious mistakes, as with the Dutchman on a ship who was asked if he was a good sailor and replied indignantly that he was not a sailor but a manager.

Several studies have shown that language fluency is a necessary condition for the adjustment of foreign students in the United States, though there is also evidence that confidence in the use of language regardless of ability is just as important (Gullahorn and Gullahorn 1966). Often there are variations in accent, dialect, or grammar—as in Black American English, or in the actual language used—as in multilingual communities. An individual may indicate a positive or negative attitude to another by shifting towards a more similar or less similar speech style (Giles and Powesland 1975). Visitors to another culture should be aware of the impression they are creating by the speech style which they use. While efforts to speak the language are usually well received, this is not always so; the French dislike the inaccurate use of their language. Taylor and Simard (1975) found that lack of interaction between English and French Canadians was less due to lack of language skills than to attitudes; language helped to preserve ethnic identity.

Most cultures have a number of forms of polite usage, which may be misleading. These may take the form of exaggeration or modesty. Americans ask questions which are really orders or requests ("Would you like to . . . ?"). In every culture, in many situations, there are special forms of words, or types of conversation, which are thought to be appropriate—to ask a girl for a date, to disagree with someone at a committee, to introduce people to each other, and so on. Americans prefer directness, but Mexicans regard openness as a form of weakness or treachery, and think one should not allow the outside world to penetrate their thoughts. Frankness by Peace Corps volunteers in the Philippines leads to disruption of smooth social relationships (Brein and David 1971).

There are cultural differences in the sequential structure of conversations. The nearly universal question–answer sequence is not found in some African cultures where information is precious and not readily given away (Goody 1978). In Asian coun-

Table 1 Accuracy of Recognition of Nonverbal Cues for Emotions and Interpersonal Attitudes by English, Italian, and Japanese, Expressed in Percentages

Judges	Performers			
	English	Italian	Japanese	Average
English	60.5	55	36	50
Italian	52	61.5	29	47
Japanese	54	56	43	51
Average	56	57	36	

From Shimoda, Argyle, and Ricci Bitti 1978.

tries the word "no" is rarely used, so that "yes" can mean "no" or "perhaps." Saying "no" would lead to loss of face by the other, so indirect methods of conveying the message may be used, such as serving a banana (an unsuitable object) with tea to indicate that a marriage was unacceptable (Cleveland, Mangone, and Adams 1960). The episode structure of conversations varies a lot: Arabs and others have a "run-in" period of informal chat for about half an hour before getting down to business.

Some of these differences are due to different use of nonverbal signals. Erickson (1976) found that White Americans interviewing Blacks often thought the interviewee wasn't attending or understanding, and kept rewording questions in simpler and simpler forms. In several cultures "thank you" is signalled nonverbally; in China this is done at meals by rapping lightly on the table.

Nonverbal Communication (NVC)

It is now known that NVC plays several essential parts in social interaction—communicating attitudes to others, e.g., of like-dislike, expressing emotions, and in supporting speech by elaborating on utterances, providing feedback from listeners, and managing synchronizing. Although nonverbal signals are used in similar ways in all cultures, there are also differences and these can easily produce

misunderstanding (Argyle 1975). Triandis, Vassiliou, and Nassiakou (1968) observed that friendly criticism may be interpreted as hatred, and very positive attitudes as neutral, by someone from another culture. Several studies have found that if people from culture A are trained to use the nonverbal signals of culture B (gaze, distance, etc.), they will be liked more by members of the second culture (e.g., Collett 1971).

The face is the most important source of NVC. Similar basic emotional expressions are found in all cultures, and are at least partially innate. However, Chan (1979) has found that the Chinese express anger and disgust by narrowing the eyes, the reverse of that found in the United States. There are also different display rules, prescribing when these expressions may be shown, where one may laugh, cry, and so on (Ekman, Friesen, and Ellsworth 1972). We carried out an experiment on the intercultural communication of interpersonal attitudes, in which judges decoded videotapes, the main cues being face and voice. As Table 1 shows, Japanese subjects found it easier to decode British and Italian than Japanese performers, probably because Japanese display rules forbid use of negative facial expressions (Shimoda, Argyle, and Ricci Bitti 1978). This shows that the Japanese are indeed relatively "inscrutable," but it is not yet known whether they make use of alternative channels, such as posture, for transmitting information normally conveyed by the face. There are also some variations of facial expression within cultures, between different regions and social classes. Seaford (1975) reports the use of a "pursed smile" facial dialect in the state of Virginia.

Gaze also is used in a similar way in all cultures but the amount of gaze varies quite widely. Watson (1970) studied the gaze of pairs of students from different countries. The highest levels of gaze were shown by Arabs and Latin Americans, the lowest by Indians and northern Europeans. When people from different cultures met, if the other had a low level of gaze he was seen as not paying attention, impolite, or dishonest, while too much gaze was seen as disrespectful, threatening, or insulting. Some cultures have special rules about gaze, such as not looking at certain parts of the body, or at certain people. Gaze may have a special meaning, as when old ladies with squints are believed to have the evil eye (Argyle and Cook 1976).

Spatial behavior varies between cultures. Watson and Graves (1966) confirmed earlier observations that Arabs stand much closer than Americans (or western Europeans), and found that they also adopt a more directly facing orientation. When an Arab and an American meet it would be expected that the American would move backwards, turning, in a backwards spiral, closely followed by the Arab. An elaborate set of rules about distance is found in India, prescribing exactly how closely members of each caste may approach other castes. There are also rules for spatial behavior in different situations—far greater crowding is allowed in lifts and buses, football matches, and parties. There are other cultural differences in the use of space. Americans establish temporary territorial rights in public places, but Arabs do not consider that people have such rights, e.g., to the seat they are sitting on.

Bodily contact is widely practiced in some cultures, but allowed only under very restricted conditions in others. "Contact" cultures include Arab, Latin American, south European, and some African cultures, and they also have high levels of gaze. In non-contact cultures, bodily contact is confined to the family, apart from greeting and parting, and various professional actions, like those of actors and tailors. Bodily contact outside these settings is taboo, and a source of considerable anxiety.

Gestures, bodily movements, and posture vary widely between cultures. There are few if any universal gestures. Some gestures are used in one culture, not in others; there are probably more gestures in Italy than anywhere else; and the same gesture can have quite different meanings in different cultures. For example the V-sign, showing the back of the hand, which is a rude sign in Britain, simply means "2" in Greece. The pursed hand means a question in Italy, "good" in Greece, and "fear" in northern Europe (Morris et al. 1979). Many gestures are distinctive to a particular culture or cultural area and it is possible to construct "gesture dictionaries" giving the local meanings of such gestures (e.g., Saitz and Cervenka 1972). Graham and Argyle (1975) found that Italian subjects could communicate spatial information (complicated shapes) more readily when able to use their hands; for British subjects adding the hands made less difference. Greeting is performed in a great variety of ways, including the Japanese bowing, the Indian placing of the hands together, and more exotic performances in preindustrial societies (Krout 1942). Disagreement is signalled by a head-shake in Western countries, but a head-toss in Greece and southern Italy. Some cultures use special postures; where furniture is uncommon, various kinds of squatting, kneeling, or leaning on spears are common (Hewes 1957).

Nonverbal aspects of vocalization vary between cultures. Arabs speak loudly and give the impression of shouting. Americans speak louder than Europeans and give the impression of assertiveness. Speech style, especially accent, varies within cultures, and is an important clue to social class. The Japanese use the sound "hai" a lot, meaning literally "yes" but usually indicating understanding rather than agreement.

Rules

The existence of different rules in another culture is one of the main areas of difficulty in ICC. As we showed earlier, rules arise to regulate behavior so that goals can be attained and needs satisfied. Systems of rules create behavior patterns which are functional, but different sets of rules can emerge to do the same job. Here are some examples:

"Bribery." In many parts of the world it is normal to pay a commission to civil servants, salesmen, or professional people who have performed a service, although they are already receiving a salary. Sometimes there is a regular fee, e.g., 1–3 percent of sales. This is regarded locally as a perfectly normal exchange of gifts, but in Europe and North America it is often illegal and unethical. Various devices are resorted to in overseas sales, such as paying a "sales commission" to an intermediary who uses some of the money for a bribe.

"Nepotism." In Africa and other countries people are expected to help their relatives, and this is the local equivalent of social welfare. Sometimes relatives have contributed to an individual's education; when he gets a good job as a result they expect some return. If he is a civil servant or manager, such favors are regarded by others as nepotism and greatly disapproved of. In fact there are usually local rules which limit the forms which these favors can take.

Gifts. In all cultures it is necessary to present relatives, friends, or work colleagues with gifts on certain occasions, but the rules vary greatly. The Japanese spend a great deal of money on gifts, which must be bought from standard gift shops so that their value can be ascertained and a gift of the same value returned. The gift is not opened in the presence of the giver and a small token present is given immediately, in return (Morsbach 1977).

Buying and Selling. There are several alternate sets of rules here—barter, bargaining, fixed-price sales, and auction. In cultures where bargaining is used it is normal to establish a relationship first, perhaps while drinking tea, and there are conventions about how the bargaining should proceed.

Eating and Drinking. One of the main problems is that there are rules in all cultures about what may not be eaten or drunk, especially certain kinds of meat—pork, beef, dog, etc., and alcohol. There may be very strong sanctions for breaking these rules, for example for consuming alcohol in some Arab countries. There are rules about how the eating is performed—knife and fork, chopstick, right hand, etc.; and there are extensive rules about table manners—when to start eating, how much to leave, how to obtain or refuse a second helping, and so on.

Rules About Time. How late is "late"? This varies greatly. In Britain and North America one may be 5 minutes late for a business appointment, but not 15 and certainly not 30 minutes late, which is perfectly normal in Arab countries. On the other hand in Britain it is correct to be 5–15 minutes late for an invitation to dinner. An Italian might arrive 2 hours late, an Ethiopian later, and a Javanese not at all—he had accepted only to prevent his host losing face (Cleveland, Mangone, and Adams 1960). A meal in Russia at a restaurant normally takes at least 3 hours. In Nigeria it may take several days to wait one's turn at a government office, so professional "waiters" do it for you.

Seating Guests. In Britain, in middle-class circles at least, there are rules about seating people at table, when there are 6, 8, or other numbers present. In the United States there appear to be no such rules, and British visitors are commonly surprised to see familiar rules broken. In China the tables are circular and the seating rules are different again, and similar to the British though the most important person faces the door. In Japan different seating positions in a room have different status. There may also be rules about who should talk to whom, as in the "Boston switch"—hostess talks to person on her right during first course, switches to person on her left for the next course, and everyone else pairs off accordingly.

Rules Based on Ideas. Sometimes the rules of another culture are quite incomprehensible until one understands the ideas behind them. In Moslem countries there are strict rules based on religious ideas, such as fasting during Ramadan, saying prayers five times each day, and giving one-fortieth of one's money as alms (Roberts 1979). In order to visit some kinds of Australian Aboriginals it is necessary to sit at the edge of their land and wait to be invited further: To move closer would be regarded as an invasion of territory. It is necessary for them to have smoking fires (without chimneys) for religious reasons, despite possible danger to the health of those inside (O'Brien and Plooij 1977).

In addition to different rules for the same or similar situations, there may also be new situations. Black American youths play the "dozens" (ritual insulting of the other's mother), other Americans go on picnics, Chinese families go to pay respect to their ancestors, Oxford dons drink port and take a special form of dessert. There may be special ceremonies connected with engagement, marriage, childbirth, and other rites of passage.

Cultures also vary in the extent to which behavior is a function of situations, as a result of their rules and other properties. Argyle, Shimoda, and Little (1978) found that Japanese were more influenced by situations, while the British behaved more consistently, i.e., as a function of personality. This means that it is more difficult to infer the properties of personality from instances of behavior for the Japanese.

Within cultures in developing countries there are often two sets of rules and ideas, corresponding to Traditional and Modern attitudes. Inkeles (1969) found similar patterns of modernization in different countries, centered round independence from parental authority, concern with time, involvement in civil affairs, and openness to new experience. Dawson, Whitney, and Lan (1971) devised T–M scales, of which some of the core concepts were attitudes to parental authority, gift-giving, and the role of women. Modernism is highly correlated with education and social class.

In some cases it is essential for the visitor to conform to rules, for example in matters of eating and drinking. In other cases the rules may be in conflict with his own values, the practice of his home orga-

nization, or the laws of his own country, as in the case of "bribery." There may be no straightforward solution to these problems, but it is at least necessary to recognize what the local rules are, and the ideas behind them, rather than simply condemning them as wrong.

Social Relationships

The pattern of social relationships at work in the family, and with friends, takes a somewhat different form in different cultures, and different skills are needed to handle these relationships. Surveys by Triandis, Vassiliou, and Nassiakou (1968) and other research workers have shown that relationships vary along the same dimensions in all cultures—in-group/out-group, status, intimacy, and hostility or competition.

FAMILY RELATIONSHIPS

In developing countries the family is more important than in developed countries. A wider range of relatives are actively related to; relationships are closer and greater demands are made. These include helping to pay for education, helping to get jobs, and helping when in trouble. Foa and Chemers (1967) point out that in traditional societies the family is the most important source of relationships, and many different role-relationships are distinguished, but relative few outside the family. Throughout Africa and the Middle East the family takes a similar form—marriage is arranged as a contract between families, and money is paid for the bride, kinship is traced through the father and male relatives, and polygyny is accepted (Roberts 1979). In China great respect is paid to older generations: Parents are respected, large financial contributions are made to the family by unmarried children who have left home, regular visits are paid to the graves of ancestors. The family itself may take varied forms, such as having more than one wife, or a wife and concubines. The way in which different relations are grouped as similar varies: Distinctions may be based primarily on age, generation, consanguinity, or sex (Tzeng and Landis 1979). Sex roles vary: In the Arab world women traditionally do not work or drive cars, but spend most of their time at home. The reverse operates in countries like Israel, China, and Poland where women do nearly all the same jobs as men. Patterns of sexual behavior vary—promiscuity may be normal, or virginity greatly prized; businessmen visiting parts of the East are sometimes embarrassed by being offered girls as part of the hospitality. Cultures vary from complete promiscuity before and after marriage to a complete taboo on sex outside marriage (Murdoch 1949). Goody (1976) has shown that there is great control over premarital sexual behavior in societies which have advanced agriculture, where marriage is linked with property (especially land) transactions so that it is necessary to control unsuitable sexual attachments. Americans, and to a lesser extent Europeans, mix work and family life, and receive business visitors into the home; Japanese and Arabs do not.

SUPERVISION OF GROUPS

In most of the world outside Europe and North America, there is greater social distance between ranks, more deference and obedience, and a generally more authoritarian social structure. Subordinates do not speak freely in front of more senior people, and less use is made of face-to-face discussion. Melikian (1959) found that Egyptian Arabs, whether Moslem or Christian, had higher scores on authoritarianism than Americans. While the democratic–persuasive type is most effective in the United States and Europe, this is not the case elsewhere. In India the authoritarian style has been found to be more effective; in China there was no difference and in Japan authoritarian-led groups did best with a difficult task (Mann 1980). In Japan the teachers and superiors at work adopt an Oyabun–Koyun relationship, involving a paternalistic care for subordinates.

GROUPS

Ethnographic studies have shown that groups have more power over their members in a number of cultures—in Japan, China, Israel, and Russia, for example. The individual is subordinated more to the group, and a high degree of conformity is expected. America and Europe are thought to be more individualistic, and social psychological experiments have shown relatively low levels of conformity in Germany and France. It has also been found that conformity pressures are stronger in the cultures where conformity is greatest. In Japan group decisions are traditionally carried out by a kind of acquiescence to the will of the group, without voting. In some cultures there is great stress on cooperation rather than competition in groups, e.g., in the Israeli kibbutz, Mexican villages, and among Australian aboriginals (Mann 1980).

CASTES AND CLASSES

In all cultures there are hierarchical divisions of status and horizontal divisions of inclusion and exclusion. The hierarchical divisions may take the form of social classes, which can be recognized by clothes, accent as in Britain, or other ways. There may be ethnic groups which have their places in the hierarchy, as in the United States; or there may be immutable castes, as in India. This creates special problems for visitors in India: European visitors are relatively rich and clean, and so appear to be of high caste, but also eat meat even with the left hand and drink alcohol like untouchables, so a special visitor caste, of *videshis*, has been created. However, visitors to ashrams who adopt the costume of holy men do not fit this caste and cause great offense to the Indians (Wujastyk 1980). The horizontal divisions between different tribes or classes are also of great importance. In Africa it may be necessary to make up work groups from members of the same tribe, and it would be disastrous to appoint a leader from another tribe. Similar clan divisions are of course found in Scotland, and also in China (Hsu 1963). In-group versus out-group distinctions can take varied forms. Studies of helping behavior have found that fellow countrymen are usually given more help than visitors, but in Greece tourists are treated like family and friends (Triandis, Vassiliou, and Nassiakou 1968).

Motivation

Several forms of motivation have been found to differ on average between cultures. This means that typical members of another culture are pursuing different goals, and are gratified by different rewards. Sometimes the causes of these motivational differences can be found in other features of a culture. For example, societies which are constantly at war with their neighbors encourage aggressiveness in their young males (Zigler and Child 1969).

ACHIEVEMENT MOTIVATION

McClelland (1961) found that cultures differed in the level of achievement motivation, as measured by the popularity of children's stories with achievement themes; the high need for achievement (n.Ach) countries had higher rates of economic growth, and this may be due in part to the motivational difference. The United States over the last century has been high in n.Ach; underdeveloped countries have been lower. McClelland and Winter (1969) ran a training course for Indian managers, in which the latter role-played high n.Ach managers. The result was that they increased the size and turnover of their enterprises after attending the course. There is of course a wide range of individual differences within a culture, but it is worth realizing that in some areas individuals are likely to work hard to take risks in order to earn more money, improve their status, and to build up the enterprise in which they work. While in other areas people expect to be rewarded on the basis of the social position of their family or clan, not their own efforts.

ASSERTIVENESS

Assertiveness or dominance versus submissiveness is one of the main dimensions along which social behavior varies. In the United States social skills training has concentrated on assertiveness, presumably reflecting a widespread approval of and desire to acquire assertive behavior. This interest in assertiveness is strong among American women, as part of the women's movement. It has also been suggested that the absence of universally accepted rules makes it necessary to stand up for your rights rather frequently.

Americans are perceived as assertive in other parts of the world. However, there are some cultures, e.g., China and parts of Indonesia, where assertiveness is not valued, and submissiveness and the maintenance of pleasant social relations are valued more (Noesjirwan 1978). In Britain candidates for social skills training are more interested in making friends. Furnham (1979) found that European white nurses in South Africa were the most assertive, followed by Africans and Indians.

EXTRAVERSION

Surveys using extraversion questionnaires show that Americans and Canadians are more extraverted than the British (e.g., Eysenck and Eysenck 1969). What exactly this means in terms of social behavior is rather unclear. It is commonly observed that Americans are good at the early stages of a relationship, where the British can be shy and awkward. In the United States the peer group plays an important part in the life of children and adolescents; and among adults great value is placed on informal relationships (Riesman, Glazer, and Denney 1955).

In the East great value is placed on maintaining good social relationships, so that assertiveness and disagreement are avoided, or at least confined to members of the same family, clan, or group.

FACE

It is well known that in Japan, and to a lesser extent other parts of the Far East, maintaining face is of great importance. Special skills are required to make sure that others do not lose face. Foa, Mitchell, and Lekhyananda (1969) found that students from the Far East who experienced failure in an experimental task withdrew from the source of the failure message. In negotiations it may be necessary to make token concessions before the other side can give way. Great care must be taken at meetings over disagreeing or criticizing, and competitive situations should be avoided.

VALUES

These are broader, more abstract goals, the general states of affairs which are regarded as desirable. Triandis, Malpass, and Davidson (1972) studied twenty values by asking for the antecedents and consequences of eleven concepts. In parts of India they found that status and glory were valued most, whilst wealth was not valued (being associated with arrogance and fear of thieves), nor was courage or power. The Greeks valued punishment (which was associated with justice) and power. The Japanese valued serenity and aesthetic satisfaction, and disvalued ignorance, deviation, and loneliness. Szalay and Maday (cited by Triandis, Malpass, and Davidson 1972) found that Americans rated *love* and *friendship* as their most important life concerns, *health* as 5th: Koreans ranked these values as 12th, 14th, and 19th. Triandis (1971) found that "work" was regarded as a good thing in moderately difficult environments where economic development was rapid, but it was rated less favorably in easy or difficult environments.

Concepts and Ideology

Certain aspects of life in another culture may be incomprehensible without an understanding of the underlying ideas. Some of these ideas are carried by language, and knowing a language deepens understanding of the culture. The words in a language reflect and provide labels for the cognitive categories used in the culture to divide up the world. The color spectrum is divided up in different ways, and the color words reflect this in different cultures (Berlin and Kay 1969).

The same is true of every other aspect of the physical and social world, so that knowledge of the language provides knowledge of the culture. Translation of words may lead to changes of emotional association—the Australian word "Pom" doesn't only mean "British immigrant" but has negative and joking associations as well. Words in one language and culture may have complex meanings which are difficult to translate, as with the Israeli Chutzpah (= "outrageous cheek," such as exporting tulips to Holland), Russian versus Western concepts of "freedom" and "democracy," and the Japanese concept of the Oyabum–Koyum relationship.

There may be misunderstanding due to differences in thinking. Sharma (1971) notes how Western observers have criticized Indian peasants for their passivity and general lack of the "Protestant ethic," despite having produced a great increase in productivity by adapting to the Green Revolution. African languages are often short of words for geometrical shapes, so that it is difficult to communicate about spatial problems. Some words or ideas may be taboo, e.g., discussion of family planning (Awa 1979).

Some of the differences in rules which were discussed above can be explained in terms of the ideas behind them, as in the cases of "bribery" and "nepotism." Attitudes to business practices are greatly affected by ideas and ideology. Marxists will not discuss "profits"; Moslems used to regard "interest" as sinful. Surprisingly the stricter forms of Protestantism have been most compatible with capitalism and gave rise to the "Protestant ethic" (Argyle 1972).

Training Methods

Language Learning. There are many cultures where visitors, especially short-term visitors, can get by quite well without learning the language. On the other hand this probably means that they are cut off from communicating with the majority of the native population, and that they do not come to understand fully those features of the culture which are conveyed by language. Language learning can be greatly assisted by the use of a language laboratory, and by textbooks like Leech and Svartlik's *A Communicative Grammar of English*, which provide detailed information on the everyday informal use of language.

Use of Educational Methods. Despite the use of more active methods of SST in other areas, for ICC reading and lectures are currently the most widely used methods. The most sophisticated approach here has been the development of Culture Assimilators. Critical-incident surveys have been carried out on occasions when Americans have gotten into difficulty in Thailand, Greece, etc., and a standard set of difficult episodes has been written, for example:

One day a Thai administrator of middle academic rank kept two of his assistants about an hour from an appointment. The assistants, although very angry, did not show it while they waited. When the administrator walked in at last, he acted as if he were not late. He made no apology or explanation. After he was settled in his office, he called his assistants in and they all began working on the business for which the administrator had set the meeting (Brislin and Pedersen [1976] pp. 90–91).

Several explanations were offered, of which the correct one is:

In Thailand, subordinates are required to be polite to their superiors, no matter what happens, nor what their rank may be (ibid, p. 92).

and further information is added.

These episodes are put together in a tutor-text, which students work through by themselves (Fiedler et al. 1971).

There have been a number of follow-up studies of the use of culture assimilators, showing modest improvements in handling mixed cultural groups in laboratory settings, and in one case in a field setting. However, not very much field assessment has been done, the effects of training have not been very striking, and the subjects used have all been of high motivation and intelligence (Brislin and Pedersen 1976).

A similar method is the use of case studies. These are widely used for management training in international firms, the cases being based on typical managerial problems in the other culture. They play an important part in two-week courses, using educational methods. It is common to include wives and children in such courses, with special materials for them too (DiStephano 1979).

Educational methods can probably make a valuable contribution to cross-cultural training, since there is always a lot to learn about another culture. However, as with other skills, it is necessary to combine such intellectual learning with actual practice of the skills involved.

Role-Playing. Several types of role-playing have been used for ICC, though it has not been the usual form of training. One approach is to train people in laboratory situations in the skills or modes of communication of a second culture, using videotape playback. Collett (1971) trained Englishmen in the nonverbal communication styles of Arabs, and found that those trained in this way were liked better by Arabs than were members of a control group.

The American Peace Corps has used simulation techniques to train their members. Trainees have been sent to work on an American Indian reservation, for example. Area simulation sites were constructed to train members for different locations, e.g., one in Hawaii for Southeast Asian volunteers, complete with water buffalos. However, it is reported that these rather expensive procedures have not been very successful, and they have been replaced by training in the second culture itself (Brislin and Pedersen 1976).

Interaction with Members of the Other Culture. In the intercultural communication workshop trainees go through a number of exercises with members of the other culture, and use is made of role-playing and the study of critical incidents (Alther 1975). This looks like a very powerful method, but no follow-up results are available. At Farnham Castle in Britain the training courses include meetings with members of the other culture, and with recently returned expatriates.

When people arrive in a new culture they are frequently helped both by native members of the culture, and by expatriates. Bochner, McLeod, and Lin (1977) found that foreign students in Hawaii usually had friends of both kinds, who could help them in different ways.

Combined Approaches. We have seen that each of the methods described has some merits, and it seems very likely that a combination of methods would be the most effective. This might include some language instruction, learning about the other culture, role-playing, and interaction with native members of the culture. Gudykunst, Hammer, and Wiseman (1977) used a combination of several methods, though not including any language teaching, in a three-day course, and found that this led to higher reported levels of satisfaction for Naval personnel posted to Japan.

Guthrie (1966) describes one of the training schemes used by the Peace Corps, for those going to the Philippines. The training included: (1) basic linguistics, so that trainees could pick up local dialects quickly; later this was replaced by teaching specific dialects; (2) lectures by experts on different aspects of the Philippines culture; (3) physical and survival training at the Puerto Rican jungle camp; as noted earlier this was later replaced by training in the culture itself.

CONCLUSIONS

A very large number of people go abroad to work in other cultures; some of them fail to complete their mission and others are ineffective, because of difficulties of intercultural communication.

Difficulties of social interaction and communication arise in several main areas: (1) language, including forms of polite usage; (2) nonverbal communication: uses of facial expression, gesture, proximity, touch, etc.; (3) rules of social situations, e.g., for bribing, gifts, and eating; (4) social relationships, within the family, at work, between members of different groups; (5) motivation, e.g., achievement motivation and for face-saving; (6) concepts and ideology, e.g., ideas derived from religion and politics.

Several kinds of training for ICC have been found to be successful, especially in combination. These include language-learning, educational methods, role-playing, and interaction with members of the other culture.

REFERENCES

Alther, G. L. (1975) "Human relations training and foreign students," *Readings in Intercultural Communication*, Vol. 1 (Edited by Hoopes, D.). Intercultural Communications Network of the Regional Council for International Education, Pittsburgh.

Argyle, M. (1972) *The Social Psychology of Work*. Penguin Books, Harmondsworth.

Argyle, M. (1975) *Bodily Communication*. Methuen, London.

Argyle, M. and Cook, M. (1976) *Gaze and Mutual Gaze*. Cambridge University Press, Cambridge.

Argyle, M., Shimoda, K. and Little, B. (1978) "Variance due to persons and situations in England and Japan," *British Journal of Social and Clinical Psychology*, 17, 335–7.

Awa, N. E. (1979) "Ethnocentric bias in developmental research," *Handbook of Intercultural Communication* (Edited by Asante, M. K., Newmark, E., and Blake, C. A.). Sage Publications, Beverly Hills, Calif.

Berlin, B. and Kay, P. (1969) *Basic Color Terms*. University of California Press, Berkeley, Calif.

Bochner, S., McLeod, B. M. and Lin, A. (1977) "Friendship patterns of overseas students: A functional model," *International Journal of Psychology*, 12, 277–94.

Brein, M. and David, K. H. (1971) "Intercultural communication and the adjustment of the sojourner," *Psychological Bulletin*, 76, 215–30.

Brislin, R. W. and Pedersen, P. (1976) *Cross-Cultural Orientation Programs*. Gardner Press, New York.

Chan, J. (1979) *The Facial Expressions of Chinese and Americans*. Unpublished Ph.D. thesis, South Eastern University, Louisiana.

Chemers, M. M., Fiedler, F. E., Lekhyananda, D., and Stolurow, L. M. (1966) "Some effects of cultural training on leadership in heterocultural task groups," *International Journal of Psychology*, 1, 301–14.

Cleveland, H., Mangone, G. J. and Adams, J. G. (1960) *The Overseas Americans*. McGraw-Hill, New York.

Collett, P. (1971) "On training Englishmen in the non-verbal behaviour of Arabs: An experiment in intercultural communication," *International Journal of Psychology*, 6, 209–15.

Dawson, J., Whitney, R. E. and Lan, R. T. S. (1971) "Scaling Chinese traditional–modern attitudes and the GSR measurement of 'important' versus 'unimportant' Chinese concepts," *Journal of Cross-Cultural Psychology*, 2, 1–27.

DiStephano, J. J. (1979) "Case methods in international management training," *Handbook of Intercultural Communication* (Edited by Asante, M. K., Newmark, E. and Blake, C. A.). Sage Publications, Beverly Hills, Calif.

Ekman, P., Friesen, W. V. and Ellsworth, P. (1972) *Emotion in the Human Face: Guidelines for Research and a Review of Findings*. Pergamon Press, New York.

Erickson, F. (1976) "Talking down and giving reasons: Hyper-explanation and listening behavior in inter-social situations." Paper presented at the Ontario Institute for the Study of Education Conference, Toronto.

Eysenck, H. J. and Eysenck, S. B. G. (1969) *Personality Structure and Measurement*. Routledge & Kegan Paul, London.

Fiedler, F. E., Mitchell, R. and Triandis, H. C. (1971) "The culture assimilator: An approach to cross-cultural training," *Journal of Applied Psychology*, 55, 95–102.

Foa, U. and Chemers, M. (1967) "The significance of role behavior differentiation for cross-cultural interaction training," *International Journal of Psychology*, 2, 45–57.

Foa, U. G., Mitchell, T. R. and Lekhyananda, D. (1969) "Cultural differences in reaction to failure," *International Journal of Psychology*, 4, 21–6.

Furnham, A. (1979) "Assertiveness in three cultures: Multidimensionality and cultural differences," *Journal of Clinical Psychology*, 35, 522–7.

Giles, H. and Powesland, P. F. (1975) *Speech Style and Social Evaluation*. Academic Press, London.

Goody, E. N. (1978) "Towards a theory of questions," *Questions and Politeness* (Edited by Goody, E. N.). Cambridge University Press, Cambridge.

Goody, J. (1976) *Production and Reproduction*. Cambridge University Press, Cambridge.

Graham, J. A. and Argyle, M. (1975) "A cross-cultural study of the communication of extra-verbal meaning by gestures," *International Journal of Psychology*, 10, 57–67.

Gudykunst, W. B., Hammer, M. R. and Wiseman, R. L. (1977) "An analysis of an integrated approach to cross-cultural training," *International Journal of Intercultural Relations*, 1, 99–110.

Gullahorn, J. E. and Gullahorn, J. T. (1966) "American students abroad: Professional versus personal development," *The Annals of the American Academy of Political and Social Science*, 368, 43–59.

Guthrie, G. M. (1966) "Cultural preparation for the Philippines," *Cultural Frontiers of the Peace Corps* (Edited by Textor, R. B.). M.I.T. Press, Cambridge, Mass.

Hammer, M. R., Gudykunst, W. B. and Wiseman, R. L. (1978) "Dimensions of intercultural effectiveness: An exploratory study," *International Journal of Intercultural Relations*, 2, 382–93.

Hewes, G. (1957) "The anthropology of posture," *Scientific American*, 196, 123–32.

Hsu, F. L. K. (1963) *Caste, Clan and Club*. Van Nostrand, Princeton, N.J.

Inkeles, A. (1969) "Making men modern: On the causes and consequences of individual change in six developing countries," *American Journal of Sociology*, 75, 208–25.

Krout, M. H. (1942) *Introduction to Social Psychology*. Harper & Row, New York.

Leech, G. and Svartlik, J. (1975) *A Communicative Grammar of English*. Longman, London.

Mann, L. (1980) "Cross cultural studies of small groups," *Handbook of Cross-cultural Psychology*, Vol. 5 (Edited by Triandis, H.). Allyn & Bacon, Boston.

McClelland, D. C. (1961) *The Achieving Society*. Van Nostrand, Princeton, N.J.

McClelland, D. C. and Winter, D. G. (1969) *Motivating Economic Achievement*. Free Press, New York.

Melikian, L. H. (1959) "Authoritarianism and its correlation in the Egyptian culture and in the United States," *Journal of Social Issues*, 15 (3), 58–68.

Morris, D., Collett, P., Marsh, P. and O'Shaughnessy, M. (1979) *Gestures: Their Origins and Distribution*. Cape, London.

Morsbach, H. (1977) "The psychological importance of ritualized gift exchange in modern Japan," *Annals of the New York Academy of Sciences*, 293, 98–113.

Murdoch, G. P. (1949) *Social Structure*. Macmillan, New York.

Noesjirwan, J. (1978) "A rule-based analysis of cultural differences in social behaviour: Indonesia and Australia," *International Journal of Psychology*, 13, 305–16.

Oberg, K. (1960) "Cultural shock: Adjustment to new cultural environments," *Practical Anthropology*, 7, 177–82.

O'Brien, G. E. and Plooij, D. (1977) "Development of culture training manuals for medical workers with Pitjantjatjara Aboriginals," *Journal of Applied Psychology*, 62, 499–505.

Riesman, D., Glazer, N. and Denney, R. (1955) *The Lonely Crowd: A Study of the Changing American Character*. Doubleday, New York.

Roberts, G. O. (1979) "Terramedian value systems and their significance," *Handbook of Intercultural Communication* (Edited by Asante, M. K., Newman, E. and Blake, C. A.). Sage Publications, Beverly Hills, Calif.

Saitz, R. L. and Cervenka, E. J. (1972) *Handbook of Gestures: Colombia and the United States*. Mouton, The Hague.

Seaford, H. W. (1975) "Facial expression dialect: An example," *Organization of Behavior in Face-to-Face Interaction* (Edited by Kendon, A., Harris, R. M. and Key, M. R.). Mouton, The Hague.

Sharma, H. (1971) "Green revolution in India: A prelude to a red one?" Unpublished paper (cited by Awa, 1979).

Shimoda, K., Argyle, M. and Ricci Bitti, P. (1978) "The intercultural recognition of emotional expressions by three national groups—English, Italian, and Japanese," *European Journal of Social Psychology*, 8, 169–79.

Taft, R. (1977) "Coping with unfamiliar cultures," *Studies in Cross-cultural Psychology*, Vol. 1 (Edited by Warren, N.). Academic Press, London.

Taylor, D. M. and Simard, L. M. (1975) "Social interaction in a bilingual setting," *Canadian Psychological Review*, 16, 240–54.

Triandis, H. (1971) "Work and leisure in cross-cultural perspective," *Theories of Cognitive Consistency: A Sourcebook* (Edited by Abelson, R. P. et al.). Rand McNally, Chicago.

Triandis, H. (1972) *The Analysis of Subjective Culture*. Wiley, New York.

Triandis, H., Malpass, R. S. and Davidson, A. R. (1972) "Cross-cultural psychology," *Biennial Review of Anthropology*, 24, 1–84.

Triandis, H. C., Vassiliou, V. and Nassiakou, M. (1968) "Three cross-cultural studies of subjective culture," *Journal of Personality and Social Psychology*, 8 (Monograph Supplement), Part 2, pp. 1–42.

Tzeng, O. C. S. and Landis, D. (1979) "A multidimensional scaling methodology for cross-cultural research in communication," *Handbook of Intercultural Communication* (Edited by Asante, M. K., Newmark, E. and Blake, C. A.). Sage Publications, Beverly Hills, Calif.

Watson, O. M. (1970) *Proxemic Behavior: A Cross-cultural Study*. Mouton, The Hague.

Watson, O. M. and Graves, T. D. (1966) "Quantitative research in proxemic behavior," *American Anthropologist*, 68, 971–85.

Wujastyk, D. (1980) "Causing a scandal in Poona," *The Times* (London), 24 April, p. 14.

Zigler, E. and Child, I. L. (1969) "Socialization," *The Handbook of Social Psychology*, Vol. 3 (Edited by Lindzey, G. and Aronson, E.). Addison-Wesley, Reading, Mass.

Context and Meaning

EDWARD T. HALL

One of the functions of culture is to provide a highly selective screen between man and the outside world. In its many forms, culture therefore designates what we pay attention to and what we ignore.[1] This screening function provides structure for the world and protects the nervous system from "information overload."[2] Information overload is a technical term applied to information processing systems. It describes a situation in which the system breaks down when it cannot properly handle the huge volume of information to which it is subjected. Any mother who is trying to cope with the demands of small children, run a house, enjoy her husband, and carry on even a modest social life knows that there are times when everything happens at once and the world seems to be closing in on her. She is experiencing the same information overload that afflicts business managers, administrators, physicians, attorneys, and air controllers. Institutions such as stock exchanges, libraries, and telephone systems also go through times when the demands on the system (inputs) exceed capacity. People can handle the crunch through delegating and establishing priorities; while institutional solutions are less obvious, the high-context rule seems to apply. That is, the only way to increase information-handling capacity without increasing the mass and complexity of the system is to program the memory of the system so that less information is required to activate the system, i.e., make it more like the couple that has been married for thirty-five years. The solution to the problem of coping with increased complexity and greater demands on the system seems to lie in the preprogramming of the individual or organization. This is done by means of the "contexting" process. . . .

The importance of the role of context is widely recognized in the communication fields, yet the process is rarely described adequately, or if it is, the insights gained are not acted upon. Before dealing with context as a way of handling information overload, let me describe how I envisage the contexting process, which is an emergent function; i.e., we are just discovering what it is and how it works. Closely related to the high–low-context continuum is the degree to which one is aware of the selective screen that one places between himself and the outside world.[3] As one moves from the low to the high side of the scale, awareness of the selective process increases. Therefore, what one pays attention to, context, and information overload are all functionally related.

In the fifties, the United States government spent millions of dollars developing systems for machine translation of Russian and other languages. After years of effort on the part of some of the most talented linguists in the country, it was finally concluded that the only reliable, and ultimately the fastest, translator is a human being deeply conversant not only with the language but with the subject as well. The computers could spew out yards of printout but they meant very little. The words and some of the grammar were all there, but the sense was distorted. That the project failed was not due to lack of application, time, money, or talent, but for other reasons, which are central to the theme of this [article].

The problem lies not in the linguistic code but in the context, which carries varying proportions of the meaning. Without context, the code is incomplete since it encompasses only part of the message. This should become clear if one remembers that the spoken language is an abstraction of an event that happened, might have happened, or is being planned. As any writer knows, an event is usually infinitely more complex and rich than the language

From Edward T. Hall, *Beyond Culture* (Garden City, N.Y.: Doubleday & Company, 1976); pp. 85–103. Copyright © 1976, 1981 by Edward T. Hall. Reprinted by permission of Doubleday and The Lescher Agency. Professor Hall teaches at Northwestern University.

used to describe it. Moreover, the writing system is an abstraction of the spoken system and is in effect a reminder system of what somebody said or could have said. In the process of abstracting, as contrasted with measuring, people take in some things and unconsciously ignore others. This is what intelligence is: paying attention to the right things. The linear quality of a language inevitably results in accentuating some things at the expense of others. Two languages provide interesting contrasts. In English, when a man says, "It rained last night," there is no way of knowing how he arrived at that conclusion, or if he is even telling the truth, whereas a Hopi cannot talk about rain at all without signifying the nature of his relatedness to the event—firsthand experience, inference, or hearsay. This is a point made by the linguist Whorf[4] thirty years ago. However, selective attention and emphasis are not restricted to language but are characteristic of the rest of culture as well.

The rules governing what one perceives and [what one] is blind to in the course of living are not simple; at least five sets of disparate categories of events must be taken into account. These are: the subject or activity, the situation, one's status in a social system, past experience, and culture. The patterns governing juggling these five dimensions are learned early in life and are mostly taken for granted. The "subject", or topic one is engaged in has a great deal to do with what one does and does not attend. People working in the "hard" sciences, chemistry and physics, which deal with the physical world, are able to attend and integrate a considerably higher proportion of significant events observed than scientists working with living systems. The physical scientist has fewer variables to deal with; his abstractions are closer to the real events; and context is of less importance. This characterization is, of course, oversimplified. But it is important to remember that the laws governing the physical world, while relatively simple compared to those governing human behavior, may seem complex to the layman, while the complexity of language appears simple to the physicist, who, like everyone else, has been talking all his life. In these terms it is all too easy for the person who is in full command of

a particular behaviorial system, such as language, to confuse what he can *do* with a given system, with the unstated rules governing the way the system operates. The conceptual model I am using takes into account not only what one takes in and screens out but what one does not know about a given system even though one has mastered that system. The two are *not* the same. Michael Polanyi[5] stated this principle quite elegantly when he said, "The structure of a machine cannot be defined in terms of the laws which it harnesses."

What man chooses to take in, either consciously or unconsciously, is what gives structure and meaning to his world. Furthermore, what he perceives is "what he intends to do about it." Setting aside the other four dimensions (situation, status, past experience, and culture), theoretically it would be possible to arrange all of man's activities along a continuum ranging from those in which a very high proportion of the events influencing the outcome were consciously considered to those in which a much smaller number were considered. In the United States, interpersonal relations are frequently at the low end of the scale. Everyone has had the experience of thinking that he was making a good impression only to learn later that he was not. At times like these, we are paying attention to the wrong things or screening out behavior we should be observing. A common fault of teachers and professors is that they pay more attention to their subject matter than they do to the students, who frequently pay too much attention to the professor and not enough to the subject.

The "situation" also determines what one consciously takes in and leaves out. In an American court of law, the attorneys, the judge, and the jury are compelled by custom and legal practice to pay attention only to what is legally part of the record. Context, by design, carries very little weight. Contrast this with a situation in which an employee is trying to decipher the boss's behavior—whether he is pleased or not, and if he is going to grant a raise. Every little clue is a story in itself, as is the employee's knowledge of behavior in the past.

One's status in a social system also affects what must be attended. People at the top pay attention to different things from those at the middle or the bottom of the system. In order to survive, all organizations, whatever their size, have to develop techniques not only for replacing their leader but for switching the new leader's perceptions from the internal concerns he focused on when he was at the lower and middle levels to a type of global view that enables the head man or woman to chart the course for the institution.

The far-reaching consequences of what is attended can be illustrated by a characteristic fault in Western thinking that dates back to the philosophers of ancient Greece. Our way of thinking is quite arbitrary and causes us to look at ideas rather than events—a most serious shortcoming. Also, linearity can get in the way of mutual understanding and divert people needlessly along irrelevant tangents. The processes I am describing are particularly common in the social sciences; although the younger scientists in these fields are gradually beginning to accept the fact that when someone is talking about events on one level this does not mean that he has failed to take into account the many other events on different levels. It is just that one can talk about only a single aspect of something at any moment (illustrating the linear characteristic of language).

The results of this syndrome (of having to take multiple levels into account when using a single-level system) are reflected in a remark made by one of our most brilliant and least appreciated thinkers in modern psychiatry, H. S. Sullivan,[6] when he observed that as he composed his articles, lectures, and books the person he was writing to (whom he projected in his mind's eye) was a cross between an imbecile and a bitterly paranoid critic. What a waste. And so confusing to the reader who wants to find out what the man is really trying to say.

In less complex and fast-moving times, the problem of mutual understanding was not as difficult, because most transactions were conducted with people well known to the speaker or writer, people with similar backgrounds. It is important for conversationalists in any situation—regardless of the area of discourse (love, business, science)—to get to know each other well enough so that they realize what each person is and is not taking into account. This is crucial. Yet few are willing to make the very real effort—life simply moves too fast—which may explain some of the alienation one sees in the world today.

Programming of the sort I am alluding to takes place in all normal human transactions as well as those of many higher mammals. It constitutes the unmeasurable part of communication. This brings us to the point where it is possible to discuss context in relation to meaning, because what one pays attention to or does not attend is largely a matter of context. Remember, contexting is also an important way of handling the very great complexity of human transactions so that the system does not bog down in information overload.

Like a number of my colleagues, I have observed that meaning and context are inextricably bound up with each other. While a linguistic code can be analyzed on some levels independent of context (which is what the machine translation project tried to accomplish), *in real life the code, the context, and the meaning can only be seen as different aspects of a single event*. What is unfeasible is to measure one side of the equation and not the others.[7]

Earlier, I said that high-context messages are placed at one end and low-context messages at the other end of a continuum. A high-context (HC) communication or message is one in which most of the information is either in the physical context or internalized in the person, while very little is in the coded, explicit, transmitted part of the message. A low-context (LC) communication is just the opposite; i.e., the mass of the information is vested in the explicit code. Twins who have grown up together can and do communicate more economically (HC) than two lawyers in a courtroom during a trial (LC), a mathematician programming a computer, two politicians drafting legislation, two administrators writing a regulation, or a child trying to explain to his mother why he got into a fight.

Although no culture exists exclusively at one end of the scale, some are high while others are low. American culture, while not on the bottom, is toward the lower end of the scale. We are still considerably above the German-Swiss, the Germans, and the Scandinavians in the amount of contexting needed in everyday life. While complex, multi-institutional cultures (those that are technologically advanced) might be thought of as inevitably LC, this is not always true. China, the possessor of a great and complex culture, is on the high-context end of the scale.

One notices this particularly in the written language of China, which is thirty-five hundred years old and has changed very little in the past three thousand years. This common written language is a unifying force tying together half a billion Chinese, Koreans, Japanese, and even some of the Vietnamese who speak Chinese. The need for context is experienced when looking up words in a Chinese dictionary. To use a Chinese dictionary, the reader must know the significance of 214 radicals (there are no counterparts for radicals in the Indo-European languages). For example, to find the word for star one must know that it appears under the sun radical. To be literate in Chinese, one has to be conversant with Chinese history. In addition, the spoken pronunciation system must be known, because there are four tones and a change of tone means a change of meaning; whereas in English, French, German, Spanish, Italian, etc., the reader need not know how to pronounce the language in order to read it. Another interesting sidelight on the Chinese orthography is that it is also an art form.[8] To my knowledge, no low-context communication system has ever been an art form. Good art is always high-context; bad art, low-context. This is one reason why good art persists and art that releases its message all at once does not.

The level of context determines everything about the nature of the communication and is the foundation on which all subsequent behavior rests (including symbolic behavior). Recent studies in sociolinguistics have demonstrated how context-dependent the language code really is. There is an excellent example of this in the work of the linguist Bernstein,[9] who has identified what he terms "restricted" (HC) and "elaborated" (LC) codes in which vocabulary, syntax, and sounds are all altered: In the restricted code of intimacy in the home, words and sentences collapse and are shortened. This even applies to the phonemic structure of the language. The individual sounds begin to merge, as does the vocabulary, whereas in the highly articulated, highly specific, elaborated code of the classroom, law, or diplomacy, more accurate distinctions are made on all levels. Furthermore, the code that one uses signals and is consistent with the situation. A shifting of code signals a shift in everything else that is to follow. "Talking down" to someone is low-contexting him—telling him more than he needs to know. This can be done quite subtly simply by shifting from the restricted end of the code toward the elaborated forms of discourse.

From the practical viewpoint of communications strategy, one must decide how much time to invest in contexting another person. A certain amount of this is always necessary, so that the information that makes up the explicit portions of the message is neither inadequate nor excessive. One reason most bureaucrats are so difficult to deal with is that they write for each other and are insensitive to the contexting needs of the public. The written regulations are usually highly technical on the one hand, while providing little information on the other. That is, they are a mixture of different codes or else there is incongruity between the code and the people to whom it is addressed. Modern management methods, for which management consultants are largely responsible, are less successful than they should be, because in an attempt to make everything explicit (low-contexting again) they frequently fail in their recommendations to take into account what people already know. This is a common fault of the consultant, because few consultants take the time (and few clients will pay for the time) to become completely contexted in the many complexities of the business.

There is a relationship between the worldwide activism of the sixties and where a given culture is situated on the context scale, because some are more vulnerable than others. HC actions are by definition rooted in the past, slow to change, and highly stable. Commenting on the need for the stabilizing effect of the past, anthropologist Loren Eiseley[10] takes an anti-activist position and points out how vulnerable our own culture is:

Their world (the world of the activist), therefore, becomes increasingly the violent, unpredictable world of the first men simply because, in lacking faith in the past, one is inevitably forsaking all that enables man to be a planning animal. For man's story,[11] in brief, is essentially that of a creature who has abandoned instinct *and replaced it with cultural tradition and the hard-won increments of contemplative thought. The lessons of the past have been found to be a reasonably secure construction for proceeding against an unknown future.*[12]

Actually, activism is possible at any point in the HC–LC continuum, but it seems to have less direction or focus and becomes less predictable and more threatening to institutions in LC systems. Most HC systems, however, can absorb activism without being shaken to their foundations.

In LC systems, demonstrations are viewed as the last, most desperate act in a series of escalating events. Riots and demonstrations in the United States, particularly those involving blacks,[13] are a message, a plea, a scream of anguish and anger for the larger society to *do something*. In China (an HC culture), the Red Guard riots apparently had an entirely different significance. They were promulgated from the top of the social order, not the bottom. They were also a communication from top to bottom: first, to produce a show of strength by Mao Tsetung; second, to give pause to the opposition and shake things up at the middle levels—a way of mobilizing society, not destroying it. Chinese friends with whom I have spoken about these riots took them much less seriously than I did. I was, of course, looking at them from the point of view of one reared in a low-context culture, where such riots can have disastrous effects on the society at large.

Wherever one looks, the influence of the subtle hand of contexting can be detected. We have just spoken of the effects of riots on high- and low-context political systems, but what about day-to-day matters of perception? On the physiological level of color perception, one sees the power of the brain's need to perceive and adjust everything in terms of context. As any interior designer knows, a powerful painting, print, or wall hanging can change the perceived color of the furnishings around it. The color psychologist Faber Birren[14] demonstrated experimentally that the perceived shade of a color depends upon the color context in which it occurs. He did this by systematically varying the color of the background surrounding different color samples.

Some of the most impressive demonstrations of the brain's ability to supply the missing information—the function of contexting—are the experiments of Edwin Land, inventor of the Land camera. Working in color photography using a single red filter, he developed a process that is simple, but the explanation for it is not. Until Land's experiments, it was believed that color prints could be made only by superimposing transparent images of three separate photographs made with the primary colors—red, blue, and yellow. Land made his color photographs with two images: a black-and-white image to give light and shadow, and a single, *red* filter for color. When these two images were projected, superimposed on a screen, even though red was the only color, they were perceived in full color with all the shades, and gradations of a three-color photograph![15] Even more remarkable is the fact that the objects used were deliberately chosen to provide no cues as to their color. To be sure that his viewers didn't unconsciously project color, Land photographed spools of plastic and wood and geometric objects whose color would be unknown to the viewer. How the eye and the visual centers of the brain function to achieve this remarkable feat of internal contexting is still only partially understood. But the actual stimulus does only part of the job.

Contexting probably involves at least two entirely different but interrelated processes—one inside the organism and the other outside. The first takes place in the brain and is a function of either past experience (programmed, internalized contexting) or the structure of the nervous system (innate contexting), or both. External contexting comprises the situation and/or setting in which an event occurs, (situational and/or environmental contexting).[16]

One example of the growing interest in the relationship of external context to behavior is the widespread interest and concern about our public-housing disasters. Pruitt-Igoe Homes in St. Louis is only one example. This $26-million fiasco imposed on poor blacks is now almost completely abandoned. All but a few buildings have been dynamited, because nobody wants to live there.

Objections and defects in high-rise public housing for poor families are legion: Mothers can't supervise their children; there are usually no community service agencies nearby and no stores or markets; and quite often there is no access to any public transportation system. There are no recreation centers for teenagers and few places for young children to play. In any budget crunch, the first thing to be cut is maintenance and then the disintegration process starts; elevators and hallways turn into death traps. The case against high-rise housing for low-income families is complex and underscores the growing recognition that environments are not behaviorally neutral.

Although situational and environmental context has only recently been systematically studied, environmental effects have been known to be a factor in behavior for years. Such men as the industrialist Pullman[17] made statements that sounded very advanced at the time. He believed that if workers were supplied with clean, airy, well-built homes in pleasant surroundings, this would exert a positive influence on their health and general sense of well-being and would make them more productive as well. Pullman was not wrong in his analysis. He simply did not live up to his stated ideals. The main street of his company town, where supervisors lived, was everything he talked about. But his workers were still poorly housed. Being isolated in a company town in close proximity to the plush homes of managers made their inadequate living conditions more obvious by way of contrast, and the workers finally embarked on a violent strike. There were many other human, economic, and political needs, which Pullman had not taken into account, that led to worker dissatisfaction. Pullman's pro-

fessed idealism backfired. Few were aware of the conditions under which his laborers actually lived and worked, so that the damage done to the budding but fragile environmentalist position was incalculable and gave ammunition to the "hard-nosed," "practical" types whose minds were focused on the bottom-line figures of profit and loss.

Quite often, the influence of either programmed contexting (experience) or innate contexting (which is built in) is brushed aside. Consider the individual's spatial needs and his feelings about certain spaces. For example, I have known women who needed a room to be alone in, whose husbands did not share this particular need, and they brushed aside their wives' feelings, dismissing them as childish. Women who have this experience should not let my talking about it raise their blood pressure. For it is very hard for someone who does not share an unstated, informal need with another person to experience that need as tangible and valid. Among people of northern European heritage, the only generally accepted proxemic needs are those associated with status. However, status is linked to the ego. Therefore, while people accept that the person at the top gets a large office, whenever the subject of spatial needs surfaces it is likely to be treated as a form of narcissism. The status and organizational aspects are recognized while internal needs are not.

Yet, people have spatial needs independent of status. Some people can't work unless they are in the midst of a lot of hubbub. Others can't work unless they are behind closed doors, cut off from auditory and visual distractions. Some are extraordinarily sensitive to their environments, as though they had tentacles from the body reaching out and touching everything. Others are impervious to environmental impact. It is these differences, when and if they are understood at all, that cause trouble for architects. Their primary concern is with aesthetics, and what I am talking about lies underneath aesthetics, at a much more basic level.

As often happens, today's problems are being solved in terms of yesterday's understanding. With few exceptions, most thinking on the man-environment relationship fails to make the man-environment (M-E) transaction specific, to say nothing of taking it into account. The sophisticated architect pays lip service to the M-E relationship and then goes right on with what he was going to do anyway, demonstrating once more that people's needs, cultural as well as individual—needing a room of one's own—are not seen as real. Only the building is real! (This is extension transference again.)

Of course, the process is much more complex than most people think. Until quite recently, this whole relationship had been unexplored.[18] Perhaps those who eschewed it did so because they unconsciously and intuitively recognized its complexity. Besides, it is much easier to deal with such simple facts as a balance sheet or the exterior design of a building. Anyone who begins to investigate context and contexting soon discovers that much of what is examined, even though it occurs before his eyes, is altered in its significance by many hidden factors. Support for research into these matters is picayune. What has to be studied is not only very subtle but is thought to be too fine-grained, or even trivial, to warrant serious consideration.

One hospital administrator once threw me out of his office because I wanted to study the effects of space on patients in his hospital. Not only was he not interested in the literature, which was then considerable, but he thought I was a nut to even suggest such a study. To complicate things further, proxemics research requires an inordinate amount of time. For every distance that people use, there are at least five major categories of variables that influence what is perceived as either correct or improper. Take the matter of "intrusion distance" (the distance one has to maintain from two people who are already talking in order to get attention but not intrude). How great this distance is and how long one must wait before moving in depends on: what is going on (activity), your status, your relationship in a social system (husband and wife or boss and subordinate), the emotional state of the parties, the urgency of the needs of the individual who must intrude, etc.

Despite this new information, research in the social and biological sciences has turned away from context. In fact, attempts are often made to consciously exclude context. Fortunately, there are a few exceptions, men and women who have been willing to swim against the main currents of psychological thought.

One of these is Roger Barker, who summarized twenty-five years of observations in a small Kansas town in his book *Ecological Psychology*.[19] Starting a generation ago, Barker and his students moved into the town and recorded the behavior of the citizens in a wide variety of situations and settings such as classrooms, drugstores, Sunday-school classes, basketball games, baseball games, club meetings, business offices, bars, and hangouts. Barker discovered that much of people's behavior is situation-dependent (under control of the setting), to a much greater degree than had been supposed. In fact, as a psychologist, he challenged many of the central and important tenets of his own field. In his words:

The view is not uncommon among psychologists that the environment of behavior is a relatively unstructured, passive, probabilistic arena of objects and events upon which man behaves in accordance with the programming he carries about within himself. . . . When we look at the environment of behavior as a phenomenon worthy of investigation for itself, and not as an instrument for unraveling the behavior-relevant programming within persons, the situation is quite different. From this viewpoint the environment is seen to consist of highly structured, improbable arrangements of objects and events which coerce behavior in accordance with their own dynamic patterning. . . . We found . . . that we could predict some aspects of children's behavior more adequately from knowledge of the behavior characteristics of the drugstores, arithmetic classes, and basketball games they inhabited than from knowledge of the behavior tendencies of particular children. . . . (emphasis added) (p. 4)

Later Barker states,

The theory and data support the view that the environment in terms of behavior settings is much more than a source of random inputs to its inhabitants, or of inputs arranged in fixed array and flow patterns. They indicate, rather, that the envi-

ronment provides inputs with controls that regulate the inputs in accordance with the systemic requirements of the environment, on the one hand, and in accordance with the behavior attributes of its human components, on the other. This means that the same environmental unit provides different inputs to different persons, and different inputs to the same person if his behavior changes; and it means, further, that the whole program of the environment's inputs changes if its own ecological properties change; if it becomes more or less populous, for example. (p. 205)[20]

Barker demonstrates that in studying man *it is impossible to separate the individual from the environment in which he functions.* Much of the work of the transactional psychologists Ames, Ittelson, and Kilpatrick,[21] as well as my earlier work,[22] leads to the same conclusion.

In summary, regardless of where one looks, one discovers that a universal feature of information systems is that meaning (what the receiver is expected to do) is made up of: the communication, the background and preprogrammed responses of the recipient, and the situation. (We call these last two the internal and external context.)

Therefore, what the receiver actually perceives is important in understanding the nature of context. Remember that what an organism perceives is influenced in four ways—by status, activity, setting, and experience. But in man one must add another crucial dimension: *culture.*

Any transaction can be characterized as high-, low-, or middle-context [Figure 1]. HC transactions feature preprogrammed information that is in the receiver and in the setting, with only minimal information in the transmitted message. LC transactions are the reverse. Most of the information must be in the transmitted message in order to make up for what is missing in the context (both internal and external).

In general, HC communication, in contrast to LC, is economical, fast, efficient, and satisfying; however, time must be devoted to programming. If this programming does not take place, the communication is incomplete.

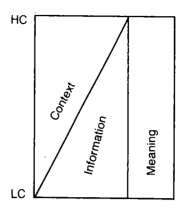

Figure 1

HC communications are frequently used as art forms. They act as a unifying, cohesive force, are long-lived, and are slow to change. LC communications do not unify; however, they can be changed easily and rapidly. This is why evolution by extension is so incredibly fast; extensions in their initial stages of development are low-context. To qualify this statement somewhat, some extension systems are higher on the context scale than others. A system of defense rocketry can be out of date before it is in place and is therefore very low-context. Church architecture, however, was for hundreds of years firmly rooted in the past and was the material focus for preserving religious beliefs and ideas. Even today, most churches are still quite traditional in design. One wonders if it is possible to develop strategies for balancing two apparently contradictory needs: the need to adapt and change (by moving in the low-context direction) and the need for stability (high-context). History is replete with examples of nations and institutions that failed to adapt by holding on to high-context modes too long. The instability of low-context systems, however, on the present-day scale is quite new to mankind. And furthermore, there is no reservoir of experience to show us how to deal with changes at this rate.

Extensions that now make up most of man's world are for the most part low-context. The question is, how long can man stand the tension between himself and his extensions? This is what *Future*

Shock[23] and *Understanding Media*[24] are all about. Take a single example, the automobile, which completely altered the American scene in all its dimensions—exploded communities, shredded the fabric of relationships, switched the rural-urban balance, changed our sex mores and churchgoing habits, altered our cities, crime, education, warfare, health, funerals. (One undertaker recently experimented with drive-in viewing of the corpse!) In summary:

The screens that one imposes between oneself and reality constitute one of the ways in which reality is structured.

Awareness of that structure is necessary if one is to control behavior with any semblance of rationality. Such awareness is associated with the low-context end of the scale.

Yet there is a price that must be paid for awareness—instability; obsolescence, and change at a rate that may become impossible to handle and result in information overload.

Therefore, as things become more complex, as they inevitably must with fast-evolving, low-context systems, it eventually becomes necessary to turn life and institutions around and move toward the greater stability of the high-context part of the scale as a way of dealing with information overload.

NOTES

1. *The Hidden Dimension* discusses this quality of culture in more detail.

2. Meier (1963)

3. Man also imposes a selective screen between the conscious part of his mind and the unconscious part. Sullivan (1947) and Freud (1933)

4. Whorf (1956)

5. Polanyi (1968)

6. Sullivan (1947)

7. The linguist Noam Chomsky (1968) and his followers have tried to deal with the contexting feature of language by eliminating context and going to so-called "deep structure." The results are interesting but end up evading the main issues of communication and to an even greater extent stress ideas at the expense of what is actually going on.

8. For further information on Chinese, see Wang (1973).

9. Bernstein (1964)

10. Eiseley (1969)

11. I do not agree with Eiseley's generalizing about all of mankind, because activism, like everything else, has to be taken in context. As we will see, LC cultures appear to be more vulnerable to violent perturbations than HC cultures.

12. Saul Bellow's (1974) article on the role of literature in a setting of changing times is also relevant to this discussion. Bellow makes the point that for some time now there has been a conscious effort on the part of avant-garde Western intellectuals to obliterate the past. "Karl Marx felt in history the tradition of all dead generations weighing like a nightmare on the brain of the living. Nietzsche speaks movingly of 'it was,' and Joyce's Stephen Dedalus also defines history as a 'nightmare from which we are trying to awaken.'" Bellow points out, however, that there is a paradox that must be met, for to do away with history is to destroy one's own part in the historical process. It is reasonably certain, however, that what these men were trying to do was to redefine context in order to reduce its influence on men's actions. Simply to do away with the past would lead to an incredibly unstable society, as we shall see.

13. Black culture is much higher on the context scale than white culture, and one would assume from our model that riots do not have the same meaning for blacks as they do to the white society in which the blacks are imbedded.

14. Birren (1961)

15. For further details on this fascinating set of experiments, see Land (1959).

16. These distinctions are completely arbitrary and are for the convenience of the writer and the reader. They do not necessarily occur in nature. The inside-outside dichotomy has been struck down many times, not only by the perceptual transactionalists (Kilpatrick, 1961) following in Dewey's footsteps but in my own writings as well. Within the brain, experience (culture) acts on the structure of the brain to produce mind. It makes little difference *how* the brain is modified; what is important is that modification does take place and is apparently continuous.

17. Buder (1967)

18. See Hall (1966) for a comprehensive treatment of man's relationship to the spaces he builds as well as a bibliography on the subject.

19. Barker (1968) and Barker and Schoggen (1973)

20. The interested reader will find it worthwhile to consult Barker's works directly.

21. Kilpatrick (1961)

22. Hall (1966)

23. Toffler (1970)

24. McLuhan (1964)

BIBLIOGRAPHY

Barker, Roger G. *Ecological Psychology*. Stanford, Calif.: Stanford University Press, 1968.
————, and Schoggen, Phil. *Qualities of Community Life*. San Francisco: Jossey-Bass, 1973.
Bellow, Saul. "Machines and Story Books," *Harper's Magazine*, Vol. 249, pp. 48–54, August 1974.
Bernstein, Basil. "Elaborated and Restricted Codes: Their Social Origins and Some Consequences." In John J. Gumperz and Dell Hymes (eds.). The Ethnography of Communication, *American Anthropologist*, Vol. 66, No. 6, Part II, pp. 55–69, 1964.
Birren, Faber. *Color, Form and Space*. New York: Reinhold, 1961.
Buder, Stanley. "The Model Town of Pullman: Town Planning and Social Control in the Gilded Age," *Journal of the American Institute of Planners*, Vol. 33, No. 1, pp. 2–10, January 1967.
Chomsky, Noam. *Language and Mind*. New York: Harcourt, Brace & World, Inc., 1968.
Eiseley, L. "Activism and the Rejection of History," *Science*, Vol. 165, p. 129, July 11, 1969.
Freud, Sigmund. *New Introductory Lectures on Psychoanalysis*. New York: W. W. Norton & Company, Inc., 1933.
Hall, Edward T. "Art, Space and the Human Experience." In Gyorgy Kepes (ed.). *Arts of the Environment*. New York: George Braziller, Inc., 1972.
————. *The Hidden Dimension*. Garden City, N.Y.: Doubleday, 1966.
————. "Human Needs and Inhuman Cities." In *The Fitness of Man's Environment, Smithsonian Annual II*. Washington, D.C.: Smithsonian Institution Press, 1968. Reprinted in *Ekistics*, Vol. 27, No. 160, March 1969.
Kilpatrick, F. P. *Explorations in Transactional Psychology* (contains articles by Adelbert Ames, Hadley Cantril, William Ittelson, and F. P. Kilpatrick). New York: New York University Press, 1961.
McLuhan, Marshall. *Understanding Media*. New York: McGraw-Hill, 1964.
Meier, Richard. "Information Input Overload: Features of Growth in Communications-Oriented Institutions," *Libri* (Copenhagen), Vol. 13, No. 1, pp. 1–44, 1963.
Polanyi, M. "Life's Irreducible Structure," *Science*, Vol. 160, pp. 1308–12, June 21, 1968.
Sullivan, Harry Stack. *Conceptions of Modern Psychiatry*. New York: William Alanson White Psychiatric Foundation, 1947.
Toffler, Alvin. *Future Shock*. New York: Bantam Books, 1970.
Wang, William. "The Chinese Language," *Scientific American*, Vol. 228, No. 2, February 1973.
Whorf, Benjamin Lee. *Language, Thought, and Reality*. New York: The Technology Press of M.I.T. and John Wiley, 1956.

Relevance and Application of Intercultural Communication Theory and Research

FELIPE KORZENNY

Theory and research in culture and communication are essential for self-understanding, the development of relationships, the conduct of business, and ultimately for the preservation of our species and habitat. This paper will first examine the relationship between communication and culture. Second, the reader will find a section that addresses the influence of intercultural theory and research on practice. Third, and to conclude, this paper will point to several reasons why the study of communication and culture is important.

CULTURE AND COMMUNICATION

In a general and abstract fashion, the study of culture can be said to be the study of communication. Communication is said to be the glue of society. In a planetary metaphor, communication is the gravitational force that keeps the planets in a certain relation to each other. Culture, in a parallel fashion, is the mechanism that allows human beings to make sense of the world, and to deal with it. Culture is a

This original essay appears here for the first time. All rights reserved. Permission to reprint must be obtained from the author and the publisher. The major concepts in this paper were presented at the Spotlight Program "Why Study Culture?" at the Sixth Annual Intercultural and International Communication Conference at the University of Miami, Florida, February, 1989. Felipe Korzenny teaches at San Francisco State University.

mix of manifest and latent patterns of behavior and relationships among human beings, patterns that allow humans to function and strive in the pursuit of order and survival. Culture is a social product and is the result of humans originating interaction, that is, communication processes. While it is true that not all cultural manifestations are communication expressions *per se*, the factors that lead to cultural manifestations must be communication processes.

In the practice of human communication, then, we create, change, and/or reinforce culture. Journalists, broadcasters, artists, speech writers, producers, directors, communication teachers, and all of us who interact with others influence culture, although to different extents and for different reasons. It is clear, however, that the modification of culture is a relatively slow process. Cultural change is usually slow because the acquisition of generally accepted ways of doing things requires widespread acceptance; once a cultural pattern has been widely communicated and adopted, however, it becomes relatively stable. We humans have the tendency to cling to our culture as to our clothing—we fear being naked. Our culture is like a security blanket; it is that with which we are familiar and comfortable. The culture one identifies with has been infused in one's being since early in life, and to each person it seems to be the most logical, consistent, and appealing way of life. Our culture constitutes an important set of tools that enables daily living, providing us with assumptions and established routines that reduce the need for constant reinvention and, in so doing, allowing for what we call progress. Culture, however, runs in the background, and it seldom makes itself explicit. The practice of intercultural communication, therefore, may entail the modification of culture for more adaptive living, making culture explicit so individuals may better understand themselves and others in a particular context.

THE INFLUENCE OF THEORY AND RESEARCH ON PRACTICE

Communication is an essential part of culture and a condition for it. Intercultural communication, a very broad umbrella title for the study of communication and culture, has made great progress in the past twenty years. The field proper is only about that old. Perhaps the most important contribution of intercultural communication theory and research has been an agenda-setting function. Currently it is acceptable and understandable to speak of intercultural training for those who need to interact with other cultures; it is unquestionable that teachers need to have intercultural skills to succeed in the most challenging task of educating a multicultural student body; and it is now in vogue to speak of training for a multicultural work force. Journalists today seem to accept the notion of cultural sensitivity and respect in covering and reporting culturally diverse communities. Advertising and marketing specialists dedicate large budgets and attention to culturally different markets. Diplomatic efforts are beginning to explore and utilize such intercultural communication constructs as *face*, *uncertainty reduction*, and *high- versus low-context communication*. In the United States, we have long assumed a common traditional past, involving the notion of an undifferentiated melting pot, but this assumption has been replaced with the image of a multicultural society. In this latter image, cultural differences need to be addressed rather than ignored, and the professionalization of intercultural practice is a necessity. The large number of bibliographic contributions in the past twenty years, as well as the emergence of intercultural communication divisions, interest groups, and associations, have contributed to making intercultural communication practice a universal need.

Academic interest and pursuit, in this case, has led and played an important role in the awakening of the need for practice, and this has not been easy. In contrast to other areas of endeavor, intercultural communication practice faces human barriers of great magnitude, such as the following:

1. *Natural but endemic ethnocentrism* which, below the surface, negates the importance of intercultural practice. This ethnocentrism is manifest in such statements as: "I already know that! I am not a racist! I know how to deal with those people." It is very difficult for most of us to accept the fact that we naturally give preference to the in-group over the out-group. It is, however, an innate tendency of humans to attribute increased importance to those who are closer to the self. Perceived similarity along multiple dimensions, including ethnic background, values, beliefs, costumes, and patterns of relationships, is the basis for evaluating others. We are most likely to attribute positive traits to those similar to us, but because to do so is, paradoxically, a societal taboo, we deny it. The denial of ethnocentrism may be one of the most crucial barriers to intercultural communication because such denial prevents confrontation, clarification, and acceptance. Accepting that ethnocentrism is natural and endemic should be an important first step in the realization that in this turbulent period, when space and time are dramatically shrunk, we must overcome ethnocentrism for survival.

2. *Assumed similarity.* Culture is like water for the fish: We are in it and are part of it but we do not see it. A great temptation exists to assume that others are just like us, and if they are different it is because they have not developed, or because they are defective (or of a superior kind, whatever the case may be). The external manifestations of culture—food, buildings, dress—are too obvious to ignore. Implicit or subjective culture is invisible, but it is the dimension of culture that is most likely to affect human interaction. The values, beliefs, attitudes, behavioral patterns, and role relationships that different cultures hold dear are difficult to detect by members of each culture as well as by those who are alien. Making culture explicit will therefore help us understand ourselves in contrast to others. The expertise to make culture explicit does not come easily, and that is a role that intercultural communication professionals can assume.

3. *Lack of immediate rewards.* In the field of diffusion of innovations, preventive innovations are known to face important difficulties—they do not have obvious consequences; for example, if you use a seat belt you do not observe yourself being safer.

One of the main difficulties of the application of intercultural communication theory and research is that few, if any, rewards are immediate, and it is difficult for most of us to delay gratification. For instance, it takes a long time to detect the benefits of an intercultural communication workshop. Intercultural communication skills and sensitivity are likely to be rewarded in the long term through better understanding and consequent good will, as well as material gains. Reports of the "bizarre," on the other hand, are readily rewarded with attention and money. Showing short-term profits, for example, is seen as true accomplishment by scattered shareholders. Currently, therefore, in our economic system, we have seen dramatic shortsightedness in business; meaningless takeovers appear to be more important than the cultivation of long-term business strategies. In contrast, intercultural communication training and research would be most likely to reward long-term strategies in the cycle of economic productivity.

4. *Cost and effort beyond expectations.* It is usual to assume that intercultural communication skills and practice are easy to come by. Books and cultural "capsules" exist that provide "quick-and-easy" prescriptions, but intercultural communication is just not that easy, unfortunately. In the first place, the multivariate and complex nature of intercultural communication makes effective, fast-and-easy solutions very difficult to find. It is important to remember that research and development projects in the physical sciences are frequently funded at the level of several million dollars. In the social sciences in general, and communication in particular, it is difficult to find research and development projects funded at the $100,000 level. The implication can thus be drawn that electronic components are more important and complex than humans. The temptation is to get rid of the "human problem" quickly so that we can proceed with business. In truth, however, human behavior is highly complex, and it is not until we acknowledge its importance in the productive cycle of our social system that we will be realistic in our expectations.

THE IMPORTANCE OF THE STUDY OF CULTURE AND COMMUNICATION

There are several benefits derived from the study of culture and communication. The following generalizations and assertions highlight the importance of intercultural communication for practitioners.

Intercultural communication provides remediation of the cultural filter that information processors impose on the content. Culture in this role is of extreme importance since only limited effects of the media can be expected, due to selective exposure, attention, perception, and recall. Clearly, a large part of these phenomena are culturally mediated. One of the main findings in media research within a "plural" perspective has been that media effects are highly dependent on the background and social context of the receivers, or, better stated, processors of information. This fact is seen in current attempts at revitalizing American pragmatism in communication through symbolic interactionism, coordinated management of meaning, and other means. The way diverse cultural groups interpret information is not straightforward. For example, the reason why black viewers seem to be more lenient about drug-related issues and crime, as my research shows, can very well be due to the meshing of the context of the blacks as processors with the media portrayals observed. In other words, people are likely to interpret information according to the circumstances of their immediate lives. My research on international news effects has clearly demonstrated that there is no monolithic media impact but a diversity of interpretations. This lack of homogeneity contradicts the claims of many mass-oriented scholars, who have traditionally argued that the U.S. media is homogenous and that consequently it homogenizes its audiences. The conceptualization of communication processors, and the recognition of audiences as plural collections of individuals and not masses, should prove useful in future pragmatic endeavors.

Cultural understanding avoids the pitfalls of early development communication research. Early development communication efforts ignored the value and usefulness of other cultures: It was assumed that only Western life styles were "modern" or "productive." With that bias, the application of stereotyped remedies became an obsession, and the outcome was frequently failure. "Just make those people more modern, more rational" seemed to be the motto. Only recently has the understanding of social information processing modes and information needs resulted in well-tailored efforts, geared to alleviate social problems. Examples are Radio Netherlands rural journalism programs in Ecuador, where rural journalists are trained to serve their own communities, and integrated farming and research systems, where farmers contribute to their own agricultural research. When one is able to understand the function of cultural traits for the members of a culture, one is able to appreciate those traits. The idea that Western values are held by all people is now being questioned by academics and increasingly by practitioners.

The study of culture helps us understand ourselves. If we accept the premise that we learn by contrast, then intercultural communication research and theory provides us with the mirror that projects an image, which can be pleasing or displeasing but which sets us in the context of human interaction. We must believe that we are only able to "know," to understand, ourselves in the context of other social beings and the diversity that now pervades our world. How can we evaluate our actions or beliefs without a point of comparison? Literature dealing with communication and culture has been largely anecdotal. Currently, as more research becomes available, contrasts of different ethnic groups and nationalities are being substantiated or negated. My research on cross-cultural comparisons of Anglo-Americans, Hispanics, Asians, and blacks has confirmed or disconfirmed many of those anecdotal accounts, and I believe that this type of comparative research serves as a mirror in which we can find ourselves in comparison to others. We are different, but understanding the differences may allow us to appreciate them, and, consequently, to be able to better tailor our messages and strategies to promote

understanding. As our differences become evident, our "selves" thus become more knowable to us, and we become less prejudiced.

Prejudice in the media is a manifestation of the beliefs of those who are in charge. Intercultural communication theory and research can assist in allowing individuals to become aware of their own prejudices. A prejudiced media, however, can only reinforce the status quo. The realization of prejudice does not eliminate it but provides individuals with the departing point for managing ethnocentrism, and, indeed, perhaps the acceptance and recognition of prejudice is the best point of departure for its effective social management. As previously discussed, a view of the world that contains wider categories for the classification of cultural experiences may assist in the promotion of collaboration among culturally diverse individuals. These sensitizing efforts can best be achieved by communication professionals who have themselves been trained in intercultural communication theory and research. The media, with its ample power of message distribution, may, under the proper management, begin to help audiences question prejudice.

Communication rules are seldom explicit; they must be uncovered. As the fish in the water is unaware of the water, we are unaware of the cultural rules that dictate patterns of interaction. Cross-cultural understanding, then, requires that the rules of cultural "others" and "our own" be made explicit. Edward T. Hall[1] has made an important contribution in arguing that "going beyond culture" is necessary for communication to take place among the culturally diverse, but to go beyond culture, it is necessary to first know it. Once we are able to transcend culture, we are in the position to strive toward convergence in achieving understanding. It is as if open confrontation functions as a prerequisite for harmony among the culturally diverse. But the confrontation of orientations must be planned for, with the intention of achieving cooperation.

Establishing an intercultural relationship requires attention to the subtle aspects of culture. Advertising, marketing, counseling, teaching, public service, and news coverage require the cultural sensitivity that only truly bicultural/multicultural individuals can have. So, more than being understood, for successful practice culture needs to be lived. This is easier said than done, however. Those catering to the tastes and needs of diverse cultural groups need to immerse themselves in those cultures, obtain the collaboration of cultural informants, and sincerely attempt to serve the needs of those individuals. Lip service and pro forma research are not successful long-term alternatives. The provision of services and products to culturally different persons entails the communication positioning of that service or product in terms that address the reality of the other culture. Selling expensive hotel rooms to individuals who culturally prefer to stay with friends and family when traveling, for example, is simply absurd. Bicultural or multicultural individuals are in the best position to serve as bridges, but these intercultural persons are difficult to find and training for these skills is not readily available. Our understanding of intercultural communication should provide the means to produce these needed cultural interpreters.

Although knowledge of a culture provides the cognitive tools for understanding, only acting in a culture can provide the tools for appropriate emotional and motor responses. While we are in a different cultural environment, we are operating in a distorted psychological space and do not know it. It seems as if continuous bumping against the walls of the new culture is one of the most effective learning processes. Studying a culture in books or movies may not be enough, because motor behavioral shaping takes place independently from verbal behavior. In a book I may learn that "those different" people value individualism, and I may be able to describe such a value. Most likely, however, I will not feel comfortable with individualism until I incorporate it into my behavioral repertoire in particular contexts—that is, until I experience the reward of individualism in a particular situation. To be able to function within a culture, therefore, one has to experiment within it. Basically one needs to approach cultural learning with reserved optimism, as one needs to learn how to accept failure, and this learning can be seen as a benefit of cultural shock, if one is prepared for it. It is better to know in advance that the task of intercultural communication will be difficult, because then the encounter with reality will be less severe than if one expects no difficulties.

The study of culture and communication will become more important, but the nature of the individual culture and the problems analyzed will be different. Customized cultures are likely to evolve as individuals become increasingly isolated from traditional human contact and their choices of channels multiply dramatically. The media choices available will enable subsets of individuals to share with each other a culture or cultural domains that do not resemble cultures of the past—these will be electronic cultures. As humans increasingly have more and more choices of media channels, their ability to control the cultural inputs will be greater. New cultures will emerge that encompass individuals who may have never been with each other physically. Other, older cultures may be reinforced through the availability of multiple cultural manifestations on recorded media. As interpersonal contact decreases, a new diversity may emerge that needs to be understood. Further, it looks like there is no going back, although perhaps in the relatively distant future a knowledge navigator will re-enable human interaction and return individuals to the idyllic global village envisioned by Marshall McLuhan.

The study of communication and culture can prevent war. Appropriate interpretations of actions can certainly lead to the reduction of tensions. Faulty attributions of intention, on the other hand, tend to be dominant causes of friction and stress across nations and cultural groups. How do individuals from different cultures reduce uncertainty in negotiation? What are the face-saving strategies common to different cultures? What are the conflict styles that characterize diverse cultures? Are there universal human principles that can provide a framework for mediation and understanding? How can international negotiators become intercultural persons? These and other questions, likely to be answered through the study of intercultural communication, are perhaps the most ambitious practical contribution that this field can make.

NOTES

1. Hall, Edward T. (1967). *Beyond Culture*. Garden City, N.Y.: Anchor Books.

CONCEPTS AND QUESTIONS
FOR CHAPTER 1

1. Porter and Samovar have asserted that people are not yet prepared for life in a global village. What does that mean? Do you agree or disagree with that assertion? Why?

2. How does the concept of a global village affect your view of international relations and your ability to relate to world events?

3. What does Barnlund mean by the "collective unconscious" and how does it relate to intercultural communication?

4. In what ways are intercultural communication and communication alike? In what ways are they different?

5. What is meant by social perception, and how does it relate to intercultural communication?

6. What is the relationship between culture and perception?

7. What are the six categories of intercultural communication difficulties discussed by Argyle? How do cultural differences within these areas affect intercultural communication?

8. How does Hall's discussion of high- and low-context communication relate to some of the underlying premises about intercultural communication?

9. What is meant by the term *cultural value*? How are these values manifest within a given culture?

10. How do the two major religious orientations differ? What effect could these differences have on intercultural communication?

11. How would someone from an extremely different cultural background respond on a first visit to your city? To your home?

12. What influences have theory and research had on the practice of intercultural communication?

13. Korzenny claims natural but endemic ethnocentrism is a barrier to intercultural communication. What does he mean by this?

14. Explain Korzenny's statement that culture is like water to a fish.

15. If the United States is to emerge into a pluralistic, multicultural society, what contribution can you make in preparing for this society?

PART TWO

Socio-Cultural Backgrounds: What We Bring to Intercultural Communication

All persons are puzzles until at last we find in some word or act the key to the man, to the woman; straightaway all their past words and actions lie in light before us.

—*Emerson*

One of the most important aspects of human communication is the fact that the experiential backgrounds participants bring to a communication experience and the social context in which that communication takes place will affect their behavior during the encounter. Psychologists A. H. Hastorf and H. Cantril underscore this issue when they note that each person acts according to the personal uniqueness he or she brings to the occasion. Think about those countless situations when you and some friends shared an experience and found that there were major differences in your reactions. What you deemed dull your companions found exciting; what you considered pointless they found meaningful. The messages received were the same for all participants; yet, because each of you has a unique personality, you experienced a variety of feelings, sensations, and responses. Each of you brought a different background to the event and as a result attributed an individual meaning to the shared experience. In short, the event meant what it did to you because of your own unique past history.

We thus contend that in order to understand any communication encounter you must appreciate the idea that there is much more to communication than the mere analysis of messages. Messages and the responses individuals make to them are products of their unique past experiences, which greatly contribute to the "immutable barriers in nature" between each individual's thoughts.

Individual past experience takes on added significance when we introduce the many dimensions of culture. Individuals are influenced not only by personal experiences but more importantly by their culture as well. As we detailed in Part One, culture refers to those cumulative deposits of knowledge, beliefs, views, values, and behaviors acquired by a large group of people and passed on from one generation to the next. In this sense, culture, in both conscious and unconscious ways, not only teaches how to think and what to think about but also dictates such values as what is attractive and what is ugly, what is good and what is evil, and what is appropriate and what is not. In addition, culture teaches such things as how close to stand next to strangers, how to greet friends, when to speak and when to remain silent, and even the various ways in which you can display your anger. When you are interacting with others and become disturbed by their actions, you can, for instance, cry, become physically violent, shout, or remain silent. Each of these behaviors is a manifestation of what you have learned; it is largely influenced by your culture.

These cultural influences affect your ways of perceiving and acting; they contain the societal experiences and values that are passed from generation to generation. Because these behaviors are so much a part of your persona, there is a danger that you might forget they are culturally diverse. This is why a person from Japan, for example, might remain silent if disturbed by someone's actions while an Israeli or an Italian will more likely verbalize such displeasure.

Whatever the culture, you can better understand your behavior and the reactions of others if you realize that what you are hearing and seeing is a reflection of that culture. As you might predict, this understanding is greatly facilitated when your cultural experiences are similar to those of the people with whom you are interacting. Conversely, when different and diverse backgrounds are brought to a communication encounter, it is often difficult to share internal states and feelings. In this section we focus on those difficulties by examining some of the experiences and perceptual backgrounds found in a variety of foreign cultures, as well as those found in a number of American co-

cultures. We also give a detailed examination of how cultural diversity affects the social context in which communication takes place and its effects on the interaction.

2

International Cultures: Understanding Diversity

Communication among members of international cultures poses one of the most perplexing intercultural communication problems. How we are to understand others when they come from different sections of the global village is a most difficult question. We need only to look around the world at any particular moment in time to find disagreement, strife, and fighting—the locations may change, but the problems persist. Nations become prominent in the news, and what happens within them and between them directly affects the entire world. Although few of us at present are directly involved with these countries, we may be in contact with their students who are studying in the United States; they may be our classmates or our students.

To help us better understand people from international cultures, we must learn to appreciate their diversity. This means that we must pass through a state of toleration for that which is different and develop true appreciation of the diversity, from which will come a perspective to help us learn how to interact with those people with whom we do come in contact. This chapter offers articles that will introduce us to the diversity in cultural values as well as in specific international cultures.

Understanding how people in other cultures view their world is crucial to successful intercultural communication. World view establishes how people view themselves, each other, and their places in the universe and serves as an underlying pattern for interaction within a culture: You interact with others according to how you view one another.

Perhaps one of the greatest cultural dichotomies in interaction patterns is found between North Americans and East Asians. In her article "The Impact of Confucianism on Interpersonal Relationships and Communication Patterns in East Asia," June Ock Yum paints for us an intriguing picture of Confucianism's effect on how people view and interact with one another. She traces the various major components of Confucian philosophy and how they tend to determine East Asian patterns of interaction. As a counterpoint to her discussion, Yum makes continuous comparisons to prevalent North American interaction patterns so you can easily understand the differences between the two cultures.

Nemi C. Jain shifts our attention to the Indian subcontinent as he provides a glimpse of Hindu culture in his article "World View and Cultural Patterns of India." Jain demonstrates how the Hindu world view and traditions of reincarnation, *dharma*, stages of life, caste system, and spirit of tolerance, which have persisted over thousands of years, permeate the Indian culture. This provides a basis for the perceptual frames of reference common to all of India and a feeling for what it is to be Hindu.

Continuing our excursion around the globe, we move next to the continent of Africa. In their article "Cultural Patterns of the Maasai," Lisa Skow and Larry A. Samovar give us a thoughtful and insightful view of the Maasai culture, which has shunned almost all Western influences and has tried to remain "pure" African. Unlike many other African cultures, it has almost completely rejected Western forms of government, dress, language, music, and religion. Skow and Samovar give us a clear view of the culture by tracing its history, values, and world view. They then discuss Maasai verbal and nonverbal processes and show how they are influenced by the prevailing Maasai culture.

We turn next to an examination of the Arabic culture. Janice Walker Anderson's article "A Comparison of Arab and American Conceptions of 'Effective' Persuasion" details for you Arabic orientations toward discourse. She shows the differences between Arabic and American concepts of persuasion and the cultural diversity in persuasive strategies.

In the last article, ". . . So Near the United States: Notes on Communication Between Mexicans and North Americans," John Condon analyzes the cultural relations between North Americans and Mexicans, concentrating on differences in how they perceive things in the context of working relationships.

The Impact of Confucianism on Interpersonal Relationships and Communication Patterns in East Asia

JUNE OCK YUM

INTRODUCTION

New communication technology has removed many of the physical barriers against communication between the East and the West, but there remain philosophical and cultural barriers, which are not well understood. The increased opportunity for interaction between different cultural groups, however, has sensitized some scholars to the need to study Eastern perspectives on communication.

Most cross-cultural studies of communication simply describe foreign communication patterns and then compare them to those of North America, rarely going beneath the surface to explore the source of such differences. This paper goes beyond these limitations and explores the philosophical roots of the communication patterns in East Asian countries, before comparing them to those of North America. The assumption here is that communication is a basic social process and that, as such, it is influenced by the philosophical foundations and value systems of the society in which it is found.

There is always a danger in generalizing certain cultural patterns to large geographical areas. Even

This original essay appears here in print for the first time. All rights reserved. Permission to reprint must be obtained from the author and the publisher. Professor Yum teaches at Towson State University, Towson, Maryland.

though we often refer to "Eastern" or "Asian" perspectives, there are many patterns, sometimes contradictory, within the region. For instance, the popular notion that Asians are more spiritual than Westerners might apply to India but not to China, Korea, or Japan. Nakamura (1964) has maintained that the Chinese and the Japanese are much more nonmetaphysical than Westerners. For this reason, this paper is limited to the Far Eastern countries of China, Korea, and Japan, those that have been most influenced by Confucian philosophical principles. Other countries that have been influenced by Confucianism are expected to have similar characteristics. For instance, Vietnam, the only country in Southeast Asia to have been influenced more by China than India, also exhibits the strong emphasis on social relationships and devotion to the hierarchical family relations that are the essence of Confucian doctrines (Luce & Sommer, 1969).

SOCIAL RELATIONSHIPS VERSUS INDIVIDUALISM

If one has to select the main difference between East Asian and North American perspectives on communication, it would be the East Asian emphasis on social relationships as opposed to the North American emphasis on individualism. According to Hofstede (1980), individualism-collectivism is one of the main dimensions that differentiate cultures. He defined individualism as the emotional independence of individual persons from groups, organizations, or other collectivities. Parsons, Shils, and Olds (1951) have suggested that self-orientation versus collectivity orientation is one of the five basic pattern variables that determine human action. Self-orientation occurs when a person gives "priority in a given situation to his own private interests, independently of their bearings on the interests or values of a given collectivity" (Parsons, Shils, & Olds, 1951, p. 81), as opposed to taking directly into account the values and interests of the collectivity before acting.

The individualism-collectivism dichotomy, however, is not identical to the difference between the East Asian emphasis on social relationships and

North American emphasis on individualism. In East Asia, the emphasis is on proper social relationships and their maintenance rather than any abstract concern for a general collective body. In a sense, it is a collectivism only among those bound by social networks. For example, a recent study on the Chinese value system found that the Confucian value of reciprocity and proper relationships was not correlated with Hofstede's individualism-collectivism dimension (Chinese Culture Connection, 1987). Hui and Triandis (1986) have recommended that collectivism be treated in two different ways: (1) as a concern for a certain subset of people and (2) as a concern for a generalized collectivity of people.

In the 1830s, the French social philosopher Alexis de Tocqueville coined the term *individualism* to describe the most notable characteristic of American people. Bellah, Madsen, Sullivan, Swidler, and Tipton (1985, pp. vii, 142) agree that individualism lies at the very core of American culture, contending that "individualism . . . has marched inexorably through our history" and that "we believe in the dignity, indeed the sacredness, of the individual. Anything that would violate our right to think for ourselves, judge for ourselves, make our own decision, live our lives as we see fit, is not only morally wrong, it is sacrilegious." According to Varenne (1977), there is but one system of principles regulating interpersonal relationships in America and that is individualism.

Even though many Americans feel they must get involved, they are also committed to individualism, including the desire to cut free from the past and define one's own self. Thus, the primary mode of American involvement is choosing organizations that one can voluntarily join or voluntarily withdraw from. Varenne (1977, p. 53) said that Americans perceive social structure "not as a system made up of different groups considered to be in a symbiotic relationship, but rather of different individuals who come together to do something."

Considering this cultural orientation, it is not surprising that the dominant paradigm of communication is an individualistic one. Each communicator is perceived to be a separate individual engaging in diverse communicative activities to maximize his or her own self-interest, usually by means of some form of persuasion.

In contrast, the most notable characteristic in East Asia is the emphasis on social relationships. Hall and Beadsley (1965) have maintained that, compared to East Asian countries, North America is in the Stone Age when it comes to social relationships. This East Asian preoccupation with social relationships stems from the doctrines of Confucianism.

CONFUCIANISM

In the philosophical and cultural history of East Asia, Confucianism has endured as the basic social and political value system for over 1,000 years. One reason (and indication) that Confucianism has had such a profound impact is that it was adopted as the official philosophy of the Yi dynasty for 500 years in Korea, of the Tokugawa shogunate in Japan for 250 years, and of many dynasties in China.

Confucianism was institutionalized and propagated both through the formal curricula of the educational system and through the selection process of government officials. Confucian classics were required textbooks in the school systems throughout the history of China, Korea, and Japan before modern educational curricula were implemented. Government officials used to be selected through national exams that mostly examined the knowledge and the level of understanding of Confucian philosophy.

Another reason why Confucianism has exerted a much stronger impact than the other religious, philosophical systems of East Asia (such as Buddhism and Taoism) is that it is a pragmatic and present-oriented philosophy. When a student named Tzu-lu asked Confucius about serving spirits, Confucius said, "If one cannot yet serve men, how can he serve the spirits?" Asked about death, Confucius replied, "If you do not understand life, how can you understand death?" (McNaughton, 1974, p. 145). Max Weber commented, "Confucianism is extremely rationalistic since it is bereft of any form of metaphysics and in the sense that it lacks traces of nearly any religious basis. . . . At the same time, it is more realistic than any other system in the sense that it lacks

and excludes all measures which are not utilitarian" (quoted by Nakamura, 1964, p. 16).

Confucianism is a philosophy of human nature that considers proper human relationships as the basis of society. In studying human nature and motivation, Confucianism sets forth four principles from which right conduct arises: *jen* (humanism), *i* (faithfulness), *li* (propriety), and *chih* (wisdom or a liberal education).

The cardinal principle, *jen* (humanism), almost defies translation since it sums up the core of Confucianism. Fundamentally it means warm human feelings between people. *Jen* is like a seed from which spring all the qualities that make up the ideal man. In addition, *jen* refers to the possession of all these qualities to a high degree. The actual practice or embodiment of *jen* in our daily lives is closely related to the concept of reciprocity. Confucius said that practicing *jen* is not to do to another man what you yourself don't want. In his own words: "If there's something that you don't like in the person to your right, don't pass it on to the person on your left. If there's something you don't like in the person to your left, don't pass it on to the person on your right" (McNaughton, 1974, p. 29).

It is suggested that Confucius himself once picked out reciprocity (*shu*) as the core of his thought. Confucius said, "There has never been a case where a man who did not understand reciprocity was able to communicate to others whatever treasures he might have had stored in himself" (McNaughton, 1974, p. 28). Therefore, practicing *jen* implies the practice of *shu*, which in turn means to know how it would feel to be the other person; to become like-hearted, and to be able to empathize with others.

The second principle of Confucianism is *i*, meaning faithfulness, loyalty, or justice. As the definition suggests, this principle also has strong implications for social relationships. Like *jen*, *i* is a difficult concept to translate. It may be easier to understand *i* through its opposite concept, which is personal or individual interest and profit. *I* is thus that part of human nature that allows us to look beyond personal, immediate profit and to elevate ourselves to the original goodness of human nature that bridges ourselves to other people (Yum, 1987). According to the principle of i, human relationships are not based on individual profit but rather on the betterment of the common good.

If *jen* and i are the contents of the Confucian ethical system, *li* (propriety, rite, respect for social forms) is its outward form. As an objective criterion of social order, *li* was perceived as the rule of the universe and the fundamental regulatory etiquette of human behavior. Mencius suggested that *li* originated from deference to others and reservation of oneself. Confucius said that *li* follows from *jen*, that is, from being considerate to others. Only when people overcome themselves and so return to propriety can they reach humanness. On the other hand, propriety without humanness was perceived to be empty and useless.

THE IMPACT OF CONFUCIANISM ON INTERPERSONAL RELATIONSHIP PATTERNS

At least three of the four principles of Confucianism deal directly with social relationships. Under such a strong influence, East Asian countries have developed interpersonal relationship patterns that are quite different from the individualistic pattern of North America. Figure 1 illustrates these five differences.

Particularistic Versus Universalistic Relationships

Human relationships under Confucianism are not universalistic but particularistic. As we described earlier, the warm human feelings of *jen* are exercised according to one's relationship with another person. Ethics in Confucian thought, therefore, are based on relationships and situations rather than on some absolute good, and they are not applicable to the larger society as a whole. Instead of applying the same rule to everybody with whom they interact, East Asians differentially grade and regulate relationships according to the level of intimacy, the

status of the persons involved, and the particular context. The East Asian countries have developed elaborate social interaction patterns for those whose social position and relationship to oneself is known, but there is no universal pattern that can be applied to someone who is not known.

From a North American point of view, applying different rules to different people and situations may seem to violate the sacred code of fairness and equality that accompanies the individualistic values. In North America, human relationships are not particularized. Rather, one is supposed to treat each person as an integral individual and apply general and objective rules. For instance, it is quite common in America for people to say "Hi" or "Good morning" to anybody they encounter during their morning walk, or to strike up a conversation with another person waiting in line. If you said "Hello" or "Good morning" to a stranger in Korea, you would be looked upon as a rather odd person.

Long-Term Asymmetrical Reciprocity Versus Short-Term Symmetrical or Contractual Reciprocity

Reciprocity as an embodiment of *jen* is the core concept in Confucianism, just as individualism is the core concept of the North American culture. While people may voluntarily join together for specific purposes in North America, each individual remains equal and independent; thus people join or drop out of clubs without any serious group sanctions. Commitments and obligations are often perceived as threats to one's autonomy or freedom of action. Relations are symmetrical-obligatory—that is, as nearly "paid off" as possible at any given moment—or else contractual—the obligation is to an institution or to a professional with whom one has established some contractual base (Condon & Yousef, 1975).

In contrast, Confucian philosophy views relationships as complementary or asymmetrical and reciprocally obligatory. In a sense, a person is forever

Figure 1 Comparison Between the North American and the East Asian Orientations
to Interpersonal Relationship Patterns

East Asian Orientations	North American Orientations
1. Particularistic	Universalistic
Particular rules and interaction patterns are applied depending upon the relationship and context	General and objective rules are applied across diverse relationships and context
2. Long-term and asymmetrical reciprocity	Short-term and symmetrical reciprocity or contractual reciprocity
3. Sharp distinction between in-group and out-group members	In-group and out-group distinction is not as sharp
4. Informal intermediaries	Contractual intermediaries
Personally known intermediaries Frequently utilized for diverse relationships	Professional intermediaries Utilized only for specific purposes
5. Personal and public relationships often overlap	Personal and public relationships are often separate

indebted to others, who in turn are constrained by other debts. Under this system of reciprocity, the individual does not calculate what he or she gives and receives. To calculate would be to think about immediate personal profits, which is the opposite of the principle of mutual faithfulness, *i*. It is somewhat unusual in Korea, for example, for a group of friends, colleagues, or superior and subordinates to go "Dutch" and split the bill for dinner or drinks. Rather, each person takes turns and pays for the whole group. In North America, people generally insist on "paying their own way." The practice of basing relationships on complementary obligations creates warm, lasting human relationships but also the necessity to accept the obligations accompanying such relationships.

In-group/Out-group Distinction

North American culture does not distinguish as strongly between in-group members and out-group members as East Asian countries do. Allegiance to a group and mobility among groups are purely volun-

tary, so that the longevity of membership in and loyalty to a particular group are both limited.

Mutual dependence as prescribed by the Confucian principle of *i*, however, requires that one be affiliated and identify with relatively small and tightly knit groups of people over long periods of time. These long-term relationships work because each group member expects the others to reciprocate and also because group members believe that sooner or later they will have to depend on the others. People enmeshed in this kind of network make clear distinctions between in-group and out-group members. For example, linguistic codes for in-group members are often different from those for out-group members. What is inside the group and what is outside it have drastically different meanings.

Informal Intermediaries Versus Contractual Intermediaries

Because the distinctions between in-group and out-group members are so strict, it is imperative to have an intermediary to help one initiate a new relationship in East Asia. Confucian emphasis on propriety *(li)* also dictates that one has to follow proper rituals in establishing a new relationship, and an intermediary is part of such rituals. The intermediary has an in-group relationship with both parties and so can connect them. One strategy is for the intermediary to bring up an existing relationship that links the two parties, for example, explaining that "you are both graduates of so-and-so college" or "you are both from province A." Alternatively, the intermediary can use his or her own connections with them to create an indirect sense of in-groupness, for example, explaining that one is "my junior from high school" and the other "works in the same department as I do."

Intermediaries in the United States, however, are mostly professional or contractual in nature: lawyers, negotiators, marriage counselors, and the like. The intermediary is an objective third person who does not have any knowledge of the parties' characteristics other than those directly related to the issue at hand. Also, the intermediary deals with each party as a separate, independent individual. Using personal connections to attain a desired goal does occur in the United States, but such a practice may be frowned on as nepotism and may also be perceived as giving up one's own individual freedom.

Overlap of Personal and Public Relationships

The Confucian concept of *i* leads to a strong distaste for a purely business transaction, carried out on a calculated and contractual basis. Therefore, in East Asian countries there is a tendency to mix personal with public relationships. Even though the obvious purpose of a meeting is for business, both parties feel more comfortable if the transaction occurs on a more personal, human level. According to the principles of social reciprocity, there are several steps to follow if you want to develop an effective business relationship in Korea (Lee, 1983): (1) have frequent contacts over a relatively lengthy period of time, (2) establish a personal and human relationship, (3) if possible, create some common experiences such as

sports, drinking, or travel, (4) foster mutual understanding in terms of personality, personal situations, and the like, and (5) develop a certain level of trust and a favorable attitude. The goal is to diminish the clear distinction between a personal relationship and a public relationship. It is implied that if one develops a warm personal relationship, a good public relationship will follow, because it is based on trust and mutual reciprocity. Such qualities are expected to endure rather than be limited to the business deal of the moment.

In the United States, there is a rather sharp dichotomy between private and public life. Since the primary task of the individual is to achieve a high level of autonomous self-reliance, there is an effort to separate the two lives as much as possible. Since the notion of "organizational man" is contradictory to the self-reliant individual, there is a certain level of anxiety about becoming an organizational man (Bellah et al, 1985). Some also perceive private life as a haven from the pressure of individualistic, competitive public life, and as such it must be protected.

THE IMPACT OF CONFUCIANISM ON COMMUNICATION PATTERNS

Confucianism's primary concern with social relationships has strongly influenced communication patterns in East Asia. In general, it has strengthened patterns that help to build and maintain proper human relationships. Figure 2 compares East Asia and North America in terms of communication patterns.

Process- Versus Outcome-Oriented Communication

Since the main function of communication under Confucian philosophy is to initiate, develop, and maintain social relationships, there is a strong emphasis on the kind of communication that promotes such relationships. For instance, it is very important in East Asia to engage in small talk before initiating

Figure 2 Comparison Between the North American and the East Asian Orientations to Communication Patterns

East Asian Orientations	North American Orientations
1. Process orientation	Outcome orientation
Communication is perceived as a process of infinite interpretation	Communication is perceived as the transference of messages
2. Differentiated linguistic codes	Less differentiated linguistic codes
Different linguistics codes are used depending upon persons involved and situations	Linguistic codes are not as extensively differentiated as East Asia
3. Indirect communication emphasis	Direct communication emphasis
The use of indirect communication is prevalent and accepted as normative	Direct communication is a norm despite the extensive use of indirect communication
4. Receiver centered	Sender centered
Meaning is in the interpretation	Meaning is in the messages created by the sender
Emphasis is on listening, sensitivity, and removal of preconception	Emphasis is on how to formulate the best messages, how to improve source credibility, and how to improve delivery skills

business and to communicate personalized information, especially information that would help place each person in the proper context. Communication is perceived to be an infinite interpretive process (Cheng, 1987), which cannot be compartmentalized into sender, message, channel, and receiver. It presumes that each partner is engaged in an ongoing process and that the relationship is in flux.

In contrast, when the main function of communication is to actualize autonomy and self-fulfillment, as in North America, the outcome of the communication is more important than the process. With short-term, discontinuous relationships, communication is perceived to be an action that is terminated after a certain duration and then replaced by a new communication. Tangible outcomes in terms of friends gained, opponents defeated, and self-fulfillment achieved become the primary function of communication.

Differentiated Versus Less Differentiated Linguistic Codes

East Asian languages are very complex and are differentiated according to social status, the degree of intimacy, age, sex, and the level of formality. There are also extensive and elaborate honorific linguistic systems in East Asian languages (Brown and Levinson, 1978; Ogino, Misono, and Fukushima, 1985). These differentiations are manifested not only in referential terms but also in verbs, pronouns, and nouns. They result from Confucian ethical rules that place the highest value on proper human relationships (*i*) and on propriety (*li*). McBrian (1978) has argued that language forms an integral component of social stratification systems, and the hierarchical Confucian society is well represented by the highly stratified linguistic codes in Korea.

Martin (1964) has proposed that one of the main differences between English, Japanese, and Korean is the levels of speech. In both Korean and Japanese, there are two axes of distinction: the axis of address and the axis of reference. The axis of address is divided into plain, polite, and honorific while the axis of reference is divided into humble and neutral (Martin, 1964). An honorific form is used to refer to the receiver's action, while a humble form is used to refer to the sender's action—the reverse would not be appropriate. The most deferential form of speech combines the honorific address form for receiver and the humble form of self-reference.

The English language also employs different codes depending upon intimacy and status difference between the speaker and listener. In general, however, English forms of address are reasonably well described by a single binary contrast: first name (FN) versus title plus last name (TLN) (Brown & Ford, 1964). Certain European languages also contrast the familiar and formal forms, such as *tu* and *vous* in French. The use of FN or TLN can either be reciprocal (both sides use the same form of address) or nonreciprocal (one side uses FN and the other side uses TLN). Status and intimacy also play a role in greetings. For example, "Hi" is more common to intimates and to subordinates while "Good morning" is for distant acquaintances and superiors (Brown & Ford, 1964). In contrast, Ogino, Misono, and Fukushima (1985), working in Japan, found 210 different word forms, through 8 address situations, which can be put into 20 different categories. Moreover, in modern American English practice, the distance between the mutual FN and mutual TLN represents only a very small increment of intimacy, sometimes as small as five minutes of conversation. In East Asian communication situations, the distance between very honorific languages and very informal ones is quite large and more often than not cannot be altered even after a long acquaintance.

In English, the speech level is defined mainly by address forms, while in Korean or Japanese, pronouns, verbs, and nouns all have different levels. Thus, in English "to eat" is "to eat" regardless of the person addressed. In the Korean language, how-

ever, there are three different ways of saying "to eat": *muk-da* (plain), *du-shin-da* (polite), and *chap-soo-shin-da* (honorific). Different levels of a verb are often accompanied by different levels of a noun: Rice may be *bap* (plain), *shik-sa* (polite), or *jin-ji* (honorific).

In English, the pronoun "you" is used to refer alike to the old and young, to the president of the country and to the child next door. In East Asian languages, there are different words for "you" depending upon the level of politeness and upon the relationship. There is also the compulsory or preferential use of a term of address instead of the pronoun, as when one says: *Jeh sh Wang.Shin.shen.de shu .ma?* (literally, "Is this Mr. Wang's book?") instead of "Is this your book?" (Chao, 1956, p. 218). Actual role terms, such as professor, aunt, student, and so forth, are used in place of the pronoun "you" even in two-partner communication because they clarify and accentuate the relationships between the two communicators better than the simple second person reference. Since Confucianism dictates that one should observe the proprieties prescribed by a social relationship, the generalized "you" does not seem to be appropriate in most communication situations in East Asian countries.

This differentiation of linguistic codes in East Asian cultures bears out the familiar psycholinguistic principle that for language communities the degree of lexical differentiation of a referent field increases with the importance of that field to the community (Brown & Ford, 1964). The importance of social relationships in Confucian societies has therefore promoted the differentiation of linguistic codes to accommodate highly differentiated relationships.

Emphasis on Indirect Communication Versus Emphasis on Direct Communication

Most cultures have both direct and indirect modes of communication. Metaphor, insinuations, innuendos, hints, and irony are only a few examples of the kinds of indirect communication that can be found in most linguistic communities. According to Searle (1969), indirect speech acts occur when the speaker communicates to the hearer more than he or she actually says by referring to some mutually shared background information and by relying on the hearer's powers of rationality and inference. Brown and Levinson (1978) have suggested that indirect speech acts are universal because they perform a basic service in strategies of politeness.

Even though the indirect mode of communication seems to be universal, however, the degree to which it is elaborated varies from culture to culture. For instance, the Malagasy speech community values an indirect style (Keenan, 1974), while certain Sabra culture prefers a straight-talking (*dugri*) style (Katriel, 1986). Rosaldo (1973) maintained that the Euro-American association of direct talk with a scientific and democratic attitude may not hold true in different cultural contexts. In Ilongot society, for example, direct talk is perceived as authoritarian and exclusionary while indirect language is perceived as accommodating and sensitive to individual wishes.

Brown and Levinson (1978) have suggested that politeness phenomena in language (indirectness is just one of them) derive from the notion of "face," the public self-image that every member wants to claim for himself or herself. According to Katriel (1986), indirect speech acts are the result of predominant concern for the other person's face. The Confucian legacy of consideration for others and concern for proper human relationships has led to the development of communication patterns that preserve one another's face. Indirect communication helps to prevent the embarrassment of rejection by the other person or disagreement among partners, leaving the relationship and each other's face intact. Lebra (1976) suggested that "defending face" is one of the main factors influencing Japanese behavior. She listed a number of concrete mechanisms for defending face, such as mediated communication (asking someone else to transmit the message), refracted communication (talking to a third person in the presence of the hearer), and acting as a delegate (conveying one's message as being

from someone else), which are all indirect forms of communication.

The use of the indirect mode of communication in East Asia is pervasive and often deliberate. In comparing Japanese and American organizations, it has been noted that American employees strive to communicate with each other in a clear, precise, and explicit manner, while Japanese often deliberately communicate in a vague and indirect manner (Hirokawa, 1987; Pascale & Athos, 1981). The extensive nature of indirect communication is exemplified by the fact that there are sixteen evasive "maneuvers" that can be employed by the Japanese to avoid saying no (Imai, 1981).

It has also been suggested that there is a significant difference in the level of indirectness between North American and East Asian communication patterns. An American might say "The door is open" as in indirect way of asking the hearer to shut the door, while in Japan, instead of saying "The door is open," one often says "It is somewhat cold today." This is even more indirect, because no words refer to the door (Okabe, 1987). Operating at a still higher level of indirection, one Japanese wife communicated to her husband her discord with her mother-in-law by slight irregularities in her flower arrangements (Lebra, 1976).

One of Grice's maxims for cooperative conversation is "manner," which suggests that the speaker should avoid obscurity of expression and ambiguity (Grice, 1975). This direct communication is a norm in North America, despite the extensive use of indirect communication. Grice's principle would not be accepted as a norm, however, in East Asia. Okabe (1987) has shown that in Japan, the traditional rule of communication, which prescribes not to demand, reject, assert yourself, or criticize the listener straightforwardly, is a much more dominant principle than Grice's maxim of manner.

Reischauer (1977, p. 136) concluded that "the Japanese have a genuine mistrust of verbal skills, thinking that these tend to show superficiality in contrast to inner, less articulate feelings that are communicated by innuendo or by nonverbal means." Thus, even though both North American and East Asian communication communities employ indirect communication, its use is much more prevalent and accepted as normative in the former than the latter.

Receiver Versus Sender Centeredness

North American communication very often centers on the sender, and until recently the linear, one-way model from sender to receiver was the prevailing model of communication. Much emphasis has been placed on how senders can formulate better messages, improve source credibility, polish their delivery skills, and so forth. In contrast, the emphasis in East Asia has always been on listening and interpretation.

Cheng (1987) has identified infinite interpretation as one of the main principles of Chinese communication. The process presumes that the emphasis is on the receiver and listening rather than the sender or speech making. According to Lebra (1976, p. 123), "anticipatory communication" is common in Japan, in which, instead of the speaker's having to tell or ask for what he or she wants specifically, others guess and accommodate his or her needs, sparing him or her embarrassment. In such cases, the burden of communication falls not on the message sender but on the message receiver. A person who "hears one and understands ten" is regarded as an intelligent communicator. To catch on quickly and to adjust oneself to another's position before his or her position is clearly revealed is regarded as an important communication skill. One of the common puzzles expressed by foreign students from East Asia is why they are constantly being asked what they want when they are visiting in American homes. In their own countries, the host or hostess is supposed to know what is needed and serve accordingly. The difference occurs because in North America it is important to provide individual freedom of choice; in East Asia, it is important to practice anticipatory communication and to accommodate accordingly.

With the emphasis on indirect communication, the receiver's sensitivity and ability to capture the under-the-surface meaning and to understand im-plicit meaning becomes critical. In North America, an effort has been made to improve the effectiveness of senders through such formal training as debate and public speech, whereas in East Asia, the effort has been on improving the receiver's sensitivity. The highest sensitivity is reached when one empties the mind of one's preconceptions and makes it as clear as a mirror (Yuji, 1984).

DISCUSSION

This paper compared the East Asian emphasis on social relationships with the North American emphasis on individualism. These two emphases produce very different patterns of interpersonal relationships and communication. The conclusions drawn in this paper are not absolute, however. Each culture contains both orientations to some degree. It is simply more probable that East Asians would exhibit certain patterns of communication, such as indirect communication, more often than North Americans, and vice versa.

The North American preoccupation with individualism and related concepts, such as equality, fairness, and justice, and its far-reaching influences on the whole fiber of society are well documented. On the other hand, the importance of social relationships as a key to the East Asian countries has been recognized only recently. For instance, investigations of Japanese management styles have found that one of the fundamental differences between Japanese and American management is the personalized, interdependent relationships among employees and between managers and employees in Japan. These human relationships are related to loyalty and high productivity. It is not uncommon to explain such relationships away as merely a result of other organizational practices, such as life-long employment. If one looks under the surface, however, one realizes that it is derived from a thousand-year-old Confucian legacy, and that similar human relationship patterns are found outside of large organizations. Consequently, attempts to transplant such a management style to North America with its philosophical and cultural orientation of individualism cannot be entirely satisfactory. The culture itself would have to be modified first.

There has been increasing concern in North America about the pursuit of individualism at the expense of commitment to larger entities such as the community, civic groups, and other organizations. It has been suggested that modern individualism has progressed to such an extent that most Americans are trapped by the language of individualism itself and have lost the ability to articulate their own need to get involved (Bellah et al., 1985). Although individualism has its own strength as a value, individualism that is not accompanied by commitments to large entities eventually forces people into a state of isolation, where life itself becomes meaningless.

If human beings are fundamentally social animals, it is necessary to balance the cultural belief system of individualism with the need to get involved with others. Americans have joined voluntary associations and civic organizations more than any other citizens of the industrialized world. However, such recent phenomena as the "me" generation and young stockbrokers who pursue only personal gain at the expense of their own organizations or the society as a whole can be perceived as pathological symptoms of individualism driven to its extreme. Bellah et al. (1985, p. 284) have maintained that "social ecology is damaged not only by war, genocide, and political repression. It is also damaged by the destruction of the subtle ties that bind human beings to one another, leaving them frightened and alone." They strongly argue that we need to restore social ecology by making people aware of our intricate connectedness and interdependence.

The emphasis of Confucianism on social relationships is conducive to cooperation, warm relaxed human relations, consideration of others, and group harmony, but it has costs as well. Under such social constraints, individual initiative and innovation are slow to appear, and some individuals feel that their individuality is being suffocated. Because of the sharp distinction between in-groups and out-groups, factionalism may be inevitable. Within such well-defined sets of social relationships, people

have a well-developed sense of obligation but a weak sense of duty to impersonal social entities.

Ironically, the solution for both the North American problems of excessive individualism and the excessive adherence to in-groupness in East Asia is the same: to be receptive to others. For the North Americans, this means accepting the limitations of self-reliance, becoming committed to a group, and putting the common good ahead of personal wants. For the East Asians, this means making their group boundaries more flexible and accepting outsiders with humanness and commitment to the common good.

There have been substantial changes in the East Asian societies since World War II. There has been an irrepressible influx of Western values; imported films and television programs are ubiquitous. However, it is not easy to change several hundred years of Confucian legacy. In Japan, for example, a greater proportion of young people than old expressed a preference for a boss endowed with the virtues of humanness and sympathy over a more efficient boss who would not ask for extra devotion (Dore, 1973). A similar finding was reported in Korea. When Korean workers, mostly in manufacturing plants, were asked their reasons for changing jobs, those who answered "a better human relationship and more humane treatment" still outnumbered those who answered "better payment" (Kim, 1984).

It seems inevitable, however, that the East Asian countries will see an increasing number of people who do not have traditional, binding relationships as the society moves further toward industrialization and higher mobility. The task will be to find a way for such people to cope with life without the protection of close in-group memberships and to learn to find satisfaction in expressing individual freedom and self-reliance.

REFERENCES

Bellah, R., Madsen, R., Sullivan, W., Swidler, A., and Tipton, S. (1985). *Habits of the Heart: Individualism and Commitment in American Life*. New York: Harper & Row.

Brown, R. W., and Ford, M. (1964). "Address in American English." In D. Hymes (Ed.), *Language in Culture and Society*. New York: Harper & Row.

Brown, R., and Levinson, S. (1978). "Universals in Language Usage: Politeness Phenomena." In E. Goody (Ed.), *Questions and Politeness*. Cambridge: Cambridge University Press.

Chao, Y. R. (1956). "Chinese Terms of Address." *Language, 32*, 217–241.

Cheng, C. Y. (1987). "Chinese Philosophy and Contemporary Communication Theory." In D. L. Kincaid (Ed.), *Communication Theory: Eastern and Western Perspectives*. New York: Academic Press.

Chinese Culture Connection. (1987). "Chinese Values and the Search for Culture-Free Dimensions of Culture." *Journal of Cross-Cultural Psychology, 18*, 143–164.

Condon, J., and Yousef, F. (1975). *An Introduction to Intercultural Communication*. New York: Bobbs-Merrill.

Dore, R. (1973). *British Factory, Japanese Factory: The Origins of National Diversity in Industrial Relations*. Berkeley and Los Angeles: University of California Press.

Grice, P. H. (1975). "Logic and Conversation." In P. Cole and J. L. Morgan (Eds.), *Studies in Syntax*. Vol. 3. New York: Academic Press.

Hall, J., and Beadsley, R. (1965). *Twelve Doors to Japan*. New York: McGraw-Hill.

Hirokawa, R. (1987). "Communication Within the Japanese Business Organization." In D. L. Kincaid (Ed.), *Communication Theory: Eastern and Western Perspectives*. New York: Academic Press.

Hofstede, G. (1980). *Culture's Consequences*. Newbury Park, Calif.: Sage.

Hui, C. H., and Triandis, H. C. (1986). "Individualism-Collectivism: A Study of Cross-Cultural Research." *Journal of Cross-Cultural Psychology, 17*, 225–248.

Imai, M. (1981). *Sixteen Ways to Avoid Saying No*. Tokyo: Nihon Keizai Shimbun.

Katriel, T. (1986). *Talking Straight: Dugri Speech in Israeli Sabra Culture*. Cambridge: Cambridge University Press.

Keenan, E. (1974). "Norm Makers, Norm Breakers: Uses of Speech by Men and Women in a Malagasy Community." In R. Bauman and J. Sherzer (Eds.), *Explorations in the Ethnography of Speaking*. Cambridge: Cambridge University Press.

Kim, S. U. (1984). *"Kong-jang no-dong-ja-ye ee-jik iyu"* ("Reasons for Changing Jobs Among Factory Workers"). Hankook Daily Newspaper, May 2 (in Korean).

Lanham, R. (1974). *Style: An Anti-Text Book*. New Haven, Conn.: Yale University Press.

Lebra, T. S. (1976). *Japanese Patterns of Behavior*. Honolulu: The University Press of Hawaii.

Lee, K. T. (1983). *Hankook-in ye u-shik koo-jo* (Cognitive Patterns of Korean People). Seoul, Korea: Shin-Won Moon-Wha Sa (in Korean).

Luce, D., and Sommer, J. (1969). *Viet Nam—the Unheard Voices*. Ithaca, N.Y.: Cornell University Press.

McBrian, C. (1978). "Language and Social Stratification: The Case of a Confucian Society." *Anthropological Linguistics, 2*, 320–326.

McNaughton, W. (1974). *The Confucian Vision*. Ann Arbor: University of Michigan Press.

Martin, S. E. (1964). "Speech Levels in Japan and Korea." In D. Hymes (Ed.), *Language in Culture and Society*. New York: Harper & Row.

Nakamura, H. (1964). *Ways of Thinking of Eastern Peoples*. Honolulu: East-West Center Press.

Ogino, T., Misono, Y., and Fukushima, C. (1985). "Diversity of Honorific Usage in Tokyo: A Sociolinguistic Approach Based on a Field Survey." *International Journal of Sociology of Language, 55*, 23–39.

Okabe, K. (1987). "Indirect Speech Acts of the Japanese." In D. L. Kincaid (Ed.), *Communication Theory: Eastern and Western Perspectives*. New York: Academic Press.

Parsons, T., Shils, E., and Olds, J. (1951). "Categories of the Orientation and Organization of Action." In T. Parsons and E. A. Shils (Eds.), *Toward a General Theory of Action*. Cambridge, Mass.: Harvard University Press.

Pascale, R., and Athos, A. (1981). *The Art of Japanese Management: Application for American Executives*. New York: Warner Communications.

Reischauer, E. (1977). *The Japanese*. Cambridge, Mass.: Harvard University Press.

Rosaldo, M. (1973). "I Have Nothing to Hide: The Language of Ilongot Oratory." *Language in Society*, *11*, 193–223.

Searle, J. R. (1969). *Speech Acts*. Cambridge: Cambridge University Press.

Varenne, H. (1977). *Americans Together: Structured Diversity in a Midwestern Town*. New York and London: Teachers College Press.

Yuji, A. (Trans. N. Chung). (1984). *Ilbon-in ye usik koo-jo* (Japanese Thought Patterns). Seoul, Korea: Baik Yang Publishing Co. (in Korean).

Yum, J. O. (1987). Korean Philosophy and Communication. In D. L. Kincaid (Ed.), *Communication Theory: Eastern and Western Perspectives*. New York: Academic Press.

World View and Cultural Patterns of India

NEMI C. JAIN

If I were asked under what sky the human mind . . . has most deeply pondered over the greatest problems of life, and has found solutions of some of them which well deserve the attention even of those who have studied Plato and Kant—I should point to India. And if I were to ask myself from what literature we . . . who have been nurtured almost exclusively on the thoughts of Greeks and Romans, and of one Semitic race, the Jewish, may draw the corrective which is most wanted in order to make our inner life more perfect, more comprehensive, more universal, in fact more truly human a life, not for this life only, but a transfigured and eternal life—again I should point to India.

—*Max Muller[1]*

For more than 3,000 years, the peoples of the Indian subcontinent have been seeking the deepest truths about the nature of reality and the self, exploring the depths of human consciousness. India's most brilliant thinkers have been preoccupied with the quest for perfection, for a way to transform this ordinary, limited, and imperfect human life into its potential greatness. Their insights and discoveries have shaped one of the world's richest and most long-lived cultures.[2]

Indian culture has a continuous history that extends over 5,000 years. Very early, India evolved a

This essay was prepared especially for this sixth edition. All rights reserved. Permission to reprint must be obtained from the publisher and the author. Professor Jain teaches in the Department of Communication and is a Research Fellow in the Center for Asian Studies at Arizona State University.

distinctive culture and religion, Hinduism, which was modified and adjusted as it came into contact with outside elements. In general, Hinduism is an amorphous body of beliefs, philosophies, worship practices, and codes of conduct. It is hard to define Hinduism or to say precisely whether it is a religion or not in the usual sense of the word. In its present form it embraces many beliefs and practices, as it did in the past, often opposed to and contradicting each other. Its essential spirit seems to be "live and let live." The very nature of Hinduism leads to a greater tolerance of other religions among its adherents, as they tend to believe that the highest divine powers complement each other for the well-being of humanity and the world. The qualities of resilience, absorption, and respect for alternative ways of reaching the same goals are perhaps the major characteristics that have generated vitality in Hinduism for millennia. In spirit, Indian culture has maintained the essential unity of the indigenous doctrines and ideas of Hinduism, which has enabled it to withstand many vicissitudes and to continue to mold the lives of millions of people in India and abroad.[3]

Like any other culture, the Indian culture is complex and consists of many interrelated beliefs, values, norms, social systems, and material cultural items. It has a world view comprising existential postulates that deal with the nature of reality, the organization of the universe, and the ends and purposes of human life. In spite of the multiethnic, multilingual, and highly stratified nature of contemporary Indian society, India is united by a set of cultural patterns that are widely shared among the Hindus, who comprise about 80 percent of India's population of over 850 million. The major aim of this article is to outline the Indian world view and some of the basic cultural patterns that have persisted over the thousands of years of Indian history, patterns that influence many aspects of Indian social institutions and affect the communication and thought patterns of millions of Hindus in India and abroad. More specifically, this article will describe briefly the following aspects of Indian culture: (1) world view, (2) reincarnation, (3) *dharma*, (4)

stages of life, (5) the caste system, and (6) the spirit of tolerance.

Each of these cultural patterns includes several specific assumptions, beliefs, values, and norms that are closely interrelated and represents a continuum; within the same culture, variations of the pattern normally occur. Contradictions among cultural patterns are probably universal throughout societies, but, despite internal variations and contradictions, there is an overall integration to the patterns of Hindu Indian culture. It is possible to simplify its description by isolating the various cultural patterns and considering them one at a time.

WORLD VIEW

World view refers to a set of interrelated assumptions and beliefs about the nature of reality, the organization of the universe, the purposes of human life, God, and other philosophical issues that are concerned with the concept of being. In short, our world view helps us locate our place and rank in the universe.[4] A culture's world view includes both implicit and explicit assumptions underlying the values, norms, myths, and behavior of its people.

Indian world view is very complex. India's great sages and philosophers for the last several thousand years have sought to understand the deepest level of reality and to satisfy the deep human longing for spiritual fulfillment. They were impressed with our capacity for thought, feeling, imagination, and action, and with the ability to enter creatively into the shaping of our own humanness. They sought a link between the dynamic energy of reality in its deepest levels and the ground of human existence. This quest generated the basic Indian wisdom that the fundamental energizing power of the cosmos and the spiritual energy of human beings are one and the same.

At the deepest levels of our existence, we share in the very energies and powers that create and structure the universe itself. Because of our participation in the ultimate energy and power of reality, it is possible to transform our superficial, suffering, and limited existence into a free and boundless one in which life is experienced at its deepest and most profound level. This spiritual transformation has constituted the ultimate aim in life for most of the Indian people over the ages.[5]

The Indian world view has been shaped by this underlying belief of participation in the ultimate reality and the aim of spiritual transformation of human existence. We need to explore the origins and development of this world view in order to understand it fully and to understand its influence on other cultural patterns of India. Indian world view involves at least seven sets of assumptions, beliefs, and concepts: (1) undivided wholeness, (2) levels of reality, (3) the normative dimension of existence, (4) the boundlessness of ultimate reality, (5) the profundity of existence, (6) gods and goddesses as limited symbols of the ultimate reality, and (7) the limitations of ordinary means of knowledge.[6]

Undivided Wholeness

According to Hinduism, the world of distinct and separate objects and processes is a manifestation of a more fundamental reality that is undivided and unconditioned. This undivided wholeness constituting the ultimate level of reality is called by various names: *Brahman, Ātman, Puruṣa, Jīva,* Lord, and so on. What is especially important about this belief is that the ultimate reality is not seen as separate, apart from ordinary things and events, but as the inner being and ground of everyday existence. This belief, developed initially in the Vedas and Upaniṣads, became an integral part of Hinduism, Jainism, Buddhism, and Yoga systems.[7]

Levels of Reality

Within the undivided wholeness or the totality of existence, there are various levels of reality or orders of being. These range from nonexistence to empirical existence limited by space and time, to consciousness limited only by the conditions of awareness, to an indescribable level that is beyond all conditions and limits whatever. The deeper the level of reality, the more fully it participates in the truth of being and the greater its value.[8] One of

the clearest examples of the tendency to distinguish between levels of reality occurs in the Taittirīya Upaniṣad, where five different levels of reality comprising the "Self" are identified:

At the lowest level the Self is material and is identified with food. At the next level the Self is identified with life: "Different from and within that which consists of the essence of food is the Self consisting of life." Identifying a still higher level of reality, the text goes on to say, "Different from and within that which consists of the essence of life is the Self which consists of mind (rudimentary forms of awareness that humans share with other animals)." Next, a fourth level of reality is recognized. Here is a still deeper source of consciousness and existence: the Self said to be of the nature of understanding (vijnana). Finally, Self is identified with joy as the fifth and ultimate level of reality. Joy (ānanda) or bliss is regarded as the root or source of all existence, the foundation of higher consciousness, lower consciousness, life, and matter.[9]

The Normative Dimension of Existence

The deepest level of reality, which grounds all the other levels, is normative. It poses an "ought" for life that stems from the heart of existence. According to Hinduism, norms for right living are an integral part of the fabric of existence—they are not derived from human reason and are not imposed on life from the outside. The foundation of these norms is much deeper than reason; it emanates from the very nature and expression of reality at its deepest level. Human reason only interprets and applies the norms of true or right living. This is why in India it is generally recognized that a person who is true to the inner norms of existence has incredible power.

In the West, norms for human behavior are usually conceived as rationally derived to fulfill human needs and aspirations. In India, on the other hand, human existence is regarded as a manifestation and expression of a deeper reality, which constitutes its ground and measure. The fundamental norm of the universe (*rta*) is the orderly coursing of this deeper reality in its central being. Moral and social rules are partial expressions of this highest norm. The normative dimensions of the interconnected reality refer to the Hindu concept of *dharma* which will be discussed later in this article.[10]

The Boundlessness of Ultimate Reality

At the deepest level, existence is boundless. There are no limits and all possibilities may coexist without excluding or compromising each other. Time is endless, space is endless, the number of gods and goddesses is endless, and so on. Indian mythology especially celebrates the idea that opposites exist together, enriching each other, with all of their differences arising simultaneously in a totally unrestricted universe of infinite freedom and richness.[11]

The Profundity of Existence

The profundity of reality at the ultimate level is such that reason is incapable of apprehending it. Human reason is an effective faculty for guiding our investigations of the empirical world and for understanding the rules of our practical and theoretical activities. But since reason operates by differentiating and comparing, it is incapable of comprehending the deepest dimensions of reality that are beyond all divisions and differences. This sense of the profundity of reality underlies Indian mysticism and encourages the emphasis upon meditation and Yoga systems.[12]

Gods and Goddesses as Limited Symbols of the Ultimate Reality

Indian gods and goddesses, from Vedic times to the present, are usually viewed as symbols of the ultimate reality rather than the ultimate reality itself. The ultimate level of reality is undivided; it has no form and no name. What can be given a name and form is not the ultimate. As symbols, gods and god-desses participate partially in the higher reality that they symbolize, pointing to the fullness of that reality. No number of symbols can exhaust the fullness of the ultimate, so there is no limit to the number of gods. This is why a Hindu can say in the same breath that there are millions of gods, only one god, and no gods, for the last two statements mean, respectively, that all gods symbolize the one ultimate reality and that this reality cannot be captured entirely by a symbol. But that a deity is not the ultimate reality does not mean that it is unreal. On the contrary, because the deity as symbol participates in the deeper levels of reality, its reality is greater than that of our ordinary existence. By identifying with the deity in love and through rituals, the power of this deeper level of reality becomes available for a spiritual transformation of life. It is this perspective of deity that underlies Hindu theism and devotionalism.[13]

The Limitations of Ordinary Means of Knowledge

Hindus believe that ordinary means of acquiring knowledge—human senses, human reason, and empirical methods—cannot penetrate the profound and undivided ultimate level of reality. For this reason they put great emphasis on developing extraordinary means. Through concentration and meditation, direct insight into the true nature of reality at its most profound level becomes possible. The limitations of knowledge mediated through sensory and conceptual filters are overcome in this direct and immediate knowledge through transempirical and transrational insight.[14]

REINCARNATION

In Hinduism, the Supreme Being is the impersonal *Brahman*, the ultimate level of reality, a philosophical absolute, serenely blissful, beyond all limitations either ethical or metaphysical. The basic Hindu view of God involves infinite being, infinite consciousness, and infinite bliss. *Brahman* is also conceived of as the Supreme Soul of the universe. Every living soul is a part, a particular manifestation, of the *Brahman*. These individual souls seem to change from generation to generation, but actually only the unimportant, outer details change—a body, a face, a name, a different condition or status in life. The *Brahman*, however, veiled behind these deceptive "realities," is continuous and indestructible. This hidden self or *ātman* is a reservoir of being that never dies, is never exhausted, and is without limit in awareness and bliss. *Ātman*, the ultimate level of reality at the individual level, is the infinite center of every life. Body, personality, and *ātman* together make up a human being.[15]

The eternal *ātman* is usually buried under the almost impenetrable mass of distractions, false ideas, illusions, and self-regarding impulses that compose one's surface being. Life is ordinarily lived at a relatively superficial level, a level at which the ultimate reality is experienced only in fragmented and limited forms. These fragmented and partial forms of existence are actually forms of bondage, restricting access to the full power or energy of life flowing from the deepest level of reality. The aim of life is to cleanse the dross from one's being to the point where its infinite center, the eternal *ātman*, will be fully manifest.

The Hindu belief in reincarnation affirms that individual souls enter the world and pass through a sequence of bodies or life cycles. On the subhuman level, the passage is through a series of increasingly complex bodies until at last a human one is attained. Up to this point, the soul's growth is virtually automatic. With the soul's graduation into a human body, this automatic, escalator mode of ascent comes to an end. The soul's assignment to this exalted habitation is evidence that it has reached self-consciousness, and with this estate comes freedom, responsibility, and effort. Now the individual soul, as a human being, is fully responsible for its behavior through the doctrine of *karma*—the moral law of cause and effect. The present condition of each individual life is a product of what one did in the previous life; and one's present acts, thoughts, and decisions determine one's future states.[16]

This concept of *karma* and the completely moral universe it implies carries two important psychological corollaries. First, it commits the Hindu who understands it to complete personal responsibility.

Each individual is wholly responsible for his or her present condition and will have exactly the future he or she is now creating. Conversely, the idea of a moral universe closes the door to all appeals to chance or accident: In this world there is no chance or accident. *Karma* decrees that every decision must have its determinate consequences, but the decisions themselves are, in the last analysis, freely arrived at. Or, to approach the matter from the other direction, the consequences of a person's past decisions condition his or her present lot, as a card player is dealt a particular hand but is left free to play that hand in a number of ways. This means that the general conditions of life—rank, station, position—are predetermined by one's past *karma*. However, individual humans as carriers of a soul are free throughout their life span to make choices and to determine actions independently of the soul.[17]

According to Hinduism, the aim of life is to free oneself progressively from the exclusive identification with the lower levels of the self in order to realize the most profound level of existence. Since at this deepest level the self is identical with ultimate reality—the *Brahman*—once this identity has been realized there is nothing that can defeat or destroy the self. Thus, the soul puts an end to the process of reincarnation and merges with the *Brahman*, from whence it originated in the first place. This state for an individual soul is called *moksha* or *nirvana*.

DHARMA

The concept of *dharma* is another unique feature of Hinduism and Indian culture. *Dharma* refers to a code of conduct that guides the life of a person both as an individual and as a member of society. It is the law of right living, the observance of which secures the double objectives of happiness on earth and salvation. The life of a Hindu is regulated in a very detailed manner by the laws of *dharma*. Personal habits, social and family ties, fasts and feasts, religious rituals, obligations of justice and morality, and even rules of personal hygiene and food preparation are all conditioned by it.

Dharma is the binding law that accounts for the cohesion in the Hindu society throughout the history of India. Since *dharma* is a social value with a strong sense of morality, harmony is achieved when everyone follows his or her *dharma*. It is not subjective in the sense that the conscience of the individual imposes it, nor external in the sense that the law enforces it. It is the system of conduct that the general opinion, conscience, or spirit of the people supports. *Dharma* does not force people into virtue but trains them for it. It is not a fixed code of mechanical rules but a living spirit that grows and moves in response to the development of the society.[18]

Dharma is only one of the four aims of human life, which according to the classical Indian philosophy, have constituted the basis for Indian values. The other three* are wealth (*artha*), enjoyment (*kāma*), and liberation (*moksha*). The pursuit of wealth and enjoyment is regulated by *dharma*. Although much of the Western world regards Indians as having deliberately chosen poverty as a way of life, this is not true. The *Panctantra*, a popular collection of Indian wisdom, puts it this way: "The smell of wealth (*artha*) is quite enough to wake a creature's sterner stuff. And wealth's enjoyment even more. Wealth gives constant vigour, confidence and power. Poverty is a curse worse than death. Virtue without wealth is of no consequence. The lack of money is the root of all evil."[19]

Hinduism also recognizes the importance of enjoyment or *kāma* in human life. The concept of *kāma* is used in two ways in the Indian literature. In the narrower sense, *kāma* is sexual desire or love, symbolized by *Kāma*, the love god. *Kāma Sutra*, along with a number of other texts, is devoted to *kāma* in this sense, providing instruction on how to obtain the greatest sexual pleasures. As a basic human aim, *kāma* goes beyond this narrower sense of sexual enjoyment to include all forms of enjoyment, including the enjoyment of fame, fortune, and power. Again, the common stereotype that presents the Indian people as so single-mindedly intent on pursuing religious salvation that there is no room for laughter, fun, or games gives us a false picture. Traditionally and currently, stories, games, festivals, and parties filled with music, laughter, and fun are highly prized by most of the people. As a recog-

nized basic aim in life, *kāma* legitimizes the human need for enjoyment; it recognizes that not only are wealth and various goods necessary for life but they are to be enjoyed in life as a way of fulfilling human nature. As in the case of *artha* or wealth, however, only those activities aiming at *kāma* that are in accord with *dharma* are allowed. Enjoyment at the pain and expense of other creatures or persons is not allowed. Sexual activity is to be restricted to one's spouse; drugs and intoxicating beverages are regarded as wrong and sinful because of the injury they do.[20]

The fourth aim, that of *moksha* or liberation, has priority over the other three (*artha, kāma,* and *dharma*). It is the aim of *moksha* that guides one's efforts to realize identity with the ultimate reality. But *moksha* does not repudiate the other aims; indeed, it calls for fulfilling these aims as a preparation for achieving complete freedom and fulfillment. Even when the distinction between worldly and spiritual existence becomes prominent, there is a tendency to see the distinction in terms of higher and lower levels of the same reality rather than to postulate two different and opposed realities.[21]

Dharma has two sides that are interdependent: the individual and the social. The conscience of the individual requires a guide, and one must be taught the way to realize one's aims of life and to live according to spirit and not sense. The interests of society require equal attention. *Dharma*, on the social level, is that which holds together all living beings in a harmonious order. Virtue is conduct contributing to social welfare, and vice is the opposite. *Dharma* is usually classified according to the requirements of one's position in society and stage in life, for these represent the main factors of time, place, and circumstance that determine one's own specific *dharma*. Thus, *varna dharma* refers to the duties attending one's caste or social class and position; for example, studying, teaching, and preaching are the primary duties of *Brahmins*. *Āshrama dharma* refers to the duties attending one's particular stage in life. For example, the householder stage requires marriage, raising a family, producing the goods necessary for society according to one's occupation, giving to those in need, and serving the social and political needs of the community. For a fuller understanding of *dharma* appropriate for different stages of life, we need to examine the Indian concept of stages of life. Also, we need to understand the caste system, which influences *dharma* and other social norms.

Hinduism also recognizes a *universal dharma* that applies to a person regardless of caste, social class, or stage in life. For example, telling the truth, avoiding unnecessary injury to others, not cheating, and so on are common *dharmas* that all human beings share. There are some *dharmas* that are determined by particular circumstances and therefore cannot be identified in advance. But the rule for determining the specific requirements of action in unusual and unpredictable situations is that the higher dharmas and values should always prevail. Noninjury and compassion are basic moral principles in deciding cases of conflicting moral duties, and one must never engage in behavior that is detrimental to spiritual progress.[22]

STAGES OF LIFE

The concept of *dharma* at the individual level recognizes four stages in each person's life: (1) *brahmacharya* or student stage, (2) *grahastha* or householder stage, (3) *vānaprastha* or retirement stage, and (4) *sannyās* or renunciation stage. In the first stage of *brahmacharya*, a child learns the requirements of *dharma* early in life and develops the appropriate attitudes and character that will allow him to consistently do his *dharma* for the rest of his life. At this student stage, the obligations of temperance, sobriety, chastity, and social service are firmly established in the minds of the young. All have to pass through this discipline, irrespective of caste, class, wealth, or poverty.

The second stage, beginning with marriage, is that of the householder or *grahastha*. At this stage, the individual normally undertakes the obligations of family life, becoming a member of a social body and accepting its rights and requirements. Self-support, thrift, and hospitality are enjoined, and the individual's energies and interests turn naturally outward. There are three fronts for fulfilling human aims—one's family, one's vocation, and the community to which one belongs—and normally the person will be interested in all three. This is the time for satisfying the first three human aims: wealth or *artha* through vocation, enjoyment or *kāma* primarily through the family, and *dharma* through one's responsibilities as a citizen.[23]

In the third stage of *vānaprastha* or retirement, the individual is required to control his or her attachment to worldly possessions. This stage begins when the duties of the householder stage have been fulfilled. At this stage, one needs to suppress all the conceits that entered through the accidents of the second stage (such as pride of birth or property, individual genius, wealth, fame, or good luck) and cultivate a spirit of renunciation. It is the time for working out a philosophy for oneself, the time of transcending the senses to find and dwell at one with the timeless reality that underlies the dream of life in this world.[24] This period of "retirement" from social life is one of asceticism aimed at achieving the self-control and spiritual strength needed to attain *moksha*. Honored and respected by nearly everyone, these "retired persons" or "forest dwellers" are sometimes sought out for their wise counsel, and therefore they constitute a vital part of the society.

The fourth stage, that of *sannyāsa* or renunciation, is one of complete renunciation of worldly objects and desires. At this stage, a person is a disinterested servant of humanity who finds peace in the strength of spirit. A *sannyāsin* lives identified with the eternal self and beholds nothing else. "He no more cares whether his body falls or remains, than does a cow what becomes of the garland that someone has hung around her neck; for the faculties of his mind are now at rest in the Holy Power, the essence of bliss."[25] At this final stage of life, one attempts to fulfill the ultimate aim of human life, *moksha* or liberation.

The concept of life stages (*āśramas*) and the basic human aims to be fulfilled at different stages embody the recognition that biological, economic, and social needs are legitimate and must be fulfilled in order to go beyond them. But it is also recognized in Indian philosophy that because of the deeper nature of human existence, the thirst for freedom and fulfillment cannot be satisfied by pursuing the lower needs of life. Their acquisition only increases the thirst for more and more of these material goods.

THE CASTE SYSTEM

The caste system is a unique feature of Indian culture. No Indian social institution has attracted as much of the attention of foreign observers, nor has any other Indian institution been so grossly misunderstood, misrepresented, and maligned. Even the word *caste*, which is derived from the Portguese *casta* (color), is a misnomer connoting some specious notion of color difference as the foundation of the system. It is a curious fact of intellectual history that caste has figured so prominently in Western thought.

The caste system began in India about 3,000 years ago. During the second millennium B.C., a host of Aryans possessing a different language and culture and different physical features (tall, fair-skinned, blue-eyed, straight-haired) migrated into India. The clash of differences that followed eventually established the caste system because the Aryans took for themselves the kinds of work thought to be most desirable: They became the rulers, the religious leaders, the teachers, and the traders. The other people were forced to become servants for the Aryans or to do less pleasing kinds of work. The outcome of this social classification and differentiation was a society clearly divided into four castes, hierarchically, from higher to lower:

1. *Brahmins*—seers or priests who perform such duties as teaching, preaching, assisting in the sacrificial processes, giving alms, and receiving gifts

2. *Kashtryās*—administrators and rulers responsible for protecting life and treasures

3. *Vaisyās*—traders, businesspeople, farmers, and herders

4. *Sūdras*—artisans such as carpenters, blacksmiths, and laborers.

In the course of time, a fifth group developed that was ranked so low as to be considered outside and beneath the caste system itself. The members of this fifth "casteless" group are variously referred to as "untouchables," "outcastes," "scheduled castes," or (by Mahatma Gandhi) *Harijans*—"children of God." People in this group inherit the kinds of work that in India are considered least desirable, such as scavenging, slaughtering animals, leather tanning, and sweeping the streets.[26]

The caste system began as a straightforward, functional division of Indian society. It was later misinterpreted by priests as permanent and immutable as the word of God. Accordingly, the caste system was justified in terms of the "immutable and inborn" qualities of individuals, the unchangeable result of "actions in previous incarnations," and the unalterable basis of Hindu religion.

The caste system applies only to the Hindu segment of the Indian society. The particular caste a person belongs to is determined by birth—one is born into the caste of his or her parents. Each caste has its appropriate status, rights, duties, and *dharma*. There are detailed rules about communication and contact among people of different castes. A caste has considerable influence on the way of life of its members; most important relationships of life, above all marriage, usually take place within the caste.

After India's independence in 1947, discrimination based on caste has been outlawed. In urban areas it is common for persons to cross caste lines in choosing their occupations, and intercaste marriages are also becoming quite popular. In rural areas, however, caste still is a major influence in one's life.

THE SPIRIT OF TOLERANCE

An outstanding feature of Indian culture is its tradition of tolerance. According to Hinduism, the reality or existence at the deepest level is boundless. No description, formula, or symbol can adequately convey the entire truth about anything. Each perspective provides a partial glimpse of reality, but none provides a complete view. Different partial—

even opposing—viewpoints are regarded as complementing each other, each contributing something to a fuller understanding of reality.

Traditionally, Indian thinkers have been willing to adopt new perspectives and new positions, without, however, abandoning old positions and perspectives. The new is simply added to the old, providing another dimension to one's knowledge. The new dimension may render the old less dominant or important, but it does not require the latter's rejection. The traditional storehouse of Indian ideas is like a four-thousand-year-old attic to which things were added every year but which were never once cleaned out.[27]

Indian culture believes in universal tolerance and accepts all religions as true. It is believed that the highest truth is too profound to allow anyone to get an exclusive grasp on it. When no beliefs can be said to be absolutely true, no beliefs can be declared absolutely false. Indian culture is comprehensive and suits the needs of everyone, irrespective of caste, creed, color, or sex—it has universal appeal and makes room for all.

India's spirit of tolerance has been developed in the Jaina theory of *syādvāda*, the theory of "may be." According to this theory, no absolute affirmation or denial is possible. As all knowledge is probable and relative, the other person's point of view is as true as one's own. In other words, one must show restraint in making judgments—a very healthy principle. One must know that one's judgments are only partially true and can by no means be regarded as true in absolute terms. This understanding and spirit of tolerance have contributed to the advancement of Indian culture, helping to bring together the divergent groups with different languages and religious persuasions under a common culture.[28]

In summary, this article has discussed six basic cultural patterns of India: world view, reincarnation, *dharma*, stages of life, the caste system, and the spirit of tolerance. These are integral parts of Hinduism and Indian culture, and they have a significant influence on the personality, values, beliefs, attitudes, and communication behavior of Hindus in India and abroad. An understanding of Indian world view and cultural patterns, and of the influence of these cultural patterns on communication behavior, will improve the quality of intercultural communication between people of India and other cultures.

NOTES

1. Cited from Huston Smith. (1958). *The Religions of Man*. New York: Harper & Row, p. 13.

2. John M. Koller. *The Indian Way*. (1982). New York: Macmillan, p. v.

3. H. V. Sreenivasa Murthy and S. U. Kamath. (1973). *Studies in Indian Culture*. Bombay: Asia Publishing House, pp. 4–5.

4. Larry A. Samovar, Richard E. Porter, and Nemi C. Jain. (1981). *Understanding Intercultural Communication*. Belmont, Calif.: Wadsworth, p. 46.

5. Koller, p. 6.

6. Koller, p. 6. This entire description of Indian world view has drawn heavily on Koller's account.

7. Koller, p. 6.

8. Koller, p. 6 and pp. 101–102.

9. Cited from Koller, p. 101.

10. Koller, p. 7 and pp. 62–63.

11. Koller, p. 7.

12. Koller, p. 7

13. Koller, pp. 7–8 and pp. 212–255.

14. Paul Hiebert. (1983). "Indian and American World Views: A Study in Contrasts," in Giri Raj Gupta (Ed.), *Religion in Modern India*. New Delhi: Vikas Publishing House, pp. 399–414.

15. Smith, pp. 24–25.

16. Smith, pp. 67–68.

17. Smith, pp. 68–69.

18. S. Radhakrishnan. (1979). *Indian Religions*. New Delhi: Vision Books, pp. 61–62.

19. Koller, p. 65.

20. Koller, pp. 65–66.

21. Koller, pp. 66–69.

22. Koller, p. 62.

23. Smith, pp. 55–56.

24. Smith, pp. 57–58.

25. Smith, p. 59.

26. S. N. Chopra. (1977). *India: An Area Study.* New Delhi: Vikas Publishing House, pp. 27–29.

27. Koller, pp. 8–9.

28. Murthy and Kamath, p. 5.

Cultural Patterns
of the Maasai

LISA SKOW
LARRY A. SAMOVAR

For many years critics of intercultural communication have charged that the field focuses on a handful of cultures while seriously neglecting others. For example, the literature abounds with material concerning Japan and Mexico, but there is very little to be found if one seeks to understand the cultures of India or black Africa. As economics and politics force a global interdependence, it behooves us to examine cultures that were previously excluded from our scrutiny.

The motivation for such analysis can take a variety of forms. Our desire for more information might be altruistic, as we learn that 40,000 babies die of starvation each day in developing countries. Or we may decide that we need to know about other cultures for more practical reasons. Strong ties with African countries can lead to economic, educational, and technological exchanges beneficial to individuals on both sides of the globe. Regardless of our motives, the 1990s and beyond will offer countless examples that demand that we look at cultures that we have ignored in the past. This article is an attempt to explore one of those cultures, specifically, that of the Maasai of East Africa.

If we accept the view of culture held by most anthropologists, it becomes nearly impossible to discover all there is to know about any one group of

This original article appears here in print for the first time. All rights reserved. Permission to reprint must be obtained from the authors and the publisher. Lisa Skow is a former Peace Corps volunteer and a graduate of San Diego State University. Larry Samovar teaches at San Diego State University.

people. That is to say, how does one decide what is important about a culture if Hall (1976) is correct when he writes, "there is not one aspect of human life that is not touched and altered by culture" (p. 14)? The decision as to what to include and exclude in any analysis of a culture is usually based on the background of the researcher. Someone interested in the music of a culture would obviously look at the portion of the culture relating to that specific topic and, in a sense, abstract only part of the total phenomenon called culture.

A researcher interested in intercultural communication is also faced with the problem of what to select from the total experiences of a people. What, in short, do we need to know if our goal is to understand the behavior of another culture? One answer to this question is found in the work of Samovar and Porter (1988). They have proposed a model of intercultural communication that can be used as a guide in selecting what aspects of culture need to be incorporated into any discussion of intercultural communication. This article will address the three major components of that model: perception, verbal processes, and nonverbal processes.

BACKGROUND

The East African countries of Kenya and Tanzania know firsthand about Western culture. They have lived through Western government, language, culture, and, unfortunately, oppression. Even today, more than two decades after each country received its independence, Western culture still has a profound influence on the people of Kenya and Tanzania. However, because there are so many different ethnic groups in these countries, it has not had the same impact and influence on each group. The Kikuyu of Kenya have adopted Western culture with such enthusiasm that one wonders what are "proper" Kikuyu traditions and customs and what are Western influences. On the other end of the Western continuum are the Maasai of southern Kenya and northern Tanzania, who have, for a number of reasons, rejected much of the culture presented by the West. They have largely shunned West-

ern forms of government, dress, language, music, religion, and frequently even assistance. The Maasai are often referred to as "true Africans" because of their "purity"—a purity of which they are very proud.

Africa may be changing at an extraordinarily fast pace, but the Maasai are one group of people who seem content to continue their own way of life. This article hopes to offer some insight into that way of life.

PERCEPTION

One of the basic axioms of intercultural communication, and one that is part of the Samovar and Porter (1988) intercultural model, is that culture and perception work in tandem. That is to say, our cultural experiences determine, to a large extent, our view of the world. Those experiences that are most important are transmitted from generation to generation as a means of assuring that the culture will survive beyond the lifetime of its current members. Therefore, to understand any culture it is necessary to examine those experiences that are deemed meaningful enough to be carried to each generation. One way to study those experiences is through the history of a culture. The history of any culture can offer insight into the behaviors of the culture as well as explain some of the causes behind those behaviors. Let us therefore begin our analysis of the Maasai people by looking at those aspects of their history that link current perceptions to the past.

History

While the history of any culture is made up of thousands of experiences, there are often a few significant ones that serve to explain how that culture might view the world. In the case of the Maasai, there are three historical episodes that have greatly influenced their perception of themselves, other people, and events. These historical occurrences center on their creation, fierceness, and reaction to modernization.

The history of the Maasai is the history of a people with an oral tradition. Like all cultures who practice the oral tradition, the content and customs that are transmitted are largely found within the stories, poetry, and songs of the people. To the outsider they appear vague and only loosely based on facts. Some historians, along with the aid of Maasai elders, have attempted to link the stories and folklore with the available information about the Maasai's past, a past that helps explain many of the perceptions and values held by the Maasai.

Most accounts of the origin of the Maasai as a unique culture begin with the belief that they were part of a larger group that was migrating south during a severe drought (Kipury, 1983). The group found themselves trapped in a deep valley so they constructed a bridge that was to transport them out of the valley. Folk tales and history go on to tell the story of how the bridge collapsed before all the people escaped. Those who were left behind are now thought to be the Somali, Borana, and Rendile peoples. Those who managed to escape the dryness of the valley went on to be the true Maa-speaking people.

While the above rendition of early Maasai history is uncertain in answering questions regarding the origins of the Maasai, it does reveal one very important aspect of how history and perception are linked. This story helps explain how the Maasai perceive themselves compared to other tribes. It also helps an outsider understand the strong feelings of pride that are associated with the Maasai culture. For the Maasai, the story of their origin, even if it is speculation, tells them they are better than other tribes of East Africa who did not come from the north nor escape across the bridge—regardless of how long ago that arrival might have been.

The Maasai's history of warfare and conflict is yet another source of knowledge about the perception of themselves and non-Maasai. Before the advent of colonialism in the latter part of the nineteenth century, other tribes in Kenya such as the Kikuyu, Akamba, and Kalenjin were often attacked by the Maasai. The attacks were fierce and usually resulted in their enemies being forced from their lands. Some Maasai, particularly the elders, still see themselves as the conquerors of other tribes, and even today, the Maasai still have the reputation of being warlike. Non-Maasai Kenyans may warn visitors of the "terrible" Maasai and their propensity for violence. A former colleague of one of the authors often expressed her distrust of the Maasai, believing that they would harm her simply because she was from the Kikuyu tribe. She had heard about the Maasai's fierceness and their dislike of other tribes who dressed in Western clothes. Whether entirely accurate or not, this perception of them as warlike influences both the behavior of the Maasai and the behavior of those who come in contact with them.

A third historical period that has shaped the perceptions of the Maasai is the preindependence period of Kenya. Because the Maasai occupied vast areas of land in Kenya, the British colonialists turned an eye toward acquiring this valuable property. Through numerous agreements, great parcels of land were turned over to the colonialists. The Maasai were settled on new tracts of land that were much less desirable than the ones they were leaving, and they soon began to realize that not only were they giving up their prime land but they were also seeing a number of promises made by the colonialists being broken. In response to these two conclusions, the Maasai adopted an attitude of passive resistance to all Western innovations and temptations to become "modern." While most other parts of Kenya were altering their culture through education and technology, the Maasai had become disillusioned with those who were seeking to alter their way of life, and hence they refused to change (Sankan, 1971).

The rejection of cultural conversion by the Maasai has had immense consequences on them and the people around them. On one hand it has caused the government and other tribes to perceive them as stubbornly traditional, backward, uneducated, and isolated. However, for the Maasai, resistance to change is yet another indication of their strength and long history of power. Other more Westernized tribes, such as the Kikuyu, feel the Maasai are backward and not in tune with changing Kenya. Ironically, the Kikuyu seem to have a love-hate relationship with the Maasai: scorn for their refusal to be more modern yet respect for their retaining their traditional customs.

Values

What a culture values, or doesn't value, also helps determine how that culture perceives the world. Therefore, understanding what the Maasai regard as good or bad, valuable or worthless, right or wrong, just or unjust, and appropriate or inappropriate can help explain the communication behavior of their culture.

Children. For a Maasai man or woman to be without children is a great misfortune. The Maasai strongly believe that children continue the race, and more important, they will preserve the family—hence, children are highly valued. The Maasai embrace the idea that a man can "live" even after death if he has a son who can carry on his name, enjoy his wealth, and spread his reputation. In addition, they value children because they offer the senior Maasai a continuous supply of workers. The Maasai have a saying that illustrates this point: "More hands make light the work." Children supply those hands. Unfortunately, this value is in direct conflict with the Kenyan government's family planning program to curb Kenya's dangerously high population growth. While the central government tries to emphasize the need to control the population, for the Maasai the man with the most children, no matter how poor he is, is the wealthiest and happiest of all men.

Cattle. The Maasai culture revolves around the cow, on which they greatly depend for their food, clothing, housing, fuel, trade, medicine, and ceremonies. Cattle have given the Maasai their traditionally nomadic life style. The more cattle a man has the more respected he is. Cattle are usually killed only on designated occasions such as for marriage and circumcision ceremonies or when special guests visit. The Maasai believe that all cattle were originally given to them by God. There is even a folk tale that tells of the Maasai descending to earth with cattle by their sides. This belief justifies their taking cattle from other tribes, even if it is in violation of the law.

Groups. Families and life-stage groups are at the core of the Maasai community. Because children are so highly valued, the family must be strong and central in their lives. An overwhelming portion of a Maasai child's education is still carried out in the home, with the grandparents, not the schools, providing the content of the culture.

Life-stage groups are specifically defined periods in the lives of all Maasai, particularly males. Traditionally, all men must go through four stages of life: childhood, adolescence (circumcision), moranship (warriorhood—junior and senior), and elderhood (junior and senior). Women must pass through childhood, circumcision, and then marriage. Each of these stages places a strong emphasis on the group. Attempts to get Maasai students to raise their hands and participate in formal classrooms are often futile. Drawing attention to oneself in a group setting is unacceptable because the tribe and the life-stage group are far more valuable than the individual (Johnstone, 1988).

Elders: Male and Female. Maasai children must give respect to any person older than themselves, whether a sibling, grandmother, or older member of the community. They must bow their heads in greeting as a sign of humility and inferiority. Even young circumcised men and women (aged fifteen to twenty-five years) must bow their heads to male elders, particularly if the elders are highly respected in the community.

The Maasai believe the older you become the wiser you become and that a wise individual deserves a great deal of deference and respect. Part of the strong emphasis placed on elders is that the Maasai hold their history in such high regard, and it is the oldest members of the tribe who know most of the history. Young people cannot know the "truth" until they progress through each of the life-stage groups.

For Maasai youths getting older indicates a change in social status. When male Maasai students return from a school holiday with their heads shaved, this indicates that they have just gone through circumcision and initiation into another life-stage. They have become men and are instantly perceived by other students and themselves as different, even older, and deserving of more respect.

Pride. Pride for the Maasai means having the virtues of obedience, honesty, wisdom, and fairness. A man may be an elder in name only, for if he does not exhibit these characteristics, he is not a respected man in the community. A woman's pride is often defined by how well she keeps her home, by whether she is an obedient wife, and by the number of children she has.

Outsiders, whether black or white, perceive the Maasai loftiness and pride as a kind of arrogance. The Maasai themselves, because they are traditionally pastoralists, still look down on strictly agricultural tribes such as the Kikuyu.

Their strong sense of pride is also fueled by their view of themselves as warriors. As noted earlier, they have always been feared by other tribes and the colonialists. Their folklore is replete with tales of their fighting with incredible fearlessness, even when their primitive weapons faced their enemies' modern bullets. For them the battles were to preserve the "true African" way of life and to protect their cattle.

Beauty. Beauty is yet another value that is important to the Maasai. Both men and women adorn themselves with elaborate beads, body paint, and other jewelry. Maasai children, especially girls, begin wearing jewelry almost from the moment of birth. One of the primary duties a woman has is to make necklaces, bracelets, bangles, belts, and earrings for her husband, children, friends, and herself. Adornment is also a way for a woman to attract a husband, and Maasai women are very meticulous in selecting jewelry for special celebrations. Maasai warriors still spend much of their day painting themselves with red ochre, and they also plait and braid their hair, which is grown long as a sign of warriorhood.

Beauty and bodily adornment are so valued in the Maasai culture that they have distinctive jewelry and dress to wear during certain periods of each life-stage. For example, one can tell if a boy has just recently been circumcised because he wears a crown of bird carcasses. Thus, we can conclude that beauty is more than superficial for the Maasai; it is a reflection of a very important value that often steers perception in one direction or another.

World View

The world view of a culture is yet another factor that greatly modifies perception. In the Samovar and Porter (1988) model, world view deals with a culture's orientation toward such things as God, humanity, the universe, death, nature, and other philosophical issues that are concerned with the concept of being. In short, it is that perception of the world that helps the individual locate his or her place and rank in the universe. It influences nearly every action in which an individual engages. Our research would tend to agree with this observation. The Maasai's world view has three components that greatly control their life and hence their perception of the universe: coexistence with nature, religion, and death.

Nature. For the Maasai, nature must always be held in the highest regard. They believe that their very existence depends solely on nature's benevolence. Their life style is one that sees them interacting with the elements: Without rain their cattle will die, and in a sense so will they, for as we pointed out earlier, cattle supply most of the basic needs of the Maasai.

The Maasai also embrace the view that nature cannot be changed; it is too powerful. But they do acknowledge that nature itself changes without their intervening, and what they must do is change as nature fluctuates. Adapting to nature is most evident in the Maasai's seminomadic life style. They carry coexistence to the point where they will not kill or eat wild animals unless they pose a threat or there is a severe drought. For the Maasai cultivating and hunting are seen as destructive to nature: Cultivation forces humans to deal directly with nature, changing and altering it to their specifications and needs; hunting for food is seen as something even worse, for then nature is not only being changed but it is being destroyed (Rigby, 1985).

Religion. The second aspect of world view, religion, is closely tied to the Maasai perception of nature. The Maasai have one god called "Engai," but this god has two very distinct personalities and therefore serves two purposes: "Engai Narok," the black god, is benevolent and generous and shows himself through rain and thunder; "Engai Nanyokie," the red god, is manifested in lightning. To the Maasai, God encompasses everything in nature, friendly or destructive (Saitoti and Beckwith, 1980). In fact, the word "Engai" actually means "sky." Cattle accompanied the Maasai people to earth from the sky and thus cattle are seen as mediators between humans and God as well as between humans and nature. Therefore, herding is traditionally the only acceptable livelihood, since it is God's will. Not to herd would be disrespectful to Engai and demeaning to a Maasai (Salvadon and Fedders, 1973).

There is a Maasai proverb that states, "The one chosen by God is not the one chosen by people" (Rigby, 1985, p. 92). Thus, not surprisingly, the Maasai have no priests or ministers; there is no one who represents God or purports to speak for God. There are "laiboni" who are considered the wisest of the elders and often cast curses and give blessings, but they do not represent God or preach. The Maasai have no religious writings, only oral legends, therefore the elders are important in the religious life of the people.

What is most significant is that God (Engai) is found in nature. Some Maasai households rise at dawn to pray to the sun, which is seen as a manifestation of Engai. God is found in many other forms in nature for the Maasai: rain, grass, and even a particularly beautiful stone. God *is* nature and cannot be artificially symbolized in a cross or a building. Since nature is God, people must live in harmony with God and the Maasai must work together. This is a different view of God than the one offered by Christianity, in which God is separate from humans and is even from a different world.

Death. The third aspect of the Maasai world view is how they perceive death. As with most cultures, death brings sorrow to those left behind by the deceased; however, cultures differ in how they respond to death. The response of the Maasai directly coincides with their belief in the coexistence of nature and human beings; therefore, except for the "laiboni" (wise man), all corpses are left out in the open to be devoured by hyenas and other scavengers. The assumption behind this action is clear, at least to the Maasai, who believe that after they have had a full life and enjoyed the benefits of nature, it is only fitting that their bones go back to the earth so they can be used to prepare the land for future life. For the Maasai there is a circular, mutually beneficial relationship between nature and humanity.

VERBAL PROCESSES

In the most basic sense, language is an organized, generally agreed upon, learned symbol system used to represent human experiences within a geographic or cultural community. Each culture places its individual imprint on words—how they are used and what they mean.

Language is the primary vehicle by which a culture transmits its beliefs, values, and norms. Language gives people a means of interacting with other members of their culture and a means of thinking, serving both as a mechanism for communication and as a guide to social reality. Anyone interested in studying another culture must therefore look at the way a culture uses language and also the experiences in their environment they have selected to name. Research on the Maasai culture reveals two language variables that offer a clue into the workings of this particular group of people: their use of metaphors and their reliance on proverbs.

Metaphors

Wisdom in the Maasai culture is marked not just by age and prudence but also by language use. Elders make decisions at tribal meetings based on speeches offered by various members of the group. The most successful speakers are those whose eloquence is embellished and ornate. The metaphor offers the gifted speaker a tool to demonstrate his mastery of words. Heine and Claudi (1986) explain the importance of metaphor to the Maasai when they write:

Maa people frequently claim that their language is particularly rich in figurative speech forms. Non-literal language, especially the use of metaphors, is in fact encouraged from earliest childhood on, and the success of a political leader depends to quite a large extent on the creative use of it (p. 17).

Because of the value placed on metaphors, Johnstone (1988) writes, "Whenever there were big meetings to decide important matters, the men always spoke in proverbs, metaphors, and other figurative language." Messages are full of elaborate symbolism—blunt and simple words are rarely used.

The information in Table 1, developed by Heine and Claudi (1986), helps clarify some of the types of metaphors employed by the Maasai. These few examples demonstrate how most of the metaphors in the Maa language reflect what is important in their culture. For example, the use of the umbilical cord to refer to a very close friend is indicative of the value placed on childbirth and of the strong bonds between members of the same age-set. In addition, an age-set generation is formally established when a select group of elders kindles the fire on the day that a new generation of boys will be circumcised (Heine & Claudi, 1986). These age-sets form both a unique governing body and a social hierarchy in all Maasai communities.

Proverbs

Like metaphors, proverbs are an integral part of the Maasai language. Massek and Sidai (1974) noted that "a Maasai hardly speaks ten sentences without using at least one proverb" (p. 6). These proverbs have common elements and themes that are directly related to the Maasai value system.

Proverbs convey important messages to the members of a culture because they often deal with subjects that are of significance. Therefore, the assumption behind examining the proverbs is a simple one—discover the meaning of the proverb and you will understand something of what is important to its user. This axiom is exceptionally true for the Maasai, for here one encounters proverbs focusing on respect, parents, children, wisdom, and proper conduct. Let us look at some of these proverbs as a way of furthering an understanding of the Maasai culture.

1. "Meeta enkerai olopeny." (The child has no owner.) Maasai children are expected to respect all elders, not just those in the immediate family. It is very common for children to refer to older men as "Father" and to older women as "Mother."

2. "Memorataa olayoni oataa menye." (One is never a man while his father is still alive.) Even as junior elders, Maasai men do not always leave their father's homestead. It is not until a man attains the full status of senior elder that he usually establishes his own home with his wife (wives) and children. In addition, the very name of male children is indicated with the word "ole," which means "son of," placed

Table 1

Category	Maasai Word	Basic Meaning	Metaphorical Meaning
Object + Animal	Olmotonyi	Large bird	Eagle shoulder cape
Person + Animal	Enker	Sheep	Careless, stupid person
Person + Object	Sotua	Umbilical cord	Close friend
Quality + Object	Olpiron	Firestick	Age-set generation

between the first and last names. A Maasai male is very often characterized by his father's name and reputation.

3. "Eder olayioni o menye, neder entito o notanye." (A boy converses with his father while a girl converses with her mother.) This proverb is representative of both the restricted relationships between the opposite sexes in a family and the strict divisions of labor found in the Maasai culture. Young girls learn to do household chores at an early age, and by age seven their brothers are responsible for tending the family herd.

4. "Menye marrmali, menye maata." (Father of troubles, father without.) In the Maasai culture there is a conviction that a man with no children has more problems than a man with many children. They believe that even a man with a fine herd of cattle can never be rich unless he also has many children. This proverb simply serves to underscore those facts.

5. "Ideenya taa anaa osurai oota oikati." (You are as proud as lean meat with soot on it.) Being proud is a well-known characteristic of the Maasai. So strong is this value that the Maasai are often criticized by other African tribes. To sustain the reality and the perception of pride, a Maasai must always add to his accomplishments, and courageous acts and large families are two common behaviors that present an image of a proud person. It should be noted, however, that foolish pride is looked down upon as a sign of arrogance.

6. "Medany olkimojino obo elashei." (One finger does not kill a louse.) The need to cooperate is crucial to the Maasai culture, and this proverb reinforces that belief. As noted earlier, the Maasai community is a highly communal one, one that is well-structured and based on group harmony and decision making. The family unit is particularly dependent on cooperation and accord. On most occasions wives care for each other's children. Cattle are kept together and shared, with ownership only a secondary consideration.

In this section on proverbs we see the connection between what a culture talks about and what it embraces and acknowledges to be true. This link between words and behavior only serves to buttress the belief that verbal symbols represent a device by which a culture maintains and perpetuates itself.

NONVERBAL PROCESSES

Nonverbal systems represent yet another coding system that individuals and cultures use as a means of sharing their realities. Like verbal symbols, nonverbal codes are learned as part of the socialization process—that is, each culture teaches its members the symbol and the meaning for the symbol. In the case of the Maasai, there are a number of nonverbal messages that, when understood, offer the outsider some clues as to the workings of this foreign culture.

Movement and Posture

The Maasai show their pride and self-regard by the way they carry themselves. They are tall and slender and have a posture that reflects an appearance of strength and vigor. There is, at first glance, a regal air about them and at times they appear to be floating. "The morans [warriors], especially, walk very erect and relatively slowly. It's like they are in so much command of their environment that they are absolutely at ease" (Johnstone, personal correspondence, 1988).

The posture and movement of Maasai women also mirrors an attitude of pride and self-assurance. They are also tall and slender and a have a gait that is slow and self-confident. Their heads are held high as a way of emphasizing their confidence and superiority over other tribes.

Paralanguage

The Maasai people utilize a number of sounds that have special meanings. The most common is the "eh" sound, which is used extensively, even though the Maasai language is ornate and metaphorical. When uttered, the sound is drawn out and can have a host of different interpretations; it can mean "yes,"

"I understand," or "continue." Although similar to the English regulators "uh huh" and "hmmm," "eh" is used more frequently and appears to dominate short, casual conversations among the Maasai.

Touching

While public touching between the sexes among the Maasai is usually limited to a light handshake, same-sex touching is common. Simple greetings between the sexes consist of a very light brush of the palms; in fact, so light is the touch, the hands appear barely to touch. If two women are good friends, however, they may greet each other with a light kiss on the lips. If they have not seen each other recently, they may embrace and clutch each other's upper arms. Men will frequently drape their arms around each other while conversing. When children greet an elder, they bow their heads so that the elder may place his or her hand on the young person's head, which is a sign of both respect and fondness. There is a great deal of affection to be found among the Maasai, and touching is one way of displaying that affection.

Time

The meaning cultures attach to time also reveals something of their view toward life and other people. The Maasai are unique in their treatment of time. Unlike the Westerner, for the Maasai there is always enough time: Their life is not governed by the clock; they are never in a hurry. This casual attitude produces a people who are self-possessed, calm, and most of all, *patient*.

Children are taught very early that there is never a need to rush. The vital chore of tending the family cattle requires that children stay alert and attentive to the herd's needs and safety, but such a chore also requires eight to ten hours of patient solitude.

This endless display of patience by the Maasai people is in direct contrast to time-conscious Americans. For example, public transportation in Kenya is not run on a firm schedule; buses and "matatus" (covered pick-up trucks) leave for their destinations when they are full. As do most Kenyans, the Maasai

understand this. Inquiries from Americans as to when a vehicle will be departing are often answered with "just now." "Just now," however, can mean anywhere from five minutes to an hour.

Even though the present is fully enjoyed, the Maasai culture is very past-oriented. This strong tie to the past stems from the view that wisdom is found not in the present or the future, but rather in the past. The future is governed by the knowledge of the elderly, not by the discoveries of the young. The insignificance of the future is apparent in how the Maasai perceive death: There is nothing after death unless one is a "laiboni" (wise man).

Space

Space, as it relates to land and grazing, is truly communal. Traditionally nomadic pastoralists, the Maasai did not regard any land as theirs to own but rather perceived all land as theirs to use. Rigby (1985) explains that the pastoral Maasai "do not conceive of land as 'owned' by any group, category, community or individual" (p. 124). He explains, however, that today most Maasai practice a subtle marking of territory. Each clan now has its own area and for the most part, clan boundaries are observed. Yet concepts of "land rights" and "trespassing" are still viewed as Western notions.

The Maasai's perception of private space is very different from Western perceptions. Maasai do not need or ask for much private space while in public settings. Lining up in a systematic order, and taking one's turn, is not part of the Maasai experience—public facilities, therefore, at least to the outsider, often appear disorderly. It is not uncommon to see a vehicle designed to hold fifteen packed with thirty occupants, and none of them complaining. For the Maasai, space is like time—there is always enough of it.

CONCLUSION

It has been the intent of this article to offer some observations about the Maasai culture. It is our contention that by knowing something about the perceptions and language systems of a culture, one can better understand that culture. This increased understanding provides us with a fund of knowledge that can be helpful in formulating messages directed to a group of people different from ourselves. It can also aid in interpreting the meanings behind the messages we receive from people who appear quite different from us. As Emerson wrote, "All persons are puzzles until at last we find some word or act, the key to the man, to the woman; straightaway all their past words and actions lie in light before us."

REFERENCES

Hall, E. (1976). *Beyond Culture*. Garden City, N.Y.: Anchor Books.

Heine, B., and Claudi, U. (1986). *On the Rise of Grammatical Categories*. Berlin, West Germany: Dietrich Reimer Verlag.

Johnstone, J. (1988, March 30). Personal correspondence.

Kipury, N. (1983) *Oral Literature of the Maasai*. Nairobi, Kenya: Heinemann Educational Books.

Massek, A. O., and Sidai, J. O. (1974). *Eneno oo Lmaasai—Wisdom of the Maasai*. Nairobi, Kenya: Transafrica Publishers.

Rigby, P. (1985). *Persistent Pastoralists: Nomadic Societies in Transition*. London, England: Zed Books.

Saitoti, T. O., and Beckwith, C. (1980). *Maasai*. London, England: Elm Tree Books.

Salvadon, C., and Fedders, A. (1973). *Maasai*. London, England: Collins.

Samovar, L. A., and Porter, R. E. (1988). "Approaching Intercultural Communication." In L. A. Samovar and R. E. Porter (Eds.), *Intercultural Communication: A Reader*. (5th ed.) Belmont, Calif.: Wadsworth.

Sankan, S. S. O. (1971). *The Maasai*. Nairobi, Kenya: Kenya Literature Bureau.

A Comparison of Arab and American Conceptions of "Effective" Persuasion

JANICE WALKER ANDERSON

This rhetorical analysis will illustrate that Americans and Saudis have different "rules" for political debate. "The rhetoric used in the Western world to describe the Arab-Israeli conflict is a prime example of the use of language, not as a means of illuminating reality," Abdel-Wahab El-Messiri (quoted by D. Ray Heisey, 1970) asserted, "but as a way of evading issues and complex historical totalities" (p. 12). In our modern global village, different conceptions of persuasion meet through the mass communication process.

Although mass media reports on events in the Middle East translate the words used by Arab leaders, the reports seldom explain the different cultural standards in Arab societies for evaluating reasonableness. "We can say that what is 'reasonable,'" intercultural communication scholars Condon and Yousef (1975) explain, "is not fully separable from cultural assumptions" (p. 213). This analysis indicates some of the differences between Arab and American cultural orientations toward what constitutes "effective" persuasion.

As Richard Barton (1982) argued in "Message Analysis in International Mass Communication Research," "the study of international media processes

From *The Howard Journal of Communications*, Vol. 2, No. 1 (Winter 1989–90), pp. 81–114. Reprinted by permission of the publisher. Janice Walker Anderson is in the Communication Department, College at New Paltz, State University of New York.

lags behind the general trend in mass communication study of systematically investigating the formal qualities of media discourse" (p. 82). This study is intended as a first step toward addressing a gap in current research on international mass communications.

This paper compares the rhetorical tactics in a Saudi Government advocacy advertisement, or paid editorial, with those in a Mobil Oil Corporation advocacy advertisement. . . . Advocacy advertisements promote ideas rather than products and usually argue one side of a controversial social or political issue.[1] Both paid editorials examined in this study explain to the American public the rationale behind the Arab's oil boycott in 1973. The two advocacy ads employ radically different rhetorical tactics to accomplish similar objectives.

First, the analysis will provide a brief overview of some essential aspects of Arab orientations toward discourse. Then, it will briefly set the historical context for the ads. Finally, it will compare the rhetorical tactics in the two advocacy advertisements and summarize the different basic assumptions about persuasion implicit in each artifact.

ARAB ORIENTATIONS TOWARD DISCOURSE

Before beginning the analysis, it is first necessary to acquaint American readers with some of the basics of Arab and Moslem orientations toward argumentation. "While only a small percentage (about 10%) of present-day Arabs are Bedouins," Gudykunst and Kim explain in *Communicating with Strangers*, "contemporary Arab culture holds the Bedouin ethos as an ideal to which, in theory at least, it would like to measure up" (p. 50). While values such as materialism, success, activity, progress, and rationality are featured in American culture, Arab societies revolve around the core values of "hospitality, generosity, courage, honor, and self-respect" (p. 50).

As H. Samuel Hamod indicated in "Arab and Moslem Rhetorical Theory and Practice," storytellers performed a vital function for the Bedouin tribes because few people could read or write: "[T]heir tribal storytellers functioned as historians and moralists in recounting battles and instances of outstanding bravery and cunning" (p. 97). These storytellers, or what we today might call poets, performed important political functions by establishing a means for interpreting and directing action. As A. J. Almaney and A. J. Alwan (1982) explained, a poet's poems "might arouse a tribe to action in the same manner as . . . [a politician] in a modern political campaign. . . . He was both a molder and agent of public opinion" (p. 79). Some attributed magical powers to these storytellers because they controlled the power of language which could act upon the human emotions and rouse the people to action.

To this day, poets are held in the highest esteem in Arab societies. As a result, many educated Arabs will attempt to write poetry at some time in their careers. In 1983, for example, Sheik Mani Said al-Otaiba, an oil minister from the United Arab Emirates, wrote a poem about OPEC's (Organization of Petroleum Exporting Companies) troubles maintaining oil production quotas. The *New York Times* reported that this poem "seemed to cause more hard feelings among his colleagues than the discord over prices" (Lewis, p. 6).

The reporter, Paul Lewis, discounted the importance of the Sheik's poem, asserting that his most important contribution was a passage in his dissertation "which marked him as one of the first Arabs to say publicly that it was the Nixon Administration that encouraged [OPEC] to quadruple world oil prices in 1973 by suggesting the West had few, if any, alternatives" (p. 6). In this instance, Lewis underestimated the importance that Arabs ascribe to poetry. It frequently functions in a political context to motivate action, and, as such, it is accorded as much weight as a scholarly dissertation.

In addition, Arab cultures connect inspired language and religion. Arabic plays an important religious role in Islamic societies. All Muslims, regardless of their nationality, must use Arabic in their daily prayers. The language of the Quran is considered a miracle in itself because it was produced by the Prophet Mohammed, who was illiterate. Consequently, Muslims believe that the Quran cannot be faithfully translated into other languages (Almaney & Alwan, p. 79).

The power of words lay not in their ability to reflect human experience, but in their ability to transcend it, to reach toward that which lay beyond human experience—the divine. To this day, the Quran stands as the ultimate book of style and grammar for Arabs. The cultural equivalent in the West would be using the King James version of the Bible as our style manual.

The Arab's appreciation for the persuasive power of the rhythm and sound of words leads to a style that relies heavily on devices that heighten the emotional impact of a message. Certain words are used in speaking that have no denotative meaning. "These are 'firm' words because the audience knows the purpose behind their use, and the words are taken as a seal of definiteness and sincerity on the part of the speaker" (Hamod, p. 100). Other forms of assertion, such as repetition and antithesis, are also quite frequent. Emphatic assertions are expected, Almaney and Alwan explain: "If an Arab says exactly what he means without the expected assertion, other Arabs may still think he means the opposite" (p. 84).

Hamod explains the reasoning behind the Arab's emphasis on stylistic concerns. "He who speaks well is well educated; he who is well educated is more qualified to render judgments and it is his advice we should follow. Eloquence and effectiveness were equated" (p. 98). An Arab writer establishes credibility by displaying ability and artistry with the language.

SETTING THE HISTORICAL CONTEXT

Both advocacy ads faced a potentially hostile American audience in presenting their views about the Middle East. The advocacy ads appeared in 1973, the year of the first oil crisis. "The press at the time," Anthony Sampson (1975), oil industry analyst, explained, "were sympathetic to the Israelis" (p. 100).

Mobil's ad, "The U.S. stake in Middle East peace: I," appeared in June of 1973 when another war was brewing in the Middle East. "This ad turned out to be one of the most controversial messages we've ever run," Herbert Schmertz (1986), Mobil's vice president for public affairs explained:

The issue at hand was simply the future of America's oil supply, which boiled down to the need for recognizing the strategic importance of Saudi Arabia. Our critics accused us of running this ad at the behest of the Saudis, but there was no truth to this charge (p. 168).

The *New York Times* editorial board was so concerned about the content of Mobil's ad that they did not allow it to appear in Mobil's normal position on the op-ed page. Instead, the ad was buried in the second section of the newspaper, where it was more likely to be obscured by product ads.

The Saudi ad, entitled, "An Open Letter to the American People," appeared six months later. The Saudi ad ran in the *Washington Post* two months after the 1973 war in the Middle East began.[2] The ad appeared on New Year's Day just as the consequences of the oil boycott were beginning to be felt within the United States.

Although the Saudi ad was attributed to Mr. Omar Sakkaf, Saudi minister of state for foreign affairs, he was not necessarily the sole author. In a telephone interview, Dr. Mohammed Al-Zafer, a former Saudi diplomat to the United States and now deputy director of King Khaled University in Saudi Arabia, explained that Mr. Sakkaf died about five years ago. In describing the generation of the ad, Dr. Al-Zafer stated that diplomats stationed in the United States speak fluent English. However, they would not prepare statements for publication without "having them checked ahead of time." By attributing the ad to the minister of state of foreign affairs, the Saudis indicated that it was an accurate reflection of their perspective on events in the Middle East. It is not unreasonable to assume the author(s) of the ad were probably educated, cosmopolitan Saudi officials familiar with both English and Arabic.

COMPARISON OF
RHETORICAL STRATEGIES

The two ads demonstrated quite different responses to the hostile audience that they faced. Most immediately, the ads employed different strategies for framing their arguments. In addition, they used contrasting organizing principles. Finally, the ads provided different kinds of justifications for action.

Framing the Argument

Mobil's ad, "The U.S. stake in Middle East peace: I," employed an inductive opening. Instead of launching immediately into a discussion of foreign affairs, the author(s) first defined a domestic problem immediate to their readers. The opening five paragraphs of the ad documented the growing gap between domestic oil production and trends in energy consumption.

Because oil and natural gas supplied over three-quarters of the United States' energy, the author(s) asserted: "Our society cannot live without adequate oil supplies . . . much less continue as an industrial society." Although domestic consumption was increasing, domestic production was declining so that foreign oil already provided one third of the United States' energy needs. "In another seven years, or less," Mobil author(s) predicted, "we will be relying on foreign sources for more than half of our oil."

Our need for increased energy supplies provided the rationale for Mobil's discussion of the Middle East. Because only the Middle East had sufficient oil reserves to meet U.S. demand, the ad concluded: "Like it or not, the United States is dependent on the Middle East even just to maintain our present living standards in the years immediately ahead."

In framing its argument, the Mobil author(s) demonstrated a typically American tendency to assume that "the world is rational in the sense that . . . events . . . can be explained and the reasons for particular occurrences can be determined" (Stewart, p. 35). Statistics described the "objective" reality of energy demand. These rational "facts" created the

necessity for action. "For Americans," Stewart explains, "the world is composed of facts—not ideas. Their process of thinking is generally inductive, beginning with facts and then proceeding to ideas" (p. 22).

The introduction of the Saudi ad, in contrast, was not concerned with the facts of energy supply and demand. It focused on competing perspectives. This "Open Letter to the American People" obliquely addressed the concerns of five distinct audiences: the American people, the American press, the "American friends of Israel," other Arab nations, and the "world in general." The first five paragraphs of the ad acknowledged the subgroups whose competing perspectives created the complexity of the political dynamics of the Middle East.

This complexity was reflected through the use of parallel structure to express contrasting ideas:

We, the Arabs, wish you a Happy New Year. Your holiday season might have been marred by the hardships of the energy crisis. Ours is haunted by the threat of death and continued aggression.

The antithesis highlighted the contrast in perspectives between the American people and the Arab people. It implicitly addressed the contrast between American materialistic values and Arab values of honor and self-respect. On the broad level of justice between nations of the world, economic hardships such as gas lines paled in comparison to displacement from a homeland.

The language structure of the opening appealed to a human tendency to respond to the rhythm of language, to enjoy, as Kenneth Burke pointed out, seeing the completion of a "form." Although American readers might not understand the content of the antithesis, they would unconsciously respond to the rhythm. The Saudi author(s) employed parallel structure to draw readers into their interpretation of the world. The literacy device illustrated the author(s)' sophistication with the language, thereby establishing their credibility through traditional means within Arab cultures.

By emphasizing the contrast between American and Arab perspectives, the opening simultaneously minimized the contrast between the Arab countries of Syria, Egypt, Jordan, and Saudi Arabia. "We, the Arabs" imposed a unitary perspective based on linguistic, religious, and cultural commonalities, not on national boundaries. "North Americans value individual centeredness and self-reliance," Gudykunst and Kim explain, "the Arabic attitude is one of mutual dependence" (p. 126). The Saudi author(s) would not perceive distinctions between individual Arab nations as particularly salient in the way that North Americans would.

But it is not in bitterness that we address this message to you and it is our hope that there will be no bitterness in you as you read it.

As though acknowledging that the American public might read the initial literary flourish as a stark exaggeration, the author(s) followed one verbal flourish with another designed to soften the impact of the first. This parallel structure emphasized commonalities. It indicated that the assertion in the opening was not intended to offend the American people. Overstatement simply indicated the sincerity of the author(s)' intentions and the seriousness of the topic. "To Arabs," Gudykunst and Kim explain, ". . . a soft tone implies weakness or even deviousness" (p. 161).

We have been under continuous attack from the American Press—with notable exceptions—for two decades, and we must confess we are unable to understand the reasoning behind this overwhelming hostility. We lived in Palestine for two thousand years, and when we resisted displacement by a foreign state, the Americans branded us aggressors.

The parallel structure was broken as this paragraph introduced two additional contrasting perspectives: the American media's portrayal of Arabs as aggressors versus the Arabs' view of themselves as victims. This paragraph employed a cultural commonplace meaningful within the Arab community. The two-thousand-year context the Saudi author(s) established and the use of the name "Palestine" emphasized the Israelis' role as interlopers. In this paragraph, the Saudi author(s) echoed the com-

ments of Abdel-Wahab El-Messiri, arguing that the American media did not excel in describing "complex historical totalities."

"But let that pass," the fourth paragraph continued, once again backing away from the emotional tone that had been established, again indicating to the American audience that statements of Arab beliefs were not intended to initiate a hostile reaction. This single-sentence paragraph signaled a transition to a new topic:

In the past year, we have made considerable concessions, given up much of what is rightfully ours, for the sole purpose of promoting peace in the Middle East and the world in general. These concessions appear to have had no effect whatsoever on the American attitude. Indeed, wild accusations against the Arabs are increasing in volume and intensity, and all of them are so baseless that we have begun to wonder if the American people really know what the Arabs want.

The Saudi author(s) asserted the Arabs' bewilderment at the reaction of Americans toward Arabs and repeated the question that prompted the letter: "Do the American people know what we are asking for?"

The opening of the Saudi ad alluded to a range of subgroups implicit in the international mass media audience. The introduction played upon the theme of competing perspectives on events in the Middle East. Parallel structure highlighted the contrasts. A break in the rhythm indicated a redefinition offered to the American people; Arabs were victims of displacement by a foreign state, not aggressors as the American media portrayed them. While the Saudi author(s) made an effort to accommodate Americans who might not know how to interpret the assertions offered, the primary focus of the introduction was on establishing a perspective for interpretation, on naming the victims and aggressors in the region rather than on explaining principles of supply and demand.

Organizing Principles

As a result, the Saudi author(s) were not concerned with the linear development of factual premises.

The organizing principle of the Saudi ad was on the implicit level of metaphoric association, not on the level of explicit meaning. The unifying thread through the opening of the Saudi ad was the portrayal of the Arabs as victims. The unifying theme in the next section of the ad was the portrayal of the Israelis as aggressors.

Rather than mention the most recent conflict in 1973, the ad turned back to the 1967 Six-Day War. The Saudi author(s) did not provide historical explanations of the conflicts in the region. Instead, the ad simply quoted UN Resolution 242, which called for a "just and lasting peace in the Middle East based on the 'withdrawal of Israel Armed Forces from territories occupied in the recent conflict' and 'termination of all claims or states of belligerency.'" The term "recent" was used equivocally. Did it refer to the last few months or to the last five years?

"This is what we are asking for," the next paragraph of the ad explained. The simple language structure of this statement reinforced the impression that the Arabs' demands were similarly uncomplicated. By quoting an official UN resolution that the United States had approved, the ad implied that world opinion sided with the Arabs. Yet, the equivocal language in the ad made it vague in terms of the Arabs' specific demands.

The next paragraph documented that United States officials had previously criticized Israeli expansionism in the region: "President Lyndon Johnson stated in September, 1968, that 'boundaries cannot and should not reflect the weight of conquest.'" The subsequent paragraph continued the parallel structure that had been established in this section: "This is what we are asking for, and we want nothing more."

Parallel structure and repetition were employed quite consistently in the next two paragraphs: "Israel says it wants peace. So do we. Israel says it wants security. So do we." The problem was that Israel wanted peace and the Arab lands it occupied in 1967: "Israel wants peace and *lebensraum*, security and Arab land, and Israel cannot have both," the ad explained. "Leben" is a traditional drink among Arabs that consists of coagulated sour milk. If viewed as a *double entendre*, between German and Arabic, Israel wanted the milk of Arab land as well as peace. An American might translate the phrase as Israel wanted to have its cake and eat it too.

The ad consistently alternated between long, complicated paragraphs and short, single-sentence paragraphs. The variety between complexity and simplicity combined with parallel structure and repetition made the ad quite rhythmic. One result of this method of organization, however, was that an American reader needed a broad knowledge of the conflicts in the region. Those who did not share the author(s)' historical perspective would have to read between the lines.

Americans are accustomed to greater explicitness in message design, while Arabs are more accustomed to reading implicit meanings. Intercultural communication scholars use the term "contexting" to "describe the perceptual process of recognizing, giving significance to, and incorporating contextual cues in interpreting the total meaning of any stimulus in a particular communication transaction" (Gudykunst & Kim, p. 120). American culture (low context) places greatest emphasis on explicit meaning. Arab cultures (high context), on the other hand, make greater use of subtle, contextual clues in interpreting messages. In explaining what the Arabs wanted, the Saudi author(s) demonstrated a cultural tendency to rely on an implicit understanding of the history of conflicts in the region.

In comparison to the Saudi ad, Mobil's argument marched forward with the precision of a military parade. The ad operated almost exclusively in the realm of explicit meaning. Each paragraph advanced the argument one step further, and there was little variety in the length of these paragraphs. Establishing a rhythm was less important than supporting premises with factual references and statistics. By using such a structure, the Mobil author(s) consistently narrowed the range of feasible options for dealing with the situation.

The opening five paragraphs of Mobil's ad established the "facts" of America's energy needs. The next section of the ad documented the "facts" about oil supplies. After dismissing other possible oil sources such as Venezuela, the North Sea, and Mexico, the author(s) concentrated on Saudi Arabia because this country had more oil than any other nation in the world. Its "reserves can support an increase in production from the present level of about 8 million barrels a day to 20 million barrels daily," the author(s) explained. Saudi Arabia's huge oil reserves made it central to America's future economic growth.

Mobil's position as the major oil company with the smallest domestic reserves and the largest reliance on Saudi oil meant that Mobil's continued economic health depended on the Saudis (Sampson, p. 202). The "fact" of Mobil's significant self-interest in Middle Eastern oil was not mentioned. Instead, the Mobil author(s) attempted to generalize the company's concerns to the oil industry and to the nation as a whole. The lockstep logic of Mobil's argument obscured the company's unique constraints that made it particularly vulnerable to a boycott of Middle Eastern oil.

Overall, Mobil's argument was quite linear in its organization. Increased oil supplies were necessary for continued economic growth. Only the Middle East had sufficient reserves to meet increased energy needs in the United States. We needed Middle Eastern oil more than they needed our money. Therefore, we could no longer ignore Arab political concerns. Each premise was supported with statistics or examples. The step-by-step progression foreclosed from consideration alternatives such as conservation, alternative energies, or non-Middle Eastern sources of oil.

In organizing their argument, the Mobil authors reflected the cause-effect thinking that Stewart asserts is typical of Americans. As he explains, "In the ideal form, the world is seen as a unilateral connection of causes and effects projecting into the future. Since the American focuses on the future rather than the present or the past, the isolation of the critical cause becomes paramount" (p. 35). The critical cause for the Mobil author(s) was access to supplies of Saudi Arabian oil.

The majority of the Mobil ad operated in the realm of explicit meaning. Implicit meaning and stylistic devices were only employed in the ending call-to-action. This ending was cast in general terms to avoid specifically mentioning either the Israelis or the Palestinians:

So we say: It is time now for the world to insist on a settlement in the Middle East. . . . A settlement that will bring justice and security to all the peoples and all the states in that region. Nobody can afford another war in the Middle East. Nobody. Nobody.

The repetition in this section emphasized the seriousness of Mobil's concern. Who could object to a call for peace and justice for all peoples in the region? Only those who read between the lines and recognized that such a general statement might include the Palestinians.

Types of Justifications

Mobil's ad conspicuously avoided discussing the political implications of economic decisions until after its detailed delineation of oil supplies and demand. "If our country's relations with the Arab world . . . continue to deteriorate," the author(s) warned, "Saudi Arabia may conclude it is not in its interest to look favorably on U.S. requests for increased petroleum supplies." Mobil executives were concerned because "we will need the oil more than Saudi Arabia will need the money."

Without specifying what political concerns might motivate Saudi Arabia, Mobil concentrated on examining the Saudi's economic constraints. Development programs in Saudi Arabia could proceed without increased production because of the country's small population and large foreign reserves already over three billion dollars, the ad explained. Since the Saudis had no financial incentive to increase oil production, the Mobil author(s) concluded: "It is therefore time for the American people to begin adapting to a new energy age, to a vastly changed world situation, to the realities with which we will have to learn to live."

Rather than deal in the treacherous realm of political affairs, the Mobil author(s) chose the terra firma of economic concerns. Throughout the ad, Mobil offered eminently practical justifications that revolved around economic necessities. The ad twice reminded Americans that they needed to act in order to preserve their current lifestyles. Americans, Stewart asserts, assume that "the things worthy of effort are material" (p. 35).

Similarly, in explaining the Saudis' motivations, the Mobil author(s) did not concentrate on the Arabs' political concerns. Instead, Mobil executives outlined the economic resources of Saudi Arabia that allowed it to enforce its political views. Mobil's practical, economic justification did not allow room for considering abstract concepts such as justice or honor.

Justice and national honor, however, were central concerns in the Saudi ad. The Arabs initiated the boycott, the ad explained, because "our national interests demanded it." The use of the personal pronoun "our" once again reinforced the identity among all Arab nations. "In the Arab world honorable behavior is that 'which is conducive to group cohesion.' . . . [S]hameful behavior is that which tends to disrupt, endanger, impair, or weaken the social aggregate" (Patai quote by Gudykunst & Kim, p. 51).

The United States had used economic boycotts in the past, the Saudi ad reminded readers. The Arabs had been provoked into a boycott when the United States, "which had repeatedly assured us of our rights to our lands, made massive arms deliveries to the Israelis to help them remain in our lands." Although the Arabs wanted peace, they could not allow Israel to take their lands. "Nor would any just people anywhere in the world expect us to do so." The ad concluded: "We are asking the American people, especially the American friends of Israel, to understand this and to help us attain the peace we are after."

Throughout the ad, the Saudi author(s) offered justifications based on national honor and self-respect. The ad briefly acknowledged but did not discuss the economic consequences of the oil boycott, which tripled oil prices in the space of a few months and triggered one of the largest transfers of wealth in the century. In the face of displacement from a homeland, pragmatic, economic concerns such as the price of oil were secondary.

The Saudis' abstract justifications for their actions were predicated upon the past. Previous grievances against the Arabs constrained the present and limited the future. A past orientation was central to the Saudis' explanation of the boycott. The purpose of the boycott was "not to impose a change in U.S. policy in the Middle East but to demand the *implementation* of U.S. policy in the Middle East, as it has been repeatedly defined." The distinction between imposing a change in U.S. policy and asking for an existing policy to be implemented was a fine one, but it grounded the Saudis' statement that the oil boycott was not an attempt to "blackmail" the American people.

In demanding that past policies be implemented, the Saudis attributed their own orientation to the Americans, neglecting the fact that each new American political administration established new foreign policy priorities. Richard Nixon would not necessarily be constrained by the comments of Lyndon Johnson. The Saudis did not acknowledge that Americans lacked a historical memory similar to their own.

While the Saudis were concerned with the past, Mobil concentrated on the future. Mobil's ad frequently referred to "the coming years" or the "years immediately ahead." The primary motivation for action for the Mobil author(s) was future supplies of oil. In contrast, the Arabs, Stewart explains, believe "it is insane to attempt to predict future events; only God knows what the future will bring" (p. 88).

Interestingly, each ad assumed the other culture's orientation was synonymous with its own. Mobil talked about the Saudis' future economic motives, while the Saudis turned to the United States' previous foreign policy statements and appealed to Americans' sense of national honor and justice. Each ad demonstrated rhetorical ethnocentrism in attributing its orientation to the other culture.

CONCLUSION

As this analysis has indicated, the differences between these two ads go far beyond superficial contrasts between a florid style and a plain style (Glenn,

Witmeyer, & Stevenson, 1977). While Mobil imposed a unitary perspective based on "objective facts," the Saudi ad concentrated on illustrating competing interpretations of reality. Images that clarified an emotional climate were most important for the Saudi author(s); statistics clarifying "objective" reality were most important in the Mobil ad. Mobil's author(s) concentrated on practical, economic justifications predicated on future events; the Saudi author(s) emphasized abstract justifications that focused on the past. In sum, the ads were mirror images of each other in terms of their selections of rhetorical tactics.

These different rhetorical tactics implied different conceptions about the nature of reality. The Mobil author(s), employing traditional Neo-Aristotelian conceptions of argumentation, assumed an objective reality that could be accurately known and verified by systematic observation. The author(s) attempted to muster factual data and logical proof to support their argument that Arab concerns should be accorded a greater role in American foreign policy. "Reasonableness" was determined by the argument's consistency in replicating the structure of objective reality. The goal of Mobil's argument was to explain how the world of energy supply and demand worked. The advocacy advertisement's reliance on linear progression, practical justifications, and a focus on the future as an extension of the present sprang from the assumption of an objective reality.

The Saudi ad, on the other hand, focused not on objective reality, but on reality as apprehended and mediated through the intensifying and distorting prism of language. The Saudi author(s) assumed that reality could not be separated from the structure of language through which we understand reality. Consequently, they focused on naming the victims and aggressors in the region. Establishing the Arab's perspective for interpretation was more important than explaining principles of oil supply and demand. "Effectiveness" in this case was determined by the author(s)' ability to employ the rhythm and sounds of the language to advance an evaluative perspective, thereby controlling the prism through

which reality was viewed.[3] Considered in such a light, the Saudi author(s) were remarkably effective.

Despite these different orientations toward the role of discourse in society, the ads were similar in their use of strategic ambiguity. The Saudis ignored the economic consequences of the oil boycott, while Mobil was obscure when it came to discussing its self-interest in the region and in considering the feasibility of other alternatives, such as conservation. The Saudis projected an image of Arabs as a unified group rather than competing nations and ignored their contributions to aggression in the region. Each ad concealed "facts" that it did not wish to emphasize. The ads were equally cognizant of the ability of language to conceal as well as to reveal. In this sense, both ads were equally self-serving.

While the Saudi author(s) made efforts to accommodate American readers, these attempts at adaptation were likely to go unrecognized by American readers lacking an understanding of different cultural rules for political debate. A Neo-Aristotelian would argue that the Saudi ad was sloppy at best, devious at worst. Arguable premises were introduced but not developed. The ad circled around issues rather than proceeding in a linear fashion from one topic to the next. Americans, with their preference for "rational," cause-effect arguments, were likely to view such an approach as deliberately deceptive.

Arabs, on the other hand, criticized Americans because they lacked the sense of historical perspective that motivated Arabs. An Arab would view Americans' insistence on a unitary perspective based on "objective" facts as deliberately deceptive in neglecting the broader historical context behind the immediate issues. It is this American lack of a sense of "historical totalities" that contributes to Arab complaints that American portrayals are arrogant, one-sided, and simplistic.

In the end, this analysis illustrates in specific detail how "the truism of one nation becomes an argument for another" (Starosta, p. 231). Each approach to political debate makes legitimate assumptions about the nature of persuasive power. Yet, given the vastly different assumptions about the role of persuasion in society, it is not surprising that misunderstandings occur between Americans and Arabs, even when the same "language" is used. Communicating across a cultural gap requires more than just a knowledge of respective vocabularies. It also requires an understanding of the different cultural rules for what constitutes "reasonable" political debate.

NOTES

1. In the United States, advocacy advertisements mushroomed in the early seventies, as executives complained about media bias against business. By purchasing their own space, business representatives circumvented the typical editorial process, taking their case directly to the public through their own editorials. Advocacy advertising became a frequent adjunct to more traditional forms of political lobbying, offering executives total control over the final message. For a more detailed discussion of the genre, see Sethi's *Advocacy Advertising and Large Corporations* or Heath and Nelson's *Issues Management: Corporate Public Policy Making in an Information Society*.

2. The territory in the Middle East that Israel now occupies was originally called Palestine, a name taken from the Philistines who occupied the coastal part of the country in the twelfth century B.C. A Hebrew kingdom established in 1000 B.C. was subsequently controlled by Assyrians, Babylonians, Egyptians, Persians, Macedonians, Romans, and Byzantines. The Arabs took control of Palestine from the Byzantine Empire in A.D. 634–40. The Arabs maintained control until the twentieth century, when Britain captured Jerusalem in 1917.

Jewish immigration to the area increased throughout Britain's time of control, as British Foreign Secretary Arthur Balfour promised support for a Jewish state in Palestine. Discussions on partitioning the area were tabled during World War II. In 1946, the Jewish population in the region numbered 678,000 compared to 1,269,000 Arabs. Unable to resolve the problem, Britain turned it over to the United Nations in 1947, which voted for partition in the face of strong Arab opposition.

War began with the founding of the State of Israel in 1948. A cease-fire was negotiated in 1949, which increased Israeli territory by fifty percent. The simmering conflict erupted again in 1956 with the Suez crisis and in 1967, when Israel increased its territory two hundred percent by occupying the Golan Heights, the West Bank of the Jordan river, the Old City of Jerusa-

lem, and parts of the Sinai Peninsula. These occupied territories provided the impetus for the 1973 war, which began on October sixth, Yom Kippur, the Israelis' holiest day of the year. Initial Arab gains were reversed, and a cease-fire was negotiated two weeks later.

3. This dichotomy in metaphysical first principles has been identified and discussed in detail by a variety of theorists. Walter J. Ong (1980), for example, contrasted the linear conventions of a written culture with the holistic perspective of an oral culture. Jacqueline De Romilly (1975), in *Magic and Rhetoric in Ancient Greece*, argued that these different formulations of the wellspring of symbolic power coexisted in ancient Greece. John Poulakos (1984) in *Rhetoric, the Sophists and the Possible* provides an excellent contrast between the perspective offered by Aristotelian and sophistic rhetoric. He examines the basic assumptions of each rhetoric in light of modern philosophers such as Nietzsche, Heidegger, and Foucault. What has not typically been done, however, is to illustrate how different basic assumptions about the nature of rhetoric and reality play themselves out in actual discourse.

REFERENCES

Al-Zafer, Mohammed. (1985, Dec.). Telephone interview with author.

Almaney, A. J., & Alwan, A. J. (1982). *Communicating with the Arabs: A handbook for the business executive*. Prospect Heights, IL: Waveland Press.

Barton, R. L. (1982). Message analysis in international mass communication research. In M. Mander (Ed.), *Communication in transition* (pp. 81–101). New York: Praeger.

Condon, J., and Yousef, F. (1975). *An introduction to intercultural communication*. New York: Bobbs-Merrill.

De Romilly, J. (1975). *Magic and rhetoric in ancient Greece*. Cambridge, MA: Harvard University Press.

Glenn, E. A., Witmeyer, D., & Stevenson, K. A. (1977). Cultural styles of persuasion. *International Journal of Intercultural Relations*, **1**(3), 52–66.

Gudykunst, W., & Kim, Y. (1984). *Communicating with strangers: An approach to intercultural communication*. Reading, MA: Addison-Wesley.

Hamod, H. S. (1963). Arab and Moslem rhetorical theory. *Central States Speech Journal*, **14**, 97–102.

Heath, R., & Nelson, R. (1986). *Issues management: Corporate public policy making in an information society.* Beverly Hills: Sage.

Heisey, R. D. (1970). The rhetoric of the Arab-Israeli conflict. *Quarterly Journal of Speech*, **46**, 12–21.

Hur, K. K. (1984). A critical analysis of international news flow research. *Critical Studies in Mass Communication*, **1**, 365–378.

Kressel, N. (1987). Biased judgments of media bias: A case study of the Arab-Israeli dispute. *Political Psychology*, **8**, 211–227.

Lewis, P. (1983, March 20). An oil minister's poem stole the show. *New York Times*, Sec. 6, p. 6.

The Mobil Oil Corporation. (1973, June 30). The U.S. stake in Middle East peace: I. *New York Times*, Sec. 2, p. 30.

Ong, W. J. (1957). Grammar today: "Structure" in a vocal world. *Quarterly Journal of Speech*, **53**, 399–407.

Ong, W. J. (1980). Literacy and orality in our times. *Journal of Communication*, **30**, 197–204.

Ong, W. J. (1981). McLuhan as teacher: The future is a thing of the past. *Journal of Communication*, **31**, 129–135.

Poulakos, J. (1984). Rhetoric, the sophists and the possible. *Communication Monographs*, **51**, 215–226.

Sakkaf, O. (1973, Dec. 31). Open letter to the American people. *Washington Post*, Sec. 1, p. 9.

Sampson, A. (1975). *The seven sisters.* New York: Viking Press.

Schmertz, H. with Novak, W. (1986). *Good-bye to the low profile: The art of creative confrontation.* Boston: Little, Brown.

Sethi, S. P. (1977). *Advocacy advertising and large corporations.* Lexington, MA: Lexington Books.

Shaheen, J. G. (1988, Feb. 29). The media's image of Arabs. *Newsweek*, p. 10.

Starosta, W. (1984). On intercultural rhetoric. In W. Gudykunst & Y. Y. Kim (Eds.), *Methods for intercultural communication research.* (pp. 229–238). Beverly Hills: Sage.

Stewart, E. (1972). *American cultural patterns: A cross-cultural perspective.* Yarmouth, ME: Intercultural Press.

"... So Near the United States": Notes on Communication between Mexicans and North Americans

JOHN CONDON

"Poor Mexico," said Porfirio Diaz, "so far from God, so near the United States." In the years since Mexico's last pre-Revolutionary president said these words the nations on both sides of the border have been greatly altered. Some might speculate on the resulting changes in Mexico's proximity to the Lord, but none would deny that geographically and commercially Mexico has never been so near the United States. The cultural distance, however, is something else, for in many respects the cultural gaps between these societies are as great as ever. Thus when President Kennedy said during his highly successful visit to Mexico in 1962 that "geography has made us neighbors, tradition has made us friends," many Mexicans thought it more accurate to say that "geography has made us close but tradition has made us more distant than ever."

Not that there has been any shortage of contact between people of these two cultures. The fifteen hundred mile border that spans the continent is crossed in both directions by more people than any other international border on the globe. These in-

From *The Bridge*, Spring 1980. Reprinted by permission of the publisher. John Condon has taught at Northwestern University and the International Christian University in Tokyo. He is currently a communication consultant in San Diego, California.

clude millions of tourists annually who venture south into Mexico to make up more than 80 percent of that nation's primary source of revenue, tourism. It also includes the countless numbers of workers, both legally admitted and undocumented, business people, students and tourists, too, who cross from Mexico into the United States. Quite apart from this daily traffic, the cultural presence of each society is to be found across the border. The capital city of Mexico is that nation's, and soon the world's, largest metropolis; but the second largest number of Mexicans reside in Los Angeles. And it is worth recalling that scarcely a century and a half ago half of the land that had been Mexico became a part of the United States, a fact remembered more in Mexico than north of the border. Intercultural contact is hardly a phenomenon of the jet age.

Information about and from each society has never been greater than one finds today. Studies show that the average Mexico City daily newspaper contains a greater percentage of news about the United States than the average *New York Times* reports about all the rest of the world combined. North American foods, fashions, products, and loan words are enough in evidence in the cities of Mexico to make the casual visitor overlook some significant differences in values and beliefs. Indeed, many veteran observers of relations between Mexicans and North Americans believe that the increase in superficial similarities actually contributes to culture-based misunderstandings.

. Insights into contrasting cultural assumptions and styles of communication cannot be gained without an appreciation of the history and geography of the two societies. One quickly learns that where there are intersections, such as the major river that marks a good part of the border or the major war that literally gave shape to each nation, the interpretations and even the names are different in each society. The name "America" itself is one that many Mexicans feel should not be limited to the United States of America alone, particularly since culturally the "anglo" culture is a minority among the nations of the Americas. "North America" and "North American" may be more appreciated.

North Americans trace their history from the time of the first English settlers. The people already living on the continent possessed no great cities or monuments to rival anything in Europe, and they held little interest for the European colonists so long as they could be displaced and their land cultivated. The North American Indian has remained excluded from the shaping of the dominant culture of the new nation just as he had been excluded from the land. With political independence and the continuous arrival of immigrants, largely from Northern Europe, the nation took shape in a steady westward pattern. The outlook was to the future, to new land and new opportunities. The spirit was of optimism.

When the Spanish soldiers arrived in Mexico in the sixteenth century they found cities and temples of civilizations that had flourished for thousands of years. In what some have called a holy crusade, the Spanish attempted to destroy the old societies and reconstruct a new order on top. In religion, in language, in marriage, there was a fusion of Indian and European which was totally different from the pattern in the United States. While Cortés is no hero in Mexico—there are no statues of him anywhere in the country—the fusion of European and native American cultures is a source of great pride, not only in Mexico but extending throughout the Latin American republics. This is the spirit of *la raza* which serves in part to give a sense of identification with other Latin Americans and a sense of separateness from those of the anglo world.

There are other contrasts to be noted as well. The land that became the United States was for the most part hospitable and, for much of the country's history, seemingly endless. Less than a fifth of the land in Mexico, in contrast, is arable.

The images which the people on each side of the border hold of the other differ. Mexico's image of the United States was to a great extent shaped in Europe, formed at a time when European writers had little good to say about the anglo-American world. Even today when Mexicans speak of the ideals of freedom and democracy, their inspiration is more likely to be French than North American. The rivalry between England and Spain, compounded by the religious hostility between Protestants and Catholics, influenced in a comparable way the North American's image of Mexico.

Finally, by way of introduction, we should note that regional differences are pronounced and of importance in understanding the people of Mexico. Social and economic differences vary considerably, and even in langauge, with perhaps 150 different languages still spoken in the country, there are truly "many Mexicos." Thus it is not surprising that for years there has been a serious interest among Mexicans to find "the Mexican." Some say this search for identity began even before the Conquest, for the sixteenth century Spaniard was himself unsure of his identity: he arrived in Mexico less than 25 years after driving out the last of the Moors from his own homeland.

An early Adlerian analysis of "the Mexican" by Samuel Ramos found the essence of the Mexican national character in the *pelado*, "the plucked one," at the bottom of the pecking order. While the Ramos thesis has been considered over the years, some of the same themes of doubt and frustration and of a tragic outlook on life continue in contemporary Mexican interpretations.

The history of relations between the United States and Mexico has not been one of understanding and cooperation, though many persons on both sides of the border are working toward those ends. Even under the best of conditions and with the best of intentions, Mexicans and North Americans working together sometimes feel confused, irritated, distrustful. The causes lie not within either culture but rather can be best understood interculturally. Here are four perspectives.

INDIVIDUALISM

In the North American value system are three central and interrelated assumptions about human beings. These are (1) that people, apart from social and educational influences, are basically the same; (2) that each person should be judged on his or her own individual merits; and (3) that these "merits," including a person's worth and character, are re-

vealed through the person's actions. Values of equality and independence, constitutional rights, laws and social programs arise from these assumptions. Because a person's actions are regarded as so important, it is the comparison of accomplishments— Mr. X compared to Mr. X's father, or X five years ago compared to X today, or X compared to Y and Z— that provides a chief means of judging or even knowing a person.

In Mexico it is the uniqueness of the individual which is valued, a quality which is assumed to reside within each person and which is not necessarily evident through actions or achievements. That inner quality which represents the dignity of each person must be protected at all costs. Any action or remark that may be interpreted as a slight to the person's dignity is to be regarded as a grave provocation. Also, as every person is part of a larger family grouping, one cannot be regarded as a completely isolated individual.

This contrast, which is sometimes expressed as the distinction between "individualism" in the case of the North American, and "individuality" in the case of the Mexican, frequently leads to misunderstandings in intercultural encounters ranging from small talk to philosophical arguments.

Where a Mexican will talk about a person's inner qualities in terms of the person's soul or spirit (*alma* or *espiritu*), North Americans are likely to feel uncomfortable using such words to talk about people. They may regard such talk as vague or sentimental, the words seeming to describe something invisible and hence unknowable, or at the very least "too personal." The unwillingness to talk in this way only confirms the view held by many Mexicans that North Americans are insensitive. "Americans are corpses," said one Mexican.

Even questions about the family of a person one does not know well may discomfit many North Americans, since asking about a person's parents or brothers or sisters may also seem too personal. "I just don't know the person well enough to ask about his family," a North American might say, while the Mexican may see things just the opposite: "If I don't ask about the person's family, how will I really know him?"

The family forms a much less important part of an individual's frame of reference in the United States than is usually the case in Mexico. Neighbors, friends, or associates, even some abstract "average American," may be the basis for the comparison needed in evaluating oneself or others. "Keeping up with the Joneses" may be important in New York or Chicago, but keeping up with one's brother-in-law is more important in Mexico City. In the same way, the Mexican depends upon relatives or close friends to help "arrange things" if there is a problem, or to provide a loan. While this is by no means rare in the United States, the dominant values in the culture favor institutions which are seen as both efficient and fair.

So it is that tensions may arise between Mexicans and North Americans over what seems to be a conflict between trusting particular individuals or trusting abstract principles. In a business enterprise, the North American manager is likely to view the organization and its processes as primary, with the role of specific people being more or less supportive of that system. People can be replaced if need be; nobody is indispensable. When one places emphasis on a person's spirit or views an organization as if it were a family, however, then it seems just as clear that nobody can be exactly replaced by any other person.

Both North Americans and Mexicans may speak of the need to "respect" another person, but here too the meanings of the word respect (or respeto) differ somewhat across the cultures. In a study of associations with this word conducted in the United States and Mexico, it was found that North Americans regarded "respect" as bound up with the values of equality, fair play and the democratic spirit. There were no emotional overtones. One respects others as one might respect the law. For Mexicans, however, "respect" was found to be an emotionally charged word involving pressures of power, possible threat and often a love-hate relationship. The meaning of respect arises from powerful human relationships such as between father and son or *patrón* and *péon*, not a system of principles to which individuals voluntarily commit themselves.

STRAIGHT TALK

Last year the leaders of both the United States and France visited Mexico. A prominent writer for the distinguished Mexican daily, *Excelsior*, commented on their visits and on the words they spoke. Interpreting the impressions they made on Mexicans, the writer alluded to cultural differences. President Carter was seen as following the anglo-saxon values of his culture as he spoke bluntly of realities. President Giscard d'Estaing, as a product of a cultural tradition which was more familiar to that of Mexico, spoke in a style far more grand, and if his words were in some way further from realities they were at least more beautiful. When all was said and done and the two leaders returned to their capitals, the writer concluded, the world had been little changed as a result of their visits but the French leader's words had at least made his Mexican listeners feel better for a while.

The ceremonial speaking of heads of state actually shows fewer differences between Mexican and North American styles than do routine conversations. It is not simply that two styles, plain and fancy, contrast; rather, persons from each culture will form judgments about the personality and character of the other as a result. The Mexican is far more likely to flatter, tease or otherwise attempt to charm another than is the North American whose culture has taught him to distrust or poke fun at anyone who "really lays it on."

Often the problem is heightened when there is a difference in the sex, status, or age of the two persons in conversation. Mexicans may want to maximize those differences while North Americans often make a great effort to minimize them. North Americans may at present be most sensitive to the way in which a businessman talks to a businesswoman, lest he be accused of "sexism," but the same values apply to "making too much" of one's age or status. Thus the very style which is called for in one culture may be regarded as quite uncalled for in the other culture. North Americans are often suspicious of one who seems effusive in praise; they are also likely to make light of one who seems too enamored of titles. Mexicans, on the other hand, value one who has the wit and charm to impress another. Nor are titles or other indications of one's status, age, or ability to be slighted. The owner of an auto repair shop may defer to a mechanic who is older and more experienced as *maestro*; doctors, lawyers and other professional people will take their titles seriously. To make light of them is to challenge one's dignity.

THE TRUTH

During the world congress held in Mexico for the International Women's Year, some first time visitors experienced the kind of problem that many North Americans have long complained about in Mexico. The visitors would be told one thing only to discover that what they were told seemed to bear no resemblance to the facts. A delegate who would ask where a meeting was being held might be given clear directions, but upon reaching the destination she would find no such meeting. "It was not that the Mexicans were unfriendly or unhelpful—just wrong!" North American managers working with Mexicans have sometimes voiced similar complaints: An employee says something is finished when in fact it has not even been begun.

Rogelio Díaz-Guerrero, head of the psychology department of the National University of Mexico and a foremost interpreter of Mexican behavior patterns, offers this explanation. There are two kinds of "realities" which must be distinguished, objective and interpersonal. Some cultures tend to treat everything in terms of the objective sort of reality; this is characteristic of the United States. Other cultures tend to treat things in terms of interpersonal relations, and this is true of Mexico. This distinction, we may note, bears some resemblance to the distinction made by the *Excelsior* columnist.

Viewed from the Mexican perspective, a visitor asks somebody for information which that person doesn't know. But wanting to make the visitor happy and enjoy a few pleasant moments together, the Mexican who was asked does his best to say something so that for a short while the visitor is made happy. It is not that Mexicans have a monopoly on telling another person what that person wants to hear: Perhaps in all cultures the truth is sometimes altered slightly to soften the impact of a harsh word or to show deference to one's superior. It is the range of situations in which this occurs in Mexico and the relatively sharper contrast of "truth-telling" standards in U.S.-Mexican encounters that is so notable.

In value, if not always in fact, North Americans, have given special importance to telling the truth. The clearest object lessons in the lives of the nation's two legendary heroes, Washington and Lincoln, concern honesty, while the presidents who have been most held in disrepute, Harding and Nixon, are held up to scorn because of their dishonesty.

Francisco Gonzales Pineda has written at length about lying. Starting from premises similar to those offered by Samuel Ramos mentioned earlier, including the idealization of manliness of the *pelado*, Gonzalez Pineda says that a Mexican must be able to lie if he is to be able to live without complete demoralization. He says that general recognition of this has made the lie in Mexico almost an institution. He describes variations of lies in different regions of Mexico, including the capital in which he says the use of the lie is socially acceptable in all its forms. He contrasts the Mexican style of lie to that which is used by North Americans. In the United States the lie is little used aggressively or defensively or to express fantasy. The more common form of defense is the expression of the incomplete truth or an evasion of truth. There are stereotyped expressions which are purposefully ambiguous and impersonal, so lacking in emotional content that they do not conflict with the emotional state of the liar.

Whether or not one supports the interpretation of Gonzalez Pineda, an examination of difficulties between North Americans and Mexicans is to be found in the broad area of matching words, deeds and intentions. The North American in a daily routine has a much narrower range of what he considers permissible than is found in similar situations in Mexico.

TIME

If a culture is known by the words exported, as one theory has it, then Mexico may be best known as the land of *mañana*. Differences in the treatment of time may not be the most serious source of misunderstanding between people of the two cultures but it is surely the most often mentioned. Several issues are actually grouped under the general label of "time."

In Edward Hall's influential writings on time across culture, he has distinguished between "monochronic" (M-time) and "polychronic" (P-time) treatments of time; these correspond to the North American and Mexican modes respectively. M-time values take care of "one thing at a time." Time is lineal, segmented. (American football is a very "M-time" game.) It may not be that time is money but M-time treats it that way, with measured precision. M-time people like neat scheduling of appointments and are easily distracted and often very distressed by interruptions.

In contrast, P-time is characterized by many things happening at once, and with a much "looser" notion of what is "on time" or "late." Interruptions are routine, delays to be expected. Thus it is not so much that putting things off until *mañana* is valued, as some Mexican stereotypes would have it, but that human activities are not expected to proceed like clock-work. It should be noted in this regard that the North American treatment of time appears to be the more unusual on a world scale. This writer discovered that even in Japan, a culture not known for its imprecision or indolence, U.S. business people were seen by Japanese colleagues as much too time-bound, driven by schedules and deadlines which in turn thwarted an easy development of human relationships.

North Americans express special irritation when Mexicans seem to give them less than their undivided attention. When a young woman bank teller, awaiting her superior's approval for a check to be cashed, files her nails and talks on the phone to her boyfriend, or when one's taxi driver stops en route to pick up a friend who seems to be going in the same direction, North Americans become very upset. North Americans interpret such behavior as showing a lack of respect and a lack of "professionalism," but the reason may lie more in the culturally different treatment of time.

Newly arrived residents seem to learn quickly to adjust their mental clocks to *la hora Mexicana* when it comes to anticipating the arrival of Mexican guests at a party; an invitation for 8:00 may produce guests by 9:00 or 10:00. What takes more adjusting is the notion that visitors may be going to another party first and yet another party afterwards. For many North Americans this diminishes the importance attached to their party, much as the teller's action diminishes the respect shown the customer. The counterpart of this, Mexicans' irritation with the North American time sense, is in their dismay over an invitation to a party which states in advance the time when the party will be over. This or subtler indications of the time to terminate a meeting before it has even gotten underway serve as further proof that Americans are slaves to the clock and don't really know how to enjoy themselves.

The identification of common problem areas in communication across cultures is always incomplete; there are always other interpretations and, since culture is a whole, the selection of "factors" or "themes" is never completely shown in its entire context. Nevertheless, a common effort to appreciate differences across cultures is essential, particularly in the relations between people of the United States and Mexico.

It is not an exaggeration to say that if North Americans cannot learn to communicate more effectively with Mexicans, our capacity to function in cultures elsewhere in the world will be doubted. Many of the well-springs of Mexican culture flow freely elsewhere, not only in other Latin American states but in such distant lands as the Philippines.

CONCEPTS AND QUESTIONS
FOR CHAPTER 2

1. How are cultural values formed?

2. What are the differences between instrumental values and terminal values? How does each of these value sets affect intercultural communication?

3. In what ways does a social relationship orientation affect communication behavior differently than does an individualism orientation?

4. What are the four Confucian principles of right conduct? How do they contribute to communicative behavior?

5. How do East Asian concepts of in-group/out-group differ from those of North Americans? How might these differences affect intercultural communication?

6. How does Confucianism affect linguistic codes?

7. What unique perspectives of world view are inherent in the Hindu culture of India?

8. How might the Hindu perspective of the universe and of humankind's role in the universe affect intercultural communication between Indians and North Americans?

9. What historical antecedents of Maasai culture contribute to their current world view?

10. How does the Maasai's orientation to children affect their world view?

11. In what ways might the Maasai world view affect intercultural communication?

12. How does the Maasai use of metaphor differ from North American use? How could this difference affect intercultural communication?

13. How do Arab concepts of advocacy differ from those of North Americans?

14. How do North American and Arab rhetorical strategies differ? How might these differences affect business negotiations?

15. How do differences in thinking patterns affect intercultural communication?

16. In what areas of interaction are there major problems between Mexican and North American cultures? How can these differences affect intercultural interactions?

17. How do North American and Mexican views of individualism differ? How might these differences affect intercultural communication?

3

Co-Cultures: Living
in Two Cultures

In Chapter 2, we focused on international cultures, that is, cultures that exist beyond the immediate borders of the United States. There are also numerous domestic co-cultures composed of various religious, economic, ethnic, age, gender, and racial compositions within U.S. society itself. These diverse co-cultures have the potential to bring exotic experiences to a communication encounter, but because they are much more visible than foreign cultures, Americans often take their presence for granted. Yet if you are not aware of and do not understand the unique cultural experiences of these people, you can have serious communication problems. The articles in this chapter have been selected to introduce you to some of the major U.S. co-cultures and to examine some of the cultural experiences and dynamics inherent in them. Admittedly there are many more co-cultures than we have included here. Our selection was based on three considerations. First, limited space and the necessity for efficiency prohibited a long list of co-cultures. Second, we decided to include some social communities that are often in conflict with the larger society. And third, we wanted to emphasize the co-cultures with which you are most likely to interact.

As the United States continues to become pluralistic and develop into a multicultural society, there will be an increased need and opportunity for effective communication between the various co-cultures that make up the society. Effective communication can only come about with the removal of stereotypes and the development of an understanding of what each culture is really like. Frequently, stereotypes and prejudices lead to assumptions about members of co-cultures that are false and frequently hurtful to other people's feelings.

To introduce this chapter, Arturo Madrid, in his article "Diversity and Its Discontents," tells us something about the negative aspects of being a member of a co-culture—the constant misperceptions and false assumptions with which one must deal and the resentment one feels as being perceived as the *other*. Madrid points out specifically the ignorance people have about Hispanic culture and how people mistake him as an immigrant although his ancestors' presence in what is now the United States predates Plymouth Rock.

Edith A. Folb in "Who's Got the Room at the Top?" discusses the concept of *intracultural* communication. This is communication between members of the same dominant culture who hold slightly different values. Folb sees the crucial characteristics of this form of communication as the interrelationships of power, dominance, and nondominance as they are manifest in the particular cultures. She carefully examines these variables as they apply to blacks, native Americans, Mexican-Americans, women, the aged, the physically challenged, and other groups that have been "caste marked and more often negatively identified when it comes to issues of power, dominance, and social control."

The U.S. population is aging. This phenomenon has sometimes been referred to in the popular press as the greying of America. For the first time in our history, more than half of the population is over thirty-five years of age. As this trend continues, new social problems emerge that must be solved to prevent an age-versus-youth division in our society. Carl W. Carmichael, in his essay "Intercultural Perspectives of Aging," asserts that aging presents both a communication and a cultural problem because the aging process is related to the beliefs, attitudes, and stereotypes about aging as well as to the interaction patterns prevalent in the culture. Carmichael then examines these aspects of the U.S. culture and compares them to similar characteristics of the Japanese culture. Since the increasing proportion of elderly members of the population is a new cultural experience for the United States, the culture must adapt and develop processes to accommodate it.

In recent years it has become apparent that disabled persons are a co-culture in our society. While there are approximately eleven million disabled Americans between the ages of sixteen and sixty-four, they often find themselves either cut off from

or misunderstood by the mainstream culture. The essay by Dawn O. Braithwaite looks at some of the reasons for this isolation in "Viewing Persons with Disabilities as a Culture." More specifically, she examines how disabled persons view their communication relationships with able-bodied persons. Braithwaite interviewed fifty-seven physically disabled adults, and she learned that they go through a process of redefinition. She found that redefinition involves four steps: (1) redefinition of the disabled as members of a "new" culture, (2) redefinition of self by the disabled, (3) redefinition of disability for the disabled, and (4) redefinition of disability for the dominant culture. By becoming familiar with these steps, we can improve our communication with members of the disabled co-culture.

There is a co-culture in the United States whose existence may come as a surprise to you. This is the Deaf culture, which comprises a class of people who identify with one another as being culturally deaf. These are people who interact primarily with other deaf people and who share the same language, beliefs, values, and traditions. In her article "On Communicating with Deaf People," Kathy Jankowski details for us the characteristics of the Deaf culture—the language, nonverbal behavior, values, socialization patterns, and traditions. She then examines stereotypes held about the deaf and gives helpful suggestions for effective intercultural communication.

Recently much attention has been paid to a social community previously taken for granted. Because women are so much a part of one's perceptual field, and hence part of one's daily life, it was seldom perceived that the experience of being female was a viable area of investigation. The resurgence of feminism in the last two decades has, however, prompted a reexamination of what it means to be a member of that particular co-culture and particularly how that community is different from the male-dominated society. One of the major differences is how they communicate. These differences, and some of the reasons behind them, are the major concern of the article by Judy C. Pearson, "Gender and Communication: An Intimate Relationship." She points out how they are related, traces how gender differences begin to be formed very early in life, and treats verbal and nonverbal patterns of communication in detail. Pearson also examines the problems created by gender-driven variations in communication and perception. Stereotyping and male bias are examples of some of the more common problems impeding gender communication.

In our final article, Randall E. Majors, in his article "America's Emerging Gay Culture," offers innumerable insights into the cultural experience of the homosexual. There can be little doubt that in recent years the gay culture has emerged as one of the most vocal and visible groups on the American scene. It has, as do most co-cultures, special patterns of communication. Majors investigates the dimensions of these patterns as they relate to the gay neighborhood, gay social institutions, gay symbols, and gay meeting behavior, providing immeasurable insight into the gay co-culture.

Diversity and Its Discontents

ARTURO MADRID

My name is Arturo Madrid. I am a citizen of the United States, as are my parents and as were my grandparents, and my great-grandparents. My ancestors' presence in what is now the United States antedates Plymouth Rock, even without taking into account any American Indian heritage I might have.

I do not, however, fit those mental sets that define America and Americans. My physical appearance, my speech patterns, my name, my profession (a professor of Spanish) create a text that confuses the reader. My normal experience is to be asked: And where are YOU from?

My response depends on my mood. Passive-aggressive I answer: "From here." Aggressive-passive I ask: "Do you mean where am I originally from?" But ultimately my answer to those follow-up questions that will ask about origins will be that we have always been from here.

Overcoming my resentment I will try to educate, knowing that nine times out of ten my words fall on inattentive ears. I have spent most of my adult life explaining who I am not.

I am, however, very clearly the *other*, if only your everyday, garden-variety, domestic *other*. I've always known that I was the *other*, even before I knew

From *Black Issues in Higher Education*, Vol. 5, No. 4, May 1988, pp. 10–11, 16. Reprinted by permission of the publisher, Cox, Matthews & Associates, Inc. Arturo Madrid is President of the Tomas Rivera Center, Claremont Graduate School. This article was excerpted from the Fourth Annual Tomas Rivera Lecture at the 1988 National Conference of the American Association of Higher Education, Washington, D.C.

the vocabulary or understood the significance of otherness.

I grew up in an isolated and historically marginal part of the United States, a small mountain village in the state of New Mexico, the eldest child of parents native to that region and whose ancestors had always lived there. In those vast and empty spaces people who look like me, speak as I do, and have names like mine predominate. But the *americanos* lived among us: the descendants of those nineteenth century immigrants who dispossessed us of our lands; missionaries who came to convert us and stayed to live among us; artists who became enchanted with our land and humanscape; refugees from unhealthy climes, crowded spaces, unpleasant circumstances; and of course, the inhabitants of Los Alamos. More importantly, however, they—*los americanos*—were omnipresent in newspapers, newsmagazines, books, on radio, in movies and ultimately, on television.

Despite the operating myth of the day, school did not erase my *otherness*. It did try to deny it, and in doing so only accentuated it. To this day what takes place in schools is more socialization than education, but when I was in elementary school and given where I was, socialization was everything. School was where one became an American. Because there was a pervasive and systematic denial by the society that surrounded us that we were Americans. That denial was both explicit and implicit. I remember the implicit denial, our absence from the larger cultural, economic, and social spaces; the one that reminded us constantly that we were the *other*. And school was where we felt it most acutely.

Quite beyond saluting the flag and pledging allegiance to it, becoming American was learning English . . . and its corollary: not speaking Spanish. I do not argue that learning English was not appropriate. On the contrary. Like it or not, and we had no basis to make any judgments on that matter, we were Americans by virtue of having been born Americans, and English was the common language of Americans. And there was a myth, a pervasive myth, to the effect that if we only learned to speak English well and particularly without an accent—we would be welcomed into the American fellowship.

The official English movement folks notwithstanding, the true test was not our speech, but rather our names and our appearance, for we would always have an accent, however perfect our pronunciation, however excellent our enunication, however divine our diction. That accent would be heard in our pigmentation, our physiognomy, our names. We were, in short, the *other*.

Being the *other* is feeling different; it is awareness of being distinct; it is consciousness of being dissimilar. Otherness results in feeling excluded, closed out, precluded, even disdained and scorned.

Being the *other* involves a contradictory phenomenon. On the one hand being the *other* frequently means being invisible. On the other hand, being the *other* sometimes involves sticking out like a sore thumb. What is she/he doing here?

If one is the *other*, one will inevitably be seen stereotypically; will be defined and limited by mental sets that may not bear much relation to existing realities.

There is sometimes a darker side to otherness as well. The *other* disturbs, disquiets, discomforts. It provokes distrust and suspicion. The *other* frightens, scares.

For some of us being the *other* is only annoying; for others it is debilitating; for still others it is damning. For the majority otherness is permanently sealed by physical appearance. For the rest otherness is betrayed by ways of being, speaking or of doing.

The first half of my life I spent down-playing the significance and consequences of otherness. The second half has seen me wrestling to understand its complex and deeply ingrained realities; striving to fathom why otherness denies us a voice or visibility or validity in American society and its institutions; struggling to make otherness familiar, reasonable, even normal to my fellow Americans.

Yet I also have experienced another phenomenon; that of being a missing person. Growing up in Northern New Mexico I had only a slight sense of us being missing persons. Hispanos, as we called (and call) ourselves in New Mexico, were very much a part of the fabric of the society and there were Hispano professionals everywhere about me: doctors, lawyers, schoolteachers and administrators. My people owned businesses, ran organizations and were both appointed and elected public officials.

My awareness of our absence from the larger institutional life of the society became sharper when I went off to college, but even then it was attenuated by the circumstances of history and geography. The demography of Albuquerque still strongly reflected its historical and cultural origins, despite the influx of Midwesterners and Easterners. Moreover, many of my classmates at the University of New Mexico were Hispanos, and even some of my professors. I thought that would also be true at U.C.L.A., where I began graduate studies in 1960. Los Angeles already had a very large Mexican population, and that population was visible even in and around Westwood and on the campus. But Mexican American students were few and mostly invisible and I do not recall seeing or knowing a single Mexican American (or for that matter Black, Asian or American Indian) professional on the staff or faculty of that institution during the five years I was there.

Needless to say persons like me were not present in any capacity at Dartmouth College, the site of my first teaching appointment, and of course were not even part of the institutional or individual mindset. I knew then that we—a we that had come to encompass American Indians, Asian Americans, Black Americans, Puerto Ricans and Women—were truly missing persons in American institutional life.

Over the past three decades the *de jure* and *de facto* segregation that have historically characterized American institutions have been under assault. As a consequence minorities and women have become part of American institutional life, and although there are still many areas where we are not to be found, the missing persons phenomenon is not as pervasive as it once was. However, the presence of the *other*, particularly minorities, in institutions and in institutional life is, as we say in Spanish, *a flor de tierra*: spare plants whose roots do not go deep, a surface phenomenon vulnerable to inclemencies of an economic, or political or social nature.

Some of us entered institutional life through the front door; others through the back door; and still others through side doors. Many, if not most of us,

came in through windows, and continue to come in through windows. Of those who entered through the front door, some never made it past the lobby; others were ushered into corners and niches. Those who entered through back and side doors inevitably have remained in back and side rooms. And those who entered through windows found enclosures built around them. For despite the lip service given to the goal of the integration of minorities into institutional life, what has frequently occurred instead is ghettoization, marginalization, isolation.

Not only have the entry points been limited, but in addition the dynamics have been singularly conflictive. Rather than entering institutions more or less passively, minorities have of necessity entered them actively, even aggressively. Rather than taking, they have demanded. Institutional relations have thus been adversarial, infused with specific and generalized tensions.

The nature of the entrance and the nature of the space occupied have greatly influenced the view and attitudes of the majority population within those institutions. All of us are put into the same box; that is, no matter what the individual reality, the assessment of the individual is inevitably conditioned by a perception that is held of the class. Whatever our history, whatever our record, whatever our validations, whatever our accomplishments, by and large we are perceived unidimensionally and dealt with accordingly.

Over the past four decades America's demography has undergone significant changes. Since 1965 the principal demographic growth we have experienced in the United States has been of peoples whose national origins are non-European. This population growth has occurred both through births and through immigration. Conversely, as a consequence of careful tracking by government agencies, we now know that the birth rate of the majority population has decreased.

There are some additional demographic changes which should give us something to think about. Black Americans are now to be found in significant numbers in every major urban center in the nation. Hispanic Americans now number over 15,000,000 persons, and American Indians, heretofore a small and rural population, are increasingly more numerous and urban. The Asian American population, which has historically consisted of small and concentrated communities of Chinese, Filipino and Japanese Americans, has doubled over the past decade, its complexion changed by the addition of Cambodians, Koreans, Hmongs, Vietnamese, et al.

Thus for the next few decades we will continue to see a growth in the percentage of non-European origin Americans as compared to EuroAmericans. To sum up, we now live in the most demographically diverse nation in the world and one that is growing increasingly more so.

One of my purposes here today is to address the question of whether a goal (quality) and a reality (demographic diversity) present a dilemma to one of the most important of American institutions: higher education.

Quality, according to the Oxford English Dictionary, has multiple meanings. One set defines quality as being an essential character, a distinctive and inherent feature. A second describes it as a degree of excellence, of conformity to standards, as superiority in kind. A third makes reference to social status, particularly to persons of high social status. A fourth talks about quality as being a special or distinguishing attribute, as being a desirable trait. Quality is highly desirable in both principle and practice. We all aspire to it in our own person, in our experiences, and of course we all want to be associated with people and operations of quality.

But let us move away from the various dictionary meanings of the word and to our own sense of what it represents and of how we feel about it. First of all we consider quality to be finite; that is, it is limited with respect to quantity; it has very few manifestations; it is not widely distributed. I have it and you have it, but they don't. We associate quality with homogeneity, with uniformity, with standardization, with order, regularity, neatness. Certainly it's always expensive. We tend to identify it with those who lead, with the rich and the famous. And, when you come right down to it, it's inherent. Either you've got it or you ain't.

Diversity, from the Latin *divertere*, meaning to turn aside, to differ, is the condition of being differ-

ent or having differences; is an instance of being different. Its companion word, diverse, means differing, unlike, distinct; having or capable of having various forms; composed of unlike or distinct elements.

Diversity is lack of standardization, of orderliness, homogeneity. Diversity introduces complications, is difficult to organize, is troublesome to manage, is problematical. The way we use the word gives us away. Something is *too* diverse, is *extremely* diverse. We want a *little* diversity.

When we talk about diversity we are talking about the *other*, whatever that *other* might be: someone of a different gender, race, class, national origin; somebody at a greater or lesser distance from the norm; someone outside the set; someone who doesn't fit into the mental configurations that give our lives order and meaning.

In short, diversity is desirable only in principle, not in practice. Long live diversity, . . . as long as it conforms to my standards, to my mind set, to my view of life, to my sense of order.

The United States, by its very nature, by its very development, is the essence of diversity. It is diverse in its geography, population, institutions, technology, its social, cultural, and intellectual modes. It is a society that at its best does not consider quality to be monolithic in form, finite in quantity, or to reside inherently in class. Quality in our society proceeds in large measure out of the stimulus of diverse modes of thinking and acting; out of the creativity made possible by the different ways in which we approach things.

One of the principal strengths of our society is its ability to address on a continuing and substantive basis the real economic, political and social problems that have faced and continue to face us. What makes the United States so attractive to immigrants are the protections and opportunities it offers; what keeps our society together is tolerance for cultural, religious, social, political, and even linguistic difference; what makes us a unique, dynamic and extraordinary nation are the power and creativity of our diversity.

The true history of the U.S. is the one of struggle against intolerance, against oppression, against xenophobia, against those forces that have prohibited persons from participating in the larger life of the society on the basis of their race, their gender, their religion, their national origin, their linguistic, and cultural background. These phenomena are not only consigned to the past. They remain with us and frequently take on virulent dimensions.

If you believe, as I do, that the well-being of a society is directly related to the degree and extent to which all of its citizens participate in its institutions, then you will have to agree that we have a challenge before us. In view of the extraordinary changes that are taking place in our society we need to take up the struggle again, unpleasant as it is. As educated and educator members of this society we have a special responsibility for assuring that all American institutions, not just our elementary and secondary schools, our juvenile halls, or our jails, reflect the diversity of our society. Not to do so is to risk greater alienation on the part of a growing segment of our society; is to risk increased social tension in an already conflictive world; and, ultimately, is to risk the survival of a range of institutions that for all their defects and deficiencies, provide us the opportunity and the freedom to improve our individual and collective lot.

Let me urge you, as you return to your professional responsibilities and to your personal spaces, to reflect on these two words—quality and diversity—and on the mental sets and behaviors that flow out of them. And let me urge you further to struggle against the notion that quality is finite in quantity, limited in its manifestations, or is restricted by considerations of class, gender, race or national origin; or that quality manifests itself only in leaders and not in followers, in managers and not in workers; or that it has to be associated with verbal agility or elegance of personal style; or that it cannot be seeded, or nurtured, or developed.

Who's Got the Room at the Top? Issues of Dominance and Nondominance in Intracultural Communication

EDITH A. FOLB

"If a phenomenon is important, it is perceived, and, being perceived, it is labeled." So notes Nathan Kantrowitz, sociologist and student of language behavior. Nowhere is Kantrowitz's observation more apparent than in that realm of communication studies concerned with the correlates and connections between culture and communication—what the editors of this text have termed "intercultural communication." Our contemporary technology has brought us into both literal and voyeuristic contact with diverse cultures and customs, from the Stone Age Tasaday to the computer age Japanese. Our domestic liberation movements, moreover, have forced upon our consciousness the existence and needs of a multiplicity of groups within our own nation. So, the phenomenon of culture-linked communication is pervasively before us. And, as scholars concerned with culture and communication, we have tried to identify and characterize what we see. This attempt to "label the goods," as it were, has generated a profusion of semantic labels and categories—international communication, cross-cultural communication, intercultural communication, intracultural communication, trans-racial communication, interracial communication, interethnic communication. What we perceive to be important, we label.

Some may chide us for our penchant for classifications—an example of Aristotelian excessiveness, they may say. However, I see it as a genuine attempt to understand what we do individually and collectively, what we focus on within the field of communication studies. I believe this effort to characterize what we do serves a useful function: It continually prods us to examine and expand our vision of what culture-linked communication is, and, at the same time, it helps us bring into sharper focus the dimensions and differences within this area of study. As Samovar and Porter (1982) remind us, "There is still a great need to specify the nature of intercultural communication and to recognize various viewpoints that see the phenomenon somewhat differently" (p. 2). It is my intention in this essay to attempt what the editors of this text suggest, to look at the correlates and connections between culture and communication from a different point of view, one that examines the properties and issues of dominance and nondominance in communicative exchange. The essay is speculative and sometimes polemical. And the focus of my interest and discussion is the realm of intracultural communication.

THE CONCEPT OF INTRACULTURAL COMMUNICATION

The label "intracultural communication" is not unknown within the field of communication studies, although it is one that has not been widely used. Sitaram and Cogdell (1976) have identified intracultural communication as "the type of communication that takes place between members of the same dominant culture, but with slightly differing values" (p. 28). They go on to explain that there are groups ("subcultures") within the dominant culture who hold a minimal number of values that differ from the mainstream, as well as from other subgroups. These differences are not sufficient to identify them as separate cultures, but diverse enough to set them

apart from each other and the culture at large. "Communication between members of such subcultures is *intracultural communication*" (Sitaram and Cogdell, 1976, p. 28).

In another vein, Sarbaugh (1979) sees intracultural communication as an indicator of the degree of cultural experience shared (or not shared) by two people—the more culturally homogeneous the participants, the greater the level of "intraculturalness" surrounding the communicative act. For Sitaram and Cogdell, then, intracultural communication is a phenomenon that operates within a given culture among its members; for Sarbaugh, it is a measure of homogeneity that well may transcend country or culture.

Like Sitaram and Cogdell, I see intracultural communication as a phenomenon that functions within a single, designated culture. However, like Sarbaugh, I am concerned with the particular variables within that context that importantly influence the degree and kind of cultural homogeneity or heterogeneity that can and do exist among members of the culture. Furthermore, the variables of particular interest to me are those that illuminate and underscore the interrelationship of power, dominance, and nondominance in a particular culture.[1] Finally, I believe that the concept of hierarchy, as it functions within a culture, has a deep impact on matters of power, dominance, and nondominance and, therefore, on both the form and content of intracultural communication.

As a backdrop for the discussion of dominance and nondominance in an intracultural context, I would like to formulate a frame of reference within which to view the discussion.

A FRAME OF REFERENCE FOR INTRACULTURAL COMMUNICATION

Society and Culture

Thomas Hobbes, the seventeenth-century political philosopher, left us an intriguing legacy in his work, *Leviathan*. He posited a hypothetical starting point for humankind's march to political and social organization. He called it "the state of nature." In this presocietal state, the biggest club ruled. Kill or be killed was the prevailing modus operandi. Somewhere along the evolutionary road, our ancestors began to recognize a need to change their ways—if any of them were to survive for very long. The principle of enlightened self-interest became the name of the game. Our forebears, however grudgingly, began to curb their inclination to kill, maim, steal, or otherwise aggress upon others and joined together for mutual survival and benefit. The move was one of expediency, not altruism. "Do unto others as you would have them do unto you," whatever its religious import, is a reiteration of the principle of enlightened self-interest.

So, this aggregate of beings came together in order to survive, and, in coming together, gave up certain base instincts, drives, and predilections. "Society" was formed. Those who may scoff at this postulated state of nature need only remember back to the United States' final pullout from Vietnam. The media showed us, in all too brutal detail, the rapidity with which a society disintegrates and we return to the force of the club.

But let us continue with the telling of humankind's tale. It was not sufficient merely to form society; it must be maintained. Controls must be established to ensure its stability. Thus, the social contract was enacted. It was, indeed, the social contract that ensured mutual support, protection, welfare, and survival for the society's members.

However, social maintenance and control did not ensure the perpetuation of the society as an intact entity, carrying along its cumulative and collective experiences, knowledge, beliefs, attitudes, the emergent relationship of self to other, to the group, to the universe, to matters of time and space. That is, it did not ensure the perpetuation of society's accoutrements—its culture. Institutions and structures were needed to house, as it were, the trappings of culture. So, culture was not only embodied in the precepts passed on from one generation to another, but also in the artifacts created by society to safeguard its culture. Looked at in a different light, culture is both a blueprint for continued societal

survival as well as the pervasive cement that holds the social mosaic together. Culture daily tells us and shows us how to be in the universe, and it informs future generations how to be.[2]

From the moment we begin life in this world, we are instructed in the cultural ways that govern and hold together our society, ways that ensure its perpetuation. Indeed, the social contract that binds us to our society and our culture from the moment of birth is neither of our own choice nor of our own design. For example, we are labeled by others almost immediately—John, Sandra, Pearl, David. Our genders are determined at once and we are, accordingly, swaddled in appropriate colors and treated in appropriate ways.[3]

As we grow from infancy to childhood, the socialization process is stepped up and we rapidly internalize the rules of appropriate and inappropriate societal behavior. Religion, education, recreation, health care, and many other cultural institutions reinforce our learning, shape and regulate our behavior and thought so they are orderly and comprehensible to other members of our society. Through the socialization process the human animal is transformed into the social animal. Thus, society is maintained through instruction and indoctrination in the ways of the culture.

But the question that pricks and puzzles the mind is: Whose culture is passed on? Whose social order is maintained? Whose beliefs and values are deemed appropriate? Whose norms, mores, and folkways are invoked?

Hierarchy, Power, and Dominance

In most societies, as we know them, there is a hierarchy of status and power. By its very nature, hierarchy implies an ordering process, a sense of the evaluative marketing of those being ordered. Our own vernacular vocabulary abounds with references to hierarchy and concomitant status and power: "top dog," "top banana," "king pin," "king of the mountain."

High status and attendant power may be accorded to those among us who are seen or believed to be great warriors or hunters, those invested with magical, divine, or special powers, those who are deemed wise, or those who are in possession of important, valued and/or vital societal resources and goods. Of course, power and high status are not necessarily—or even usually—accorded to these specially designated members of the society in some automatic fashion. Power, control, and subsequent high status are often forcibly wrested from others and forcibly maintained. Not everyone abides by the social contract, and strong-arm rule often prevails, as conquered, colonized, and enslaved people know too well.

Whatever the basis for determining the hierarchy, the fact of its existence in a society assures the evolution and continued presence of a power elite—those at the top of the social hierarchy who accrue and possess what the society deems valuable or vital. And, in turn, the presence of a power elite ensures an asymmetrical relationship among the members of the society. In fact, power is often defined as the ability to get others to do what you want and the resources to force them to do your bidding if they resist—the asymmetrical relationship in its extreme form.

But the perpetuation of the power elite through force is not the most effective or efficient way of ensuring one's position at the top of the hierarchy. It is considerably more effective to institute, encourage, and/or perpetuate those aspects of culture—knowledge, experiences, beliefs, values, patterns of social organization, artifacts—that subtly and manifestly reinforce and ensure the continuation of the power elite and its asymmetrical relationship within the society. Though we may dismiss Nazism as a malignant ideology, we should attend to the fact that Hitler well understood the maintenance of the power elite through the manipulation and control of culture—culture as propaganda.

Though I would not imply that all power elites maintain themselves in such an overtly manipulative way, I would at least suggest that the powerful in many societies—our own included—go to great lengths to maintain their positions of power and what those positions bring them. And to that end, they support, reinforce, and, indeed, create those particular cul-

tural precepts and artifacts that are likely to guarantee their continued power. To the extent that the culture reflects implicitly or expressly the needs and desires of the power elite to sustain itself, it becomes a vehicle for propaganda. Thus, cultural precepts and artifacts that govern such matters as social organization and behavior, values, beliefs, and the like can often be seen as rules and institutions that sustain the few at the expense of the many.

So, we come back to the question of whose rules, whose culture? I would suggest that when we in communication studies refer to the "dominant culture" we are, in fact, not talking about numbers. That is why the label "minorities" is misleading when we refer to cultural groups within the larger society. Blacks in South Africa and women in the United States are not numerical minorities—but they are not members of the power elite either. In fact, when we talk about the concept of dominant culture, we are really talking about power—those who *dominate* culture, those who historically or traditionally have had the most persistent and far-reaching impact on culture, on what we think and say, on what we believe and do in our society. We are talking about the culture of the minority and, by extension, the structures and institutions (social, political, economic, legal, religious, and so on) that maintain the power of this minority. Finally, we are talking about rules of appropriate and inappropriate behavior, thought, speech, and action for the many that preserve power for the few. Dominant culture, therefore, significantly reflects the precepts and artifacts of those who dominate culture and is not necessarily, or even usually, a reference to numbers, but to power.

So, coming full circle, I would suggest that our socialization process, our social introduction to this aggregate of people who form society, is an introduction to a rule-governed milieu of asymmetrical societal organization and relationship, and the communicative behaviors and practices found there are likewise asymmetrical in nature. As the witticism goes, "All men (perhaps even women) are created equal—some are just more equal than others."

Given this frame of reference, I would now like to explore some definitions and concepts that, I believe, emerge from this perspective. It is my hope that the discussion will provide the reader with another way to look at intracultural communication.

A NOMENCLATURE
FOR INTRACULTURAL
COMMUNICATION

The Concept of
Nondominance

As already indicated, I view intracultural communication as a phenomenon that operates within a given cultural context. However, my particular focus, as suggested, is not a focus on numbers but an attention to dominance, nondominance, and power in the cultural setting. That is, how do nondominant groups intersect and interact with the dominant culture membership (with those who enact the precepts and support the institutions and systems of the power elite)? For purposes of discussion and analysis, I will take most of my examples from the geopolitical configuration called the United States.

By "nondominant groups" I mean those constellations of people who have not historically or traditionally had continued access to or influence upon or within the dominant culture's (that is, those who dominate culture) social, political, legal, economic, and/or religious structures and institutions. Nondominant groups include people of color, women, gays, the physically challenged,[4] and the aged, to name some of the most prominent. I use the expression "nondominant" to characterize these people because, as suggested, I am referring to power and dominance, not numbers and dominance. Within the United States, those most likely to hold and control positions of real—not token—power and those who have the greatest potential ease of access to power and high status are still generally white, male, able-bodied, heterosexual, and youthful in appearance if not in age.[5]

Nondominant people are also those who, in varying degrees and various ways, have been "invisible" within the society of which they are a part and at the same time bear a visible caste mark. Furthermore, it is this mark of caste identity that is often consciously or habitually assigned low or negative status by members of the dominant culture.

The dimensions of invisibility and marked visibility are keen indicators of the status hierarchy in a given society. In his book, *The Invisible Man*, Ralph Ellison instructs us in the lesson that nondominant people—in this instance, black people—are figuratively "invisible." They are seen by the dominant culture as no one, nobody and therefore go unacknowledged and importantly unperceived.[6] Furthermore, nondominant peoples are often relegated to object status rather than human status. They are viewed as persons of "no consequence," literally and metaphorically. Expressions such as, "If you've seen one, you've seen them all"; "They all look alike to me"; "If you put a bag over their heads, it doesn't matter who you screw" attest to this level of invisibility and dehumanization of nondominant peoples, such as people of color or women. Indeed, one need only look at the dominant culture's slang repertory for a single nondominant group, women, to see the extent of this object status: "tail," "piece of ass," "side of beef," "hole," "gash," "slit," and so on.

At the same time that nondominant peoples are socially invisible, they are often visibly caste marked. Though we tend to think of caste in terms, say, of East Indian culture, we can clearly apply the concept to our own culture. One of the important dimensions of a caste system is that it is hereditary—you are born into a given caste and are usually marked for life as a member. In fact, we are all born into a caste, we are all caste marked. Indeed, some of us are doubly or multiply caste marked. In the United States, the most visible marks of caste relate to gender, race, age, and the degree to which one is able-bodied.

As East Indians do, we too assign low to high status and privilege to our people. The fact that this assignment of status and privilege may be active or passive, conscious or unconscious, malicious or unthinking does not detract from the reality of the act. And one of the major determinants of status, position, and caste marking relates back to who has historically or traditionally had access to or influence upon or within the power elite and its concomitant structures and institutions. So, historically blacks, native Americans, Chicanos, women, the old, the physically challenged have at best been neutrally caste marked and more often negatively identified when it comes to issues of power, dominance, and social control.[7]

Low status has been assigned to those people whom society views as somehow "stigmatized." Indeed, we have labels to identify such stigmatization: "deviant," "handicapped," "abnormal," "substandard," "different"—that is, different from those who dominate. As already suggested, it is the white, male, heterosexual, able-bodied, youthful person who both sets the standards for caste marking and is the human yardstick by which people within the United States are importantly measured and accordingly treated. As Porter and Samovar (1976) remind us, "We [in the United States] have generally viewed racial minorities as less than equal; they have been viewed as second class members of society—not quite as good as the white majority—and treated as such. . . . Blacks, Mexican Americans, Indians, and Orientals are still subject to prejudice and discrimination and treated in many respects as colonized subjects" (p. 11). I would add to this list of colonized, low-status subjects women, the physically challenged, and the aged. Again, our language is a telling repository for illuminating status as it relates to subordination in the social hierarchy: "Stay in your place," "Don't get out of line," "Know your place," "A woman's place is chained to the bed and the stove," "Know your station in life" are just a few sample phrases.

It is inevitable that nondominant peoples will experience, indeed be subjected to and suffer from, varying degrees of fear, denial, and self-hatred of their caste marking. Frantz Fanon's (1963) characterization of the "colonized native"—the oppressed native who has so internalized the power elite's perception of the norm that he or she not only serves and speaks for the colonial elite but is often more critical and oppressive of her or his caste than is the colonial—reveals this depth of self-hatred and denial.

In a parallel vein, the concept of "passing" which relates to a person of color attempting to "pass for" white, is a statement of self-denial. Implicit in the art of passing is the acceptance, if not the belief, that "white is right" in this society, and the closer one can come to the likeness of the privileged caste, the more desirable and comfortable one's station in life will be. So, people of color have passed for white—just as Jews have passed for Gentile or gay males and females have passed for straight, always with the fear of being discovered "for what they are." Physical impairment, too, has been a mark of shame in this country for those so challenged. Even so powerful a figure as F.D.R. refused to be photographed in any way that would picture him to be a "cripple."

If the act of passing is a denial of one's caste, the process of "coming out of the closet" is a conscious acceptance of one's caste. It is an important political and personal statement of power, a vivid metaphor that literally marks a rite of passage. Perhaps the most striking acknowledgement of one's caste marking in our society relates to sexual preference. For a gay male or lesbian to admit their respective sexual preferences is for them to consciously take on an identity that our society has deemed abnormal and deviant—when measured against the society's standard of what is appropriate. They become, quite literally, marked people. In an important way, most of our domestic liberation movements are devoted to having their membership come out of the closet. That is, these movements seek not only to have their people heard and empowered by the power elite, but to have them reclaim and assert their identity and honor their caste. Liberation movement slogans tell the story of positive identification with one's caste: "Black is beautiful," "brown power," "Sisterhood is powerful," "gay pride," "I am an Indian and proud of it."

The nature and disposition of the social hierarchy in a given society, such as the United States, is reflected not only in the caste structure, but also in the class structure and the role prescriptions and expectations surrounding caste and class. Although the power structure in the United States is a complex and multileveled phenomenon, its predominant, generating force is economic. That is, the power elite is an elite that controls the material resources and goods in this country as well as the means and manner of production and distribution. Though one of our national fictions is that the United States is a classless society, we have, in fact, a well-established class structure based largely on economic power and control. When we talk of lower, middle, and upper classes in this country, we are not usually talking about birth or origins, but about power and control over material resources, and the attendant wealth, privilege, and high status.

There is even a kind of status distinction made within the upper-class society in this country that again relates to wealth and power, but in a temporal rather than a quantitative way—how long one has had wealth, power, and high-class status. So, distinctions are made between the old rich (the Harrimans, the Gores, the Pews) and the new rich (the Hunt family, Norton Simon, and their like).

Class, then, is intimately bound up with matters of caste. Not all, or even most, members of our society have the opportunity—let alone the caste credentials—to get a "piece of the action." It is no accident of nature that many of the nondominant peoples in this country are also poor peoples. Nor is it surprising that nondominant groups have been historically the unpaid, low-paid, and/or enslaved work force for the economic power elite.

Finally, role prescriptions are linked to both matters of status and expectations in terms of one's perceived status, class, and caste. A role can be defined simply as a set of behaviors. The set of behaviors we ascribe to a given role is culture-bound and indicative of what has been designated as appropriate within the culture vis-à-vis that role. They are prescriptive, not descriptive, behaviors. We hold certain behavioral expectations for certain roles. It is a mark of just how culture-bound and prescriptive these roles are when someone is perceived to behave inappropriately—for example, the mother who gives up custody of her children in order to pursue her career; she has "stepped out of line."

Furthermore, we see certain roles as appropriate or inappropriate to a given caste. Though another of our national myths—the Horatio Alger myth—tells us that there is room at the top for the industrious, bright go-getter, the truth of the matter is that there is room at the top if you are appropriately caste

marked (that is, are white, male, able-bodied, and so on). The resistance, even outright hostility, nondominant peoples have encountered when they aspire to or claim certain occupational roles, for example, is a mark of the power elite's reluctance to relinquish those positions that have been traditionally associated with privileged status and high caste and class ranking. Though, in recent years, there has been much talk about a woman Vice-President of the United States, it has remained just talk. For that matter, there has not been a black Vice-President or a Hispanic or a Jew. The thought of the Presidency being held by most nondominant peoples is still "unspeakable."

The cultural prescription to keep nondominant peoples "in their place" is reinforced by and reinforces what I refer to as the "subterranean self"— the culture-bound collection of prejudices, stereotypes, values, and beliefs that each of us embraces and employs to justify our world view and the place of people in that world. It is, after all, our subterranean selves that provide fuel to fire the normative in our lives—what roles people ought and ought not to perform, what and why certain individuals are ill- or well-equipped to carry out certain roles, and our righteously stated rationalizations for keeping people in their places as we see them. Again, it should be remembered that those who dominate the culture reinforce and tacitly or openly encourage the perpetuation of those cultural prejudices, stereotypes, values, and beliefs that maintain the status quo, that is, the asymmetrical nature of the social hierarchy. Those who doubt the fervent desire of the power elite to maintain things as they are need only ponder the intense and prolonged resistance to the Equal Rights Amendment. If women are already "equal," why not make their equality a matter of record?

The foregoing discussion has been an attempt to illuminate the meaning of nondominance and the position of the nondominant person within our society. By relating status in the social hierarchy to matters of caste, class, and role, it has been my intention to highlight what it means to be a nondominant person within a culture that is dominated by the cultural precepts and artifacts of a power elite. It has also been my intention to suggest that the concept of "dominant culture" is something of a fiction, as we in communication studies traditionally use it. Given my perspective, it is more accurate to talk about those who dominate a culture rather than a dominant culture per se. Finally, I have attempted to point out that cultural dominance is not necessarily, or even usually, a matter of the numbers of people in a given society, but of those who have real power in a society.

Geopolitics

The viewpoint being developed in this essay highlights still another facet of dominance and nondominance as it relates to society and the culture it generates and sustains—namely, the geopolitical facet. The United States is not merely a territory with certain designated boundaries—a geographical entity—it is a geopolitical configuration. It is a country whose history reflects the clear-cut interrelationship of geography, politics, economics, and the domination and control of people. For example, the westward movement and the subsequent takeover of the Indian nations and chunks of Mexico were justified by our doctrine of Manifest Destiny, not unlike the way Hitler's expansionism was justified by the Nazi doctrine of "geopolitik." It is no accident that the doctrine of Manifest Destiny coincides with the rapid growth and development of U.S. industrialization. The U.S. power elite wanted more land in which to expand and grow economically, so it created a rationalization to secure it.

Perhaps nowhere is a dominant culture's (those who dominate culture) ethnocentrism more apparent than in the missionary-like work carried on by its members—whether it be to "civilize" the natives (that is, to impose the conquerors' cultural baggage on them), to "educate them in the ways of the white man," or to "Americanize" them. Indeed, the very term *America* is a geopolitical label as we use it. It presumes that those who inhabit the United States are the center of the Western hemisphere, indeed its only residents.[8] Identifying ourselves as "Americans" and our geopolitical entity as "America," in light of the peoples who live to the north and south

of our borders speaks to both our economic dominance in this hemisphere and our ethnocentrism.

Identifying the United States in geopolitical terms is to identify it as a conqueror and controller of other peoples, and suggests both the probability of nondominant groups of people within that territory and a polarized, even hostile relationship between these groups and those who dominate culture. What Rich and Ogawa (1982) have pointed out in their model of interracial communication is applicable to most nondominant peoples: "As long as a power relationship exists between cultures where one has subdued and dominated the other — hostility, tension, and strain are introduced into the communicative situation" (p. 46). Not only were the Indian nations[9] and parts of Mexico conquered and brought under the colonial rule of the United States, but in its industrial expansionism, the United States physically enslaved black Africans to work on the farms and plantations of the South. It also economically enslaved large numbers of East European immigrants, Chinese, Irish, Hispanics (and more recently, Southeast Asians) in its factories, on its railroads, in its mines and fields through low wages and long work hours. It coopted the cottage industries of the home and brought women and children into the factories under abysmal conditions and the lowest of wages.

Indeed, many of the nondominant peoples in this country today are the very same ones whom the powerful have historically colonized, enslaved, disenfranchised, dispossessed, discounted, and relegated to poverty and low-caste and class status. So, the asymmetrical relationship between the conqueror and the conquered continues uninterrupted. Although the form of oppression may change through time, the fact of oppression—and coexistent nondominance—remains.

It has been my desire throughout this essay to speculate about the complex ways in which society, culture, position, and place in the societal hierarchy affect and are affected by the matters of dominance, power, and social control. To this end, I have chosen to identify and characterize configurations of people within a society not only along a cultural axis but along a socioeconomic and a geopolitical axis as well. I have tried to reexamine some of the concepts and definitions employed in discussions of culture-linked communication in a different light. And I have chosen the issues and conditions surrounding dominance and nondominance as points of departure and return. As I said at the beginning of this essay, the content is speculative, exploratory, and, hopefully, provocative. Above all, it is intended to encourage dialogue and exchange about the conditions and constraints surrounding intracultural communication.

NOTES

1. See Folb (1980) for another perspective on the intersection of power, dominance, and nondominance as they operate within a discrete microcultural group, the world of the black ghetto teenager.

2. For a fascinating account of how and what kind of culture is transmitted from person to person, see Margaret Mead's *Culture and Commitment* (1970).

3. Mary Ritchie Key's book, *Male/Female Language* (1975), provides an informative discussion of the ways in which females and males are catalogued, characterized, and compartmentalized by our language. She illuminates its effects on how we perceive ourselves, as well as discussing how others perceive us through the prism of language.

4. The semantic marker "physically challenged" is used in lieu of other, more traditional labels such as "handicapped," "physically disabled," or "physically impaired," because it is a designation perferred by many so challenged. It is seen as a positive, rather than a negative, mark of identification.

5. In a country as youth conscious as our own, advanced age is seen as a liability, not as a mark of honor and wisdom as it is in other cultures. Whatever other reservations people had about Ronald Reagan's political aspirations in 1980, the one most discussed was his age. His political handlers went to great lengths—as did Reagan himself—to "prove" he was young in spirit and energy if not in years. It was important that he align himself as closely as possible with the positive mark of youth we champion and admire in this country.

6. It is no mere coincidence that a common thread binds together the domestic liberation movements in this country. It is the demand to be seen, heard, and empowered.

7. See Nancy Henley's *Body Politics* (1977) for a provocative look at the interplay of the variables power, dominance, and sex as they affect nonverbal communication.

8. The current bumper sticker, "Get the United States Out of North America," is a pointed reference to our hemispheric self-centeredness.

9. Neither the label "Indian" nor the label "native American" adequately identifies those people who inhabited the North American continent before the European conquest of this territory. Both reflect the point of view of the labeler, not those so labeled. That is why many who fought for the label "native American" now discount it as not significantly different from "Indian."

REFERENCES

Fanon, Frantz. (1963). *Wretched of the Earth*. New York: Grove Press.

Folb, Edith A. (1980). *Runnin' Down Some Lines: The Language and Culture of Black Teenagers*. Cambridge, Mass.: Harvard University Press.

Porter, Richard E., and Larry A. Samovar. (1976). "Communicating Interculturally." In Larry A. Samovar and Richard E. Porter (Eds.), *Intercultural Communication: A Reader* (2nd ed.) Belmont, Calif.: Wadsworth.

Rich, Andrea L., and Dennis M. Ogawa. (1982). "Intercultural and Interracial Communication: An Analytical Approach." In Larry A. Samovar and Richard E. Porter (Eds.), *Intercultural Communication: A Reader* (3rd ed.) Belmont, Calif.: Wadsworth.

Samovar, Larry A., and Richard E. Porter (Eds.). (1982). *Intercultural Communication: A Reader* (3rd ed.) Belmont, Calif.: Wadsworth.

Sarbaugh, L. E. (1979). *Intercultural Communication*. Rochelle Park, N.J.: Hayden Book Co.

Sitaram, K. S., and Roy T. Cogdell. (1976). *Foundations of Intercultural Communication*. Columbus, Ohio: Merrill.

Intercultural Perspectives of Aging

CARL W. CARMICHAEL

In the United States, concern for older people has grown considerably during the last two decades. Evidence of this concern ranges from the emergence of more than 200 departments of gerontology in institutions of higher education to the passing of hundreds of congressional bills and the creation of numerous government programs to aid the elderly. Yet all of this attention has barely put a dent in the problems of growing old in a youth-oriented culture.

Of course, problems of aging have been prevalent in virtually every society. Whereas the nature of those problems and the treatment of the aged vary widely from culture to culture, the fact that this subpopulation is viewed as a *problem* does not vary. In keeping with the theme of this book, we discuss three aspects of aging. First, we look at how communication relates to aging in several important ways; second, although people normally think of aging as something that happens to an individual, we show that it is very much a cultural phenomenon; and third, we point out that the intercultural aspects of aging are interesting and useful areas of study for the communication scholar.

COMMUNICATION ASPECTS OF AGING

The field of gerontology has focused on a particular population subgroup, and it has used a "social problem" orientation. The study of aging and the problems of the aged have necessarily been an interdisciplinary venture. Unfortunately, until recently, communication has not been included as one of the traditional subdisciplines. However, the kind of knowledge and the kind of perspective found in communication studies would obviously be useful in dealing with this social problem. Certainly, one can argue that any social problem or cultural phenomenon cannot be fully understood unless one studies the communication systems that relate to it. But, more specifically, many of the problems of the aged are communication problems, and they should be studied as such.[1]

The relevance and the value of communication to aging begins at the very heart of how the field of communication has defined itself. Two of the major conceptual aspects of communication are: (1) information processing and (2) human interaction—interpersonally or through the media. Many of the traditionally studied problems of aging relate to one of these aspects, and an analysis from this communication perspective leads to new areas of study that have great potential in gerontological theory development.

Information Processing

Communication—whatever the setting, the level, or the type—inherently involves the processing of information. The individual human organism encodes, decodes, packages, distorts, and relays information, as do the group, the business organization, the social system, and the culture. Some of the oldest and most researched theories of aging relate to information processing.

Recent research on changes in memory function as a result of aging has led to a reevaluation of widely held beliefs previously confirmed by earlier research.[2] Similarly, the deterioration of intelligence was always assumed to be a normal function of aging, but this assumption is now controversial thanks to recent findings and improved research techniques.[3] Questions relating to linguistic function or language facility are now being asked by gerontologists.[4] The processing of nonverbal cues has been the focus of two papers delivered at recent

This original essay appeared in print for the first time in the fifth edition. All rights reserved. Permission to reprint must be obtained from the publisher and the author. Professor Carmichael teaches at the University of Oregon.

national meetings of the Gerontological Society and the Speech Communication Association.[5]

One of the most serious communication problems faced by older people is the reduction of information to process because of age-related sensory losses. Under normal conditions of aging, older people can expect noticeable decreases in the sensory abilities—hearing, vision, touch, and smells.[6] Furthermore, some abnormal conditions that severely impair one's health are age-related, and they result in serious communication problems. For example, strokes often damage the speech centers in the brain; arteriosclerosis can reduce the oxygen supply to the brain and thus affect the information processing functions. Surely the communication process is significantly affected when any of these normal or pathological changes in information processing occur. How the process is affected and how improvements can be made are socially relevant research questions for the communicologist.

Human Interaction

While the field of communication, in its broadest sense, can include the study of computer systems and even animal behavior, the bulk of the research and writing has been focused on human interaction. Most current definitions of communication contain the concept of interaction (transaction, linking, and so on), and most communicologists are primarily, if not exclusively, concerned with interaction on the human level. In our coursework and in our research, we have studied every type of setting—from the classroom to the business conference room— and every size of group—the dyad, the triad, the small group, the assembly, the social system. Yet almost none of this tremendous accumulation of knowledge relates specifically to older people.

There is no reason to believe that the basic, human need to communicate—to interact with other human beings for socializing, decision making, or whatever—should change with age. Older people are subject to the same communication anxieties, the same communication needs, the same communication dependencies, and the same communication problems in relationships as younger people

are, and their needs occur in the same kinds of settings—from the family (perhaps now a redefined unit for them) to the classroom. Some older people use the media more than younger people do, and some even use it as a substitute for dwindling interpersonal communication.[7]

CULTURAL ASPECTS OF AGING

There are times when everyone feels very much alone; we are born, struggle for survival, and go to our graves alone. Yet while that feeling may be justified, the reality is that we do not and cannot live in a social vacuum in this complex, interpersonally interdependent culture. Our lives are inextricably interwoven with many other individuals and institutions. We cannot escape the rules, the laws, the social conditioning, the media—the basic socialization process of our culture.

The aging process may appear at first to be a uniquely individual experience, but that is simply not the case. The aging process is very much related to such cultural phenomena as attitudes toward aging, beliefs about aging, and stereotypes of aging found within the culture. Also, the aging individual is greatly affected by cultural mechanisms and policies that determine such daily needs as health care and employment. Mandatory retirement is an example of a formalized policy that demonstrates that integrating older people into the mainstream of society is not a cultural goal.

Attitudes

In recent years numerous studies have been conducted to discover what the attitudes of our culture are toward older people and the aging process. I myself have reviewed nearly 300 such studies.[8] The subjects in these studies ranged in age from the very young (preschoolers) to the very elderly (those in their nineties). While the findings are far too diverse to relate in detail here, one general conclusion prevails: From the teenage years on, the attitudes of people in our culture toward growing old are fairly negative. They don't begin that way, as many of the studies with younger children reveal, but something in our culture changes our attitudes to negative ones around the age of puberty. Communicologists must now seek to learn how these attitudes are communicated, what factors reinforce them, and how they can be changed.

The phenomenon at issue here should be of great concern to us. Although the concept of attitude has been difficult to define, it usually refers to some kind of a cognitive evaluation. An attitude is how we feel about something, how much we like or don't like something. Unquestionably, how we *feel* about older people and the aging process—the prevailing attitudes toward aging in our culture—relates to how we *treat* our elderly, as well as to how we are affected by the aging process ourselves as individuals.

Beliefs

A broad set of beliefs, or misbeliefs, about aging exists in our culture. Cultural communication, from generation to generation, has perpetuated myths of aging that have become so widely accepted they are all but impossible to change, even in the face of recent scientific evidence to the contrary. Consider a few salient examples and check your own beliefs in each case:

When people get old, they can expect increased memory loss.

You can't teach an old dog new tricks.

Intelligence declines in old age.

One of the worst problems in old age is loneliness.

People become more religious when they grow old.

Older people have no interest in sex.

The list could go on; however, these examples are typical of beliefs that are not only widely accepted in our culture but have been disputed by recent gerontological research. Some findings have even received popular coverage in the media, such as the CBS Special, "Sex After Sixty." Yet, such false beliefs are so firmly grounded in the American culture that change does not come easily, and many older people are quite directly affected by them. In fact, one could argue quite legitimately that one of the worst problems our culture imposes on its aging members is this false set of beliefs. Psychologically induced states of "oldness" may occur as a result of the self-fulfilling prophecy phenomenon and a belief system that abounds with myths, or at least half-truths, that are more applicable to the very elderly years than they are at the relatively younger ages of sixty or sixty-two when the word *old* becomes appropriate in our culture. It is quite possible that many older people have aged prematurely by adopting the age-related characteristics they have come to believe must exist after a certain age.

Stereotyping

In some ways, the stereotyping process is a necessary evil. On the positive side, it enables communication efficiency in the sense that communication about a person or a group of people can be simplified by identifying the group in terms of its most basic, widely believed characteristics. One might argue that whether or not those beliefs are accurate is irrelevant as long as they come from the belief system of the communication receivers. Yet, this process, by its very nature, invites inaccuracy. So, on the negative side, people who are stereotyped are identified *only* in terms of those common-denominator characteristics that are believed, but are not necessarily true, and that relate to a whole category of people, but not necessarily to an individual.

Stereotyping requires cooperation on a cultural level. When an actor portrays an old man, he turns to the most convenient symbols of "oldmanness" his culture provides: white hair, stooped posture, a cane, a hearing aid, and a harsh, raspy voice. Note that the culture provides these symbols and, therefore, the actor is able to communicate the image of this character efficiently to an audience from that culture.

The problem for older people in this regard is obvious. Negative stereotypes, or at least inaccurate ones, are perpetuated by this process. The image that younger people have of their elders, the image that older people have of themselves, is affected by the stereotypes we see through the media and elsewhere. The burning question, of course, is who is at fault? Is the actor guilty of perpetuating a negative image? Or does he merely reflect cultural beliefs that just happen to be inaccurate and negative? When Carol Burnett plays her famous crotchety old woman role, should she be faulted for portraying characteristics that are unduly negative and not true of most older women? Or should she be commended for cleverly choosing characteristics that are true of at least some older women and hilariously funny to most of her viewers?

While those questions may be unanswerable, at least we must consider the problems produced for older people by the stereotyping process. The stereotypes of aging come from a cultural belief system that is highly inaccurate. That these images can sometimes be portrayed as funny by a comedian is no solace for one who tries to age gracefully in a culture that sees the aging person as ugly, wrinkled, stooped, deranged, decrepit, slow, sexless, and crotchety.

Integration Not a Cultural Goal

Unquestionably, the United States has not been successful in integrating the elderly into the mainstream of American culture. As individuals, we may feel great compassion for the plight of our elderly and advocate strongly that people should remain in active roles and be a viable part of our culture as long as they live; but as a society we have acted collectively to make it difficult for this integration to take place. In fact, many of our cultural policies are unmistakably intended to militate against the integration of the aged into the mainstream of society.

The most blatant example of such a policy is mandatory retirement. In our culture one's occupation often becomes one's identity. "What do you do?" is an almost rote conversation opener in the United States because we evaluate others in terms of

their occupational roles. One's job is also a major social outlet. For many people, most of their primary social affiliations are occupationally related, whether they are the breadwinners or the breadwinners' spouses. The typical person in our culture depends on the workplace to meet the normal needs of affiliation and social attachment. The loss of one's job can be a devastating disruption in the fulfillment of these needs. Such is the case when workers reach retirement age and discover they are no longer part of the social system at the office or the mill.

This article is not the place to debate the complicated issues relating to retirement. In fact, the problem is not retirement *per se* but the fact that retirement is mandatory at a given age. The point here is that mandatory retirement is a government-imposed, cultural mechanism, the intent of which is to remove people above a certain age from the job market. In our culture, when someone is removed from the job market, he or she is well on the way to being removed from the mainstream of society. Thus the goal in the United States seems to be to eliminate older people from the active roles that contribute to society rather than attempt to integrate them into the culture. Interestingly enough, we find considerable cultural variance on this issue. For example, the oriental cultures, though practices are rapidly changing in recent years, have a long history and tradition of utilizing the resources of their older citizens and integrating them more fully into the culture than do Western cultures.[9] This issue is just one of many that invites intercultural comparisons.

INTERCULTURAL ASPECTS OF AGING

Gerontologists have long been aware of the usefulness of comparing cultures in the study of aging. The International Association of Gerontology, founded in 1950, sponsors an international congress every three years. One of the most significant publications on the intercultural aspects of aging, *International Handbook on Aging: Contemporary*

Developments and Research, contains articles on twenty-eight different countries. These articles reveal such demographic information about the elderly as population proportions and life expectancies, and they review the major programs, social services, medical care systems, and so on for the aged in each of these major cultures.[10] A noteworthy observation from this book is that, although the study of aging has experienced a golden age in the United States in the last fifteen years, research in other cultures is not being done primarily by Americans. The list of contributors to the *International Handbook* shows that most research is being conducted by people from their own cultures and represents a variety of disciplines—none of which is communication.

Cross-cultural comparisons have enabled us to explore significant gerontological phenomena that necessarily go beyond cultural boundaries. Some areas that have been compared include demographic characteristics, treatment of the aged—both physically and mentally—roles and statuses of older people, types of programs available for the aged, and relationships among aspects of the aging process and numerous cultural characteristics such as socioeconomic factors, educational policies, social policies and values, and social conditions. One major research effort in intercultural aspects of aging resulted in the observation that many age-related phenomena are interwoven with factors of modernization.[11] Such cross-cultural research has also led to the conclusion that there is a relationship between the numbers and proportions of older people in modernizing societies and the development of study, analysis, and education about aging.[12]

Intercultural Comparisons

We could choose any of the twenty-eight countries included in the *International Handbook* to exemplify the usefulness of cross-cultural comparisons in the area of communication and aging. In the interest of brevity, we will select only one.

Numerous types of comparisons have been made between Japan and the United States in the postwar years, but only recently, beginning in the mid-1970s, have we found gerontologists from the United States studying aging in Japan. Our research on aging in Japan is so recent that drawing conclusions is premature, but we cannot help but be intrigued by the fact that we are getting two distinctly different viewpoints about what it is like to become old in Japan.[13]

The catalyst in this discussion is Erdman Palmore's book, *The Honorable Elders*.[14] From beginning to end, the posture of this book is a very positive one, as the title indicates. After spending a sabbatical leave at the Gerontological Institute in Tokyo, Palmore came to the conclusion that there is much the United States can learn from Japan in the area of aging—that the old Confucian-related beliefs of giving great respect to the elderly and allowing them to grow old with dignity still persist and that there are only minor problems connected with aging in Japan.

Briefly, Palmore focuses on two major issues: (1) that the aged enjoy a high status in Japan and (2) that the Japanese elderly are well integrated into the social networks of their culture. He supports these notions with statistics from the prime minister's office, by personal observations of behavior, and by cultural studies. Palmore states that the high status of the aged in Japan is evidenced by (1) the honorific language used in speaking to or about the elderly; (2) family traditions in the household—elders being served first, getting special seats, walking in front, or being first in the bath; and (3) public declarations of respect for the aged—specifically referring to the 1963 National Law for Welfare of the Elders, which states that:

The Elders shall be loved and respected as those who have for many years contributed toward the development of society, and a wholesome and peaceful life shall be guaranteed to them. In accordance with their desire and ability, the elders shall be given opportunities to engage in suitable work or to participate in social activities.

Palmore also notes the Japanese annual national holiday in September devoted to respecting the elders in the family.

Palmore's second major issue is the integration of the aged in Japanese society. He focuses on three levels of social integration—in the family, in the work force, and in the community—and he concludes that "Japan is an exception to the general rule that industrialization causes a sharp decline in status and integration of the aged" and that "Japan demonstrates that the aged need not suffer from prejudice and discrimination in modern society."

However, a considerably different perspective can be seen in the writings of other scholars.[15] Douglas Sparks conducted a study that focused mostly on retirement problems in Japan—certainly an area worth considering since retirement is one of the major adjustment problems for the aged in modern industrial societies.[16] Sparks argues that retirement is an especially serious problem in Japan. It usually occurs at age fifty-five, or twenty years short of one's statistical life expectancy, which has increased dramatically from forty-five years before World War II to seventy-five years today. Pension systems are grossly inadequate, according to Sparks. Some companies give a lump sum equivalent to two or three years' salary, hardly enough to sustain the retiree for twenty years. Public pension plans pay only a few hundred dollars a year, and benefits do not begin until age sixty (sixty-five if employed). Therefore, the Japanese retiree must depend on the family for support or get another job, but postretirement jobs, as Sparks points out, typically mean a significant decline in status and responsibility.

David Plath explores the problems of aging in Japan from a broader sociological perspective.[17] He describes the cultural shifts from the Meiji Age (1868–1912), when Japan was becoming a modern nation, to the era between the world wars when the vertical society prevailed and when the Confucian values of paternalism and great respect for the elderly returned, to the postwar era of becoming a modern industrialized state—with its problems for the elderly. Plath's analysis includes such deeply imbedded cultural phenomena as (1) the concept of *obasute* (pronounced oh-boss-tay), literally meaning "discarding granny," death before dependence in old age; (2) the high suicide rate among the elderly in Japan—both statistically and in terms of the

belief systems; (3) the discrepancy between the attitudes of younger people toward the care of the aged and the views expressed by the aged themselves; (4) the financial plight of the aged in Japan; and (5) the advent of nursing homes as a solution.

This more negative picture portrayed by Sparks and Plath is confirmed by my own research, conducted in Japan in 1976 and 1978, and by a prominent Japanese gerontologist Daisaku Maeda, in a more recent publication.[18] I learned from interviews with housewives in Hiroshima, Osaka, and Tokyo that respect for elders in Japan has decreased considerably in recent decades. Lack of respect for the elderly was expressed frequently as the reason for the 1963 legislation and the special holiday in September to honor the old people in the family. Maeda agrees with Plath's conclusions, quoting from them throughout his article, but he presents a slightly more positive picture on some sociological dimensions; he cites surveys indicating that 80 percent of Japanese elders are "satisfied" with their lives and circumstances.

The marked contrast between the two discrepant positions represented by Palmore and Plath may actually reveal a discrepancy that currently exists in the Japanese culture between the reality of the problems of aging in contemporary Japan and deeply rooted cultural beliefs that survive through tradition. It would be extremely interesting to analyze this social problem in the communication classroom. Since any problem that can be characterized as social will find its expression in the communication systems of the culture within which it is found, a study of these communication systems should reveal the nature and extent of the social problem. This method of finding the extent of the problem may be especially important in cultures where the social problem may be a negative reflection on the culture or where the problem is in conflict with religious or ethnic belief systems within the culture. The latter may be the case in Japan in considering the problems of aging.

One interesting example of a socially significant theme that can be traced in the literature and communication systems is the concept of *obasute*. Plath and others who have studied this concept have traced it to the sixth century. A mountain west of Tokyo is named *obasute*; according to legend, old people are sent there, never to return. Throughout these many centuries, this Japanese legend has been repressed by the Confucian dictates of respect and honor for the aged, which are the opposite of *obasute*. In the 1950s *obasute* emerged as a theme in a widely read short story by Niwa Fumio; its descriptive title has been translated as "The Hateful Age."[19] Students may ask why this story was so popular, or why this theme found its way into other stories in the popular media, including "The Oak Mountain Song," some award winning movies within the last couple of years, and a No drama titled "Obasute."[20] What can we conclude from the current popularity, in the communication media, of a theme that depicts old age as despicable and its solution as abandonment? Should we believe the Confucian expressions of respect and honor for the elderly that are gathered in polite interviews, or should we listen to the statements of the people in the communication systems of the culture?

SOME CONCLUSIONS

Our culture has chosen to ignore many of the normal communication needs of our older citizens. After retirement, social contacts decrease. For some, this process is a slow one that begins at retirement and continues through the young-old years (sixty to seventy-two), but for others the change occurs abruptly at retirement because most of their friendships were job related. Through the middle-old years (seventy-two to eighty), most older people experience the deaths of their closest friends and, perhaps, their spouses. Then, ultimately, in the old-old years (eighty and older), most old people experience considerable aloneness or, worse yet, institutionalization—a cultural mechanism to care for the infirmed elderly that has been described by some as inhumane.

Some of the needs of older people get widespread attention, especially the medical and economic needs. But our culture has not shown any concern for the communication needs of the el-

derly. The major communication mechanisms that our culture provides for the older person are the media, but how much of the content of the media is geared to the older audience?

It may well be that many older people in our culture are communication starved. Many may experience a state of communication deprivation that is affecting other aspects of their lives, including such social psychological phenomena as life satisfaction, self-esteem, or even the will to live. If so, as a culture we have not responded to this problem.

Cross-cultural comparisons show that the United States may have one of the worst records for integrating the aging population into the mainstream of its culture. This problem is very much a *communication* problem. It could be solved in part by changing the retirement system and allowing at least part-time employment for older people. Perhaps some assistance could come in the form of increased educational opportunities for the aged, or more organizations for them to join, or even more attention in the media. But the problem isn't just one of employment, or education, or clubs. On a cultural level, we must change our attitudes, beliefs, stereotypes, values, and the public policies that affect the aged. Such change begins on the individual level, but it eventually permeates the communication systems of the whole culture.

NOTES

1. For a more elaborate discussion of this point, see Carl W. Carmichael, "Communication and gerontology: Interfacing disciplines," *Western Speech Communication*, XL, Spring 1976, pp. 121–129.

2. For example, see Jack Adamowicz, "Visual short-term memory and aging," *Journal of Gerontology* 31 (1976), 39–46.

3. For example, see Paul Baltes and K. W. Schaie, "Aging and IQ: The myth of the twilight years," *Psychology Today* (March 1974), pp. 35–40.

4. For example, see Frain Pearson, *Language Facility and Aging*, Ph.D. dissertation, University of Oregon, 1976.

5. Carl W. Carmichael, Jean McGee, and Melissa Barker, "Nonverbal communication and the aged," paper presented at annual conference of The Gerontological Society, San Diego, Calif., 1980; and Carl W. Carmichael, "Nonverbal aspects of aging," paper presented at annual conference of Speech Communication Association, Chicago, 1986.

6. For literature reviews on individual senses, see James Birren and K. W. Schaie, *Handbook of the Psychology of Aging* (New York: Van Nostrand Reinhold, 1977).

7. For example, see Marshall J. Graney, "Media use as a substitute activity in old age," *Journal of Gerontology* 29 (1974), pp. 322–327.

8. Carl W. Carmichael, "Attitudes toward aging throughout the life span," *Journal of the Communication Association of the Pacific* VIII (August 1979), pp. 129–151.

9. Erdman Palmore, "The status and integration of the aged in Japanese society," *Journal of Gerontology* 30 (1975), pp. 199–208; and Erdman Palmore, "What can the USA learn from Japan about aging?" *The Gerontologist* (February 1975), pp. 64–67.

10. Erdman Palmore (ed.), *International Handbook on Aging: Contemporary Developments and Research* (Westport, Conn.: Greenwood Press, 1980).

11. Donald Cowgill and Lowell Holmes (eds.), *Aging and Modernization* (New York: Appleton-Century-Crofts, 1972); and Donald Cowgill, "Aging and modernization: A revision of the theory," in J. Gubrium, *Late Life* (Springfield, Ill.: Charles C. Thomas, 1974).

12. Donald Cowgill and R. A. Orgren, "The international development of academic gerontology," in H. Sterns, *Promoting the Growth of Gerontology in Higher Education* (Belmont, Calif.: Wadsworth, 1979).

13. For a summary of areas appropriate for comparison, see Aaron Lipman, "Conference on the potential for Japanese-American cross-national research on aging," *The Gerontologist* (June 1975), pp. 248–253. Contrasting perspectives also can be seen by comparing such articles as Merle Broberg, Dolores Melching, and Daisaku Maeda, "Planning for the elderly in Japan," *The Gerontologist* (June 1975), pp. 242–247; Michael P. Mealey, "Twilight years in the land of the rising sun," *Modern Healthcare* (June 1975), pp. 52–58; and Daisaku Maeda, "Growth of old people's clubs in Japan," *The Gerontologist* (June 1975), pp. 254–256.

14. Erdman Palmore, *The Honorable Elders* (Durham, N.C.: Duke University Press, 1975).

15. Carl W. Carmichael, "Aging in Japan and America: A communication perspective," *Journal of the Association of the Pacific*, VII (Fall 1978).

16. Douglas Sparks, "The still rebirth: Retirement and role discontinuity," in David W. Plath, *Adult Episodes in Japan* (Leiden, The Netherlands: E. J. Brill, 1975), pp. 64–74.

17. David W. Plath, "Japan: The after years," in Cowgill and Holmes, *Aging and Modernization* (1972), pp. 133–150.

18. Daisaku Maeda, "Japan," in Palmore, *International Handbook on Aging: Contemporary Developments and Research*, pp. 251–270.

19. Niwa Fumio, "The hateful age (Iyagarase no nenrei)," translated by Ivan Morris, in Morris, *Modern Japanese Stories: An Anthology* (Rutland, Vt. and Tokyo: Charles H. Tuttle Publishing Co., 1962), p. 340.

20. Ito Sei, "On 'The Oak Mountain Song,'" *Japan Quarterly* IV (April-June 1957), pp. 233–235.

Viewing Persons with Disabilities as a Culture

DAWN O. BRAITHWAITE

Jonathan is an articulate, intelligent, thirty-five-year-old man who has used a wheelchair since he became a paraplegic when he was twenty years old.[1] He recalls taking an ablebodied woman out to dinner at a nice restaurant. When the waitress came to take their order, she patronizingly asked his date, "And what would *he* like to eat for dinner?" At the end of the meal the waitress presented Jonathan's date with the check and thanked her for her patronage. Although it may be hard to believe the insensitivity of the waitress, this incident is not an isolated one. Rather, such an experience is a common one for persons with disabilities.

There has been a growing interest in the important area of health communication among communication scholars, with a core of researchers looking at communication between ablebodied persons and those with disabilities. Disabled persons are becoming an increasingly large and active minority in our culture due to (1) an increase in the number of persons who live long enough to develop disabilities and (2) advances in medical technology that allow those with disabilities to survive their illnesses and injuries. In the past disabled persons were kept out of public view, but today they are mainstreaming into all facets of modern society. All of us have or will have contact with persons with disabilities of some kind, and many of us will find family, friends, coworkers, or even ourselves part of the disabled culture. Says Marie, a college student who became a quadraplegic after diving into a swimming pool, "I knew there were disabled people around, but I never thought this would happen to me. I never even knew a disabled person before I became one. If before this happened, I saw a person in a wheelchair, I would have been uncomfortable and not known what to say."

The purpose of this essay is to discuss several aspects of communication between ablebodied and disabled individuals as a cultural communication phenomenon. To better understand communication between ablebodied and disabled persons, we must view disabled persons as a *culture* (Emry and Wiseman, 1987). That is, we must recognize that persons with disabilities develop certain unique communicative characteristics that are not shared by the majority of ablebodied individuals in U.S. society.

This essay presents research findings from a series of interviews with persons who have visible physical disabilities. First, we introduce the communication problems that can arise between persons in the ablebodied culture and those in the disabled culture. Second, we discuss some problems with the way research into communication between ablebodied and disabled persons has been conducted. Third, we present results from the interviews. These results show persons with disabilities engaged in a process whereby they critique the prevailing stereotypes of the disabled held by the ablebodied and engage in a process that we call *redefinition*. Finally, we discuss the importance of these findings for both scholars and students of intercultural communication.

COMMUNICATION BETWEEN ABLEBODIED AND DISABLED PERSONS

Persons with disabilities seek to overcome the barriers associated with physical disability because disability affects all areas of an individual's life: behavioral, economic, and social. When we attempt to understand the effects of disability, we must differentiate between disability and handicap. Many aspects of disability put limitations on an individual because one or more of the key life functions, such as self-care, mobility, communication, socialization, and employment, is interrupted. Disabilities are often compensated for or overcome through assisting devices, such as wheelchairs or canes, or through training. Disabilities become handicaps when the disability interacts with the physical or social environment to impede a person in some aspect of his or her life (Crewe and Athelstan, 1985). For example, a disabled individual who is paraplegic can function in the environment with wheelchairs and curb cuts, but he or she is handicapped when buildings and/or public transportation are not accessible to wheelchairs. When the society is willing and/or able to help, disabled persons have the ability to achieve increasingly independent lives (Cogswell, 1977; DeLoach and Greer, 1981).

Many physical barriers associated with disabilities can be detected and corrected, but the social barriers resulting from disabilities are much more insidious. Nowhere are the barriers more apparent than in the communication between ablebodied persons and persons with disabilities. When ablebodied and disabled persons interact, the general, stereotypical communication problem that is present in all new relationships is heightened, and both persons behave in even more constrained and less spontaneous ways, acting overly self-conscious, self-controlled, and rigid because they feel uncomfortable and uncertain (Belgrave and Mills, 1981; Weinberg, 1978). While the ablebodied person may communicate verbal acceptance to the person with the disability, his or her nonverbal behavior may communicate rejection and avoidance (Thompson, 1982). For example, the ablebodied person may speak with the disabled person but stand at a greater distance than usual, avoid eye contact, and cut the conversation short. Disability becomes a handicap, then, for persons with disabilities when they interact with ablebodied persons and experience discomfort when communicating; this feeling blocks the normal development of a relationship between them.

Most ablebodied persons readily recognize that what we have just described is representative of their own communication experiences with disabled persons. Ablebodied persons often find themselves in the situation of not knowing what is expected of them or how to act; they have been taught both to "help the handicapped" and to "treat all persons equally." For example, should we help a person with a disability open a door or should we help them up if they fall? Many ablebodied persons have offered help only to be rebuffed by the person with the disability. Ablebodied persons greatly fear saying the wrong thing, such as "See you later!" to a blind person or "Why don't you run by the store on your way home?" to a paraplegic. It is easier to avoid situations where we might have to talk with a disabled person rather than face discomfort and uncertainty.

Persons with disabilities find these situations equally uncomfortable and are well aware of the discomfort of the ablebodied person. They are able to describe both the verbal and nonverbal signals of discomfort and avoidance that ablebodied persons portray (Braithwaite, Emry, and Wiseman, 1984). Persons with disabilities report that when they meet ablebodied persons, they want to get the discomfort "out of the way," and they want the ablebodied person to see them as a "person like anyone else," rather than focus solely on the disability (Braithwaite, 1985, 1989).

PROBLEMS WITH THE PRESENT RESEARCH

When we review the research in the area of communication between ablebodied and disabled persons, three problems come to the forefront. First, very little is known about the communication behavior of disabled persons. A few researchers have studied disabled persons' communication, but most of them study ablebodied persons' reactions to disabled persons (most of these researchers are themselves ablebodied). Second, most researchers talk *about* persons with disabilities, not *with* them. Disabled persons are rarely represented in the studies; when they are, the disabled person is most often "played," for example, by an ablebodied person in a wheelchair. Third, and most significantly, the research is usually conducted from the perspective of the ablebodied person; that is, what can persons with disabilities *do* to make ablebodied persons feel more comfortable. It does not take into consideration the effects on the person with the disability. Therefore, we have what may be called an *ethnocentric bias* in the research, which focuses on ablebodied/disabled communication from the perspective of the ablebodied majority, ignoring the perspective of the disabled minority.

We shall discuss the results of an ongoing study that obtains the perspectives of disabled persons concerning their communication with ablebodied persons. To date, fifty-seven in-depth interviews have been conducted with physically disabled adults about their communication with ablebodied persons in the early stages of relationships. Here we are concerned with understanding human behavior from the disabled person's own frame of reference. This concern is particularly important in the area of communication between ablebodied and disabled persons and, as we have said, previous research has been conducted from the perspective of ablebodied persons; disabled persons have not participated in these studies. Doing research by talking directly to the person with the disability helps to bring out information important to the individual, rather than simply getting the disabled person's reaction to what is on the researcher's mind. This research represents a unique departure from what other researchers have been doing because the focus is on the perspective of the disabled minority.

PROCESS OF REDEFINITION

When discussing their communication with ablebodied persons, disabled persons' responses often deal with what we call *redefinition*. That is, in their communication with ablebodied persons and among themselves, disabled persons engage in a process whereby they critique the prevailing stereo-

types held by the ablebodied and create new definitions: (1) of the disabled as members of a "new" culture; (2) of self by the disabled; (3) of disability for the disabled; and (4) of disability for the dominant culture.

Redefinition of the Disabled as Members of a "New" Culture

Persons with disabilities report seeing themselves as a minority or a culture. For some of the subjects, this definition crosses disability lines; that is, their definition of *disabled* includes all persons who have disabilities. For others, the definition is not as broad and includes only other persons with the same type of disability. Most persons with disabilities, however, do define themselves as part of a culture. Says one person:

It's (being disabled) like West Side Story. *Tony and Maria; white and Puerto Rican. They were afraid of each other; ignorant of each others' cultures. People are people.*

According to another man:

First of all, I belong to a subculture because of the way I have to deal with things being in the medical system, welfare. There is the subculture . . . I keep one foot in the ablebodied culture and one foot in my own culture. One of the reasons I do that is so that I don't go nuts.

Membership in the disabled culture has several similarities to membership in other cultures. Many of the persons interviewed likened their own experiences to those of other cultures, particularly to blacks and women. When comparing the disabled to both blacks and women, we find several similarities. The oppression is biologically based, at least for those who have been disabled since birth; one is a member of the culture by being born with cerebral palsy or spina bifida, for example. As such, the condition is unalterable; the disability will be part of them throughout their lifetime.

For those persons who are not born with a disability, membership in the culture can be a process that emerges over time. For some, the process is a slow one, as in the case of a person with a degenerative disease that may develop over many years and gradually become more and more severe. If a person has a sudden-onset disability, such as breaking one's neck in an accident and waking up a quadraplegic, the movement from a member of the dominant culture—"normal person"—to the minority culture—disabled person—may happen in a matter of seconds. This sudden transition to membership in the disabled culture presents many challenges of readjustment in all facets of an individual's life, especially in communication relationships with others.

Redefinition of Self by the Disabled

How one redefines oneself, then, from normal or ablebodied to disabled, is a process of redefinition of self. While blacks struggle for identity in white society and women struggle for identity in a male-dominated society, the disabled struggle for identity in an ablebodied world. One recurring theme from the participants in this study is "I am a person like anyone else" (if disabled since birth) or "I'm basically the same person I always was" (if a sudden-onset disability). The person who is born with a disability learns the process of becoming identified as "fully human" while still living as a person with a disability. The individual who is disabled later in life, Goffman (1963) contends, goes through a process of redefinition of self. For example, the subjects born with disabilities make such statements as, "I am not different from anyone else as far as I am concerned" or "Disability does not mean an incomplete character." Persons whose disabilities happened later say "You're the same person you were. You just don't do the same things you did before." One man put it this way:

If anyone refers to me as an amputee, that is guaranteed to get me madder than hell! I don't deny the leg amputation, but I am me. I am a whole person. One.

During the redefinition process, individuals come to terms with both positive and negative ramifications of disability. Some subjects report that "disability is like slavery to me." In contrast, one woman reports:

I find myself telling people that this has been the worst thing that has happened to me. It has also been one of the best things. It forced me to examine what I felt about myself . . . confidence is grounded in me, not in other people. As a woman, not as dependent on clothes, measurements, but what's inside me.

One man expresses his newfound relationship to other people when he says, "I'm more interdependent than I was. I'm much more aware of that now." This process of redefinition is evident in what those interviewed have to say.

Redefinition of Disability for the Disabled

A third category of redefinition occurs as persons with disabilities redefine both disability and its associated characteristics. For example, in redefining disability itself, one man said, "People will say, 'Thank god I'm not handicapped.' And I'll say, 'Let's see, how tall are you? Tell me how you get something off that shelf up there!'" This perspective is centered on the view of the disability as a characteristic of the person rather than the person himself; it recognizes disability as situational rather than inherent or grounded in the person. In this view, everyone is disabled to some extent: by race, gender, height, or physical abilities, for example.

Redefinition of disability can be seen in the use of language. Says one subject who objected to the label *handicapped person*: "Persons with a handicapping condition. You emphasize that person's identity and then you do something about the condition." This statement ties into viewing one's self as a person first. Research reveals movement from the term *handicapped* to *disability* or *disabled*, although a wide variety of terms are used by these subjects to talk about the self. Another change in language has been the avoidance of phrases such as "polio victim" or "arthritis sufferer." Again the emphasis is on the person, not the disability. "I am a person whose arms and legs do not function very well," says one subject who had polio as a child.

There have also been changes in the terms that refer to ablebodied persons. Says one man:

You talk about the ablebodied. I will talk about the nonhandicapped . . . It's a different kind of mode. In Michigan they've got it in the law: "temporarily ablebodied."

It is common for the persons interviewed to refer to the majority in terms of the minority: "nondisabled" or "nonhandicapped," rather than "ablebodied" or "normal." More than the change in terminology, the phrase "temporarily ablebodied" or TABS serves to remind ablebodied persons that no one is immune from disability. The persons interviewed also used TABS as a humorous reference term for the ablebodied as well. "Everyone is a TAB." This view jokingly intimates, "I just got mine earlier than you . . . just you wait!"

In addition to redefining disability, the disabled also redefine "assisting devices":

Now, there were two girls about eight playing and I was in my shorts. And I'll play games with them and say, "which is my good leg?" And that gets them to thinking. Well, this one (pats artificial leg) is not nearly as old as the other one!

Says another subject:

Do you know what a cane is? It's a portable railing! The essence of a wheelchair is a seat and wheels. Now, I don't know that a tricycle is not doing the exact same thing.

Again, in these examples, the problem is not the disability or the assisting device, such as a cane, but how one views the disability or the assisting device. These assisting devices take on a different meaning for the persons using them. Subjects expressed frustration with persons who played with their wheelchairs: "This chair is not a toy, it is part of me. When you touch my chair, you are touching me." One woman, a business executive, expanded on this by

saying, "I don't know why people who push my chair feel compelled to make car sounds as they do it."

Redefinition of Disability for the Dominant Culture

Along with the redefinitions that concern culture, self, and disability comes an effort to try to change society's view of the disabled and disability. Persons with disabilities are attempting to change the view of themselves as helpless, as victims, or merely sick. One man says:

People do not consider you, they consider the chair first. I was in a store with my purchases on my lap and money on my lap. The clerk looked at my companion and said, "Cash or charge?"

This incident with the clerk is a story that has been voiced by every person interviewed in some form or another, just as it happened to Jonathan at the restaurant with his date. One woman who has multiple sclerosis and uses a wheelchair told of her husband accompanying her while she was shopping for lingerie. When they were in front of the lingerie counter, she asked for what she wanted, and the clerk repeatedly talked only to her husband saying, "And what size does she want?" The woman told her the size and the clerk looked at the husband and said, "and what color?" Persons with disabilities recognize that ablebodied persons often see them as disabled first and persons second (if at all), and they expressed a need to change this view. Says a man who has muscular dystrophy:

I do not believe in those goddamned telethons . . . they're horrible, absolutely horrible. They get into the self-pity, you know, and disabled folk do not need that. Hit people in terms of their attitudes and then try to deal with and process their feelings. And the telethons just go for the heart and leave it there.

Most of the subjects indicate they see themselves as educators or ambassadors for all persons with disabilities. All indicate they will answer questions put to them about their disabilities, as long as they determine the other "really wants to know, to learn." One man suggests a solution:

What I am concerned with is anything that can do away with the "us" versus "them" distinction. Well, you and I are anatomically different, but we're two human beings! And at the point we can sit down and communicate eyeball to eyeball . . . the quicker you do that, the better!

Individually and collectively, persons with disabilities do identify themselves as part of a culture. They are involved in a process of redefinition of disability, both for themselves and for the ablebodied.

CONCLUSIONS

This research justifies the usefulness of viewing disability from an intercultural perspective. Persons with disabilities do see themselves as members of a culture, and viewing communication between ablebodied and disabled persons from this perspective sheds new light on the communication problems that exist. Emry and Wiseman (1987) argue that intercultural training should be the focus in our perceptions of self and others: They call for unfreezing old attitudes about disability and refreezing new ones. Clearly, from these findings, that is exactly what persons with disabilities are doing, both for themselves and for others.

Of the fifty-seven persons with disabilities interviewed, only a small percentage had any sort of education or training concerning communication, during or after rehabilitation, that would prepare them for changes in their communication relationships due to their disabilities. Such education seems especially critical for those who experience sudden-onset disabilities because their self-concepts and all of their relationships undergo sudden, radical changes. Intercultural communication scholars have the relevant background and experience for this kind of research and training, and they can help make this transition from majority to minority an easier one (Emry and Wiseman, 1987; Smith, 1989).

As for ablebodied persons who communicate with disabled persons, this intercultural perspective leads to the following suggestions:

Don't assume that persons with disabilities cannot speak for themselves or do things for themselves. *Do assume* they can do something unless they communicate otherwise.

Don't force your help on persons with disabilities. *Do let* them tell you if they want something, what they want, and when they want it. If a person with a disability refuses your help, don't go ahead and help anyway.

Don't avoid communication with persons who have disabilities simply because you are uncomfortable or unsure. *Do remember* they probably feel the same way you do.

Do treat persons with disabilities as *persons first*, recognizing that you are not dealing with a disabled person but with a *person* who has a disability.

NOTE

1. The names of all the subjects have been changed to protect their privacy.

REFERENCES

Belgrave, F. Z., and Mills, J. (1981). "Effect upon Desire for Social Interaction with a Physically Disabled Person of Mentioning the Disability in Different Contexts." *Journal of Applied Social Psychology, 11* (1), 44–57.

Braithwaite, D. O. (1985). "Impression Management and Redefinition of Self by Persons with Disabilities." Paper presented at the annual meeting of the Western Speech Communication Association, Denver, Col.

Braithwaite, D. O. (1989). "An Interpretive Analysis of Disabled Persons' Impression Management Strategies in Response to Perceived Discomfort and Uncertainty of Ablebodied Others." Paper presented at the annual meeting of the Western Speech Communication Association, Spokane, Wash.

Braithwaite, D. O., Emry, R. A., and Wiseman, R. L. (1984). "Ablebodied and Disablebodied Persons' Communication: The Disabled Persons' Perspective." ERIC ED 264 622.

Cogswell, Betty E. (1977). "Self Socialization: Readjustment of Paraplegics in the Community." In R. P. Marinelli and A. E. Dell Orto (Eds.), *The psychological and social impact of physical disability.* New York: Springer.

Crewe, N., and Athelstan, G. (1985). *Social and Psychological Aspects of Physical Disability.* Minneapolis: University of Minnesota, Department of Independent Study and University Resources.

DeLoach, C., and Greer, B. G. (1981). *Adjustment to Severe Disability.* New York: McGraw-Hill.

Emry, R., and Wiseman, R. L. (1987). "An Intercultural Understanding of Ablebodied and Disabled Persons' Communication." *International Journal of Intercultural Relations, 11,* 7–27.

Goffman, E. (1963). *Stigma: Notes on the Management of Spoiled Identity.* New York: Simon & Schuster.

Smith, D. H. (1989). "Studying Health Communication: An Agenda for the Future." *Health Communication, 1* (1), 17–27.

Thompson, T. L. (1982). "Disclosure as a Disability-Management Strategy: A Review and Conclusions." *Communication Quarterly, 30,* 196–202.

Weinberg, N. (1978). "Modifying Social Stereotypes of the Physically Disabled." *Rehabilitation Counseling Bulletin, 22* (2), 114–124.

On Communicating with Deaf People

KATHY JANKOWSKI[1]

I am deaf (actually, I am "Deaf," rather than "deaf," but more about that in a moment). If I ask you to close your eyes and think about "a deaf person," it is possible that your mental image will resemble someone elderly who has lost his or her hearing late in life, perhaps someone very much like one of your own grandparents. Or maybe you will think about a TV commercial or entertainment program in which someone who is hard of hearing gets laughs by frequently misinterpreting others' messages, or manifests an uncanny ability to eavesdrop on others' conversations by lipreading.

After you read this article, I hope your image of what "a deaf person" is like will have changed a bit. I hope you will understand, for example, that people who lose their hearing as mature adults are likely to have interacted primarily with hearing people throughout their lives, and probably do not consider being deaf to be a particularly crucial part of their self-concepts. These are not, however, the deaf people that I am concerned with here. Instead, our focus will be on a lesser known group, those who are "culturally deaf." Culturally deaf people interact primarily with other deaf people, sharing the same language, beliefs, values, and traditions. In America, culturally deaf people communicate among each other in a language called American Sign Language (ASL). As I hope to demonstrate, our experience of our own lives is probably very different from the image that most hearing people have of this experience.

Before we continue, I need to establish one convention, first proposed by James Woodward (1972), that will make it easier for you to understand the rest of this article. Whenever I refer to someone as Deaf with a capital "D," I am talking about someone who is a part of the Deaf culture. If I refer to someone who is "deaf" with a small "d," I mean only that the person is audiologically deaf, which usually means that he or she does not have enough residual hearing to be able to understand human speech.

Like most cultures, the Deaf culture encompasses language, nonverbal behavior, values, socializing patterns, and traditions. We will explore each of these features in this article, and we will also discuss at more length the kind of stereotypes of Deaf people held by hearing people, because these greatly affect the nature and quality of communication between the two cultures.

Most Deaf Americans are visually indistinguishable from their hearing counterparts. They have no native dress, no single set of religious beliefs, and usually no clearly defined neighborhoods or ghettoes. So it may seem odd to you to even think of Deaf Americans as a separate culture—but we are precisely that.

LANGUAGE

Probably the one feature of our lives more than any other that makes us into a culture is our language. You already know that Deaf people use sign language to communicate, but many hearing people assume incorrectly that our sign language is merely a visual, word-for-word (or even letter-by-letter) depiction of English. The truth is that ASL is a separate language, with its own syntax, structure, and semantics. The structure of ASL has been likened to Latin, Russian (Baker and Padden, 1978), and Navajo (Padden and Humphries, 1988). The differentiating factor is that ASL is not a spoken language. Hearing people use their voices to express themselves and their ears to receive messages; Deaf people use

their hands, facial expressions, and body movements to express themselves and their eyes to receive messages (Kannapell, 1985).

In ASL, one handshape can be used to convey different meanings with a slight variation or movement or location of the hands; meaning is simultaneously conveyed too with facial expressions, as well as posture of the head and upper body. For example, holding up a hand with all five fingers can mean "fine" when placed on the chest, and the same sign and location can mean "swell" with a wriggling of the fingers and a change in facial expression. You need to be as precise about your ASL signing as you would be with your word choice in a spoken language. Slight changes will make the sign that means "Oh, I finished that!" into "I absolutely loathe him!" That same sign for "finish" can likewise be modulated with expression and movement to ask "Are you finished?" or to assert, "I'm finished," or even to order someone to "stop it!" To cite another example, the same hand and body movement can be "modulated" with different facial expressions to mean either "she's fine," or "sure, that's fine," or even "I've never been better!"

For a majority of Deaf Americans, English is actually their second language, so one of the things to keep in mind when communicating with Deaf people is to treat them like anyone else whose native language might be different from your own. Minimally, this means showing a respect for the rules and structure of the other person's language. Do not be shocked when English idioms or attempts to sign in strict, literal English word order (rather than following the rules of ASL) lead to misunderstandings, especially when dealing with Deaf people who are not truly bilingual (possessing fluency in both ASL and English). A hearing teacher who signs that she is GOING-TO-A-LECTURE when she really means that she is GOING-TO-LECTURE may confuse her students. (They might even begin to wonder why the teacher is still there talking—isn't she missing the lecture she wanted to attend?) Similarly, if you tell a story about how a certain group of people experienced a BLOOD-BATH, signing each word as a separate English language concept, your listeners will not experience empathy for the plight of those people but will be shocked at their extraordinarily odd, even perverse, grooming habits. Then too, it is highly idiomatic in English to issue a long list of things, then to alert the listener that the end is finally approaching by inserting the words "AND NOT TO MENTION" between the last and the next to last item. The Deaf person, like any non-native English speaker, may take the words "and not to mention" quite literally and wonder why the last item in the series is to be treated as taboo, why it should not be mentioned. The point is that ASL syntax and structure are not the same as English, so to equate native signing with mere "English on the hands" is to demean and insult many Deaf people and thus to make this particular kind of intercultural communication all the more difficult. Deaf people also have different values and norms about how language is supposed to be used in general. Whereas the hearing culture seems to value the use of euphemisms as an indication of politeness, for example, Deaf people value directness and candor. It is not at all unusual for a Deaf person to exclaim to a friend that she or he has certainly put on some weight. In the hearing culture, such a direct confrontation might be seen as graceless, or even mean.

One further example of the differences between hearing and Deaf value systems with respect to language is especially relevant to anyone who has ever taken a public speaking course. The chances are that your public speaking teacher taught you about the importance of the speech's introduction: It should be graceful, not abrupt. Depending upon the situation, you might begin with a joke, a compliment for the hosts, a reference to a common experience just shared by everyone in the room, or with a remark about something the previous speaker just said. Only after the audience is "warmed up" and ready to listen should you tell them exactly what your topic is. This rule applies with even more force if you are delivering a persuasive speech, and especially if your audience is not a friendly one. In Deaf culture, the accepted norm for formal speaking occasions is quite different. Directness is valued highly: A completely unadorned introduction, something that might translate into English as "my topic

is _____," is generally most appropriate. This is not to suggest that Deaf people prefer a skeleton of a speech to the full-blown event; indeed, Deaf audiences demand the use of an abundance of examples for each point illustrated, probably even more so than their hearing counterparts. But Deaf people do not value "beating around the bush"; they prefer that the speaker get to the point quickly.

To understand another linguistic difference between hearing and Deaf cultures, it is important to recognize a key difference between spoken and signed languages generally. Both kinds of languages employ what might commonly be called "body language," such as facial expression, eye gaze, eyebrow raising and lowering, head tilts, torso shifts, and the like. In English and other spoken languages, however, whatever information speakers relay through body language is like the icing on the cake. It is not the heart of the message itself; at most it is a way of commenting upon the message. But in ASL and other countries' sign languages, this use of the body often *is* the message. A raised eyebrow might distinguish a question from a statement; the swing of a finger might make the singular into a plural; a slight shift in posture may change the present tense into the past. "Body language," in ASL, often carries important linguistic, cognitive, and indeed, grammatical information. This essential fact about ASL is often misunderstood by hearing people in ways that may make for unsatisfactory intercultural encounters.

Imagine sitting in a restaurant. Nearby are what appear to be two people scowling and signing at what seems to be a fast pace. You may interpret this to be an argument between two Deaf people; in fact, it is more likely that the two Deaf people are engrossed in a serious discussion or simply recreating a scene from an earlier occurrence. At the risk of oversimplifying, when a hearing person talks about her boss having gotten "mad" earlier in the day, the word alone carries the important message—one need not make an angry face. But in ASL, an angry face may be part of the composition of the sign for "MAD." Hearing people may mistakenly believe that Deaf people are awfully emotional and high strung!

NONVERBAL BEHAVIOR

We have already seen that some of the problems presented in intercultural communication between Deaf and hearing people come from a misunderstanding of where the language ends and the embellishment we call "body language" begins. In any culture, many norms exist governing nonverbal behaviors in communication, everything from use of time and space to what constitutes appropriate attire (Hall, 1969).

One variable that clearly separates Deaf and hearing cultures is eye contact. At one level, this is not only obvious but utterly predictable. The scene of the husband and wife who fight because he "never listens to her" (that is, does not pay attention, does not look at her, seems to be preoccupied with other tasks) but can nonetheless repeat every word she says is so often depicted that it is a cliché. The same encounter could not be depicted in regard to a Deaf couple—he would not be able to repeat every sign she made unless he looked at her (at least peripherally). Successful communication in ASL or any spatial language requires visual contact. Eye contact is not, to repeat an earlier metaphor, just the icing on the cake. It is not something we do just to be polite—we do it because it is a necessary part of the communication act itself. Deaf people, therefore, probably value eye contact even more than hearing people. Even when a Deaf person who uses her voice communicates with a hearing person (who would thus not need to actually "see" the message in order to understand it), the same norm holds true. Because Deaf culture is such a visual one, a hearing person who fails to reciprocate eye contact may be perceived as rude.

Differing norms surrounding touch can also cause intercultural miscommunications. Perhaps because Deaf people touch each other as a means of getting attention, they tend not to be so hypersensitive or squeamish about touch as hearing people sometimes seem to be. More than in the hearing culture, we hug a friend as a form of greeting and again upon leavetaking. Another greeting ritual used to demonstrate joviality is the "back-slap."

Deaf people use visual cues to obtain another person's attention. Switching lights on and off, waving, stamping the floor, throwing light objects, and tapping a person's shoulder are all acceptable ways to secure a Deaf person's attention. There is even a "chain tap" used by Deaf students in which they tap the person next to them and each person taps the next person until the specific person they want to talk to is reached. This is not to imply, however, that a person entering a predominantly Deaf scene will encounter flashing lights, flying objects, and a room full of waving hands. Rather, there are unwritten rules about getting attention, with a time and a place for each method. For instance, in the classroom, only the teacher can switch lights to get attention. Tapping another person can be done by touching shoulders or legs (if sitting), but not on the face. Waving hands in itself has a variety of rules. If the person you want to talk to is nearby, the hand-waving motion is smaller and specified in that person's direction, whereas if the person you want is further away, a more extravagant type of wave is needed.

VALUES

Values constitute what people within a culture believe and how they perceive the world, and thus values influence behavioral patterns. Values, likewise, play a role in Deaf culture and are manifested in both socializing patterns and in traditions.

Socializing Patterns

The majority of Deaf people (90 percent) have hearing parents, who for the most part have little or no knowledge of Deaf culture and are not fluent in ASL, which often results in the alienation of Deaf people from their families (Woodward, 1972). Hearing parents, upon finding out they have a deaf child, are often at a loss as to what should be done. Frequently, they rely upon the advice of medical doctors, audiologists, or educators who may or may not have adequate information about deafness. The advice often given to parents is to make their children as "hearing" as possible by teaching them to speak and lipread. This occurs despite the traditional failure of educational approaches using primarily speech and lipreading to educate deaf children.

For these and a number of other reasons, hearing parents often do not learn ASL, nor are they able to carry on a fluent conversation with their Deaf children. Most develop home-made gestures or use basic signs to communicate. Picture a Deaf child sitting at a dinner table in which a lively conversation ensues about the newest candidate to join the presidential race. Imagine then the frustration of a Deaf child asking what all the excitement was about and in response receiving a sentence or two summarizing the entire thirty-minute discussion. Or picture a Deaf child asking the reason why everyone was laughing and being told simply that someone had made a joke.

There is great variability, of course, in the ease or difficulty with which hearing families communicate with their Deaf members, but it is almost certain that the Deaf child will not receive the same amount of information as hearing members. The frustration that these children experience leads to further alienation from the family and also to stronger bonding with other Deaf children, bonding that usually begins in the residential school and continues throughout adult life. Consequently, residential schools for the Deaf, as well as sports organizations and clubs organized by Deaf people, hold special meaning within the Deaf community and are highly valued. Residential schools are often the first introduction to Deaf culture and ASL for Deaf children of hearing parents. It is in the dormitories of these schools that Deaf children freely interact with each other and as a result become encultured (Padden and Humphries, 1988).

When Deaf children become adults, they continue the pattern of maintaining close ties with other Deaf people. Sports events with Deaf participants are thus very large draws for participants and fans alike who primarily attend to socialize. During the summer, Deaf people flock to softball games, at which picnics are often held, and during the fall, they join bowling leagues. In the spring, they attend basketball and racquetball tournaments. Staff members or hearing visitors at bowling alleys or other host sites are often astonished at seeing the large numbers of Deaf people milling around, often filling up the place.

Most major cities in America have at least one "Deaf club," an organization that provides a regular social outlet for community members and sponsors numerous events. These social gatherings are highly valued by Deaf people as places where they are free to mingle with others without the many communicative and cultural restrictions they often face in daily life. Most Deaf people socialize primarily with other Deaf people, and between 85 and 95 percent marry Deaf spouses (Fay, 1898; Rainer, Altshuler, and Kallman, 1972).

Socializing is so highly cherished as a pastime that even business meetings cannot commence without Deaf people first having the opportunity to chat and to catch up on the latest news. Hearing people who are unfamiliar with this procedure often show impatience, requesting that they "get on with the meeting." This socializing ritual is not limited to the beginning of the function but is also evident at the end with the "long good-bye." Deaf people are known to remain at social functions long after the function is over, continuing to socialize—they very often will have said "good-bye" several times before they actually leave. Although this phenomenon also occurs with hearing people, it is a prominent occurrence with Deaf people almost every time there is a social function, including a visit to friends' homes.

Traditions

Traditions are an important part of Deaf culture. Deaf stories and jokes are passed down from generation to generation, from Deaf families, alumni of schools for the deaf, and Deaf clubs (Kannapell, 1985). Those in residential schools often pass down stories about administrators, faculty, and staff from years past. There are even "ghost" stories about haunted sites on campuses. The importance of passing down folklore in the Deaf culture is attributed to the fact that ASL is an unwritten language, which means Deaf people rely on signed stories rather than written documentation.

Gallaudet University, the world's only liberal arts college for deaf people (whether culturally Deaf or not), also the scene of the 1988 student protest for the university's first deaf president, has its fair share of such stories. One involves a former dean of women named Elizabeth Peet, who was reputedly very prim and proper. Dean Peet always segregated the male and female students at Gallaudet when they swam in the pool—the boys would go swimming first and have to leave the swimming pool before the girls could swim. But before the girls could even touch the pool, the water had to be drained and filled again with fresh water. Why? So that the girls would not get pregnant!

Deaf folklore is a tradition that takes on many forms. Many Deaf people play with signs much the way hearing people play with words (Kannapell, 1985). They include sign plays, success stories, ABC stories, narratives, jokes, and other folklore. ABC stories, for instance, are a creative form of telling stories in which the entire alphabet is used to weave together a tale. The "A" handshape (a loosely closed fist, with the thumb resting against the side of the index finger) might begin one such story as a knock on a door. The door opens, an action depicted by a movement of the "B" handshape (the open palm). But no one is inside, so the sign for "SEARCHING" is made with the "C" handshape (the slightly cupped palm, in this case moving back and forth in front of the searcher's eyes), and on it goes until the entire alphabet has been exhausted. There are Western stories, ghost stories, car racing stories, and many others.

Deaf and hearing humor is very different. The title of one recent article by Rutherford (1985)—"Funny in Deaf—Not in Hearing"—says it all. Hearing jokes are often not funny to Deaf people because they tend to be aurally based and center on the hearing perspective that is most closely related to sound, that is, rhymes, word plays, and puns. Deaf humor, on the other hand, is strongly based on visual perceptions. For instance, Deaf people might laugh hysterically at a horror scene because distorted expressions actors and actresses display can seem funny, especially when the background "scary" noises are not heard (Bienvenu, 1989a).

Deaf jokes also can serve as a source of Deaf empowerment. If the real world is one in which our deafness is used against us, the world painted by our humor allows us to survive, even flourish, sometimes by using people's hearing status against them. One such joke tells of a young couple who go to a motel on their honeymoon. The husband decides he needs to get something from the store and leaves. When he returns, he realizes he has forgotten their room number. It is late at night, and it is virtually impossible to distinguish among the rooms. What to do? He thinks for a moment, then walks to his car and leans heavily and repeatedly on the horn. The lights quickly come on in all the rooms—except one, of course. Aha—now he knows where his wife is waiting for him!

STEREOTYPES

An overview of Deaf people and their culture would not be complete without a discussion of stereotypes often held by people with little or no knowledge of Deaf culture. A lack of understanding about Deaf culture has led to a host of negative labels attributed to Deaf people. Deaf people have been labeled contradictorily by psychologists and other medical professionals as being aggressive and submissive, disobedient and shy, passionate and detached (Lane, 1988). The prevalent view from hearing society is that Deaf people are victims of pathology, that they are "disabled," have "communication disorders," and in general have "hearing problems."

Often, to the astonishment of hearing people, Deaf people do not feel "disabled." The ethnocentrism of many hearing people leads them to believe that Deaf people, upon being given a choice, would flock to seek new cures that would make them hear (for example, the cochlear implant). But the truth of the matter is that very few culturally Deaf people would ever want to change. Those who would embrace a "cure" tend to be either people who lost their hearing later in life and have little or no contact with Deaf people or parents who seek to "normalize" their children.

"Hearing impaired" is another label used by hearing people because they believe it to be a polite way of describing Deaf people. The term "hearing impaired" is even listed in the Associated Press style book of correct terminology, which is geared to promote the use of nonracist, nonsexist language (Bienvenu, 1989b). On the contrary, many Deaf people find the phrase offensive because of its implication that to be Deaf is to be "diseased" or "suffering" (Bienvenu, 1989b; Jordan, 1990).

Hearing people also often make the assumption that all Deaf people can learn to talk or wish to learn, but while there are a number of Deaf people who can speak well, there are far more who cannot or do not wish to do so. The fact is that many Deaf people have gone through years of intensive speech training. As Deaf adults, they often realize the futility of these many years of wasted efforts and do not appreciate the "help" that these hearing people profess to offer.

Another stereotype is that Deaf people are helpless: They need help in stores, restaurants, or other public places. Hearing people with limited signing ability have been known to "rush to the rescue" by attempting to interpret for the Deaf person. Even though this gesture is well intended, it is best not to offer help unless Deaf people specifically ask for it. Deaf people have developed survival skills in communicating with hearing people in public places thus far, and any effort to help may only hinder the process.

An awareness of these stereotypes will enable hearing people to develop a better understanding of Deaf people and will serve as a beginning guide for developing effective intercultural strategies.

DEVELOPING EFFECTIVE INTERCULTURAL INTERACTION

Researchers in the field of intercultural communication, including Arensberg and Niehoff; Barna; Bris-

lin and Pedersen; Gudykunst, Hammer, and Wiseman; Bochner; Cleveland and Mangone; and others (cited in Ruben, 1977), have suggested a number of behaviors to foster effective intercultural communication. They have been identified as the capacity (1) to communicate respect; (2) to be nonjudgmental; (3) to personalize one's knowledge and perceptions; (4) to display empathy; (5) to be flexible; (6) to take turns; and (7) to be tolerant of ambiguity. Let us see how these characteristics relate to interacting with Deaf people.

To communicate respect to Deaf people includes acknowledging their language and culture. Instead of encouraging Deaf people to speak and lipread when they have demonstrated a reluctance to do so, hearing people could show their respect by accepting whatever means of communication the Deaf person suggests: writing, using an interpreter, or any other means. Respect also includes the willingness to communicate directly with the Deaf person, rather than turning to another person standing nearby to secure help in communicating.

To be nonjudgmental is not to evaluate a Deaf person's worth on his or her ability to speak. All too often, Deaf people have related tales in which they were passed over for promotions or jobs in favor of Deaf people who spoke well. The ability to speak also has no relationship to their intelligence level, a misconception often held. It also means listening to the Deaf person and accepting his or her experiences at face value. Often hearing people will disregard a Deaf person's opinion in favor of those espoused by hearing people about Deaf people. In fact, many times hearing people are sought out as experts in the "field of deafness" even though this phenomenon rarely occurs in today's society with other minority communities.

Although Deaf people share a language and culture, they are still individuals with various experiences and backgrounds. Hearing people should be willing to broaden their knowledge base and be sensitive enough to perceive differences, rather than relying on erroneous stereotypes possibly shaped by the media or misinformation. Thus, a hearing person who has met a Deaf person should not expect the same behavior from the next Deaf person she or he meets, because each is unique and will react and communicate according to his or her own personal experiences. The Deaf person will also probably have had a different type of experience growing up in American society from that of the hearing person and will thus perceive the world differently. Hearing people cannot expect Deaf people to see the world and have the same values as they do.

The ability to show empathy is an important factor in effective communication with Deaf people. Ironically, people who are able to empathize with other minorities are often unable to carry over this empathy to Deaf people. For instance, people may readily accept the fact that native Americans have their own language but will ask Deaf people what ASL is and show skepticism when told that Deaf people have a culture as well. These same people do not question what the Navajo language or culture entails, or even what English is, for that matter, or whether other minorities have a culture. The best means of displaying empathy is to listen to Deaf people and accept them for what they are.

In showing the capacity to be flexible, keeping an open mind is instrumental. If hearing people can be receptive to new ideas, and to new ways of thinking, it will become easier to get along with Deaf people. It helps to keep in mind that Deaf people have had different experiences and are often more direct and have different communication patterns. In being flexible, hearing people should therefore not take offense if such behaviors are demonstrated. Rather, they can accept this behavior as cultural and in doing so enhance their appreciation of the diversity of cultures in this world.

Hearing people can have the patience to take turns, to give Deaf people the opportunity to finish conversations. Some hearing people assume they can explain things better because of the "communication barrier" and will proceed with the conversation as if the Deaf person were not there: Hearing mothers do this to their Deaf children; hearing co-workers do this to Deaf employees; and on it goes. Allowing the Deaf person to explain or to talk at his or her own pace will enable a more pleasant relationship.

Deaf people are accustomed to being in situations where hearing people cannot tolerate ambiguity. For instance, if a Deaf person signs with another person, the hearing person who does not know sign language will become impatient and demand to know what the conversation is about. These same hearing people will not have second thoughts about carrying on a conversation in spoken English with another hearing person in front of Deaf people without offering any explanation of what their conversation is about. Often hearing people will become nervous in interactions with Deaf people and either give up and leave, carry on very limited conversations, or giggle nervously and turn to another person for help.

CONCLUSION

The Deaf community, portrayed by this article as a culture little known to most people, is a uniquely American entity. Deaf people are a cultural group in which American Sign Language is the primary language, and, as with any culture, they share nonverbal behaviors, values, socializing patterns, and traditions. In the general perception of Deaf people, stereotypes abound. It was suggested here that striving toward the seven skills identified by Ruben (1977) might serve to bridge the communication gap between Deaf and hearing cultures so that hearing people can vastly enrich and broaden their perception of the world by learning to appreciate the Deaf culture that is all around them.

NOTE

1. The author wishes to thank M. J. Bienvenu, Co-Director of the Bicultural Center, and Dr. Barbara Kannapell, a Deaf Culture Consultant, for their helpful suggestions and input. A special thank you to Carla Mathers and Dr. Paul Siegel for their careful and thorough editing of the manuscript.

REFERENCES

Baker, C., and Padden, C. (1978). *American Sign Language: A Look at Its History, Structure, and Community.* Silver Spring, Md.: TJ Publishers.

Baker-Shenk, C. (1983). "A Microanalysis of the Non-manual Components of Questions in American Sign Language." Unpublished doctoral dissertation, University of California, Berkeley.

Baker-Shenk, C. (1985). "The Facial Behavior of Deaf Signers: Evidence of a Complex Language." *American Annals of the Deaf, 130,* 297–304.

Bienvenu, M. J. (1989a). "Reflections of American Deaf Culture in Deaf Humor." *The Bicultural Center News, 17,* 1–3.

Bienvenu, M. J. (1989b). An Open Letter to Alumni, Students of Gallaudet, and Friends. *The Bicultural Center News, 18,* 1–2.

Fay, E. A. (1898). *Marriages of the Deaf in America.* Washington, D.C.: Volta Bureau.

Hall, E. T. (1969). *The Hidden Dimension.* Garden City, N.Y.: Anchor Press, Doubleday.

Jordan, I. K. (1990). "Together We Stand." *The Bicultural Center News, 21,* 5.

Kannapell, B. (1985). *Orientation to Deafness: A Handbook and Resource Guide.* Washington, D.C.: Gallaudet.

Lane, H. (1988). "Paternalism & Deaf People: An Open Letter to Mme. Umuvyeyi." *Sign Language Studies, 60,* 251–270.

Padden, C., and Humphries, T. (1988). *Deaf in America: Voices from a Culture.* Cambridge, Mass.: Harvard University Press.

Rainer, J. D., Altshuler, K. Z., and Kallman, F. J. (1972). *Family and Mental Health Problems in a Deaf Population.* New York: State Psychiatric Institute, Columbia.

Ruben, B. D. (1988). "Human Communication and Cross-Cultural Effectiveness." In L. A. Samovar and R. E. Porter (Eds.), *Intercultural Communication: A Reader* (5th ed.) Belmont, Calif.: Wadsworth. (Reprinted from *International and Intercultural Communication Annual,* 1977, *4,* 98–105.)

Rutherford, S. (1985). "Funny in Deaf—Not in Hearing." In M. McIntire (Ed.), *Proceedings of the 1985 RID Convention.* Silver Springs, Md.: RID Publications.

Woodward, J. (1972). "Implications for Sociolinguistics Research Among the Deaf." *Sign Language Studies, 1,* 1–7.

Gender and Communication: An Intimate Relationship

JUDY C. PEARSON

Are men or women more likely to use the words "puce," "aquamarine," "ecru," and "mauve"? If a speaker discussed such matters as "carburetors," "pistons," "overhead cams," and "cylinders," would you guess that the speaker was male or female? Is the chief executive officer of a Fortune 500 company more likely to be a man or a woman? In almost any organization, are men or women more likely to be chosen as secretaries? Every day you make observations and predictions about people's gender on the basis of their communicative behaviors and the roles they play in our culture. You are not unfamiliar, therefore, with the relationship between gender and communication, but you may not realize that a great deal of theorizing and research has gone into this topic.

Although interest in the relationship between biological sex and communication may be traced to the beginning of this century (Stopes, 1908), the past two decades have produced the bulk of the research on gender and communication. The relationships among women, men, and communication are complex and bear careful scrutiny. This essay will consider some of the issues that allow us to conclude that an intimate relationship exists between gender and communication.

This article was written especially for this sixth edition. All rights reserved. Permission to reprint must be obtained from the author and the publisher. Ms. Pearson is a Professor of Interpersonal Communication at Ohio University, Athens, Ohio.

HOW ARE GENDER AND COMMUNICATION RELATED?

In order to understand how gender and communication are related, we must understand the history of the research in this area. You may have already observed that we are using the term "gender" rather than the more familiar word "sex." The choice of the word "gender" is deliberate and important for our discussion. Before the mid-1970s, the term "sex" was used to refer to biological differences that existed between people. Studies that considered "sex differences" simply categorized people on the basis of their biological differences and observed differences in communicative behavior. For example, we observed that women smile more frequently than men (Argyle, 1975), that men speak more loudly than do women (Markel, Prebor, and Brandt, 1972), that women are more likely to be observed or watched than are men (Argyle and Williams, 1969), and that men are more likely than women to interrupt others (Zimmerman and West, 1975).

In 1974, Sandra Bem created a new conceptualization of sex. Before this time, people were categorized on masculinity and femininity measures as being more or less of each of these measures. In other words, masculinity was placed at one end of the continuum and femininity was placed at the other end, as illustrated below.

MASCULINITY   FEMININITY

An individual, through a series of questions, would be categorized as either masculine or feminine or somewhere between these two extremes. We should observe, however, that the more masculine one indicated that he or she was, the less feminine he or she would be. An individual could not be high in both masculinity and femininity nor low in both categories.

In private conversations, Bem has explained that she felt limited by this conceptualization of masculinity and femininity. She perceived herself as possessing a number of masculine traits and a number of feminine traits. In other words, she felt that she should score high in both masculinity and femininity. Instead, when she was categorized, her score indicated that she was somewhere between masculinity and femininity and was thus viewed as neither feminine nor masculine.

In the Bem Sex Role Inventory, Bem (1974) created a new way to measure and conceive of sex roles. She suggested that masculinity and femininity are separate dimensions and that one might be high in masculinity and low in femininity (masculine), low in masculinity and high in femininity (feminine), high in masculinity and high in femininity (androgynous), or low in masculinity and low in femininity (undifferentiated). This view is depicted in the following figure.

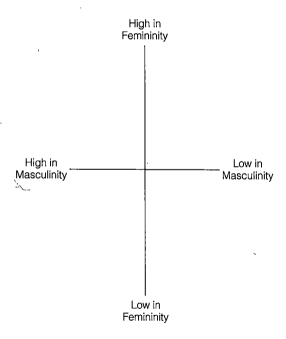

Although Bem's conceptualization may appear to be a fairly simplistic change, her perspective radically altered the way women and men were categorized. In the past, women and men were viewed as different because of biological traits. Bem suggests that people should be categorized on the extent to which they have internalized societal standards for masculine and feminine behaviors. Thus, a biological male might be seen as highly feminine or a biological female might be viewed as very masculine. As sex became a psychological, rather than a physical, variable, we began to talk about gender rather than sex. Sex refers to biological differences between people; gender refers to internalized predispositions about masculine and feminine roles. As you will see, these differences are critical for our understanding of gender and communication.

Communication Creates Gender

Communication is related to gender in two ways. First, to a large extent, communication creates gender. How does communication create gender? Our communicative exchanges tell us what our roles are and encourage or discourage us from internalizing predispositions that relate to masculinity or femininity. Early theorists, such as William James, Charles Cooley, John Dewey, and I. A. Thomas, all contributed to a theory that George Herbert Mead (1934) originated. That theory—symbolic interactionism—has important implications for us. Mead felt that people were actors, not reactors. He suggested that people develop through three stages. The preparatory phase includes the stage in which infants imitate others by mirroring. The baby may wash off a surface, put on mommy's or daddy's shoes, or pat the dog, though the child does not necessarily understand the imitated acts.

In the play stage, the child actually plays the role of others. She may pretend to be mommy, daddy, the postal carrier, a fire fighter, a nurse, or a doctor. Each role is played independently; the behaviors are not integrated into a single set of role behaviors. In other words, the child does not play a superwoman who is a mother, a wife, a runner, an airplane pilot, a writer, and a teacher.

In the game stage, the child responds simultaneously in a generalized way to several others. The child generalizes a composite role by considering all others' definitions of self. The person thus develops a unified role from which he or she sees the self, a perception that is the overall way that other people see the individual. People unify their self-concepts by internalizing this composite view, so that the self-picture emerges from years of symbolically interacting, or communicating, with others.

Your integrated self will tend toward the behaviors others encourage you to perform and will tend away from behaviors that others discourage you from performing. From the time we are born, we are treated differently because of our genitalia. We dress male and female babies in different kinds and colors of clothing. Parents respond differently to male and female infants (Bell and Carver, 1980). We describe male and female babies with different adjectives: boys are strong, solid, and independent, while girls are loving, cute, and sweet. People describe identical behavior on the part of infants differently if they are told the infant is a "boy" or a "girl" (Condry and Condry, 1976). Preschool children observe commercials and cartoons on television, are read books, and play with toys in which "appropriate" sex roles are depicted.

Gender is Related to Our Communicative Behaviors

A second way that gender and communication are related is in our specific use of verbal and nonverbal codes. You know that different roles invite different languages. For example, terms like "bits," "RAM," "ROM," "motherboard," "modem," "memory," "monitor," "hard disk," "CPT," "CRT," and "CPU" are common in language about computers. Similarly, words like "coma," "carcinoma," "cardiovascular," "chemotherapy," "colostomy," and "capillary" are common in the language of medicine.

Masculine and feminine individuals use different languages, and they put their words together differently. Maybe you never considered that sex roles place people in different subcultures, just as race and age do. All subcultures create special languages. (Adolescents, for instance, purposefully talk in ways that their parents do not understand. "Cool" and "neat" are succeeded by "tubular," "groaty to the max," "I'm so sure," and "mega-hard," which in turn are supplanted by "rad," "wick," or "in your dreams.") Feminine and masculine people similarly establish their own way of talking as a result of being separate subcultures. Why do subcultures establish separate languages? At least two reasons may be offered: (1) A special language is developed in order to conduct its function or business and (2) a special language allows a subculture to symbolize its identity as a subculture. Feminine people may be more likely to know color terms such as "ecru" and "mauve" because they use these terms in their work, just as masculine types may use terms related to motors and engines in their work. Furthermore, feminine individuals might overuse adjectives to demonstrate that they are part of a feminine subgroup; masculine individuals may rely upon four-letter swear words to clarify their subculture.

A caveat is in order. When subcultures develop separate languages, they often understand each other's language; they may even use the alternative language when they are in their own subculture. For example, we might associate traditional four-letter swear words with masculine individuals, but feminine types understand the terms and may use them as well—in the exclusive company of other feminine persons. Masculine individuals may not touch each other in a caring way in mixed company, but they certainly rely on hugging, stroking, and touching on the football field.

Similarly, people may feel free to engage in out-of-role behavior when they are within the safety of an established relationship but not in the company of acquaintances and strangers. Dindia, Fitzpatrick, and Williamson (1986), for instance, showed that wives are more likely to behave in a submissive manner with males to whom they are not married although they behave in a dominant way with their own spouses.

On the other hand, recent evidence suggests that women and men may be more likely to engage in gender-linked language with members of their own sex and less likely to do so with members of the opposite sex. Mulac, Wiemann, Widenmann, and Gibson (1988) demonstrated this finding and suggested that women and men both tend to reflect the language of the person with whom they are speaking. This interactive effect suggests that male and female language may approach convergence, rather than divergence, in mixed-sex groups. Their research demonstrates that not only the speaker's gender but also the gender of the listener may be essential to include in predictions about the relationship between gender and communication.

With these considerations in mind, what are a few of the differences between the two subcultures? Feminine people can be generally characterized as more expressive, nurturing, and relational. For example, Bonaguro and Pearson (1986) determined that feminine individuals are more animated than masculine and undifferentiated identities and more relaxed than androgynous and masculine individuals. Serafini and Pearson (1984) similarly showed that feminine types are more likely to be relational. The feminine identity is generally higher in empathy, caring, and nurturing (McMillan, Clifton, McGrath, and Gale, 1977; Wiggins and Holzmuller, 1981), warmth (Tellegen and Lubinski, 1983), and expressiveness, which includes blends of interpersonally related traits (Spence, 1983). Feminine females report that they self-disclose, or provide personal information, less than do androgynous females; masculine men have lower disclosure scores than do androgynous men (Greenblatt, Hasenauer, and Freimuth, 1980).

Although women have been consistently shown to smile more than men, one's masculinity or femininity affects this nonverbal behavior, too (LaFrance and Cramen, 1980; Halberstadt, Hayes, and Pike, 1988). Further, people perceive smiling behavior to be indicative of higher levels of femininity and friendliness (Halberstadt and Saitta, 1987) and of politeness and warmth (Deutsch, LaBaron, and Fryer, 1987).

By contrast, masculine individuals tend to be more instrumental and dominant. Masculine individuals are more argumentative (Rancer and Dierks-Stewart, 1985) and higher on dominance (Tellegen and Lubinski, 1983). They score higher on assertiveness, which includes independence, decisiveness, and dealing with self-assertiveness (Spence, 1983). Finally, masculine types are more apt to be goal-oriented (Serafini and Pearson, 1984).

Although masculinity has generally been associated with high self-esteem (see, for example,

Whitley, 1983; Whitley, 1988), recent examinations have shown that while masculinity is highly correlated with positive adjustment measures such as self-esteem, lower anxiety, and lower loneliness, it is also related to less desirable traits such as Type A behavior and aggression (Payne, 1987). The strong relationship between masculinity and self-esteem may thus be viewed as a mixed bag. (For a comprehensive review of gender and sex differences in communication behaviors, see Pearson, 1985.)

WHAT PROBLEMS EXIST IN GENDER AND COMMUNICATION?

As you might guess, the area of gender and communication is in upheaval. At least three problems exist that account for our difficulty in coming to grips with effective and appropriate communication across these subcultures. First, people still assume that gender and sex are synonyms for the same commodity. Second, we often confuse our perceptions of behavior with actual behavior. Third, both communication and our American culture have a masculine bias.

Gender and Sex Are Presumed to Be Synonymous

While gender and sex are highly related (men are more likely to be masculine than are women and women are more likely to be feminine than are men), they were never identical constructs and have become increasingly disparate in recent times. Furthermore, a great number of people are androgynous (possess both male and female qualities) or are undifferentiated (possess neither male nor female qualities). Let us consider how recent changes have impacted on the differences in the conceptions of gender and sex.

Our world and the roles of women and men are undergoing rapid changes, but our interactions do not acknowledge these changes. To a great extent we tend to live in the past. We behave on the basis of the naturalistic fallacy: "What is (or has been) is

what should be." For example, if you ask people in Iowa how farming should be performed, they will tell you that it should occur on relatively small sets of acreage owned by individual families. If you ask people in New York who should control the major networks, they will tell you it should be persons trained in telecommunications and broadcast journalism. But family farms are nearly a thing of the past and NBC and ABC are owned, operated, and controlled by large multinational corporations.

Our changing world also creates an inability to keep up and to "know" people. We increasingly communicate with people on the basis of cultural and sociological information, and we categorize them simplistically on the basis of surface or demographic cues (biological sex) rather than knowing them interpersonally (on the basis of unique and idiosyncratic personal characteristics, including their gender role). In days gone by, you might have communicated only with members of your own community and family. You would have known a great deal about the men and women with whom you interacted. You would have known that you do not talk about sex with your aunt, that you should hug your grandparents, and that you must treat your teachers with respect. You might not have traveled to other cities, states, and nations. Today such travel is commonplace, and you are called upon to interact quickly with strangers and acquaintances in a wide variety of new settings.

We make errors in our assessments of other people in brief encounters for a variety of reasons. For instance, we may rely upon implicit personality theory, which suggests that our own experience and assumptions about human nature are shared by others. We assume that everyone has a high achievement motivation and competes to win, and we do not understand that many people develop a fear of failure. We may make the fundamental attribution error, which is the tendency to underestimate situational influences on behavior and to attribute behavior to internal personal characteristics. You assume that the bartender in the place where you drink beer is cold and closed mouthed, and you do not recognize that her job description and her negative past experiences with others in bars invite such decorum.

In our interactions with women and men, we are most likely to err, however, on the basis of four other errors in person perception. The first error occurs when we stereotype (apply a generalized belief about some group of people to individuals belonging to that group without considering differences among group members). For example, we assume that all men are cold and unfeeling because one men's group has shown these characteristics. The second error occurs when we rely upon social roles (assume that persons possess characteristics associated with their roles in society). For instance, we assume that all mothers are nurturing. The third problem arises when we make logical errors (assume that because a person has one characteristic he or she will have other characteristics that "go together"). For instance, we assume that women who dress like "ladies" will also talk like them. The fourth misconception comes when we engage in wishful thinking (seeing others as we would like them to be rather than as they are). For example, we assume our husbands will be like our fathers.

Perceptions of Behavior Are Confused with Actual Behavior

A second problem is that we often confuse our perceptions of behavior with actual behavior. In other words, we may view a behavior as negative when displayed by a woman, but we may judge the same behavior to be positive when enacted by a man. For instance, a businesswoman might be labeled "aggressive, pushy, and argumentative," while her male counterpart may be viewed as "ambitious, assertive, and independent." Countless studies have demonstrated that when women and men engaged in identical behavior, the behavior was devalued for the woman. For example, Goldberg (1968), in a classic study, showed that an identical essay was given a higher grade when respondents believed it to be written by a man and a lower grade when respondents believed it to be written by a woman. Further-

more, both women and men demonstrated their prejudice toward women.

One reason that we confuse perceptions with behaviors comes from the literature on gender and communication itself. In all areas of inquiry, we must ask the question that Whitney Houston made famous in her song, "How will I know?" In the area of social science, and especially in gender and communication, this question is particularly critical. Social science research can rely on self-perceptions, perceptions of others, or on actual behavioral observations. In some cases, researchers have relied upon the perceptions of others to determine how women and men communicate. For instance, people were asked if they believed that women or men speak more often. Although later behavioral research suggested that men talk more than women (Swacker, 1975), most people, when asked, guessed that women talked more than men. Similarly, in research on whether masculine or feminine managers are viewed as more successful, researchers have often asked subordinates and others in the work environment whose perceptions, although they might be valuable, may also be value-laden, relying more on stereotypes than on actual observations.

Some research on gender and communication has relied upon individuals' self-reports or their self-perception. People have made estimates of their own communicative behaviors, but as we have learned more recently, our self-reports may be based more on our notions of the ideal, or of a prototype that we hold, than on our actual behaviors (Hample, 1984; Pavitt and Haight, 1986). Or we may be responding on the basis of social-desirability. In addition, because of the passage of time, we often forget how we behaved (Sulloway and Christensen, 1983).

Some recent research has begun to measure people's actual communicative behaviors to determine the extent to which women and men communicate differently or similarly. Although these research reports are fewer in number than are the studies that have relied upon perceptions or self-report data, they suggest that the differences between women and men may be fewer than we once believed, that they may be based on factors other than biological sex as suggested above, and that the rationale offered may be different than we originally posited.

For example, if you ask most people if women or men use more profanity, hostility, and expletives, they would probably guess that men use more of these forms. However, Staley (1978) tested that commonsense view. She asked students between the ages of eighteen and forty-seven to complete a questionnaire that listed a series of emotional situations. In each case, she asked the respondents to report the expletive they would use, to predict the expletive a member of the opposite sex would use, and to define each expletive that they provided. Surprisingly, she found that men and women averaged about the same number of expletives per questionnaire. She did find a great difference in predicted response, however. Men predicted far fewer expletives for women and women predicted far more expletives for men. Both women and men judged the female expletive use as weaker than male expletive use, even when the terms were identical. Staley thus demonstrated that women and men may be more alike than different on the usage of expletives; nonetheless, people still perceive their behavior differently.

None of these methods of learning about gender and communication is inherently superior to the others, but we should note that each provides us with different answers. Sometimes we wish to know how an individual perceives himself or herself. In other cases, we may find others' perceptions of people as important. Often, we wish to determine the actual behavior in which people engage. Always, we want to be clear that our means for making assessments are consistent with our research goal. Perhaps more important, we wish to ensure that people do not confuse perceptions with behaviors.

Our Culture and Our Communication Have a Masculine Bias

A third problem that is relevant to gender and communication is that both communication and our culture have a male bias. An increasing amount of research demonstrates that the symbols we use to communicate are man-made. The language that we use was created primarily by men and for men—the words we have available reflect male experience and encourage male domination.

Kramarae (1981) has proposed that female/male communication can best be understood in terms of the muted group theory. This theory suggests that women are a muted (or silenced) group because of their exclusion from the creation of human symbols. Basically, she explains that males perceive the world and then create symbols to represent their experience. Since women's experiences are different and they are not allowed to create an alternative set of symbols, women are muted. Eventually, women learn to use the male symbols, but they are only useful insofar as women are willing to see the world through "male eyes."

What are some obvious examples of man-made words? We might consider the language of business. Although the business world may be viewed as an area that is open to both women and men, when you listen carefully you find that it is primarily a "male club." Many business clichés, for example, come straight from sports—a traditionally male activity. If you want to be successful, you have to "keep your eye on the ball," be a "boy wonder," "keep your head down," be a "team player," be a "pinch hitter," and "tackle the job." What do you avoid? You don't want to be in the "penalty box," "under fire," "under the gun," in the "cellar," a "disqualified player," "caught with your pants down," or have a "jock mentality."

We can also build the argument that language is male dominated when we deal with the so-called generic pronouns. When we talk about generic people, which pronoun do we choose? In general, people use the male form to refer to both men and women. We use "he," "his," and "him" to refer to men unless they refer to both men and women. We never use "she" and "her" to refer to women, and to women and men. We may ask why these forms are not equally appropriate.

Language does not serve all of its users equally well. Women are left out far more often than men, but both men and women find that language limits the expression of our experience. Students of gender and communication have created "sexlets," which are sniglets about male and female experience for which our language has no words. A few examples may provide you with an illustration of words that are not currently within our everyday usage. First, from the women came "sexpectations"—when a man takes a woman out for a nice dinner, maybe a movie, and then expects sex at the end of the evening—and "PMS'ed off"—the frustration women feel with their boyfriends who always claim that when they're angry, they must be expecting their period. The men suggested "chronoloneliness"—how one male stated that he felt when he had not seen his girlfriend for a long time—and "condomnesia"—the moment, mostly in high school, when you finally get your girlfriend ready for the big moment and she asks if you have protection and you must admit that you forgot.

Our research has similarly been flawed in that it has encouraged a masculine bias. The American culture, as-we-observed, is one which is masculinist. In other words, male values, attitudes, and perspectives dominate. Our government, our industry, and most public organizations are headed by men. Even our private associations, including friendships and family life, are dominated-by-men. As a result our investigations of women in male-dominated cultures have been, at the very least, biased. Wood, McMahan, and Stacks (1984) observe:

the contexts for the bulk of study on women's communication are invariably male-contexts—task groups, businesses, organizations. The tendency to study masculine activities and environments, then, achieves two outcomes. First, it constitutes an implicit argument for the importance of masculine issues, enterprises, and settings and a corresponding argument for the unimportance of feminine concerns, activities, and contexts. Second, it distorts descriptions, assessment, and understanding of women's communication by consistently observing it in alien environments (p. 41).

The placement of our inquiry, then, has encouraged the continuation of a male-dominated social order. Deaux (1984) observes, "Some tasks may not be neutral arenas in which to test possible differences" (p. 107). We are wise to heed the words of Kramarae (1981), who observed, "Social scientific research is not impersonal, apolitical, and factual, but interpretative" (p. vi).

HOW CAN WE SOLVE THE PROBLEMS OF GENDER AND COMMUNICATION?

Can we solve the dilemmas we face in the area of gender and communication? We can if we are willing to engage in three practices. First, we must separate our perceptions of the behaviors of ourselves or of other people from the behaviors that we, or they, actually exhibit. Second, we need to view sex and gender as distinctive constructs. Third, we need to understand the role of the masculinist culture and how it shapes both our perceptions and our behaviors.

Separate Our Perceptions of Behaviors from Actual Behaviors

We must recognize that our perceptions of another person's behavior may vary dramatically with his or her actual behavior. At the very minimum, we must be clearly cognizant of the level of our discussions. When we observe, predict, and evaluate the behavior of others, we must understand how our own attitudes, values, and perceptions intervene.

The area of organizational communication provides an example. Within the past decade, researchers have begun to examine the role of women-as-leaders-and-managers. In general, in organizational research, we tend to use outcome variables such as productivity to determine the influence of independent variables like information availability, upward and downward communication, and openness. However, when the influence of gender in the organization is investigated, people's *perceptions*-of-them-in-their positions are used. For instance, we do not study whether productivity increases or decreases when women serve as managers; instead we ask others if they prefer to work for a man or a woman. Given the current state of affairs, it is not difficult to guess which sex they prefer.

Research on gender and communication is no better. Too often we assume that male communication is standard. We begin with a male model of communication and then we look at a female's communication to see how it differs from the male, or we study women's communication in clearly male contexts—like the male workplace. We also assume that women's behaviors determine their effectiveness. In other words, we don't take into account that women are often devalued simply because they are women. The most competent woman may be viewed negatively simply because she is a woman.

View Sex and Gender as Distinctive Constructs

Second, we need to view sex and gender differentially. We are in the midst of a paradigm shift concerning sex and gender. Intercultural communication students are familiar with the notion of "passing," in which members of lower-status groups sometimes attempt to "pass" as members of higher-status groups. (For instance, light-skinned blacks sometimes attempt to "pass" as white.) In the same way, many women in our contemporary society have attempted to "pass" as men. For example, a number of female managers have become successful by adopting masculine characteristics. Similarly, female graduate students will often try to outperform their male counterparts. In the professional ranks, too, including medicine and the law, women regularly are more masculine in their behavior than are the men with whom they work.

There are more dual-career couples now than single-career couples. While some of us may applaud the opportunities that women are provided to work outside the home as well as within it, we should recognize what is occurring. Often, biologically, the dual-career marriages include a man and a woman, but behaviorally, the couple is made up of two masculine types.

Changes in our social groupings encourage us to consider "sex" and "gender" as separate constructs.

We cannot assume that women are "feminine" nor that men are "masculine." In some instances, just the opposite is the case.

Understand the Role of the Masculinist Culture

Third, we need to understand the role of the masculinist culture and how it shapes both our perceptions and our behaviors. Men are in charge of our culture, and masculine values and traits are generally viewed as superior to feminine values and traits. When women "pass" as men, they may gain momentary success in the workplace at low-level positions, but they may never become the CEO of a Fortune 500 company. Furthermore, they may be losing far more by discarding their feminine side. Masculine behaviors have been shown to lead to disability and physical destruction; for example, heart attacks, strokes, and many forms of cancer are more prevalent in men than in women. As women have gained opportunities and experiences, however, their rates of death from these diseases have similarly increased. We must understand the inherent sexism that defines our American culture and the values that are associated with the masculine perspective. Furthermore, we must consider whether we wish to continue the status quo.

SUMMARY

In this essay you learned about some of the theorizing and research that has gone on in the area of gender and communication. You determined how gender and communication are related, the problems that have occurred in considering gender and communication, and how we might solve some of those problems in our everyday interactions as well as in our research on this topic. Gender and communication have been shown to share an intimate relationship.

REFERENCES

Argyle, M. (1975). *Bodily Communication*. New York: International Universities Press.

Argyle, M., and Williams, M. (1969). "Observer or Observed? A Reversible Perspective in Person Perception." *Sociometry, 32*, 396–412.

Bell, N. J., and Carver, W. (1980). "A Reevaluation of Gender Label Effects: Expectant Mothers' Responses to Infants." *Child Development, 51*, 925–927.

Bem, S. (1974). "The Measurement of Psychological Androgyny." *Journal of Consulting and Clinical Psychology, 42*, 155–162.

Bonaguro, E. W., and Pearson, J. C. (November 1986). *The Relationship Between Communicator Style, Argumentativeness, and Gender.* Paper presented to the Speech Communication Association, Chicago, Ill.

Condry, J., and Condry, S. (1976). "Sex Differences: A Study of the Eye of the Beholder." *Child Development, 47*, 812–819.

Deaux, K. (1984). "From Individual Differences to Social Categories." *American Psychologist*, 105–116.

Deutsch, F. M., LeBaron, D., and Fryer, M. M. (1987). "What Is in a Smile?" *Psychology of Women Quarterly, 11*, 341–351.

Dindia, K., Fitzpatrick, M. A., and Williamson, R. (November 1986). *Communication and Control in Spouse Versus Stranger Interaction.* Paper presented to the Speech Communication Association, Chicago, Ill.

Goldberg, P. (1968). "Are Women Prejudiced against Women?" *Transaction, 6*, 28.

Greenblatt, L., Hasenauer, J., and Freimuth, V. (1980). "Psychological Sex Type and Androgyny in a Study of Communication Variables." *Human Communication Research, 6*, 117–129.

Halberstadt, A. G., Hayes, C. W., and Pike, K. M. (1988). "Gender and Gender Role Differences in Smiling and Communication Consistency." *Sex Roles, 19*, 589–604.

Halberstadt, A. G., and Saitta, M. B. (1987). "Gender, Nonverbal Behavior, and Dominance: A Test of the Theory." *Journal of Personality and Social Psychology, 53*, 257–272.

Hample, D. (1984). "On the Use of Self-Reports." *Journal of the American Forensic Association, 20*, 140–153.

Kramarae, C. (1981). *Women and Men Speaking.* Rowley, Mass: Newbury House Publishers.

LaFrance, M., and Carmen, B. (1980). "The Nonverbal Display of Psychological Androgyny." *Journal of Personality and Social Psychology, 38*, 36–49.

Markel, N., Prebor, L., and Brandt, J. (1972). "Biosocial Factors in Dyadic Communication: Sex and Speaking Intensity." *Journal of Personality and Social Responsibility, 23*, 686–690.

McMillan, J., Clifton, A. K., McGrath, D., and Gale, W. S. (1977). "Women's Language: Uncertainty or Interpersonal Sensitivity and Emotionality?" *Sex Roles, 3*, 545–559.

Mead, G. H. (1934). *Mind, Self, and Society.* Chicago: University of Chicago Press.

Mulac, A., Wiemann, J. M., Widenmann, S. J., and Gibson, T. W. (1988). "Male/Female Language Differences and Effects in Same-Sex and Mixed-Sex Dyads: The Gender-Linked Language Effect." *Communication Monographs, 55*, 315–335.

Pavitt, C., and Haight, L. (1986). "Implicit Theories of Communicative Competence: Situational and Competence Level Differences in Judgments of Prototype and Target." *Communication Monographs, 53*, 221–235.

Payne, F. D. (1987). "'Masculinity,' 'Femininity,' and the Complex Construct of Adjustment." *Sex Roles, 17*, 359–374.

Pearson, J. C. (1985). *Gender and Communication.* Dubuque, Iowa: William C. Brown Company.

Rancer, A., and Dierks-Stewart, K. (1985). "The Influence of Sex and Sex-Role Orientation on Trait Argumentativeness." *The Journal of Personality Assessment, 49*, 61–70.

Serafini, D., and Pearson, J. (1984). "Leadership Behavior and Sex Role Socialization: Two Sides of the Same Coin." *The Southern Speech Communication Journal, 49*, 396–405.

Spence, J. T. (1983). "Comment on Lubinski, Tellegen, and Butcher's 'Masculinity, Femininity, and Androgyny Viewed and Assessed as Distinct Concepts.'" *Journal of Personality and Social Psychology, 44*, 440–446.

Staley, C. (1978). "Male-Female Use of Expletives: A Heck of a Difference in Expectations." *Anthropological Literature, 20*, 367–380.

Stopes, C. C. (1908). *The Sphere of "Man": In Relation to That of "Woman" in the Constitution.* London: T. Fisher Unwin.

Sulloway, M., and Christensen, A. (1983). "Couples and Families as Participant Observers of Their Interaction." *Advances in Family Intervention, Assessment, and Theory, 3,* 119–160.

Swacker, M. (1975). "The Sex of the Speaker as a Sociolinguistic Variable." In B. Thorne and N. Henley (Eds.), *Language and Sex: Difference and Dominance.* Rowley, Mass.: Newbury House Publishers.

Tellegen, A., and Lubinski, D. (1983). "Some Methodological Comments on Labels, Traits, Interaction, and Types in the Study of 'Femininity' and 'Masculinity': Reply to Spence." *Journal of Personality and Social Psychology, 44,* 447–455.

Whitley, B. E., Jr. (1983). "Sex Role Orientation and Self-Esteem: A Critical Meta-Analytic Review." *Journal of Personality and Social Psychology, 44,* 765–778.

Whitley, B. E., Jr. (1988). "Masculinity, Femininity, and Self-Esteem: A Multitrait-Multimethod Analysis." *Sex Roles, 18,* 419–431.

Wiggins, J. S., and Holzmuller, A. (1981). "Further Evidence on Androgyny and Interpersonal Flexibility." *Journal of Research in Personality, 15,* 67–80.

Wood, J. T., McMahan, E. M., and Stacks, D. W. (1984). "Research on Women's Communication: Critical Assessment and Recommendations." In D. L. Fowlkes and C. S. McClure (Eds.), *Feminist Visions: Toward a Transformation of the Liberal Arts Curriculum.* University, Ala.: University of Alabama Press.

Zimmerman, D., and West, C. (1975). "Sex Roles, Interruptions and Silences in Conversation." In B. Thorne and N. Henley (Eds.), *Language and Sex: Difference and Dominance.* Rowley, Mass.: Newbury House Publishers.

America's Emerging Gay Culture

RANDALL E. MAJORS

A gay culture, unique in the history of homosexuality, is emerging in America. Gay people from all walks of life are forging new self-identity concepts, discovering new political and social power, and building a revolutionary new life style. As more people come out, identify themselves as gay, and join with others to work and live as openly gay people, a stronger culture takes shape with each passing year.

There have always been homosexual men and women, but never before has there emerged the notion of a distinct "culture" based on being gay.[1] A useful way to analyze this emerging gay culture is to observe the communication elements by which gay people construct their life styles and social institutions. Lesbians and gay men, hereafter considered together as gay people, are creating a new community in the midst of the American melting pot.[2] They are building social organizations, exercising political power, and solidifying a unique sense of identity—often under repressive and sometimes dangerous conditions. The following essay is an analysis of four major communication elements of the American gay culture: the gay neighborhood, gay social groups, gay symbols, and gay meeting behavior. These communication behaviors will demonstrate the vibrancy and joy that a new culture offers the American vision of individual freedom and opportunity.

This article was written especially for this sixth edition. All rights reserved. Permission to reprint must be obtained from the author and the publisher. Mr. Majors teaches at California State University, Hayward.

THE GAY NEIGHBORHOOD

Most cultural groups find the need to mark out a home turf. American social history has many examples of ethnic and social groups who create their own special communities, whether by withdrawing from the larger culture or by forming specialized groups within it. The utopian communities of the Amish or Shakers are examples of the first, and ghetto neighborhoods in large urban areas are examples of the latter.

This need to create a group territory fulfills several purposes for gay people. First, a gay person's sense of identity is reinforced if there is a special place that is somehow imbued with "gayness." When a neighborhood becomes the home of many gay people, the ground is created for a feeling of belonging and sharing with others. Signs of gayness, whether overt symbols like rainbow flags or more subtle cues such as merely the presence of other gay people on the street, create the feeling that a certain territory is special to the group and hospitable to the group's unique values.

How do you know when a neighborhood is gay? As with any generality, the rule of thumb is that "enough gay people in a neighborhood and it becomes a gay neighborhood." Rarely do gay people want to paint the streetlamps lavender, but the presence of many more subtle factors gives a gay character to an area. The most subtle cues are the presence of gay people as they take up residence in a district. Word spreads in the group that a certain area is starting to look attractive and open to gay members. There is often a move to "gentrify" older, more affordable sections of a city and build a new neighborhood out of the leftovers from the rush to the suburbs. Gay businesses, those operated by or catering to gay people, often develop once enough clientele is in the area. Social groups and services emerge that are oriented toward the members of the neighborhood. Eventually, the label of "gay neighborhood" is placed on an area, and the transformation is complete. The Castro area in San Francisco, Greenwich Village in New York, New Town in Chicago, the Westheimer district in Houston, and West Hollywood or Silver Lake in Los Angeles are examples of the many emergent gay neighborhoods in cities across America.[3]

A second need fulfilled by the gay neighborhood is the creation of a meeting ground. People can recognize and meet each other more easily when a higher density of like population is established. It is not easy to grow up gay in America; gay people often feel "different" because of their sexual orientations. The surrounding heterosexual culture often tries to imprint on everyone sexual behaviors and expectations that do not suit gay natures. Because of this pressure, gay people often feel isolated and alienated, and the need for a meeting ground is very important.[4] Merely knowing that there is a specific place where other gay people live and work and play does much to anchor the psychological aspect of gayness in a tangible, physical reality. A gay person's sense of identity is reinforced by knowing that there is a home base, or a safe place where others of a similar persuasion are nearby.

Gay neighborhoods reinforce individual identity by focusing activities and events for members of the group. Celebrations of group unity and pride, demonstrations of group creativity and accomplishment, and services to individual members' needs are more easily developed when they are centralized. Gay neighborhoods are host to all the outward elements of a community—parades, demonstrations, car washes, basketball games, petition signing, street fairs, and garage sales.

A critical purpose for gay neighborhoods is that of physical and psychological safety. Subcultural groups usually experience some degree of persecution and oppression from the larger surrounding culture. For gay people, physical safety is a very real concern—incidences of homophobic assaults or harassment are common in most American cities.[5] By centralizing gay activities, some safeguards can be mounted, as large numbers of gay people living in proximity create a deterrence to violence. This may be informal awareness of the need to take extra precautions and to be on the alert to help other gay people in distress or in the form of actual street patrols or social groups, such as Community United Against Violence in San Francisco. A sense of psychological safety follows from these physical measures. Group consciousness raising on neighborhood safety and training in safety practices create a sense of group cohesion. The security inspired by the group thus creates a psychic comfort that offsets the paranoia that can be engendered by alienation and individual isolation.

Another significant result of gay neighborhoods is the political reality of "clout."[6] In the context of American grassroots democracy, a predominantly gay population in an area can lead to political power. The concerns of gay people are taken more seriously by politicians and elected officials representing an area where voters can be registered and mustered into service during elections. In many areas, openly gay politicians represent gay constituencies directly and voice their concerns in ever-widening forums. The impact of this kind of democracy-in-action is felt on other institutions as well: police departments, social welfare agencies, schools, churches, and businesses. When a group centralizes its energy, members can bring pressure to bear on other cultural institutions, asking for and demanding attention to the unique needs of that group. Since American culture has a strong tradition of cultural diversity, gay neighborhoods are effective agents in the larger cultural acceptance of gay people. The gay rights movement, which attempts to secure housing, employment, and legal protection for gay people, finds its greatest support in the sense of community created by gay neighborhoods.

GAY SOCIAL GROUPS

On a smaller level than the neighborhood, specialized groups fulfill the social needs of gay people. The need for affiliation—to make friends, to share recreation, to find life partners, or merely to while away the time—is a strong drive in any group of people. Many gay people suffer from an isolation caused by rejection by other people or by their own fear of being discovered as belonging to an unpopular group. This homophobia leads to difficulty in identifying and meeting other gay people who can help create a sense of dignity and caring. This is par-

ticularly true for gay teenagers who have limited opportunities to meet other gay people.[7] Gay social groups serve the important function of helping gay people locate each other so that this affiliation need can be met.

The development of gay social groups depends to a large degree on the number of gay people in an area and the perceived risk factor. In smaller towns and cities, there are often no meeting places, which exacerbates the problem of isolation. In some small towns a single business may be the only publicly known meeting place for gay people within hundreds of miles. In larger cities, however, an elaborate array of bars, clubs, social groups, churches, service agencies, entertainment groups, stores, restaurants, and the like add to the substance of a gay culture.

The gay bar is often the first public gay experience for a gay person, and it serves as a central focus for many people. Beyond the personal need of meeting potential relationship partners, the gay bar also serves the functions of entertainment and social activity. Bars offer a wide range of attractions suited to gay people: movies, holiday celebrations, dancing, costume parties, live entertainment, free meals, boutiques, and meeting places for social groups. Uniquely gay forms of entertainment, such as drag shows and disco dancing, were common in gay bars before spreading into the general culture. Bars often become a very central part of a community's social life by sponsoring athletic teams, charities, community services, and other events as well as serving as meeting places.

The centrality of the bar in gay culture has several drawbacks, however. Young gay people are denied entrance because of age restrictions, and there may be few other social outlets for them. A high rate of alcoholism among urban gay males is prominent.[1] With the spread of Acquired Immune Deficiency Syndrome (AIDS), the use of bars for meeting sexual partners has declined dramatically as gay people turn to developing more permanent relationships.[8]

Affiliation needs remain strong despite these dangers, however, and alternative social institutions arise that meet these needs. In large urban areas, where gay culture is more widely developed, social groups include athletic organizations that sponsor teams and tournaments; leisure activity clubs in such areas as country-and-western dance, music, yoga, bridge, hiking, and recreation; religious groups such as Dignity (Roman Catholic), Integrity (Episcopal), and the Metropolitan Community Church (MCC); volunteer agencies such as information and crisis hotlines and charitable organizations; and professional and political groups such as the Golden Gate Business Association of San Francisco or the national lobby group, the Gay Rights Task Force. A directory of groups and services is usually published in urban gay newspapers, and their activities are reported on and promoted actively. Taken together, these groups compose a culture that supports and nourishes a gay person's life.

GAY SYMBOLS

Gay culture is replete with symbols. These artifacts spring up and constantly evolve as gayness moves from an individual, personal experience into a more complex public phenomenon. All groups express their ideas and values in symbols, and the gay culture, in spite of its relatively brief history, has been quite creative in symbol making.

The most visible category of symbols is in the semantics of gay establishment names. Gay bars, bookstores, restaurants, and social groups want to be recognized and patronized by gay people, but they do not want to incur hostility from the general public. This was particularly true in the past when the threat of social consequences was greater. In earlier days, gay bars, the only major form of gay establishment, went by code words such as "blue" or "other"—the Blue Parrot, the Blue Goose, the Other Bar, and Another Place.

Since the liberalization of culture after the 1960s, semantics have blossomed in gay place names. The general trend is still to identify the place as gay, either through affiliation (Our Place or His 'N' Hers), humor (the White Swallow or Uncle Charley's), high drama (the Elephant Walk or Backstreet), or sexual

suggestion (Ripples, Cheeks, or Rocks). Lesbians and gay men differ in this aspect of their cultures. Lesbian place names often rely upon a more personal or classical referent (Amanda's Place or the Artemis Cafe), while hypermasculine referents are commonly used for gay male meeting places (the Ramrod, Ambush, Manhandlers, the Mine Shaft, the Stud, or Boots). Gay restaurants and nonpornographic bookstores usually reflect more subdued names, drawing upon cleverness or historical associations: Dos Hermanos, Women and Children First, Diana's, the Oscar Wilde Memorial Bookstore, and Walt Whitman Bookstore. More commonly, gay establishments employ general naming trends of location, ownership, or identification of product or service similar to their heterosexual counterparts. The increasing tendency of businesses to target and cater to gay markets strengthens the growth and diversity of gay culture.

A second set of gay symbols are those that serve as member-recognition factors. In past ages such nonverbal cues were so popular as to become mythical: the arched eyebrow of Regency England, the green carnation of Oscar Wilde's day, and the "green shirt on Thursday" signal of mid-century America. A large repertoire of identifying characteristics has arisen in recent years that serves the functions of recognizing other gay people and focusing on particular interests. In the more sexually promiscuous period of the 1970s, popular identifying symbols were a ring of keys worn on the belt, either left or right depending upon sexual passivity or aggressiveness, and the use of colored handkerchiefs in a rear pocket coded to desired types of sexual activity. Political sentiments are commonly expressed through buttons, such as the "No on 64" campaign against the LaRouche initiative in California in 1986. The pink triangle as a political symbol recalls the persecution and annihilation of gay people in Nazi Germany. The lambda symbol, an ancient Greek referent, conjures up classical images of gay freedom of expression. Stud earrings for men are gay symbols in some places, though such adornment has evolved and is widely used for the expression of general countercultural attitudes. The rainbow and the unicorn, mythical symbols associated with supernatural potency, also are common signals of gay enchantment, fairy magic, and spiritual uniqueness to the more "cosmic" elements of the gay community.

Another set of gay symbols to be aware of are the images of gay people as portrayed in television, film, literature, and advertising. The general heterosexual culture controls these media forms to a large extent, and the representations of gay people in those media take on a straight set of expectations and assumptions. The results are stereotypes that often oversimplify gay people and their values and do not discriminate the subtleties of human variety in gay culture. Since these stereotypes are generally unattractive, they are often the target of protests by gay people. Various authors have addressed the problem of heterosexual bias in the areas of film and literature.[9] As American culture gradually becomes more accepting of and tolerant toward gay people, these media representations become more realistic and sympathetic, but progress in this area is slow.

One hopeful development in the creation of positive gay role models has been the rise of an active gay market for literature. Most large cities have bookstores that stock literature supportive of gay culture. A more positive image for gay people is created through gay characters, heros, and stories that deal with the important issues of family, relationship, and social responsibility. This market is constantly threatened by harsh economic realities, however, and gay literature is not as well developed as it might be.[10]

Advertising probably has done the most to popularize and integrate gay symbols into American culture. Since money making is the goal of advertising, the use of gay symbols has advanced more rapidly in ad media than in the arts. Widely quoted research suggests that gay people, particularly men, have large, disposable incomes, so they become popular target markets for various products: tobacco, bodycare products, clothing, alcohol, entertainment, and consumer goods. Typical gay-directed advertising in these product areas includes appeals based upon male bonding, such as are common in tobacco and alcohol sales ads, which are attractive to both straight and gay men since they stimulate the bonding need that is a part of both cultures.

Within gay culture, advertising has made dramatic advances in the past ten years, due to the rise of gay-related businesses and products. Gay advertising appears most obviously in media specifically directed at gay markets, such as gay magazines and newspapers, and in gay neighborhoods. Gay products and services are publicized with many of the same means as are their straight counterparts. Homoerotic art is widely used in clothing and body-care product ads. The male and female body are displayed for their physical and sexual appeal. This eroticizing of the body may be directed at either women or men as a desirable sexual object, and perhaps strikes at a subconscious homosexual potential in all people. Prominent elements of gay advertising are its use of sexuality and the central appeal of hypermasculinization. With the rise of sexual appeals in general advertising through double entendre, sexual punning, subliminal seduction, and erotic art work, it may be that gay advertising is only following suit in its emphasis on sexual appeals. Hugely muscled bodies and perfected masculine beauty adorn most advertising for gay products and services. Ads for greeting cards, billboards for travel service, bars, hotels, restaurants, and clothing stores tingle to the images of Hot 'N' Hunky Hamburgers, Hard On Leather, and the Brothel Hotel or its crosstown rival, the Anxious Arms. Some gay writers criticize this use of advertising as stereotyping and distorting of gay people, and certainly, misconceptions about the diversity in gay culture are more common than understanding. Gay people are far more average and normal than the images that appear in public media would suggest.

GAY MEETING BEHAVIOR

The final element of communication in the gay culture discussed here is the vast set of behaviors by which gay people recognize and meet one another. In more sexually active days before the concern for AIDS, this type of behavior was commonly called cruising. Currently, promiscuous sexual behavior is far less common than it once was, and cruising has evolved into a more standard meeting behavior that helps identify potential relationship partners.

Gay people meet each other in various contexts: in public situations, in the workplace, in gay meeting places, and in the social contexts of friends and acquaintances. Within each context, a different set of behaviors is employed by which gay people recognize someone else as gay and determine the potential for establishing a relationship. These behaviors include such nonverbal signaling as frequency and length of interaction, posture, proximity, eye contact, eye movement and facial gestures, touch, affect displays, and paralinguistic signals.[11] The constraints of each situation and the personal styles of the communicators create great differences in the effectiveness and ease with which these behaviors are displayed.

Cruising serves several purposes besides the recognition of other gay people. Most importantly, cruising is an expression of joy and pride in being gay. Through cruising, gay people communicate their openness and willingness to interact. Being gay is often compared to belonging to a universal—though invisible—fraternity or sorority. Gay people are generally friendly and open to meeting other gay people in social contexts because of the common experience of rejection and isolation they have had growing up. Cruising is the means by which gay people communicate their gayness and bridge the gap between stranger and new-found friend.

Cruising has become an integral part of gay culture because it is such a commonplace behavior. Without this interpersonal skill—and newcomers to gay life often complain of the lack of comfort or ease they have with cruising—a gay person can be at a distinct disadvantage in finding an easy path into the mainstream of gay culture. While cruising has a distinctly sexual overtone, the sexual subtext is often a symbolic charade. Often the goals of cruising are no more than friendship, companionship, or conversation. In this sense, cruising becomes more an art form or an entertainment. Much as the "art of conversation" was the convention of a more genteel cultural age, gay cruising is the commonly accepted vehicle of gay social interaction. The sexual element, however, transmitted by double meaning, clever punning, or blatant nonverbal signals, remains a part of cruising in even the most innocent of circumstances.

In earlier generations, a common stereotype of gay men focused on the use of exaggerated, dramatic, and effeminate body language—the "limp wrist" image. Also included in this negative image of gay people was cross-gender dressing, known as "drag," and a specialized, sexually suggestive argot called "camp."[12] Some gay people assumed these social roles because that was the picture of "what it meant to be gay," but by and large these role behaviors were overthrown by the gay liberation of the 1970s. Gay people became much less locked into these restraining stereotypes and developed a much broader means of social expression. Currently, no stereotypic behavior would adequately describe gay communication style—it is far too diverse and integrated into mainstream American culture. Cruising evolved from these earlier forms of communication, but as a quintessential gay behavior, cruising has replaced the bitchy camp of an earlier generation of gay people.

The unique factor in gay cruising, and the one that distinguishes it from heterosexual cruising, is the level of practice and refinement the process receives. All cultural groups have means of introduction and meeting, recognition, assessment, and negotiation of a new relationship. In gay culture, however, the "courtship ritual" or friendship ritual of cruising is elaborately refined in its many variants and contexts. While straight people may use similar techniques in relationship formation and development, gay people are uniquely self-conscious in the centrality of these signals to the perpetuation of their culture. There is a sense of adventure and discovery in being "sexual outlaws," and cruising is the shared message of commitment to the gay life style.[13]

CONCLUSION

These four communication elements of gay culture comprise only a small part of what might be called gay culture. Other elements have been more widely discussed elsewhere: literature, the gay press, religion, politics, art, theater, and relationships. Gay culture is a marvelous and dynamic phenomenon, driven and buffeted by the energies of intense feeling and creative effort. Centuries of cultural repression that condemned gay people to disgrace and persecution have been turned upside down in a brief period of history. The results of this turbulence have the potential for either renaissance or cataclysm. The internalized fear and hatred of repression is balanced by the incredible joy and idealism of liberation. Through the celebration of its unique life style, gay culture promises to make a great contribution to the history of sexuality and to the rights of the individual. Whether it will fulfill this promise or succumb to the pressures that any creative attempt must face remains to be seen.

NOTES

1. Several good reviews of famous homosexuals include the following: Barbara Grier and Coletta Reid, *Lesbian Lives* (Oakland, Calif.: Diana Press, 1976); Noel I. Garde, *Jonathan to Gide: The Homosexual in History* (New York: Nosbooks, 1969); and A. L. Rowse, *The Homosexual in History* (Metuchen, N.Y.: Scarecrow Press, 1975).

2. The relative differences and similarities between gay men and lesbians is a hotly debated issue in the gay/lesbian community. For the purposes of this paper, I have chosen to speak of them as a single unit. For an introduction to this issue, see Celia Kitzinger, *The Social Construction of Lesbianism* (Newbury Park, Calif.: Sage Publications, 1987).

3. An excellent analysis of the role of the Castro in California's gay culture is in Frances FitzGerald, *Cities on a Hill* (New York: Simon and Schuster, 1986). An entertaining source that discusses gay neighborhoods across America is Edmund White, *States of Desire: Travels in Gay America* (New York: E. P. Dutton, 1980).

4. For more information on the problems of gay self-identity, see Don Clark, *(The New) Loving Someone Gay* (Berkeley: Celestial Arts, 1987) and George Weinberg, *Society and the Healthy Homosexual* (New York: Doubleday, 1973).

5. A discussion of violence and its effects on gay people is in Dennis Altman, *The Homosexualization of America: The Americanization of Homosexuality* (New York: St. Martin's Press, 1982), pp. 100–101.

6. For a discussion of emerging gay politics, see Peter Fisher, *The Gay Mystique* (New York: Stein and Day, 1972) and Laud Humphreys, *Out of the Closets: The Sociology of Homosexual Liberation* (Englewood Cliffs, N.J.: Prentice-Hall, 1972).

7. Problems of young gay people are discussed in Mary V. Borhek, *Coming Out to Parents* (New York: Pilgrim Press, 1983) and in story form in Mary V. Borhek, *My Son Eric* (New York: Pilgrim Press, 1979) and Aaron Fricke, *Reflections of a Rock Lobster* (New York: Alyson, 1981).

8. Gay relationships are discussed in Betty Berzon, *Permanent Partners: Building Gay and Lesbian Relationships That Last* (New York: E. P. Dutton, 1988) and David P. McWirter and Andrew M. Mattison, *The Male Couple* (Englewood Cliffs, N.J.: Prentice-Hall, 1984).

9. The treatment of gay people in literature is discussed in Barbara Grier, *The Lesbian in Literature* (Iowa City, Iowa: Naiad, 1988); George-Michel Sarotte, *Like a Brother, Like a Lover* (New York: Doubleday, 1978); Ian Young (Ed.), *The Male Homosexual in Literature: A Bibliography* (Metuchen, N.Y.: Scarecrow Press, 1975); and Roger Austen, *Playing the Game: The Homosexual Novel in America* (Indianapolis: Bobbs-Merrill Press, 1977). Gay people in films are discussed in Parker Tyler, *Screening the Sexes: Homosexuality in the Movies* (New York: Holt, Rinehart & Winston, 1972) and Vito Russo, *The Celluloid Closet: Lesbians and Gay Men in American Film* (New York: Harper & Row, 1980).

10. The emergence of positive roles is discussed in Betty Berzon, *Positively Gay* (Los Angeles: Mediamix Associates, 1979).

11. An excellent reference source for more information on gay communication research is Wayne R. Dynes, *Homosexuality: A Research Guide* (New York: Garland, 1987). He covers nonverbal communication in his section on "Social Semiotics," pp. 372 ff.

12. Camp is discussed in Susan Sontag, "Notes on Camp," *Against Interpretation* (New York: Dell, 1969). For a dictionary of antique camp language, see Bruce Rodgers, *The Queen's Vernacular: A Gay Lexicon* (New York: Simon and Schuster, 1972).

13. Altman discusses cruising in *The Homosexualization of America*, p. 176.

CONCEPTS AND QUESTIONS
FOR CHAPTER 3

1. By what means can you approach interaction with members of co-cultures without making assumptions that are harmful to their sense of self-worth?

2. Arturo Madrid has pointed out the difficulties members of co-cultures face in becoming full-fledged members of American institutions. How would you propose to solve that problem?

3. How did Madrid address the concept of cultural diversity?

4. Can you think of other co-cultures that fall into Edith Folb's category of nondominant groups?

5. How do you suppose someone from a foreign culture would respond to one of our co-cultures? Be specific.

6. What major problems will develop in American society as the population continues to age?

7. What does Carl Carmichael mean when he suggests that integration of the elderly is not a cultural goal in the United States?

8. How does becoming disabled change a person's communication patterns?

9. What are some of the cultural problems inherent in communication between able-bodied and disabled persons?

10. How does American Sign Language differ from English in terms of its grammar and syntax? With what other languages has it been found to have similarities?

11. What are the seven communicative behaviors that Kathy Jankowski recommends be developed in order to foster effective intercultural communication with the Deaf culture?

12. How does growing up female affect one's perceptions and ultimately one's communication behaviors?

13. What does Judy Pearson mean when she says "communication creates gender"?

14. What function does gay communicative behavior serve?

15. In what ways have gay people adopted specific nonverbal behaviors that signify the manifestation of their co-culture?

16. Do you believe that co-cultures seeking to practice their own ways of life ought to be permitted this freedom? What are the limits of this behavior?

17. In what different ways have racial and ethnic co-cultures been treated in the United States?

18. How does the history of a co-culture offer us insight into its communication behaviors?

4

Cultural Contexts: The Influence of the Setting

Communication does not occur in a vacuum. All communication takes place in a social setting or environment that impacts on the communication event. We call this the social context because the setting is never neutral; it influences how the participants behave. We have all learned culturally appropriate patterns of communicative behavior for the various social contexts in which we normally find ourselves. But, as in other aspects of intercultural communication, the patterns of behavior appropriate to various social contexts are culturally determined and, therefore, diverse. When we find ourselves in unfamiliar contexts without an internalized set of rules to govern our behavior, or when we are interacting with someone who has internalized a different set of rules, communication problems often arise.

The growth of international business during the last thirty years has been startling. Overseas transactions that involved millions of dollars annually are now worth multibillions of dollars. In addition, the international business community has experienced a more profound change—business has become multinational, and organizational units include participants from a wide variety of cultures. In fact, study of the multinational organization has become a subtopic within the fields of intercultural and organizational communication. Successful businesspeople functioning in international business and world markets must learn about approaches to business practices that may be vastly different from their own or those they studied in school.

Because of this economic growth and internationalization of business, the businessperson no longer has the luxury of dealing exclusively with people who possess the same cultural background and experiences. In this global economy, one's clients, peers, subordinates, and even supervisors are frequently from a different country and culture. Such aspects as gift giving, methods of negotiation, decision making, policy formulation, management structure, and patterns of communication are subject to cultural differentiation.

While the internationalization of business was taking place, changes also were happening within the United States. This country was moving toward a pluralistic, multicultural, and intercultural society. As a result, the U.S. population has become culturally diverse, and we often find ourselves engaged in intercultural communication in many social contexts. The workplace, the schools, social service agencies, and health services, among others, are contexts that have become especially intercultural.

In this chapter we will look at a series of essays that deal with cultural diversity in communication context. We focus on a combination of international and domestic settings in which knowledge and appreciation of cultural diversity is important if successful intercultural communication is to occur.

The Japanese approach to business and multinational organizations is one of special interest, not only because of the financial impact the Japanese have on the world economy, but also because of the unique ways in which they perceive the business context and the consequent implications for communicating within multinational organizations. Lea P. Stewart, in her article "Japanese and American Management: Participative Decision Making," examines Japanese and American management processes and their differing styles of decision making and conferencing through an analysis and description of their nature and characteristics. She concludes with an observation that, although Japanese companies are highly successful, we must first wonder whether we want to measure success in terms similar to those used by Japanese society before we start a wholesale application of Japanese management to U.S. corporations.

All business activities involve many forms of communication, but there are two forms that are crucial to successful businesses: discussion and negotiation. These often are difficult enough when dealing within one's own culture, but when these forms involve intercultural communication there is added difficulty due to the influence of culture on communication styles. The next two articles will examine cultural diversity in both of these forms of interaction. First, in his article, "Contrasts in Discussion Behaviors of German and American Managers," Robert A. Friday examines the effect of culture on this form of communication. Friday traces cultural expectations of both German and American managers across a number of dimensions, points out the differences, and shows how they can lead to misunderstandings and ineffective communication.

In the next article, Susan A. Hellweg, Larry A. Samovar, and Lisa Skow lead us through an investigation of cultural diversity in negotiating behavior. In "Cultural Variations in Negotiation Styles," they highlight negotiation styles used by such cultures as the French, Japanese, Chinese, Brazilians, and Arabic cultures of the Middle East. They present a detailed description of various communication styles and cultural variations in decision making and show how sensitivity to cultural diversity is essential to successful intercultural business negotiations.

A culturally diverse communication context that may occur in a variety of locations, such as the workplace, the schools, health care services, and social services, is counseling in the multicultural setting. In the article "The Cultural Grid: A Framework for Multicultural Counseling," Anne and Paul Pedersen develop what they call the cultural grid as a theoretical framework, which combines personal and cultural perspectives of social system variables. The cultural grid can thus be used to describe a distinctive cultural orientation in each communication situation and to suggest how specific behaviors, expectations, and values are related to social system variables.

A multicultural society impacts strongly on the health care setting because cultural beliefs about health and disease are very diverse. Such a simple question as "How do you catch a cold?" can elicit a variety of answers, ranging from standing in a draft to being the victim of a supernatural spell, depending on one's cultural background. In her article

"The Role of Culture in Health and Disease," Kim Witte introduces you to a number of ethnomedical systems that are culturally unique beliefs and knowledge about health and disease. Through her discussion of Hispanic folk medicine, she gives considerable insight into the Hispanic ethnomedical system. She continues with a discussion of intercultural communication in health care systems and concludes with an example involving Bolivian Indians of how health care communication may be improved interculturally.

The classroom environment is one of those settings that specifically influences intercultural interaction. The rules, assumptions, values, customs, practices, and procedures of a given culture strongly affect the conduct of classroom activity. While many people naively believe that all classrooms are pretty much alike, Janis F. Andersen and Robert Powell take the position that learning environments are culturally diverse and that they alter the communication patterns of people within those environments. In their article "Intercultural Communication and the Classroom," they support this assertion by highlighting intercultural differences in classroom settings, teacher-student relationships, nonverbal behaviors, what is taught, and how it is taught.

We end our discussion of cultural contexts with a completely different yet significant intercultural context: the courtroom. Wayne A. Beach, in his article "Intercultural Problems in Courtroom Interactions," explores courtrooms and their culture to determine how "fair and impartial treatment" can be a part of the legal process when defendants need interpreters to function as mediators between themselves and the judges, lawyers, and jurors. Relying on transcribed segments of video-recorded court proceedings, Beach looks at traditional notions of differences between cultures and how these differences produce problems for Spanish-speaking defendants.

Japanese and American Management: Participative Decision Making

LEA P. STEWART

In recent years, Japanese management techniques have been proclaimed by both scholars and lay authors as the salvation of American business. Perhaps because of popular books such as *Theory Z* by William Ouchi (1981) and *The Art of Japanese Management* by Richard Tanner Pascale and Anthony G. Athos (1981), it seems that everyone has heard of the wonders of Japanese management. According to Ouchi, corporations such as Hewlett-Packard, Eli Lilly, and Dayton-Hudson are using his Theory Z approach to management. Given the glowing success stories described by Ouchi and others, it would seem that American industry could profit from the widespread application of these techniques. This may or may not be true. The danger lies in applying techniques based on Japanese management without critically examining them. This is easy to do because, as one searches for information on this approach, one finds that the vast majority of articles portray the Japanese system in a favorable light. Yet, there are some authors who criticize, or at least express concern about, Japanese management techniques. This paper will review some of these articles to provide a more balanced look at an approach to management that everyone seems to be talking about.

Table 1

	United States	*Japan*
Employment	Short term, market oriented	Long term, career oriented
Management values	Openness and accountability	Harmony and consensus
Management style	Action oriented, short term horizons	Perfectionism in long term, paralysis in short term
Work values	Individual responsibility	Collective responsibility
Control processes	Formalized and explicit	Not formalized, implicit
Learning systems	External consultants and universities	Internal consultants and company training

The differences between U.S. and Japanese management are summarized in Table 1, adapted from McMillan (1980).

Americans and Japanese live in quite different conceptual worlds. Whereas Americans regard responsible individuality as a virtue and view lack of autonomy as a constraint, the Japanese regard individuality as evidence of immaturity and autonomy as the freedom to comply with one's obligations and duties (Fox, 1977). According to Fox, the "traditional Japanese male employee is born into an intricate web of obligations and relationships in which ridicule is unbearable and the ideal is to 'blend selflessly into a system of otherdirectedness' " (p. 77). This socially committed male is chosen from the graduating class of one of the best universities to become a manager in a Japanese company for life. As a Japanese manager who abhors unpleasant face-to-face confrontations and discord, he will manage through a system of apparent consensus building (Tsurumi, 1978).

This consensus-building system, the *ringi* system, is one of the most talked about virtues of the Japanese system. There is evidence, however, that this system is not dedicated to true consensus. Fox (1977) describes the *ringi* system as a process in which a proposal prepared by middle management is circulated to affected units of the organization for review, revision, and approval. When each unit has attached its approval seal to the proposal, it goes to

the appropriate higher-level authority for final approval and implementation. Although the system involves numerous group meetings and much delay, once final approval is granted, the organization moves surprisingly quickly to implement it. Fox claims that this system should be labeled "consensual understanding" instead of decision making by consensus. According to Fox:

It is not uncommon for the ringisho *to be merely the formalization of a suggestion from higher management which has had the benefit of considerable prior discussion before being drafted. Apparently, not many* ringisho *are drastically revised en route to the top or vetoed when they get there. And considerable discretion is retained by management to prescribe in detail when and by whom they will be implemented* (pp. 79–80).

Although Fox believes the *ringi* system is not true decision making by consensus, he does believe the system nurtures commitment and, thus, "recalls the work of Lewin, Maier, Coch and French, and Likert who demonstrated the effectiveness of participative decision making in American organizations long ago" (p. 85). Krauss (1973) sees many parallels between the management styles of successful U.S. companies dedicated to participative decision making and the Japanese system. Tsurumi (1978) takes a more critical view and characterizes the decision-making process inside Japanese corporations as "personality-based." He claims that "the art of consensus-building is to sell ideas and decisions to others" (p. 60). This criticism echoes the claims of American critics who have challenged participative decision making. Often American employees are allowed only limited participation (see French et al., 1964, for a classic application of participation in a manufacturing plant), or are allowed to participate in making only insignificant decisions. Participation is often used to make an employee *feel* that he or she is taking part in the decision-making process even if the employee's input does not actually have an effect on the process.

Pascale (1978) reinforces the similarity in decision-making style between American and Japanese managers in an extensive study of communication practices in U.S. and Japanese corporations. Pascale found that managers in Japanese firms engage in over 30 percent more face-to-face contacts each day than do managers in U.S. firms. In addition, compared to U.S. managers, Japanese managers score themselves higher on decision quality and substantially higher on implementation quality. Yet, there is no significant difference in the style of decision making used by Japanese and U.S. managers. Japanese managers do not use a consultative decision-making process more often than do American managers. Pascale argues that the Japanese manager's tendency to use more face-to-face contacts is more efficient because the Japanese language does not lend itself to mechanical word processing and most written communication has to be done by hand, which is a lengthy process. In addition, face-to-face communication is encouraged by the crowded Japanese work setting in which many levels of the hierarchy are located in the same open work space. Thus, the nature of the Japanese language and of the work setting may be the major determinants of the Japanese manager's communication style. This face-to-face style, in turn, leads to higher perceived decision quality and higher perceived implementation quality.

The dominance of face-to-face communication may account for the perception that there is more openness about major decisions in Japanese firms and "more desire to explore and learn together"

(McMillan, 1980). While Japanese managers are not actually using a consultative decision-making style, they are talking to their workers a great deal. This increased face-to-face contact is interpreted by observers of the system as openness. Systematic research into the content of these face-to-face interactions is needed to determine if Japanese managers are being "open" with their subordinates or merely answering questions and giving advice.

No matter how decisions are actually made within Japanese corporations, there is no doubt that Japanese companies are highly successful. McMillan attributes the phenomenal success of Japanese industry to high productivity due to the "best technology-oriented hardware, which combines the newest processes available, an emphasis on quality control and cost-volume relationships, and, where necessary, automation and robot technology" (p. 28)—in essence, machines. McMillan argues that the Japanese have invested a great deal in developing and maintaining advanced hardware systems and are reaping the benefits of this technology. Fox (1977), on the other hand, takes a more human approach to the success of the Japanese system. He claims that the Japanese system has accomplished so much due to "dedicated, self-sacrificing workers, spurred by a sense of urgency" (p. 80). Supposedly these workers are rewarded by lifetime employment, but this is not actually the case.

Permanent employment (the *nenko* system) operates mainly in the larger Japanese firms and applies to a minority of Japanese workers (Oh, 1976). It is reserved for male employees in government and large businesses (Drucker, 1978). The limitation of the the *nenko* system and its benefits to perhaps 30 percent of the nonagricultural Japanese labor force, according to Oh, "appears to be essential to the continued survival of the *nenko* system, and is probably its greatest cost to Japanese society" (p. 15). The benefits of the *nenko* system, however, are not limitless for those who are covered by it. Although a manager can expect yearly raises and bonuses since wages are based at least partly upon seniority, lifetime employment for most managers ends at age fifty-five, pensions rarely exceed two or three years of salary, and government social security benefits are nominal (Fox, 1977). To keep this system in operation and to assure a flexible supply of workers, the Japanese system considers 20 to 30 percent of its workers as "temporary" (Fox, 1977). Women, by definition, are temporary employees (Drucker, 1978) and are "consistently discriminated against with regard to pay, benefits, and opportunity for advancement" (Fox, 1977, p. 79). Even Ouchi (1981) admits that "Type Z organizations have a tendency to be sexist and racist" (p. 77).

To avoid the stigma of becoming a temporary worker or a manual laborer, Japanese children are pressured at increasingly younger and younger ages to learn enough to be admitted to the most prestigious schools. According to Drucker (1978), since "career opportunities are dependent almost entirely on educational attainment" (p. 33), the pressure starts with the child's application to nursery school. As the pressure is becoming more intense, Drucker notes, the suicide rate among teenagers and even preteens is reaching alarming proportions. Perhaps partly because of this pressure, young people in Japan are starting to defect from the traditional values (Fox, 1977). Although McMillan (1980) discounts its effect, he notes that "a growing minority of young people are impatient with the career employment system and the age-related wage practice" (p. 29). Oh (1976) claims that management tends to cultivate these grievances among younger workers to keep them from unifying with older workers to oppose management. Whether or not these grievances will become strong enough to challenge traditional management practices remains to be seen.

After careful examination, Japanese management appears to be a system of contradictions. Managers spend a great deal of time in face-to-face communication with workers, but they do not use consultative decision making more than American managers. The *ringi* system gives the appearance of consensus seeking, but it is actually more of an information dissemination system. The Japanese are rewarded for their educational attainments, so they are pressured into starting on the path toward the best schools at increasingly earlier ages. "Permanent" employment ends at age fifty-five. Undoubt-edly, the Japanese system has produced successful corporations, but, as Sethi (1973) notes, "Do we want to measure success in terms similar to those used by the Japanese society?" (p. 14). This question must be answered before we start the wholesale application of Japanese management to U.S. corporations.

REFERENCES

Drucker, P. F. (1978). "The Price of Success: Japan Revisited." *Across the Board, 15* (8), 28–35.

Fox, W. M. (1977). "Japanese Management: Tradition Under Strain." *Business Horizons, 20* (4), 76–85.

French, J. R. P., Ross, I. C., Kirby, S., Nelson, J. R., and Smyth, P. (1958). "Employee Participation in a Program of Industrial Change." *Personnel, 35* (6), 16–29. Reprinted in W. C. Redding and G. A. Sanborn (Eds.), *Business and Industrial Communication*. New York: Harper & Row, 1964, 372–387.

Krauss, W. P. (1973). "Will Success Spoil Japanese Management?" *Columbia Journal of World Business, 8* (4), 26–30.

McMillan, C. (1980). "Is Japanese Management Really So Different?" *Business Quarterly, 45* (3), 26–31.

Oh, T. K. (1976). "Japanese Management—A Critical Review." *Academy of Management Review, 1,* 14–25.

Ouchi, W. G. (1981). *Theory Z*. New York: Avon Books.

Pascale, R. T. (1978). "Communication and Decision Making Across Cultures: Japanese and American Comparisons." *Administrative Science Quarterly, 23,* 91–110.

Pascale, R. T., and Athos, A. G. (1981). *The Art of Japanese Management*. New York: Warner Books.

Sethi, S. P. (November 24, 1973). "Drawbacks of Japanese Management." *Business Week,* 12–13.

Tsurumi, Y. (1978). "The Best of Times and the Worst of Times: Japanese Management in America." *Columbia Journal of World Business, 13* (2), 56–61.

Contrasts in Discussion Behaviors of German and American Managers

ROBERT A. FRIDAY

AMERICAN MANAGERS' EXPECTATION

Business Is Impersonal

In any business environment, discussion between colleagues must accomplish the vital function of exchanging information that is needed for the solution of problems. In American business, such discussions are usually impersonal.[1] Traditionally the facts have spoken for themselves in America. "When facts are disputed, the argument must be suspended until the facts are settled. Not until then may it be resumed, for all true argument is about the meaning of established or admitted facts" (Weaver, 1953) in the rationalistic view. Much of post-WWII American business decision making has been based on the quantitative MBA approach which focuses on factual data and its relationship to the ultimate fact of profit or loss, writing strategy plans, and top-down direction. After all of the facts are in, the CEO is often responsible for making the intuitive leap and providing leadership. The power and authority of the CEO has prevailed in the past 40 years, with no predicted change in view (Bleicher & Paul, 1986, p. 10–11). Through competition and contact with West Germany and Japan, the more personal approach is beginning to enter some lower level decision-

making practices (Peters & Waterman, 1982, pp. 35–118).

Another reason for the impersonal nature of American business is that many American managers do not identify themselves with their corporations. When the goals and interests of the corporation match up with those of the American manager, he or she will stay and prosper. However, when the personal agenda of the American manager is not compatible with that of the corporation, he or she is likely to move on to attain his or her objective in a more conducive environment. Most American managers can disassociate themselves from their business identity, at least to the extent that their personal investment in a decision has more to do with their share of the profit rather than their sense of personal worth.

In contrast, "the German salesman's personal credibility is on the line when he sells his product. He spends years cultivating his clients, building long-term relationships based on reliability" (Hall, 1983, p. 67). This tendency on the part of Germans is much like American business in the early part of this century.

The cohesiveness of the employees of most German businesses is evidenced in the narrow salary spread. Whereas in the United States the ratio of lowest paid to highest paid is approximately 1 to 80, in Germany this ratio is 1 to 25 (Hall, 1983, p.74).

GERMAN MANAGERS' EXPECTATION

Business Is Not as Impersonal

The corporation for most Germans is closely related to his or her own identity. German managers at Mobay are likely to refer to "Papa Bayer" because they perceive themselves as members of a corporate family which meets most of their needs. In turn, most German managers there, as elsewhere, have made a lifelong commitment to the larger group in both a social and economic sense (Friday & Biro, 1986–87). In contrast to the American post-WWII

From *International Journal of Intercultural Relations*, Vol. 13, 1989, pp. 429–445. Reprinted by permission of Pergamon Press, Inc. and the author.

trend is "the German postwar tradition of seeking consensus among a closely knit group of colleagues who have worked together for decades [which] provides a collegial harmony among top managers that is rare in U.S. corporations" (Bleicher & Paul, 1986, p. 12). Our interviews suggested that many German managers may enter a three-year-plus training program with the idea of moving on later to another corporation. This move rarely occurs.

While a three-year training program appears to be excessively long by American standards, one must understand that the longer training program works on several levels that are logical within the German culture. The three or more years of entry level training is a predictable correlation to the German and USA relative values on the Uncertainty Avoidance Index[2] (Hofstede, 1984, p. 122). The longer training period is required to induct the German manager into the more formal decision-making rules, plans, operating procedures, and industry tradition (Cyert & March, 1963, p. 119), all of which focus on the short-run known entities (engineering/reliability of product) rather than the long-run unknown problems (future market demand).

On another level the "strong sense of self as a striving, controlling entity is offset by an equally strong sense of obligation to a *code* of decency" (McClelland, Sturr, Knapp, & Wendt, 1958, p. 252). Induction into a German company with an idealistic system of obligation requires a longer training period than induction into an American company in which the corporate strategy for productivity is acquired in small group and interpersonal interaction.[3] The German manager who moves from one corporation to another for the purpose of advancement is regarded with suspicion partly because of his lack of participation in the corporate tradition, which could prove to be an unstabilizing factor.

Our preliminary interview results suggested uncertainty avoidance (Hofstede, 1984, p. 130) in everyday business relationships, especially the German concern for security. For example, most of the transfer preparation from the German home office to the USA consists of highly detailed explanations of an extensive benefits package. Since the German manager sees a direct relationship between his or her personal security and the prosperity of his or her company, business becomes more personal for him or her. Similarly, Americans who work in employee-owned companies are also seeing a clear relationship between personal security and the prosperity of their company.

AMERICAN MANAGERS' EXPECTATION

Need to Be Liked

The American's need to be liked is a primary aspect of his or her motivation to cooperate or not to cooperate with colleagues. The arousal of this motivation occurs naturally in discussion situations when direct feedback gives the American the desired response which indicates a sense of belongingness or acceptance. The American "envisions the desired responses and is likely to gear his actions accordingly. The characteristic of seeing others as responses is reflected in the emphasis on communication in interaction and in the great value placed on being liked. . . . American's esteem of others is based on their liking him. This requirement makes it difficult for Americans to implement projects which require an 'unpopular' phase" (Stewart, 1972, p. 58).

For Americans, the almost immediate and informal use of a colleague's first name is a recognition that each likes the other. While such informality is common among American business personnel, this custom should probably be avoided with Germans. "It takes a long time to get on a first-name basis with a German; if you rush the process, you may be perceived as overly familiar and rude. . . . Germans are very conscious of their status and insist on proper forms of address. Germans are bewildered by the American custom of addressing a new acquaintance by his first name and are even more startled by our custom of addressing a superior by first name" (Hall, 1983, p. 57–58). When such matters of decorum are overlooked during critical discussions, an "unpopular phase" may develop.

The need to be liked is culturally induced at an early age and continued throughout life through regular participation in group activities.

They [Americans] are not brought up on senti- ments of obligation to others as the Germans are, but from kindergarten on they regularly partici- pate in many more extracurricular functions of a group nature. In fact, by far the most impressive result . . . is the low number of group activities lis- ted by the Germans (about 1, on the average) as compared with the Americans (about 5, on the av- erage). In these activities the American student must learn a good deal more about getting along with other people and doing things cooperatively, if these clubs are to function at all (McClelland et al., 1958, p. 250).

This cultural orientation in relation to group par- ticipation will be revisited later in the closing dis- cussion on "learning styles, training, instruction, and problem solving."

GERMAN MANAGERS' EXPECTATION

Need to Be Credible

The German counterpart to the American need to be liked is the need to establish one's credibility and position in the hierarchy. The contrast between American informality and mobility and German for- mality and class structure are a reflection of the dif- ference between these two needs. In the absence of a long historical tradition, Americans have devel- oped a society in which friendships and residence change often, family histories (reputations) are un- known, and, therefore, acceptance of what one is doing in the present and plans to do in the future is a great part of one's identity. In order to maintain this mobility of place and relationships, Americans rely on reducing barriers to acceptance through informality.

Germans, with their strong sense of history, tra- dition, family, and life-long friendships, tend to move much less often, make friendships slowly, and keep them longer than Americans. Because one's family may be known for generations in Germany, the family reputation becomes part of one's own identity, which in turn places the individual in a sta- ble social position.[4]

The stability of the social class structure and, thus, the credibility of the upper class in Germany is largely maintained through the elitist system of higher education.

Educational achievement has been a major factor in determining occupational attainment and so- cioeconomic status in the post-World War II era. University education has been virtually essential in gaining access to the most prestigious and re- munerative positions. Some of the most enduring social divisions have focused on level of education (Nyrop, 1982, p. 113).

A German's education most often places him or her at a certain level which, in turn, determines what they can and can't do. In Germany, one must present credentials as evidence of one's qualification to per- form *any* task (K. Hagemann, personal communica- tion, May–September, 1987). Thus, the German so- cietal arrangement guarantees stability and order by adherence to known barriers (credentials) that con- firm one's credibility. In Germany, loss of credibility would be known in the manager's corporate and so- cial group and would probably result in truncated advancement (not dismissal since security is a high value).

The rigid social barriers established by educa- tion and credentials stand in direct contrast to the concepts of social mobility in American society. "Our social orientation is toward the importance of the individual and the equality of all individuals. Friendly, informal, outgoing, and extroverted, the American scorns rank and authority, even when he/ she is the one with the rank. American bosses are the only bosses in the world who insist on being called by their first names by their subordinates" (Kohls, 1987, p. 8). When Germans and Americans come together in discussion, the German's drive is to establish hierarchy, the American's is to dis- solve it.

AMERICAN MANAGERS' EXPECTATIONS

Assertiveness, Direct Confrontation, and Fair Play

In comparing Americans with Japanese, Edward Stewart relates the American idea of confrontation as "putting the cards on the table and getting the information 'straight from the horses mouth'. It is also desirable to face people directly, to confront them intentionally" (Stewart, 1972, p. 52). This is done so that the decision makers can have all of the facts. Stewart contrasts this intentional confrontation of Americans to the indirection of the Japanese, which often requires the inclusion of an intermediary or emissary in order to avoid face to face confrontation and thus, the loss of face. However, this view may leave the American manager unprepared for what he or she is likely to find in his or her initial discussion with a German manager.

The American manager is likely to approach his or her first discussion with German managers in an assertive fashion from the assumption that competition in business occurs within the context of cooperation (Stewart, 1972, p.56). This balance is attained by invoking the unspoken rule of fair play.

Our games traditions, although altered and transformed, are Anglo-Saxon in form; and fair play does mean for us, as for the English, a standard of behavior between weak and the strong—a standard which is curiously incomprehensible to the Germans. During the last war, articles used to appear in German papers exploring this curious Anglo-Saxon notion called "fair play," reproduced without translation—for there was no translation.

Now the element which is so difficult to translate in the idea of "fair play" is not the fact that there are rules. Rules are an integral part of German life, rules for behavior of inferior to superior, for persons of every status, for every formal situation. . . . The point that was incomprehensible was the inclusion of the other person's weakness inside the rules so that "fair play" included in it a state-

ment of relative strength of the opponents and it ceased to be fair to beat a weak opponent.

. . . Our notion of fair play, like theirs [British], includes the opponent, but it includes him far more personally . . . (Mead, 1975, p. 143–145).

I am not implying that the American is in need of a handicap when negotiating with Germans. It is important to note however, that the styles of assertiveness under the assumption of American equality (fair play) and assertiveness under the assumption of German hierarchy may be very different. The general approach of the German toward the weaker opponent may tend to inspire a negative reaction in the American, thus reducing cooperation and motivation.

GERMAN MANAGERS' EXPECTATIONS

Assertiveness, Sophistication, and Direct Confrontation

The current wisdom either leaves the impression or forthrightly states that Americans and Germans share certain verbal behaviors which would cause one to predict that discussion is approached in a mutually understood fashion.

If North Americans discover that someone spoke dubiously or evasively with respect to important matters, they are inclined to regard the person thereafter as unreliable, if not dishonest. Most of the European low-context cultures such as the French, the Germans, and the English show a similar cultural tradition. These cultures give a high degree of social approval to individuals whose verbal behaviors in expressing ideas and feelings are precise, explicit, straightforward, and direct (Gudykunst & Kim, 1984, p. 144).

Such generalizations do not take into account the difference between *Gespräch* (just talking about—casually) and *Besprechung* (discussion in the more formal sense of having a discussion about an issue). *Besprechung* in German culture is a common form of social intercourse in which one has high level discussions about books, political issues, and other weighty topics. This reflects the traditional German values which revere education. Americans would best translate *Besprechung* as a high level, well evidenced, philosophically and logically rigorous debate in which one's credibility is clearly at stake—an activity less familiar to most Americans.

The typical language of most Americans is not the language many Germans use in a high level debate on philosophical and political issues.

In areas where English immigrants brought with them the speech of 16th and 17th century England, we find a language more archaic in syntax and usage than [sic] present-day English. Cut off from the main stream, these pockets of English have survived. But the American language, as written in the newspapers, as spoken over the radio (and television), . . . is instead the language of those who learned it late in life and learned it publicly, in large schools, in the factory, in the ditches, at the polling booth. . . . It is a language of public, external relationships. While the American-born generation was learning this public language, the private talk which expressed the overtones of personal relationships was still cast in a foreign tongue. When they in turn taught their children to speak only American, they taught them a one-dimensional public language, a language oriented to the description of external aspects of behavior, weak in overtones. To recognize this difference one has only to compare the vocabulary with which Hemingway's heroes and heroines attempt to discuss their deepest emotions with the analogous vocabulary of an English novel. All the shades of passion, laughter close to tears, joy tremulous on the edge of revelation, have to be summed up in such phrases as: 'They had a fine time.' Richness in American writing comes from the invocation of objects which themselves have overtones rather than from the use of words which carry with them a linguistic aura. This tendency to a flat dimension of speech has not been reduced by the maintenance of a classical tradition (Mead, 1975, pp. 81–82).

Since many Americans tend not to discuss subjects such as world politics, philosophical and ethical issues with a large degree of academic sophistication, a cultural barrier may be present even if the Germans speak American style English. In a study of a German student exchange program, Hagemann observed that "it was crucial for the Germans, that they could discuss world-politics with their American counterparts, found them interested in environmental protection and disarmament issues and that they could talk with them about private matters of personal importance. . . . If they met Americans who did not meet these demands the relationships remained on the surface" (Hagemann, 1986, p. 8).

This tendency not to enter into sophisticated discussions and develop deeper relationships may be a disadvantage for many Americans who are working with Germans (see Figure 1). In addition, in a society in which one's intellectual credibility[5] establishes one's position in the group and thus determines what one can and can't do, *Besprechung* can become quite heated—as is the case in Germany.

FOCUS: WHEN *BESPRECHUNG* AND DISCUSSION MEET

The management style of German and American managers within the same multinational corporation is more likely to be influenced by their nationality than by the corporate culture. In a study of carefully matched national groups of managers working in the affiliated companies of a large U.S. multinational firm, "cultural differences in management assumptions were not reduced as a result of working for the same multinational firm. If anything, there was slightly more divergence between the national groups within this multinational company than originally found in the INSEAD multinational study" (Laurent, 1986, p. 95).

On the surface we can see two culturally distinct agendas coming together when German and American managers "discuss" matters of importance. The American character with its need to remain impersonal and to be liked avoids argumentum ad hominem. Any attack on the person will indicate disrespect and promote a feeling of dislike for the other,

Figure 1 Development of Discussion Behavior At a Glance

American	Focus	German
Impersonal—act as own agent—will move on when business does not serve his/her needs or when better opportunity arises	Relationship to Business	Not as impersonal—corporation is more cohesive unit—identity more closely associated with position, and security needs met by corporation
Need to be liked—expressed through informal address and gestures	Personal Need	Need for order and establishment of place in hierarchy—expressed through formal address and gestures
Short-term—largely informal—many procedures picked up in progress	Orientation to Corporation	Long-term training—formal—specific rules of procedure learned
Based on accomplishment and image—underlying drive toward equality	Status	Based on education and credentials—underlying drive toward hierarchy
Assertive, tempered with fair play—give benefit of doubt or handicap	Confrontation	Assertive—put other in his/her place
Discussion about sports, weather, occupation: what you do, what you feel about someone. Logical, historical analysis rarely ventured. Native language sophistication usually low.	Common Social Intercourse	Besprechung—rigorous logical examination of the history and elements of an issue. Politics favorite topic. Forceful debate expected. Native language sophistication high.

thus promoting the "unpopular phase," which, as Stewart indicates, may destroy cooperation for Americans.

In contrast, the German manager, with his personal investment in his position and a need to be credible to maintain his or her position, may strike with vigor and enthusiasm at the other's error. The American manager with his lack of practice in German-style debate and often less formal language, education, and training, may quickly be outmaneuvered, cornered, embarrassed, and frustrated. In short, he or she may feel attacked. This possible reaction may be ultimately important because it can be a guiding force for an American.

Beyond the question of character is the more fundamental question of the guidance system of the individual within his or her culture and what effect changing cultural milieu has on the individual guidance system. I define guidance system as that which guides the individual's actions. In discussing some of the expectations of German and American managers, I alluded several times to what could be con-

strued as peer pressure within small groups. How this pressure works to guide the individual's actions, I will argue in the next section, has great implications for developing programs for American success in Germany.

Viewed as systems of argumentation, discussion and *Besprechung* both begin a social phase even though Americans may at first view the forcefulness of the Germans as anti-social (Copeland & Griggs, 1985, p. 105). However, a dissimilarity lends an insight into the difference in the guidance systems and how Germans and Americans perceive each other.

American discussion, with the focus on arriving at consensus, is based on the acceptance of value relativism (which supports the American value of equality and striving for consensus). The guidance system for Americans is partly in the peer group pressure which the individual reacts to but may not be able to predict or define in advance of a situation. Therefore, some Americans have difficulty articulating, consciously conceiving, or debating concepts

Figure 2 Manager Background At a Glance

American	Focus	German
Peer pressure of immediate group—reluctant to go beyond the bounds of fair play in social interaction—backdrop is social relativism	Guidance System	Peer pressure from generalized or larger social group—forceful drive to conform to the standard—backdrop is consistent and clearly known
Generally weaker higher education—weak historical perspective and integrated thought—focus is on the future results—get educational requirements out of the way to get to major to get to career success	Education	Higher education standards generally superior, speak several languages, strong in history, philosophy, politics, literature, music, geography, and art
More group oriented—social phase develops into team spirit—individual strengths are pulled together to act as one	Problem Solving	More individualized and compartmentalized—rely on credentialed and trained professional
Informal awareness—get the hang of variations—often unconscious until pointed out	Learning	Formal awareness—specific instruction given to direct behavior—one known way to act—highly conscious

in their guidance system but rather prefer to consider feedback and adjust their position to accommodate the building of consensus without compromising their personal integrity.

German *Besprechung*, with the focus on arriving at truth or purer concepts, rejects value relativism in support of German values of fixed hierarchy and social order. The German *Besprechung* is argumentation based on the assumption that there is some logically and philosophically attainable truth. The guidance system for Germans is composed of concepts which are consciously taken on by the individual over years of formal learning (a la Hall) and debate. While a German makes the concepts his/her own through *Besprechung*, his/her position is not likely to shift far from a larger group pressure to conform to one hierarchical code.

The peer pressure of the immediate group can often become a driving force for Americans. The irony is that many Germans initially perceive Americans as conformists and themselves as individualists, stating that Americans can't act alone while Germans with their clearly articulated concepts do act alone. Americans, on the other hand, often initially

perceive Germans as conformists and themselves as individualists stating that Germans conform to one larger set of rules while Americans do their own thing.

LEARNING STYLES, TRAINING, INSTRUCTION, AND PROBLEM SOLVING

Education and Training

The ultimate function of group process in American corporations is problem solving and individual motivation (being liked). For Germans motivation is more of a long term consideration such as an annual bonus or career advancement. Problem solving for Germans is more compartmentalized and individualized.

The contrasting elements discussed earlier and outlined in both "At a Glance" summaries (Figures 1 and 2) indicate that considerable cultural distance may have to be traveled by Germans and Americans before they can be assured that cooperation and motivation are the by-products of their combined efforts. The contrasting elements are, of course, a result of the organization and education—the acculturation—of the minds of Germans and Americans. In this section I will examine the different cultural tendencies from the perspective of Hall's definitions of formal and informal culture and discuss some implications for intercultural training and education.

The first level of concern is general preparation for the managerial position. As an educator I must take a hard look at the graduates of our colleges and universities as they compare to their German counterparts. I am not attempting to imply that Germans are better than Americans. All cultural groups excel in some area more than other cultural groups.

Germans are better trained and better educated than Americans. A German university degree means more than its U.S. equivalent because German educational standards are higher and a smaller percentage of the population wins college entrance. Their undergraduate degree is said to be on par with our master's degree. It is taken for granted that men and women who work in business offices are well educated, able to speak a foreign language, and capable of producing coherent, intelligible, thoughtful communications. German business managers are well versed in history, literature, geography, music and art (Hall, 1983, p. 58).

Americans tend to focus on the present as the beginning of the future, whereas Germans tend to "begin every talk, every book, or article with background information giving historical perspective" (Hall, 1983, p. 20). While Hall makes a strong generalization, a contrary incident is rare. American college graduates are not known for having a firm or detailed idea of what happened before they were born. While some pockets of integrated, sophisticated thinking exist, it is by no means the standard. Indeed, many American college students are unable to place significant (newsworthy) events within an over-all political/philosophical framework two months after the occurrence.

In contrast, college educated Germans tend to express a need to know *why* they should do something—a reasoning grounded in a logical understanding of the past. Compared to the rigorous German theoretical and concrete analysis of past events, Americans often appear to be arguing from unverifiable aspirations of a future imagined. While such vision is often a valuable driving force and the basis for American innovation and inventiveness, it may not answer the German need to explicitly know why and, thus, may fall short (from a German perspective) in group problem solving when these two cultures are represented. From the educational perspective, one must conclude that more than a few days of awareness training is needed before successful discussions can result between German and American managers, primarily because of what is not required by the American education system. The contrary may also be true in the preparation of Germans to work with Americans. Tolerance for intuitive thinking may well be a proper focus in part of the German manager's training prior to working with American managers.

Formal and Informal Culture

The unannounced and largely unconscious agenda of small group process among Americans is usually more subtle than the German formal awareness but equally as important. American individuals come together in the initial and critical social phase, "size up" each other, and formally or informally recognize a leader. In a gathering of hierarchical equals the first to speak often emerges as the leader. At this point the embers of team spirit warm once again. As the group moves through purpose and task definition, members define and redefine their roles according to the requirements of the evolving team strategy. Fired with team spirit, inculcated through years of group activity and school sports, the group produces more than the sum of their individual promises.

"In the United States a high spontaneous interest in achievement is counterbalanced by much experience in group activities in which the individual learns to channel achievement needs according to the opinions of others. ... Interestingly enough, the American 'value formula' appears to be largely unconscious or informally understood, as compared to the German one, at any rate" (McClelland et al., 1958, p. 252). Though this observation is 30 years old, it still appears to be quite accurate. The use of modeling (imitation) as a way of acquiring social and political problem-solving strategies is also a way of adjusting to regionalisms. In taking on different roles, Americans become adept at unconsciously adjusting their character to meet the requirements of different situations. In short, says Hall, "Compared to many other societies, ours does not invest tradition with an enormous weight. Even our most powerful traditions do not generate the binding force which is common in some other cultures. ... We Americans have emphasized the informal at the expense of the formal" (Hall, 1973, p. 72).

The German learning style is often characterized by formal learning as defined by Hall (Hall, 1973, p. 68). The characteristics of German frankness and directness are echoed in Hall's example of formal learning: "He will correct the child saying, 'Boys don't do that,' or 'You can't do that,' using a tone of voice indicating that what you are doing is unthinkable. There is no question in the mind of the speaker about where he stands and where every other adult stands" (Hall, 1973, p. 68). German formal awareness is the conscious apprehension of the detailed reality of history which forms an idealistic code of conduct that guides the individual to act in the national interest as if there was no other way.[6]

American informal awareness and learning is an outgrowth of the blending of many cultural traditions, in an environment in which people were compelled to come together to perform group tasks such as clearing land, building shelter, farming, and so on. The reduction of language to the basic nouns and functions was a requirement of communication for the multilingual population under primitive conditions. Cultural variations will always be a part of the vast American society. Americans have had to "get the hang of it" precisely because whatever *it* is, *it* is done with several variations in America.

In a sense, the informal rules such as "fair play" are just as prescriptive of American behavior as the system of German etiquette is prescriptive of much of German social interaction, including forms of address (familiar *Du* and the formal *Sie*). Even the rules for paying local taxes, entering children in schools, or locating a reputable repair person vary by local custom in America and can only be known by asking.[7] The clear difference is that the rules are not overtly shared in America.

The American expectations or informal rules for group discussion are general enough to include the etiquette of American managers from different ethnic backgrounds. As long as notions of equality, being liked, respect, fair play, and so on guide behaviors things run smoothly. "Anxiety, however, follows quickly when this tacit etiquette is breached. ... What happens next depends upon the alternatives provided by the culture for handling anxiety. Ours include withdrawal and anger" (Hall, 1973, p. 76). In the intercultural situation, the American who participates informally in group behavior may feel that something is wrong but may not be able to consciously determine the problem. Without the ability of bringing the informal into conscious awareness, which is a function of awareness and education, many Americans may flounder in a state of confusion, withdrawal and anger.

CONCLUSION

What should become apparent to intercultural trainers working with companies that are bringing German and American personnel together is that they are working with two populations with distinct learning and problem-solving styles. The American is more likely to learn from an interactive simulation. Within the situation the American can "get the hang of" working with someone who has a German style. Trainers and educators of American managers know that the debriefing of the role play, which brings the operative informal rules in to conscious awareness, is the focus of the learning activity. The short-term immersion training so often used today can only supply some basic knowledge and limited role-play experience.

What must never be forgotten in the zeal to train American managers is that their basic guidance system in America is a motivation to accommodate the relative values of the immediate group. While the general cultural awareness exercises that begin most intercultural training may make Americans conscious of their internal workings, much more attention must be given to inculcate an understanding of German social order and the interaction permitted within it.

Knowledge of the language and an in-depth orientation to the culture for the overseas manager and spouse should be mandatory for American success in Germany and German success in the United States. "The high rate of marital difficulties, alcoholism and divorce among American families abroad is well known and reflects a lack of understanding and intelligent planning on the part of American business" (Hall, 1983, p. 88). In our pilot program we became quite aware of the fact that German spouses require much more preparation for a sojourn to America. American short-term planning is in conflict with the long-term preparation needed for most Americans who are going to work with Germans. In Germany the role of the spouse (usually the female) in business includes much less involvement than in the United States. We suspect this has much to do with the lack of attention to spouse preparation that we have observed thus far.

RECOMMENDATION

Long-term programs should be established that provide cultural orientation for overseas families at least three or four years before they start their sojourn with beginning and increasing knowledge of the language as a prerequisite for entry. Such programs should

• attend to the general instructional deficiencies of Americans in the areas of history, philosophy, and politics as studied by Germans,

• prepare Germans to expect and participate in an informal culture guided by value relativism in a spirit of equality,

• incorporate cultural sharing of German and American managers and their families in social settings so

the sojourners can come together before, during, and after their individual experiences to establish a formal support network.

Segments of such programs could be carried on outside the corporate setting to allow for a more open exchange of ideas. In America, colleges and universities could easily establish such programs. Many American colleges and universities which have served as research and development sites for business and industry are also developing alternative evening programs to meet the educational needs in the community. Also, corporate colleges are an ideal setting for extended in-house preparation. In such learning environments, professors can come together with adjunct faculty (private consultants and trainers) to produce a series of seminars which combine lecture instruction, small group intercultural interaction, networking, media presentations, contact with multiple experts over time, and even a well planned group vacation tour to the sojourner's future assignment site.

Part of the programs should be offered in the evening to avoid extensive interference with the employee's regular assignments and to take advantage of the availability of other family members who should be included in intercultural transfer preparation. Cost to the corporation would be greatly reduced in that start-up funds could be partly supplied through federal grants, travel costs would be lessened, and program costs would be covered under regular tuition and materials fees. As a final note, I strongly recommend that such programs for American managers be viewed as graduate level education since they will be entering a society in which education is a mark of status.

NOTES

1. Future references to America and Americans should be understood as referring to the North Eastern United States and the citizens thereof, while references to Germany and Germans should be understood as West Germany and the citizens thereof.

2. Actual German values were 65, with a value of 53 when controlled for age of sample, while the actual

USA values were 46, with a value of 36 when controlled for age of sample.

3. For a quick overview of how small group and interpersonal communication is related to corporate success in America see Peters and Austin, 1985, pp. 233–248.

4. These comparative descriptions correspond to the German social orientation and the American personal orientation discussed by Beatrice Reynolds (1984, p. 276) in her study of German and American values.

5. "In Germany, power can be financial, political, entrepreneurial, managerial or intellectual; of the five, intellectual power seems to rank highest. Many of the heads of German firms have doctoral degrees and are always addressed as 'Herr Doktor.'" (Copeland & Griggs, 1985, p. 120). While there may be exceptions to this rule, exceptions are few and hard to find.

6. "Yet this rigidity has its advantages. People who live and die in formal cultures tend to take a more relaxed view of life than the rest of us because the boundaries of behavior are so clearly marked, even to the permissible deviations. There is never any doubt in anybody's mind that, as long as he does what is expected, he knows what to expect from others" (Hall, 1973, p. 75). "In Germany everything is forbidden unless it is permitted" (Dubos, 1972, p. 100).

7. The perplexing problem for German executives who are new in the United States is that in Germany everything is known thus, *you should not have to ask* to find your way around. But in the USA where change is the watch word, *one has to ask to survive.*

REFERENCES

Bleicher, K., & Paul, H. (1986). Corporate governance systems in a multinational environment: Who knows what's best? *Management International Review,* **26,** (3) 4–15.

Copeland, L., & Griggs, L. (1985). *Going international: How to make friends and deal effectively in the global marketplace.* New York: Random House.

Cyert, R. M., & March, J. G. (1963). *A behavioral theory of the firm.* Englewood Cliffs, N.J.: Prentice-Hall.

Dubos, R. (1972). *A god within.* New York: Charles Scribner's Sons.

Friday, R. A., & Biro, R. (1986–87). [Pilot interviews with German and American personnel at Mobay Corporation (subsidiary of Bayer), Pittsburgh, PA]. Unpublished raw data.

Gudykunst, W. B., & Kim, Y. (1984). *Communicating with strangers: An approach to intercultural communication.* Reading, Mass.: Addison-Wesley.

Hagemann, K. (1986). *Social relationships of foreign students and their psychological significance in different stages of the sojourn.* Summary of unpublished diploma thesis, University of Regensburg, Regensburg, Federal Republic of Germany.

Hall, E. T. (1973). *The silent language.* New York: Doubleday.

Hall, E. T. (1983). *Hidden differences: Studies in international communication—How to communicate with the Germans.* Hamburg, West Germany: Stern Magazine Gruner + Jahr AG & Co.

Hofstede, G. (1984). *Culture's consequences: International differences in work-related values.* Beverly Hills: Sage Publications.

Kohls, L. R. (1987). *Models for comparing and contrasting cultures,* a juried paper, invited for submission to National Association of Foreign Student Advisors, June, 1987.

Laurent, A. (1986). The cross-cultural puzzle of international human resource management. *Human Resource Management,* **25,** 91–103.

McClelland, D. C., Sturr, J. F., Knapp, R. N., & Wendt, H. W. (1958). Obligations of self and society in the United States and Germany. *Journal of Abnormal and Social Psychology,* **56,** 245–255.

Mead, M. (1975). *And keep your powder dry.* New York: William Morrow.

Nyrop, R. F. (Ed.) (1982). *Federal republic of Germany, a country study.* Washington, D.C.: U.S. Government Printing Office.

Peters, T., & Austin, N. (1985). *A passion for excellence.* New York: Warner Communication.

Peters, T., & Waterman, R. (1982). *In search of excellence.* New York: Warner Communication.

Reynolds, B. (1984). A cross-cultural study of values of Germans and Americans. *International Journal of Intercultural Relations*, **8**, 269–278.

Stewart, E. C. (1972). *American cultural patterns: A cross-cultural perspective.* Chicago: Intercultural Press.

Weaver, R. M. (1953). *The ethics of rhetoric.* South Bend, IN.: Rengery/Gateway.

Cultural Variations in Negotiation Styles

SUSAN A. HELLWEG
LARRY A. SAMOVAR
LISA SKOW

As we enter the 1990s, it seems hardly necessary to document the truth of Marshall McLuhan's prophecy about the global village. Nowhere is this international interdependence more evident than in the business arena. From a Toyota plant in Kentucky to a U.S. trade deficit that is now measured in hundreds of billions of dollars, the foreign influence on "doing business" is all around us. Newspapers and magazines abound with stories detailing how, if the United States is to survive, it must learn to adapt to an economic challenge that does well beyond its own boundaries. Earlier calls to engage in a financial battle with Japan have now been replaced with concerns that are far more universal. For example, the twelve-nation European Economic Community (EEC) may completely restructure Europe as a world-class power. Additionally, the six countries of the Association of Southeast Asian Nations (ASEAN) will soon become a major source of influence in the global marketplace.

Adapting to this new marketplace has been difficult for the United States. While talk concerning the

This original article appears here in print for the first time. All rights reserved. Permission to reprint must be obtained from the publisher and the authors. Susan Helwig and Larry Samovar teach at San Diego State University. Lisa Skow is a graduate of San Diego State University.

Pacific Rim, the "twenty-four-hour stock market," and the need for joint ventures can be heard in nearly every corporate office, the facts seem to tell a story of a country that was not prepared to share the rewards of economic power.

When World War II ended, most of the world was decimated. Not only were financial institutions in disarray, but most countries had to fight the war at their front door; hence buildings, including banks, were destroyed. Such was not the case with the United States. We emerged from the war as the only superpower. Economically, we were in control. We set the tempo everywhere. Back in the early 1950s, America monopolized high tech and the majority of the world's automobiles and television sets. Then only a small portion of America's industries faced foreign competition. Even in the 1960s we were the world's largest exporter of manufactured goods. We represented only 5 percent of the world's population, yet we ruled over a vast economic empire.

What has transpired throughout the world in the last twenty years has dramatically changed this picture. For whether we like it or not, it is now a fact of life that the United States must share economic dominance with Japan, West Germany, Great Britain, the Netherlands, Korea, Canada, and a long list of other countries that also compete for a portion of the world's economic bounty. Like all cultures, our deep sense of ethnocentrism has kept us, until recently, from admitting to the economic revolution that was unfolding before us.

The purpose of this chapter is to highlight negotiation styles used by members of other cultures, ones that American business people must be aware of in their future dealings around the globe. With this knowledge, they can adapt to the styles reflected in other cultures; knowledge of only American negotiation techniques is no longer enough to compete successfully in the global marketplace. We have selected three of the most common problems that plague Americans when they attempt to negotiate with other countries. These problems can best be summarized as cultural variations concerning (1) rules for conducting business, (2) the selection of negotiators, and (3) methods of decision making.

CULTURAL VARIATIONS IN CONDUCTING BUSINESS

All cultures explicitly and implicity instruct their members as to the procedural rules that should be followed in both their public and private affairs. From greetings to appropriate dress, members of a culture know the rules for that culture. Most rules for behavior are learned at a low awareness level and hence are acted out with a regularity that hides them even from the user. There are not only general rules that are unique to a culture, but there are also a series of specific cultural codes that help define a particular context. It is our contention that not knowing the rules that apply to the business environment can hinder the international negotiation process. We will now look at some cross-cultural rules for doing business that are often misunderstood by Americans.

Negotiation Atmosphere

American negotiators assume an attitude of "economic gain" in the negotiation process. They expect others to display what they conceive of as "American professionalism," including an aggressive approach toward that which is to be negotiated (Scott, 1981). As they tend to be uninterested in establishing long-term relationships in this context, they view socializing as unimportant. Rather, the American norm is to conduct business in an efficient manner; while compromises may be part of the outcome, in the eyes of the American negotiators, prestige is achieved by their ability to maneuver a debate. In keeping with the notion of American professionalism, they are more likely to presume trust of their counterparts at the onset of negotiations (Graham, 1987).

The French in contrast to Americans, are likely to distrust their counterparts at first. Their negotiations are conducted through formal hospitality. As the French are represented by a heavily bureaucratic government with a history of involvement in international negotiations, they see themselves as more experienced negotiators (Fisher, 1980).

The Japanese believe that socializing is integral to the negotiation process. They are concerned with establishing-long-term business/personal relationships through such transactions—the Japanese view a contract as the beginning of an adaptive process rather than as the end of one. Negotiators from this culture rely on the trust established between the parties involved and on an implicit understanding (Fisher, 1980).

Like the Japanese, Chinese negotiators feel that mutual interests and friendships are important in the negotiation process, so socialization during the contract-agreement process is an expectation. Favorable terms are anticipated from friends; the nature of the relationship between the parties involved is critical to the Chinese. Trust is acquired between negotiators through favorable direct experience. Contracts are not considered as binding by the Chinese as the trust between those involved (Weiss and Stripp, 1985).

In the Middle East, personal relationships are also an important part of negotiations. Hospitality is a first priority in their business transactions (Weiss & Stripp, 1985), and negotiations are initiated with prenegotiation social graces. Trust and respect must be secured for successful negotiations (Scott, 1981).

The general business approach utilized by Brazilians and Mexicans is similar to the approach taken by Middle Eastern negotiators. Since Brazilians cannot rely on a legal system "to iron things out," they focus on establishing and maintaining personal relationships in business transactions (Graham and Herberger, 1983). For Mexicans, the public forum is not considered the appropriate place to consummate negotiations. Likewise, formal negotiations are not viewed by Mexicans as a time for objective analysis and pragmatic matters (Fisher, 1980).

Detail: Depth Versus Breadth

American negotiators assume that many small agreements will be consummated before the final agreement. Members of American negotiating teams want "the facts" pertaining to the negotiation only. Like the French, Americans put considerable emphasis on written agreements or contracts, be-

lieving that American integrity is at stake (Fisher, 1980). They are more concerned with quantity versus quality and with issues that deal with the amount of time involved, rather than with details that might be important to their counterparts (Moran and Harris, 1982).

Believing that much detail is comprehended implicitly in negotiation processes, the Japanese identify fewer specific issues and are less detail oriented than their American counterparts. "The Japanese tend to avoid any appearance of a petty focus on details in negotiations, striving to reach a broad agreement where details are not clearly spelled out" (March, 1985, p. 57). The Japanese rely primarily on general, brief written agreements. They believe that agreed-upon "principles" between negotiators are important, not the specifics of an agreement, principles that are designed to "guide" the agreement relationship (Weiss and Stripp, 1985).

Like the Japanese, the Chinese also prefer written agreements that would probably appear general to American and French negotiators; they leave room for "trust and common sense" (Weiss and Stripp, 1985). The Chinese tend to bargain away details at the negotiation table, preferring to use generalities (Fisher, 1980). Middle Eastern and Mexican negotiators prefer agreements that are bound by an oral understanding; they believe the written agreement is secondary and only represents the strong bond of the oral obligation (Weiss and Stripp, 1985). Thus, like Japanese and Chinese negotiators, a detailed, written agreement is not central to the negotiation process in the Middle East and Mexico.

Communication Style

According to Scott (1981), Americans tend to convey warmth, sincerity, confidence, and positiveness in their communication. March (1985) suggests that Americans are always ready to engage in bargaining. Americans often engage in compromise activity in the negotiation context. Negotiators from the United States tend to automatically assume that English will be spoken in the sessions. The use of translators may put the American participants at a disadvantage since the other side is likely to know a fair amount of English and will have more time to contemplate what is taking place during the translation period. American negotiators tend to be more interested in logical arguments than in the people they are dealing with. They may employ threats, warnings, and continual pushiness, even if their counterparts are signaling "no" (Graham and Herberger, 1983). Americans tend to express their ideas bluntly, silence being perceived as uncomfortable and indicative of trouble.

According to Graham, Campbell, and Meissner (1988), Americans employ a negotiating style similar to that of the British, but less silence is utilized and they are more egalitarian. The British interrupt less in their negotiations than their American counterparts and they have a polite yet indistinct style of negotiating. Scott (1981) describes British negotiators as kind, friendly, sociable, agreeable, flexible, and responsive.

The Japanese appear to be easily persuadable because of their seemingly accepting, passive mien, and they show little reaction to their counterparts during negotiations save for nodding. Japanese negotiators take long pauses, appear not to be rushed, and expect patience from other participants and no interruptions. The Japanese keep their emotions in check (Zimmerman, 1985), but seek simple symbolic expression (Morrison, 1972). According to Yotsukura (1977), the Japanese process 10 percent of a message through its verbal or overt expression and the other 90 percent through personal meaning. The Japanese encourage covert, fragmented expression. The fact that their language leads to a variety of interpretations through its ambiguity leads to frequent communication failures. Furthermore, Japanese verbal expression is encased in layers of indirectness through such phrases as "I think," "perhaps," "probably," and "maybe" (Ishii, 1985; Okabe, 1973; Yotsukura, 1977).

Silence is also part of the Japanese negotiation process. They are more evasive with their feelings and ideas than their Western counterparts. Harmony is crucial to their negotiations; they desire to achieve smoothness in all their transactions, both business and personal, and they may therefore ap-

pear standoffish or inscrutable to the other side (Fisher, 1980). The Japanese are most polite as negotiators and because of their behaviors in this context, they are among the least aggressive among cultures. Their communication is more frequently positive than expressive of "no's" and commands (Graham, Campbell, and Meissner, 1988).

The Chinese tend to be suspicious of Western negotiators. They do not wish to openly confront conflict and therefore shun any proposal-counterproposal style of negotiating. The Chinese must not be forced to withdraw from a stand, due to a possible loss of face (Scott, 1981). Chinese negotiators make concessions slowly and refrain from small talk. They do not accept hypothetical examples (Weiss and Stripp, 1985).

Unlike the Japanese, the French employ frequent "no" communication and often insist on using their own language in the negotiation settings (Scott, 1981). Said to be the most "difficult" of Europeans, French negotiators may be long-winded and rationalize a great deal without bargaining or compromising. They tend to put forth all their information and establish principles of reasoning first; new information is not easily accepted by them. They may thus be perceived as inflexible by opposing negotiation teams (Fisher, 1980). According to Weiss and Stripp (1985), the French relish debate and welcome and respect dissent. They are confrontational and competitive—to the French, negotiation involves a search for well-reasoned arguments.

For Germans, strength lies in the bidding stage of negotiation. They do not tend to compromise. German negotiators are generally clear, firm, and assertive in their expression—once a bid is put forth, it becomes sacrosanct and they are less likely to accept other possibilities (Scott, 1981). The Germans may not ask many questions in the negotiation process but will disclose a great deal and may frequently interrupt (Graham, Campbell, and Meissner, 1988).

In sharp contrast to American negotiators, "rhetoric and the grand idea are pursued" by Mexican negotiators (Fisher, 1980, p. 20). These negotiators do not see any advantage in frank talk. They may play the weaker side because of the perception that

Americans have sympathy for the disadvantaged, the side that needs special consideration, but at the same time they are still extremely wary of patronizing assistance or concessions. Compromise to them threatens dignity in the negotiation process. Mexican negotiators prefer the deductive approach; they start with a general proposal, define the issues, and then make conclusions with the little detail or evidence used. More emphasis is placed upon contemplation and intuition. Mexicans stand closer than Americans and Japanese; they use more physical contact to show confidence (Fisher, 1980).

Brazilian negotiators are very aggressive by American standards, use a lot of commands, and employ a high frequency of "no's" and "you's." They do not engage in silence tactics, frequent touching, or facial gazing (Graham, Campbell, and Meissner, 1988). Brazilians may compete with each other for the floor and often appear to Americans to be rude and poor listeners (Graham and Herberger, 1983).

CULTURAL VARIATIONS IN SELECTING NEGOTIATORS

Our research and experience has led us to conclude that Americans also fail to understand the type of person they will be facing at the negotiating table. Like language, person perception is culturally based. While in the United States and Mexico one might consider a dynamic speaker to be a highly credible source, in Japan such a person is not to be trusted. Because of cultural variations in person perception, status, rank, and so on, not all cultures select the same type of individual to attend negotiating sessions. A few cultural differences in personnel selection will help illustrate this second variation in negotiation styles.

Younger negotiators (in the thirties or even twenties) are more common among American teams than in other cultures. Women may be included although few hold top-level positions (Greenwald, 1983). Technical expertise is a critical concern in the selection of American negotiation representatives. The social background, education, and age of candidates have little to do with their selection as negotiating team members or leaders.

Americans believe that relying on social status for such selection is unreasonable. In the international arena, team members from the United States make the assumption that they are world leaders and advisors, solicited or unsolicited (Fisher, 1980). Using a "John Wayne" type of strategy, American negotiators often believe they can do it alone and handle any negotiation situation. This strategy saves money on personnel and Americans pride themselves on having full authority to make decisions (Graham and Herberger, 1983).

French negotiation team members are usually selected on the basis of their social and professional status (Fisher, 1980). In addition, Weiss and Stripp (1985) report that French team members are selected based on social, professional, academic, and family ties. Similarity in personality and background among French negotiators is important and appears to be influential in the negotiation process. Among German negotiators similarity does not seem to be an important factor. And while the status and role of negotiators is crucial among British negotiators, similarity among them has been found to have little effect (Campbell, Graham, Jolibert, and Meissner, 1988).

The average age of Japanese business negotiators is the late thirties, with the leader being at least in his forties. Women are not usually participants on a Japanese negotiation team (Greenwald, 1983). Selection of negotiators is based largely on status and knowledge (Weiss and Stripp, 1985), with age seniority being the single most important criterion used in the selection of team leaders (Fisher, 1980). Chinese negotiators expect to deal with someone of authority and high status, and they feel slighted if they do not negotiate with such individuals (Scott, 1981).

Middle Eastern negotiators select negotiation team members similarly to the Japanese. The oldest member is usually the leader and younger members may even be ignored on Iranian teams (Soderberg, 1985). Negotiators from Saudi Arabia are generally selected on the basis of status and loyalty. Americans have commented that Saudis like to work alone when negotiating and take credit for accomplishments while passing blame on to others. The first person to enter the room often has the highest rank in Saudi negotiations and titles are frequently used (Weiss and Stripp, 1985).

Personal qualities and connections are often the criteria for selection on Mexican negotiating teams. Group dynamics depend upon the social relationships among team members. Who holds authority on these teams is not always apparent; a subordinate present with a team member (for example, personal secretary) may indicate authority. Even personal secretaries to high authorities may be given more respect than an official who does not have *palanca* (leverage). Authority tends to be inherent in the individual on the team, not in the individual's position (Fisher, 1980).

CULTURAL VARIATIONS IN DECISION MAKING

There are vast cultural differences in how people think, apply forms of reasoning, and make decisions. Unless individuals have had experiences with people from other cultures who follow different patterns of thought, most will assume everyone thinks in much the same manner. In the Western view, we believe that we can discover truth if we just apply the correct steps of the scientific method. We believe that if we follow the Aristotelian modes of reasoning all problems will be solved. The Eastern version, best illustrated by Taoist thought, holds that truth, not the individual, is the active agent and ways of knowing take a variety of forms. Even the simple Western notion of introduction, body, and conclusion is not found in most of the world. In short, cultural variations in decision making represent yet another problem facing American negotiators.

Problem-Solving Process

American negotiators view negotiation sessions as problem-solving sessions, even if no real problem exists. They tend to compartmentalize issues, focusing on one issue at a time, instead of negotiating many issues together. They are preoccupied with who makes the decisions on the opposing side, to

whom they should be directing their proposals. Americans see themselves in the negotiating setting as universal problem solvers, working in everyone's best interests (Fisher, 1980). They rely on rational thinking and concrete data in their negotiations (Weiss and Stripp, 1985) and utilize a factual inductive style of persuasion (Glenn, Witmeyer, and Stevenson, 1977).

The French have no problem with open disagreement—they debate more than they bargain and are less apt than Americans to be flexible for the sake of agreement. Decisions are made with self-assurance. They start with a long-range view of their purposes, as opposed to Americans, who work with more short-range objectives (Fisher, 1980). The French are generally conservative, safe decision makers. Decisions are centrally made and by top authorities (Weiss and Stripp, 1985).

The Western concept of decision making is not applicable to the Japanese, who depend heavily on middle-level expertise; subordinates brief superiors who in turn use their influence to negotiate and make decisions. The Japanese use a consensus-building, direction-taking process where everyone affected by the decision is included in the process. For the Chinese, on the other hand, decision-making is more authoritative than consensual; decisions are made by higher authorities without the inclusion of subordinates (Weiss and Stripp, 1985). The Japanese allow little room for flexibility in their negotiations, and they are slow in producing conclusions but fast in implementation. They stick to a decision once it is made (Fisher, 1980). The Japanese will not often ask for more than they need, although they may offer less than they can eventually offer. Proposal-counterproposal negotiating with the Japanese is not effective because their teams take so long to make decisions. Japanese negotiators make decisions on the basis of detailed information rather than persuasive arguments. Informal agreements and then written agreements are reached among all concerned.

Middle-Easterners can be described as having an intuitive-affective approach to persuasion. Broad issues that do not appear to be directly related to the issue at hand are brought up; issues are linked to gether on the basis of whether or not the speaker likes the issues. Personal bias is often exercised (Glenn, Witmeyer, and Stevenson, 1977). Negotiation teams from Saudi Arabia do not make decisions on the basis of empirical reasoning; while subordinates are consulted informally, the leader always makes the final decision, and Saudis expect the top man to negotiate with them (Weiss and Stripp, 1985).

The Mexicans use a centralized decision-making process. They view authority as being inherent within the individual, not his position; delegating of authority by an individual would be seen as a surrendering of assets. Making trade-offs is common for Mexican negotiators, including additional issues that are not part of the business at hand (Fisher, 1980).

Organizational Structure

For Americans the task-related stage is the most important for successful negotiations, where the most information is given (Adler, Graham, and Gehrke, 1987). But Americans tend to move toward the persuasion (bargaining) stage too quickly, not spending enough time gathering information. Americans usually approach negotiations sequentially, taking one thing at a time. For Americans, concessions on individual issues lead to the final agreement (Graham and Herberger, 1983). Negotiation outcomes to Americans depend upon events at the negotiation table, not the role of the negotiator or prenegotiation socializing (Campbell, Graham, Jolibert, and Meissner, 1988).

The French engage in a lateral-style of negotiation; the whole deal is covered each step of the way. First comes the outline agreement, then the principal agreement, and then the headings agreement (Scott, 1981).

The Japanese do not discuss bargaining tactics. Prenegotiations move slowly and cautiously. The Japanese do not openly disagree during formal negotiations; they would consider this distasteful and embarrassing. They often use mediators during negotiations, and they basically take one position throughout the process; adjustments or modifications can be made once the final agreement is decided upon. American negotiators might see this as

devious (Fisher, 1980). A seller may often express regret and apologies before offering a request. The Chinese state their proposition in the beginning and do not enhance it if the opposing side raises doubts (Weiss and Stripp, 1985). Concessions may come only at the end with negotiators from the Far East (Graham and Herberger, 1983).

Prenegotiation is crucial for successful Middle Eastern negotiations; it is only after respect and trust have been acquired that the hard negotiations will take place. Establishing a comfortable climate and spending time on the exploratory phase of negotiations are therefore crucial (Scott, 1981).

For Mexicans also the beginning stage of negotiations is used for social discourse and gaining trust among participants. This phase is crucial to them for successful and harmonious negotiations (Weiss and Stripp, 1985). In negotiations with Brazilians, the first stage of the process, nontask-sounding (where pleasantries and nonbusiness information are exchanged) may be lengthened if the Brazilians feel that the other side is impatient. Such impatience may lead them to be apprehensive about beginning information-seeking that starts the actual business negotiations. Brazilians offer high prices and eventually make concessions (Graham and Herberger, 1983).

CONCLUSION

Most of the reasons why Americans overlook cultural differences are traceable to strong feelings of ethnocentrism that influence how they send and receive messages. What makes ethnocentrism such a powerful and insidious force in communication is that it often exists invisibly (for example, we only study Western philosophers) and is usually invisible in its manifestations (for example, we approach problems with a Western orientation). The fact that many other cultures also demonstrate these feelings of conscious and unconscious superiority makes ethnocentrism especially difficult to control in the negotiating context.

It is our contention that sensitivity to cultural differences must begin before negotiation teams confront their counterparts from other countries. Most critics seem to agree that currently our universities are contributing to ethnocentric behavior instead of reducing it, by training people to do things "the American way" (Graham and Herberger, 1983, p. 161), a way, as we have argued, that may hinder international negotiations.

◆

REFERENCES

Adler, N. J., Graham, J. L., and Gehrke, T. S. (1987). "Business Negotiations in Canada, Mexico, and the United States." *Journal of Business Research*, *15*, 411–429.

Campbell, N. C. G., Graham, J. L., Jolibert, A., and Meissner, H. G. (1988). "Marketing Negotiations in France, Germany, the United Kingdom, and the United States." *Journal of Marketing*, *52*, 49–62.

Fisher, G. (1980). *International Negotiation: A Cross-Cultural Perspective*. Chicago, Ill.: Intercultural Press, Inc.

Glenn, E. S., Witmeyer, D., and Stevenson, K. A. (1977). "Cultural Styles of Persuasion." *International Journal of Intercultural Relations*, *1* (3), 52–66.

Graham, J. L. (1987). "Deference Given the Buyer: Variations Across Twelve Cultures." In F. Lorange and F. Contractor (Eds.), *Cooperative Strategies in International Business*. Lexington, Mass.: Lexington Books.

Graham, J. L., Campbell, N., and Meissner, H. G. (1988). *Culture, Negotiations, and International Cooperative Ventures*. Unpublished manuscript.

Graham, J. L., and Herberger, R. A., Jr. (1983). "Negotiators Abroad—Don't Shoot from the Hip." *Harvard Business Review*, *61*, 160–168.

Greenwald, J. (1983, August 1). "The Negotiation Waltz." *Time*, pp. 41–42.

Hall, E. T. (1977). *Beyond Culture*. New York: Anchor Books.

Ishii, S. (1985). "Thought Patterns as Modes of Rhetoric: The United States and Japan." In L. A. Samovar and R. E. Porter (Eds.), *Intercultural Communication: A Reader* (4th ed.) Belmont, Calif.: Wadsworth.

March, R. (1985, April). "East Meets West at the Negotiating Table." *Winds*, pp. 47–55.

Moran, R. T., and Harris, P. R. (1982). *Managing Cultural Synergy*. Houston: Gulf.

Morrison, J. L. (1972). "The Absence of a Rhetorical Tradition in Japanese Culture." *Western Speech*, *36*, 89–102.

Okabe, R. (1973). "Yukichi Fukuzawa: A Promulgator of Western Rhetoric in Japan." *Quarterly Journal of Speech*, *59*, 186–195.

Scott, B. (1981). *The Skills of Negotiating*. New York: Wiley.

Soderberg, D. C. (1985). *A Study of the Influence of Culture on Iranian and American Negotiations*. Unpublished master's thesis, San Diego State University, San Diego, Calif.

Weiss, S. E., and Stripp, W. (1985). *Negotiating with Foreign Businesspersons: An Introduction for Americans with Propositions on Six Cultures*. Working paper no. 1, New York University, Graduate School of Business Administration.

Yotsukura, S. (1977). "Ethnolinguistic Introduction to Japanese Literature." In W. C. McCormack and S. A. Wurm (Eds.), *Language and Thought: Anthropological Issues*. Hague, The Netherlands: Mouton.

Zimmerman, M. (1985). *How to Do Business with the Japanese*. New York: Random House.

The Cultural Grid:
A Framework for
Multicultural Counseling

ANNE PEDERSEN
PAUL PEDERSEN

From a practical standpoint, the interview is the most commonly used method for gathering and evaluating information about an individual (Zima, 1983; Goodale, 1982). Culturally intentional interviewing is the 'key' to effective counseling in the typical day of persons dealing one-on-one with employees, colleagues, superiors, customers, suppliers, students, teachers and the outside public (Ivey, Ivey & Semik Downing, 1987).

Is this almost unquestioned dependence on the interview for organizational and personal change justified? The evidence, at least occasionally, suggests that the counseling interview is not entirely reliable (Meehl, 1954; Egan, 1985, p. 61). First, the interviewer's ability to collect and refine information in an accurate manner for decision-making is influenced by her/his own culturally bound filter. Second, the interviewer is subjected to situational pressures, changing personal preference for a particular interview style, and lack of cultural awareness or certainty. There is considerable margin for error due to personal and cultural aspects of the interview as an evaluation tool.

Should the interview, then, be eliminated as a technique from which to guide personal and orga-

From *International Journal for the Advancement of Counselling*, Vol. 12 (1989), pp. 299–307. Reprinted by permission of Kluwer Academic Publishers. Anne and Paul Pedersen teach at Syracuse University.

nizational change? The anwer is certainly 'no.' The very pervasiveness of interviewing indicates that it fulfills a basic human need for both the interviewer and the person being interviewed. The interview provides an opportunity for both parties to 'know' the persons with whom they will work. While the interview should not be discarded, it should certainly be used with care.

The multicultural situation is especially complicated and most likely to test the counselor's abilities in face-to-face interviews. Working across cultures, counselors often must make decisions with incomplete data and/or with little experience in judging the quality of limited information. Data that are available from one culture may not be comparable to similar data in a different culture. In addition, it is well documented that some persons prefer to establish a personal relationship through face-to-face contact with others before getting on with the task. This individual interaction provides a valuable basis for the subsequent adjustment or socialization process.

How might concepts from counseling enhance the decision making ability of counselors in a cross cultural situation? The purpose of this paper is to describe a cross cultural counseling approach to the interview. Although traditional objectives of counseling are complicated by cultural differences, the interview provides a means to understand complex cultural relationships. The first step in cross cultural counseling is the differentiation between 'cultural' and 'personal' aspects of misunderstandings in the multicultural-counseling-interview (Pedersen, 1988).

EXPECTATIONS AND BEHAVIORS

In the process of counseling, there has been a marked tendency to presume that complex cultural factors first must be simplified to obtain concise criteria for prediction and decision making. For that reason, the entire constellation of potentially salient social system variables which shape our behavior are condensed to a few, obvious concrete categories such as educational level, nationality, or minority identity. Our natural tendency is to construct simplified labels of complex reality such as right and wrong, good and bad in order to manage that reality more conveniently without necessarily considering the cultural context. When we behave rationally with regard to the label we have just created, we assume the behavior is appropriately generalizable to the "real" outside world. It is dangerous to confuse labels with reality.

Normative behaviors, such as appearance appropriate to the person's qualifications, become criteria for judgment in isolation from other factors. As a consequence of reducing a complicated culture to a few obvious behaviors and disregarding the culturally learned expectation and values which give each behavior meaning, misinterpretations occur.

Sometimes the expectations by the counselor and the client are quite different. This preference for simplicity, then, often masks both the degree of similarity and difference between the client or the counselor. Without understanding the culturally learned *expectations*, it is nearly impossible to accurately interpret *behavior* by either the client or counselor. Culture has made a profound contribution to our understanding of human behavior by complicating explanations of personal development and interpersonal contact.

Some counselors are better able to manage complexity than others. The more skilled create several dimensions in a range of alternatives to explain a situation and are able to see connections among different possibilities. This ability has been identified as a necessity in the field of physics (Bohr, 1950). Bohr proposed the principle of complementarity. This states that many phenomena can only be understood from several perspectives. Light, for example, may be regarded both as a particle and as a wave. Both quantum and wave theories are necessary to explain the real nature of light. In the same manner, a satisfactory understanding of cross-cultural interaction requires a broad, rather than a narrow, focus; tolerance for initial ambiguity; avoidance of premature conclusions; and the ability to operate with multiple perspectives and differentiation of thought (Triandis, 1975).

In recognizing complexity as a friend rather than as an enemy of multicultural counseling, it is neces-

sary to consider the many social system variables and psychological perspectives that contribute to behavior. Only then can the counseling interview select those elements which are salient for each situation and point in time.

The process of differentiation implies a change in human growth and development. A comprehensive model to assess multicultural interaction will need the capacity to capture the dynamic factors that influence a person's behavior and intentions. Such a model encourages the more fluid analysis typical of analogical judgment, yet foster the creation of orderly categories to help the interviewer interpret relationships.

Rather than refer to a person's 'culture' as an external factor, which is simple but vague and abstract, an accurate assessment must locate "culture" *in the person* where it can be understood with reference to the intended expectations and values. A skilled interviewer will accurately identify the salient social system variable influencing a client's expectations and values to explain the attendant behaviors.

Pedersen and Pedersen (Hines and Pedersen, 1982; Pedersen and Pedersen, 1985; Pedersen, 1988) have developed a Cultural Grid to help the interviewer organize this complicated but not chaotic information. The cultural grid is a heuristic framework proposed for counselors to:

1. represent a unique personal cultural orientation;

2. identify and describe the cultural aspect of a situation; and

3. form hypotheses about cultural vs. personal differences

The cultural grid framework suggests a network of behaviors, expectations and values on the one hand and social system variables on the other hand. This framework might be useful for understanding an individual's 'personal cultural orientation' to make a *particular* decision in a *certain* way at a *certain* time. If you were to fill in this grid for a particular decision you have made your world understand how your decision was culturally influenced.

The Cultural Grid provides an open-ended range of conceptual social system categories for organiz-

Cognitive perspective

Social system variable	Role behavior	Expectation	Value-Meaning

Demographic
   race
   gender
   age
   other			

Ethnographic
   nationality
   ethnicity
   language			

Status level
   economic
   social
   educational			

Affiliation
   formal
   non-formal
   informal			

Figure 1 The *Cultural Grid*: Personal cultural orientation.

ing the complex and dynamic variables of a person's context. These categories provide a conceptual map for the interviewer to explain how the interviewee's behaviors fit with expectation and value.

As an example of how the Cultural Grid might be useful in understanding the role of culture in counseling in connection with a course in cross cultural counseling where the cultural grid was taught, students are asked to analyze the role of culture in the interview by filling in the categories of the Cultural Grid. The following excerpts provide an example from one such analysis (Fohs, 1982).

The differing Social System Variables between us are:

1. *Age*—He is 45 and I am 29. This did not seem to affect our interaction.

2. *Economic Class*—He is from the lower socio-economic strata and I am from the middle. He has experienced the feeling of no hope and I have not. Much of any difference here may be mitigated by the fact that he is now somewhat in the middle strata.

3. *Affiliation*—He does not perceive himself to be at all limited to his actions by his disability, at least at close quarters (he's visually disabled). This did not seem to have any effect on our interaction.

At this point in time this individual is very close to, if not already completely bicultural. If he functions effectively within his role he has the potential of being a cultural interpreter. However, there is also the possibility that he might find himself in a position of not being completely trusted by either camp if he enacts his strategy for change. I see this as a possibility, not necessarily a probability.

Many things are changing in his life right now. Because of his new job he will now be making the

Table 1 Client Characteristics

Role Behavior	Expectations	Value, Meaning
Working in a job that involves change agentry.	· Other people will derive hope and will have reason to go out and improve. He will feel a sense of accomplishment. ·	Other people will *see* these people trying to improve themselves and will have better opinions of them and will reach out to give them the help they need.

economic transition to the middle class. To an extent, he has already started the social transition, and yet he would also like to maintain his present social network as well. His being in between may also be an issue right now as well. He gave an illustration of this indirectly when he told me about a comment by a girl client of his that she would not be able to associate with his daughters because they will be 'high classed people.' This seemed to affect him quite a bit; although he is determined not to see this happen, the fear of this possibility is in his mind.

THE CULTURAL GRID AND ANALYSIS OF MISUNDERSTANDING BETWEEN PERSONS

In discriminating between cross 'cultural' conflict and that type of misinterpretation more appropriately rooted in 'personal' difference, it is useful to consider the implications of similarity and difference in behavior and expectation *between* two individuals. Given that similarity of behavior and expectation are not always possible, or perhaps even desirable, it is necessary to consider the importance of accurate interpretation and mutual agreement of expectations in the analysis of personnel interaction. Both persons may rightly agree to disagree if each accurately understands the other person's intention.

Cultural misunderstanding and conflict occur when two persons with differing cultural orientations assume that they share the same experiences

for a situation but choose different behavior to convey their intentions. Each inaccurately interprets the other's behavior from the viewpoint of her/his own cultural experience. Different behaviors may or may not indicate similar expectations.

By contrast, a personal conflict is more likely to be the result of disagreement in expectations. For example, two sales persons, a Japanese and an Australian, meet in Hong Kong. The Japanese has a flexible set of greeting *behaviors* from which to choose according to the situation. At home with certain elders, he/she may bow. On other occasions, a half bow and an extension of the hand may be chosen. Long accustomed to business transactions with Commonwealth nations, (s)he may simply offer a hand, followed by a business card as he/she is *expected*. Both know which initial greeting *behavior* is intended to convey the expectation of politeness to the other. However, one chooses not to perform in this manner for reasons of her/his own. Owing to occupational status or perceived inequality of resources, one may delay extending the hand. In this case, the behavior patterns are quite similar, but the expectations for the outcome are different. Obvious cultural differences mask a personal disagreement.

Personal misunderstandings are a reality of daily life across all occupations. This type of situation may be more complicated than necessary when it occurs between persons of more obviously differing cultural orientations. Through matching behaviors and expectations from the Cultural Grid, the interviewer has waking criteria to evaluate performance and propose intervention.

Behavior

	SAME	DIFFERENT
SAME		
DIFFERENT		

Expectation

Figure 2 Summary of interaction between two personal cultural orientations.

IMPORTANCE OF ANALYSIS
TO COUNSELING

Unless the cross cultural misunderstanding or conflict is identified and distinguished from the elements of personal conflict, the following *negative* chain of events may occur:

1. The different behaviors will suggest that expectations may also be different;

2. As different behaviors persist, the two persons may conclude that they do *not* share the same expectations;

3. One of the two persons may choose to modify behaviors to match the other person, due perhaps to power constraints of the most powerful partner. However, the sense of shared expectations will become more and more divergent;

4. Both partners may ultimately resort to total conflict where both expectations and behaviors are different and misunderstood;

5. Both partners will conclude that there is a low level of agreement between them;

6. Neither partner will be aware that there is also a low level of accuracy in their communication.

If the cross cultural nature of the situation is identified and distinguished as separate from personal hostility, the following *positive* chain of events is likely to occur:

1. The different behaviors will be understood as expressions of shared expectations;

2. The two or more persons will conclude that they do share the same expectations in spite of their different behaviors;

3. One or both of the two persons may choose to modify their behavior to match the other person so that both the expectations and the behaviors will be similar;

4. Both partners may ultimately move toward a more harmonious situation where both the expectations and the behaviors are similar;

5. Both partners may conclude there is *either* a high or a low level of agreement between them;

6. Both partners will be aware that there is a high level of accuracy in their communication.

The Cultural Grid was used to analyze an interview transcript with a 78 year old Irish widow and grandmother who was chronically ill and had lived in a private care facility for some years. To understand her personal cultural orientation the counselor must understand many other factors than age, marital status and the nature of her illness. (Pedersen and Pedersen, 1989). A content analysis of the interview emphasized the importance of 'independence' as a foundation value. There was some conflict between her view of herself based on her extremely active and full past life and her view of herself in the present situation. She was unwilling to give up her image as an independent and self-sufficient person in exchange for the view of herself reflected by others who describe her as 'aged.' Understanding her personal cultural orientation and the expectations behind her behaviors could help her counselor accurately interpret those behaviors which follow from independence and self sufficiency from her perceptual viewpoint. At different points in the interview, social system variables from different aspects of her self identity became salient making it difficult for the counselor to interpret her behaviors from *her* personal cultural orientation. Each aspect of her past and present culture adds a richness to the understanding of her cultural identity beyond the singular description of 'aged.'

CONCLUSION

There is good reason to believe that counseling fulfills a need for both the counselor and the client beyond the gathering of information. This is particularly true in the multicultural situation. Concepts derived from the Cultural Grid provide structure for the process of the interview. They also produce criteria for the evaluation both of individual performance and personnel interaction.

Culturally learned values and expectations are essential data in the appropriate interpretation of performance. The Cultural Grid is a heuristic framework that might help the interviewer distinguish between cultural and personal aspects of a situation. Through the understanding of the complex interaction of social system variables with behaviors, expectations, and values, it is possible for the counselor to more accurately assess the cultural context. While much research on the Cultural Grid is needed an accurate understanding of behavior from the client's personal cultural orientation is the necessary first step in the multicultural counseling process.

REFERENCES

Bohr, N. (1950). On the notion of causality and complementarity. *Science* 11: 51–54.

Egan, G. (1985). *Change Agent Skills in Helping and Human Service Settings* Monterey, CA: Brooks/Cole.

Fohs, M. (1982). Tape transcript submitted for credit, Syracuse University, unpublished manuscript.

Goodale, J. G. (1982). *The Fine Art of Interviewing*. Englewood Cliffs, N.J.: Prentice-Hall.

Hines, A. & Pedersen, P. (March, 1982). The Cultural Grid: Management guidelines for a personal cultural orientation. *The Cultural Learning Institute Report* Honolulu, HI: East West Center.

Ivey, A., Ivey, M. & Simek-Downing. (1987). *Counseling & Psychotherapy* Englewood Cliffs, N.J.: Prentice-Hall.

Meehl, P. E. (1954). *Clinical vs. Statistical Prediction* Minneapolis, MN: University of Minnesota Press.

Pedersen, A. & Pedersen, P. (1985). In: Samovar, L. & Porter, R. (eds.), *Intercultural Communication: A Reader* Belmont, CA: Wadsworth.

Pedersen, A. & Pedersen, P. (1989). *The Place of Age in Culture: An Application of the Cultural Grid*, unpublished manuscript.

Pedersen, P. (1988) *A Handbook to Develop Multicultural Awareness*. Washington, DC: AACD.

Triandis, H. C. (1975). Cultural training, cognitive complexity and interpersonal attitudes. In: Brislin, R. & Bocner, S. & Linner, W. (eds.), *Cross Cultural Perspectives on Learning* New York: Wiley.

Zima, J. P. (1983). *Interviewing: Key to Effective Management* Chicago: Science Research Associates.

The Role of Culture in Health and Disease

KIM WITTE

How do you get a cold? Do you "catch it" from standing in a cold draft? Are you being punished by the gods, having bad luck, or simply "run down"? Perhaps you caught a virus or perhaps you are the victim of a supernatural spell.

Your answer probably depends on your cultural background. Each culture has certain beliefs about health and disease that explain how and why one gets sick. Tribal peoples from Southeast Asia may believe that they are being punished, so they ask the shaman to intervene on their behalf and talk to the gods. Mexicans or South Americans may believe they are the victims of bad luck or that someone cast an evil spell on them. They seek help from curanderos (folk healers). White Americans might believe that they have "caught" the cold from a draft or from a virus and they go to a physician for treatment.

Culturally based beliefs about health and illness influence our interactions with people from other cultures—especially in health care settings. Cultural beliefs are subtle and may be unknown to the health practitioner but obvious to the patient. The chances for miscommunication, noncooperation with medical treatments, and even poor health outcomes increase when the health practitioner and patient view health and disease differently. A person's socialization and cultural background form the framework from which he or she communicates, although we tend to assume that other people

have similar definitions of the words we use to communicate. Our nonverbal communication also is culturally based. In some cultures, one must not look one's perceived superior (for example, a physician) in the eye. In other cultures, this behavior indicates the person is not listening.

Only by understanding other cultures' views of health and disease can the health needs of diverse populations representing different cultural groups be served. Intercultural communication specialists can help physicians, health care organizations (for example, hospitals), and public health officials understand and communicate effectively with patients. By incorporating traditional medical beliefs of a given culture with modern medical practices, physicians can help patients achieve optimal health within the patient's cultural framework. By framing medical diagnoses and treatments in language and terms the patient understands, the physician increases patients' understanding and willingness to comply with medical regimens. Conversely, if the physician fails to understand the patient's cultural framework, the patient may not understand the treatment nor adhere to the doctor's recommendations. For example, suppose a patient has been diagnosed with hypertension but feels fine. One of the patient's health beliefs is that, if one feels fine, medicine is unnecessary. If the physician does not counter this belief, the patient may not take the medicine and may thus jeopardize his or her health. The focus in this chapter, then, will be on patients from different cultures and their interaction with mainstream American health care professionals.

ETHNOMEDICAL SYSTEMS

Ethnomedical systems are the culturally unique beliefs and knowledge about health and disease held by the culture's members (both health experts and nonexperts) (McElroy & Townsend, 1985). Disease is defined as an objective phenomenon of organic malfunction (for example, bacterial infection, viral attack, injury). Illness is an individual's perception of "not feeling well." Someone can have a disease yet not feel ill (for example, hypertension); on the other hand, one can feel ill but not have a disease (psychosomatic illnesses). Usually, however, one experiences disease and illness simultaneously (the flu, cancer, infection). The biomedical perspective of Western medicine focuses more on objective, physiological processes of disease while non-Western medical systems tend to focus more on subjective perceptions of illness. No one medical system is right or correct; rather, each system provides a unique approach to understanding health and disease.

Several ethnomedical systems exist in today's world, and these will be our focus. It is important to note that as people become more assimilated into certain societies (for example, Western industrial societies), previous cultural beliefs about health and illness fade and new beliefs acquired through acculturation become more prominent. Therefore, when ethnomedical systems are discussed here, it is assumed that persons are still embedded in their respective cultures (they have not acculturated to another culture).

Medical systems serve multiple functions in culture: (1) They explain why disease or illness occurs; (2) they support moral cultural norms; and (3) they serve to control aggression.

When explaining why illnesses occur, it is important to remember that all medical systems are "logical." That is, the prescribed cure relates to the perceived cause of the illness. In Western medical systems (the United States, for example), the streptococcus bacteria is thought to cause illness and is treated with antibiotics. In non-Western societies, the treatment also is logically related to the cause: If Arctic Indians are experiencing soul loss (an illness), the treatment is confession and sacrifice; if a member of a primitive tribe breaches a taboo and becomes ill as a result, the treatment also is confession; if spirit intrusion is believed to be causing the illness, exorcism will cure it.

Disease and illness can be examined from multiple levels of causation (Clark, 1983). *Immediate* causes of disease include viruses or malignancies. *Underlying* causes of disease include exposure to infection, poor sanitation, or weak immunization systems. Finally, bad luck, stress, or "God's will" characterize *ultimate* causes of disease. Western

medical systems focus most on immediate causes of disease and to a lesser extent on underlying causes, while non-Western medical systems typically focus on ultimate causes of disease and health. Metaphysical, supernatural, and religious beliefs play a large role in views on health and disease in many cultures.

Disease also has been used as a form of social control to support moral norms of a culture (Foster and Anderson, 1978). When the plague struck Europe, the prevailing notion was that one had better be good to avoid getting sick. In animistic cultures, disease comes from spirits of the dead. For example, the Lugbara people of the Congo believe that the dead are listening to the words of the living, and if the dead don't like what they hear, they cause illness in the living. Thus, the people are motivated to conform to a certain code of behavior.

Finally, disease has been used to control aggression (Foster and Anderson, 1978). In many cultures, hostility toward the perceived disease agent is one means to vent aggressive tendencies. For instance, the Ifaluk people of Micronesia believe that illness is caused by ghosts called alus, and they deploy aggression against the ghosts instead of each other. Likewise, Navajo Indians believe that witchcraft is the cause of illness. Other villages are always the source of this witchcraft so violence against them is acceptable, whereas violence within the tribe would not be acceptable.

Most ethnomedical systems fall into one of three categories: (1) personalistic systems; (2) naturalistic systems; and (3) scientific systems (Foster and Anderson, 1978). Non-Western medical systems focus on either naturalistic or personalistic etiologies of disease, in which the person is viewed holistically. A body part cannot be treated separately from the mind—if one gets the flu, both the body and mind are treated through herbal treatments and confession. Scientific medical systems focus on the measurable aspects of disease such as physiological processes, and psychosocial elements often are not considered. Ethnomedical systems often are not simply personalistic or naturalistic but contain elements of each and may be viewed on a continuum as relatively more or less personalistic, naturalistic, or scientific.

Personalistic Medical Systems

Personalistic medical systems view supernatural beings (gods), nonhumans (ghosts, ancestors, evil spirits), or certain people (sorcerers) as causing disease. Personalistic ethnomedical systems prevail among primitive peoples, including African tribes south of the Sahara, tribal Pacific Islanders, and North and South American Indians. The ill person is viewed as the victim of some alien power. Shamans chant or perform ritual dances to negotiate with the demons or gods to come out of the sick person and heal him or her; Yanomamo shamans of Venezuela take hallucinogenic drugs in order to speak with the demons and persuade them to leave the stricken person (McElroy and Townsend, 1985).

Naturalistic Medical Systems

In naturalistic medical systems, illness is explained in impersonal, systemic terms—health prevails when there is equilibrium in the body. Humoral pathology (ancient Greece), traditional Chinese medicine, Ayurvedic medicine (India), Hispanic folk medicine (Mexico, Central and South America), and Inani medicine (Arabic) are all examples of naturalistic medical systems. Humoral pathology and Hispanic folk medicine will be discussed here.

Humoral Pathology. This was developed by Hippocrates in 460 b.c. and is the foundation for many cultures' current medical practices (McElroy and Townsend, 1985). It is based on the principle of balance. Hippocrates believed that the body contained four humors (or liquids) and that optimal health was achieved when these humors were in balance and in correct proportion to each other. The four bodily humors were blood, phlegm, yellow bile, and black bile and each had a certain quality based on the dimensions of hot, cold, moist, or dry. Blood was thought to be hot and moist, phlegm was cold and moist, yellow bile was hot and dry, and black bile was cold and dry. Illness occurred when there was an excess or deficiency of any humor. In addition, certain seasons and personality types were associated with certain humors—during the winter,

phlegm was thought to increase, and during the summer, yellow bile was thought to be more prevalent. Thus, the excess of phlegm in the winter had to be reduced in order to restore balance (and health) to the body. People who had sanguine (cheerful, optimistic) personalities were thought to have an excess of blood and people who had melancholy (depressed) personalities were thought to have an excess of black bile.

Standard Hippocratic treatment was to remove excess humors by bleeding, purging, vomiting, or starvation. To replace deficient humors, diet and herbal medicines were administered. In order to treat a patient, a Hippocratic physician needed to (1) know the personality type of the patient (Did the person naturally have an excess of yellow bile—A choleric (ill-tempered, active) personality?); (2) determine which humor was at the moment deficient or excessive in quantity (Which humor characterized this particular illness?); and (3) match these findings with the dominant humor of the season (Was it summer (excess of yellow bile)?). Based on this knowledge, the physician would decide what treatment was needed to restore balance to the patient.

A modern form of humoral pathology is contained in the adage "feed a cold, starve a fever." The idea is that we need to balance a cold by feeding someone hot chicken soup. Conversely, we need to balance the "hot" fever by withholding any food (food would add to the heat) and offering the ill person cool drinks. Another example of modern humoral medicine is the admonishment to "wear your jacket so you won't catch cold." Can we really "catch cold"? Physicians would say no, that only a combination of exposure to viruses and weakened immunizations would cause us to contract a cold. Many of today's ethnomedical systems are similar to, or based on, Hippocrates's view that bodily fluids or elements must be kept in balance for proper health.

Hispanic Folk Medicine. Practiced today in Mexico and some Central and South American countries, this is a "hot-cold" theory of disease. Similar to humoral medicine, it is believed that health is maintained through the balance of hot and cold elements. The symbolic quality of a substance determines whether it is hot or cold, not the actual temperature. Foods, herbs, medicines, and emotional states are considered to be either hot or cold. Cold elements can enter the body through the air or through cold foods; hot elements enter the body from exposure to the sun, from cooking (being near a hot stove), from bathing in warm water, sleeping, reading, or being pregnant. When the body becomes imbalanced (more hot or more cold), illness occurs. Like Hippocratic treatments, "hot" illnesses are treated with cold remedies (enemas, purging, cold herbal remedies) to restore balance to the body. "Cold" illnesses are treated with hot herbal remedies, hot food, or hot plasters. Hispanic women who have just given birth in a hospital (a "hot" experience) may request cilantro, a "cold" food, to restore balance to the body. Likewise, a Hispanic experiencing a "hot" illness will be reluctant to take penicillin, which is thought of as a "hot" treatment.

Other causes of Hispanic folk illness are strong emotions, such as fright or rage, which result in physical-emotional illnesses. Because the mind and body are viewed as inseparable, there is no distinction between emotional, somatic, or physical illnesses. *Susto* is seen primarily in women and is caused by "awesome fright" (Maduro, 1983). *Bilis* primarily afflicts men and results from extreme rage, usually caused by frustration or poor treatment by others, when the victim becomes so angry that he "boils over." Symptoms include vomiting, diarrhea, headaches, and nightmares (Maduro, 1983). Emotional upsets causing *bilis* or *susto* are thought to be caused by an "imbalance of yellow bile" (Maduro, 1983). The treatment for both is to resocialize or reintegrate the patient back into the culture. The folk healer, or curandero, often helps to perform this function.

Curanderos (or curanderas) perform a variety of spiritual, homeopathic (herbal), and scientific medical treatments. The patient is viewed holistically with physiological, psychological, and social concerns addressed simultaneously. A social illness holds the same stature as a physical illness. The cur-

andero is believed to have "the gift" or "the call" to be a healer and may have been apprenticed at a young age. She or he performs a wide repertoire of treatments, including therapy to those who are psychologically troubled, administration of herbal treatments (in line with hot/cold illnesses) or scientific medicines (aspirin), massage and manipulation of the body, and spiritual remedies (such as confession or praying to a saint, for Roman Catholics). A personalistic cause of illness in Hispanic folk medicine is that disease is sent as a punishment by God or a saint. Many Hispanics believe that God is the ultimate healer and seek the intervention of Catholic saints to heal the sick. In general, however, patients are viewed as innocent victims of malevolent or hostile forces in the environment.

Several core values among Hispanics influence their interactions with health professionals. Interactions between physicians and patients are expected to be personalized and marked with trust (*personalismo*). A health practitioner should vigorously shake a Hispanic patient's hand to establish a warmth and friendliness. At the same time, *respeto* (respect) also is very important: Hispanics are taught to treat others with respect and defer to the opinions of others who are older or more experienced. Physicians are at the same level of authority as priests and should thus act more formal and authoritative in the medical consultation. Other core values of Hispanic culture are *cooperacion* (focus on cooperation as opposed to competition), familism (family is more important than the individual), and interdependence (again, group is more important than person). The role of the extended family is very important when caring for Hispanic patients. The eldest member has the most authority and respect and must be consulted before any medical treatments can take place. Responsibility for the healing of a person lies with the family, which provides social, emotional, and physical resources to the ill person.

By understanding these cultural values and Hispanic folk beliefs about the causation and treatment of illness, modern medical practitioners can improve communication, patient satisfaction, and patient adherence to prescribed medical regimens. If the physician states the illness and treatment in terms the patient is familiar with and can understand, the patient's health is likely to improve. Likewise, unnecessary medical expenditures or treatments can be avoided if the physician is acquainted with folk illnesses such as *susto* or *bilis*. A culturally sensitive health practitioner can then refer the patient to the curandero. ·

Scientific Medical Systems

Western medicine is based on scientific or modern medicine. Spectacular advances in health have been made with the onset of scientific medicine; for example, polio has been virtually eradicated in the United States. Deaths from cancer have plummeted as more than 80 percent of victims now survive beyond five years. Scientific medicine emphasizes objective, physical, or chemical data. This dichotomy in modern medicine stems from Cartesian Dualism (Friedman and DiMatteo, 1979), with its basic belief that the mind and body are separate. The premise that underlies modern medical approaches is that science can study only what it can measure, rather than unmeasurable psychosocial concerns. The body and physiological processes can be studied "objectively," but the mind is a subjective phenomenon that cannot be measured accurately.

Modern medicine in the United States has been criticized as ignoring the whole person and as being too fragmentive (Helman, 1984). Physicians practicing scientific medicine have been likened to auto mechanics—patients go in to get a body part fixed, and then are released, much as an automobile gets a tune-up or new tires. An example of this process is the business executive who has a heart attack. An ultimate cause of the heart attack may have been too much stress at work. Until recently, physicians would "fix" the heart (perhaps with a coronary bypass) and send the patient home to recover for six weeks and then go back to work. Little attention was paid to the social environment, a major contributor to the heart attack. The focus has been on curing, which the scientific medical system does very well, as opposed to healing, which has been neglected. Recently, Western medicine has adopted a more ho-

listic approach, and physicians now may consider psychosocial dimensions in medical treatments. In addition, alternative forms of medicine are becoming more acceptable in mainstream society. For example, many health insurance companies now will pay for chiropractic treatments.

The "culture" of scientific medicine is what the modern physician brings to a medical consultation. Physicians practicing modern medicine in the United States are a relatively homogeneous group of upper-middle-class to upper-class white males (Cockerham, 1982). Such values as individualism, rationality, and a belief in technological and scientific superiority represent U.S. physicians' cultural viewpoints, while folk beliefs are often looked upon with disdain.

INTERCULTURAL COMMUNICATION IN HEALTH CARE SETTINGS

Several potential problems surface when treating patients of differing cultural beliefs in modern medical settings such as hospitals or clinics. Proxemics, beliefs about etiquette, modesty, or time, and verbal communication all influence interactions between health care practitioners and patients (Hartog and Hartog, 1983).

Prevailing standards of etiquette and modesty in one culture may differ greatly from standards in other cultures. In the United States, the patient usually is consulted for medical treatments. In other countries, the eldest family member must be consulted (for example, in Mexico and Middle Eastern countries). Following an introduction, a health care practitioner should always ask patients how they like to be addressed. "Mrs. Brown, I'm Dr. Smith. How would you like me to address you?" is a safe protocol to use, although some patients will wonder why one needs to ask in the first place. Calling someone "honey" or "pop" may offend patients who do not expect such intimacy and familiarity from their physicians.

Standards of physical modesty vary greatly from culture to culture, with some parts of the body viewed as sacred. Gypsies believe that the upper part of the body is sacred and the lower part is profane (Hartog and Hartog, 1983). One cannot touch the knee and then touch the head without violating the Gypsy. Many medical diagnoses depend on the patient explaining what hurts, itches, or burns, and where the pain is. In numerous cultures, male patients may be reluctant to discuss "male" problems with female physicians. It is better to pair same-sex physicians with patients of different cultures to improve communication and, hence, ability to diagnose.

Time is viewed differently by other cultures. In the United States, punctuality is very important and people seek to "get down to business" immediately, an approach that may offend people from Latin American or Middle Eastern cultures. In these cultures, one must first establish the relationship, find out how the patient and family are doing, and then proceed with the medical consultation. In terms of proxemics, members of different cultures are comfortable at different conversational distances. Conversational distance for Middle Easterners, for example, is about two feet apart (Lipson and Meleis, 1983). For Americans, the comfortable distance for a conversation is about five feet apart (Lipson and Meleis, 1983). An American physician attending to a Middle Eastern patient may be perceived as distant and rude because of his or her perceived "stand-offishness." Not knowing a particular culture's views on etiquette, modesty, proxemics, or time can undermine physician-patient rapport and hinder the healing process.

Verbal communication problems may occur with the use of interpreters, when English is used as a second language, or when words themselves have magical meanings (Hartog and Hartog, 1983). Interpreters native to the patient's culture may intentionally or unintentionally distort information. For example, interpreters may wish to "protect" the patient from bad news from the physician and tell the patient only part of what the doctor says. Likewise, if an interpreter does not consider some of the patient's symptoms to be significant, these symptoms may not be translated. Different meanings for words compound the English as a second language problem. Even people who speak English but represent different cultures face this problem. (Hartog and Hartog (1983) cite the example of Americans saying "I feel stuffed" after a big meal, which to Britons means to have had sexual intercourse.) One must attempt to reach beyond the euphemisms given for certain illnesses or disease (especially those of a sexual nature), to diagnose and treat the medical problem. Finally, some people will be wary of naming certain illnesses for fear of "catching" them (for example, cancer). The presentation of information also should be adapted to cultural styles. Americans, for example, usually want all of the information available whereas Middle Easterners typically prefer to receive negative information in stages. Health care practitioners must walk a fine line between informing and panicking the patient.

Bolivian Indian Example

When communicating medical knowledge and treatments with patients representing different ethnomedical systems, it is important to incorporate their views on health and illness in the treatment. Bolivian physicians and nurses did just this in a public health campaign targeted toward Andean Indians in Bolivia to treat diarrhea and dysentery—a major cause of infant mortality (for a full explication of the method, see Bastien, 1987). A workshop to develop the campaign was held with doctors and nurses from small peasant clinics. The goal of the workshop was to teach doctors and nurses how to analyze benefits and deficits in traditional and modern medicine and to focus on essential items of behavior change in order to improve doctor-patient communication, with the end goal being improved health for their patients. Participants at the workshop did three things: (1) They generated both modern and traditional terms for the name, symptoms, causes, and treatment of diarrhea and dysentery; (2) they selected a focal point for the campaign (one behavior that was essential and appropriate in changing health-related behaviors); and (3) they developed a lesson plan to carry out this goal.

First, the various names of diarrhea and dysentery were generated. Bolivian peasants had many names for diarrhea, ranging from the least severe, *aika*, to the most severe, *wila curso* (dysentery). By listing the names, it became apparent that the reason an earlier health campaign run by the Bolivian Ministry of Health had failed was that the posters used the word *aika* instead of *wila curso*. The Andean Indians knew that they could treat *aika* themselves so they ignored the posters; however, the Andean Indians did recognize the seriousness of *wila curso* and often took victims to medical clinics. Symptoms of diarrhea were similar for both modern and traditional medicine (fever, frequent bowel movements). Perceived causes of the disease for Indians were fright, change, anger, or cold, but modern medicine saw the causes as germs, bacteria, parasites, or viruses. Finally, folk treatments were listed (cinnamon, chocolate, sitting on hot llama dung) and compared with modern medical treatments (such as oral rehydration therapy). Treatments were logically related to the perceived cause. If the cold was thought to have caused the diarrhea, parents may have sat their children on warm sheep dung to counteract the perceived excess of "cold." A key problem in definitional terms is that although diarrhea or dysentery causes severe dehydration and potentially death, it is primarily thought of by Bolivian Indians as a wet disease, with wet symptoms. This is because the victim is perceived to have a "surplus of fluids" and needs to be dried out.

Instead of educating the Indians about bacterial and viral causes of disease (which had been done previously, to no avail), physicians and nurses were taught to select a focal point for the campaign (1) that was pivotal to health and (2) that the peasants were able to do. One could argue that people don't need to believe that bacteria causes illness to treat the illness. In addition, the physicians and nurses thought that beliefs about causation of illness were too embedded in the peasant's culture to change. Therefore, they thought that time might better be spent focusing on treatments that are practical and feasible. They decided on the following focal points to teach the patients: (1) Diarrhea is serious; (2) it can and often does cause death; and (3) it should be treated with a combination of rehydration formula and native treatments. The goal of Bastien (1987) was to convince health care practitioners to utilize traditional beliefs and practices in order to promote basic and essential modern medicine techniques (oral rehydration therapy).

The final step was to develop a lesson plan that physicians and nurses could use when communicating with their patients on diarrhea and its treatment. The lesson had to be framed in terms of the Bolivian Indians' belief schemas and it had to motivate them to change their behavior. The main obstacle to overcome was the belief that diarrhea was a wet disease, which necessitated that the belief be restructured. One of the participating nurses recalled an Andean legend familiar to the Bolivian Indians about three mountains, two of whom were male and in love with the maiden mountain, who scorned them both. The legend stated that the two male mountains fought, that one knocked off the other's crest, and that the other sent gophers to drain it of water. The original purpose of the story was to explain why one mountain is pock-marked and why the other is without a crest (Bastien, 1987). This legend was restructured to serve as a teaching tool. The restructured legend emphasized the seriousness of diarrhea and the symptoms of dehydration (sunken eyes, no tears) and outlined how to prepare and administer rehydration formula. The revised legend is contained in the box.

In modern medical terms, the legend is explained as follows:

Sajama is comparable to people with diarrhea who are losing their fluids and dying. The gophers are like bacteria multiplying and causing holes in our bodies. The fox is like those who tell us that we should stop drinking when we have diarrhea. This does us more harm than good. The Condor is like the person who prepares suero casero *for people with diarrhea. This is prepared with one liter of boiled water, two soupspoons of sugar, and one-fourth of a small spoon each of salt and bicarbonate of soda. It is necessary to give this in small amounts, every five minutes, until the person is cured of diarrhea. The hawks and eagles are like the fathers and mothers who clean the house so that their children do not get diarrhea. This is followed by having the audience memorize the for-*

mula for suero casero *by repeating the parts of the legend where the Condor gathers the ingredients: one liter of boiled water from Illimani, two soup-spoons of sugar from Wyana Potosi, and so on.*

Comic books depicting the restructured legend were created, which were distributed to community health workers and have been credited with reducing the rate of deaths attributed to diarrhea.

This example illustrates how cultural beliefs and practices can be utilized in public health campaigns. The frustration often encountered when traditional and modern medical practices clash can be eliminated by merging and incorporating essential and appropriate elements from each. This three-step approach of defining terms, selecting a focal point, and developing a lesson plan has also been used with success in other health communication campaigns.

CONCLUSION

Much research has been conducted establishing the fact that information alone does not result in behavior change. For a medical treatment to work, it must be framed in terms of the patient's reality and world view. Physicians must present health information and treatments so that the patient can understand why and how these treatments lead to better health. Bastien (1987) emphasizes that traditional cultural medical practices not essential to health should be left intact. Behavioral change interventions to improve health should be conducted within the patient's cultural framework, with cultural beliefs incorporated into the diagnosis and treatment of disease. However, it is important to note that every ethnomedical system has scientifically valid treatments and therapies (McElroy and Townsend, 1985). Herbal treatments, sweat baths, or dietary taboos all have therapeutic value and can be just as lifesaving as invasive surgical procedures or modern drugs. In fact, many of today's drug treatments have their basis in natural herbs. By taking time to understand patients' cultural viewpoints of health and illness, health care practitioners may be able to improve patients' health, and ultimately to save lives.

REFERENCES

Bastien, J. W. (1987). "Cross-Cultural Communication Between Doctors and Peasants in Bolivia." *Social Science and Medicine, 24* (12), 1109–1118.

Clark, M. M. (1983). "Cultural Context of Medical Practice." *The Western Journal of Medicine, 139* (6), 2–6.

Cockerham, W. C. (1982). *Medical Sociology.* Englewood Cliffs, N.J.: Prentice-Hall.

Foster, G. M., and Anderson, B. G. (1978). *Medical Anthropology.* New York: Wiley.

Friedman, H. S., and DiMatteo, M. R. (1979). "Health Care as Interpersonal Process." *Journal of Social Issues, 35* (1), 1–11.

Hartog, J., and Hartog, E. A. (1983). "Cultural Aspects of Health and Illness Behavior in Hospitals." *The Western Journal of Medicine, 139* (6), 106–112.

Helman, C. (1984). *Culture, Health, and Illness.* Bristol, England: John Wright and Sons, Ltd.

Lipson, J. G., and Meleis, A. I. (1983). "Issues in the Health Care of Middle Eastern Patients." *The Western Journal of Medicine, 139* (6), 50–57.

McElroy, A., and Townsend, P. K. (1985). *Medical Anthropology in Ecological Perspective.* Boulder, Colo.: Westview Press.

Maduro, R. (1983). "*Curanderismo* and Latino Views of Disease and Curing." *The Western Journal of Medicine, 139* (6), 64–70.

Acknowledgments: I am grateful to Dr. Don Brownlee, Dr. Garth Ludwig, and Margaret Schneider for their helpful contributions to this manuscript.

ANDEAN INDIAN LEGEND RESTRUCTURED

Near the Chilean border are three mountains, Sajama, Sabaya, and Cariquina. In times past, *Tata* Sajama and *Tata* Sabaya were young men (*Way-nakuna*) who fell in love with Cariquina, a beautiful young maiden. They courted her with flowers grown on their loins and sent to her on the wings of eagles. When she became sick, they sent her leaves of *nencia* (gentian) to soothe her ills.

As time passed, Sajama and Sabaya became jealous of each others' love for Cariquina. Each wanted to marry her. Their disputes resounded in lightning bolts and thunder. Their discussions caused icy winds. Skilled in the sling, Sajama whirled it around his head until it caused a tornado, and letting it go, he hurled a great rock at the *uma pacha* (head place) of Sabaya. The rock crashed into Sabaya's crest, knocking it off, and causing it to tumble down the valley. Sabaya looked like a big tooth, instead of a mountain.

Smoldering in revenge, Sabaya put a spell on Sajama with a *mesa negra* (misfortune table). The hex was that gophers drill holes all over Sajama. Rapidly, gophers appeared on Sajama. They multiplied and drilled more holes. Sajama began losing water through the gopher holes. Daily, Sajama became drier and drier as the water drained from his body.

One day, Tiwula, the fox, ran up the side of Sajama's back. Sajama beckoned to Tiwula, crying out, "Save me, all my water is flowing out to the river's bottom!"

"You must stop drinking," the fox replied, "because this makes the water flow out!"

Indeed, the fox didn't want Sajama to get well so that he could continue to hunt and eat the gophers.

The other animals became alarmed. They loved *Tata* Sajama as a father who had given them food and shelter, so they beckoned Condor. Condor flew immediately to Sajama.

Sajama was dying and barely able to speak because his tongue and throat were dry. His eyes were sunken and he cried without tears. Barely conscious, he pleaded:

"I'm dying from lack of water, please save me!"

"I'll be right back with medicine!" Condor said. Then Condor flew to Mt. Illimani who gave him a liter of crystalline-pure water; next to Illampu who gave him two soupspoons of sugar, then to Wyana Potosi who gave him one-fourth of a small spoon of salt; and finally to the Valley of Cochabamba where Mt. Tunari gave him one-fourth of a small spoon of baking soda. Each time, Condor mixed these ingredients in the liter of pure water.

After he returned to Mt. Sajama, Condor gave him a swallow of this medicine every five minutes. He did this slowly and carefully so that Sajama would not vomit. Because Sajama was a young man, Condor gave him two liters a day. Condor made many trips to the mountains for the cure. He also asked the eagles and hawks to hunt the gophers.

Within a week, Sajama was cured and the gophers disappeared. Later that year, Sajama married Cariquina. Condors, eagles, and hawks attended the wedding. Sajama then told Condor to provide the herders of alpacas and llamas with the same cure, because many die each year in similar fashion!

Source: Bastien, J. W. (1987). "Cross-Cultural Communication Between Doctors and Patients in Bolivia." *Social Science and Medicine, 24* (12), 1109–1118. Reprinted by permission of the publisher, Pergamon Press, Oxford, England. Joseph W. Bastien is affiliated with the University of Texas at Arlington.

Intercultural Communication and the Classroom

JANIS F. ANDERSEN
ROBERT POWELL

Nearly two decades ago, anthropologist Edward Hall[1] argued that culture is a hidden dimension. He explained that culture penetrates our perceptual system, thus masking the basic aspects of our existence that are immediately obvious to an outsider. Hall's position is now a basic tenet of intercultural communication,[2] but acknowledging it does little to expose the many ways that culture influences our perceptions and communication. One context where culture obscures our vision is in the classroom environment. In the United States, the impact of culture on education is growing in importance. At no time in history has such a culturally diverse population of students participated in our educational system. Students from Asia, Mexico, Latin America, and the Philippines are enrolled in U.S. classrooms. Each of these students brings culturally based rules and expectations about education and classroom behavior. Our task in this essay is to lift the veil of culture that obscures our understanding of the classroom environment. The first part of this essay addresses the issue comparatively by illustrating how educational practices vary around the world. The second part explores the way in which student culture within the United States may influence instructional communication.

THE IMPORTANCE OF CULTURE

Many people tend to think that all classrooms and instructional practices are pretty much the same. If we asked you to imagine classroom interaction in central Illinois, southern California, northern New York, or even France, Brazil, or the Philippines, you would picture a classroom with which you are most familiar. You may picture different kinds of people in the different locations, but your overall image is not likely to vary. Maybe you envision nattily dressed students at some Ivy League school, or you see blond-haired, suntanned students in shorts and tee shirts in southern California, but the rest of the image reflects your own educational experiences. If you are from the United States, you probably visualize a classroom with rows of desks for students and a lectern in the front of the room where the instructor spends most of the time imparting information.

The point is that people tend to think that the learning environment with which they are most familiar is representative of learning environments in general. Furthermore, even if these culturally based environmental images do not generalize as we suggest, they are often held up as models for what a learning environment should be. Culture provides us with a heritage and a set of expectations about educational settings. If you were asked to create a classroom context and to structure the interaction to provide the best possible learning situation, chances are you would create something very similar to the classroom in which you are now sitting. This claim may seem remarkable. You may not find the current situation ideal, but your images of a proper learning environment are inextricably linked to your familiarity with and experience in learning environments. Think for a moment about the movement for year-long schedules for elementary and secondary schools. Many of the criticisms about a year-long schedule have little to do with education and much to do with the way schools are supposed to be structured. In this country, we expect to begin school in September and get out in June. Family vacations, part-time work, camp, swimming lessons, and athletic activities are organized around a nine-month school year and a three-month summer vacation. Any deviation from this expected norm is disruptive. Teachers tend to teach the way they were taught; parents treat their children the way they were treated. The entire educational system, together with the rules and procedures for effective classroom interaction, reflects a cultural dictate rather than a universal mandate.

CULTURAL VARIANCE
IN INSTRUCTION

This section highlights some cultural differences in educational practices, differences that are useful not so much for understanding other cultures but for facilitating heightened awareness of our own culture. Much systematic, in-depth study of an individual culture, its institutions, and its people is necessary for us to know enough about another culture's educational system to seriously improve our instructional encounters with someone from that culture. However, the discussion that follows allows insights into our own educational system. Hall[3] believes that we can never really understand another's culture but being aware of its diversity is a tremendous aid in understanding our own culture better. Further, by studying culture's role in education, we can put our own educational assumptions into perspective and perhaps better understand our educational practices and procedures.

Educational Systems

If asked to describe a generic educational system, we might begin by talking about a classroom, a teacher, and some students. However, even these seemingly basic components reflect cultural assumptions. Classrooms are a relatively recent innovation; they are still not used for teaching children in preliterate societies. Socrates, Plato, and Aristotle disseminated their teachings without the benefit of a blackboard and the comfort—or discomfort—of a classroom building. And the students of these teachers did quite well even though they did not take notes and their teachers did not provide hand-outs or study guides. In the early 1970s the Metro School in Chicago was a complete high school without walls.[4] The classes met in museums, libraries, bookstores, and other interesting places. Teachers taught a sociology class by having students walk the length of Halsted Street through numerous ethnic neighborhoods, where students ate in restaurants, visited families, and observed street activity.

Teachers

Teachers, as we think of them, also reflect a cultural bias. In the United States, it was not until around the Civil War period (1860s) that women replaced men as teachers.[5] Today many cultures still refuse to entrust the education of their young to professional women. One distinguishing characteristic of education in preliterate societies is that kin are responsible for educating the young. Deciding which category of kin will assume which responsibility is highly systematized; being related in a certain way is a teaching credential for a specific content area. Instead of learning art from Mrs. Ruiz, home economics from Mrs. Sullivan, and woodworking from Mr. Yang, children learn pottery from their father's sister, cooking from their mother, and toolmaking from their mother's father.

Many of us think of teachers as being older than their students, but cultural anthropologist Margaret Mead states that this pattern reflects a culturally determined, postfigurative learning paradigm.[6] In postfigurative societies older people disseminate their knowledge to younger, less experienced, and less knowledgeable individuals; configurative cultures adopt primarily peer learning patterns; and prefigurative societies learn from their younger members who are more up to date. The one-room schoolhouses of the early 1900s relied mainly on configurative or peer instruction. Due to teacher shortages and interest in team learning, the utilization of configurative learning strategies emerged again in the United States in the 1980s.[7] Prefigurative learning patterns are used in complex industrial societies where rapid technological and scientific advances quickly outdate previously acquired knowledge. Thus, many fifty-year-old executives attend special seminars on computer technology that are taught by people twenty or thirty years younger than they are.

Learning

Our acceptance of prefigurative learning patterns permits and encourages younger students to inform or even disagree with older teachers. In many cultures, however, Asian, for example, students would seldom disagree with a teacher. In traditional Asian societies, wisdom comes with age and all important learning is postfigurative. In some societies the teacher is a revered individual who is teaching sacred truth. The task of the student is to absorb knowledge.

In the United States, a teacher may consider knowledge more relative or negotiable. Lively class discussions play an important role in these types of learning contexts. Questions such as "You agree with that, don't you?" are intended to evoke classroom interaction and not compliance. Immigrants from Cambodia, Vietnam, or Korea may not join into the interaction because of their cultural experiences.

The Asian pattern of teacher-student interaction was made evident to one instructor while discussing the role of self-disclosure in the development of intimate relationships. The instructor argued that self-disclosure is central to the development of intimacy. His Anglo students were quick to discuss the role of self-disclosure in interpersonal relationships but the Asian students in the class merely listened and took notes. When the teacher directly asked one of the Asian students if self-disclosure was used in his culture, he replied that it was not and went on to explain that in his country (Korea) feelings of intimacy were understood, not explicitly communicated. In fact, he added, it would be rude to state explicitly how you felt about someone. The instructor learned two valuable lessons. The first was that self-disclosure is not central to the development of intimacy across cultures and the second was that Asian students are unlikely to openly and spontaneously disagree with a teacher.

Teacher-Student Relationships

The teacher-student relationship is culturally mandated. The primary school system is highly informal in an Israeli kibbutz with close social relationships between teachers and students.[8] Students move from their desks at will to sharpen pencils or to get drinks, they talk among themselves while writing, readily criticize teachers if they feel the teachers are wrong, and address teachers by their first names.

A typical classroom in the Soviet Union provides a sharp contrast to the one in the kibbutz. Students sit in rows of desks that face the teacher; they rise when a teacher enters the room; they stand at attention when asking or answering a question; and they sit with their arms folded when listening to a lesson.[9] The teacher is in complete control of the classroom.

Classroom Rituals

Rituals and patterns of classroom interaction vary from culture to culture. Obviously we picture students speaking their native languages in classroom interactions throughout the world, and we might picture all students raising their hands to ask or answer a question. In fact, mathematics is taught in English in the Philippines, since the Filipino language does not have sufficient technical terms for mathematics instruction.[10] In Jamaica, primary school students flap or snap their fingers to signal that they know the answer. In Trinidad, students put their index and middle fingers on their forehead with the inside facing out to ask permission to be excused.[11] Some cultures do not have a way for students to signal a desire to talk to a teacher; in these cultures, students speak only after the teacher has spoken to them. There is virtually no classroom interaction in Vietnamese culture, and in Mexican culture all classroom interaction is tightly controlled and directed by the teacher.[12]

The classroom in an Israeli kibbutz is very noisy and interaction is spontaneous.[13] In sharp contrast, Chinese classrooms are so quiet that North Americans teaching there often find the silence unnerving.[14] Cultures reflecting a Buddhist tradition hold that knowledge, truth, and wisdom come to those whose quiet silence allows the spirit to enter. Classrooms in the United States tend to reflect more of a Socratic ideal, where teacher and student interact a great deal in pursuit of knowledge.

Intelligence Assessment

The ways intelligence and learning are measured are certainly related to culture. In the United States a single score may be used to index a student's intelligence. Consider, for example, the importance that standardized test scores have in this country—students' academic futures are dramatically affected by their verbal and math SAT scores. In Iran a child might be considered bright if he has memorized the Koran and mastered the Arabic language.[15] Howard Gardner points out that different cultures cultivate the development of an assortment of intelligences.[16]

Formal Education Value

The value placed on formal education also has a cultural dimension. Education is a high national priority in Japan, for example. The Japanese believe that the best way to ensure their future is to develop their most valued natural resource—their people. In 1980, more students graduated from the twelfth grade in Japan than in any country in the world, and this trend will continue into the next decade.[17]

Competition to get into Japanese colleges and universities is especially keen. Almost four applications are submitted for each college opening. The entrance examinations for universities are as important as the World Series or the Super Bowl in our country. With such a commitment to education, it is not surprising that the Japanese are world leaders in technology.

Time Value

Our use of time and our view of time also reflect a cultural bias that alters our educational process. Punctuality is revered in the United States. Students who turn their work in late are considered less intelligent than those who work more quickly, and we designate certain time periods for certain educational tasks. Yet these clock-oriented values reflect a Western "monochronic" view of time. One time-related problem that is overlooked involves testing: Students are often graded on how many questions they can answer correctly in a designated period of time. This grading philosophy is a disadvantage for students raised in Hispanic cultures who have not been conditioned to use every moment in a productive task-oriented manner. The following idioms show the contrast between Western and Hispanic views of time. For Westerners the "clock races," for Hispanics, el reloj anda (the clock walks).

In contrast to the Western monochronic view of time, American Indians have a "polychronic" view of time. These individuals do things when they think the time is right, not when the calendar says it's a certain date. In many cultures, classes end when the subject matter has been thoroughly discussed rather than when the clock designates the end of the period. In the United States, we measure education itself in time—years spent in school—and it is only recently that our system has allowed credit to be given for knowledge when one has not spent the requisite time in the classroom. The entire notion of education as a timed process, however, is a product of nineteenth-century Western thought.[18]

Nonverbal Behavioral Differences

Many nonverbal behaviors are culturally learned, and the literature on nonverbal behavior is replete with examples of cross-cultural differences in interpreting these behaviors.[19] These differences are also manifest in classroom environments. In the United States we show respect to teachers by looking at them when they talk to us, but in Jamaica looking at teachers is a sign of disrespect, while not looking at them is a sign of respect. Black Americans and many West African cultures also reflect the Jamaican pattern.[20]

In Italian classrooms, teachers and students touch each other frequently, and children greet a teacher with a kiss on both cheeks while putting their arms around the teacher. On the other hand, Chinese and Japanese children show complete emotional restraint in classrooms.[21] In short, our entire communication transaction, with its verbal and nonverbal messages, systematic patterns, and socialized rituals, is a reflection of our culture.

CULTURE AND INSTRUCTIONAL PRACTICES IN THE UNITED STATES

Now that we have discussed some of the more glaring cultural differences characterizing educational processes, we would like to shift our attention and focus on some of the ways that culture impacts communication and instruction in the United States. Specifically, we will examine how students from diverse cultural and ethnic backgrounds interact in the classroom and how they feel about certain types of teacher communication behaviors.

Academic Advisement

The expectations that students have about academic advisement appears to be influenced by culture. Collier[22] assessed communication in the advisement relationships between Anglo advisors and Asian-American, African-American, and Latino students. She asked students to describe a conversation with an Anglo advisor in which she or he behaved inappropriately and ineffectively. Thus, culturally based expectations about appropriate communication from the Anglo advisor were obtained. A significant number of Asian and Latino students felt the references to their accents were inappropriate. Asian-Americans felt that embarrassing criticism and openness were inappropriate. African-Americans described distance and hostility as inappropriate. Latinos cited distance and lack of individual concern as inappropriate behaviors. Collier also found some similarities across the groups. Asian-Americans, African-Americans, and Latinos mentioned behav-

iors such as mismanagement of time (being late, rushing the student), interrupting the student, and not nonverbally attending to the student as inappropriate.

Collier concludes her research by providing a taxonomy of rules for Anglo advisors. Following are the rules she provides for politeness, cultural appropriateness, relational appropriateness, and approaching tasks in advisement contexts.

1. **Politeness rules:** With Asian-Americans, manage time appropriately, attend nonverbally, allow mutual talk time, greet warmly, pronounce names accurately, and avoid foul language. With African-Americans, allow mutual talk time, manage time appropriately, show recognition and respect for the student as an individual, attend appropriately, and greet warmly. With Latinos, attend appropriately through verbal and nonverbal means, allow mutual talk time, be courteous, greet warmly, manage time appropriately and pronounce names as accurately as possible.[23]

2. **Culturally appropriate rules:** Avoid overgeneralizing and stereotyping or criticizing students' ability or preparation for college, avoid negative comments about accents, and allow adequate time for all students.[24]

3. **Relationally appropriate rules:** With Asian-Americans, show respect, don't use or ask for too much openness, and avoid confronting or embarrassing the advisee. With African-Americans, be friendly and direct, show respect for the individual student, and allow trust to build slowly. With Latinos, take time to show concern and friendliness, and show support and empathy verbally and nonverbally.[25]

4. **Rules for approaching the task:** With Asian-Americans, provide adequate advice throughout the meeting, allow a mutual role in decision making, and be direct. With African-Americans, provide adequate advice throughout the meeting, allow a mutual role in decision making, be direct, and check out information to avoid mistakes. With Latinos, establish the relationship first through a warm greet-

ing and small talk and then provide adequate advice, allow a mutual role in decision making, and check out information to avoid mistakes.[26]

Teacher Behavior

Judgments about teacher classroom communication are also affected by culture. Powell and Collier[27] studied the effects of teacher immediacy on students from Latino, Anglo, Asian-American, and African-American ethnic groups. According to Mehrabian,[28] nonverbal immediacy behaviors signal accessibility and openness to communication. Eye contact, smiling, physical proximity, and relaxed body posture are examples of immediacy behaviors. The authors found that Asian students did not feel that it was appropriate for a teacher to be in close proximity to the students. The teacher who stands too close to the Asian student may engender feelings of tension and embarrassment rather than openness and receptivity; the Asian student may prefer a more distant and formal relationship.

In a related study, Collier and Powell[29] studied the relationship between teacher immediacy and teacher effectiveness over a period of time. The authors found differences across the groups they examined. Immediacy early in the course was most important for the Latino group. In contrast, African-Americans indicated that immediacy was more important later in the course. Immediacy had fairly stable effects for Anglos and Asians.

The results of these studies suggest that the behaviors that we assume are effective communication strategies for teachers have cultural implications. A behavior that may have positive effects for one group may have negative effects for others.

SUMMARY

In an informative and interesting book on intercultural behavior, Geert Hofstede explores the differences in thinking and action among people from forty different nations.[30] He argues that people have mental programs based on their cultural experiences that are both developed and reinforced by schools and other social institutions. Many of these patterns are so subtle that people fail to realize that things can be another way. By highlighting intercultural differences in educational environments, we begin to realize that nothing about the educational process is absolute. Every component reflects a cultural choice, conscious or unconscious, about whom to educate, how, when, in what subjects, for what purpose, and in which manner. Perhaps this realization will not only increase our tolerance but also increase our awareness of and sensitivity to the new multicultural classroom that is forming in the United States.

NOTES

1. Edward T. Hall. (1969). *The Hidden Dimensions.* Garden City, N.Y.: Anchor Books.

2. Larry Samovar, Richard Porter, and Nemi Jain. (1981). *Understanding Intercultural Communication.* Belmont, Calif.: Wadsworth.

3. Hall, 1969.

4. *Chicago Sun Times*, December 6, 1972.

5. Jules Henry. (1970). "Cross Cultural Outline of Education." In Joan I. Roberts and Sherrie C. Adinsanya (Eds.), *Educational Patterns and Cultural Configurations.* New York: David McKay.

6. Margaret Mead. (1970). *Culture and Commitment: A Study of the Generation Gap.* Garden City, N.Y.: Natural History Press, Doubleday & Company.

7. D. A. Kolb. (1984). *Experiential Learning: Experience as a Source of Learning and Development.* Englewood Cliffs, N.J.: Prentice-Hall.

8. M. Spiro. (1958). *Children of the Kibbutz.* Cambridge, Mass.: Harvard University Press.

9. Nigel Grant. (1979). *Soviet Education.* New York: Penguin Books.

10. Josefine R. Cortes. (1980). "The Philippines." In T. Neville Postelethwaite and R. Murray Thomas (Eds.), *Schooling in the Asian Region.* New York: Pergamon Press.

11. Aaron Wolfgang. (1979). "The Teacher and Nonverbal Behavior in the Multicultural Classroom." In Aaron

Wolfgang (Ed.), *Nonverbal Behavior, Application and Cultural Implications.* New York: Academic Press.

12. Julie Becker. (1983). "A Cross-Cultural Comparison of Interaction Patterns in the Classroom." Master's thesis, San Diego State University.

13. M. Spiro. (1958). *Children of the Kibbutz.* Cambridge, Mass.: Harvard University Press.

14. Wolfgang, p. 167.

15. Howard Gardner. (1983). *Frames of Mind.* New York: Basic Books.

16. Gardner.

17. Thomas P. Rohlen. (1983). *Japan's High Schools.* Los Angeles: University of California Press.

18. James J. Thompson. (1973). *Beyond Words: Nonverbal Communication in the Classroom.* New York: Citation Press.

19. See, for example, Edward Hall. (1959). *The Silent Language.* Greenwich, Conn.: Fawcett Publications; Loretta Malandro and Larry Barker. (1983). *Nonverbal Communication.* Reading, Mass.: Addison-Wesley; Marianne LaFrance and Clara Mavo. (1978). *Moving Bodies: Nonverbal Communication in Social Relationships.* Monterey, Calif.: Brooks/Cole.

20. Wolfgang, p. 167.

21. Wolfgang, p. 169.

22. Mary Jane Collier. (1988). "Competent Communication in Intercultural Unequal Status Advisement Contexts." *Howard Journal of Communications*, Vol. 1, pp. 3–22.

23. Collier, p. 16.

24. Collier, p. 16.

25. Collier, p. 17.

26. Collier, pp. 17–18.

27. Robert G. Powell and Mary Jane Collier. "The Effects of Teacher Immediacy on Judgments of Teaching Effectiveness for Students from Different Ethnic Backgrounds." Manuscript submitted for publication.

28. Albert Mehrabian. (1981). *Silent Messages: Implicit Communication of Emotions and Attitudes.* Belmont, Calif.: Wadsworth.

29. Mary Jane Collier and Robert Powell. "Ethnicity, Instructional Communication and Classroom Systems." Accepted for publication in *Communication Quarterly.*

30. Geert Hofstede. (1980). *Culture's Consequences: International Differences in Work-Related Values.* Newbury Park, Calif.: Sage Publications.

Intercultural Problems in Courtroom Interaction

WAYNE A. BEACH

Nearly all English-speaking U.S. citizens have faced difficulties communicating in courtroom settings. Litigants are often intimidated by the formality of court proceedings, even though they are shown "how" to behave in court (Pollner, 1979; Atkinson, 1979), and numerous constraints are placed on questioning and answering throughout the interrogation and testimony (Atkinson and Drew, 1979). As lawyers exert control and witnesses typically defer to their authority, it is not uncommon for witnesses to become frustrated because they cannot "tell their complete story" regarding a past incident (O'Barr, 1982, p. 114). Moreover, the presence of "eavesdropping" third parties, such as judges, juries, and observers, is not necessarily conducive to disclosing what may be considered private information in a public setting. Even in more informal plea bargaining sessions, defendants are not always aware of their role in the proceedings or the nature of the plea being negotiated for them (Maynard, 1984). For these reasons and more, it becomes obvious that while the U.S. legal system is explicitly designed to aid and protect lay persons, it can nevertheless be a foreign environment for communication.

The question can thus be raised: Within such a "foreign communicative environment," how is it possible to accomplish "social justice" and "fair and impartial treatments" for all litigants?

This essay was prepared especially for this sixth edition. All rights reserved. Permission to reprint must be obtained from the publisher and the author. Wayne A. Beach teaches at San Diego State University.

If English is your native language, and you have participated within and/or directly observed U.S. court proceedings, you can likely identify with the sense of "displacement" emerging from being constrained, uninformed, intimidated, and perhaps even frustrated with how a particular case is bureaucratically managed and legally processed. But can you imagine how these problems might increase in both frequency and complexity for non-English-speaking participants, those lacking sufficient fluency to comprehend and participate (more or less "competently") in routine court proceedings?

The plight of these litigants has not been totally disregarded. Throughout the 1970s, for example, increased attention was given to the communication problems faced by non-English-speaking people in the courts. In 1976 the state of California led the way in trying to solve these problems by commissioning a unique study of the language needs of those who do not speak English. In 1978 the U.S. Congress finally passed a law entitled the Court Interpreters Act, requiring translations for all litigants requesting and/or in need of such a service. At both the state and national levels, it was clear that litigants incapable of understanding the language and the proceedings of the courts were denied a basic American right: to reasonably confront one's accuser and/or adversary *face-to-face* as guaranteed by the Sixth Amendment. Thus it has become customary for courts to provide translators/interpreters in each and every case involving non-English-speaking litigants.

To this date little is known about the emergent *communication* difficulties of routine translations and interpretations. While it has become customary to provide these services, it is by no means sufficient to assume that communication problems are automatically resolved and remedied. The purpose of this article is to address several of these difficulties as displayed in the *interactional organization* of court proceedings. We shall pay attention to basic and potential problems evident when Spanish-speaking defendants interact with judges and lawyers through court interpreters. Data are drawn from an ongoing collection of video-recorded court proceedings.[1] Before turning directly to a discussion of these data, however, it may prove useful to address three constituent components of "culture": *language, knowledge*, and *context*. In so doing, it becomes possible to grasp more fully not only *intercultural* communication processes but also *interactional* resolutions to intercultural problems.

LANGUAGE, KNOWLEDGE, AND CONTEXT

The communication of cultures may be understood in and through members' methods of assembling social contexts and creating social order. Viewed as context building, the concern is with *how* everyday interactions rely on their social knowledge to get practical activities done *together* (Beach, 1982, 1983). In other words, our study of communication and culture should transcend individual (monadic) concerns and focus instead on an understanding of *sequences* of collaboratively produced interactions (Beach, 1989). As Goffman (1961) repeatedly envisioned, our research efforts should rest *not* with men and their moments but rather with moments and their men—that is, with social occasions and their organizing properties. Thus social occasions may be framed as organized displays of cultural *practices*, used and relied upon to create a "situated condition for adequate, practical comprehension" (Coulter, 1979, p. 173). Because language (verbal and nonverbal) is the major vehicle for accomplishing communication, language functions both *in* context and *as* context (Ochs, 1979), simultaneously constructing and being constructed by the social occasion. In this sense, the title of Mishler's (1979) article, "Meaning in Context: Is There Any Other Kind?", is more than simply a rhetorical question. Rather, it is a referent for understanding how contexts get "workably built in endless ways" (Sacks, Schegloff, and Jefferson, 1974).

Regardless of the contexts within which intercultural communication has been studied, a widely accepted orientation is to provide explanations of such phenomena as misunderstandings, embarrassing moments, and competing perspectives (for example, "reality disjunctures," see Pollner, 1975), by invoking differences in "background knowledge" as the reason for certain actions. In most simple terms, when explaining how and why members of different cultures engage in certain communication activities, one makes reference to the following kinds of phenomena: attitudes, values, beliefs, needs, residual experiences (memory, tradition, and folklore), perceptions, interpretations, morals, and ethics. These features comprise that which counts as knowledge, and there is little doubt as to their importance in connecting thought and culture. But have you ever *seen* any of these phenomena? Do these features hold significance apart from the way they are displayed in and through interaction? More importantly, what features do intercultural interactions *themselves* have available as they encounter one another face-to-face?

The point is that while differences in cultural background and knowledge are normal and inevitable, the problems emerging from such differences are evident in the language practices employed to resolve these problems within intercultural interaction. More specifically, problems that occur when Spanish-speaking defendants appear in an English court emerge *from the interaction itself*. Only by looking at the interactions among judges, lawyers, defendants, and interpreters is it possible to describe and explain if and when problems exist in the process of trials, hearings, and arraignments.

ANALYZING ENGLISH- AND SPANISH-SPEAKING INTERACTIONS IN COURT

Throughout the following segments, readers are encouraged to carefully inspect and compare the turn-by-turn organization of data drawn from actual (naturalistic) courtroom interactions involving English- and Spanish-speaking defendants. By so doing, it becomes possible to gain an initial appreciation for how "understanding" is achieved through a series of practical, collaboratively produced courtroom activities. At times the negotiation of understanding appears altogether routine and void of specific difficulties. Yet understanding can itself be problematic, in which cases attention should be given to how (that is, the methods through which) judges, defendants, and interpreters seek resolutions to such troubles.

This preliminary analysis might begin with the question: In what interactional environments might intercultural problems and misunderstandings occur?

English-Speaking Defendants

One point of departure is to first locate and examine the work of *questions* and *answers* when defendants are called in front court to enter a plea of *guilty* or *not guilty* to an alleged criminal activity. Consider a basic interaction between an English-speaking defendant (ED) and a judge (J):[2]

1. T1/ELAC:D5 ((simplified transcripts))

> J: Do you understand the nature of the charge and the rights which *we've been discussing*.

> ED: ((nods)) I do

Through ED's affirmation, it is apparent that the defendant recognized J's prior turn as one designed to assess ED's understanding of the "charge"/"rights" and responded appropriately; that is, a question projects and receives an answer:

1a. J: Question (Understanding Check)

> ED: Answer (Affirmation of Understanding)

ED's ability to provide a relevant response displays a competency in courtroom interaction, and thus the right to "speak for one's self" in matters of guilt and innocence. Such an ability makes available to ED, as a resource, both direct and immediate access to the floor. Access of this type would be particularly useful if, for example, in (1) ED had understood the charge but *not* the rights discussed. Had this been the case, ED could have immediately specified such partial understanding and/or sought clarification of the problem(s) addressed.

A specific instance appears in (2) below, where an English-speaking defendant is able to achieve clarification and thereby enhance understanding by self-initiating access to the floor:

2. T1:ELAC:D3

> J: Do you understand the *two* charges.

> ED: ((nods)) *Yes*

> J: Do you understand the rights which I've summarized.

1→ED: [Wait the first?]

        (0.2)

2→ED: First charge is what.

> J: Driving under the influence of alcho *hol*

3→ED: [Sec]

        ond charge?

> J: It's the *new* legislation ((continues))

Although Ed initially responds affirmatively to J's query and understanding check, upon J's continuation ED (in 1→) displays that in fact a sufficient understanding of the charges had *not* been obtained. In overlap with J's moving onto "rights," ED is able to seek clarification and by so doing initiate repair of the "charges." As evident in (2→) ED *recycles* prior turn by paraphrasing ("First charge is what."), a normal device for insuring that information contained within prior overlapping utterance (1→) is comprehended adequately (cf. Schegloff, 1987). In next turn J provides the information sought through ED's clarification ("Driving under the influence of alcho*hol*). The sufficiency of J's response to ED's initial clarification is evident as ED moves on (in overlap) to "Second charge?" (3→), to which J once again offers the information sought.

Segment (2) begins to illustrate how problems with understanding "charges" can be quickly repaired by participants speaking the same language, that is, the "language of the court." To simplify, the interactional work in (2) above mirrors (1) through the first two turns-at-talk (understanding check/affirmation), but then moves onto repairing an understanding ED noticeably treats as problematic:

2a. T1/ELAC:D3

> J: Question (Understanding Check/Charges)

> ED: Answer (Affirmation of Understanding)

> J: Question (Understanding Check/Rights)

ED: Question (Clarification/Repair)

ED: Question (Recycled Clarification/Repair)

   J: Answer (Informative Response/First Charge)

ED: Question (Clarification/Repair)

   J: Answer (Informative Response/Second Charge)

Segments (1–2a) begin to indicate how it is possible for judges and English-speaking defendants to converse and get a plea entered. To summarize, when an English-speaking defendant is called to front court to enter a plea, the following interactional resources are available for negotiating and resolving problematic understandings:

1. Direct and immediate (i.e., non-mediated) access to the floor;

2. Self-initiated clarification and repair by defendant;

3. The ability of participants, whether J or ED, to recognize what questions project and, in turn, to provide relevant next answers.

Spanish-Speaking Defendants

As noted previously, defendants unable to speak the "language of the court" are assisted by court interpreters (I). With the addition of a third, mediating party, many of the interactional resources available to English-speaking defendants are suspended due to the need for "translation." In such cases, Spanish-speaking defendants (SD) and judges must address one another *through* the court interpreter. Thus, defendants and judges *cannot* address one another directly and immediately so as to accomplish, for example, clarification and repair. Even basic question/answer sequences must become "expanded" to accommodate court-interpreted activities:

3. T1:ELAC:D1 ((simplified transcripts))

   J: Been able to get the temporary *li*cense?

   I: *((Espanol, 2.6))*

  SD: ((nodding)) *((Espanol, 1.2))*

   I: Yes

In this four-turn exchange—the simplest of its kind—I's eventual answer ("Yes") to J's initial query is a consequence of *two inserted turns* (cf. Schegloff, 1972): I's translation of J's query, and SD's affirmative response. Clearly, what took only two turns-at-talk between J and ED (that is, Q-A) now requires a *minimum of four contiguous turns among three interactants* (Q-Q-A-A):

3a.   J: Question (Informational Query)

     I: Question (Repeated/Translated) ⎫ Insertion
   SD: Answer (Affirmative Response) ⎭ Sequence

     I: Answer (Repeated/Translated)

And due to the fact that J and SD do not speak "directly" with one another, it is within this sequential environment that the *accuracy* of translation must be taken into account. It is reasonable to inquire, for example, whether J's question was "heard" by SD the way it was asked, and whether SD's answer was paraphrased by I exactly as it was constructed. While no apparent problems emerged in (3) above, a final analysis cannot be rendered until and unless "Espanol" was itself carefully transcribed and translated by researchers. Due to the relatively quiet nature of I and SD's talk, however, this is not possible with the video-recordings employed herein. Nevertheless, from (3–3a) the *potential* for problematic understandings is readily apparent.

A related, potentially problematic issue involves the basic assumption in conversational turn-taking that, overwhelmingly, one person speaks at a time with little or no gap or overlap (cf. Sacks, Schegloff, and Jefferson, 1974). In this manner, what single speakers say can be attended to without "competition" from other speakers. Throughout nonmediated conversations, therefore, *simultaneous speech* routinely occasions efforts to restore order, such that one person regains undisputed control of the floor. In contrast, turn-taking involving court interpreters is frequently possible only within a speech exchange system where, by explicit order and consent of the court, the "one-at-a-time" pattern of interaction is necessarily suspended: Judges, interpreters, and defendants must orient to simultaneous talk (multiple voices) as both normal and inevitable.

An inspection of what problems might arise throughout such simultaneous/translated talk can begin with (4):

4. T1:ELAC:D2

> J: Would you. > sho:w us your p*lan*: pl ease
>
> I: ((Espa
> [   ]
> nol, 0.4)) =
>
> SD: = ((Espanol, 0.6))
>
> 1→ J: How do you in*tend* to pay these people back. =
>
> 2→ I: = ((Espanol, 0.5))
>
> 3→ D: ((Espanol, 3.3   ))
>
> 4→ I: [*You]*told me not to bring *any* kind of plan.*
>
> • ((Four turns-at-talk between I and SD deleted as J
> • searches records))
>   (5.2)
>
> > J: I have that on Oc*to*ber thirty one. you had sh*own* us that you had go*tt*:en insurance ((continues to read record))

Until (1 →), this segment evolves in a manner not unlike (3–3a) above (Q-Q-A-A), namely: J asks a question (Q); I restates/translates J's question to SD (Q); and SD appears to offer an answer (A). However, spoken simultaneously with SD's "answer," J asks a *second* question in (1 →). This is problematic for the interpreter for at least two reasons: First, J's question occurs in the same "slot" where I would normally provide a translated answer to J, so as to complete the Q-Q-A-*A* sequence. In essence, J's second question essentially *deletes* the possibility of I's delivering SD's answer; and second, in (2 →) I is faced with contradictory and thus *conflicting* tasks: To offer to J SD's previously deleted answer? To withhold SD's answer for the moment and proceed to translate J's second question?

Though exactly what I and D are doing in (2 →) and (3 →) above cannot be determined unequivocally, in

(4 →) it can be seen that I's translation of SD's answer involves a partial restatement of J's initial query. Does this mean that J's second question (in 1 →), was overlooked by I and/or SD? Was SD's initial answer, deleted by J in (1 →), eventually delivered by I in the course of this exchange? It is just these decision points that comprise the moment-by-moment contingencies of mediated courtroom interaction, and, in turn, exactly these kinds of uncertainties that remain for analysts to investigate.

CONCLUSION

Suffice it to say that considerably more complex segments of interaction emerge during court proceedings involving non-English-speaking defendants and court interpreters. The data above only begin to sketch how the potential for misunderstandings and for routine problems of comprehension is greater when a court interpreter is required. This is not to say that, for all practical purposes, sufficient understandings fail to be negotiated in all cases involving non-English-speaking defendants, nor that court interpreters lack basic competencies in working as mediators/translators on an ongoing basis in courts. On the contrary, assessments of court interpreters' skills have yielded results suggesting that "verbatim accuracy" of translations consistently meet or excel standards set for "optimum efficiency" (Quinones, 1986, p. 4). *Yet the ability to translate with verbatim accuracy does not necessarily take into account the inherent complexities and constraints involved in the interactional organization, distribution, and allocation of turns-at-talk among participants speaking the same and/ or different languages.* A focus on such skills need not, and frequently fails to systematically address how people cope interactionally with being called into court, accused of wrongdoing, and therefore treated as "societal deviants." Clearly, being called into court is itself a stigma of sorts; that is, the reputations of the defendants are at least challenged and possibly spoiled by having to defer to court authority in a public setting (Goffman, 1963).

Such constraints are highlighted by the following set of questions:

1. What happens when the judge *and* the defendant speak simultaneously to the interpreter? Does the interpreter give preference to translating the judge's message or respond to (and/or possibly delay) the defendant's query? Several observed instances suggest that preference is given to the judge's message, while the defendant's message is temporarily and/or permanently disregarded.

2. Do defendants requiring interpreters have the same access to the floor, and thus to the judge, as do English-speaking defendants? What evidence would suggest that they do or do not? If they do not, as has been evidenced with the previously examined interactional segments, what remedies would better insure the ability of the legal system to satisfy Sixth Amendment rights for *all* defendants? How might these remedies be implemented, for example, through training court interpreters and non-English-speaking defendants to recognize and deal with the interactional constraints of mediated turn-taking?

The questions raised here focus attention on potential problems inherent in the context of the courtroom where intercultural communication encounters are routine. At the very least, it is clear that the answers to these questions reside in the methods by which courtroom interactions are accomplished—turn-by-turn, face-to-face. Because language is the vehicle through which social justice and "fair and impartial treatments" are meted out, we need to pay attention to the way language structures (and is structured by) those constraints inherent in court proceedings. In this sense, language is both the container and the reflection of one's knowledge of the social world. By paying close, analytic attention to talk sequences, we can see how people orient to, make sense of, and construct social realities of the contexts in which they are placed. If and when intercultural encounters create communication problems, the evidence for such problems must ultimately be generated from the collaborative actions of the interacting members— that is, *how* problems emerge interactionally. Such

is also the case for remedies to such problems, for language possesses the unique ability to simultaneously create and resolve troubles inherent to intercultural experiences.

NOTES

1. These data were collected at the East Los Angeles Municipal Court, where nearly 70 percent of the cases require court interpreters.

2. The transcription notation system employed for the trial segments is an adaptation of Gail Jefferson's work in conversation analysis (see Atkinson and Heritage, 1984, pp. ix–xvi; Beach, 1989, pp. 89–90). The symbols are described as follows:

Colon(s). An extended sound or syllable is noted by a colon (:). A single colon indicates a short prolongation (e.g., "Uh:h"). Longer sound extensions are indicated by more than one colon (e.g., "de::scribe");

Underlining. Vocalic emphasis of syllables, words, or phrases (e.g., "at*tack*ed you was the *eyes*");

Single Parentheses Enclosing Numbers or Periods Within an Utterance. Speakers often pause during an utterance. If the pause is too short to be timed it is indicated by enclosing a period within parentheses (e.g., "is the *only* thing that (.) made you believe that (.) the photograph"). Intervals of longer duration are indicated by seconds and tenths of seconds (e.g., "Um:m (1.2) on that occasion (0.4) preliminary hearing (0.2)");

Single Parentheses Enclosing Numbers Between Utterances. Intervals between same or different speaker's utterance are so noted:

W: Yes.
   (2.6)
P: Uh:h (1.6) did you

Single Parentheses Enclosing Utterances or Blank Spaces. Indicates transcriptionist doubt as to words or sounds transcribed as best possible (e.g., "cuz I (left early).", or when undecipherable and/or when names of interactants are anonymous (e.g., "start work or do ya (   )?").

Double Parentheses Enclosing Words. Are employed when providing details of the scene (e.g., "((angered)) When you see somebody").

Periods. A falling vocal tone is indicated by a period. Such tones do not necessarily occur at the end of a sentence, though they may (e.g., "I'm not sure.")

Question Marks. Indicate a rising inflection, not necessarily a question (e.g., "you saw the suspect's footwear?")

Asterisk. A passage of talk noticeably softer and/or quieter than surrounding talk (e.g., "*Yes.")

Equal Signs. Suggest latching of adjacent utterances, with no interval and no overlap between utterances:

D: three o'clock? =
*W: = Some*time

Single Brackets. When overlapping utterances do not start simultaneously, the point at which an ongoing utterance is joined by another is marked with a single left-hand bracket:

P: after they occurred (0.4) or wor se
W: [   ]
                      Wo rse

Exclamation Points. An animated, though not necessarily exclamatory, tone (e.g., "don't you think you'd recognize 'em!!!")

Hyphens. Indicate a halting, abrupt cut off of a word or sound (e.g., "wi- dirty bu- shoes on").

REFERENCES

Atkinson, J. M. (1979). "Sequencing and Shared Attentiveness to Court Proceedings." In G. Psathas (Ed.), *Everyday Language: Studies in Ethnomethodology.* New York: Irvington.

Atkinson, J. M., and P. Drew. (1979). *Order in Court: The Organization of Verbal Interaction in Judicial Settings.* Atlantic Highlands, N.J.: Humanities Press.

Atkinson, J. M., and M. Heritage (Eds.). (1984). *Structures of Social Action: Studies in Conversation Analysis.* Cambridge: Cambridge University Press.

Beach, W. A. (1982). "Everyday Interaction and Its Practical Accomplishment: Progressive Developments in Ethnomethodological Research." *Quarterly Journal of Speech, 68,* 314–327.

Beach, W. A. (1983). "Background Understandings and the Situated Accomplishment of Conversational Telling-Expansions." In R. Craig and K. Tracy (Eds.), *Conversational Coherence: Form, Structure, and Strategy.* Newbury Park, Calif.: Sage Publications.

Beach, W. A. (1985). "Temporal Density in Courtroom Interaction: Constraints on the Recovery of Past Events in Legal Discourse." *Communication Monographs, 52,* 1–18.

Beach, W. A. (Ed.) (1989). "Sequential Organization of Conversational Activities." *Western Journal of Speech Communication, 53,* special issue.

Coulter, J. (1979). "Beliefs and Practical Understanding." In G. Psathas (Ed.), *Everyday Language: Studies in Ethnomethodology.* New York: Irvington.

Goffman, E. (1961). *Encounters.* Indianapolis: Bobbs-Merrill.

Goffman, E. (1963). *Stigma: Notes on the Management of Spoiled Identity.* Englewood Cliffs, N.J.: Prentice-Hall, Inc.

Maynard, D. W. (1984). *Inside Plea Bargaining: The Language of Negotiation.* New York: Plenum Press.

Mishler, E. G. (1979). "Meaning in Context: Is There Any Other Kind?" *Harvard Educational Review, 49,* 1–19.

O'Barr, W. M. (1982). *Linguistic Evidence: Language, Power, and Strategy in the Courtroom.* New York: Academic Press.

Ochs, E. (1979). "Introduction: What Child Language Can Contribute to Pragmatics." In E. Ochs and B. Schiefflen (Eds.), *Developmental Pragmatics.* New York: Academic Press.

Pollner, M. (1975). "The Very Coinage of Your Brain: The Resolution of Reality Disjunctures." *Philosophy of the Social Sciences, 5,* 411–430.

Pollner, M. (1979). "Explicative Transactions: Making and Managing Meaning in Traffic Court." In G. Psathas (Ed.), *Everyday Language: Studies in Ethnomethodology.* New York: Irvington.

Quinones, M. O. (1986). "Interpreters Are Indispensable." *The Polyglot, 21,* 1–12.

Sacks, H., E. Schegloff, and G. Jefferson (1974). "A Simplest Systematics for the Organization of Turn-Taking for Conversation." *Language, 59,* 696–735.

Schegloff, E. (1972). "Notes on a Conversational Practice: Formulating Place." In J. Schenkein (Ed.), *Studies in the Organization of Conversational Interaction.* New York: The Free Press.

Schegloff, E. A. (1987). "Recycled Turn Beginnings: A Precise Repair Mechanism in Conversation's Turn-Taking Organization." In G. Button and J. R. E. Lee (Eds.), *Talk and Social Organisation.* Clevedon, England: Multilingual Matters.

CONCEPTS AND QUESTIONS
FOR CHAPTER 4

1. What does Stewart mean when she refers to *ringi*?

2. How do imported Japanese management techniques affect communication in the conduct of the multinational business organization in the United States?

3. How do peer group relations in multinational/multicultural business organizations differ from those in U.S. business organizations?

4. As an employee of a U.S. company, you have just been assigned to the international division and will soon take a position as a department manager at a facility in Germany. What differences in the cultural context of the workplace might you expect to encounter? How would you prepare yourself for the new assignment?

5. How would you approach a business discussion with a German managerial counterpart knowing the German impersonal approach to business?

6. How would you reconcile the American need to be liked with the German need to be credible if you were undertaking a discussion of management techniques with a German business counterpart?

7. What is the German concept of *Besprechung*, and how does it apply to business discussions?

8. What are the three major problems associated with international negotiations?

9. How does the American perspective of the negotiation atmosphere differ from the perspective held by other cultures?

10. In what ways does the American communication style differ from that of the Japanese, the French, and the Mexican?

11. What is the cultural grid and how can you use it personally to improve your ability to be an intercultural communicator?

12. What influence does culture have on the context of the classroom?

13. How does the culturally defined role of the teacher affect the classroom context?

14. How has your culture shaped the expectations for your classroom behavior?

15. What are personalistic medical systems and how do they differ from naturalistic medical systems?

16. What communication problems might a health care provider working within a scientific health care system orientation encounter when dealing with patients coming from a personalistic or naturalistic orientation? What should he or she do to minimize these problems?

17. What cultural functions are served by medical systems?

18. What problems arise when a non-English-speaking person must defend him- or herself in a U.S. courtroom?

19. How does the introduction of translators into the courtroom process affect the normal proceedings?

20. Does the use of a translator assure that a non-English-speaking defendant will obtain a "fair and impartial" trial?

PART THREE

Intercultural Interaction: Taking Part in Intercultural Communication

If we seek to understand a people we have to put ourselves, as far as we can, in that particular historical and cultural background. . . . One has to recognize that countries and people differ in their approach and their ways, in their approach to life and their ways of living and thinking. In order to understand them we have to understand their way of life and approach. If we wish to convince them, we have to use their language as far as we can, not language in the narrow sense of the word, but the language of the mind.

—Jawaharlal Nehru

In this part we are concerned with taking part in intercultural communication. Our interest focuses on both verbal and nonverbal forms of symbolic interaction. As we pointed out in introducing Part Two, meanings reside within people, and symbols serve as stimuli to which these meanings are attributed. Meaning-evoking stimuli consist of both verbal and nonverbal behaviors. Although we consider these forms of symbolic interaction separately for convenience, we hasten to point out their interrelatedness. As nonverbal behavior accompanies verbal behavior, it becomes a unique part of the total symbolic interaction. Verbal messages often rely on their nonverbal accompaniment for cues that aid the receiver in decoding the verbal symbols. Nonverbal behaviors not only serve to amplify and clarify verbal messages but can also serve as forms of symbolic interaction without verbal counterparts.

When we communicate verbally, we use words with seeming ease, because there is a high consensus of agreement about the meanings our words evoke. Our experiential backgrounds are similar enough that we share essentially the same meanings for most of the word symbols we use in everyday communication. But even within our culture we disagree over the meanings of many word symbols. As words move farther from sense data reality they become more abstract, and there is far less agreement about appropriate meanings. What do highly abstract words such as *love, freedom, equality, democracy,* or *good time* mean to you? Do they mean the same things to everyone? If you are in doubt, ask some friends; take a poll. You will surely find that people have different notions of these concepts and consequently different meanings for these words. Their experiences have been different, and they hold different beliefs, attitudes, values, concepts, and expectations. Yet all, or perhaps most, are from the same culture. Their backgrounds, experiences, and concepts of the universe are really quite uniform. When cultures begin to vary, much larger differences are found.

Culture exerts no small influence over our use of language. In fact, it strongly determines just what our language is and how we use it. In the narrowest sense, language is a set of symbols (vocabulary) that evoke more or less uniform meanings among a particular population and a set of rules (grammar and syntax) for using the symbols. In the broadest sense, language is the symbolic representation of a people, and it includes their historical and cultural backgrounds as well as their approach to life and their ways of living and thinking.

What comes to be symbolized and what the symbols represent are very much functions of culture. Similarly, how we use our verbal symbols is also a function of culture. What we think about or speak with others about must be capable of symbolization, and how we speak or think about things must follow the rules we have for using our language. Because the symbols and rules are culturally determined, how and what we think or talk about are, in effect, a function of our culture. This relation between language and culture is not unidirectional, however. There is an interaction between them—what we think about and how we think about it also affect our culture.

As we can see, language and culture are inseparable. To be effective intercultural communicators requires that we be aware of the relationship between culture and language. It further requires that we learn and know about the culture of the person with whom we communicate so that we can better understand how his or her language represents that person.

Another important aspect of verbal symbols or words is that they can evoke two kinds of meanings: *denotative* and *connotative*. A denotative meaning indicates the referent or the "thing" to which the symbol refers. For example, the denota-

tive meaning of the word *book* is the physical object to which it refers; or, in the case of the set of symbols *"Intercultural Communication: A Reader,"* the referent is the book you are now reading. Not all denotations have a physical correspondence. As we move to higher levels of abstraction, we often deal with words that represent ideas or concepts, which exist only in the mind and do not necessarily have a physical basis. For example, much communication research is directed toward changes in attitude. Yet attitude is only a hypothetical construct used to explain behavior; there is no evidence of any physical correspondence between some group of brain cells and a person's attitudes.

The second type of meaning—connotative—indicates an evaluative dimension. Not only do we identify referents (denotative meaning), we place them along an evaluative dimension that can be described as positive-neutral-negative. Where we place a word on the dimension depends on our prior experiences and how we "feel" about the referent. If we like books, we might place *Intercultural Communication: A Reader* near the positive end of the dimension. When we are dealing with more abstract symbols, we do the same thing. In fact, as the level of abstraction increases, so does our tendency to place more emphasis on connotative meanings. Most will agree that a book is the object you are holding in your hand, but whether books are good or bad or whether this particular book is good or bad or in between is an individual judgment based on prior experience.

Culture affects both denotative and connotative meanings. Consequently, a knowledge of how these meanings vary culturally is essential to effective intercultural communication. To make the assumption that everyone uses the same meanings is to invite communication disaster.

There are other ways in which culture affects language and language use. We tend to believe that our way of using language is both correct and universal and that any deviation is wrong or substandard. This belief can and does elicit many negative responses and judgments when we encounter someone from another culture whose use of language deviates from our own specifications.

What all of these examples are trying to point out should be quite obvious—language and culture are inseparable. In fact, it would be difficult to determine which is the voice and which is the echo. How we learn, employ, and respond to symbols is culturally based. In addition, the sending and the receiving of these culturally grounded symbols are what enable us to interact with people from other cultures. Hence, it is the purpose of this part of the book to highlight these verbal and nonverbal symbols to help you understand some of the complexities, subtleties, and nuances of language.

5

Verbal Processes: Thinking and Speaking

Some people have suggested that our most unique feature is our ability, as a species, to receive, store, manipulate, and generate symbols. All 5.5 billion of us deal with past, present, and future experiences by using language; we make sounds and marks on paper that stand for something. In short, language is that special, simple, and yet magical instrument that lets us share our internal states with others.

It is the premise of this chapter that a culture's use of language involves much more than words and phrases. Forms of reasoning, techniques of problem solving, and specialized linguistic devices such as metaphors, similes, and analogies are all part of a culture's approach to language. Hence, to understand the language of any culture demands that you look beyond the vocabulary, grammar, and syntax. This philosophy has guided us in our selection of readings. We urge you to view language from this larger perspective as you read the articles in this chaper; this eclectic outlook toward language will help you understand the interaction patterns of cultures that are different from your own.

We begin with an essay by Devorah A. Lieberman, "Ethnocognitivism and Problem Solving," that advances the claim that thinking, problem solving, and language are not only interrelated but are grounded in culture. She maintains that "consideration and understanding of differences among cultures in cognitive processing and presentation styles in regard to problem solving" is essential for successful intercultural communication. To assist that understanding, she examines a number of cultures that employ diversified problem-solving techniques. She then compares these styles with the patterns of thought used in North America. She also offers cultural contrasts concerning the role of left- and right-brain hemispheres on problem solving. Lieberman concludes with an appeal to North American teachers to accept the idea that cultural diversity in classrooms also means cultural diversity in patterns of reasoning, problem solving, and language.

Our assertion that a culture's verbal processes encompass more than vocabulary is also reflected in the second selection, in which we are concerned with differences in how culture influences the ways people speak and argue in public settings. For example, the Chinese and Japanese views of dialogue and debate are contrary to those of North Americans. Many of these cultural distinctions are pointed out by Carl B. Becker in his article, "Reasons for the Lack of Argumentation and Debate in the Far East." Becker does not take the position that one approach to logic, thought patterns, and speech is superior to another, but rather he explains *why* the Chinese and Japanese tend to avoid public argumentation and debate. Like so many cultural values, the roots of this behavior are found in the deep structure of both cultures. Therefore, maintains Becker, to understand why Far Eastern cultures withdraw from public debate, we need to look at the social history, linguistic features, and philosophy and religion of China and Japan.

Continuing our theme that language goes beyond words, we present a selection that declares a direct connection between perception and language, a point of view that is at the heart of the Sapir-Whorf hypothesis of "linguistic relativity." This classic and sometimes controversial hypothesis maintains that each language embodies and imposes upon its users and their culture a particular view of reality that functions not only as a device for reporting experience but also, and more significantly, as a way of defining experience. To help explain this argument and its ramifications, Harry Hoijer introduces the basic assumptions, usability, and plausibility of linguistic relativity.

As we noted in the introduction of this part, language involves attaching meanings to word symbols, whether they are sounds or marks on a piece of paper. If those symbols have to be translated, as in a foreign language, numerous problems arise. Without accurate translations those trying to communicate often end up simply exchanging meaningless sounds. What usually happens is that the interpretations lack a common vocabulary and familiar referents. For mutual understanding, we

need more than an examination of linguistics. The process of translation, as our next essay explains, involves a whole set of extra-linguistic criteria. If we are to understand the internal state of someone who speaks a language different from our own, we must appreciate these added criteria. Susan Bassnett-McGuire introduces us to these often overlooked issues in her essay "Translation Studies." She begins by distinguishing three types of translation: (1) intralingual translation, or rewording (an interpretation of verbal signs by means of other signs in the same language), (2) interlingual translation or translation proper (an interpretation of verbal signs by means of some other language), and (3) intersemiotic translation or transmutation (an interpretation of verbal signs by means of non-verbal sign symbols). Bassnett-McGuire then shows how the process of decoding and recoding transcends the linguistic elements. She increases our appreciation of translation as she reminds us of the problems of equivalence and how we need to understand questions of what is lost and what is gained. She concludes by reviewing some problems associated with linguistic and cultural untranslatability, difficulties that arise when there is no lexical or syntactical substitute in the second language. What makes this essay so helpful is the author's abundant use of examples to clarify all of the issues she advances.

Although Bassnett-McGuire shows us some of the difficulties encountered in translation, she does not deal with problems faced when one individual must transform the thoughts of another individual from one language into another. To overcome many of these problems, a translator is often asked to become part of an intercultural event. This act of introducing a third party often creates another set of problems, many of which are discussed by Jan Carol Berris in her essay "The Art of Interpreting." Berris makes a distinction between translation and interpreting, and she looks at a host of potential problems that can impede intercultural communication. Among the more serious issues is the problem of not having enough interpreters for long sessions. She also discusses the importance of proper preparation, the differences between precise translations and simple paraphrasing, and nonverbal communication and its role in interpretative events.

All cultures introduce new members into their group by employing a rather elaborate symbol system. We are born with the tools to learn these systems, so passing on culture by speaking and listening is universal, but what is not universal is a culture's knowledge of the skills necessary to read and write. Literacy entails more than learning how to read and write; it influences thinking patterns, perceptions, cultural values, communication styles, and social organizations as well. Because we often interact with people who have no written language, it is useful to know something of how cultures such as the Hmong of Laos share experiences. So many Asian refugees have migrated to the United States that it seems appropriate to look at this culture, as Robert Shuter does in his essay "The Hmong of Laos: Orality, Communication, and Acculturation."

The purpose of this chapter is to introduce you to the various forms of verbal communication found among and between cultures. Our use of language not only gives us the gift of sharing ideas and information with those we encounter, but language is one of the primary ways we learn our culture.

In this book we encourage you to see that there are almost as many communication styles as there are cultures. The overriding assumption is that if you know something about the way other people communicate, how they use language, you can improve the quality of your communication with them and your understanding of their behavior. This study of language is important because one's language is a model of one's culture; language functions as a reflection of a culture's unique experiences. In no instance is this point more vivid than in the black community. Here the study of language not only reveals something about that group's view of the world, but it is also an examination of how past experiences find their way to the present. In our next essay, "The Need to Be: The Socio-Cultural Significance of Black Language," Shirley N. Weber uses black language to show how the African people attempted to adjust to slavery, an adjustment that is still being acted out today. She isolated five aspects of black language that she suggests might "help others understand and appreciate black language styles and the reasons blacks speak the way they do, in hopes of building respect for cultural differences."

Ethnocognitivism and Problem Solving

DEVORAH A. LIEBERMAN

Intercultural communication theory is grounded in the concept that participants in any interaction bring with them a system of symbols and meanings (Schneider, 1976) that shapes their perceptions of a shared phenomenon. Based on this approach to intercultural communication, much of the research in the field and the teaching of intercultural communication in our own college classrooms has claimed that differences (for example, in values, beliefs, attitudes, frames of reference) are the basic variables that influence these perceptions (Kohls, 1984). However, few intercultural communication scholars have addressed specific differences among cultures in their approach to solving problems. (Condon and Yousef (1975) and Samovar and Porter (1988) are notable exceptions.) A great deal of research has addressed the different ways cultures vary in values, beliefs, and ways of classifying, but "there is a lack of research addressing differences in problem solving by culture. This research needs to be done" (Cole and Scribner, 1974, p. 174). The "cultural differences in problem solving" debate among ethnocognitivists (Bogen, Dezare, TenHouten, and Marsh, 1972; Cole and Scribner, 1974) ranges from whether there is inherent cultural difference in cognition abilities to whether cultures merely teach culture-specific cognitive processes. Based upon the assumption that cultures reason and problem solve quite differ-

ently, this essay has a twofold purpose. First, it explores the possible reasons for and approaches to differences among cultures in problem solving and cognitive processing. Second, it examines generic teaching styles that reinforce and perpetuate culture-specific problem-solving approaches.

CULTURE AND PROBLEM-SOLVING APPROACHES

Cognitive processes are universal cerebral means employed to handle a specific task or problem at hand. According to Luria (1966), everyone has the same cognitive components but learns to use them differently throughout life. Cole and Scribner (1974), supporting Luria, contend that it is the cultural influence that conditions the alternative cognitive processes chosen to complete tasks or problem solve. Each culture teaches, trains, and molds those within its system for what it considers the most appropriate methods for problem solving. Anthropological research has traditionally examined culture and problem solving from a group, content-observation, field-description approach. Psychological research has examined cognition, elementary functions, process, the individual laboratory, and explanation (Cole, 1985). This chapter integrates these two approaches (culture and cognition), examining problem-solving approaches in different cultures, which range from concrete and participative to abstract and individualistic.

PROBLEM SOLVING OF KPELLE, FIJI, POMO, AND TROBRIAND

Following are four examples of cultures that use problem-solving techniques acquired through observation and group participation: Kpelles of Liberia, Fijians, native Americans, and Trobriands. Each is a relatively high-context culture (Hall, 1976), gathering information from the immediate environment and employing concrete approaches to attend to unsolved tasks. In each, there seems to be little leeway for inferential problem solving.

The Kpelle rice farmers are from central Liberia. They work together clearing land and raising rice and in the forest gathering materials for buildings, tools, and medicine. The researcher seated two of the Kpelles at a table facing one another with a small partition between them. In front of each man were ten sticks (pieces of wood of different kinds). Each stick had a match with a stick in the other pile. The researcher chose one stick from one man, and the man was told to describe the stick so that the other Kpelle farmer could choose the matching stick from his pile. The procedure continued until they had described and selected all ten sticks.

The partition was lifted and the men compared the two rows of sticks and described and discussed errors. The barrier was replaced, and they repeated the entire process of choosing one stick and describing it to the other man. Examples of the descriptions on the first trial were: "one of the sticks," "not a large one," "piece of bamboo," "one stick," and "one of the thorny." Examples of the descriptions on the second trial were: "one of the sticks," "curved bamboo," "large bamboo," and "has a thorn."

The problem-solving technique of "hit and miss" description used to transfer information did not take into account the precise information the other person needed to know to choose the stick. These farmers, through observation of one another, always participate together in tasks and do not need to share the information the other person lacks. All information is observable and available to all individuals (Cole, Gay, and Glick, 1969). In this high-context culture, where information is gathered from the environment, the Kpelles thus problem solve in a concrete manner.

Griffin (1983) found that the Fijian language does not allow for creative or abstract problem solving as there is inadequate verbal coding to identify a new problem. Thus, when a problem arises that has not previously been confronted, the Fijian is "unable to think out new rules, verbalize problems and generate options" (p. 60). Anxiety and frustration often follow as outlets for the problem-solving barrier.

Another concrete approach to reasoning is evident in the native American culture (Freedle, 1981).

When Pomo native Americans were asked to recall a story and could not remember a piece of information, their response was that they could not recount the story at all. Thus, a subject's recall was either null or perfect. Similarly, a problem could either be perceived as solvable or not, depending on information availability. All pieces of the puzzle were required for problem solving to occur. Other native American languages (for example, Hopi and Navajo) also lend themselves to concrete rather than abstract thinking, leading to less analytic and more absolute problem solving.

The Trobriand, also concrete in language, do not problem solve from the cause-and-effect approach that is associated with linear-thinking cultures. They do not have the traditional stimulus-response system; thus, when they are confronted with a problem, the solution approach is present oriented. As the language has no "to be" verbs, the concept of delayed gratification or a solution emerging in the future, does not exist. Trobriand students present an example of a negative consequence of the differences in problem solving among cultures. They have been refused entrance to colleges because the autobiographical sketches accompanying their applications were assessed as showing a lack of purposefulness and ability to plan. They were considered inadequate in character as well as intellect (Lee, 1950).

PROBLEM SOLVING IN MAINSTREAM CULTURES

Kaplan (1966) examined problem-solving approaches and patterns of thought in mainstream cultures. He concluded that English-speaking persons from the United States were more linear and direct than Semitic, Asian, Romance, or Russian speakers. The Semitic individuals solved problems using a combination of tangential and semidirect approaches. Asians employed a circular approach. Romance cultures used a more consistently circuitous approach, and Russians employed a combination of direct and circuitous approaches.

Each culture teaches the patterns of thought and problem-solving approaches that are most appropriate when one is confronted with particular situations (Condon and Yousef, 1975). These patterns have been identified by various authors as universalistic, nominalistic, hypothetical, intuitional, organismic, dialectical, temporal, axiomatic, affective, inductive/deductive, analytic, global, sequential, concrete sequential, and abstract random (Condon and Yousef, 1975; Felder and Silverman, 1988; Pribram, 1949). Particular patterns predominate within specific cultures. For example, the U.S. method is predominantly factual-inductive (ascertain facts, find similarities, and formulate conclusions); the U.S.S.R. patterns are predominantly axiomatic-deductive (move from general principle to particulars, which can be easily deduced); and Arab cultures' ways of thinking are predominantly intuitive-affective (facts are secondary to emotions).

An extension of the cognitive process for problem solving is an individual's style of presentation. Confronted with a problem, an individual from the United States might respond with two or three specific alternative solutions. The U.S. culture perpetuates either thinking in threes (for example, "Tom, Dick, and Harry," "I came, I saw, I conquered" and (when telling a joke) "and then the third man came up and said") or in dichotomies (for example, either/or; right/wrong; good/bad). Conditioning to perceive a situation or problem from a particular style as well as from a particular perspective dictates the appropriate response (Condon and Yousef, 1975). Though individuals have the ability to use any process, each culture continuously stresses only two or three particular approaches. Even though these styles and patterns are idiosyncratic to the individual, "they must be heavily influenced by cultural transmission" (Collins and Dedre, 1987, p. 263).

ETHNOCOGNITIVISM AND HEMISPHERICITY

Intercultural communication theory addressing cultural patterns of thought and problem-solving approaches has only scratched the surface of cognitive functioning and differences among cultures. Springer and Deutsch (1985) contend that different languages (whether oriented toward concrete or abstract thought) are very likely responsible for differential hemispheric involvement (hemisphere dominance in the brain). They maintain that particular cognitive functions are hemisphere specific. Thus, if a culture produces individuals who exhibit predominant problem-solving patterns and these patterns are associated with a particular hemisphericity, then it follows that ethnocognitivism (thought patterns dominant within a culture) and hemisphericity should be a greater consideration in the examination of intercultural interactions.

The left hemisphere has traditionally been associated with the following processes: verbal, analytic, symbolic, abstract, temporal, rational, digital, logical, and linear. The right hemisphere has traditionally been associated with processes such as nonverbal, synthetic, concrete, analogic, nontemporal, nonrational, spatial, intuitive, and holistic (Edwards, 1979).

The "cultural cognition" paradox asks whether a culture trains its individuals to have dominant left or right hemispheres or whether cultures are inherently left- or right-hemisphere dominant (Paredes and Hepburn, 1976). Springer and Deutsch (1985) resolve the paradox by suggesting that "every human brain is capable of more than one kind of logical process, but cultures differ with respect to the processes used with various situations" (p. 188). Recent research (Tsunoda, 1978, cited in *Science*, 1980) suggests that the Japanese brain actually functions differently from the Western brain. Tsunoda claims that the Japanese left hemisphere processes nonverbal human sounds, animal sounds, and Japanese instrumental music, while the right hemisphere processes Western instrumental music. (Previous research claimed all nonverbal sounds (human, animal, and musical) were processed in the right hemisphere.) Also, he continues, Westerners process emotion in the right hemisphere and Japanese process emotion in the left hemisphere. He claims that the language first learned develops the person's patterns of thought and influences "the way the brain's two halves process language" (*Science*, p. 25). For example, Western children raised in the Japanese culture speaking Japanese "typically acquire Japanese brains" (p. 25) and vice versa concerning Japanese children raised in Western culture and speaking English. Very little of this research has been translated from Japanese into English, and understandably "much more work is needed to determine if cultural differences in hemispheric utilization are real and, if so, to what they are attributable" (Springer and Deutsch, 1985, p. 242). Though this research has not yet been corroborated, it raises exciting questions regarding culture, hemisphericity, and problem solving.

CULTURE, HEMISPHERICITY, AND EDUCATION

Given the potential for cultural influence on brain development and hemisphere dominance, it is essential to understand the responsibility educational systems have toward understanding their effect on developing students' patterns of thought, approaches to problem solving, and, in turn, communication styles. For example, Blakeslee (1980) contends that the U.S. educational system has not realized that it is almost entirely teaching its students to process information and formulate responses using traditionally accepted left-hemisphere skills (for example, linear, analytic, rational, and nonemotional thought). Qualities of the right hemisphere, often termed the unconscious hemisphere, are not only suppressed but are often associated with less important or irrelevant qualities. "Because we operate in such a sequential world [U.S.] and because the logical thought of the left hemisphere is so honored in our culture, we gradually damp out, devalue, and disregard the input of our right hemispheres. It is not that we stop using it altogether; it just becomes less and less available to us because of established patterns" (Prince, 1978, p. 57). Blakeslee (1980, p. 76) goes so far as to contend that "there is a decadence in the field of higher education that is the natural result of an ignorance of the unconscious side of the brain. . . . The system thus feeds itself and becomes more and more scholarly and less and less intuitive."

Thus, as patterns of thought develop accompanying world view, the educational system is encouraging a world view and world interpretation con-structed by the individual and the culture (Ong, 1973). Numerous researchers suggest patterns of reasoning and problem solving that are encouraged in the classroom (Kolb, 1984; Kaplan and Kaplan, 1981). Though they differ in their specific approaches, each asserts that classroom education reinforces the dominant world view and thought patterns that are condoned and rewarded by a particular culture.

Felder and Silverman (1988) claim that most U.S. college students, either of traditional college age or beyond, need teaching methods that stress right-hemisphere visual information. However, the information in U.S. classrooms is presented predominantly through auditory methods (lecturing) or a visual representation of auditory information (words and mathematical symbols written in texts and handouts, on transparencies, or on a chalkboard). Silverman (1987) found that students retain 10 percent of what they read, 26 percent of what they hear, 30 percent of what they see, 50 percent of what they see and hear, 70 percent of what they say, and 90 percent of what they say while doing something. Helgesen (1988) claims that the teacher usually teaches in the style in which he or she has been trained (traditionally left-hemisphere in the United States) and that the student tries to match his or her learning style to that of the teacher, which often leads to learning some material, missing some material, and tuning out. Numerous educators suggest that teachers learn to "understand the duality of their students' minds" (Blakeslee, 1980, p. 59) and in this way stimulate both the verbal and nonverbal parts of the brain.

Lesser (1976) asserts that students "who share a common cultural background will also share, to a certain extent, common patterns of intellectual abilities, thinking styles and interests" (p. 137). He maintains that we will not have a successful multicultural educational system until we first examine the cultural diversity in the U.S. classroom and address the thinking patterns and problem-solving styles of these cultures. He states, "We are facing a self-declared moratorium on research, and until the times change, we will know less and less about the connections that exist between cultural conditions and cognitive growth" (p. 162). Following Cole's (1976) suggestions regarding education, culture, hemisphericity, and thought patterns, materials presented in a culturally diverse classroom taught in different contexts to appeal to different students, using a variety of materials, would facilitate student learning.

CONCLUSION

Whether the intercultural interactants are in the classroom, socializing, or in a business environment, cultural differences in cognitive processing and problem solving are inherent within the interaction. Understanding of differences among cultures in cognitive processing and presentation styles in regard to problem solving is a major step toward successful intercultural communication.

REFERENCES

Blakeslee, T. R. (1980). *The Right Brain: A New Understanding of the Unconscious Mind and Its Creative Powers.* New York: Anchor Press.

Bogen, J., Dezare, W., TenHouten, W., and Marsh, J. (1972). "The Other Side of the Brain. IV: The a/p Ration," *Bulletin of the Los Angeles Neurological Societies, 37,* 49–61.

Cole, M. (1976). "Commentary: Cultural Differences in the Contexts of Learning." *Individuality in Learning.* San Francisco: Jossey-Bass.

Cole, M. (1985). "The Zone of Proximal Development: Where Culture and Cognition Create Each Other." In J. Wertsch (Ed.), *Culture, Communication and Cognition: Vygotskian Perspectives.* Cambridge: Cambridge University Press.

Cole, M., Gay, J., and Glick, J. (1969). "Communication Skills Among the Kpelle of Liberia." Paper presented at the Society for Research in Child Development Meeting, Santa Monica, Calif.

Cole, M., and Scribner, S. (1974). *Culture and Thought: A Psychological Introduction.* New York: Wiley.

Collins, A., and Dedre, G. (1987). "How People Construct Mental Models." In D. Holland and N. Quinn (Eds.), *Cultural Models in Language and Thought.* New York: Cambridge University Press.

Condon, J., and Yousef, F. (1975). *An Introduction to Intercultural Communication.* Indianapolis: Bobbs-Merrill.

Edwards, B. (1979). *Drawing on the Right Side of the Brain.* Los Angeles: J. P. Tarcher.

Felder, R., and Silverman, L. (1988). "Learning and Teaching Styles in Engineering Education." *Engineering Education,* pp. 674–681.

Ficsher, J. (1961). "Art Styles as Cultural Cognitive Maps." *American Anthropologist, 63* (1), 79–93.

Freedle, R. (1981). "The Need for a Cross-Cultural Perspective." In J. Harvey (Ed.), *Cognition, Social Behavior and the Environment.* Hillsdale, N.J.: Erlbaum.

Griffin, C. (1983). "Social Structure, Speech and Silence: Fijian Reactions to the Problems of Social Change." In W. Maxwell (Ed.), *Thinking: The Expanding Frontier.* Philadelphia: The Franklin Institute Press.

Hall, E. (1976). *Beyond Culture.* New York: Doubleday.

Helgesen, M. (1988). *Natural Style and Learning Style Preferences: Their Effect on Teaching and Learning.* Urbana-Champaign: Instruction and Management Services, University of Illinois.

Kaplan, R. (1966). "Cultural Thought Patterns in Inter-cultural Education." *Language Learning, 16* (1 and 2), 1–20.

Kaplan, S., and Kaplan, R. (1981). *Cognition and Environment.* New York: Pergamon Press.

Kohls, L. (1984). *Survival Kit for Overseas Living* (rev. ed.) Yarmouth, Me.: Intercultural Press.

Kolb, D. (1984). *Experiential Learning.* Englewood Cliffs, N.J.: Prentice-Hall.

Lee, D. (1950). "Codifications of Reality: Lineal and Nonlineal." *Psychosomatic Medicine, 12* (2), 89–97.

Lesser, G. (1976). "Cultural Differences in Learning and Thinking Styles." *Individuality in Learning.* San Francisco: Jossey-Bass.

Lieberman, D., Kosokoff, S., and Kosokoff, J. (1988). "What Is Common About Common Sense?" *ORTESOL.*

Luria, A. R. (1966). *Higher Cortical Function in Man.* New York: Basic Books.

Ong, W. (1973). "Word as View and World as Event." In M. Prosser (Ed.), *Intercommunication Among Nations and Peoples.* New York: Harper & Row.

Paredes, J., and Hepburn, K. (1976). "The Split Brain and the Culture-and-Cognition Paradox." *Current Anthropology, 17,* 121–127.

Pribram, K. (1949). *Conflicting Patterns of Thought.* Washington, D.C.: Public Affairs Press.

Prince, G. (1978). "Putting the Other Half of the Brain to Work." *Training: The Magazine of Human Resources Development, 15,* 57–61.

Samovar, L., and Porter, R. (Eds.). (1988). *Intercultural Communication: A Reader* (5th ed.) Belmont, Calif.: Wadsworth.

Schneider, D. (1976). "Notes Toward a Theory of Culture." In K. Basso and H. Silby (Eds.), *Meanings in Anthropology.* Albuquerque: University of New Mexico Press.

Silverman, L. (1987). "Global Learners: Our Forgotten Gifted Children." Paper presented at the seventh World Conference on Gifted and Talented Children, Salt Lake City, Utah.

Springer, S., and Deutsch, G. (1985). *Left Brain, Right Brain.* New York: Freeman.

Tsunoda, T. (1978). *The Japanese Brain Function.* (Cited in Sibatani, A. (1980), "It May Turn Out That the Language We Learn Alters the Physical Operation of Our Brains." *Science,* pp. 24–26.)

Reasons for the Lack of Argumentation and Debate in the Far East

CARL B. BECKER

China and Japan have been much in the spotlight recently, for their political and economic dominance in Asia. Japan is already counted among the world's industrial leaders, and China is also undergoing rapid modernization. Both countries have adopted the forms of Western governments, media, and communications-systems. Yet communications on a person-to-person level operate under very different premises than in the West. Western Asia-watchers expect that Asian languages are very different from Western languages, and then try to compensate by careful translation-and-interpretation techniques. What they often fail to understand until too late, however, is that both the content of the dialogue and the assumptions about what represents acceptable and proper communications-are very different in the Orient than in the West.

In particular, the use of public-speaking for the debating of conflicting viewpoints, especially popular in election years in the West, has generally been unacceptable in the Orient. This essay will examine the attitudes of Chinese and Japanese towards speech communication in public settings. While there are many differences between China and Japan apparent today, they share common cultural backgrounds and assumptions in the areas which we shall consider as contributing to their common

From *International Journal of Intercultural Relations* 10 (1986), 75–92. Reprinted by permission of the publisher. Carl B. Becker is Assistant Professor of Asian Curriculum Research and Development at the University of Hawaii.

aversion to public debate. We shall focus specifically on three areas of oriental culture which have tended to discourage argumentation: (1) social history, (2) linguistic features, and (3) philosophy and religion. A longer [article] might identify important subtle distinctions between China and Japan on each of these subjects, but for the purposes of our study, we shall argue that the same factors have functioned in both societies to downplay the importance of argumentation and debate.

SOCIAL HISTORY

China and Japan have been densely populated, labor-intensive rice-growing cultures since ancient times. Their survival depended upon the peaceful cooperation of people in each community for the irrigation and planting of rice. The people were unable or unwilling to change their vocations and residential areas, for both geographic and political reasons, so there was little change in their life-patterns from year to year. The cycles of planting and harvest continued inexorably, and there was little room for radical experimentation with new methods of agriculture, for if a new method failed, some of the populace would likely starve. When travel and change were thus minimized, experience could be accumulated only through the repetitions of years, and the one who had the most experience was naturally the village elder. When a flood or plague threatened the community, the elder was the one consulted about what worked best against such problems when they last occurred some decades previously.

Through such historical evolution, China and Japan developed hierarchical societies in which the very notion of two people being absolutely equal became almost inconceivable. Age became equated with authority, and even twins addressed each other as "older brother" and "younger brother," depending on who emerged a few minutes earlier. Age and rank became the unquestioned basis for distinction of inferior and superior. Once the superior person had been identified by age and rank, his word was taken as law, without further logical examination. . . . Such societies left little room for the development

of ideals like "liberty, equality, or individuality" (Nakamura 1964, pp. 205–207). Authority and obligation proceeded not from reason, but from the superior status of the elderly and the superior power of the landed class. . . .

Since the individual could not be heard nor recognized on his own, . . . there developed the additional tendency towards standardization over individuality. Free thought and individual expression were discouraged, giving way to the safer and surer domain of classical quotation. This attitude can already be seen by the time of Confucius, 2,500 years ago. Throughout Chinese history, there were purges and book-burnings, when all but the few texts approved by officialdom were destroyed, and possession of contraband books carried the death penalty (Goodrich 1935, pp. 39–42). Thus the thought control of Mao's China was nothing new to the Chinese. In such circumstances, safe ritual phrases tend to take over from self-expression. This influence continues to be pervasive even today in both cultures. Speeches at weddings are among the few times that an oriental is ever expected to address a large number of people. Research has shown that these speeches are almost invariably composed of standardized phrases within standardized formulae and structures (Saito 1973). Japanese word processors have prestored a hundred set greetings and phrases from which the operator can compile complete letters without ever thinking up a sentence of his own. Thus there is little self-expression expected even within these most mundane and politically innocent occasions.

Conversely, in the world of politics, the uses of speech were more frequently ad hominem than rational. More than once did outlying states lose favor with or risk invasion from China and Japan by improperly addressing their interlocutors. Jobs could be forfeit by injudicious criticism, while political favors might be curried through flattery. Political friends and enemies were divided along personal rather than ideological lines. One of the greatest intellects of nineteenth century Japan, Yukichi Fukuzawa, wrote that it was hard for him to comprehend the system of Western political parties and amicable argumentation:

It was beyond my comprehension to understand what these [political enemies] were fighting for, and what was meant, anyway, by "fighting" in peace time . . . these "enemies" were to be seen at the same table, eating and drinking with each other. I could not make much sense out of this (Fukuzawa 1934, pp. 142–44).

In Chinese and Japanese eyes, taking opposite sides of an argument necessarily meant becoming a personal rival and antagonist of the one who held the other side. The more important concomitant of this idea was that if one did not wish to become a lifelong opponent of someone else, he would not venture an opinion contrary to the other person's opinions in public.

Even the legal system was set up in such a way that it avoided direct confrontations and made no demands on logical brief building. While private property rights existed, no freedoms nor personal rights were guaranteed by law, and all power rested with the court (Nakamura 1964, p. 214).

Chinese court procedure was not characterized by the development of judicial dialogue between the accused and the accuser. The reason is that the Chinese judge was not an arbitrator between two groups, but an official who took evidence from both sides, and then sent out his own underlings to examine the truth of the statements made by both sides (Nakamura 1964, p. 189).

The danger of "frame-ups" in such a system must be obvious, although they are not unknown to the judicial systems of the West, either. The more important consequence from the viewpoint of communication theory is that there never developed a "spirit of controversial dialogue," nor a "tradition of free public debate."

In this political tradition, *truth* is taken to mean a quality of manhood, not the accuracy of propositions alone. Men could be arrested and imprisoned on the basis of suspicious character; even today, Chinese and Japanese police may detain and interrogate people for "suspicious behavior" in "unsavory neighborhoods." At the same time, few people are convicted on technicalities if their overall character

testimony is good. Sino-Japanese thought had no standards for matching propositions with other propositions (coherence) or with other states of affairs in the world ("correspondence tests of truth"). Rather, they maintained the idea that a man whose actions and character followed through on his commitments, and were in line with his way of speaking, was a "true man" or a "man of truth." Instead of the affirmation or negation of particular propositions, Chinese and Japanese thought starts with the "aura," "feeling," or "ring" of truth which is embodied, not in a particular set of hieroglyphs or spoken sounds, but the whole being of the person (Scharfstein 1974, p. 139). . . .

FEATURES OF LANGUAGE

Some of the reasons militating against public argumentation can be traced to social and historical conditions, as we have seen, but other reasons must be sought in the nature of the Chinese and Japanese languages themselves, through which the Chinese and Japanese view and interpret their world.

The Chinese (and thence Japanese) written language was pictographic in origin, like the picture writing on an American-Indian tepee, but it was written not on tepees but on tortoise-shell fragments. Now a person could fit only a few intelligible pictures—or hieroglyphs derived from pictures—on one tortoise shell fragment. It became somewhat like composing a telegram: One chose the bare minimum necessary to convey his message, and trusted the other party to decipher it. The length of one line was generally about four pictures; even when paper and other writing surfaces became available, the four-character sentence remained the standard. Thus, a typical written dialogue might run:

Confucius: I no desire talk.

Disciple: If master no talk, what can disciple(s) learn?

Confucius: Does Heaven say anything? (= Heaven rules without language.) (*Analects*, XVII, 9.)

This excerpt is translated in this literal way, not to mock, but to demonstrate the cryptic and ambiguous style inherent in Chinese. Even the Chinese philosophers were acutely aware of the shortcomings of their own language to reflect anything like the richness of human experience (as we shall examine in greater detail in the section, "Philosophy and Religion").

To this day, the Chinese language remains an efficient but highly ambiguous medium, which makes few distinctions necessary for in-depth debates or discussions. Chinese has no copulas, no plurals, and no tenses unless they are deliberately and awkwardly inserted. Since its contact with Chinese, Japanese language has moved in the same direction (Waley 1958, p. 63). Lacking singulars and plurals, capitalization and tenses, many medieval philosophers got into arguments which Russell could show to be mere pseudo-problems, because neither side was speaking about the same subject. One school would write poems or treatises to show that principles were discernible within temporal events, and the other that Principle was eternal and not instantiated in physical objects. Since Principle and principles are the same word, both schools carried on long and fruitless debates ending only in frustration and embarrassment, unaware that both sides could be right because each was using the same words in very different ways (Ching 1974).

The problem is complicated in Japanese by the fact that the Japanese who originally imitated the Chinese hieroglyphic script and vocabulary were tone deaf. All four Chinese tones of a given phoneme were condensed into the same Japanese sound. Sixteen unique two-syllable Chinese words all came to have the same pronunciation in Japanese. This extreme plethora of homonyms in Japanese handicaps Japanese speech communication further. The more Chinese loan-words the speaker uses, the more he must pause to either verbally or pictorially (on blackboard or palm of his hand) distinguish the word he is using from numerous homonyms. This 'method, of course, detracts from the elegance and flow of the spoken language. The only alternative is to simply *assume* that the listeners all imagine the same single meaning of the homonym that the speaker intends. In either event, we have a reinforcement of the idea that precision is cumber-

some and inelegant, while ordinary speech is necessarily vague and depends heavily on the cooperative imagination and sympathy of the listener.

Like most other languages, Chinese vocabulary acquires new meanings through a process of accretion and meaning extension. In English, for example, the word *fire* means combustion, then to ignite, then to shoot a gun, then to release from employment. Through the centuries, the Chinese superimposed on a few thousand hieroglyphs some tens of thousands of extended meanings. Indeed, this was the only way to get hieroglyphs for words like "idea" or "unified theory of relativity." The problem with this process is that the pictograph remains the same throughout the centuries, so that in addition to new meanings, the old, more graphic and concrete meanings are still largely preserved. These in turn overlay (or underlie) every more abstract or theoretical expression (Waley 1958, p. 60). Thus Chinese and Japanese develop homonyms in another way, using the same character as well as the same pronunciation in two very different ways, and leaving the interpretation totally open to the reader or listener. Some scholars conclude that written Chinese, read aloud, "was almost too ambiguous to be understood" (Scharfstein 1974; cf. Graham 1964, pp. 54–55).

While these ambiguities enabled many subtle double entendres and poetic turns of phrase, they too reinforced the notion that language was a vehicle for art and not for conveying information; for elegant play, but not for clarifying problems. Nakamura enumerates many specific examples of the confusions in hieroglyphics and syntax, concluding that Chinese has been "an awkward medium for expressing abstract thought" (Nakamura 1964, p. 188). The same can certainly be said of Korean and Japanese. It is no coincidence that, unlike Sanskrit, Greek, and Latin, the Chinese language never produced scholars either conscious enough or interested enough in their own grammar to examine the way syntax and sentences function (Nakamura 1964).

The tremendous ambiguities and difficulties implicit in ancient hieroglyphic languages, reviewed in the previous section, have led over the centuries to language taking on very different functions in the Orient than those it has in the West. This area of scholarship has been all but ignored by Western scholars, although it is painfully obvious to Anglo-American expatriates functioning in oriental languages.

In China and Japan, communication is less of a process of mutually gathering and exchanging information ("How are you? What's happening?") than an affirmation of inevitably shared human conditions ("Sure is hot today. Makes you hot to work in the sun, doesn't it?"). A large part of the language activity of any oriental dinner or drinking party consists of parroting of each other's sentiments in the same words; as the evening wears on, singing and chanting take the place of speech. While the Westerner in such situations tends to feel that such behavior indicates the lack of anything further to talk about, the Oriental feels that in singing and chanting he has achieved true togetherness with his fellows, which in his mind transcends the importance of exchanging ideas. When the oriental climbs staircases, hefts burdens, reaches home, begins to eat, smashes a tennis ball—and in any number of similar situations—he is expected to say or shout words. These words are addressed to no one and communicate nothing; the Japanese will say them even when he is alone or when no one is listening. Some of these words may have psychological functions of demarcating the time of one activity from another; others are little more than animal grunts and cries given phonemic pronunciations. . . . In many situations, the oriental language is used less to communicate than to commune, congratulate, emote, and to begin and end activities.

One fascinating consequence of the extreme ambiguity and noncommunicative roles of oriental languages is that Chinese and Japanese communication assumes a kind of telepathic intuition which has gone all but ignored in Western studies of communication. Japanese and Chinese languages have many words for their intuitive, nonverbal "stomach-to-stomach" or "heart-to-heart" communication, which serves as the ground for all verbal communication and can exist independently of words and phrases altogether (Ryu 1974). In addition to leaving

off subjects and pronouns, it is not uncommon for the grammatical objects of sentences (be they ideas or physical things) to be indicated by unreferenced pronouns (like the English "that"). A professor may enter a classroom and ask, "Make it?" Only the person whom the professor has in mind is expected to respond, and he is expected to know exactly what the object of the professor's inquiry is. That oriental languages function in this way is further illustrated by the difficulties that orientals have in learning English—in their omission of subjects, objects, and specific referents until trained to include them. That their cultures function as efficiently as they do is testimony to the well-nigh telepathic sensitivity of each person to the unvoiced intentions of each speaker.

This sensitivity may be due in part to the fact that these cultures have been relatively homogeneous and have possessed single languages for thousands of years. It may be due to the pressures of close-knit families and densely packed societies to preserve harmony through concern with others' feelings. It may be partly due to the fact that hieroglyphic language users sort language into the right hemispheres of their brains (Westerners generally put language in the left, linear-logical hemispheres)—and right hemispheres have been linked to intuition, art, and telepathy (cf. Sasanuma 1980; Sibatani 1980; Tsunoda 1973; Tzeng 1978; Walker 1981). The intuitive/telepathic abilities of some orientals in communication may strike some Westerners as almost incredible, but are taken for granted as a necessary part of their successful communication process.

Still another problem inherent in Chinese and Japanese is their lack, not only of formal logical systems, but indeed of a principle of noncontradiction. One can add characters to a sentence in order to negate it, but adding two of them does not make a double negation, as a Western observer might wish; nor return the sentence to its unnegated meaning. . . .

Historians of logic might challenge such assertions by pointing out that Sanskrit (Indian) Buddhism had a highly developed mathematical logic by the time of Christ, when Buddhism was just beginning to be introduced to the Chinese. Since China and Japan adopted Buddhism, should we not also expect them to have adopted many of its logical rules? In fact, however, the Chinese butchering of Indian logical texts almost defies imagination. The dean of Japanese Buddhist historians observes:

In the history of Buddhist logic in China, we can observe several striking phenomena. First, very few logical works were ever translated. . . . Interest in Buddhist logic was very slight among the Chinese. Secondly, only logical works of the simplest kind were translated. . . . Indian works on epistemology of logical theory were not translated. . . .

Indian logic was accepted only in part, and even the part that was accepted was not understood in the sense of the Indian originals. Hsuantsang, who introduced Indian logic, seems not to have fully understood it. . . . In developing his arguments, he violated the rules of Indian logic. . . .

Ts'u-en's work, which was regarded as the highest authority in China and Japan, contains many fallacies in philosophical and logical analysis. He apparently did not understand the Indian rule that the middle term should be distributed by the major term. . . . He confused ratio essendi and ratio cognoscendi. . . . in doing this, he simply made a mechanical classification, and his explanation is self-contradictory as well as at odds with the original meaning (Nakamura 1964, p. 192).

The account could go on and on, but the point should be clear by now. Even the highest authorities on logic in China literally did not know what they were talking about, and frequently contradicted themselves *without being bothered by it!* However, this failure is less to be blamed on the stupidity and mechanical translation methods of the scholars than on the intractable opacity and ambiguity of the Chinese language itself. In Chinese, the fine distinctions and mathematical rules of Sanskrit simply were untranslatable, did not apply, and seemed to make no difference.

From all these features of Chinese and Japanese language: Their telegraphic terseness and consequent ambiguities; their many homonyms; their inabilities to make fine distinctions and abstractions; the use of language in noncommunicative ways and

of intuition for communication; and in their lack of logical rules and constraints; we gain further insights as to why public discussion and debate were considered inconclusive if not futile. Unlike Indian and Western traditions, the Chinese had no internal standards for determining when one set of arguments were better than another, so even if debates had occurred, they could neither be governed nor judged by a consistent logic. Thus, these whole languages and cultures tend to frustrate the Western assumptions that reasonable men in free communication can arrive at truer conclusions, either about the natural world or the desirability of a given policy, than can a single man without discussion.

PHILOSOPHY AND RELIGION

We have already alluded to reasons for oriental respect for age and hence antiquity. Few cultures have so valued the study of classical philosophical and religious texts as have China, Korea, and Japan. In fact, for centuries, examinations on the classical texts constituted the major screening method and stepping stone to political offices in China and Korea. Although there were several antagonistic schools of thought in ancient China, which have dominated the cultural and philosophical scene in the Orient ever since, they each held similarly negative views of speech and language. Let us turn our attention respectively to Confucianism, Taoism, and Buddhism, and finally to an opposition school which favored logic and language, to examine their ideas on speech communication.

Confucius is often known as the father of Chinese philosophy and culture, although he in turn relied heavily upon odes and classics composed centuries before the sixth century B.C. in which he lived. From Confucius' reliance on ancient sources to vindicate his own teachings, we may again observe the recurring theme that it is preferable to copy old solutions to problems rather than inventing and discussing new ones. Confucius' emphasis is continually on being humble and respectful, rather than bold, assertive, or innovative. He sets up a trilemma which virtually precludes the use of persuasive speech:

To be importunate with one's lord will mean humiliation; to be importunate with friends will mean estrangement (IV, 24).
To speak to a man incapable of benefitting is wasting words (XV, 8). (Analects—Lau translation, 1979, standard verse numbering.)

Even from the format of Confucius' *Analects* themselves, we may observe that Confucius' remarks never run to a paragraph, but usually only to a fleeting fortune-cookie response to a disciple's inquiry. Of course Confucius was aware that there were times when appropriate speech was indispensable, but for the most part, the preceding verses manifest his reticence to speak (cf. *Analects*, XVI, 8). As Confucian biographer Herlee Creel puts it, "Confucius was always markedly contemptuous of eloquence and of ornate language" (Creel 1953, p. 27). This contempt is so often seen that some scholars speculate that Confucius was in fact a poor, tongue-tied speaker, jealous and therefore critical of those with rhetorical eloquence.

Confucius established for China the ideal of the gentleman, or "superior man"—not necessarily someone from the upper classes, but one who has properly cultivated himself in virtue and righteousness. Then how does Confucius envisage the ideal man speaking? Confucius says:

The superior man is diligent in duty but slow to speak (I, 14).
The superior man is slow to speak but quick to act (IV, 24).
In antiquity [the ideal time], men were loath to speak (IV, 22).

. . . Central to Confucius' philosophy was the principle of *hsin*—that one's words should always be in accordance with that which one does, lives, and practices. It is not that the Confucian cannot speak at all, but that he must always speak with discretion only of that which he is prepared to act upon or commit himself to (cf. Lau, "Introduction," *Analects* 1979, p. 25). Naturally, this principle put a damper on bold or persuasive speech.

The superior man acts before speaking and speaks according to his action (II, 13).

Immodest statements are hard to live up to. . . . A superior man is ashamed of his words outstripping his deeds (XIV, 20, 27).

In Confucius' idea of *hsin*, we can again discern the Chinese idea of the identity of the man and the ideas he voices. Words are not to be treated as sounds, ideas, or propositions which exist independently of their utterers, to be judged by critical linguistic analysis. They are inextricably interrelated to the person who utters them. Their truth depends on his character, and his truth depends on the character of his words. Thus it becomes impossible to scrutinize or criticize an idea without casting aspersions on the character of the person who voices it. Since one of our primary duties is to be respectful to men (*Analects* I, 13), then we should sooner allow their mistakes to pass uncriticized than exhibit a lack of proper respect for their words and hence their selves (*Analects* XIV, 29). Confucius taught that ordinary men were to learn from the life and deeds of the superior man, and not from his logic or language.

In overview, then, Confucius opposed eloquent and clever speech, advocating hesitancy over brilliance, and he grounded this criticism of speech deeply within his philosophy of the ideal man. This Confucian attitude still persists widely in East Asia.

The ancient Taoist school of Chinese philosophy is best represented by the *Tao-te Ching* of Lao-tzu and by Chuang-tsu. In contrast to the Confucian concerns with public behavior, etiquette, and politics, the Taoists were more interested in man's finding peace within himself and within nature. The Taoists tended to be hermits and recluses whom, even sympathetically, we should have to call quietistic. It is hardly surprising that we find further opposition to speech and rhetoric within the Taoist philosophy. The classic text of the *Tao-te Ching* advocates silence from the beginning:

The sage spreads doctrines without words (2).
Nature says few words, but the whirlwind [windbag] lasts less than a single morning (23).

It revels in a juxtaposition of opposites:

The greatest skill seems clumsy and the greatest eloquence stutters (45).
He who knows does not talk; he who talks does not know.
Keep your mouth shut (56).

Such radical statements are not designed merely to shock the hearer nor to take issue with all authority. Like Confucius' opposition to speech, the Taoists' is also grounded in their philosophy, although their reasons are different from Confucius'. The Taoists were acutely aware of the artificiality of names and labels, the inability of their hieroglyphic language to capture the fullness of experience, and the inappropriateness of most linguistic distinctions to the real world. Thus we are told:

The Tao that can be named is not the eternal Tao (1).
As soon as there are names, know that it is time to stop (32).

The sage, however, remains at peace, because he does not distinguish good and bad, desirable and undesirable, proper and improper:

Common folk make distinctions and are clear cut. I [the sage] alone make no distinctions (20).

Thus, within Taoism, language and precision are thought to be the root of contention and dissatisfaction, therefore a barrier to contentment and sagehood. . . .

The philosophy of Taoism may appear attractive to people tired of competition, and to those resigned in the face of authoritarian administrations. But Taoism provides no solutions to social problems, and is thorough going in its rejection of both speech and communication.

Zen (Chinese: Ch'an) Buddhism first became known in America for its curious tales about the sound of one-hand, and of monks beating one another instead of answering questions. In fact, Zen Buddhism was a uniquely un-Indian Chinese creation, "in persistent and often violent opposition to words, and then to the intellect which deals exclusively in words" (Suzuki 1953, p. 36). Zen became the leading school of Chinese Buddhism by the

eleventh century, and the philosophy of the Japanese upper-classes by the fourteenth century. Zen accepted the pervasive relativism of Chuang-tzu, as can be seen in such statements as "he who drinks water alone knows if it is cold or warm." It agreed with the Taoist notions that fundamental principles are inexpressible in language; and thus that many questions are also unanswerable (cf. Fung 1948, pp. 257, 262). Zen proclaimed itself in China as a "separate transmission of the *dharma* [true teachings] outside scriptures and not dependent on words or phrases" (deBary 1972, p. 208).

The Rinzai school of Zen particularly denounced eloquent speech:

Even though your eloquence be like a rushing torrent, it is nothing but hell-producing karma *[activity]. . . . Students become attached to words and phrases. . . . and cannot gain enlightenment (deBary 1972, p. 227).*

Rinzai Zen inveighs against studying the words of the past classics; it calls words "dreams and illusions," and it specifically criticizes those who spend their days "in idle talk" about rights and wrongs, landowners and thieves, laws and politics (deBary 1972, p. 230).

In Zen, truth is thought to be intuited only in silent meditation and incommunicable through language. This is one reason that Zen masters frequently beat their logically minded disciples, or give them insoluble language-tangles called *koans* to contemplate until they realize the futility of discursive reason. To their students' logical inquiries, some masters respond with cries, some with blows. Some lift tea trays or put their sandals on their heads. Many simply remain silent to the most serious and important of questions, or walk out of the room (Suzuki 1961, pp. 294–296). Hundreds of such examples have been compiled into the classic literature of Zen, which itself disavows classic literature and scripture. Zen in turn became the model for *bushido*, the martial code of the Japanese *Samurai*, which was drummed into the heads and hearts of the educated classes for centuries in Japan. While Westerners may be fascinated or bemused by Zen anecdotes of cries and cat-cutting, we must not forget that such tales also represent the deep-seated religious rejection of logic and denial of rational communication in China and Japan.

It is not true that there never existed logicians and debaters in China. The *Ming-chia* (literally, "School of Names") philosophers were a class of lawyers analogous in role and history to the Sophists of Greece. They early became known for their debates about whether white horses were horses and whether criminals were men. In fact, these were very logical arguments designed to demonstrate (1) that there are distinctions within classes of objects, as among horses and among men; (2) that a man sets himself apart from other men by committing criminal deeds; (3) that in so doing, he sacrifices his human right to life and liberty, and therefore (4) capital punishment is justifiable, for taking the life of a criminal is not the same as taking the life of an ordinary man. To the average man, however, the state had the power to kill or free criminals without needing such justifications, and the debates of the *Ming-chia* seemed purest sophistry. As Chuang-tzu criticized: "They can subdue others' mouths but cannot win their hearts" (Chan 1963, p. 233).

Even in their own day, the *Ming-chia* were loathed by other scholars. Historian Ssu-ma T'an wrote (around 110 B.C.):

The School of Names conducted minute examinations of trifling points in complicated and elaborate statements, which made it impossible for others to refute their ideas (Quoted in Fung 1948, p. 81).

Some *Ming-chia* lawyers were indeed highly successful in getting their own suspects sentenced or acquitted, and were at the same time accused of turning wrong into right. The typical reaction of both people and government was summarized by philosopher Han Fei-tzu: "When discussion of hardness and whiteness appear [the standard examples of *Ming-chia* logic], then the governmental laws lose their effect" (Fung 1948, p. 82). Popular as well as official opinion militated against *Ming-chia*; their school was consequently short lived, and their name remained more as an epithet for vacuous language manipulation than as a respectable title of a

school of logicians. Thus the history of Chinese and Japanese thought is dominated by three major philosophico-religious schools: Confucian, Taoist, and Buddhist; and all of them opposed debate, public speech, and even communication. The single small school famous for debate and logical argumentation soon defeated its own purposes; by being too good at argument, it lost the trust of the people and government forever.

CONCLUSIONS

There are tremendous barriers—socio-historical, linguistic, and philosophical—to the acceptance of argumentation and debate as methods for the consideration of new proposals or as strategies for sociopolitical change in East Asia. In addition to the many problems reviewed here, there are also the practical problems of education, of martial law, of industrial as well as international rivalries, and of the lack of speech and communication courses in Asian schools and universities. All these factors militate against the rapid rise of public argumentation and debate in the near future.

Many Westerners may be convinced of the importance of logic, and of its superiority to emotive intuition. Yet we need to be careful not to discard those areas of human life and communication in which intuition may be extremely valuable, in our efforts to quantify and mathematize. We may agree with Habermas that an ideal speech situation requires equality of participants, freedom from social coercion, suspension of privilege, and free expression of feeling [rather than self-censorship] (cf. Burleson and Kline 1979, pp. 412–428). But we should realize that this is at best a very Western ideal, both impractical and even theoretically inconceivable to traditionally educated Chinese and Japanese.

We desire to understand our powerful East Asian neighbors, and to do so, we propose to communicate. It is true that they may have many ideas to learn from our forms and modes of argumentation and debate. At the same time, we should not forget the long and relatively peaceful histories they have experienced, entirely without the benefit of our methods of discussion and rhetoric. Before imposing our own models of communication upon them in another gross display of insensitivity and cultural imperialism, let us remind ourselves that our own presuppositions about ideal communications are also culture-bound. In mutual respect, while we make our communications methods and studies available to those in the Far East, let us seek to understand their own respective culture contexts. It is hoped that this article will have made a start in that direction.

REFERENCES

Analects (1979). (D. C. Lau, Trans.). Harmondsworth, England: Penguin Books.

Becker, C. B. (1983). "The Japanese Way of Debate." *National Forensic Journal*, 1 (2), 141–147.

Burleson, B., and S. Kline. (1979). "Habermas' Theory of Communication: A Critical Explanation." *Quarterly Journal of Speech*, 65, 412–428.

Chan, W. T. (1963). *A Sourcebook in Chinese Philosophy*. Princeton: Princeton University Press.

Ching, J. (1974). "The Goose Lake Monastery Debate." *Journal of Chinese Philosophy*, 1 (2), 161–177.

Chuang-Tzu. See Chan, pp. 179–210.

Confucius. See *Analects*.

Creel, H. (1953). *Chinese Thought from Confucius to Mao Tse-tung*. Chicago: The University of Chicago Press.

deBary, W. T. (ed.). (1972). *The Buddhist Tradition in India, China, and Japan*. New York: Random House/Vintage Books.

Fukuzawa, Y. (1934). *Autobiography of Fukuzawa Yukichi*. (E. Kiyooka, Trans.). Tokyo: Hokuseido.

Goodrich, L. C. (1935). *The Literary Inquisition of Ch'ien-lung*. Baltimore: ACLS/Waverly Press.

Graham, A. C. (1964). "The Place of Reason in the Chinese Philosophical Tradition." In R. Dawson (ed.), *The Legacy of China*. London: Oxford University Press.

Nakamura, H. (1964). *Ways of Thinking of Eastern Peoples*. P. Weiner (ed.). Honolulu: East-West Center Press.

Ryu, S. (1974). *A Study of the Concept of* hara *and a Japanese Philosophy of Communication*. Senior Thesis for International Christian University, Tokyo.

Saito, I. (1973). *A Rhetorical Analysis of Japanese Wedding Speeches*. Senior Thesis for International Christian University, Tokyo.

Sasanuma, S. (1980). "The Nature of the Task-Stimulus Interaction in the Tachistoscopic Recognition of *Kanji* and *Kana*." *Brain and Language*, 9, 298–306.

Scharfstein, B. A. (1974). *The Mind of China*. New York: Delta.

Shigeta, H. (1973). *An Experimental Study of Ambiguity in Japanese and American Speaking Behavior* (Chap. 3). Senior Thesis for International Christian University, Tokyo.

Sibatani, A. (1980). "The Japanese Brain." *Science*, 80, 1 (8), 24–27.

Suzuki, D. T. (1953). "Zen: A Reply to Hu Shih." *Philosophy East and West*, 3, 36.

Suzuki, D. T. (1953). *Zen Buddhism*. (W. Barrett, Ed.). Garden City, N.Y.: Doubleday/Anchor.

Suzuki, D. T. (1961). *Essays in Zen Buddhism* (first series). New York: Grove Press.

Tao-Te Ching. (1964). (D. C. Lau, Trans.). Harmondsworth, England: Penguin Books.

Tsunoda, T. (1971). "The Difference of Cerebral Dominance of Vowel Sounds among Different Languages." *Journal of Auditory Research*, 11, 305.

Tsunoda, T. (1973). "Functional Differences between Right-Cerebral and Left-Cerebral Hemispheres." *Brain and Language*, 2, 152–170.

Tzeng, O. J. L. (1978). "Cerebral Lateralization of Function and Bilingual Decision Processes." *Brain and Language*, 5 (1), 56–71.

Tzeng, O. J. L. (1979). "Visual Lateralization Effects in Reading Chinese Characters." *Nature*, 282, 499–501.

Waley, A. (1958). *The Way and Its Power*. New York: Grove Press.

Walker, L. C. (1981). "The Ontogeny of the Neural Substrate for Language." *Human Evolution*, 10, 429–441.

The Sapir-Whorf Hypothesis

HARRY HOIJER

The Sapir-Whorf hypothesis appears to have had its initial formulation in the following two paragraphs, taken from an article of Sapir's, first published in 1929.

Language is a guide to "social reality." Though language is not ordinarily thought of as of essential interest to the students of social science, it powerfully conditions all of our thinking about social problems and processes. Human beings do not live in the objective world alone, nor alone in the world of social activity as ordinarily understood, but are very much at the mercy of the particular language which has become the medium of expression for their society. It is quite an illusion to imagine that one adjusts to reality essentially without the use of language and that language is merely an incidental means of solving specific problems of communication or reflection. The fact of the matter is that the "real world" is to a large extent unconsciously built up on the language habits of the group. No two languages are ever sufficiently similar to be considered as representing the same social reality. The worlds in which different societies live are distinct worlds, not merely the same world with different labels attached.

The understanding of a simple poem, for instance, involves not merely an understanding of the single words in their average significance, but

From *Language in Culture*, edited by Harry Hoijer, Copyright 1954 by The University of Chicago. Reprinted by permission of the publisher and the author. Professor Hoijer teaches in the Department of Anthropology, University of California at Los Angeles.

a full comprehension of the whole life of the community as it is mirrored in the words, or as it is suggested by their overtones. Even comparatively simple acts of perception are very much more at the mercy of the social patterns called words than we might suppose. If one draws some dozen lines, for instance, of different shapes, one perceives them as divisible into such categories as "straight," "crooked," "curved," "zigzag" because of the classificatory suggestiveness of the linguistic terms themselves. We see and hear and otherwise experience very largely as we do because the language habits of our community predispose certain choices of interpretation. [In Mandelbaum 1949: 162]

The notion of language as a "guide to social reality" is not entirely original with Sapir. Somewhat similiar ideas, though far less adequately stated, may be found in Boas' writings, at least as early as 1911. Thus we find in Boas' introduction to the *Handbook of American Indian Languages* a number of provocative passages on this theme, to wit:

It seems, however, that a theoretical study of Indian languages is not less important than a practical knowledge of them; that the purely linguistic inquiry is part and parcel of a thorough investigation of the psychology of the peoples of the world [p. 63].

. . . language seems to be one of the most instructive fields of inquiry in an investigation of the formation of the fundamental ethnic ideas. The great advantage that linguistics offer in this respect is the fact that, on the whole, the categories which are formed always remain unconscious, and that for this reason the processes which lead to their formation can be followed without the misleading and disturbing factors of secondary explanation, which are so common in ethnology, so much so that they generally obscure the real history of the development of ideas entirely [pp. 70–71].

The Sapir-Whorf hypothesis, however, gains especial significance by virtue of the fact that both these scholars had a major interest in American Indian languages, idioms far removed from any in the Indo-European family and so ideally suited to contrastive studies. It is in the attempt to properly interpret the grammatical categories of an American Indian language, Hopi, that Whorf best illustrates his principle of linguistic relativity, the notion that "users of markedly different grammars are pointed by their grammars toward different types of observations and different evaluations of externally similar acts of observations, and hence are not equivalent as observers but must arrive at somewhat different views of the world" (1952: 11).

The purpose of this paper is twofold: (1) to review and clarify the Sapir-Whorf hypothesis, (2) to illustrate and perhaps add to it by reference to my own work on the Navajo language. . . .

The central idea of the Sapir-Whorf hypothesis is that language functions, not simply as a device for reporting experience, but also, and more significantly, as a way of defining experience for its speakers. Sapir says (1931: 578), for example:

Language is not merely a more or less systematic inventory of the various items of experience which seem relevant to the individual, as is so often naively assumed, but is also a self-contained, creative symbolic organization, which not only refers to experience largely acquired without its help but actually defines experience for us by reason of its formal completeness and because of our unconscious projection of its implicit expectations into the field of experience. In this respect language is very much like a mathematical system which, also, records experience in the truest sense of the word, only in its crudest beginnings, but, as time goes on, becomes elaborated into a self-contained conceptual system which previsages all possible experience in accordance with certain accepted formal limitations. . . . [Meanings are] not so much discovered in experience as imposed upon it, because of the tyrannical hold that linguistic form has upon our orientation in the world.

Whorf develops the same thesis when he says (1952: 5):

. . . the linguistic system (in other words, the grammar) of each language is not merely a reproducing instrument for voicing ideas but rather is itself

the shaper of ideas, the program and guide for the individual's mental activity, for his analysis of impressions, for his synthesis of his mental stock in trade. . . . We dissect nature along lines laid down by our native languages. The categories and types that we isolate from the world of phenomena we do not find there because they stare every observer in the face; on the contrary, the world is presented in a kaleidoscopic flux of impressions which has to be organized by our minds—and this means largely by the linguistic systems in our minds.

It is evident from these statements, if they are valid, that language plays a large and significant role in the totality of culture. Far from being simply a technique of communication, it is itself a way of directing the perceptions of its speakers and it provides for them habitual modes of analyzing experience into significant categories. And to the extent that languages differ markedly from each other, so should we expect to find significant and formidable barriers to cross-cultural communication and understanding. These barriers take on even greater importance when it is realized that "the phenomena of a language are to its own speakers largely of a background character and so are outside the critical consciousness and control of the speaker" (Whorf 1952: 4).

It is, however, easy to exaggerate linguistic differences of this nature and the consequent barriers to intercultural understanding. No culture is wholly isolated, self-contained, and unique. There are important resemblances between all known cultures—resemblances that stem in part from diffusion (itself an evidence of successful intercultural communication) and in part from the fact that all cultures are built around biological, psychological, and social characteristics common to all mankind. The languages of human beings do not so much determine the perceptual and other faculties of their speakers vis-à-vis experience as they influence and direct these faculties into prescribed channels. Intercultural communication, however wide the difference between cultures may be, is not impossible. It is simply more or less difficult, depending on the degree of difference between the cultures concerned.

Some measure of these difficulties is encountered in the process of translating from one language into another language that is divergent and unrelated. Each language has its own peculiar and favorite devices, lexical and grammatical, which are employed in the reporting, analysis, and categorizing of experience. To translate from English into Navaho, or vice versa, frequently involves much circumlocution, since what is easy to express in one language, by virtue of its lexical and grammatical techniques, is often difficult to phrase in the other. A simple illustration is found when we try to translate the English phrases *his horse* and *his horses* into Navaho, which not only lacks a plural category for nouns (Navaho lí·? translates equally English *horse* and *horses*) but lacks as well the English distinction between *his*, *her*, *its*, and *their*. (Navaho bìlí·? may be translated, according to context, *his horse* or *horses*, *her horse* or *horses*, *its horse* or *horses*, and *their horse* or *horses*.) These Navaho forms lí·?, bìlí·? make difficulties in English also because Navajo makes a distinction between a third person (the bì- in bìlí·?) psychologically close to the speaker (e.g., *his* [that is, a Navajo's] *horse*) as opposed to a third person (the hà- of hàlí·?) psychologically remote (e.g., *his* [that is, a non-Navaho's] *horse*).

Differences of this order, which reflect a people's habitual and favorite modes of reporting, analyzing, and categorizing experience, form the essential data of the Sapir-Whorf hypothesis. According to Whorf (1952: 27), it is in these "constant ways of arranging data and its most ordinary everyday analysis of phenomena that we need to recognize the influence . . . [language] has on other activities, cultural and personal."

The Sapir-Whorf hypothesis, it is evident, includes in language both its structural and its semantic aspects. These are held to be inseparable, though it is obvious that we can and do study each more or less independently of the other. The structural aspect of language, which is that most easily analyzed and described, includes its phonology, morphology, and syntax, the numerous but limited frames into which utterances are cast. The semantic aspect consists of a self-contained system of meanings, inex-

tricably bound to the structure but much more difficult to analyze and describe. Meanings, to reiterate, are not in actual fact separable from structure, nor are they, as some have maintained (notably Voegelin 1949: 36), to be equated to the nonlinguistic culture. Our interest lies, not in questions such as "What does this form, or form class, mean?" but, instead, in the question, "In what manner does a language organize, through its structural semantic system, the world of experience in which its speakers live?" The advantage of this approach to the problem of meaning is clear. As Bloomfield long ago pointed out, it appears quite impossible, short of omniscience, to determine precisely the meaning of any single form or form class in a language. But it should be possible to determine the limits of any self-contained structural-semantic system and the ways in which it previsages the experiences of its users.

To illustrate this procedure in brief, let us turn again to Navaho and one of the ways in which it differs from English. The Navaho color vocabulary includes, among others, five terms: lìgài, dìlxìl, lìžìn, lìčí·?, and dò·λìž, to be taken as one way of categorizing certain color impressions. Lìgài is roughly equivalent to English *white*, dìlxìl and lìžìn to English *black*, lìčí·? to English *red* and dò·λìž to English *blue* or *green*. Clearly then, the Navaho five-point system is not the same as English white-black-red-blue-green, which also has five categories. English *black* is divided into two categories in Navaho (dìlxìl and lìžìn), while Navaho has but one category (dò·λìž) for the English *blue* and *green*. We do not, it should be noted, claim either that English speakers cannot perceive the difference between the two "blacks" of Navaho, or that Navaho speakers are unable to differentiate "blue" and "green." The difference between the two systems lies simply in the color categories recognized in ordinary speech, that is, in the ordinary everyday ways in which speakers of English and Navaho analyze color phenomena.

Every language is made up of a large number of such structural-semantic patterns, some of which pertain to lexical sets, as in the case of the Navaho and English color terms, and others of which pertain to sets of grammatical categories, such as the distinction between the singular and plural noun in English. A monolingual speaker, if his reports are to be understood by others in his speech community, is bound to use this apparatus, with all its implications for the analysis and categorization of experience, though he may of course quite often select from a number of alternative expressions in making his report. To quote Sapir again (Mandelbaum 1949: 10–11):

> ... as our scientific experience grows we must learn to fight the implications of language. "The grass waves in the wind" is shown by its linguistic form to be a member of the same relational class of experiences as "The man works in the house." As an interim solution of the problem of expressing the experience referred to in this sentence it is clear that the language has proved useful, for it has made significant use of certain symbols of conceptual relations, such as agency and location. If we feel the sentence to be poetic or metaphorical, it is largely because other more complex types of experience with their appropriate symbolisms of reference enable us to reinterpret the situation and to say, for instance, "The grass is waved by the wind" or "The wind causes the grass to wave." The point is that no matter how sophisticated our modes of interpretation become, we never really get beyond the projection and continuous transfer of relations suggested by the forms of our speech. . . . Language is at one and the same time helping and retarding us in our exploration of experience, and the details of these processes of help and hindrance are deposited in the subtler meanings of different cultures.

It does not necessarily follow that all the structural-semantic patterns of a language are equally important to its speakers in their observation, analysis, and categorizing of experience. In describing a language, we seek to uncover all its structural-semantic patterns, even though many of these exist more as potentialities of the system than in actual usage. For ethnolinguistic analysis we need to know, not only that a particular linguistic pattern exists, but also

how frequently it occurs in everyday speech. We also need to know something of the degree of complexity of the pattern of expression. There are numerous patterns of speech, particularly among peoples who have well-developed arts of oratory and writing, that are little used by any except specialists in these pursuits. The patterns of speech significant to ethnolinguistic research fall clearly into the category of habitual, frequently used, and relatively simple structural-semantic devices; those, in short, which are common to the adult speech community as a whole, and are used by its members with the greatest of ease.

Not all the structural patterns of the common speech have the same degree of semantic importance. In English, for example, it is not difficult to ascertain the semantic correlates of the structural distinction between singular and plural nouns; in most cases this is simply a division into the categories of "one" versus "more than one." Similarly, the gender distinction of the English third-person singular pronouns, as between "he," "she," and "it," correlates fairly frequently with the recognition of personality and sex.

In contrast to these, there are structural patterns like that which, in many Indo-European languages, divides nouns into three great classes: masculine, feminine, and neuter. This structural pattern has no discernible semantic correlate; we do not confuse the grammatical terms "masculine," "feminine," and "neuter" with the biological distinctions among male, female, and neuter. Whatever the semantic implications of this structural pattern may have been in origin, and this remains undetermined, it is now quite apparent that the pattern survives only as a grammatical device, important in that function but lacking in semantic value. And it is perhaps significant that the pattern is an old one, going back to the earliest history of the Indo-European languages and, moreover, that it has disappeared almost completely in some of the modern languages of this family, notably, of course, in English.

In ethnolinguistic research, then, it is necessary to concentrate on those structural patterns of a language which have definable semantic correlates, and to omit those, like the Indo-European gender system, which survive only in a purely grammatical function. The assumption behind this procedure is as follows: every language includes a number of active structural-semantic categories, lexical and grammatical, which by virtue of their active status serve a function in the everyday (nonscientific) analysis and categorizing of experience. It is the study of these categories, distinctive when taken as a whole for each language, that yields, or may yield, significant information concerning the thought world of the speakers of the language.

One further point requires emphasis. Neither Sapir nor Whorf attempted to draw inferences as to the thought world of a people simply from the fact of the presence or absence of specific grammatical categories (e.g., tense, gender, number) in a given language. To quote Whorf (1952: 44) on this point: the concepts of time and matter which he reports for the Hopi

do not depend so much upon any one system (e.g., tense, or nouns) within the grammar as upon the ways of analyzing and reporting experiene which have become fixed in the language as integrated "fashions of speaking" and which cut across the typical grammatical classifications, so that such a "fashion" may include lexical, morphological, syntactic, and otherwise systematically diverse means coordinated in a certain frame of consistency.

To summarize, ethnolinguistic research requires the investigator to perform, it seems to me, the following steps:

1. To determine the structural patterns of a language (that is, its grammar) as completely as possible. Such determination should include not only a statement of the modes of utterance but as well a careful indication of the frequency of occurrence of these modes, lexical and grammatical, in the common speech.

2. To determine, as accurately as possible, the semantic patterns, if any, that attach to structural patterns. This is a task neglected by most structural

linguists who, as is repeatedly mentioned in the discussions that follow, are frequently content simply to label rather than to define both lexical units and grammatical categories. In this connection it is important to emphasize that the analyst must not be taken in by his own labels; he is to discover, where possible, just how the form, or form class, or grammatical category functions in the utterances available to him.

3. To distinguish between structural categories that are active in the language, and therefore have definable semantic correlates, and those that are not. It goes without saying that such distinction requires a profound knowledge of the language, and possibly even the ability to speak and understand it well. Mark Twain's amusing translation of a German folktale into English, where he regularly translates the gender of German nouns by the English forms "he," "she," and "it," illustrates, though in caricature, the pitfalls of labeling the grammatical categories of one language (in this case, German gender) by terms belonging to an active structural-semantic pattern in another.

4. To examine and compare the active structural-semantic patterns of the language and draw from them the fashions of speaking there evidenced. As in Whorf's analysis of Hopi (1952: 25–45), while clues to a fashion of speaking may be discovered in a particular grammatical category or set of lexical items, its validity and importance cannot be determined until its range and scope within the language as a whole is also known. Whorf's conclusions as to the nature of the concept of time among speakers of English rest not alone on the tense distinctions of the English verb (mixed as these are with many other and diverse distinctions of voice, mode, and aspect) but as well on techniques of numeration, the treatment of nouns denoting physical quantity and phases of cycles, and a host of other terms and locutions relating to time. He says (1952: 33):

The three-tense system of SAE verbs color all our thinking about time. This system is amalgamated with that larger scheme of objectification of the subjective experience of duration already noted in other patterns—in the binomial formula applicable to nouns in general, in temporal nouns, in plurity and numeration.

Taken together, the fashions of speaking found in a language comprise a partial description of the thought world of its speakers. But by the term "thought world" Whorf means

more than simply language, i.e., than the linguistic patterns themselves. [He includes] . . . all the analogical and suggestive value of the patterns . . . and all the give-and-take between language and the culture as a whole, wherein is a vast amount that is not linguistic yet shows the shaping influence of language. In brief, this "thought world" is the microcosm that each man carries about within himself, by which he measures and understands what he can of the macrocosm [1952: 36].

It follows then that the thought world, as derived from ethnolinguistic studies, is found reflected as well, though perhaps not as fully, in other aspects of the culture. It is here that we may search for connections between language and the rest of culture. These connections are not direct; we see, instead, in certain patterns of nonlinguistic behavior the same meaningful fashions that are evidenced in the patterns of the language. Whorf summarizes this facet of his researches in a discussion of "Habitual Behavior Features of Hopi Culture and Some Impressions of Linguistic Habit in Western Civilization" (1952: 37–52).

It may be helpful to outline briefly some aspects of Navaho culture, including the language, as illustration of the Sapir-Whorf hypothesis. In particular, I shall describe first some of the basic postulates of Navaho religious behavior and attempt to show how these fit in a frame of consistency with certain fashions of speaking evidenced primarily in the morphological patterns of the Navajo verb.

A review of Navaho religious practices, as described by Washington Matthews, Father Berard Haile, as many others, reveals that the Navaho conceive of themselves as in a particular relationship with the environment—physical, social, and supernatural—in which they live. Navaho man lives in a universe of eternal and unchanging forces with which he attempts to maintain an equilibrium, a kind of balancing of powers. The mere fact of living is, however, likely to disturb this balance and throw it out of gear. Any such disturbance, which may result from failure to observe a set rule of behavior or ritual or from the accidental or deliberate committal of some other fault in ritual or the conduct of daily activities, will, the Navaho believe, be revealed in the illness or unexplained death of an individual, in some other personal misfortune or bad luck to an enterprise or in some community disaster such as a food shortage or an epidemic. Whereupon, a diviner must be consulted, who determines by ritual means the cause of the disturbance and prescribes, in accordance with this knowledge, the appropriate counteracting religious ceremony or ritual.

The underlying purpose of the curing ceremony is to put the maladjusted individual or the community as a whole back into harmony with the universe. Significantly, this is done, not by the shaman or priest acting upon the individual and changing him, nor by any action, by shaman or priest, designed to alter the forces of the universe. It is done by reenacting one of a complex series of religious dramas which represent, in highly abstract terms, the events, far back in Navaho history, whereby the culture heroes first established harmony between man and nature and so made the world fit for human occupation. By re-enacting these events, or some portion of them, the present disturbance, by a kind of sympathetic magic, is compensated and harmony between man and universe restored. The ill person then gets well, or the community disaster is alleviated, since these misfortunes were but symptoms of a disturbed relation to nature.

From these numerous and very important patterns of Navaho religious behavior, it seems to me we can abstract a dominant motif belonging to the Navaho thought world. The motif has been well put by Kluckhohn and Leighton, who also illustrate it in many other aspects of Navaho culture. They call it, "Nature is more powerful than man," and amplify this in part by the Navaho premise "that nature will take care of them if they behave as they should and do as she directs" (1946: 227–28). In short, to the Navaho, the way to the good life lies not in modifying nature to man's needs or in changing man's nature but rather in discovering the proper relation of nature to man and in maintaining that relationship intact.

Turning now to the Navaho language, let us look at some aspects of the verb structure, illustrated in the following two forms:

nìńtį́ *you have lain down*
nìšíńłtį́ *you have put, laid me down*

Both these verbs are in the second person of the perfective mode (Hoijer 1946); the ń- marks this inflection. Both also have a prefix nì-, not the same but subtly different in meaning. The nì- of the first means [*movement*] *terminating in a position of rest*, that of the second [*movement*] *ending at a given point*. The second form has the causative prefix t- and incorporates the first person object, expressed in this form by ši-. The stem -tį́, common to both forms, is defined *one animate being moves*.

The theme of the first verb, composed of nì-...tį́, means *one animate being moves to a position of rest*, that is, *one animate being lies down*. In the second verb the meaning of the theme, nì-...-ł-tį́, is *cause movement of one animate being to end at a given point* and so, by extension, *put an animate being down* or *lay an animate being down*.

Note now that the first theme includes in its meaning what in English we should call both the actor and the action; these are not, in Navaho, expressed by separate morphemes. The subject pronoun prefix ń- serves then simply to identify a particular being with the class of possible beings already delimited by the theme. It functions, in short, to individuate one belonging to the class *animate being in motion to a position of rest*. The theme of the second verb, by reason of the causative l-, includes in its meaning what in English would be called action and goal. Again the pronoun ši, as a consequence, simply identifies or individuates one of a class of possible beings defined already in the

theme itself. It should be emphasized that the forms used here as illustration are in no sense unusual; this is the regular pattern of the Navaho verb, repeated over and over again in my data.

We are now ready to isolate, from this necessarily brief analysis, a possible fashion of speaking peculiar to Navaho. The Navaho speaks of "actors" and "goals" (the terms are inappropriate to Navaho), not as performers of actions or as ones upon whom actions are performed, as in English, but as entities linked to actions already defined in part as pertaining especially to classes of beings. The form which is glossed *you have lain down* is better understood you [*belong to, equal one of*] *a class of animate beings which has moved to rest*. Similarly the second form, glossed *you have put, laid me down* should read *you, as agent, have set a class of animate beings, to which I belong, in motion to a given point*.

This fashion of speaking, it seems to me, is wholly consistent with the dominant motif we saw in Navaho religious practices. Just as in his religious-curing activities the Navaho sees himself as adjusting to a universe that is given, so in his habits of speaking does he link individuals to actions and movements distinguished, not only as actions and movements, but as well in terms of entities in action or movement. This division of nature into classes of entity in action or movement is the universe that is given, the behavior of human beings or of any being individuated from the mass is customarily reported by assignment to one or other of these given divisions. . . .

REFERENCES

Boas, Franz (Ed.) (1911). "Introduction," *Handbook of American Indian Languages*, Part I. Washington, D.C., Government Printing Office.

Hoijer, Harry (1946). "The Apachean Verb, Part III: The Prefixes for Mode and Tense," *International Journal of American Linguistics*, 12:1–13— (1953); "The Relation of Language to Culture." In *Anthropology Today* (by A. L. Kroeber and others), pp. 554–73. Chicago, University of Chicago Press.

Kluckhohn, Clyde, and Dorothea Leighton (1946). *The Navaho*. Cambridge, Harvard University Press.

Mandelbaum, David G. (Ed.) (1949). *Selected Writings of Edward Sapir.* Berkeley and Los Angeles, University of California Press.

Sapir, Edward (1931). "Conceptual Categories in Primitive Languages," *Science* 74:578.

Voegelin, C. F. (1949). "Linguistics without Meaning and Culture without Words," *Word* 5:36–42.

Whorf, Benjamin L. (1952). *Collected Papers on Metalinguistics.* Washington, D.C., Department of State, Foreign Service Institute.

Translation Studies

SUSAN BASSNETT-MCGUIRE

LANGUAGE AND CULTURE

The first step towards an examination of the processes of translation must be to accept that although translation has a central core of linguistic activity, it belongs most properly to *semiotics*, the science that studies sign systems or structures, sign processes and sign functions (Hawkes, *Structuralism and Semiotics*, London 1977). Beyond the notion stressed by the narrowly linguistic approach, that translation involves the transfer of "meaning" contained in one set of language signs into another set of language signs through competent use of the dictionary and grammar, the process involves a whole set of extra-linguistic criteria also.

Edward Sapir claims that "language is a guide to social reality" and that human beings are at the mercy of the language that has become the medium of expression for their society. Experience, he asserts, is largely determined by the language habits of the community, and each separate structure represents a separate reality:

No two languages are ever sufficiently similar to be considered as representing the same social reality. The worlds in which different societies live are distinct worlds, not merely the same world with different labels attached.[1]

Sapir's thesis, endorsed later by Benjamin Lee Whorf, is related to the more recent view advanced by the Soviet semiotician, Jurí Lotman, that language

From Susan Bassnett-McGuire, *Translation Studies* (New York: Methuen, 1980), pp. 13–38. Reprinted by permission of the publisher, Routledge, London.

is a *modelling system*. Lotman describes literature and art in general as *secondary modelling systems*, as an indication of the fact that they are derived from the primary modelling system of language, and declares as firmly as Sapir or Whorf that "No language can exist unless it is steeped in the context of culture; and no culture can exist which does not have at its center, the structure of natural language."[2] Language, then, is the heart within the body of culture, and it is the interaction between the two that results in the continuation of life-energy. In the same way that the surgeon, operating on the heart, cannot neglect the body that surrounds it, so the translator treats the text in isolation from the culture at his peril.

TYPES OF TRANSLATION

In his article "On Linguistic Aspects of Translation," Roman Jakobson distinguishes three types of translation:[3]

1. Intralingual translation, or *rewording* (an interpretation of verbal signs by means of other signs in the same language).

2. Interlingual translation or *translation proper* (an interpretation of verbal signs by means of some other language).

3. Intersemiotic translation or *transmutation* (an interpretation of verbal signs by means of signs of nonverbal sign systems).

Having established these three types, of which (2) *translation proper* describes the process of transfer from SL to TL,[*] Jakobson goes on immediately to point to the central problem in all types: that while messages may serve as adequate interpretations of code units or messages, there is ordinarily no full equivalence through translation. Even apparent synonymy does not yield equivalence, and Jakobson shows how intralingual translation often has to resort to a combination of code units in order to fully

---

*Ed. note: SL: Source language, TL: Target language

interpret the meaning of a single unit. Hence a dictionary of so-called synonyms may give *perfect* as a synonym for *ideal* or *vehicle* as a synonym for *conveyance* but in neither case can there be said to be complete equivalence since each unit contains within itself a set of non-transferable associations and connotations.

Because complete equivalence (in the sense of synonymy or sameness) cannot take place in any of his categories, Jakobson declares that all poetic art is therefore technically untranslatable:

Only creative transposition is possible: either intralingual transposition—from one poetic shape into another, or interlingual transposition—from one language into another, or finally intersemiotic transposition—from one system of signs into another, e.g. from verbal art into music, dance, cinema or painting.

What Jakobson is saying here is taken up again by Georges Mounin, the French theorist, who perceives translation as a series of operations of which the starting point and the end product are *significations* and function within a given culture.[4] So, for example, the English word *pastry*, if translated into Italian without regard for its signification, will not be able to perform its function of meaning within a sentence, even though there may be a dictionary "equivalent"; for *pasta* has a completely different associative field. In this case the translator has to resort to a combination of units in order to find an approximate equivalent. Jakobson gives the example of the Russian word *syr* (a food made of fermented pressed curds) which translates roughly into English as *cottage cheese*. In this case, Jakobson claims, the translation is only an adequate *interpretation* of an alien code unit and equivalence is impossible.

DECODING AND RECODING

The translator, therefore, operates criteria that transcend the purely linguistic, and a process of decoding and recoding takes place. Eugene Nida's model

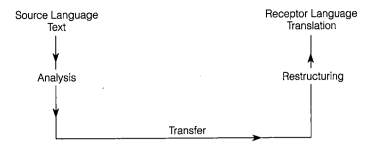

Source Language   Receptor Language
Text   Translation

Analysis   Restructuring

Transfer

of the translation process illustrates the stages involved:[5]

As examples of some of the complexities involved in the interlingual translation of what might seem to be uncontroversial items, consider the question of translating *yes* and *hello* into French, German and Italian. This task would seem, at first glance, to be straightforward, since all are Indo-European languages, closely related lexically and syntactically, and terms of greeting and assent are common to all three. For *yes* standard dictionaries give:

> French: *oui, si*
> German: *ja*
> Italian: *si*

It is immediately obvious that the existence of two terms in French involves a usage that does not exist in the other languages. Further investigation shows that whilst *oui* is the generally used term, *si* is used specifically in cases of contradiction, contention, and dissent. The English translator, therefore, must be mindful of this rule when translating the English word that remains the same in all contexts.

When the use of the affirmative in conversational speech is considered, another question arises. *Yes* cannot always be translated into the single words *oui, ja* or *si*, for French, German and Italian all frequently double or "string" affirmatives in a way that is outside standard English procedures (e.g. *si, si, si; ja, ja,* etc.). Hence the Italian or German translation

of *yes* by a single word can, at times, appear excessively brusque, whilst the stringing together of affirmatives in English is so hyperbolic that it often creates a comic effect.

With the translation of the word *hello*, the standard English form of friendly greeting when meeting, the problems are multiplied. The dictionaries give:

> French: *ça va?; hallo*
> German: *wie geht's; hallo*
> Italian: *olà; pronto; ciao*

Whilst English does not distinguish between the word used when greeting someone face to face and that used when answering the telephone, French, German and Italian all do make that distinction. The Italian *pronto* can only be used as a telephonic greeting, like the German *hallo*. Moreover, French and German use as forms of greeting brief rhetorical questions, whereas the same question in English *How are you?* or *How do you do?* is only used in more formal situations. The Italian *ciao*, by far the most common form of greeting in all sections of Italian society, is used equally on arrival and departure, being a word of greeting linked to a moment of contact between individuals either coming or going and not to the specific context of arrival or initial encounter. So, for example, the translator faced with the task of translating *hello* into French must first extract from the term a core of meaning and the stages of the process, following Nida's diagram, might look like this:

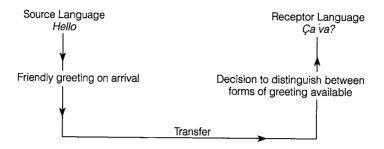

Source Language *Hello*		Receptor Language *Ça va?*
↓		↑
Friendly greeting on arrival		Decision to distinguish between forms of greeting available
↓		
└───────────	Transfer ──────────→	┘

What has happened during the translation process is that the *notion of greeting* has been isolated and the word *hello* has been replaced by a phrase carrying the same notion. Jakobson would describe this as interlingual transposition, while Ludskanov would call it a *semiotic transformation*:

Semiotic transformation (Ts) *are the replacements of the signs encoding a message by signs of another code, preserving (so far as possible in the face of entropy) invariant information with respect to a given system of reference.*[6]

In the case of *yes* the invariant information is *affirmation*, whilst in the case of *hello* the invariant is the *notion of greeting*. But at the same time the translator has had to consider other criteria, e.g. the existence of the *oui/si* rule in French, the stylistic function of stringing affirmatives, the *social context* of greeting—whether telephonic or face to face, the class position and status of the speakers and the resultant *weight* of a colloquial greeting in different societies. All such factors are involved in the translation even of the most apparently straightforward word.

The question of semiotic transformation is further extended when considering the translation of a simple noun, such as the English *butter*. Following Saussure, the structural relationship between the signified (*signifié*) or concept of butter and the signifier (*signifiant*) or the sound-image made by the word *butter* constitutes the linguistic sign *butter*.[7] And since language is perceived as a system of interdependent relations, it follows that *butter* operates within English as a noun in a particular structural relationship. But Saussure also distinguished be-

tween the syntagmatic (or horizontal) relations that a word has with the words that surround it in a sentence and the associative (or vertical) relations it has with the language structure as a whole. Moreover, within the secondary modelling system there is another type of associative relation and the translator, like the specialist in advertising techniques, must consider both the primary and secondary associative lines. For *butter* in British English carries with it a set of associations of wholesomeness, purity and high status (in comparison to margarine, once perceived only as second-rate butter though now marketed also as practical because it does not set hard under refrigeration).

When translating *butter* into Italian there is a straightforward word-for-word substitution: butter—*burro*. Both *butter* and *burro* describe the product made from milk and marketed as a creamy-coloured slab of edible grease for human consumption. And yet within their separate cultural contexts *butter* and *burro* cannot be considered as signifying the same. In Italy, *burro*, normally light coloured and unsalted, is used primarily for cooking, and carries no associations of high status, whilst in Britain *butter*, most often bright yellow and salted, is used for spreading on bread and less frequently in cooking. Because of the high status of *butter*, the phrase *bread and butter* is the accepted usage even where the product used is actually margarine.[8] So there is a distinction both between the *objects* signified by *butter* and *burro* and between the *function and value* of those objects in their cultural context. The problem of equivalence here involves the utilization and perception of the object in a given context. The *butter—burro* translation, whilst perfectly adequate on one level, also serves as a reminder of the

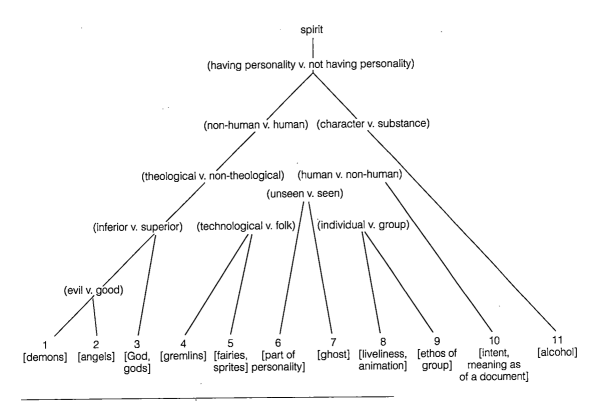

spirit
|
(having personality v. not having personality)

(non-human v. human) (character v. substance)

(theological v. non-theological) (human v. non-human)
(unseen v. seen)

(inferior v. superior) (technological v. folk) (individual v. group)

(evil v. good)

1	2	3	4	5	6	7	8	9	10	11
[demons]	[angels]	[God, gods]	[gremlins]	[fairies, sprites]	[part of personality]	[ghost]	[liveliness, animation]	[ethos of group]	[intent, meaning as of a document]	[alcohol]

Figure 1

validity of Sapir's statement that each language represents a separate reality.

The word *butter* describes a specifically identifiable product, but in the case of a word with a wider range of SL meanings the problems increase. Nida's diagrammatic sketch of the semantic structure of *spirit* (see Figure 1) illustrates a more complex set of semantic relationships.[9]

Where there is such a rich set of semantic relationships as in this case, a word can be used in punning and word-play, a form of humour that operates by confusing or mixing the various meanings (e.g. the jokes about the drunken priest who has been communing too often with the "holy spirit," etc.). The translator, then, must be concerned with the particular use of *spirit* in the sentence itself, in the sentence in its structural relation to other sentences, and in the overall textual and cultural contexts of the sentence. So, for example,

The spirit of the dead child rose from the grave

refers to 7 and not to any other of Nida's categories, whereas

The spirit of the house lived on

could refer to 5 or 7 or, used metaphorically, to 6 or 8 and the meaning can only be determined by the context.

Firth defines meaning as "a complex of relations of various kinds between the component terms of a context of situation"[10] and cites the example of the English phrase *Say when*, where the words "mean" what they "do." In translating that phrase it is the function that will be taken up and not the words themselves, and the translation process involves a decision to replace and substitute the linguistic elements in the TL. And since the phrase is, as Firth points out, directly linked to English social behavioural patterns, the translator putting the phrase into French or German has to contend with the problem of the non-existence of a similar convention in either TL culture. Likewise, the English translator of the French *Bon appetit* has a similar problem, for again the utterance is situation-bound. As an example of the complexities involved here, let us take a hypothetical dramatic situation in which the phrase *Bon appetit* becomes crucially significant:

A family group have been quarreling bitterly, the unity of the family has collapsed, unforgivable things have been said. But the celebratory dinner to which they have all come is about to be served, and the family sit at the table in silence ready to eat. The plates are filled, everyone sits waiting, the father breaks the silence to wish them all "Bon appetit" and the meal begins.

Whether the phrase is used mechanically, as part of the daily ritual, whether it is used ironically, sadly or even cruelly is not specified. On a stage, the actor and director would come to a decision about how to interpret the phrase based on their concept of characterization and of the overall meaning and structure of the play. The interpretation would be rendered through voice inflexion. But whatever the interpretation, the significance of the simple utterance cutting into a situation of great tension would remain.

The translator has to take the question of interpretation into account in addition to the problem of selecting a TL phrase which will have a roughly similar meaning. Exact translation is impossible: *Good appetite* in English used outside a structural sentence is meaningless. Nor is there any English phrase in general use that fulfils the same function as the French. There are, however, a series of phrases that might be applicable in certain situations—the colloquial *Dig in* or *Tuck in*, the more formal *Do start*, or even the ritualistically apologetic *I hope you like it*, or *I hope it's alright*. In determining what to use in English, the translator must:

1. Accept the untranslatability of the SL phrase in the TL on the linguistic level.

2. Accept the lack of a similar cultural convention in the TL.

3. Consider the range of TL phrases available, having regard to the presentation of class, status, age, sex of the speaker, his relationship to the listeners and the context of their meeting in the SL.

4. Consider the significance of the phrase in its particular context—i.e. as a moment of high tension in the dramatic text.

5. Replace in the TL the invariant core of the SL phrase in its two referential systems (the particular system of the text and the system of culture out of which the text has sprung).

Levý, the great Czech translation scholar, insisted that any contracting or omitting of difficult expressions in translating was immoral. The translator, he believed, had the responsibility of finding a solution to the most daunting of problems, and he declared that the functional view must be adopted with regard not only to meaning but also to style and form. The wealth of studies on Bible translation and the documentation of the way in which individual translators of the Bible attempt to solve their problems through ingenious solutions is a particularly rich source of examples of semiotic transformation.

In translating *Bon appetit* in the scenario given above, the translator was able to extract a set of criteria from the text in order to determine what a suitable TL rendering might be, but clearly in a different context the TL phrase would alter. The emphasis always in translation is on the *reader* or listener, and the translator must tackle the SL text in such a way that the TL version will correspond to the SL version. The nature of that correspondence may vary considerably . . . but the principle remains constant. Hence Albrecht Neubert's view that Shakespeare's Sonnet "Shall I compare thee to a summer's day?" cannot be semantically translated into a language where summers are unpleasant is perfectly proper, just as the concept of God the Father cannot be translated into a language where the deity is female. To attempt to impose the value system of the SL culture onto the TL culture is dangerous ground, and the translator should not be tempted by the school that pretends to determine the original *intentions* of an author on the basis of a self-contained text.

The translator cannot *be* the author of the SL text, but as the author of the TL text has a clear moral responsibility to the TL readers.

PROBLEMS OF EQUIVALENCE

The translation of idioms takes us a stage further in considering the question of meaning and translation, for idioms, like puns, are culture bound. The Italian idiom *menare il can per l'aia* provides a good example of the kind of shift that takes place in the translation process.[11] Translated literally, the sentence

Giovanni sta menando il can per l'aia.

becomes

John is leading his dog around the threshing floor.

The image conjured up by this sentence is somewhat startling and, unless the context referred quite specifically to such a location, the sentence would seem obscure and virtually meaningless. The English idiom that most closely corresponds to the Italian is *to beat about the bush*, also obscure unless used idiomatically, and hence the sentence correctly translated becomes

John is beating about the bush.

Both English and Italian have corresponding idiomatic expressions that render the idea of prevarication, and so in the process of interlingual translation one idiom is substituted for another. That substitution is made not on the basis of the linguistic elements in the phrase, nor on the basis of a corresponding or similar image contained in the phrase, but on the function of the idiom. The SL phrase is replaced by a TL phrase that serves the same purpose in the TL culture, and the process here involves the substitution of SL sign for TL sign. Dagut's remarks about the problems of translating metaphor are interesting when applied also to the problem of tackling idioms:

Since a metaphor in the SL is, by definition, a new piece of performance, a semantic novelty, it can clearly have no existing "equivalence" in the TL: what is unique can have no counterpart. Here the translator's bilingual competence—"le sens," as Mallarmé put it "de ce qui est dans la langue et de ce qui n'en est pas"—is of help to him only in the negative sense of telling him that any "equivalence" in this case cannot be "found" but will have to be "created." The crucial question that arises is thus whether a metaphor can, strictly speaking, be translated as such, or whether it can only be "reproduced" in some way.[12]

But Dagut's distinction between "translation" and "reproduction," like Catford's distinction between "literal" and "free" translation[13] does not take into account the view that sees translation as semiotic transformation. In his definition of translation equivalence, Popovič distinguishes four types:

1. *Linguistic equivalence*, where there is homogeneity on the linguistic level of both SL and TL texts, i.e. word for word translation.

2. *Paradigmatic equivalence*, where there is equivalence of "the elements of a paradigmatic expressive axis," i.e. elements of grammar, which Popovič sees as being a higher category than lexical equivalence.

3. *Stylistic (translational) equivalence*, where there is "functional equivalence of elements in both original and translation aiming at an expressive identity with an invariant of identical meaning."

4. *Textual (syntagmatic) equivalence*, where there is equivalence of the syntagmatic structuring of a text, i.e. equivalence of form and shape.[14]

The case of the translation of the Italian idiom, therefore, involves the determining of stylistic equivalence which results in the substitution of the SL idiom by an idiom with an equivalent function in the TL.

Translation involves far more than replacement of lexical and grammatical items between languages and, as can be seen in the translation of idioms and metaphors, the process may involve discarding the basic linguistic elements of the SL text so as to achieve Popovič's goal of "expressive identity" between the SL and TL texts. But once the translator moves away from close linguistic equivalence, the problems of determining the exact nature of the level of equivalence aimed for begin to emerge.

Albrecht Neubert, whose work on translation is unfortunately not available to English readers, distinguishes between the study of translation as a *process* and as a *product*. He states bluntly that: "the 'missing link' between both components of a complete theory of translations appears to be the theory of equivalence relations that can be conceived for both the dynamic and the static model."[15] The problem of equivalence, a much-used and abused term in Translation Studies, is of central importance, and although Neubert is right when he stresses the need for a theory of equivalence relations, Raymond van den Broeck is also right when he challenges the excessive use of the term in Translation Studies and claims that the precise definition of equivalence in mathematics is a serious obstacle to its use in translation theory.

Eugene Nida distinguishes two types of equivalence, *formal* and *dynamic*, where formal equivalence "focuses attention on the message itself, in both form and content. In such a translation one is concerned with such correspondences as poetry to poetry, sentence to sentence, and concept to concept." Nida calls this type of translation a "gloss translation," which aims to allow the reader to understand as much of the SL context as possible. *Dynamic equivalence* is based on the principle of *equivalent effect*, i.e. that the relationship between receiver and message should aim at being the same as that between the original receivers and the SL message. As an example of this type of equivalence, he quotes J. B. Phillips' rendering of *Romans* 16:16, where the idea of "greeting with a holy kiss" is translated as "give one another a hearty handshake all round." With this example of what seems to be a piece of inadequate translation in poor taste, the weakness of Nida's loosely defined types can clearly be seen. The principle of *equivalent effect* which has enjoyed great popularity in certain cultures at certain times, involves us in areas of speculation and at times can lead to very dubious conclusions. So E. V. Rieu's deliberate decision to translate Homer into English prose because the significance of the epic form in Ancient Greece could be considered equivalent to the significance of prose in modern Europe, is a case of *dynamic equivalence* applied to the formal properties of a text which shows that Nida's categories can actually be in conflict with each other.

It is an established fact in Translation Studies that if a dozen translators tackle the same poem, they will produce a dozen different versions. And yet somewhere in those dozen versions there will be what Popovič calls the "invariant core" of the original poem. This invariant core, he claims, is represented by stable, basic and constant semantic elements in the text, whose existence can be proved by experimental semantic condensation. Transformations, or variants, are those changes which do not modify the core of meaning but influence the expressive form. In short, the invariant can be defined as that which exists in common between all existing translations of a single work. So the invariant is part of a dynamic relationship and should not be confused with speculative arguments about the "nature," the "spirit" or "soul" of the text; the "indefinable quality" that translators are rarely supposed to be able to capture.

In trying to solve the problem of translation equivalence, Neubert postulates that from the point of view of a theory of texts, translation equivalence must be considered a *semiotic category*, comprising a *syntactic*, *semantic* and *pragmatic* component, following Pierce's categories.[16] These components are arranged in a hierarchical relationship, where semantic equivalence takes priority over syntactic equivalence, and pragmatic equivalence conditions and modifies both the other elements. Equivalence overall results from the relation between signs themselves, the relationship between signs and what they stand for, and the relationship between signs, what they stand for and those who use them. So, for example, the shock value of Italian or Spanish blasphemous expressions can only be rendered pragmatically in English by substituting expressions with sexual overtones to produce a comparable shock effect, e.g. *porca Madonna—fucking hell*.[17] Similarly, the interaction between all three components determines the process of selection in the TL, as for example, in the case of letter-writing. The norms governing the writing of letters vary considerably from language to language and from period to period, even within Europe. Hence a woman writing to a friend in 1812 would no more have signed her letters *with love* or *in sisterhood* as a contemporary Englishwoman might, any more than an Italian would conclude letters without a series of formal greetings to the recipient of the letter and his relations. In both these cases, the letter-writing formulae and the obscenity, the translator decodes and attempts to encode pragmatically.

The question of defining equivalence is being pursued by two lines of development in Translation Studies. The first, rather predictably, lays an emphasis on the special problems of semantics and on the transfer of semantic content from SL to TL. With the second, which explores the question of equivalence of literary texts, the work of the Russian Formalists and the Prague Linguists, together with more recent developments in discourse analysis, have broadened the problem of equivalence in its application to the translation of such texts. James Holmes, for example, feels that the use of the term equivalence is "perverse," since to ask for sameness is to ask too much, while Durišin argues that the translator of a literary text is not concerned with establishing equivalence of natural language but of artistic procedures. And those procedures cannot be considered in isolation, but must be located within the specific cultural-temporal context within which they are utilized.[18]

Let us take as an example, two advertisements in British Sunday newspaper colour supplements, one for Scotch whisky and one for Martini, where each product is being marketed to cater for a particular taste. The whisky market, older and more traditional than the Martini market, is catered to in advertising by an emphasis on the quality of the product, on the discerning taste of the buyer and on the social status the product will confer. Stress is also laid on the naturalness and high quality of the distilling process, on the purity of Scottish water, and on the length of time the product has matured. The advertisement consists of a written text and a photograph of the product. Martini, on the other hand, is mar-

keted to appeal to a different social group, one that has to be won over to the product which has appeared relatively recently. Accordingly, Martini is marketed for a younger outlook and lays less stress on the question of the quality of the product but much more on the fashionable status that it will confer. The photograph accompanying the brief written text shows "beautiful people" drinking Martini, members of the international jet set, who inhabit the fantasy world where everyone is supposedly rich and glamourous. These two types of advertisement have become so stereotyped in British culture that they are instantly recognizable and often parodied.

With the advertising of the same two products in an Italian weekly news magazine there is likewise a dual set of images—the one stressing purity, quality, social status; the other stressing glamour, excitement, trendy living and youth. But because Martini is long established and Scotch is a relatively new arrival on the mass market, the images presented with the products are exactly the reverse of the British ones. The same modes, but differently applied, are used in the advertising of these two products in two societies. The products may be the same in both societies, but they have different values. Hence Scotch in the British context may conceivably be defined as the equivalent of Martini in the Italian context, and vice versa, in so far as they are presented through advertising as serving equivalent social functions.

Mukařovský's view that the literary text has both an autonomous and a communicative character has been taken up by Lotman, who argues that a text is *explicit* (it is expressed in definite signs), *limited* (it begins and ends at a given point), and it has *structure* as a result of internal organization. The signs of the text are in a relation of opposition to the signs and structures outside the text. A translator must therefore bear in mind both its autonomous and its communicative aspects and any theory of equivalence should take both elements into account.[19]

Equivalence in translation, then, should not be approached as a search for sameness, since sameness cannot even exist between two TL versions of the same text, let alone between the SL and the TL

OBJECTIVE FIELD	SPEAKER (SENDER)	HEARER (RECEIVER)	HANDLING OF TOPIC. RUNNING OF THIRD PERSON
SITUATION 1a			ENGLISH...'HE IS RUNNING' HOPI........'WARI' (RUNNING. STATEMENT OF FACT)
SITUATION 1b OBJECTIVE FIELD BLANK DEVOID OF RUNNING			ENGLISH...'HE RAN' HOPI........'WARI' (RUNNING. STATEMENT OF FACT)
SITUATION 2			ENGLISH...'HE IS RUNNING' HOPI........'WARI' (RUNNING. STATEMENT OF FACT)
SITUATION 3 OBJECTIVE FIELD BLANK			ENGLISH..'HE RAN' HOPI........'ERA WARI' (RUNNING. STATEMENT OF FACT FROM MEMORY)
SITUATION 4 OBJECTIVE FIELD BLANK			ENGLISH...'HE WILL RUN' HOPI.........'WARIKNI' (RUNNING. STATEMENT OF EXPECTATION)
SITUATION 5 OBJECTIVE FIELD BLANK			ENGLISH...'HE RUNS' (E.G. ON THE TRACK TEAM) HOPI........ 'WARIKNGWE' (RUNNING. STATEMENT OF LAW)

Figure 2 Whorf's comparison between temporal and timeless languages

version. Popovič's four types offer a useful starting point and Neubert's three semiotic categories point the way towards an approach that perceives equivalence as a dialectic between the signs and the structures within and surrounding the SL and TL texts.

LOSS AND GAIN

Once the principle is accepted that sameness cannot exist between two languages, it becomes possible to approach the question of *loss and gain* in the translation process. It is again an indication of the low status of translation that so much time should have been spent on discussing what is lost in the transfer of a text from SL to TL whilst ignoring what can also be gained, for the translator can at times enrich or clarify the SL text as a direct result of the translation process. Moreover, what is often seen as "lost" from the SL context may be replaced in the TL context, as in the case of Wyatt and Surrey's translations of Petrarch (see pp. 56–7; 104–9).

Eugene Nida is a rich source of information about the problems of loss in translation, in particular about the difficulties encountered by the translator when faced with terms or concepts in the SL that do not exist in the TL. He cites the case of Guaica, a language of southern Venezuela, where there is little trouble in finding satisfactory terms for the English *murder*, *stealing*, *lying*, etc., but where the terms for *good*, *bad*, *ugly*, and *beautiful* cover a very different area of meaning. As an example, he points out that Guaica does not follow a dichotomous classification of *good* and *bad*, but a trichotomous one as follows:

1. *Good* includes desirable food, killing enemies, chewing dope in moderation, putting fire to one's wife to teach her to obey, and stealing from anyone not belonging to the same band.

2. *Bad* includes rotten fruit, any object with a blemish, murdering a person of the same band, stealing from a member of the extended family and lying to anyone.

3. *Violating taboo* includes incest, being too close to one's mother-in-law, a married woman's eating tapir before the birth of the first child, and a child's eating rodents.

Nor is it necessary to look so far beyond Europe for examples of this kind of differentiation. The large number of terms in Finnish for variations of snow, in Arabic for aspects of camel behaviour, in English for light and water, in French for types of bread, all present the translator with, on one level, an untranslatable problem. Bible translators have documented the additional difficulties involved in, for example, the concept of the Trinity or the social significance of the parables in certain cultures. In addition to the lexical problems, there are of course languages that do not have tense systems or concepts of time that in any way correspond to Indo-European systems. Whorf's comparison (which may not be reliable, but is cited here as a theoretical example) between a "temporal language" (English) and a "timeless language" (Hopi) serves to illustrate this aspect (see Figure 2).[20]

UNTRANSLATABILITY.

When such difficulties are encountered by the translator, the whole issue of the translatability of the text is raised. Catford distinguishes two types of *untranslatability*, which he terms *linguistic* and *cultural*. On the linguistic level, untranslatability occurs when there is no lexical or syntactical substitute in the TL for an SL item. So, for example, the German *Um wieviel Uhr darf man Sie morgen wecken?* or the Danish *Jeg fandt brevet* are linguistically untranslatable, because both sentences involve structures that do not exist in English. Yet both can be adequately translated into English once the rules of English structure are applied. A translator would unhesitatingly render the two sentences as *What time would you like to be woken tomorrow?* and *I found the letter*, restructuring the German word order and adjusting the position of the postpositive definite article in Danish to conform to English norms.

Catford's category of linguistic untranslatability, which is also proposed by Popovič, is straightfor-

ward, but his second category is more problematic. Linguistic untranslatability, he argues, is due to differences in the SL and the TL, whereas cultural untranslatability is due to the absence in the TL culture of a relevant situational feature for the SL text. He quotes the example of the different concepts of the term *bathroom* in an English, Finnish or Japanese context, where both the object and the use made of that object are not at all alike. But Catford also claims that more abstract lexical items such as the English term *home* or *democracy* cannot be described as untranslatable, and argues that the English phrases, *I'm going home*, or *He's at home* can "readily be provided with translation equivalents in most languages" whilst the term *democracy* is international.

Now on one level, Catford is right. The English phrases can be translated into most European languages and *democracy* is an internationally used term. But he fails to take into account two significant factors, and this seems to typify the problem of an overly narrow approach to the question of untranslatability. If *I'm going home* is translated as *Je vais chez moi*, the content meaning of the SL sentence (i.e. self-assertive statement of intention to proceed to place of residence and/or origin) is only loosely reproduced. And if, for example, the phrase is spoken by an American resident temporarily in London, it could either imply a return to the immediate "home" or a return across the Atlantic, depending on the context in which it is used, a distinction that would have to be spelled out in French. Moreover the English term *home*, like the French *foyer*, has a range of associative meanings that are not translated by the more restricted phrase *chez moi*. *Home*, therefore, would appear to present exactly the same range of problems as the Finnish or Japanese *bathroom*.

With the translation of *democracy*, further complexities arise. Catford feels that the term is largely present in the lexis of many languages and, although it may be relatable to different political situations, the context will guide the reader to select the appropriate situational features. The problem here is that the reader will have a concept of the term based on his or her own cultural context, and will apply that particularized view accordingly. Hence the difference between the adjective *democratic* as it appears in the following three phrases is fundamental to three totally different political concepts:

the American Democratic Party
the German Democratic Republic
the democratic wing of the British Conservative Party.

So although the term is international, its usage in different contexts shows that there is no longer (if indeed there ever was) any common ground from which to select relevant situational features. If culture is perceived as dynamic, then the terminology of social structuring must be dynamic also. Lotman points out that the semiotic study of culture not only considers culture functioning as a system of signs, but emphasizes that "the *very relation of culture to the sign and to signification* comprises one of its basic typological features."[21] Catford starts from different premises, and because he does not go far enough in considering the dynamic nature of language and culture, he invalidates his own category of *cultural untranslatability*. In so far as language is the primary modelling system within a culture, cultural untranslatability must be *de facto* implied in any process of translation.

Darbelnet and Vinay, in their useful book *Stylistique comparée du français et de l'anglais* (A Comparative French-English Stylistics),[22] have analysed in detail points of linguistic difference between the two languages, differences that constitute areas where translation is impossible. But once again it is Popovič who has attempted to define untranslatability without making a separation between the linguistic and the cultural. Popovič also distinguishes two types. The first is defined as

A situation in which the linguistic elements of the original cannot be replaced adequately in structural, linear, functional or semantic terms in consequence of a lack of denotation or connotation.

The second type goes beyond the purely linguistic:

A situation where the relation of expressing the meaning, i.e. the relation between the creative subject and its linguistic expression in the original does not find an adequate linguistic expression in the translation.

The first type may be seen as parallel to Catford's category of linguistic untranslatability, while into this second type come phrases such as *Bon appetit* or the interesting series of everyday phrases in Danish for expressing thanks. Bredsdorf's Danish grammar for English readers gives elaborate details of the contextual use of such expressions. The explanation of the phrase *Tak for mad*, for example states that "there is no English equivalent of this expression used to a host or hostess by the guests or members of the household after a meal."

A slightly more difficult example is the case of the Italian *tamponamento* in the sentence *C'è stato un tamponamento*.

Since English and Italian are sufficiently close to follow a loosely approximate pattern of sentence organization with regard to component parts and word order, the sentence appears fully translatable. The conceptual level is also translatable: an event occurring in time past is being reported in time present. The difficulty concerns the translation of the Italian noun, which emerges in English as a noun phrase. The TL version, allowing for the variance in English and Italian syntax, is

There has been/there was a slight accident (involving a vehicle).

Because of the differences in tense-usage, the TL sentence may take one of two forms depending on the context of the sentence, and because of the length of the noun phrase, this can also be cut down, provided the nature of the accident can be determined outside the sentence by the receiver. But when the significance of *tamponamento* is considered *vis-à-vis* Italian society as a whole, the term cannot be fully understood without some knowledge of Italian driving habits, the frequency with which "slight accidents" occur and the weighting and relevance of such incidents when they do occur. In short, *tamponamento* is a sign that has a culture-bound or context meaning, which cannot be translated even by an explanatory phrase. The relation between the creative subject and its linguistic expression cannot therefore be adequately replaced in the translation.

Popovič's second type, like Catford's secondary category, illustrates the difficulties of describing and defining the limits of translatability, but whilst Catford starts from within linguistics, Popovič starts from a position that involves a theory of literary communication. Boguslav Lawendowski, in an article in which he attempts to sum up the state of translation studies and semiotics, feels that Catford is "divorced from reality,"[23] while Georges Mounin feels that too much attention has been given to the problem of untranslatability at the expense of solving some of the actual problems that the translator has to deal with.

Mounin acknowledges the great benefits that advances in linguistics have brought to Translation Studies; the development of structural linguistics, the work of Saussure, of Hjelmslev, of the Moscow and Prague Linguistic Circles has been of great value, and the work of Chomsky and the transformational linguists has also had its impact, particularly with regard to the study of semantics. Mounin feels that it is thanks to developments in contemporary linguistics that we can (and must) accept that:

1. Personal experience in its uniqueness is untranslatable.

2. In theory the base units of any two languages (e.g. phonemes, monemes, etc.) are not always comparable.

3. Communication is possible when account is taken of the respective situations of speaker and hearer, or author and translator.

In other words, Mounin believes that linguistics demonstrates that translation is a *dialectic process* that can be accomplished with relative success:

Translation may always start with the clearest situations, the most concrete messages, the most elementary universals. But as it involves the consideration of a language in its entirety, together with its most subjective messages, through an examination of common situations and a multiplication

of contacts that need clarifying, then there is no doubt that communication through translation can never be completely finished, which also demonstrates that it is never wholly impossible either.[24]

As has already been suggested, it is clearly the task of the translator to find a solution to even the most daunting of problems. Such solutions may vary enormously; the translator's decision as to what constitutes invariant information with respect to a given system of reference is in itself a creative act. Levý stresses the intuitive element in translating:

As in all semiotic processes, translation has its Pragmatic dimension *as well. Translation theory tends to be normative, to instruct translators on the OPTIMAL solution; actual translation work, however, is pragmatic; the translator resolves for that one of the possible solutions which promises a maximum of effect with a minimum of effort. That is to say, he intuitively resolves for the so-called MINIMAX STRATEGY.*[25]

NOTES

1. Edward Sapir, *Culture, Language and Personality* (Berkeley, Los Angeles: University of California Press, 1956), p. 69.

2. Jurí Lotman and B. A. Uspensky, "On the Semiotic Mechanism of Culture," *New Literary History*, IX (2), 1978, pp. 211–32.

3. Roman Jakobson, "On Linguistic Aspects of Translation," in R. A. Brower (ed.), *On Translation* (Cambridge, Mass.: Harvard University Press, 1959), pp. 232–9.

4. Georges Mounin, *Les problèmes théoriques de la traducion* (Paris: Gallimard, 1963).

5. Eugene Nida and Charles Taber, *The Theory and Practice of Translation* (Leiden: E. J. Brill, 1969), p. 484.

6. A. Ludskanov, "A Semiotic Approach to the Theory of Translation," *Language Sciences*, 35 (April), 1975, pp. 5–8.

7. See Ferdinand de Saussure, *Course in General Linguistics* (London: Fontana, 1974).

8. Though there is also the idiomatic use of the phrase *bread and butter* that signifies basic essentials, means of livelihood, e.g. *to earn one's bread and butter*.

9. This sketch is taken from Eugene Nida, *Towards a Science of Translating. With Special Reference to Principles and Procedures Involved in Bible Translating* (Leiden: E. J. Brill, 1964), p. 107. All quotations from Nida, unless otherwise indicated, are taken from this volume.

10. J. R. Firth, *The Tongues of Men and Speech* (London: Oxford University Press, 1970), p. 110.

11. Popovič distinguishes several types of shift:
   (a) *Constitutive shift* (in translation) described as an inevitable shift that takes place as a result of differences between two languages, two poetics and two styles.
   (b) *Generic shift*, where the constitutive features of the text as a literary genre may change.
   (c) *Individual shift*, where the translator's own style and idiolect may introduce a system of individual deviations.
   (d) *Negative shift*, where information is incorrectly translated, due to unfamiliarity with the language or structure of the original.
   (e) *Topical shift*, where topical facts of the original are altered in the translation.

12. M. B. Dagut, "Can Metaphor Be Translated?" *Babel*, XXII (1), 1976, pp. 21–33.

13. J. C. Catford, *A Linguistic Theory of Translation* (London: Oxford University Press, 1965).

14. All quotations from Popovič, unless otherwise indicated, are taken from his *Dictionary*.

15. Albrecht Neubert, "Elemente einer allgemeinen Theorie der Translation," *Actes du Xe Congrès International des Linguistes*, 1967, Bucarest II, pp. 451–6.

16. See C. S. Pierce, *Collected Papers* (8 vols), ed. C. Hartshorne, P. Weiss and A. Burks (Cambridge, Mass.: Harvard University Press, 1931–58).
For a discussion of Pierce's contribution to semiotics, see T. Hawkes, *Structuralism and Semiotics* (London: Methuen, 1977), pp. 126–30.

17. One interesting aspect of languages in contact is that systems of swearing and blasphemy often become interchangeable. In the case of Chicano Spanish, the Anglo-American system has been incorporated with the traditional Spanish system.

18. Examples quoted by Raymond van den Broeck in "The Concept of Equivalence in Translation Theory: Some Critical Reflections," in James S. Holmes, José Lambert and Raymond van den Broeck (eds), *Literature and Translation* (Louvain: ACCO. 1978), pp. 29–48.

19. For a discussion of Lotman's theories, see D. W. Fokkema, "Continuity and Change in Russian Formalism, Czech Structuralism, and Soviet Semiotics," *PTL*, I (1) Jan. 1976, pp. 153–96, and Ann Shukman, "The Canonization of the Real: Juri Lotman's Theory of Literature and Analysis of Poetry," *PTL* I (2), April 1976, pp. 317–39.

20. Benjamin Lee Whorf, *Language, Thought and Reality* (Selected Writings) ed. J. B. Carroll (Cambridge, Mass.: The MIT Press, 1956), p. 213

21. Lotman and Uspensky, op. cit.

22. J. L. Darbelnet and J. P. Vinay, *Stylistique comparée du français et de l'anglais* (Paris: Didier, 1958).

23. Boguslav P. Lawendowski, "On Semiotic Aspects of Translation," in Thomas Sebeok (ed.), *Sight, Sound and Sense* (Bloomington: Indiana University Press, 1978), pp. 264–83.

24. Mounin, op. cit., p. 279.

25. Jiří Levý, *Die literarische Übersetzung. Theorie einer Kunstgattung*, tr. Walter Schamschula (Frankfurt am Main: Athenaion, 1969).

The Art of Interpreting

JAN CAROL BERRIS

Exchanges with the People's Republic of China have proliferated to a degree unimagined just a short time ago. As recently as 1977, fewer than twenty Chinese delegations visited the United States during the whole year; in 1982 delegations were averaging about 100 per month. This enormous increase in contact has necessitated a corresponding increase in the number of Chinese and Americans who can communicate in each other's language. Although many Chinese are learning English (it is by far the most important foreign language in China) and a few Americans know Chinese, interpreters are and will continue to be essential in facilitating communication between both sides.

Interpreting, as I have learned through more than a decade of experience, is a physically exhausting and often emotionally draining art. But those who work with interpreters can do a great deal to help maximize the interpreter's effectiveness and minimize his or her weaknesses.

WHAT MAKES A GOOD INTERPRETER?

Many people assume that anyone fluent in two languages can function as an interpreter. Indeed, a good command of both languages and alertness to their constant evolution is the foundation of effective interpreting. But that is only the first step. Expressing your own thoughts, choosing your own

From Robert A. Kapp (ed.), *Communicating with China* (Chicago: Intercultural Press, 1983), pp. 41–57. Reprinted by permission of the publisher and the author. Jan Berris is Vice President of the National Commission on U.S.-China Relations.

words, and picking your own sentence patterns in a foreign tongue are very different—and infinitely easier—than precisely reproducing someone else's ideas, phrases, and nuances. At the National Committee on U.S.-China Relations, we interview many people with Chinese language skills ranging from fairly good to excellent. Yet in an interpreting test, nearly all, even those who do quite well in general conversation, fall apart.

A good interpreter is more than a translator of words, since language skills are only a part of the process of communication. Biculturalism—sensitivity to cultural and social differences—is often as important as bilingualism. An interpreter must be sensitive to what is appropriate to the occasion. One of my favorite examples of this concerns a famous Western scientist who was asked to address a large Chinese audience. Before his talk, he was disconcerted to find that a number of children were playing and chattering in the aisles. His impatience increased when he realized that no one was attempting to quiet them down as he was about to begin. He exploded angrily at the interpreter, "Will you tell those little bastards to shut up!" With perfect aplomb the interpreter spoke quietly into the microphone, "Xiao pengyoumen, qing nimen shaowei anjing yidian, hao bu hao!" Which roughly translates, "Little friends, would you please be just a bit more quiet, if you don't mind."

Another important aspect of biculturalism is knowing what makes people laugh in the other culture. Humor is very difficult to translate. In fact, very often American humor just does not work in Chinese. In that case one may have to resort to the tactic of Doonesbury's interpreter Honey (who is actually modeled on one of China's best interpreters, Tang Wensheng) when she tells her audience in one frame, "I think he's about to make a joke. . . ." and in the next, "The joke has been made, and he will be expecting you to laugh at it. Go wild."

Political sensitivity is also an essential aspect of biculturalism. Several times during the past decade we have been spared unhappy incidents when interpreters wisely avoided repeating an American speaker's inadvertent use of "Republic of China" for "People's Republic of China" and translated the latter term into Chinese. No matter how often people are forewarned about this error it is still quite common, whether out of nervousness or habit—especially when one is attempting a phrase like, "the people of the People's Republic of China." Somehow that mouthful usually comes out wrong.

Bilingualism and biculturalism can be learned—though often only by a process of osmosis—during long years of study and/or living in another country. But there are other, more innate characteristics that contribute to the making of a good interpreter.

Good interpreters must have a special kind of personality, in fact, a somewhat schizophrenic one. On the one hand, they must be confident and aggressive enough to be relaxed when speaking in front of audiences large or small, presidents or prime ministers. On the other hand, they must have the ability to submerge their own egos and take on the personalities of the speakers. Frustrated actors probably make some of the best interpreters. They don't mind, in fact they enjoy, mirroring the actions and tones of the speaker or, as is quite often the case, a series of speakers with varying demeanors. Yet sometimes an interpreter can be too much of a ham. This is dangerous because while it makes for an entertaining, lively session, it usually detracts from the speaker, who should be the focus of attention.

Another theatrical talent that comes in handy is projection. Occasionally interpreters have the use of a microphone; more often they have to compete against the whir and rumble of factory machinery or city street noises. Some interpreters have a tendency to look at and speak directly to the leader of a delegation, ignoring the rest of the group. Many times I have found myself in the back of a room, waving my arms or otherwise trying to indicate to the interpreter that the people at the back cannot hear.

These personal traits often compensate for minor language problems. For instance, one interpreter with whom we have worked over the years speaks excellent Chinese, but in a classical, literary style. As an academic interested in traditional China he has not needed to be conversant with contemporary language changes. But since this particular person is also a consummate actor with exaggerated movements and facial expressions, we overlook his literary rather than vernacular language. Although he sometimes interjects too much of himself into the interpreting process, we also like to work with him because he interacts very well with the Chinese. They have great respect for his knowledge of traditional China, and they love to imitate (with great affection) his mannerisms and speech patterns.

On a more practical note, being able to do two (or more) things at one time is important. An interpreter must be listening to what the speaker is saying while thinking about the best way to render it into another language. This is obviously much more critical for simultaneous interpreters, but those who do consecutive interpreting face the problem as well. A few interpreters manage to do four things at the same time: listen; jot down key words to jog their memories; look up unknown words in a small dictionary (which usually appears magically out of a pocket); and, juggling notebook and dictionary, write down the unfamiliar word so if it is repeated later the dictionary will not have to be hauled out again. All this without diverting attention from the speaker.

And speaking of writing things down, interpreters should always carry notebooks—and use them. Even the best of memories sometimes fails. But one should be selective. Only those with super stenographic skills should attempt a verbatim transcript; otherwise they will still be on the third word while the speaker is waiting for the translation. Selected words or phrases should be sufficient to recall the full sentence.

Obviously interpreters should be matched to specific jobs; some will be better at one kind of work while others will excel at another. For technical interpreting someone who not only knows the specific jargon (that, after all, can be looked up in a dictionary) but also is familiar with the concepts behind the words is needed.

There are times when an interpreter who blends into the background is required, perhaps for high-level diplomatic negotiations. At other times, someone with a more forceful personality is required. The National Committee on U.S.-China Relations opts for the latter, since our work generally entails introducing Chinese and American counterparts to one another. Our interpreters must be observant, outgoing, and interested in others, so that in a social situation they can get a group of Americans to stop chatting with their friends and encourage them to interact with the Chinese who, more than likely, have clustered themselves in the corner or at a window to exclaim over the view. We also need interpreters who are lively and knowledgeable about the United States so they can help explain American culture and history to members of Chinese delegations. . . .

THE INTERPRETING SITUATION

Even if competent interpreters are available, many communication problems can still occur. Insuring that they do not is as much the responsibility of those relying on interpretation as it is of the interpreter. This is particularly true for an American who is conducting negotiations or substantive discussions with the Chinese and who has a clear stake in their success. But everyone involved should be aware of certain pitfalls and try to avoid them. . . .

Preparation

It is always useful for the interpreter to have some advance knowledge of the material to be translated so that unfamiliar terms can be checked and unclear concepts defined. Providing the interpreter with a copy of the text, promotional brochures about the product that is going to be sold or information about the sites to be visited is always worth the effort. If written material isn't available or if the speaker prefers to talk off-the-cuff, it is a good idea for the speaker to go over the issues that will be addressed in the discussion with the interpreter beforehand. . . .

Pacing

How long an interpreter can work without losing effectiveness depends very much on the individual.

I know a number of Americans and Chinese who can go from 8:00 in the morning until 1:00 the next morning. On the other hand, there are some people who cannot concentrate for more than a two-hour span, and need regular breaks to recharge their batteries. Obviously, knowing the interpreter's capacity in advance is very useful in planning agendas. Once discussions begin, the person in charge should look for clues that the interpreter is tiring.

Precision Versus Paraphrase

The interpreter should always be given a sense of how precise a translation is expected. For an interpreter to stay up the whole night toiling over an exact, word-for-word translation of a speech is counterproductive if the occasion does not demand it.

Another aspect of this issue is when to translate and when to leave people alone. I am of the school that believes that it is better to overtranslate than to undertranslate. There are those who feel that it is not important to translate everything that is said, especially when the conversation is not a substantive or professional one or when there are visual aids. But I think that interpreters, because they are bilingual, often forget what it is like to be in a strange land with no knowledge whatsoever of the language or culture. The non-English-speaking Chinese do not know that the spiel being given by the trainer at Sea Life Park is not all that relevant. While it might not be necessary to go into great detail in such situations, a quick paraphrase would at least give the Chinese the gist and let them know that they are not missing something really important.

Sometimes we encounter interpreters who feel the need for great precision and will take several seconds (which always seem like eons to listeners) to think of the word or phrase carrying the precise nuance of the situation. This is very commendable and certainly necessary in delicate diplomatic or business negotiations. But for general interpreting, it is more important to keep the flow of speech constant and use the closest approximation so as not to have an awkward silence (during which the speaker is apt to feel compelled to start talking again, thereby throwing the interpreter off balance).

Another kind of interpreter is the paraphraser or editor who tends to give the gist of what the speaker is saying, ignoring the details. If such actions stem from the interpreter's laziness, fatigue, or boredom, it is inexcusable. But if the interpreter "reads" the audience well enough to know that they are indeed tired or not interested, it is forgivable and indeed often desirable to speed things up a bit by omissions or condensations. For instance, before White House and Congressional tours, the National Committee escorts always tell the guides that the Chinese are generally unfamiliar with names of European sculptors, painters, and craftsmen, and with the minutiae of American history. Yet the guides cannot seem to stop themselves from cataloging who painted which portrait of a president's wife and which glass company in what year produced the goblets used by President Hayes! At such times we do not complain if the interpreters leave out some details.

In general, where one strikes a balance depends on the nature of the situation. Usually, only business or diplomatic negotiations demand a precise, word-for-word translation. In other situations, accuracy is the goal but it is permissible to paraphrase on occasion.

Supplying Background Information

Sometimes, trying to be helpful and fill in gaps in the audience's understanding, interpreters will add background information not supplied by the speaker. This is often quite useful, but the interpreter should indicate to the speaker that this has been done, especially since the speaker may have planned to give the same explanation in the very next sentence.

Length of Speech Units

Most people are not used to working with interpreters and often talk in long, rambling sentences. Forgetting to pause for translation, they leave the interpreter to scribble madly in a notebook or else to cough discreetly or in some way break into the monologue. Chinese interpreters tend to be more patient and will stand diligently taking notes until the bitter end, perhaps because they are more carefully trained or less aggressive (or more respectful of authority?) than some of their American colleagues. Occasionally the opposite will occur. In an effort to be as helpful as possible, an American speaker will give a phrase at a time, stopping in the middle of sentences and thoughts to allow the interpreter to translate. This may work in some languages, but not in Chinese. Since subject, verb, and object generally occupy different positions in many English and Chinese sentences, interpreters need to have nearly the whole sentence in hand before they set to work. Speakers should always be reminded of this problem.

Invisibility of Interpreters

Quite a few interpreters tend to speak in the third rather than in the first person. If the speaker is a proud father and wants to regale the listener with stories about his son, the interpreter should say "my son" and should not say "he says his son. . . ."

Interpreters should confine themselves to facilitating communication, and not (except in unusual situations) add their own personal comments. This is a very difficult thing to do; it is even harder when an American looks directly at the interpreter and asks questions that are meant for the delegation member: "What's the next stop on the itinerary?" "How many children do you have?" "What has impressed you most about the United States?" The interpreter knows very well that the next stop is San Francisco, that the delegation member has three children, aged 28, 24, and 18 (and even what they all do), and has heard twenty times how impressed the Chinese are with the warmth and friendliness and hospitality of Americans. But that knowledge is no excuse for not turning to the Chinese and asking once again, thus drawing the Chinese into the conversation.

Direction of Translation

It is always easier to interpret into one's native tongue from the foreign language. Diplomatic practice, however, has made the opposite the rule, based on the theory that as part of a negotiating team, an interpreter is familiar with his or her own side's position and is able to render it better than someone unfamiliar with the background. Thus when interpreters are available from both sides, it is common for American interpreters to go from English to Chinese and for Chinese interpreters to work from Chinese to English even though articulateness would be increased if this were reversed.

Numbers

Even the best Chinese and American interpreters have problems with large numbers, since the Chinese arrange digits in sets of four, as opposed to sets of three in the West. Numbers should always be checked, especially if the translation seems surprising. Writing figures down and asking the interpreter whether they are correct is the best way of guaranteeing that one hundred thousand has not become one million.

Translating Substance

It is inevitable that Americans will think and talk in their own categories, which do not necessarily have an analogue in Chinese. This can create problems, especially when the interpreter translates rather mechanistically. One way to compensate is for the Americans to learn as much as possible about China, so that they are more likely to use concepts that Chinese can understand, and, in turn, be able to better comprehend Chinese concepts.

Another dimension of this problem is the American tendency to express ideas in abstract and complex ways, while Chinese are accustomed to more concrete modes of expression. Providing a translation bridge over this gap can often prove very difficult, especially since there is no subjunctive mode in Chinese.

Questions

The above difference is particularly evident when it comes to questions. Americans often preface questions with statements and then pose their queries in a theoretical fashion. Chinese are more used to questions that are direct, down-to-earth, and pragmatic. Straightforward rather than hypothetical questions will produce better results.

Chinese, especially officials, like to listen to a whole series of questions before giving any answers. They are masters at taking eighteen different questions and then weaving one statement that conveys their message, answers those queries they wish to address, and barely touches those they wish to avoid. Americans can escape this trap by suggesting a question-by-question approach, on the grounds that the answer to one question will spark new and more interesting questions.

Nonverbal Communication

There are two ways in which body language can affect interpreter-aided communication. The first is in choosing whom one looks at. Most people tend to look at the interpreter when they really should look at the person being addressed. When listening to what is being interpreted one should try to look at the person who first said it. Doing this seems unnatural, and the Chinese are better at it than we are. Second, talking with your hands seems to aid communication. Listeners can pick up a vague idea of what it is being said even before the interpreter translates.

Helping with Problems

None of us is perfect—including interpreters. But weak points can be minimized. If the interpreter's problem is comprehension, speaking slowly will help. If it is a vocabulary problem, having a good dictionary and paraphrasing creatively are partial remedies. Once when interpreting for a Chinese delegation, I totally blanked on how to say, "The sun set." So I just said, "The sun went to sleep." They got the idea and I got a lot of laughs! Above all, interpreters should receive frequent doses of positive reinforcement and, if necessary, constructive criticism. . . .

The Hmong of Laos: Orality, Communication, and Acculturation

ROBERT SHUTER

Although human beings have inhabited this planet for between thirty thousand and fifty thousand years, the first written scripts date back to 3500 B.C. and only during the last fifteen hundred years has writing been used extensively. In fact, of three thousand reported languages currently in use, only 78 possess a written literature and hundreds may have no written component to their language.[1] Evidently orality is the foundation of all languages, with written codes emerging late in the development of most languages.

It has been argued that acquiring literacy entails more than learning how to read and write, for literacy appears to influence thinking patterns, perception, cultural values, communication style, and the social organization of societies.[2] For example, it has been reported that people from oral cultures—societies that do not have a written language—are inextricably bound to social context and are incapable of conceiving of spoken words as separate from objects or deeds.[3] Hence, unlike literates, oral people are reportedly unable to identify abstract geometric shapes or to classify objects. Instead, the shape is identified as an object familiar to them, and classification is supplanted by function (i.e., saw cuts logs). Similarly, oral and literate communication

This original essay was written for the fourth edition. All rights remain with the author. Permission to reprint must be obtained from the author. Robert Shuter teaches at Marquette University and is Director of the Center for Intercultural Communication.

may also reflect differences in social contexting, with oral people, for example, communicating in narratives bereft of detail that describe critical incidents, while literates use more sequential speech that is often abstract and nonsituational.[4]

Despite the prevalence of cultures in the developing world that are either exclusively oral or possess a high degree or orality, few field studies have been conducted on oral societies.[5] In addition, no reported research has limited its scope to the interpersonal patterns of oral people or examined how these patterns influence acculturation into a literate society, the focus of this study. Instead, reported studies on orality have been limited to ethnographic and historical analysis of oral literature and investigation of oral traditions in ancient Greece.[6]

This paper examines the influence of orality on communication and acculturation by focusing on the Hmong of Laos, a predominantly preliterate culture that has over 68,000 people living in the United States. Since many of the most recent Southeast Asian refugees who have migrated to the United States are from oral cultures, an understanding of orality in Hmong society should provide insight into the acculturation of oral people who have settled in literate societies.[7]

The immigration of the Hmong to the U.S. occurred in the late 1970s after they were attacked by Communist Laotians and Vietnamese regimes for assisting the United States during the Vietnam war. Apparently, the Hmong were trained first by the CIA and then by the American military to serve as flight personnel on bombing missions to Laos and Vietnam. They also engaged in ground surveillance and guided U.S. pilots by radio to enemy targets deep in the jungles of Laos and Vietnam. After the United States pulled out of Vietnam, Hmong villages in Laos were frequently attacked by Laotians and Vietnamese. As a result, the Hmong fled to Thailand where they lived in refugee camps.[8]

The Hmong lived isolated in the mountains of northern Laos in a traditional society characterized by slash-and-burn cultivation, a kinship-based social and political organization, and an animistic belief system consisting of spirit curing, shamanism, and ancestor worship.[9] In addition, the Hmong are essentially an oral people who had no written language until the 1950s when a missionary developed rudimentary written Hmong, which is still unfamiliar to most Hmong.

Field research for this study began in January, 1983 with the selection of 22 interviewees from the Hmong community in Milwaukee, Wisconsin where about two thousand Hmong refugees reside. Ranging in age from 31 to 68, fifteen oral and seven literate Hmong were interviewed using in-depth interview techniques.[10] Subjects were interviewed twice for approximately three hours per session; interviews were taped and then transcribed; and selected interviews were videotaped. The principal investigator conducted all interviews over eight months and was assisted by two Hmong translators.

Interviews probed various dimensions of Hmong culture, but primarily examined five research questions, the focus of the study.

1. What is the structure and content of interpersonal messages communicated in an oral society?

2. How do communicators in an oral society transmit information? Do types of communication transmission affect the selection of cultural values regarding individualism and group centeredness?

3. How do communicators in an oral society retain information?

4. Do communicators from oral societies retain distinct oral communication patterns after they become literate?

5. How do the communication patterns of an oral society affect the acculturation of oral people into a literate society?

RESULTS

Oral Hmong are narrative communicators; that is, the structure and content of their interpersonal messages is generally in the form of a story. Structurally, a typical interpersonal disclosure consists of a plot, normally a critical incident, and a cast of characters, either living or dead. Description of the event or deed is highlighted, and details about time, date, and even place are often omitted. While the content of these stories varies, the plot generally focuses on events or deeds that occurred during the communicator's day or consists of stories about past ancestors and/or memorable events.

For the older oral Hmong, the past is communicated through stories about agriculture, war, and migration—dominant historical themes—and the activities and role responsibilities of significant ancestors. Consider the following description of grandfather provided by Wang, a 68-year-old oral Hmong who has lived in the U.S. for seven years.

"My grandfather was born in Laos. He was a leader of the village when the French came to Laos. He was looked up to by the French soldiers. He was a soldier with the French in Laos."

Wang remembered his grandfather through the roles he enacted, principally soldier and village leader, and the activity he engaged in, fighting. Wang could not provide specific information about his grandfather's age, appearance, personality, or the battles in which he fought: he only seemed to know that grandfather was a leader. Similar descriptions of parents who died in Laos are provided by Hmong interviewees: "My parents taught me to be a good person. They also taught me how to do a slash and burn." Like Wang's description of his grandfather, parental memories highlighted farming or fighting activity, and never included character descriptions or other person-centered information.

Hmong communication about the present is also activity oriented and, in Laos, reportedly focused on agriculture, war, migration, climate, and cultural events like funerals, weddings, and animistic rituals. Like communication about the past, interpersonal messages transmitted in Laos generally highlighted what someone *did* and sometimes included a comment about the reactions of others.

"We talked about slash and burn and what we must do tomorrow. We talked about fighting in the war. We talked about leaving the village again. We talked about who will teach our children."

Bereft of detail, these messages focused on the main event, while time, dates, character titles, and sometimes places were normally absent from the communication.

The narrative communication style of the Hmong reflects a central world view of oral people: they tend to "totalize".[11] That is, words cannot be disconnected from deeds and events, and people cannot be separated from social context. The word and the event are one, inextricably united. As a result, the Hmong's interpersonal messages tend to be narrative, situational, activity oriented, and lacking detail, characteristics similar to the oral rhetoric of ancient Greece.[12] In contrast, the communication style of literates tends to be categorical rather than narrative, conceptual not situational. This style may reflect the contextual distance literacy bestows on the speaker, a distance that emerges from being able to think of words as being separate from objects, deeds, and events. Once disconnected from social context, the communicator can think and speak conceptually, and messages need not dwell solely on events and deeds.

Tied to social context, the Hmong culture relies strictly on people and groups to transmit information and consequently places inordinate value on these sources of information. The society is arranged sociologically and politically into groups, with clan and family the preeminent groups. In Laos the Hmong farmed in small groups, socialized in small groups and, as children, were often taught about agriculture, Hmong customs, and animistic beliefs in small groups. Without books, oral people like the Hmong learned only from others and became dependent on people and groups in the community, their only sources of information. For example, consider how the Hmong in Laos learned important cultural customs and sacred beliefs.

"Normally, when the person who knows most of the things in the community, most of the cultural things, when they realize that the man is old, people will go to his house at night and ask him to teach them. As many people that can will go to the house and learn, but they know that a lot of people can go and learn but a few can remember. So

maybe 10 or 20 will go to an elderly's house and learn at night, but probably two or three remember. And there is subject matter that they should learn at night because it is sacred, like spiritual beliefs."

Apparently, small groups were also used extensively to assist individuals to remember information, an enormous problem in oral societies. As a result, the Hmong learned all essential information about cultural events and slash-and-burn agriculture in small groups, often from an elder in the community who was known to have a good memory.

"There are so many things the old man teaches and in different ways. . . . When he realizes that he is old enough and has concerns about the next generation, he will ask the village chief and they should send some of the young men to go to his house and to work with him on the farm and learn the different types of cultural events he knows. When they are 11 to 14 they go and learn. When you and I learn together, you may remember one thing and I remember one thing; we share and discuss. In case I forget something I ask you—you may remember what I forgot. I may remember what you forgot."

In oral societies like the Hmong, learning must take place in groups since individuals do not have written material to study. Hence, individual study does not exist in an oral society, which promotes group-centered values. In contrast, literacy provides individuals with the opportunity to learn alone, since reading and writing are solitary experiences. As a result, literates are less dependent on groups for information and seem to develop a keener sense of independence than oral people. In fact, becoming literate requires individuals to separate themselves from others and instead to communicate with a new appendage—a pen or pencil. Separation from the group appears to be one of the costs of literacy and may restrict an oral person's acculturation into a literate society, an issue examined later in this paper.

As indicated earlier, memory plays a unique role in oral society: it is the only repository of the past. In

Hmong culture, for example, each clan may depend on only one or two persons who remember cultural customs and beliefs. These individuals have no title and do not belong to a particular family, social class, or caste: they are persons who are known to have an extraordinary memory, a highly valued trait.

"This is a simple society—they know each other. When they (Hmong community) learn who remembers better, that one will be famous for it, and they (Hmong community) know."

As a result, persons with excellent memories are respected and are the most credible members of the Hmong community. What appears to make these individuals unique is their retention of detail about significant customs and events, an unusual capacity in a society that communicates in narratives. For example, Hmong culture, like many oral societies, has many animistic beliefs that were practiced daily in Laos and that ranged from animal sacrifices when a new home was built to healing rituals like Kakong, an ancient verbal poem used to cure certain sicknesses and physical injuries. These shared beliefs still serve as the ideological cement that binds clan members together and distinguishes one Hmong clan from another. Not surprisingly, individuals who can remember these detailed rituals are vital members of the clan.

Because the Hmong rely strictly on memory, they usually retain deeds, events, and customs that are repeated and, hence, part of their daily activities. Moreover, the rituals that each male in Laos was supposed to retain were limited to selected activities: birth rituals, how to get married, how to arrange a wedding, funeral procedures, burying the dead, and agricultural practices. Hmong frequently communicated in Laos about these subjects, the basics of a "simple" society, and their messages tend to be repetitive, a characteristic of their present communication as well.

"Here in the United States there's a lot of difficulty in remembering, but back in Laos, in the simple society, we are able to remember. . . . In Hmong society, to me it's because it was so simple and we

use day after day most of the same thing, that helps the people to remember the different steps that we should do. For example, in the procedure of holding a ceremony or whatever, because we use day after day and it was so simple, not so complex that we could remember, but that it was so simple that we could learn easily and we can remember what we learned. And once we got it in the mind, it cannot be forgotten total."

The preceding speaker is Hmong and, though he speaks English and is literate, his message is redundant, for he repeats his thesis, that simplicity aids memory, four times in four consecutive sentences. Similar repetition patterns occur in the messages of oral and literate Hmong interviewees and they are empirical evidence of the narrative, repetitive communication style of oral communicators, a style that seems to be a product of a culture that relies on memory.

That oral and literate Hmong interviewees have similar communication styles suggests that oral stylistic patterns may not disappear after a person becomes literate. This is called residual orality, and it appears to influence more than just communication style for literate Hmong. For example, literate Hmong appear to have difficulty following written directions that explain how to perform an activity, operate a mechanical object, or assemble something. Reared in an oral culture, Hmong traditionally learned through "doing," that is, elders taught Hmong how to perform an activity by involving them in the process: learning was always experiential. For many literate Hmong, the printed word is an inadequate mode of communication, a poor substitute for the oral, experiential learning of the traditional society.

"If Hmong students used to learn by doing and if they went to school and learned just the theory, they have problems when they practice. For example, myself—when I go to school and I learn something by reading, I could understand when I read, but if I was supposed to do it by hand, I didn't know how. So I had to get help from someone in order to be able to do it."

It is difficult to determine which oral patterns of the Hmong survive literacy; nevertheless, residual orality poses additional obstacles for acculturating oral people into a literate society.

Each oral pattern of the Hmong described in this paper significantly influences their acculturation into the United States; consider their communication style, for example. Narrative and situational in nature, the Hmong communication style collides with the communication demands of a literate society that they be categorical, detailed, and, at times, abstract and conceptual. The collision takes place daily in schools and factories, government offices and social service agencies, where the Hmong are required to know birthdates, titles, time of day, definitions; in short, details and categories that are normally omitted from their communication. Lacking temporal and categorical perspective on their past and present, the Hmong cannot provide sufficiently detailed information about age, date of birth, type and dates of employment, children's birthdates—information necessary to survive in a literate society.

In schools they encounter definitions and detailed explanations of words, words that are disconnected from objects and about concepts they cannot see and touch: this is an abstract, categorical world detached from situation and nature. As a result, many older Hmong become frustrated and drop out of school, particularly the men who appear to have less experience with detail and tolerate it less than Hmong women. Females in Hmong society are responsible for cooking, a sequential, categorical activity, and for sewing, a detailed procedure consisting of putting symbolic designs on cloth. These domestic activities may account for Hmong gender differences in becoming literate, and, hence, acculturated.

Literacy threatens the very fabric of Hmong oral society, its group-centeredness, and it is another major obstacle to acculturation. For older Hmong, the very concept of independent study is alien to them, since learning always occurred in the present with cohesive groups of community people. Learning in groups of strangers, homework, independent study—hallmarks of literacy—run counter to the group-centered value of the Hmong and, as a result,

many adult Hmong have resisted literacy. For young Hmong, literacy often distances them from their families.

For example, when school-age Hmong begin public school, parents, elders, and the clan—traditionally the only sources of information—now must share their teaching role with groups of strangers: unfamiliar teachers and American peers. As Hmong students become more literate and engage in independent study, they rely less on traditional groups and more on themselves and alien others. This often divides the Hmong family: parents are disturbed by the loss of centrality and power, and often become dependent on literate children, which produces additional family tension. Sensing the consequences of schooling and literacy, Hmong elders want their children to become literate but they do not want it to affect their relationship with them, a difficult request that may impede literacy and acculturation.

Finally, residual orality poses unique acculturation problems for literate Hmong. As indicated earlier, literate Hmong, particularly adults, have difficulty following written instructions unless they are accompanied by oral explanation and demonstrations. This residual pattern, for example, may be an obstacle to certain types of job training, particularly training that is primarily theoretical. As a result, it may limit literate Hmong to occupations that are activity-oriented and taught experientially. Having fewer occupational choices, literate Hmong have less access to American jobs and to goods and services, which may impede their acculturation. Similarly, the narrative, repetitive communication style of many literate Hmong may further narrow job options, since it delays the acquisition of a mainstream American communication style, a prerequisite for employability. Stylistically different from many of their American peers, Hmong literates may have more difficulty acculturating than Southeast Asians from literate societies.

CONCLUSION

Evidently, the oral tradition of the Hmong is reflected in the structure, content, transmission, and

Table 1

	Exclusively Oral	High-Residual Orality	Low-Residual Orality
Structure of message	Narrative; critical incident; high repetition	Narrative; critical incident; high repetition	Categorical/sequential; detailed; low repetition
Content of message	Situational topics	Primarily situational topics	Abstract and situational topics
	Low in temporal and chronological data	Low in temporal and chronological data	High in temporal and chronological data
Transmission of message	Interpersonal interaction: small group interaction; value group relations	Interpersonal interaction; small group interaction; additional media secondary; value group relations	Multiple media: priority on mass media; value individualism
Retention of message	Memory	Primarily memory	Multiple media
Communication world view	Words, objects, and events inseparable	Words, objects, and events closely connected	Words, objects, and events separate

retention of interpersonal communication. And because these oral patterns seem to collide with the values of a literate society and the expected communication of literates, they seem to slow the acculturation of the Hmong into a literate society. This is significant, since a sizable percentage of recent Southeast Asian refugees, possibly as high as 80%, are either exclusively oral or predominantly oral, having grown up in rural oral villages in countries that have a written language, but few schools outside large cities. It is likely that oral patterns and acculturation problems described for the Hmong may be shared by many of the recent Southeast Asian refugees and by others who have migrated from South and Central America, the Middle East, Asia, and Africa, where there seem to be high levels of orality and residual orality.[13]

Conceptually, orality has unique implications for furthering our understanding of communication across cultures. For example, oral cultures may possess significantly different values and communication patterns from literate societies. By being able to classify cultures along an orality continuum, consist-

ing of exclusively oral, high-residual orality, and low-residual orality, a researcher should be able to predict potential intercultural misunderstandings and conflicts. To determine how to classify a culture, communication characteristics of a society can be compared with the list of oral interaction patterns in Table 1, generated from the preceding study.

The table indicates that communicators in each of the three categories may differ in five communication areas: structure of message, content of message, transmission of message, retention of message, and communication world view. In terms of the structure and content of the message, exclusively oral and high-residual oral speakers tend to be narrative communicators emphasizing situational topics, with little temporal and chronological data provided. In contrast, low-residual communicators tend to structure messages categorically and generally provide chronological and temporal information. Societies that are placed in each category also differ in the way information is normally transmitted: exclusively oral and high-residual oral cultures rely primarily on face-to-face interaction, while low-residual oral societies use multiple media to transmit messages, including print and electronic channels. Reliance on face-to-face transmission in exclusively oral and high-residual oral societies produces group-centered values; in contrast, low-residual oral societies tend to be more individualistic. Without print, exclusively oral cultures depend on memory to retain information. High-residual oral cultures also rely heavily on memory and may also employ other media as a repository of information, though they are of less importance. In contrast, low-residual oral cultures use multiple media to retain information and tend to stress print and electronic media. Finally, communicators from exclusively oral and high-residual oral cultures have varying degrees of difficulty separating spoken words from objects and events and, hence, are tied to social context. Speakers from low-residual oral societies can disconnect words from objects and events.

This paradigm can be used in a variety of ways. For example, in intercultural transactions, researchers may be able to identify areas of potential communication conflict and misunderstandings, once the communicators' cultures have been classified. Similarly, acculturation problems due to differences in degrees of orality can be isolated with greater ease. Potentially useful, this paradigm should be tested in future studies to determine with greater certainty both the communication patterns of the three types of oral societies and systematic methods for classifying world cultures.

NOTES

1. Munro E. Edmonson, *Lore: An Introduction to the Science of Fiction* (New York: Holt, Rinehart and Winston, 1971).

2. See, for example, John Foley, "The Traditional Oral Audience," *Balkan Studies* 18, 145–153; Jack Goody, *Literacy in Traditional Societies* (Cambridge, England: Cambridge University Press, 1968); Walter Ong, *Orality and Literacy* (London: Methuen, 1982); Sylvia Scriber and Michael Cole, "Literacy Without Schooling: Testing for Intellectual Effects," *Harvard Educational Review* 48, 1978, 448–461.

3. Aleksandr Romanovich Luria, *Cognitive Development: Its Cultural and Social Foundations*, ed. Michael Cole (Cambridge, Mass.: Harvard University Press, 1976).

4. Ibid.

5. See, for example, Roger Abrahams, "The Training of the Man of Words in Talking Sweet," *Language in Society* 1, 15–29; John Miles Foley, "The Traditional Oral Audience," *Balkan Studies* 18, 1977, 145–153; Aleksandr Romanovich Luria, *Cognitive Development: Its Cultural and Social Foundations*, ed. Michael Cole (Cambridge, Mass.: Harvard University Press, 1976).

6. See, for example, Ruth Finnegan, *Oral Literature in Africa* (Oxford: Clarendon Press, 1970); Eric Havelock, "The Ancient Art of Oral Poetry," *Philosophy and Rhetoric* 19, 187–202, 1979.

7. It is difficult to ascertain the exact percentage of Southeast Asian refugees who are either exclusively oral or predominantly oral. But since most of the recent refugees migrated from rural communities where there were no schools, it has been estimated that most of them are predominantly oral, particularly women, who generally did not receive education even when it was available.

8. Robert William Geddes, *Migrants of the Mountains: The Cultural Ecology of the Blue Miau (Hmong) of Thailand* (Oxford: Clarendon Press, 1976).

9. Timothy Dunnigan, "Segmentary Kinship in an Urban Society: The Hmong of St. Paul, Minneapolis," *Anthropological Quarterly*, 1981, 126–133.

10. Lewis Dexter, *Elite and Specialized Interviewing* (Evanston, Ill.: Northwestern University Press, 1971).

11. Walter Ong, *Orality and Literacy* (London: Methuen, 1982), p. 56.

12. Ibid, pp. 16–30.

13. Walter Ong first used the term residual orality and argues that contemporary cultures have different degrees of residual orality. See Walter Ong, *Orality and Literacy* (London: Methuen, 1982), pp. 28–29.

The Need to Be: The Socio-Cultural Significance of Black Language

SHIRLEY N. WEBER

"Hey blood, what it is? Ah, Man, ain't notin to it but to do it."
"Huney, I done told ya, God, he don't lak ugly."
"Look-a-there. I ain't seen nothin like these economic indicators."

From the street corners to the church pew to the board room, black language is used in varying degrees. It is estimated that 80 to 90 percent of all black Americans use the black dialect as least some of the time.[1] However, despite its widespread use among blacks at all social and economic levels, there continues to be concern over its validity and continued use. Many of the concerns arise from a lack of knowledge and appreciation for the history of black language and the philosophy behind its use.

Since the publication of J. L. Dillard's book *Black English* in 1972, much has been written on the subject of black language. Generally, the research focuses on the historical and linguistic validity of black English, and very little has been devoted to the communications and cultural functions black language serves in the black community. It seems obvious that given the fact that black English is not "formally" taught in schools to black children and, yet, has widespread use among blacks, it must serve some important functions in the black community

that represents the blacks' unique experience in America. If black language served no important function, it would become extinct like other cultural relics because all languages are functional tools that change and adapt to cultural and technological demands. If they cease to do this, they cease to exist as living languages. (The study of the English language's evolution and expansion over the last hundred years, to accommodate changing values and technological advancements, is a good example.) This article looks at the "need to be," the significance of black language to black people.

One's language is a model of his or her culture and of that culture's adjustment to the world. All cultures have some form of linguistic communications; without language, the community would cease to exist. To deny that a people has a language to express its unique perspective of the world is to deny its humanity. Furthermore, the study of language is a study of the people who speak that language and of the way they bring order to the chaos of the world. Consequently, the study of black language is really an examination of African people and of their adjustment to the conditions of American slavery. Smitherman says that black English (dialect) is

an Africanized form of English reflecting Black America's linguistic-cultural African heritage and the conditions of servitude, oppression and life in America. . . .

(It) is a language mixture, adapted to the conditions of slavery and discrimination, a combination of language and style interwoven with and inextricable from Afro-American culture.[2]

Much has been written about the origins of black language, and even though the issue seems to be resolved for linguists, the rest of the world is still lingering under false assumptions about it. Basically, there are two opposing views: one that says there was African influence in the development of the language and the other that says there was not. Those who reject African influence believe that the African arrived in the United States and tried to speak English. And, because he lacked certain intellectual and physical attributes, he failed. This hypothesis makes no attempt to examine the phonological and grammatical structures of West African languages to see if there are any similarities. It places the African in a unique position unlike any other immigrant to America. Linguistic rationales and analyses are given for every other group that entered America pronouncing words differently and/or structuring their sentences in a unique way. Therefore, when the German said *zis* instead of *this*, America understood. But, when the African said *dis*, no one considered the fact that consonant combinations such as *th* may not exist in African languages.

Countering this dialectical hypothesis is the creole hypothesis that, as a result of contact between Africans and Europeans, a new language formed that was influenced by both languages. This language took a variety of forms, depending on whether there was French, Portuguese, or English influence. There is evidence that these languages were spoken on the west coast of Africa as early as the sixteenth century (before the slave trade). This hypothesis is further supported by studies of African languages that demonstrate the grammatical, phonological, and rhythmic similarities between them and black English. Thus, the creole hypothesis says that the African responded to the English language as do all other non-English speakers: from the phonological and grammatical constructs of the native language.

The acceptance of the creole hypothesis is the first step toward improving communications with blacks. However, to fully understand and appreciate black language and its function in the black community, it is essential to understand some general African philosophies about language and communications, and then to see how they are applied in the various styles and forms of black communications.

In Janheinz Jahn's *Muntu*, basic African philosophies are examined to give a general overview of African culture. It is important to understand that while philosophies that govern the different groups in Africa vary, some general concepts are found throughout African cultures. One of the primary principles is the belief that everything has a reason for being. Nothing simply exists without purpose or consequences. This is the basis of Jahn's explanation of the four basic elements of life, which are

Muntu, mankind; Kintu, things; Hantu, place and time; and Kuntu, modality. These four elements do not exist as static objects but as forces that have consequences and influence. For instance, in Hantu, the West is not merely a place defined by geographic location, but a force that influences the East, North, and South. Thus, the term "Western world" connotes a way of life that either complements or challenges other ways of life. The Western world is seen as a force and not a place. (This is applicable to the other three elements also.)

Muntu, or man, is distinguished from the other three elements by his possession of Nommo, the magical power of the word. Without Nommo, nothing exists. Consequently, mankind, the possessor of Nommo, becomes the master of all things.

All magic is word magic, incantations and exorcism, blessings and curse. Through Nommo, the word, man establishes his mastery over things. . . .

If there were no word all forces would be frozen, there would be no procreation, no changes, no life. . . . For the word holds the course of things in train and changes and transforms them. And since the word has this power every word is an effective word, every word is binding. And the muntu is responsible for his word.[3]

Nommo is so powerful and respected in the black community that only those who are skillful users of the word become leaders. One of the main qualifications of leaders of black people is that they must be able to articulate the needs of the people in a most eloquent manner. And because Muntu is a force who controls Nommo, which has power and consequences, the speaker must generate and create movement and power within his listeners. One of the ways this is done is through the use of imaginative and vivid language. Of the five canons of speech, it is said that Inventio or invention is the most utilized in black American. Molefi Asante called it the "coming to be of the novel," or the making of the new. So that while the message might be the same, the analogies, stories, images, and so forth must be fresh, new, and alive.

Because nothing exists without Nommo, it, too, is the force that creates a sense of community among communicators, so much so that the speaker and audience become one as senders and receivers of the message. Thus, an audience listening and responding to a message is just as important as the speaker, because without their "amens" and "right-ons" the speaker may not be successful. This interplay between speaker and listeners is called "call and response" and is a part of the African world view, which holds that all elements and forces are interrelated and indistinguishable because they work together to accomplish a common goal and to create a sense of community between the speaker and the listeners.

This difference between blacks and whites was evident, recently, in a class where I lectured on Afro-American history. During the lecture, one of my more vocal black students began to respond to the message with some encouraging remarks like "all right," "make it plain," "that all right," and "teach." She was soon joined by a few more black students who gave similar comments. I noticed that this surprised and confused some of the white students. When questioned later about this, their response was that they were not used to having more than one person talk at a time, and they really could not talk and listen at the same time. They found the comments annoying and disruptive. As the lecturer, I found the comments refreshing and inspiring. The black student who initiated the responses had no difficulty understanding what I was saying while she was reacting to it, and did not consider herself "rude."

In addition to the speaker's verbal creativity and the dynamic quality of the communication environment, black speech is very rhythmic. It flows like African languages in a consonant-vowel-consonant-vowel pattern. To achieve this rhythmic effect, some syllables are held longer and are accented stronger and differently from standard English, such as DE-troit. This rhythmic pattern is learned early by young blacks and is reinforced by the various styles it complements.

With this brief background into the historical and philosophical foundation of black language, we can examine some of the styles commonly employed and their role in African-American life.

Among the secular styles, the most common is *rappin'*. Although the term *rappin'* is currently used by whites to mean simply talking (as in *rap sessions*), it originally described the dialogue between a man and a woman where the main intention is to win the admiration of the woman. A man's success in rappin' depends on his ability to make creative and imaginative statements that generate interest on the part of the woman to hear more of the rap. And, although she already knows his intentions, the ritual is still played out; and, if the rap is weak, he will probably lose the woman.

To outsiders, rappin' might not appear to be an important style in the black community, but it is very important and affects the majority of black people because at some time in a black person's life, he or she will be involved in a situation where rappin' will take place. For, in the black community, it is the mating call, the introduction of the male to the female, and it is ritualistically expected by black women. So that while it is reasonable to assume that all black males will not rise to the level of "leader" in the black community because only a few will possess the unique oral skills necessary, it can be predicted that black men will have to learn how to "rap" to a woman.

Like other forms of black speech, the rap is rhythmic and has consequences. It is the good *rapper* who *gets over* (scores). And, as the master of Nommo, the rapper creates, motivates, and changes conditions through his language. It requires him to be imaginative and capable of responding to positive and negative stimuli immediately. For instance:

R: Hey Mama, how you doing?

L: Fine.

R: Yeah, I can see! (looking her up and down) Say, you married?

L: Yes.

R: Is your husband married? (bringing humor and doubt)

The rap requires participation by the listener. Thus, the speaker will ask for confirmation that the listener is following his line of progression. The rap is an old style that is taught to young men early. And, while each male will have his own style of rappin' that will adapt to the type of woman he is rappin' to, a poor, unimaginative rap is distasteful and often repulsive to black women.

Runnin' it down is a form of rappin' without sexual overtones. It is simply explaining something in great detail. The speaker's responsibility is to vividly recreate the event or concept for the listener so that there is complete agreement and understanding concerning the event. The speaker gives accurate descriptions of the individuals involved, describing them from head to toe. Every object and step of action is minutely described. To an outsider this might sound boring and tedious. However, it is the responsibility of the speaker to use figurative language to keep the listener's attention. In a narrative of a former slave from Tennessee, the following brief excerpt demonstrates the vivid language used in runnin' it down:

I remember Mammy told me about one master who almost starved his slaves. Mighty stingy I reckon he was.

Some of them slaves was so poorly thin they ribs would kinda rustle against each other like corn stalks a-drying in the hot winds. But they gets even one hog killing time, and it was funny, too, Mammy said.[4]

Runnin' it down is not confined to secular styles. In C. L. Franklin's sermon, "The Eagle Stirreth Her Nest"—the simple story of an eagle, mistaken for a chicken, that grows up and is eventually set free—the story becomes a drama that vividly takes the listener through each stage of the eagle's development. And even when the eagle is set free because she can no longer live in a cage, she does not simply fly away. Instead, she flies from one height to the other, surveying the surroundings, and then flies away. The details are so vivid that the listener can "see" and "feel" the events. Such is the style and the effect of runnin' it down.

Another common style of black language is *the dozens*. The dozens is a verbal battle of insults between speakers. The term dozens was used during slavery to refer to a selling technique used by slavers. If an individual had a disability, he was considered "damaged goods" and was sold with eleven other "damaged" slaves at a discount rate. The term dozens refers to negative physical characteristics. To an outsider, the dozens might appear cruel and harsh. But to members of the black community, it is the highest form of verbal warfare and impromptu speaking. The game is often played in jest.

When the dozens is played, there is usually a group of listeners that serves as judge and jury over the originality, creativity, and humor of the comments. The listeners encourage continuation of the contest by giving comments like "Ou, I wouldn't take that," "Cold," "Rough," "Stale," or any statement that assesses the quality of the comments and encourages response. The battle continues until someone wins. This is determined by the loser giving up and walking away, or losing his cool and wanting to fight. When a physical confrontation occurs, the winner is not determined by the fight, but by the verbal confrontation. The dozens is so popular that a rock 'n' roll group made a humorous recording of insults between friends. Some of the exchanges were:

Say Man, your girlfriend so ugly, she had to sneak up on a glass to get a drink of water.

Man, you so ugly, yo mamma had to put a sheet over your head so sleep could sneak up on you.

The dozens, like other forms of black language, calls on the speaker to use words to create moods. More than any other form, it pits wit against wit, and honors the skillful user of Nommo.

The final secular style to be discussed is proverbial wisdom. Sayings are used in the black community as teaching tools to impart values and truths. Their use demonstrates the African-American's respect for the oral tradition in teaching and socializing the young. Popular phrases, such as "what goes around comes around," "if you make you bed hard you gon lay in it," "God don't like ugly," and "a hard head make a soft behind," are used in everyday conversation by blacks from all social, economic, and educational strata. At some time in a black child's life, the sayings are used to teach them what life expects of them and what they can expect in return. It is also used to expose the truth in an artful and less offensive manner, such as "you don't believe fat meat is greasy." In this saying the listener is being put down for having a narrow or inaccurate view of things. And while it might appear that proverbial wisdoms are static, they are constantly changing and new ones are being created. One of the latest is said when you believe someone is lying to you or "putting you on." It is, "pee on my head and tell me it's raining." Or, if someone is talking bad about you, you might say, "don't let your mouth write a check your ass can't cash." Proverbial wisdom can be found on every socioeconomic level in the black community, and it is transmitted from generation to generation. Listening to speech that is peppered with proverbial sayings might seem strange to nonblacks. But, because proverbial sayings are generally accepted as "truths" because they are taught to children at a very early age, they effectively sum up events and predict outcome.

Like the secular, the nonsecular realm places a tremendous emphasis on the creative abilities of the speaker. The speaker (preacher) creates experiences for his listeners, who are participants in the communication event. The minister calls and his audience responds, and at some point they become one. The minister actively seeks his audience's involvement and when he does not receive it, he chides and scolds them. The audience also believes that the delivery of a good sermon is dependent upon them encouraging the minister with their "amens" and "right-ons." And if the minister preaches false doctrine, the audience also feels obliged to tell him, "Uh, oh Reb, you done gone too far now!"

The language used by the minister, who is probably very fluent in standard English, is generally seasoned with black English. Seldom will you hear the term *Lord* used, but you will hear *Lawd* because the *Lord* is the man in the big house who is an overseer, but the *Lawd* is a friend who walks, talks, and comforts you. The relationship between the *Lawd* and his people is more personal than the *Lord*'s.

Also, the speaker may overaccent a word for black emphasis. In C. L. Franklin's sermon, he said,

"*extra*-ordinary sight." He then came right back and said *extraordinary*, to demonstrate that he knew how to "correctly" enunciate the word. The nonsecular style of speech is generally the most dramatic of all forms and has the highest degree of audience participation. It encompasses all the elements of black language, and of all the styles it is the most African in form.

Black language and the numerous styles that have been developed are indications of the African-American's respect for the spoken word. The language has often been called a hieroglyphic language because of the vivid picture created by the speaker for the listener about the activities or feelings taking place. To say someone is "all jawed up," or "smacking on some barnyard pimp," or "ready to hat," is more imaginative and creative than saying they had "nothin to say," or "eating chicken," or "ready to leave." The responsibility of the speaker and the listener to participate in the communication event also emphasizes the African world view, which stresses the interrelatedness of all things to each other. And finally, the dynamics of the communication, and the responsibility of man as the user of Nommo, places communication and the spoken word in the arena of forces and not static objects. The rhythm and flow of the language approximates the style and flow and unity of African life.

Despite all of the explanation of the Africanness found in black language, many continue to ask, why use it? Why do blacks who have lived in America for hundreds of years continue to speak "black"? Why do those who possess degrees of higher learning and even write scholarly articles and books in standard English continue to talk "black"?

There are many reasons for the continued use of black language. A language expresses an experience. If the experiences of a group are culturally unique, the group will need a different vocabulary to express them. If white folks in white churches don't *get happy* because they have been socialized to be quiet listeners in church, then they don't have the vocabulary that blacks have to describe levels of spiritual possession. And if they do not have curly hair, they probably do not *press* their hair or worry about *catching up* their *kitchins*. Thus, because blacks experience the world differently from other groups in America, there is a need for a language that communicates that experience.

Secondly, black language reaches across the superficial barriers of education and social position. It is the language that binds, that creates community for blacks, so that the brother in the three-piece Brooks Brothers suit can go to the local corner where folks "hang out" and say, "hey, blood, what it is?", and be one with them. Additionally, the minister's use of black language reminds the listeners of their common experiences and struggles (for example, "I been thur the storm"). Through black language, barriers that separate blacks are lowered and they are finally "home" with each other. So, for cultural identity, the code is essential to define the common elements among them.

Finally, black language usage stands as a political statement that black people are African people who have not given up a vital part of themselves in slavery: their language. They have retained the cultural link that allows them to think and to express themselves in a non-European form. As an old adage says, The namer of names is the father of things. Thus, the ability of blacks to maintain and sustain a living language shows their control over that aspect of their lives, and their determination to preserve the culture. The use of black language is the black man's defiance of white America's total indoctrination. The use of black language by choice is a reflection not of a lack of intelligence, but of a desire to retain and preserve black life styles.

The purpose of this discussion is to help others understand and appreciate black language styles and the reasons blacks speak the way they do, in hopes of building respect for cultural difference. Now the question may be asked, what does the general society do about it? Some might ask, should whites learn black English? To that question comes a resounding *no*! Black language is, first of all, not a laboratory language and it cannot be learned in a classroom. And even if you could learn definition and grammar, you would not learn the art of creative expression that is taught when you're "knee high to a duck." Thus, you would miss the elements of rhythm and style, and you would sound like invaders or foreigners.

What one should do about the language is be open-minded and not judge the speaker by European standards of expression. If you're in a classroom and the teacher is *gettin down*, don't *wig out* because the black student says "teach." Simply realize that you must become listening participants. If some *bloods* decide to use a double negative or play *the dozens*, don't assume some social theory about how they lack a father image in the home and are therefore culturally and linguistically deprived. You just might discover that they are the authors of your college English text.

The use of black language does not represent any pathology in blacks. It simply says that, as African people transplanted to America, they are a different flower whose aroma is just as sweet as other flowers. The beginning of racial understanding is the acceptance that difference is just what it is: different, not inferior. And equality does not mean sameness.

NOTES

1. Geneva Smitherman. *Talkin' and Testifyin'.* (1972). Boston: Houghton Mifflin Company, p. 2.

2. Ibid., p. 3.

3. Janheinz Jahn. *Muntu.* (1961). New York: Grove Press, Inc., pp. 132–133.

4. Smitherman, *Talkin' and Testifyin'*, p. 156.

CONCEPTS AND QUESTIONS
FOR CHAPTER 5

1. Can you think of examples that would demonstrate the validity of linguistic relativity?

2. What is meant by the sentence, "Language is a guide to social reality"?

3. Can you think of some arguments that would disprove the concept of linguistic relativity?

4. What intercultural difficulties could arise as a result of different speaking styles when American and Japanese business persons are engaged in policy development?

5. In what manner does culture influence the spoken aspects of decision making in Asian countries?

6. How does the bridge concept help us understand the role of language in intercultural communication?

7. Some people have suggested that the problems associated with translation could be solved if everyone spoke the same universal language. Evaluate this view in light of the influence culture has on language.

8. What do you consider to be the difference between translating and interpreting?

9. What are the advantages of having an interpreter who is aware of nonverbal behaviors as well as verbal behaviors?

10. Suggest ways that people might learn about the experiential aspects of other cultures that lead to unique language differences.

11. What is black language and how does it function within the black community?

12. What are the "dozens" and what purpose does this activity play in the black community?

13. Drawing from your own experiences, can you think of any examples that demonstrate the idea that cultures often use different problem-solving techniques?

14. What might be some other cultural differences in left- and right-brain hemisphere activity not mentioned by Lieberman?

15. What does Shuter mean when he writes, "Conceptually, orality has unique implications for furthering our understanding of communication across cultures"?

6

Nonverbal Interaction: Action, Sound, and Silence

Successful participation in intercultural communication requires that we recognize and understand culture's influence not only on verbal interaction but on *nonverbal* interaction as well. Nonverbal behaviors, just as do verbal behaviors, constitute messages to which people attach meaning. Because nonverbal symbols are derived from such diverse behaviors as body movements, postures, facial expressions, gestures, eye movements, physical appearance, the use and organization of space, and the structuralization of time, these symbolic behaviors often vary from culture to culture. An awareness of the role of nonverbal behaviors is crucial, therefore, if we are to appreciate all aspects of intercultural interaction.

Nonverbal behavior is largely unconscious. We use nonverbal symbols spontaneously, without thinking about what posture, what gesture, or what interpersonal distance is appropriate to the situation. These factors are critically important in intercultural communication because, as with other aspects of the communication process, nonverbal behaviors are subject to cultural variation. These nonverbal behaviors can be categorized in two ways.

In the first, culture tends to determine the specific nonverbal behaviors that represent or symbolize specific thoughts, feelings, or states of the communicator. Thus, what might be a sign of greeting in one culture could very well be an obscene gesture in another. Or what might be a symbol of affirmation in one culture could be meaningless or even signify negation in another. In the second, culture determines when it is appropriate to display or communicate various thoughts, feelings, or internal states; this is particularly evident in the display of emotions. Although there seems to be little cross-cultural difference in the behaviors that represent emotional states, there are great cultural differences in which emotions may be displayed, by whom, and when or where they may be displayed.

As important as verbal language is to a communication event, nonverbal communication is just as, if not more, important. Nonverbal messages tell us how other messages are to be interpreted. They indicate whether verbal messages are true, joking, serious, threatening, and so on. Gregory Bateson has described these "second-order messages" as meta communication, which we use as frames around messages to designate how they are to be interpreted.* The importance of meta communication can be seen from communication research indicating that as much as 90 percent of the social content of a message is transmitted paralinguistically or nonverbally.†

Chapter 6 deals with nonverbal interaction. The readings examine the influence of culture on various aspects of nonverbal behavior in order to demonstrate the variety of culturally derived nonverbal behaviors and the underlying value structures that produce these behaviors.

As in the previous chapter, which dealt with verbal language, we begin this chapter with an overview. Peter Andersen's article "Explaining Intercultural Differences in Nonverbal Communication" begins with an analysis of how culture determines our nonverbal communicative behavior. Andersen goes beyond a mere cataloging of differences in nonverbal communication and offers us insights into cultural explanations for a variety of nonverbal communication differences.

In Chapter 3 we noted that the experiences of men and women often produce some significant differences in values, attitudes, and communication patterns. One of these major differences is found in the area of nonverbal communication. More specifically, researchers have found sex differences in all the categories normally associated with nonverbal behavior. In "Sex Differences in Nonverbal Communication," Barbara Westbrook

Eakins and R. Gene Eakins review these research findings. Male-female comparisons are made for eye contact, facial expressions, posture and bearing, gestures, clothing, grooming and physical appearance, use of space, and touch. Being aware of and knowing how these sex differences in nonverbal behavior operate during interaction should be helpful to both women and men as they attempt to exchange ideas, information, and feelings with one another.

One of the major themes of this volume is that culture touches nearly every phase of the communication process. While seldom viewed in the West as an ingredient of communication, silence also affects communication. The main focus of the next essay is the special link between culture and silence. In "Silence and Silences in Cross-Cultural Perspective: Japan and the United States," Satoshi Ishii and Tom Bruneau discuss the cultural bases of silence, define the concept of silence, and then compare how the East and West use silence as a form of communication. Their analysis of East-West differences in the use of silence goes a long way toward helping us understand the problems that can exist in American-Japanese intercultural communication when the role and function of silence is not understood by both sides.

Our next essay examines a culture's use of space as yet another aspect of human interaction. The assumption behind this analysis is that our use of space is a message that transmits meaning to those around us. As noted in several selections in this chapter, our perception of space and the use we make of it are directly related to our culture. This relationship is documented and illustrated by Carol Zinner Dolphin in her article "Variables in the Use of Personal Space in Intercultural Transactions." Dolphin, like the editors of this book, conceives of a culture as more than simply the country one calls home; she therefore includes the influence of age, sex, relationships, environment, and ethnicity on the communication encounter. Dolphin concludes by presenting a number of suggestions for further research. She believes that the issues raised by these questions will increase our

*Gregory Bateson, "A Theory of Play and Fantasy," *Psychiatric Research* 2 (1955), 39–51.
†Albert Mehrabian and Morton Wiener, "Decoding in Inconsistent Messages," *Journal of Personality and Social Psychology* 6 (1967), 109–114.

understanding of the link between culture, communication, and space.

In our final essay, Edward T. Hall looks at the conscious and unconscious ways cultures use time. Hall maintains that cultures organize and respond to time in two different ways, which he refers to as Polychronic (P-time) and Monochronic (M-time). While these systems are not meant to be perceived as either/or categories, they do offer two distinct approaches to time. Cultures such as those found in the Mediterranean, Africa, and South America are P-time cultures in that they do many things at the same time, are more concerned with people and the present moment than with schedules, and believe that they are in command of time rather than being controlled by it. M-time cultures of Northern Europe and North America, on the other hand, emphasize schedules, the segmentation of time, and promptness. It is easy to imagine the potential for misunderstanding when people from these diverse orientations come together. Hall's essay helps us avoid communication problems by introducing us to the many forms these two interaction patterns take.

Explaining Intercultural Differences in Nonverbal Communication

PETER ANDERSEN

Culture has been equated with communication by a number of scholars. Culture and communication are inseparable because culture is both learned and maintained through human interaction (Andersen, Lustig, and Andersen, 1986; Prosser, 1978; Saral, 1977). Moreover, culture is primarily a nonverbal phenomenon because most aspects of one's culture are learned through observation and imitation rather than explicit verbal instruction or expression. The primary level of culture is communicated implicitly, without awareness, by primarily nonverbal means (Hall, 1984).

Intercultural communication occurs when two or more individuals with different cultural backgrounds interact. This process is rarely smooth and problem free. In most situations, intercultural interactants do not share the same language, but languages can be learned and larger communication problems occur in the *nonverbal* realm. Nonverbal communication is a subtle, multidimensional, and usually spontaneous process (Andersen, 1986). Indeed, individuals are not aware of most of their own nonverbal behavior, which is enacted mindlessly, spontaneously, and unconsciously (Andersen, 1986; Burgoon, 1985; Samovar and Porter, 1985). Since we are not usually aware of our *own* nonverbal behavior, it is extremely difficult to identify and master the nonverbal behavior of another culture. At times we feel uncomfortable in other cultures because we intuitively know something isn't right. "Because nonverbal behaviors are rarely conscious phenomena, it may be difficult for us to know exactly why we are feeling uncomfortable" (Gudykunst and Kim, 1984, p. 149).

This article reviews briefly the codes of nonverbal communication, locates culture as a part of interpersonal behavior, then discusses five main dimensions of cultural variation, including *immediacy, individualism, masculinity, power distance,* and *high* and *low context*. It is argued that each of these dimensions produces differences in a culture's communication, particularly in a culture's nonverbal communication.

NONVERBAL CODES

Most discussions of nonverbal intercultural communication take an anecdotal approach, where numerous examples of intercultural differences for each nonverbal code are discussed in detail. Recapitulation of the various nonverbal codes of intercultural communication is not a primary purpose of the present article. Thus each code will be discussed only briefly along with references that provide detailed and excellent analyses of how each nonverbal code differs interculturally.

Two of the most fundamental nonverbal differences in intercultural communication involve space and time. *Chronemics*—or the study of meanings, usage, and communication of time—is probably the most discussed and well-researched nonverbal code in the intercultural literature (Bruneau, 1979; Burgoon and Saine, 1978; Gudykunst and Kim, 1984; Hall, 1959, 1976, 1984; Malandro and Barker, 1983; Merriam, 1983). The analyses suggest that the time frames of various cultures differ so dramatically that even if only chronemic differences existed, intercultural misunderstandings would still be abundant. A second nonverbal code that has attracted considerable attention is *proxemics*, the communication of interpersonal space and distance. Research has documented that cultures differ substantially in their use of personal space, the dis-

tances they maintain, and their regard for territory, as well as the meanings they assign to proxemic behavior (Burgoon and Saine, 1978; Gudykunst and Kim, 1984; Hall, 1959, 1976; Malandro and Barker, 1983; Samovar, Porter, and Jain, 1981; Scheflen 1974).

Many intercultural differences have been reported in people's *kinesic* behavior, including their facial expressions, body movements, gestures, and conversational regulators (Burgoon and Saine, 1978; Gudykunst and Kim, 1984; Hall, 1976; Jensen, 1985; Malandro and Barker, 1983; Rich, 1974; Samovar, Porter, and Jain, 1981; Scheflen, 1974). Interpersonal patterns of tactile communication called *haptics* also reveal substantial intercultural differences (Andersen and Leibowitz, 1978; Malandro and Barker, 1983; Prosser, 1978; Samovar, Porter, and Jain, 1981).

Other important codes of nonverbal communication have attracted considerably less space in publications on nonverbal intercultural communication. *Physical appearance*, the most important nonverbal code during initial encounters, is of obvious importance because many intercultural encounters are based on stereotypes and are of short duration. Some discussion of intercultural differences in appearance is provided by Scheflen (1974) and Samovar, Porter, and Jain (1981). *Oculesics*—the study of messages sent by the eyes, including eye contact, blinks, eye movements, and pupil dilation—has received only marginal attention by intercultural communication scholars (Gudykunst and Kim, 1984; Jensen, 1985; Samovar, Porter, and Jain, 1981). Since eye contact has been called an "invitation to communicate," the way it varies cross-culturally is an important communication topic. *Vocalics* or *paralanguage*—the nonverbal elements of the voice—also has received comparatively little attention from intercultural researchers (Gudykunst and Kim, 1984; LaBarre, 1985; Rich, 1974; Scheflen, 1974; Samovar, Porter, and Jain, 1981). Music and singing—a universal form of aesthetic communication—has been almost completely overlooked in intercultural research except for one excellent study (Lomax, 1968) that identified several groups of worldwide cultures through differences and similarities in folk songs. Finally, *olfactics*—the

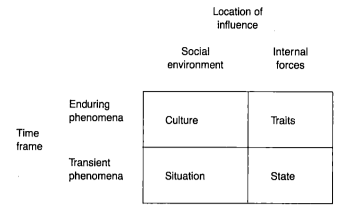

Location of
influence

		Social environment	Internal forces
Time frame	Enduring phenomena	Culture	Traits
	Transient phenomena	Situation	State

Figure 1 Sources of Influence on Interpersonal Behavior

study of the interpersonal communication via smell—has been virtually ignored in intercultural research despite its importance (Samovar, Porter, and Jain, 1981).

LOCATING CULTURE IN INTERPERSONAL BEHAVIOR

Culture is a critical concept to communication scholars because every communicator is a product of her or his culture. Culture, along with traits, situations, and states, is one of the four primary sources of interpersonal behavior (Andersen, 1987a, 1987b) (see Figure 1). Culture is the enduring influence of the social environment on one's behavior, including one's interpersonal communication behavior. Culture exerts a considerable force on individual behavior through what Geetz (1973) called "control mechanisms—plans, recipes, rules, instructions (what computer engineers call 'programs')— for the governing of behavior" (p. 44). Culture has similar powerful, though not identical, effects on all residents of a cultural system. "Culture can be behaviorally observed by contrasting intragroup homogeneity with intergroup heterogeneity" (Andersen, Lustig, and Andersen, 1986, p. 11).

Culture has been confused with personal traits because both are enduring phenomena (Andersen, 1987a, 1987b). Traits have multiple causes (An-

dersen, 1987b), only some of which are the result of culture. Culture has also been confused with the situation because both are part of one's social environment. However, culture is an enduring phenomenon whereas the situation is a transient one with an observable beginning and end. Culture is one of the most enduring, powerful, and invisible shapers of our behavior.

DIMENSIONS OF CULTURAL VARIATION

Thousands of anecdotes regarding misunderstandings caused by nonverbal behaviors between persons from different cultures have been reported. While it may be useful to know that Arabs stand closer to one another than do Americans, that the Swiss are more time-conscious than the Italians, and that Orientals value silence more than Westerners, this anecdotal approach is not sufficient. Because the number of potential pairs of cultures is huge, and because the number of possible misunderstandings based on nonverbal behavior between each pair of cultures is similarly large, millions of potential intercultural anecdotes are possible. What is needed is some way to organize and understand this plethora of potential problems in intercultural communication. Some initial research has shown that cultures can be located along dimensions that help to explain these intercultural differences. Most cultural differences in nonverbal behavior are a result of variations along the dimensions we discuss next.

Immediacy and Expressiveness

Immediacy behaviors are actions that simultaneously communicate warmth, closeness, and availability for communication; they signal approach rather than avoidance and closeness rather than distance (Andersen, 1985). Examples of immediacy behaviors are smiling, touching, eye contact, close distances, and vocal animation. Some scholars have labeled these behaviors as "expressive" (Patterson, 1983).

Cultures that display considerable interpersonal closeness or immediacy have been labeled "contact cultures" because people in these countries stand close and touch often (Hall, 1966). People in low-contact cultures tend to stand apart and touch less. According to Patterson (1983):

These habitual patterns of relating to the world permeate all aspects of everyday life, but their effects on social behavior define the manner in which people relate to one another. In the case of contact cultures, this general tendency is manifested in closer approaches so that tactile and olfactory information may be gained easily (p. 145).

It is interesting that contact cultures are generally located in warm countries and low-contact cultures in cool climates. Considerable research has shown that contact cultures include most Arab countries; the Mediterranean region including France, Greece, and Italy; Jewish people from both Europe and the Middle East; Eastern Europeans and Russians; and Indonesians and Hispanics (Condon and Yousef, 1983; Jones and Remland, 1982; Mehrabian, 1971; Montagu and Matson, 1979; Patterson, 1983; Samovar, Porter, and Jain, 1981; Scheflen, 1972). Australians are moderate in their cultural contact level, as are North Americans, although North Americans tend toward low contact (Patter-

son, 1983). Low-contact cultures include most of Northern Europe, including Scandinavia, Germany, and England; British-Americans; white Anglo-Saxons (the primary culture of the United States); and the Japanese (Andersen, Andersen, and Lustig, 1987; Heslin and Alper, 1983; Jones and Remland, 1982; Mehrabian, 1971; Montagu and Matson, 1979; Patterson, 1983; Samovar, Porter, and Jain, 1981; Scheflen, 1972).

Explanations for these latitudinal variations have included energy level, climate, and metabolism (Andersen, Lustig, and Andersen, 1987). Evidently, cultures in cool climates tend to be task-oriented and interpersonally "cool," whereas cultures in warm climates tend to be interpersonally oriented and interpersonally "warm." Even within the United States, people in warm latitudes tend to exhibit more contact than people in cold areas. Andersen, Lustig, and Andersen (1987) found a 0.31 correlation between the latitude of universities and touch avoidance. These data suggest that students at sunbelt universities are more touch-oriented than their counterparts in colder climates.

Individualism

One of the most fundamental dimensions along which cultures differ is the degree of *individualism* versus *collectivism*. This dimension determines how people live together (alone, in families, or tribes; see Hofstede, 1982), their values, and how they communicate. As we shall see, people in the United States are individualists for better or worse. We take individualism for granted and are blind to its impact until travel brings us in contact with less individualistic, more collectivistic cultures.

Individualism has been applauded as a blessing and has been elevated to the status of a national religion in the United States. Indeed, the best and worst features of our culture can be attributed to individualism. Proponents of individualism have argued that it is the basis of liberty, democracy, freedom, and economic incentive and that it serves as a protection against tyranny. On the other hand, individualism has been blamed for our alienation from one another, loneliness, selfishness, and narcissism. Indeed, Hall (1976) claimed that, as an extreme, "Western man has created chaos by denying that part of his self that integrates while enshrining the parts that fragment experience" (p. 9).

There can be little doubt that individualism is one of the fundamental dimensions that distinguish cultures one from the other. Likewise, there is little doubt that Western culture is individualistic, whereas Eastern culture emphasizes harmony among people and between people and nature. Tomkins (1984) demonstrated that an individual's psychological makeup is the result of this cultural dimension. He stated, "Human beings, in Western Civilization, have tended toward self-celebration, positive or negative. In oriental thought another alternative is represented, that of harmony between man and nature" (p. 182). Prosser (1978) suggested that the Western emphasis on individuality finds its culmination in contemporary U.S. cultures, where the chief cultural value is the role of the individual. This idea is verified in the landmark intercultural study of Hofstede (1982). In his study of individualism in forty noncommunist countries, the nine most individualistic (in order) were the United States, Australia, Great Britain, Canada, the Netherlands, New Zealand, Italy, Belgium, and Denmark—all Western or European countries. The nine least individualistic (starting with the least) were Venezuela, Colombia, Pakistan, Peru, Taiwan, Thailand, Singapore, Chile, and Hong Kong—all oriental or South American cultures. Similarly, Sitaram and Cogdell (1976) reported individuality to be of primary importance in Western cultures, of secondary importance in black cultures, and of lesser importance in Eastern and Muslim cultures.

While the United States is the most individualistic country on earth (Hofstede, 1982), regions of the United States vary in their degree of individualism. Elazar (1972) has shown that the Central Midwest and the mid-Atlantic states have the most individualistic political culture, whereas the Southeast has the most traditionalistic and least individualistic. But these differences are all relative and, by world standards, even Mississippi has an individualistic culture. Bellah et al. (1985) stated:

Individualism lies at the very core of American culture. . . . Anything that would violate our right to think for ourselves, judge for ourselves, make our own decisions, live our lives as we see fit, is not only morally wrong, it is sacrilegious (p. 142).

Indeed, our extreme individualism makes it difficult for Americans to interact with and understand people from other cultures. We are unique; all other cultures are less individualistic. As Condon and Yousef (1983) stated:

The fusion of individualism and equality is so valued and so basic that many Americans find it most difficult to relate to contrasting values in other cultures where interdependence greatly determines a person's sense of self (p. 65).

The degree to which a culture is individualistic or collectivistic has an impact on the nonverbal behavior of that culture in a variety of ways. First, people from individualistic cultures are comparatively remote and distant proximically. Collectivistic cultures are interdependent and, as a result, they work, play, live, and sleep in close proximity to one another. Hofstede (1972) cites research which suggests that as hunters and gatherers, people lived apart in individualistic nuclear families. As agricultural societies developed, the interdependent extended family began to live in close proximity in large family or tribal units. Urban-industrial societies returned to a norm of individualism, nuclear families, and lack of proximity to one's neighbors, friends, and coworkers.

Kinesic behavior tends to be synchronized in collectivist cultures. Where families work collectively, movements, schedules, and actions need to be highly coordinated (Argyle, 1975). In urban cultures, family members often do their "own thing," coming and going, working and playing, eating and sleeping on different schedules. People in individualistic cultures also smile more than people in normatively oriented cultures according to Tomkins (1984). This fact can probably be explained by the fact that individualists are responsible for their relationships and their own happiness, whereas normatively or collectively oriented people regard compliance with norms as a primary value and personal or interpersonal happiness as a secondary value. Similarly, people in collectivist cultures may suppress both positive and negative emotional displays that are contrary to the mood of the group because maintaining the group is a primary value. People in individualistic cultures are encouraged to express emotions because individual freedom is of paramount value.

Research suggests that people in individualistic cultures are more nonverbally affiliative than people in collectivist cultures. The reason for this is not intuitively obvious because individualism does not require affiliation. However, Hofstede (1982) explained that:

In less individualistic countries where traditional social ties, like those with extended family members, continue to exist, people have less of a need to make specific friendships. One's friends are predetermined by the social relationships into which one is born. In the more individualistic countries, however, affective relationships are not socially predetermined but must be acquired by each individual personally (p. 163).

In individualistic countries like the United States, affiliativeness, dating, flirting, small-talk, and initial acquaintance are more important than they are in collectivist countries where the social network is more fixed and less reliant on individual initiative. Bellah et al. (1985) maintain that for centuries in the individualistic and mobile United States, society people could meet very easily and their communication was open. However, their relationships were usually casual and transient.

Finally, in an impressive study of dozens of cultures, Lomax (1968) found that the song-and-dance styles of a country are related to its level of social cohesion and collectivism. Collectivist cultures rate high in stressing groupness and in the cohesion found in their singing styles. Collectivist cultures show both more cohesiveness in singing and more synchrony in their dance style than do individualistic cultures (Lomax, 1968). It is not surprising that rock dancing, which emphasizes separateness and "doing your own thing," evolved in individualistic cultures such as those in England and the United States. These dances may serve as a metaphor for the whole U.S. culture, where individuality is more prevalent than in any other place.

Masculinity

Masculinity is a neglected dimension of culture. Masculine traits are typically attributes such as strength, assertiveness, competitiveness, and ambitiousness, whereas feminine traits are attributes such as affection, compassion, nurturance, and emotionality (Bem, 1974; Hofstede, 1982). Cross-cultural research shows that young girls are expected to be more nurturant than boys although there is considerable variation from country to country (Hall, 1984). Hofstede (1982) has measured the degree to which people of both sexes in a culture endorse masculine or feminine goals. Masculine cultures regard competition and assertiveness as important, whereas feminine cultures place more importance on nurturance and compassion. Not surprisingly, the masculinity of a culture is negatively correlated with the percentage of women in technical and professional jobs and positively correlated with segregation of the sexes in higher education (Hofstede, 1982).

The nine countries with the highest masculinity scores, according to Hofstede (1982) (most masculine first) are Japan, Austria, Venezuela, Italy, Switzerland, Mexico, Ireland, Great Britain, and Germany. With the exception of Japan, these countries all lie in Central Europe and the Caribbean. The eight countries with the lowest masculinity scores (least masculine first) are Sweden, Norway, Netherlands, Denmark, Finland, Chile, Portugal, and Thailand—all Scandinavian or South American cultures with the exception of Thailand. Why don't South American cultures manifest the Latin pattern of machismo? Hofstede (1982) suggests that machismo occurs more often in the Caribbean region than it does in South America itself.

Considerable research suggests that androgynous patterns of behavior (those that are both feminine and masculine) result in a high degree of self-esteem, social competence, success, and intellectual development for both males and females. Nonverbal styles where both men and women are free to express both masculine (e.g., dominance, anger) and feminine (e.g., warmth, emotionality) behavior are likely to be healthy and very effective. Indeed, Buck (1984) has shown that males may harm their health by internalizing emotions rather than externalizing them as women usually do. Internalized emotions that are not expressed result in a high stress level and high blood pressure. Interestingly enough, countries considered very masculine show high levels of stress (Hofstede, 1982).

Considerable research has demonstrated significant differences in vocal patterns between egalitarian and nonegalitarian countries. Countries where women are economically important and where sexual standards for women are permissive show more relaxed vocal patterns than other countries (Lomax, 1968). Moreover, egalitarian countries show less tension between the sexes, more vocal solidarity and coordination in their songs, and more synchrony in their movement than we see in less egalitarian countries (Lomax, 1968).

It is important to note that the United States tends to be a masculine country according to Hofstede (1982) although it is not among the nine most masculine. Intercultural communicators should keep in mind that other countries may be more or less sexually egalitarian than is the United States. Similarly, most countries are more feminine (i.e., nurturant, compassionate), and people of both sexes in the United States frequently seem loud, aggressive, and competitive by world standards.

Power Distance

A fourth fundamental dimension of intercultural communication is power distance. Power distance—the degree to which power, prestige, and wealth are unequally distributed in a culture—has been measured in a number of cultures using Hofstede's (1982) power distance index (PDI). Cultures with high PDI scores have power and influence concentrated in the hands of a few rather than distributed more or less equally throughout the population. Condon and Yousef (1983) distinguish among three cultural patterns: democratic, authority-centered, and authoritarian. The PDI is highly correlated (0.80) with authoritarianism (as measured by the F-Scale) (Hofstede, 1982).

The nine countries with the highest PDI (highest first) are the Philippines, Mexico, Venezuela, India, Singapore, Brazil, Hong Kong, France, and Colombia (Hofstede, 1982)—all of which are South Asian or Caribbean countries, with the exception of France. Gudykunst and Kim (1984) report that both African and Asian cultures generally maintain hierarchical role relationships. Asian students are expected to be modest and nonverbally deferent in the presence of their instructors. Likewise, Vietnamese consider employers to be their mentors and will not question orders. The nine countries with the lowest PDI (lowest first) are Austria, Israel, Denmark, New Zealand, Ireland, Sweden, Norway, Finland, and Switzerland (Hofstede, 1982)—all of which are European, middle-class democracies located at high latitudes. The United States is slightly lower than the median in power distance. A fundamental determiner of power distance is the latitude of a country. Hofstede (1982) claims that latitude and climate are major forces in shaping cultures. He maintains that the key intervening variable is that technology is needed for survival in colder climates. This need produces a chain of events in which children are less dependent on authority and learn from people other than authority figures. Hofstede (1982) reports a 0.65 correlation between PDI and latitude! In a study conducted at forty universities throughout the United States, Andersen, Lustig, and Andersen (1987) report a − 0.47 correlation between latitude and intolerance for ambiguity and a − 0.45 correlation between latitude and authoritarianism. These findings suggest that residents of the northern United States are less authoritarian and more tolerant of ambiguity. Northern cultures may have to be more tolerant and less autocratic to ensure cooperation and survival in harsher climates.

It is obvious that power distance affects the nonverbal behavior of a culture. High PDI countries such as India, with its rigid caste system, may severely limit interaction, as in the case of India's "untouchables." More than 20 percent of India's population are untouchables—those who are at the bottom of India's five-caste system (Chinoy, 1967). Any contact with untouchables by members of other castes is strictly forbidden and considered "polluting." Obviously, tactile communication among castes is greatly curtailed by Indian culture. High PDI countries with less rigid stratification than India may still prohibit interclass dating, marriage, and contact, which are taken for granted in low PDI countries.

Social systems with large power discrepancies also produce different kinesic behavior. According to Andersen and Bowman (1985), subordinates' body tension is more obvious in power-discrepant relationships. Similarly Andersen and Bowman (1985) report that in power-discrepant circumstances, subordinates smile often in an effort to appear polite and to appease superiors. The continual smiles of many orientals may be an effort to appease superiors or to produce smooth social relations; they may be the result of being reared in a high PDI culture.

Vocalic and paralinguistic cues are also affected by the power distance in a culture. People living in low PDI countries are generally less aware that vocal loudness may be offensive to others. The vocal tones of people in the United States are often perceived as noisy, exaggerated, and childlike (Condon and Yousef, 1983). Lomax (1968) has shown that in countries where political authority is highly centralized, singing voices are tighter and the voice box is more closed, whereas more permissive societies produce more relaxed, open, and clear sounds.

High and Low Context

A final essential dimension of intercultural communication is that of context. Hall (1976, 1984) has described high- and low-context cultures in considerable detail. "A high-context (HC) communication or message is one in which most of the information is either in the physical context or internalized in the person, while very little is in the coded, explicit,

transmitted parts of the message" (Hall, 1976, p. 91). Lifelong friends often use HC or implicit messages that are nearly impossible for an outsider to understand. The situation, a smile, or a glance provides an implicit meaning that doesn't need to be articulated. In HC situations or cultures, information is integrated from the environment, the context, the situation, and from nonverbal cues that give the message a meaning that is unavailable in the explicit verbal utterance.

Low-context (LC) messages are just the opposite of HC messages; most of the information is in the explicit code (Hall, 1976). LC messages must be elaborated, clearly communicated, and highly specific. Unlike personal relationships, which are relatively HC message systems, institutions such as courts of law and formal systems such as mathematics or computer language require explicit, LC systems because nothing can be taken for granted (Hall, 1984).

Cultures vary considerably in the degree of context used in communication. The lowest-context cultures are probably the Swiss, German, North American (including the United States), and Scandinavian (Hall, 1976, 1984; Gudykunst and Kim, 1984). These cultures are preoccupied with specifics, details, and precise time schedules at the expense of context. They utilize behavior systems built around Aristotelean logic and linear thinking (Hall, 1984). Cultures that have some characteristics of both HC and LC systems include the French, English, and Italian (Gudykunst and Kim, 1984), which are somewhat less explicit than Northern European cultures.

The highest-context cultures, found in the Orient, China, Japan, and Korea, are extremely HC cultures (Elliott, Scott, Jensen, and McDonough, 1982; Hall, 1976, 1984). Languages are some of the most explicit communication systems, but the Chinese language is an implicit high-context system. To use a Chinese dictionary, one must understand thousands of characters that change meaning when combined with other characters. People from the United States frequently complain that the Japanese never get to the point; they fail to recognize that HC cultures must provide a context and setting and let the point evolve (Hall, 1984). American Indian cultures with ancestral migratory roots in East Asia are remarkably like contemporary oriental culture in several ways, especially in their need for high context (Hall, 1984). Not surprisingly, most Latin American cultures, a fusion of Iberian (Portuguese-Spanish) and Indian traditions, are also high-context cultures. Southern and eastern Mediterranean people such as Greeks, Turks, and Arabs tend to have HC cultures as well.

Communication is obviously quite different in high- and low-context cultures. First, explicit forms of communication such as verbal codes are more prevalent in low-context cultures such as the United States and Northern Europe. People from LC cultures are often perceived as excessively talkative, belaboring the obvious, and using redundancies. People from HC cultures may be perceived as nondisclosive, sneaky, and mysterious. Second, HC cultures do not value verbal communication the same way as do LC cultures. Elliot et al. (1982) found that people who were more verbal were perceived as more attractive by people in the United States, but people who were less verbal were perceived as more attractive in Korea—a high-context culture. Third, HC cultures are more reliant on and tuned in to nonverbal communication than are LC cultures. LC cultures, and particularly the men in LC cultures, fail to perceive as much nonverbal communication as do members of HC cultures. Nonverbal communication provides the context for all communication (Watzlawick, Beavin, and Jackson, 1967), but people from HC cultures are particularly affected by contextual cues. Thus facial expressions, tensions, movements, speed of interaction, location of the interaction, and other subtleties of nonverbal behavior are likely to be perceived by and have more meaning for people from high-context cultures. Finally, people from HC cultures expect more nonverbal communication than do interactants in LC cultures (Hall, 1976). People from HC cultures expect communicators to understand unarticulated feelings, subtle gestures, and environmental cues that people from LC cultures simply do not process. What is worse, both cultural extremes fail to recognize these basic differences in behavior, communication, and context, and both are quick to misattribute the causes for the other's behavior.

CONCLUSION

Reading about these five dimensions of culture cannot ensure competence in intercultural communication. The beauty of international travel, and even travel within the United States, is that it provides a unique perspective on one's own behavior and the behavior of others. Combining cognitive knowledge from articles and courses with actual encounters with people from other cultures is the best way to gain such competence.

A full, practical understanding of the dimensions along which cultures differ, combined with the knowledge of how specific communication acts differ cross-culturally, has several practical benefits. First, such knowledge will highlight and challenge assumptions about our own behavior. The structure of our own behavior is invisible and taken for granted until it is exposed and challenged through the study of other cultures and actual intercultural encounters. Indeed, Hall (1976) stated that ethnic diversity in interethnic communication can be a source of strength and an asset from which one can discover oneself.

Second, this discussion should make it clear that our attributions about the nonverbal communication of people from other cultures are often wrong. No dictionary or code of intercultural behavior is available. We cannot read people like books, not even people from our own culture. Understanding that someone is from a masculine, collectivist, or high-context culture will, however, make their behavior less confusing and more interpretable.

Finally, understanding about intercultural differences and actually engaging in intercultural encounters is bound to reduce ethnocentrism and make strangers from other cultures seem less threatening. Fear is often based on ignorance and misunderstanding. The fact of intercultural diversity should produce joy and optimism about the number of possible ways to be human.

REFERENCES

Andersen, P. A. (1985). "Nonverbal Immediacy in Interpersonal Communication." In A. W. Siegman and S. Feldstein (Eds.). *Multichannel Integrations of Nonverbal Behavior.* Hillsdale, N.J.: Lawrence Erlbaum.

Andersen, P. A. (1986). "Consciousness, Cognition, and Communication." *Western Journal of Speech Communication,* 50, 87–101.

Andersen, P. A. (1987a). "Locating the Sources of Interpersonal Behavior." *Distinguishing among Traits, States, Cultures and Situations.* Unpublished paper, San Diego State University, San Diego, Calif.

Andersen, P. A. (1987b). "The Trait Debate: A Critical Examination of the Individual Differences Paradigm in Intercultural Communication." In B. Dervin and M. J. Voigt (Eds.). *Progress in Communication Sciences,* Volume VIII. Norwood, N.J.: Ablex Publishing.

Andersen, J. F., Andersen, P. A., and Lustig, M. W. (February 1987). "Predicting Opposite-Sex Touch Avoidance: A National Replication and Extension." Paper presented at the annual convention of the Western Speech Communication Association, San Diego, Calif.

Andersen, P. A., and Bowman, L. (May 1985). "Positions of Power: Nonverbal Cues of Status and Dominance in Organizational Communication." Paper presented at the annual convention of the Interpersonal Communication Association, Honolulu, Hawaii.

Andersen, P. A., and Leibowitz, K. (1978). "The Development and Nature of the Construct Touch Avoidance." *Environmental Psychology and Nonverbal Behavior,* 3, 89–106.

Andersen, P. A., Lustig, M. W., and Andersen, J. F. (1986). "Communication Patterns Among Cultural Regions of the United States: A Theoretical Perspective." Paper presented at the annual convention of the International Communication Association, Chicago.

Andersen, P. A., Lustig, R., and Andersen, J. F. (1987). Changes in Latitude, Changes in Attitude: The Relationship Between Climate and Interpersonal Communication." Unpublished manuscript, San Diego State University, San Diego, Calif.

Argyle, M. (1975). *Bodily Communication.* New York: International Universities Press.

Bellah, R. N., Madsen, R., Sullivan, W. M., Swidler, A., and Tipton, S. (1985). *Habits of the Heart: Individualism and Commitment in American Life.* New York: Harper & Row.

Bem, S. L. (1974). "The Measurement of Psychological Androgyny." *Journal of Consulting and Clinical Psychology,* 42, 155–162.

Bruneau, T. (1979). "The Time Dimension in Intercultural Communication." In D. Nimmo (Ed.). *Communication Yearbook 3.* New Brunswick, N.J.: Transaction Books.

Buck, R. (1984). *The Communication of Emotion.* New York: The Guilford Press.

Burgoon, J. K. (1985). "Nonverbal Signals." In M. L. Knapp and G. R. Miller (Eds.). *Handbook of Interpersonal Communication.* Newbury Park, Calif.: Sage Publications.

Burgoon, J. K., and Saine, T. (1978). *The Unspoken Dialogue: An Introduction to Nonverbal Communication.* Boston: Houghton Mifflin.

Chinoy, E. (1967). *Society.* New York: Random House.

Condon, J. C., and Yousef, F. (1983). *An Introduction to Intercultural Communication.* Indianapolis, Ind.: Bobbs-Merrill.

Elazar, D. J. (1972). *American Federalism: A View from the States.* New York: Thomas P. Crowell Company.

Elliot, S., Scott, M. D., Jensen, A. D., and McDonough, M. (1982). "Perceptions of Reticence: A Cross-Cultural Investigation." In M. Burgoon (Ed.). *Communication Yearbook 5.* New Brunswick, N.J.: Transaction Books.

Geertz, C. (1973). *The Interpretation of Cultures.* New York: Basic Books.

Gudykunst, W. B., and Kim, Y. Y. (1984). *Communicating with Strangers: An Approach to Intercultural Communication.* New York: Random House.

Hall, E. T. (1959). *The Silent Language.* New York: Doubleday and Company.

Hall, E. T. (1966). *The Hidden Dimension.* New York: Doubleday and Company.

Hall, E. T. (1976). *Beyond Culture*. Garden City, N.Y.: Anchor Books.

Hall, E. T. (1984). *The Dance of Life: The Other Dimension of Time*. Garden City, N.Y.: Anchor Press.

Heslin, R., and Alper, T. (1983). "Touch: A Bonding Gesture." In J. M. Wiemann and R. Harrison (Eds.). *Nonverbal Interaction*. Newbury Park, Calif.: Sage Publications.

Hofstede, G. (1982). *Culture's Consequences* (abridged ed.). Newbury Park, Calif.: Sage Publications.

Jensen, J. V. (1985). "Perspective on Nonverbal Intercultural Communication." In L. A. Samovar and R. E. Porter (Eds.). *Intercultural Communication: A Reader*. Belmont, Calif.: Wadsworth.

Jones, T. S., and Remland, M. S. (May 1982). "Cross-Cultural Differences in Self-Reported Touch Avoidance." Paper presented at the annual convention of the Eastern Communication Association, Hartford, Conn.

LaBarre, W. (1985). "Paralinguistics, Kinesics, and Cultural Anthropology." In L. A. Samovar and R. E. Porter (Eds.). *Intercultural Communication: A Reader*. Belmont, Calif.: Wadsworth.

Lomax, A. (1968). *Folk Song Style and Culture*. New Brunswick, N.J.: Transaction Books.

Malandro, L. A., and Barker, L. (1983). *Nonverbal Communication*. Reading, Mass.: Addison-Wesley.

Mehrabian, A. (1971). *Silent Messages*. Belmont, Calif.: Wadsworth.

Merriam, A. H. (1983). "Comparative Chronemics and International Communication: American and Iranian Perspectives on Time." In R. N. Bostrom (Ed.). *Communication Yearbook 7*. Newbury Park, Calif.: Sage Publications.

Montagu, A., and Matson, F. (1979). *The Human Connection*. New York: McGraw-Hill.

Patterson, M. L. (1983). *Nonverbal Behavior: A Functional Perspective*. New York: Springer-Verlag.

Prosser, M. H. (1978). *The Culture Dialogue: An Introduction to Intercultural Communication*. Boston, Mass.: Houghton Mifflin.

Rich, A. L. (1974). *Interracial Communication*. New York: Harper & Row.

Samovar, L. A., and Porter, R. E. (1985). "Nonverbal Interaction." In L. A. Samovar and R. E. Porter (Eds.). *Intercultural Communication: A Reader*. Belmont, Calif.: Wadsworth.

Samovar, L. A., Porter, R. E., and Jain, N. C. (1981). *Understanding Intercultural Communication*. Belmont, Calif.: Wadsworth.

Saral, T. (1977). "Intercultural Communication Theory and Research: An Overview." In B. D. Ruben (Ed.). *Communication Yearbook I*. New Brunswick, N.J.: Transaction Books.

Scheflen, A. E. (1972). *Body Language and the Social Order*. Englewood Cliffs, N.J.: Prentice-Hall.

Scheflen, A. E. (1974). *How Behavior Means*. Garden City, N.Y.: Anchor Press.

Sitaram, K. S., and Cogdell, R. T. (1976). *Foundations of Intercultural Communication*. Columbus, Ohio: Charles E. Merrill.

Tomkins, S. S. (1984). "Affect Theory." In K. R. Scherer and P. Ekman (Eds.). *Approaches to Emotion*. Hillsdale, N.J.: Lawrence Erlbaum.

Watzlawick, P., Beavin, J. H., and Jackson, D. D. (1967). *Pragmatics of Human Communication*. New York: W. W. Norton.

Sex Differences in Nonverbal Communication

BARBARA WESTBROOK EAKINS
R. GENE EAKINS

. . . People talking without speaking
. . . People hearing without listening

—Paul Simon

In addition to the spoken language that we hear daily, a host of silent messages continually occurs around us. These messages make up a nonverbal code, which is used and responded to by us all. This language is not formally taught. A substantial portion of the nonverbal communication that takes place is not consciously noted. But it is an extremely important aspect of communication, for we make many important decisions on the basis of nonverbal cues.

Ray Birdwhistell estimates that in most two-person conversations the words communicate only about 35 percent of the social meaning of the situation; the nonverbal elements convey more than 65 percent of the meaning. Another estimate is that the nonverbal message carries 4.3 times the weight of the verbal message. This is not so surprising when we consider the many ways in which we communicate information nonverbally: through eye contact, facial expressions, body posture and body tension, hand gestures and body movements, the way we position ourselves in relation to another person, touch, clothing, cosmetics, and possessions.

From Barbara Eakins and R. Gene Eakins, *Sex Differences in Human Communication*. Copyright © 1978 Harper and Row Publishers, Inc. Used with permission of the publisher. Barbara Eakins teaches at the Ohio State University, and R. Gene Eakins teaches at Wright State University. Footnotes have been deleted.

Some time ago Freud said, "He that has eyes to see and ears to hear may convince himself that no mortal can keep a secret. If his lips are silent, he chatters with his finger tips; betrayal oozes out of him at every pore." To be more skillful communicators, we need to be aware of nonverbal cues and to use what has been learned to improve communication.

Micro-units of nonverbal communication, such as dropping the eyelids, smiling, pointing, lowering the head slightly, or folding the arms are often considered trivia. But some researchers believe these so-called trivia constitute the very core or essence of our communication interactions. They consider them elements in the "micropolitical structure" that help maintain and support the larger political structure. The larger political structure needs these numerous minutiae of human actions and interactions to sustain and reinforce it. These nonverbal cues fall somewhere on a continuum of social control that ranges from socialization or cultivation of minds, at one extreme, to the use of force or physical violence, at the other. There are some significant sex differences in nonverbal communication patterns and, as we shall see, they have important implications in the lives of women and men. . . .

SEX DIFFERENCES IN NONVERBAL COMMUNICATION

Women seem to be more sensitive than men to social cues. Research has shown that female subjects are more responsive to nonverbal cues, compared with verbal ones, than males. Not only have women been found to be more responsive to nonverbal stimuli, but they apparently read it with greater accuracy than males. One study used the Profile of Nonverbal Sensitivity, a test that utilizes film clips of a series of scenes involving people using body movement and facial expression and showing face, torso, both, or neither. Subjects heard scrambled voice, content-filtered speech with intonation features preserved, or no sound. They were to select the best of the written interpretations of the nonverbal cues after each scene. Females from fifth grade to adulthood obtained better scores than males, with the exception of men who held jobs involving "nurturant, artistic, or expressive" work. When body cues were included, women did better than men. Sensitivity to nonverbal cues appeared to be independent of general intelligence or test-taking skills.

One could hypothesize that nonverbal awareness is an inborn trait and that females are more sensitive and responsive to nonverbal cues from birth. However, it seems more likely that females learn to become nonverbally sensitive at an early age because of their socialization. Their greater receptivity to nonverbal cues from others may be related to their lower status in society and the necessity of this skill to their survival. Blacks, for example, have been shown to be better than whites at interpreting nonverbal signals.

When a group of teachers took the Profile of Nonverbal Sensitivity, those more sensitive to nonverbal communication scored as less authoritarian and more democratic in teaching orientation. Females were relatively better than males at interpreting negative attitudes. Since females may be placed in subordinate positions or be dependent on others in social situations more often, they may be forced to become adept at reading signs of approbation or displeasure from those on whom they depend. Perhaps more than men, they need to know what expectations for them are. Developing the ability to pick up small nonverbal cues in others quickly may be a defense mechanism or survival technique women unconsciously use. It is much more important to someone in a subordinate position to know the mood, the feelings, or intentions of the dominant one than vice versa. The office worker will immediately note and relay to other office subordinates the information that "the boss is in one of his moods again." Just a look, the manner of walk, or the carriage of the arms and shoulders may provide the clue for that anxious observer. Rare, however, is the authority figure who notices employees' moods or is even aware that they have them.

We are not taught nonverbal communication in school. Our schools emphasize verbal communication. Because we seldom examine how we send and interpret nonverbal messages, the nonverbal chan-

nel is a very useful avenue for subtly manipulating people. The manipulation does not have to be consciously perceived.

We are prevented from getting knowledge or understanding of nonverbal communication because a delineation of looks, gait, posture, or facial expression is not legitimate in describing interaction. Such items are surely not accepted as valid data in an argument. ("What do you mean, I look as if I don't approve? I said 'all right,' didn't I?") And yet nonverbal cues have more than four times the impact of verbal messages. Not only are women more sensitive to such cues, but their position in society and their socialization to greater docility and compliance may predispose them to be more vulnerable to manipulation and thus make them ideal targets for this subtle form of social control. It behooves both women and men to learn as much as possible about how nonverbal cues can affect people and can serve to perpetuate status and power relationships in society. With this concern in mind, let us examine the categories of nonverbal behavior.

Eye Contact

Research in the use of eye contact has shown sharp differences according to sex. In studies involving female and male subjects, women have been found to look more at the other person than men do. In addition, women look at one another more and hold eye contact longer with each other than men do with other men. Women look at one another more while they are speaking, while they are being spoken to, and while they are exchanging simultaneous glances. Whatever the sex of the other, women have been shown to spend more time looking at their partner than men do. What might account for this asymmetry, or difference, in looking behavior of the sexes? The usual explanation given is that women are more willing to establish and maintain eye contact because they are more inclined toward social and interpersonal relations. The gaze may be an avenue of emotional expression for women.

Another reason has been suggested for sex differences in eye behavior. Some experiments have found that in orienting their bodies in space women are more affected than men by visual cues. In other words, in tests where subjects must make judgments about horizontal and vertical position, women tend to use reference points in the environment rather than internal body cues. This physical characteristic could be generalized to social situations.

Let us consider the paradigm of asymmetrical behavior as an indicator of status. Among unequals the subordinate is the one most likely to want social approval, and it has been shown that people have more eye contact with those from whom they want approval. The kinds of clues or information women may get by observing a male's reactions or behavior are important in helping them gauge the appropriateness of their own behavior. Women may value nonverbal information from males more than males value nonverbal information from females. Furthermore, it has been found that in conversation, the listener tends to look more at the speaker, whereas the speaker often looks away while talking. Since some studies show that men tend to talk more in female-male pairs, women would spend more time listening and, therefore, probably more time looking at the other.

Also it has been shown that the more positive an attitude toward the person being addressed, the more eye contact there is. Increased eye contact with the person being addressed also occurs if that person is of higher status. In some cases males use more positive head nods, but females use more eye contact, when they are seeking approval. In an investigation involving mixed-sex pairs, when women were told their partner's eye contact exceeded normal levels, they had a more favorable evaluation of him. But when men were told their partner looked more than usual, they had a less favorable evaluation of her. These studies suggest that women may be using eye contact to seek approval and that perhaps both women and men perceive women to have less status than men. Perhaps, as one student commented, "They almost *ask* for the subordinate position by their behavior."

In our personal experience, we became acquainted with a graduate student and the woman he had just married. There was a discrepancy in educational background between the man, who was just beginning work on his Ph.D., and the woman, who had a high school education. Not only her uneasiness but her heavy reliance on nonverbal cues to her husband's reaction were evident at social gatherings. During conversations, her eyes would continually stray to his face. When speaking with her, it was difficult to establish eye contact, for during her comments or her answers to questions, her eyes would dart to her husband's face, as if to measure the appropriateness of her remark by his approbation or lack of it.

Some writers have observed that women tend to avert their gaze, especially when stared at by men. Although mutual eye contact between persons can indicate affiliation or liking, prolonged eye contact or staring can signify something quite different. Back in our youth, we sometimes engaged in "double whammy," a game in which we tried to outstare our partner. The first one to break the eyelock by looking away, dropping the eyes, or closing the eyes was the loser. It has been suggested that this kind of competitiveness is involved when two persons' gazes meet, such that "a wordless struggle ensues, until one or the other succeeds in establishing dominance." Dominance is acquiesced to and submissiveness signaled by the person who finally looks away or down. We might ask ourselves, in our last encounter with the boss, someone in very high authority, or a person whom we felt greatly "outclassed" us in position or wealth, who was the first to break the mutual gaze and glance away? Indeed, this is a "'game' . . . enacted at [subtle] levels thousands of times daily."

Jane van Lawick-Goodall has observed behavior of chimpanzees for a number of years and has noted striking similarities in the behavior of chimpanzees and people, particularly in nonverbal communication patterns. She points out how a greeting between two chimpanzees generally re-establishes the dominance status of the one relative to the other. She describes how one female chimp, "nervous Olly," greets another chimp, "Mike," to whom she may bow to the ground and crouch submissively with downbent head. "She is, in effect, acknowledging Mike's superior rank," says Goodall. This would seem to be the extreme of avoiding eye gaze with one of superior rank. Goodall also indicates that an angry chimpanzee may fixedly stare at an opponent.

Some years ago, when our oldest daughter was quite young, she asked us earnestly, "Why is it baboons don't like you to stare at them?" The family was amused at this, and it became a standing joke at our home for years. But we had been to the zoo and, young as she was, our daughter had apparently noticed that the baboons she saw reacted in a disturbed manner to staring.

Research with humans has shown that staring calls forth the same kinds of responses found in primates and that it serves as threat display. Observations of averted eye behavior in autistic children suggest that the averted glance or downcast eyes may be a gesture of submissiveness in humans. Researchers noted to their surprise that autistic children were rarely attacked by the other children, although they seemed to be "easy targets." They concluded that the autistic child's avoidance of eye contact served as a signal much like the appeasement postures used by certain gulls, for example. That is to say, turning away the gaze and avoiding eye contact seemed to restrain or check aggressive behavior or threat display.

The power of the direct stare and the strength of the message it conveys, as well as the acquiescence that turning the eyes away can signify, was illustrated to us by a humorous incident at a cocktail hour for new faculty. One young couple was eager to please and be accepted because it was the husband's first position after finishing graduate school. The wife was a hearty, direct young woman who had been reared in Iowa. She had a bluff, good-natured sense of humor and an amusing way with idioms that refused to stay tucked under the sedateness she tried in vain to assume for this "important" occasion. She was in a tight little circle with some of the tenured and dignified "old guard," when one of them commented upon the great pleasure of discovering that his young colleague had such a lovely wife. The young woman was pleased and began animatedly telling her elderly admirer she felt "as grateful as the cow who remarked to the farmer, 'Thank you for a warm hand on a cold morning.'" As she spoke, her husband fixed upon her a direct and piercing stare. The young woman then stopped her talk and turned her head slightly as she lowered her eyes and became very intent upon sipping her punch.

There may seem to be a contradiction in reporting that women tend to look at others more than men do and yet claim that they generally follow a pattern of submission in one-sided behavior interactions. But several explanations may be offered. First, more of women's looking consists of mutual eye contact. It is possible that during mutual eye contact women are the first to turn the eyes away, the signal of submission. For example, one observation in which a male stared at 60 females and males showed that females averted their gaze more often. About 40 percent of the females would return the stare, then immediately break eye contact, and then reestablish it—as many as four times in an encounter. Only one male of the group made repetitive eye contact in this way.

Second, it may be useful to identify the nature of the gaze and [to] distinguish between subordinate attentiveness and dominant staring. Women may do more looking or scanning of the other person's face for expressive cues when the other person's gaze is directed elsewhere, just as subordinates in the animal world must stay alert to cues from the powerful. But when that person returns the gaze, a woman may drop hers. Intermittent and repetitive eye contact may be the female's response to two conflicting tendencies: the inclination to avert the eyes in submission and the need to watch for visual cues from the powerful.

Third, people tend to do more looking while they are listening to another speak than when they themselves are speaking; and we have learned that women are listeners more often than talkers. So women may be doing more of their looking while listening (in the submissive role) to the other person talk.

Fourth, looking that is done by subjects in experimental lab situations may function differently from looking that occurs in more natural settings. Some informal studies of eye contact by persons passing one another in public showed 71 percent of the males established eye contact with a female but only 43 percent of the females established eye contact with a male. Other observations have shown a pattern of females averting the eyes from both female and male starers. In contrast, males generally stared back at female starers, although they avoided eye contact with other males.

Apparently two types of eye behavior characterize both dominance and submissiveness, but in different ways.

1. Dominant staring and looking away. Staring can be used by a superior in some situations to communicate power and assert dominance. But in other instances staring may not be needed. With subordinates, one can feel comfortable and secure in one's power. A superior need not anxiously scan the inferior's face for approval or feedback, but can instead look away or gaze into space as if the underling were not there.

2. Submissive watching and averting of the gaze. Careful watching by an underling can be used to communicate submission and dutiful attentiveness, as well as to gather feedback or attitude cues from the dominant. But in some cases looking is not useful or appropriate. When receiving the fixed stare of a powerful other, for example, a subordinate may signal submission by averting the eyes.

Finally, it is said that while looking directly at a man, a woman will often have her head slightly tilted. This may imply the beginning of a "presenting" gesture, or enough submission to render the stare ambivalent if not actually submissive.

It is interesting to note that in a "Dear Abby" survey on what women notice first about men and what men notice first about women, the eyes rank third for both sexes. Comments included such sentiments from women as, "The eyes tell everything," or "You can tell more about a man's character from his eyes than from anything else. His mouth can lie, but his eyes can't." Males' comments included explanations such as, "It tells me whether or not she's interested in me," or "The eyes show kindness, cruelty, warmth, trust, friendliness and compassion—or lack of it."

Facial Expression

Women have been found to be more prone to reveal their emotions in facial expressions than men. A psychologist who conducted an experiment on this subject found that men tended to keep their emotions "all bottled up." Subjects in the experiment (students) were shown slides calculated to arouse strong feelings or emotions. The pictures included scenes that were unpleasant, such as a victim with severe burns; pleasant, such as happy children; unusual, a double-exposed photograph; scenic; or sexual. While the subjects were viewing the slides, their own facial expressions were being picked up over closed-circuit television. The researchers found that it was easier to tell what kind of picture was being shown from viewing the women's facial expressions than from viewing the men's expressions. They concluded that men are "internalizers." Some of the evidence suggesting that men keep their emotions inside were the faster heart beat and greater activity of the sweat glands of males during the experiment.

It is significant to note that while preschool children were found to react differently to pictures, this difference did not seem to occur according to sex but on the basis of individual personality differences. The implication is that while they are growing up males are conditioned by society not to show or express their feelings and females are conditioned to reveal theirs more freely. While perhaps less advantageous in terms of power, it would seem to be healthier to express one's emotions.

Women have been found to be better able to remember names and faces, at least those of high school classmates. A study tested subjects from ages 17 to 47, with men and women put into nine categories, depending on the number of years since they had graduated from high school. In all categories the women's memories were superior to men's in matching names and faces. One would conclude that women are conditioned to associate names with physical characteristics more so than men.

From her study of chimpanzees, Goodall has observed that many of the submissive and aggressive gestures of the chimpanzee closely resemble our own. The chimpanzees have some facial expressions for situations that seem to provide insight when considering the human social environment. One facial expression is the "compressed-lips face" shown by aggressive chimpanzees during a charging display or when attacking others.

Another expression is the "play face" shown during periods of frolicking. The front upper teeth are exposed, and the upper lip is drawn back and up. A "full open grin" with upper and lower front teeth showing and jaws open, is displayed when a chimpanzee is frightened or excited, such as during attack or when a high-ranking male "displays" close to a subordinate. A "low open grin," with the upper lip slightly relaxed to cover the upper front teeth, is shown when the chimpanzee is less frightened or excited.

When the chimpanzee is less frightened or less excited than in the previous situations, "a full closed grin," with upper and lower teeth showing but with jaws closed, may be shown. It is also displayed by a low-ranking chimpanzee, when approaching a superior in silence. Goodall remarked, "If the human nervous or social smile has its equivalent expression in the chimpanzee it is, without doubt, the closed grin." Elsewhere it has been observed that apes use a "rudimentary smile" as an appeasement gesture or to indicate submission. It apparently signals to an aggressor that the subordinate creature intends no harm.

Some writers have pointed out that women smile more than men do, whether or not they are really happy or amused. The smile may be a concomitant of the social status of women and be used as a gesture of submission as a part of their culturally prescribed role. Supposedly the smile is an indicator of submission, particularly from women to men. Silveira indicates two instances in which women are more likely to smile: when a woman and a man greet one another, and when the two are conversing and are only moderately well acquainted. In these situations, rather than indicating friendliness or pleasure, the smile supposedly shows that no aggression or harm is intended. One study found that women tended to smile and laugh more than men during laboratory conversations. Women may have

smiled more to cover up uneasiness or nervousness or to meet social expectations. The men who smiled generally did so only after they felt comfortable and to express solidarity or union.

In an investigation of approval seeking, one member in each pair of communicators was instructed to try to either gain or avoid the approval of the other. Those who tried to gain approval used significantly more nonverbal acts, including smiles. There was no difference between the sexes in use of smiles in approval seeking. However, when subjects were instructed to behave so as to avoid the approval of the other, the women avoiding approval tended to smile more often than the men avoiding approval. Perhaps the women were unwilling to withhold this gesture because they believe smiling is expected of them socially, whatever the situation. Or it may be that the forced or ready smile was so much a part of the female subjects' socialization that they used it unconsciously, even when inappropriate for their purposes.

Research has shown that children tend to respond differently to female and male smiles. Children five to eight years old responded to women's smiles, as compared to men's smiles, in a neutral manner. Furthermore, children five to twelve years old tended to react to "kidding" messages, which included a negative statement spoken with a smile, as negative; and the negative interpretation was stronger when the speaker was a woman. Young children's different responses to the smiles of women and men in these studies probably reflect sex differences in the smiling communication patterns of adults.

In another experiment videotapes were made of parents with their children. Half the families in the sample had disturbed children and half had normal children. Ratings were made of the parents' words and smiling during interaction with their children. Results showed that fathers made more positive statements when they smiled than when they did not smile. But mothers' statements were not more positive when they were smiling than when they were not smiling, and sometimes in fact were even slightly more negative when smiling. The pattern was not related to child disturbance.

Mothers in lower-class families smiled considerably less than their middle-class counterparts. Whereas 75 percent of the middle-class mothers smiled more than once, only 13 percent of the lower-class mothers smiled more than once. There was no significant difference between lower- and middle-class fathers in amount of smiling. From the results of this study, it appears that fathers are more sincere when they smile, and they are more likely to be saying something relatively friendlier or more approving when smiling than when they are not smiling. When mothers smile at their children, they may be saying something no more evaluatively positive than when they are not smiling. One may conclude that children are probably "reading" adults accurately when they interpret more friendliness in a male's smile than in a female's smile.

What does the middle-class mother's public smile mean? The researchers suggest that the mother is trying to meet middle-class expectations for a "good" mother, which discourage open expression of negative feelings. Her culturally prescribed role calls for "warm, compliant behavior in public situations." The smile may be used as a kind of softener, or mitigator, of critical statements. Another explanation is that the woman may use a smile as "socially ingratiating behavior," rather than as an indicator of friendliness or approval. One writer suggests that both women and men are "deeply threatened" by a female who does not smile often enough and who is apparently not unhappy.

A class project by Henley featured a field study in which students smiled at about three hundred persons (half females, half males) in public and recorded whether each individual smiled back or not. Seventy-six percent of the time people returned smiles. But different patterns of smiling could be identified for each sex. Women returned smiles more often, about 89 percent of the time; and they returned smiles more frequently to males (93 percent of the time) than to other females (86 percent). Males returned smiles only 67 percent of the time to females and were even more inhibited in smiling back at other males, which they did only 58 percent of the time. Henley concluded that some short-changing occurs in the tradeoff of smiles between the sexes: "Women are exploited by men—they give 93 percent but receive in return only 67 percent."

Shulamith Firestone represents an extreme but thought-provoking view concerning the smile as a "badge of appeasement." She terms the smile "the child/woman equivalent of the shuffle," since it indicates the acquiescence to power, and she describes her youthful efforts to resocialize herself. "In my own case, I had to train myself out of that phony smile, which is like a nervous tic on every teenage girl. And this meant that I smiled rarely, for in truth, when it came down to real smiling, I had less to smile about." Firestone describes her "'dream' action": ". . . *a smile boycott*, at which declaration all women would instantly abandon their 'pleasing' smiles, henceforth smiling only when something pleased them."

Posture and Bearing

It has been observed that among nonequals in status, superordinates can indulge in a casualness and relative unconcern with body comportment that subordinates are not permitted. For example, one researcher observed that doctors in the hospital had the privilege of sitting in undignified positions at staff meetings and could saunter into the nurses' station and lounge on the station's dispensing counter. Other personnel such as attendants and nurses had to be more circumspect in their bearing. We need no handbook to tell us that in most interactions the person whom we observe sprawling out, leaning back, or propping feet up while the other maintains more "proper" bearing probably has the authority or power role.

A number of nonverbal sex differences in bearing and posture seem to parallel this asymmetry between nonequals. Birdwhistell describes some posture differences between the sexes involving leg, arm, and pelvis positioning. He believes these are among the most easily recognizable American gender identification signals. In fact, he indicates that leg angle and arm-body angle can be measured exactly. Women giving off gender signals are said to bring their legs together, sometimes even to the extent that their upper legs cross or they stand knee over knee. The American male, however, tends to keep legs apart by a 10- to 15-degree angle. Anyone who has ever participated in physical fitness exercises and assumed "attention" and "at ease" stances knows that the male stance is a more relaxed one.

As for arm-body carriage, females are said to keep their upper arms close to the trunk, while the male moves the arms 5 to 10 degrees away from the body in giving gender cues. Males may carry the pelvis rolled slightly back and females slightly forward. In movement, females supposedly present the entire body from neck to ankles as a moving whole. Males, in contrast, move the arms independently from the trunk and may subtly wag the hips with a slight right and left movement involving a twist at the rib cage. The male bearing seems the more relaxed of the two. Johnny Carson once said of Dr. Joyce Brothers, "She sits as if her knees were welded together."

That these are socialized positions may be inferred from the fact that often as women and men grow older or become ill, their gender positions may become underemphasized or indistinguishable. An elderly woman may, for example, sit relaxed with her legs apart. Because this is an inappropriate gender signal, such an action appears bizarre or may be the object of humor. Carol Burnett, portraying an old woman in one of her comedy routines, sometimes uses this position to get laughs.

Research indicates that in social situations, men assume a more relaxed posture than women, no matter what the sex of the other partner is. Males have been found to assume more asymmetric leg positions and more reclining postures than females. Generally females tend to position their bodies more directly facing the person with whom they are communicating than male communicators do.

In one study males and females were asked to imagine themselves communicating with different persons and to sit the way they would if addressing those persons. Torso lean proved to be a distinguishing difference in some cases. There is less sideways lean in communications with high-status persons. Torso lean was more relaxed, more backward, when communicators addressed persons

they disliked. Torso lean of the males was farther back than that of the females. Women used less arm openness with high-status persons than with low-status persons. Males showed no difference. Leg openness of female communicators was less than that of male communicators.

It appears from these and a number of related studies that males are generally more relaxed than females, just as higher-status persons are more relaxed than those in subordinate roles. Research also shows that communicators in general are more relaxed with females than with males. They show less body tension, more relaxed posture, and more backward lean. By their somewhat tenser postures, women are said to convey submissive attitudes. Their general bodily demeanor and bearing is more restrained and restricted than men's. But society seems to expect this. Greater circumspection in body movement appears to be required of women, even in all-female groups.

It is considered unfeminine or unladylike for a woman to "use her body too forcefully, to sprawl, to stand with her legs widely spread, to sit with her feet up, . . . to cross the ankle of one leg over the knee of the other." And depending on the type of clothing she wears, "she may be expected to sit with her knees together, not to sit cross-legged, or not even to bend over." Although restrictions on women have relaxed recently, these prescriptions of propriety still seem to be in force. Women who break them are not fully accepted.

The public posture, stance, and gait prescribed for and expected of women can be extremely awkward. In an effort to demonstrate to our classes how inconvenient some of the expected behaviors for women are, the authors have borrowed a six-item list of exercises for men for our male students to perform in class. While the result has often led to merriment over the inability of some males to deftly and convincingly perform these actions, the exercises have served to make both the women and the men aware of the extent to which many of our learned behaviors are unexamined.

The following six sets of directions illustrate the inconvenience of the public postures permitted to women:

1. Sit down in a straight chair. Cross your legs at the ankles and keep your knees pressed together.

2. Bend down to pick up an object from the floor. Each time you bend, remember to bend your knees so that your rear end doesn't stick up, and place one hand on your shirt-front to hold it to your chest.

3. Run a short distance, keeping your knees together. You will find you have to take short, high steps.

4. Sit comfortably on the floor. . . . Arrange your legs so that no one can see [your underwear]. Sit like this for a long time without changing position.

5. Walk down a city street. . . . Look straight ahead. Every time a man walks past you, avert your eyes and make your face expressionless.

6. Walk around with your stomach pulled in tight, your shoulders thrown back, and your chest out. . . . Try to speak loudly and aggressively in this posture.

Gesture

"Every little gesture has a meaning all its own." So go the lyrics of an old song. And though students of kinesics, like Birdwhistell, hasten to warn us that no position, expression, or movement ever carries meaning in and of itself, research in nonverbal communication seems to indicate that patterns of gesture can tell us a good deal about ourselves and others. An important consideration is this: "The more men and women interact in the way they have been trained to from birth without considering the meaning of what they do, the more they become dulled to the significance of their actions." Outsiders who observe a culture different from their own can sometimes spot behavioral differences, and the significance of these differences, which those engaged in the behaviors are not conscious of. Some observational studies help us get outside ourselves and draw our attention to details we might otherwise not notice.

In viewing nonverbal gestures of preschool children, one investigator discovered that girls exhibited more pronounced bodily behavior when they were with other girls than when they were with boys. When they were paired with boys, they tended to be quieter. She concluded that society's expectations of sex differences in social behavior are evident even in the very young child and that different behavior is expected from boys than from girls.

Hand gestures are generally considered to function as illustrators, and they also serve to reveal our emotional states, intentionally or unintentionally. Hand and foot movements can sometimes signal messages at variance with our words. There seems to be some indication that in approval-seeking situations, women use more gesticulations than do males. Since some studies have shown that males talk more, interrupt more, and in general dominate conversations more than females, perhaps women resort to nonverbal expression more frequently. Some have concluded that women are molded into more patterns of behavior than are men, for there are more implicit and explicit rules as to how females should act and behave. Although initiative, innovation, boldness, and action are encouraged in males, such qualities are discouraged in women. "Forced to submerge their individual impulses and energies, women tend to express themselves more subtly and covertly." The nonverbal channel may be an outlet for women's covert and more subtle expression.

Peterson did a videotape study of nonverbal communication that occurred during verbal communication between male-male, female-female, and female-male pairs. Subject pairs were university students, and each pair held a two-minute conversation on the topic of their choice. She studied number of gestures, kinds of gestures, gestures used primarily by females, and gestures used primarily by males. She focused on hand, leg, and foot movements.

She found that overall, the number of gestures displayed by males exceeded the number exhibited by females, regardless of the sex of the conversation partner. Males displayed about the same number of gestures when conversing with either sex. However, females displayed significantly more gestures with males than with other females.

As for differences between the sexes in the kinds of gestures used, she observed the following:

Females

tend to leave both hands down on chair arms more than males do

arrange or play with their hair or ornamentation more

Males

use sweeping gestures more than females

use arms to lift or move the body position more

use closed fist more

stroke chin more

sit with ankle of one leg crossing the knee of the other more

tend to exhibit greater amount of leg and foot movement

tap their feet more

In addition, certain gestures seemed to be performed exclusively by females and others by males in this study. An asterisk indicates a more frequently performed gesture.

Female

hand or hands in lap

tapping hands

legs crossed at knees*

ankles crossed, knees slightly apart

Male

stretching hands and cracking knuckles

pointing*

both feet on floor with legs apart

legs stretched out, ankles crossed

knees spread apart when sitting*

General observations that Peterson made in regard to nonverbal gestures and the sexes include the following:

1. Both males and females seemed to be more relaxed with the same sex than with the opposite sex, except in two cases where subjects knew each other previously. Subjects exhibited more nervous gestures with the opposite sex.

2. Exclusively male and exclusively female gestures seemed to be reserved for conversations with the same-sex partner. Pointing generally occurred only between males, and hands in the lap between females.

3. Some traits appeared related to gender display. Females handled their hair and clothing ornamentation a great deal more in front of men than women. Men were significantly more open with their leg position and kept their feet on the floor with legs apart when conversing with other males. With females, however, the men nearly always crossed one ankle over the other knee.

4. Both males and females tended to display a greater number and greater diversity of gestures with the opposite sex. There seemed to be more foot movement with the same sex.

Peterson believed her study indicated that nonverbal communication fills a dual role in conversation for the sexes. Gesture serves as an illustrator and supplement to the verbal channel, and it acts as a means of gender display. Since certain movements occurred exclusively in same-sex pairs, it is possible that separate nonverbal languages are occurring. There seemed to be a greater display of dominant gestures by males—closed fist, pointing, sweeping gestures. Open and dominant gestures may be signals of power and status.

Clothing, Grooming, and Physical Appearance

Physical attractiveness and the artifacts that contribute to appearance affect communication and communication responses. One study explored the use of physical attractiveness by females as a means of obtaining higher grades from male college professors. The researcher found no differences in the scores of females and males on a Machiavellian scale, which attempts to get at traits associated with those who use any means (cunning, duplicity, or whatever) to achieve a goal. He hypothesized that cultural and social norms may prevent females from using obvious exploitative or deceptive tactics, so they utilize more socially acceptable, but more covert, means and take advantage of their physical attractiveness.

After comparing faculty ratings of women's pictures with their grade-point averages and position in the family, he found a correlation between physical attractiveness, grade point average, and being firstborn and female. Women who used more exhibiting behavior were probably more memorable to professors and thus fared better on grades. They tended to sit in the front of the room more often or come to see the professor after class or during the instructor's office hours more frequently. Using a series of questions about body measurements, the researcher determined that, as he had hypothesized, the firstborn females did indeed seem more aware of and socially concerned about their looks.

In some respects, claimed the researcher, he found the results "not at all surprising," for "the suggestion that *men* live by their *brains* and *women* by their *bodies* was made as far back as Genesis." He found the implications of these results "rather frightening" since the results suggest that the male college professor is a "rather putupon creature, *hoodwinked* by the *male* students (later born) and *enticed* by the *female* students (first born)." [Italics added.] Whether the reverse is true for female college professors ought to be the subject for future research. As consolation, however, the writer noticed that when a sample of 22 faculty members was given the Machiavellian scale, their average scores, compared with the scores of students in the study, showed them to be significantly more manipulative.

In another experiment, a girl was made up to look unattractive in one setting and attractive in another. The girl read aloud and explained some questions to listeners. Results showed the attitudes of the male students were modified more by the girl in the attractive condition than in the unattractive condition. However, this result was true for a male audience only.

Several years ago, the authors videotaped two women and two men speakers giving persuasive pro and con speeches about the merits of debate. Each gave his or her speech twice: once when made up to look unattractive with nose putty; subtle, unflattering make-up touches; and poorly styled hair and again when made up to look attractive. Clothing was kept constant. The speeches were such that, in the first set, the pro speech was constructed as a cogent and well-reasoned talk and the con speech was poorly reasoned and dogmatic. In the second set, the pro speech was poorly reasoned and dogmatic, and the con speech was cogent and well-reasoned. Listeners, who were college students, took a pretest concerning their attitudes on the subject and then took a post-test following the talks.

Results showed that physical attractiveness did have a persuasive effect on both sexes in their acceptance of the views of the speakers. Both speakers of the well-reasoned talks had a greater persuasive effect when made up in their attractive state, as was anticipated. An interesting result was a difference in persuasiveness that occurred between the females and males in their unattractive states, whether they gave the poorly reasoned or well-reasoned talk. The males made up unattractively were only slightly less effective than in their attractive states. However, there was considerable difference in the influence of the females, depending on physical state. Unattractiveness in the female caused a decidedly more negative reception of her views. In fact, in one of the videotaped versions the unattractiveness of the female who delivered the cogent pro talk weighed so heavily that the attractive female who answered with the poorly reasoned and ill-constructed con speech had the greater impact on listeners. Both females and males seemed more accepting of arguments or views from an unattractive male than from an unattractive female. Males were most negative toward the unattractive female's stand. Another study showed that regardless of sex, attractive people are rated high on character in credibility scales.

In a "Dear Abby" reader survey mentioned earlier, readers were asked to indicate what they noticed first about the opposite sex. Results indicated that women noticed physique first. Added the columnist: "But nearly every female who wrote that it is the first thing she *notices* about a man also wrote that it was certainly not the most *important*." A close second was grooming, including attire. Most women who wrote that they noticed a man's physical attributes first emphasized that it is "what's on the inside" that counts. Women placed much more importance on behavior than the men did in their survey. Responses from men indicated that men noticed bosoms first. After bosoms, a woman's figure, or whole torso, ranked next in importance, with some male respondents terming themselves "leg men" or "fanny fanciers."

These studies, as well as the casual responses to the "Dear Abby" column, seem to reflect our cultural emphasis on a man's activity—what he does—and on a woman's being—how she appears. This was graphically illustrated last year at Arizona State University, where one of the authors teaches. Several men stationed themselves in front of the student union with signs numbered from 4 to 9. They proceeded to rate women on campus by holding numbered signs over the women's heads as they passed. After the university police were summoned to investigate complaints, one of the self-appointed raters explained lamely, "It seemed to me that everyone in the area enjoyed what we did, except for one woman who asked for a sign so she could rate one of us. Of course I refused."

Perhaps women in our society are expected to be more visible and to reveal more of their bodies than men are. Men are sometimes described as more modest than women. This, at least, was the view of Hollywood dress designer Edith Head during an interview. Head has dressed stars from Cary Grant to Robert Redford, and Carole Lombard to Elizabeth Taylor. "Men for the most part are annoyingly modest in the fitting room if a woman is present," she says. "Women, however, will peel off to their panties and bras with male fitters present without batting an eye." She cited Clark Gable as one who was extremely modest. He could bare his chest, but if he had to unzip his trousers and expose his shorts, "he would bluster and blush and make amusing remarks about what he had to go through for his art." Head mentioned a friend who was the head nurse in

a urology clinic. "She faces up to male modesty all day long and it's a bore. Women, for the most part, do not have false modesty about their bodies." The references to modesty in all instances refer to mixed company.

The significance of clothing should be noted in passing. Different clothing types for the sexes are believed by some to have important social ramifications. Of course, pant suits for women have been and are worn extensively today, along with skirts, yet pants remain the symbol of the male and skirts the symbol of the female. Some writers question the notion that skirts should be worn by females. The roles of both sexes are changing. Women are moving out of old patterns, acquiring more education, exercising control of their childbearing, and getting political power. Yet, say some, they are still dressed in an archaic manner, with hips, thighs, and stomach skirted protectively or defensively hidden. Specialists in the history of dress indicate that the differentiation of pants and skirts goes back many years. Skirts may have been important once to protect the one who bore children because in early ages humans were more at the mercy of the elements, dangerous animals, human enemies, and high infant mortality. Presumably then, men were in awe of women's life-giving power and felt it necessary to "protect women's gateway to birth with skirts."

The division of pants from skirts may have been made originally because men needed freedom of leg movement when hunting and working the soil. Women needed skirts to hide their children under if danger threatened, to protect their own bodies, and to form convenient carrying places to convey children or food. Moira Johnston, a clothing historian, believes that skirts later became a male constriction for females because men feared the power a woman's childbearing ability gave her. So they consigned her sexuality to hiding. Later on the skirt became a form of modesty and an attempt to conceal seductive areas.

According to Johnston, the silhouette loosens when morals are lowered, as for example in the Roaring Twenties with the loose flapper dress. After the Second World War, when women went back to the home and to childbearing, fashions became more constrictive and restrictive. Women wore clothing cinched at the waist, with long, full skirts and high-heeled shoes. In looking at the history of feminism, one writer notes the significance of clothing. Before the 1920s women's clothing was confining and cumbersome. Casting aside the old corsets and long skirts may have had more significance for women's emancipation than women's suffrage had.

Henley notes that women's clothing today is fashioned to be revealing, but it still restricts women's body movement. Women are not supposed to reveal too much, and this required guarded movement in many cases. Another concomitant of clothing designed to reveal physical features is that, unlike more loose-fitting men's clothing, there are not convenient pockets in which to carry belongings—hence women's awkward purses. Some men's clothing styles today are styled for closer fit, and this may account for the carrying bags and purselike cases made and sold for males in some places. A clothing historian hypothesized that women have not freed themselves more from skirts and other restrictive women's clothing styles because they fear "terror of disorientation, and dissolution of identity."

In reflecting upon contemporary feminine clothing styles, the authors of this book would add this thought: The popular pants suit has had a liberating effect upon females. No longer must knees be tightly drawn together when sitting. Pants allow much more freedom of movement when walking, sitting on the floor, or lounging on the arm of a chair. The traditional need to cover and protect the female genital area by posture and apparel has been reduced considerably.

The so-called unisex look in clothing has freed women's bosoms from the protective slouch and the provocative thrust. It would be interesting to do research on how attitudes of the wearer are changed when clothing habits are modified. Perhaps it is true that we are what we wear!

Use of Space

The way we use space can convey nonverbal messages. It has been observed that dominant animals and dominant human beings keep a larger buffer zone of personal space surrounding them that discourages violation than do subordinate animals and humans. Dominant persons are not approached so closely as persons of lesser status. But research has shown that women are approached by both sexes more closely than men.

In one study, university students carried tape measures with them and when approached by anyone who began a conversation, each student measured the distance nose-to-nose between themselves and each speaker. Distance between pairs varied according to sex, age, and race. It was found that generally women were approached more closely than men by both women and men. Perhaps the envelope of inviolable space surrounding women is generally less than men's, and women are perceived as less dominant. Further, compared with men, women stand more closely to good friends but farther away from those they describe just as friends. It has been suggested that perhaps women are more cautious until they have established close relationships. In addition, it has been found that less distance is maintained between women and members of both sexes when they are sitting. There are indications that compared with men, women perceive their own territory as being smaller and as being more open to influence by others. Both sexes have been found more wary of the approach of males than of females.

Studies on crowding offer some insight on differences in personal space between the sexes. One researcher observed groups of people in crowded and uncrowded rooms during one-hour periods of time. Results showed that generally men had more negative reactions to crowding. They liked others less and considered them less friendly. In general, they found the situation more unpleasant, and they became more contentious and distrustful. In contrast, women found the experience pleasanter, liked others more, and considered them friendlier than men did.

It appears that women's territory is perceived as smaller by both males and females. Women may be more tolerant of, or accustomed to, having their personal space breeched by others. This may also be an indication that they are considered to be of lower status by those with whom they interact.

Certainly control of greater territory and space is a characteristic we associate with dominance and status. Superiors have the prerogative of taking more space. They have larger houses, estates, cars, offices, and desks, as well as more personal space in body spread. Inferiors own less space and take up less space personally with their bodies. Females generally command less space. For example, a study showed that women are less likely to have a special and unviolated room in the home. The male may have his den where "nothing is to be touched." Some will counter that the woman has her terri-tory—her kitchen or sewing room. But this space is often as infinitely invadable for the woman working in it as her time while she is doing so. We are all familiar with Archie Bunker's special chair. While men may have their own chair in a house, women rarely do.

Seating arrangement is another space variable. Research shows that female/male status is evident in the way people seat themselves. At rectangular ta-bles, generally the "head" position (the seat at either end of the table) is associated with higher status. Subjects in a study were shown paper-and-pencil diagrams of rectangular tables and asked how they would locate themselves with regard to a person of higher, lower, or equal status and of either sex. When subjects were asked to choose the seat they would take upon arriving first and then to name the seat the other would then take, approx-imately twice as many females as males would sit side by side, and this was more frequent in relation to a low-status than a high-status person. When asked to choose which seat the other would take upon arriving first, respondents tended to put others at an "end" chair. This tendency was greater for a high-status male authority figure. Subjects were also told to imagine that either Professor Henry Smith or Professor Susan Smith were there. Twice as many subjects would choose the head chair for themselves when the female professor was there as when the male professor was there.

Students in one of our classes did some observa-tional studies of female and male students walking across the Arizona State University campus during peak class-change times in the heavily trafficked mall areas. They found people of both sexes tend to cut across females' paths more frequently.

When female-male pairs approach each other on the street, apparently women are expected to walk around men, according to the results of one study. Nineteen woman-man pairs were observed, and in 12 out of the 19, the woman moved out of the man's way. In only 3 cases did the man move, and in the remaining 4 instances both moved. When women approached women or men approached men, how-ever, about half of the time both moved out of each other's way. The rest of the time only one person moved.

Also in regard to space, it has been observed that women's general body comportment is restrained. Often their femininity is judged according to how little space they take up. Women condense or com-press; men expand. Whereas males use space ex-pansively, women, by the way they cross their legs, keep their elbows to their sides, and maintain a more erect posture, seem to be trying to take up as little space as possible. Novelist Marge Piercy, de-scribing a character teaching movement to a theater group, put it well:

Men expanded into available space. They sprawled, or they sat with spread legs. They put their arms on the arms of chairs. They crossed their legs by putting a foot on the other knee. They dom-inated space expansively. Women condensed. Women crossed their legs by putting one leg over the other and alongside. Women kept their elbows to their sides, taking up as little space as possible. They behaved as if it were their duty not to rub against, not to touch, not to bump a man. If con-tact occurred, the woman shrank back. If a woman bumped a man, he might choose to inter-pret it as a come-on. Women sat protectively using elbows not to dominate space, not to mark terri-tory, but to protect their soft tissues.

Touch

Touch has been the object of some investigation. Most research seems to show that females are

touched by others more than males are. Mothers have been found to touch their female children more than their male children from the age of six months on. In one study of touch, the researcher gave a questionnaire to students concerning which parts of the body are touched most often and by whom. He found that females are considerably more accessible to touch by all persons than males are. Friends of the opposite sex and mothers did the most touching.

Further investigation showed that mothers touched their sons more than fathers did, and fathers touched their daughters more than their sons. Daughters touched their fathers more than sons did, and sons touched their mothers more than they touched their fathers. In other words, fathers and sons tended to refrain from touching each other, but other touching interaction in the family was about equal. As for body regions, mothers touched daughters in more places than they did sons. Fathers touched daughters in more places than they did sons. Fathers also were touched by their daughters in more places than they were by their sons. Males touched their opposite-sex best friends in more regions than females reported touching their opposite-sex friends. So in three of the four comparisons, touch by fathers, touch by mothers, and touch by opposite-sex friends, females were touched more. The mean total being-touched score for women was higher than for men. Also, whereas women's opposite-sex friends touched them the most, men's opposite-sex friends touched them the least.

The pattern of greater touching by males has been interpreted by some as a reflection of sexual interest and greater sexual motivation of men. Henley does not accept this, since she finds research does not support greater sexuality in males than females. Rather, she regards touching as a sign of status or power. Touching is an invasion of one's personal space and involves the deference or lack of deference accorded to the space surrounding the body. Touching between intimates can symbolize friendship and affection. But when the pattern of touching is not reciprocal, and both parties do not take equal touch privileges, it can indicate power and status. An observer of the touch system in a hos-

pital noted that although the doctors mi[...] other ranks to convey support or comf[...] ranks tended to feel it would be presum[...] return a doctor's touch, and particularly to [...]

One investigation of touching involved[...] hours of observing incidents of touching i[...] Intentional touch with the hand was rec[...] well as whether the touch was returned. [...] and approximate socioeconomic status of[...] sons observed was also noted. Results sho[...] higher-status persons touched lower-stat[...] significantly more frequently. Comparing t[...] between the sexes, men touched wom[...] greater rate, when all else (age and apparen[...] economic status) was equal. When other[...] were unequal, for example if women had a[...] economic status advantage, the women wo[...] the more likely one to initiate touch.

The pattern of sexual status showed up pri[...] in outdoor settings (shopping plaza, beach, [...] campus, and so forth) rather than in indoor i[...] tion (bank, store, restaurant, doctor's office, [...] on). It was suggested that because outdoor in[...] tion is more public, it may necessitate stricter[...] tion to signals of power. Indoor interaction is[...] informal and encourages more relaxed powe[...] tionships. When people are indoors, powe[...] probably be more easily communicated by [...] cues than touching. Subtle cues, such as eye m[...] ments, gestures, and voice shifts, can conve[...] minders of status easily. But outdoors gross, la[...] physical acts, such as touching, seem to be requi[...]

Goodall describes one use of touch am[...] chimpanzees. A chimpanzee, after being threate[...] or attacked by a superior, may follow the aggres[...] around, screaming and crouching to the ground[...] holding out his or her hand. The chimpanze[...] begging a reassuring touch from the superi[...] Sometimes the subordinate champanzee will n[...] relax until he or she has been touched or patted a[...] embraced. Greetings also reestablish the dom[...] nance status of one chimpanzee in relation to t[...] other. For example, Olly would greet Mike by hol[...] ing out her hand toward him. By this gesture sh[...] was acknowledging his superior rank. Mike woul[...] touch, pat, or hold her hand and touch her head i[...]

response to her submission. These gestures of dominance and submission observed in primates seem to occur among humans as well. As with apes, the gestures used are probably used by humans to maintain and reinforce the social hierarchy by reminding lower-status persons of their position in the order and by reassuring higher-status people that those of lesser rank accept their place in the pecking order.

An informal test of the significance of touch that is not reciprocated and the authority it symbolizes would be to ask ourselves which person in each of the following pairs would be more likely to touch the other—to lay a hand on the back, put an arm around the shoulder, tap the chest, or grasp the wrist: master and servant; teacher and student; pastor and parishioner; doctor and patient; foreman and worker; executive and secretary; police and accused; lawyer and client. If status can explain touch differences in other groups, it seems reasonable to accept this as a factor in female/male touch differences as well.

A considerable amount of touching of women is so much a part of our culture that it goes virtually unnoticed. It occurs when men guide women through the door, down the stairs, into the car, across the street; when they playfully lift women; when they pat them on the head, or playfully spank them; and in many other instances. Males seem to have greater freedom to touch others. When used with objects, touching seems to connote possession. This may apply to attitudes about women as well. As Henley and Thorne express it: ". . . the wholesale touching of women carries the message that women are community property. They are tactually accessible just as they are visually and informationally accessible."

It is interesting to consider the difference in interpretation of touch by the sexes. This difference seems to support the idea that touch is used as a sign of status or power among the sexes. The difference in female/male perspective can be shown by an illustration which Henley relates. A woman was at a party one evening and saw a male friend of both her and her husband. At various times in the evening he would come up and sit with his arm around her.

This she interpreted as a friendly gesture, and she reciprocated the action with friendly intent. However, later the man approached her in private and made sexual advances. When the woman expressed surprise at his suggestions, he replied, "Wasn't that what you were trying to tell me all evening?" The point is that women do not interpret a man's touch as necessarily a sexual invitation, but men often interpret a woman's touch in that way. Touch, of course, can be either. It can be a gesture of power or of intimacy. But touch as a gesture of power will appear to be inappropriate if it is used by one not having power.

Since women are often subordinate, touching by women will be perceived as a gesture of intimacy or sexual invitation rather than power. One would not anticipate that they would be exercising power. In addition, viewing a woman's gesture as a sexual invitation is not only complimentary to the man, but it can put the woman at a disadvantage. By putting a narrower sexual interpretation on what she does and placing her in the position of a sex object, she is effectively placed outside the arena of primary social interaction.

STATUS AND NONVERBAL COMMUNICATION

We have looked at a number of nonverbal behavior differences exhibited by females and males. One theoretical thread running through much of the discussion is the concept of asymmetry, or nonreciprocality of behavior, that exists between nonequals in status. Female/male differences have been seen to roughly parallel those between superiors and subordinates in status, suggesting a status and power differential behind the socialization of the sexes. Table 1, which is based on theory and some research cited previously, categorizes behavior cues used by females and males.

To a certain extent we may say that behavior is cued. Perhaps women give gestures of submission because they have been shown gestures of dominance. In some situations some people may use gestures of dominance because they have been shown gestures of acquiescence or ingratiation by the

Table 1 Asymmetrical Nonverbal Cues

Cues	Superior [male]	Subordinate [female]
Eyes	Look or stare aggressively Look elsewhere while speaking	Lower eyes, avert eyes, look away, blink Watch speaker while listening
Face	No smile or frown Impassive, not showing emotions	Smile Expressive facial gestures, showing emotions
Posture	Relaxed, more body lean	Tense, more erect
Bearing	Loose legs, freed arms, non-circumspect positions	Tight, legs together, arms close to body
Gestures	Larger, more sweeping, forceful, such as pointing	Smaller, more inhibited
Touch	Touches other	Does not touch other or reciprocate touch, cuddles, or yields to touch
Use of space	Expands, uses more space	Condenses, contracts, takes as little space as possible
Distance	Maintains larger envelope of space Closer × Approaches closer, crowds Cuts across other's path Walks into other's path	Maintains smaller envelope of space More distant Approaches more distant, retreats, yields Gives way Moves out of the way
Clothing	Loose, comfortable	Constraining, formfitting

Source: Some of the material in this table was suggested by Nancy Henley, "Examples of Some Nonverbal Behaviors with Usage Differing for Status Equals and Nonequals, and for Women and Men," *Siscom '75: Women's (and Men's) Communication*, ed. Barbara Eakins, Gene Eakins, and Barbara Lieb-Brilhart (Falls Church, Va.: Speech Communication Association, 1976), Table 1, p. 39; and Henley, "Gestures of Power and Privilege. Examples of Some Nonverbal Behaviors with Usage Differing for Status Equals and Nonequals, and For Women and Men," *Body Politics Power, Sex and Nonverbal Communication* (Englewood Cliffs, N.J.: Prentice-Hall, 1977), Table 5, p. 181.

others with whom they interact. One writer had some sobering pronouncements to make concerning many of the so-called womanly gestures. She indicated that submission in women is conveyed by such behaviors as smiling, averting the eyes, or lowering or turning the head. Self-improvement specialists would grow pale on hearing her definition of charm: "Charm is nothing more than a series of gestures (including vocalizations) indicating submission!" Staunch feminists would probably add a hearty "amen."

Changing or manipulating the signals and indicators of power or subordination may not go very far toward transforming the inequities of society. But perhaps by becoming aware of what we are signifying or are responding to nonverbally, we can better gain control over our lives and more readily ensure that our actions and responses are more conscious, more voluntary or, at least, less automatic. We may surprise ourselves by the extent to which we can affect the patterns and relationships in our lives.

Silence and Silences in Cross-Cultural Perspective: Japan and the United States

SATOSHI ISHII
TOM BRUNEAU

A BRIEF FOCUS

Every deed and every relationship is surrounded by an atmosphere of silence. . . . Friendship needs no words—it is solitude delivered from the anguish of loneliness. Silence pervades the world, as do a multitude of kinds of silences and an entire spectrum of silencings. A cultural, social, and political nature. It is certainly not particular to any single cultural tradition. However, different cultural groups seem to stylize their forms of silence according to their own traditional wisdom, beliefs, and attitudes.

Hammarskjold (1971, p. 8)

Most people throughout the world experience some form of silence. However, the manner in which people's attitudes become socially and culturally disposed toward silence is dramatically different in different cultural groups. Northern European and North American societies, for example, are so involved in linear progression that even flashes of silence are filled with action and doing. In these cultures, silence is viewed as dark, negative, and full of "no things"—all of which are considered socially undesirable. In such cultures, silence is ritualized and ceremonialized by authoritative leader-

This essay was prepared especially for the fifth edition. All rights reserved. Permission to reprint must be obtained from the publisher and the authors. Satoshi Ishii teaches at Otsuma Women's University, Mobara, Chiba-ken, Japan. Tom Bruneau teaches at Radford University, Radford, Virginia.

ship in a wide variety of contexts. In other cultures, however, silence is *often* achieved. Here breaking silence is a necessary evil, at best; speaking is a negative act.

Silence is the mode of communication for the contemplative throughout the world—but it is more practical in some cultural and social groupings than others. For some, Lao Tsu's (1972) simple statement, "To talk little is natural" (No. 23), is obviously and experientially descriptive. Pragmatists and people in action—those mobilized in projects and active planning, in decision making, and the like—seldom experience deep silence. Pragmatists and scientific-minded people shake their heads in utter amazement that what means nothing to them can be significant to others in many different ways.

Silence belongs to the world of being—not to the world of becoming. Silence is stillness—a mental phenomenon of some duration. *Silences*, however, while connected to the deeper level of silence, belong to the world of becoming, of linear progression, of conscious and semiconscious thinking, saying, and doing. Stillness and silence-of-being appear to concern right-brained cortical processes; silence, in its social or asocial manifestations, concerns sitting still, solitude, and inaction. Silences-of-becoming appear to concern left-brained cortical processes.

Silences

Silences lie on the surface of deeper levels of silence. Silences are like interconnected rivers and lakes; silence is like the sea to which they are connected. Silences are discontinuities; they are breaks in action. Silences are often dynamic variations of processes recognized as having signification. They are stillings of process where we attempt to impose duration (Bruneau, 1985). Some cultural groups, many of them Far Eastern, are biased in favor of lengthy silences. These groups create silences more frequently than do those from some Western cultures; they interrupt processual action with long and deep silences.

When we alter continuity significantly, we create silences; when we alter expected succession, we create silences; when we stop to think, we create internal silences.

Silences are not only based in the very comprehensibility of each language of the world but are also the stuff out of which social acts, social actions, social presence, and social events are created and articulated. Thus we can speak of social silences, or interpersonal or group silences. Some lengthy group silences can be viewed as "social silences." These silences are also durational breaks in process, succession, and continuity. Customs, traditions, social mannerisms, social stability, normative actions, and the like can be viewed as they relate to habitual silences.

Silencing

The process of arresting process is *silencing*. At a basic level, silencing is the imposition of volition or will to give signification or symbolic meaning (Bruneau, 1985). At a political or social level, it is a process of using a figure to gain rhetorical import; it is a persuasive act, an exercise in enforcing norms and directing others and one's self; it is many such communicative matters. As far as social and political exigencies, events, situations, and circumstances are concerned, we can speak of those who silence and those who are silenced, those who act and those who observe, those who listen and those who speak.

We silence others to gain attention, to maintain control, to protect, to teach, to attempt to eliminate distractions, to induce reverence for authority or tradition, and to point to something greater than ourselves or our groups. Silencing is also a way of positing a ground of psychological and social neutrality, so that silences and silence can occur positively. Zones of silence, or places where extraneous noise is controlled, are sometimes created as a means of silencing others. These zones can concern authority, expertise, secrecy, thinking, and the like.

Silencing can be the essence of the language of superiority and inferiority, affecting such relationships as teacher-follower, male-female, and expert-client. The definition of much role behavior across many cultural groups concerns the manner of speech and refraining from speech. The process of

silencing can have both positive and negative effects. In some situations, quiet is demanded by others and by those who must themselves be quiet. Being quiet—effecting a self-imposed silence is often valued and rewarded in some social environments. Being quiet is often a sign of respect for the wisdom and expertise of others. The elderly of many Eastern cultural groups expect signs of respect, one of which is the silence of the young, as well as the silence of less authoritative family members. Westerners often do not understand this process: It was common several decades ago but is practiced less and less today.

Contrary to outspoken and often ego-driven Western women (even the milder ones), many women in Eastern cultures view their silent roles as very powerful. Some women see their silent roles as natural (some are unconscious of them) and cannot *imagine* speaking out unless violated personally. There is a power of control in silence and in the outward show of reticence. This power often goes unrecognized by those who value speech-as-power and by those who value assertiveness by all, equally and democratically. It is, without a doubt, a truism that many cultures of the world expect more silences from women and children.

SILENCES IN CROSS-CULTURAL PERSPECTIVE

Today's communication scholars, who often observe the Western rhetorical tradition uncritically, have been concerned primarily with verbal expressions or speaking out. The Western tradition is relatively negative in its attitude toward silence and ambiguity, especially in social and public relations. People seldom recognize that silences do have linking, affecting revelational, judgmental, and activating communicative functions in Western cultures (Jensen, 1973). Also, silences can convey all the various kinds and degrees of messages that may be described as cold, oppressive, defiant, disapproving or condemning, calming, approving, humble, excusing, and consenting (Samovar et al., 1981, p. 184). The intercultural implications of silent behaviors are diverse because the value and use of silence as communication vary markedly from one culture to another. Consequently, communication scholars ought to pay more attention to the cultural views of silence and the interpretations given to silence in communication interactions.

Since the time of ancient Greek philosophers, Western thought has emphasized bipolar values and concepts by opposing terms such as black versus white, good versus bad, and yes versus no. Speech versus silence has been researched and taught from the same bipolarization: Speech has a positive connotation and silence has a negative one. Recently, however, both Eastern and Western scholars have come to advocate relativistic viewpoints on such concepts and values: "A major misconception is . . . the common, basic assumption that silence is completely other than speech, its foreign opposite, its antagonist" (Bruneau, 1973, p. 17). Silence is not the "empty" absence of speech sound; silence creates speech, and speech creates silence; yin and yang are, in this view, counterdependent as well as dynamically concomitant. In Gestalt terms, the two function as the "figure" and the "ground," one being possible because of the other's existence, but dynamically so. Generally, silence is regarded as the ground against which the figures of speech are perceived and valued. The two should sometimes be perceived in the reverse way; silence should be treated as the figure against which the ground of speech functions. Most people, especially in Western cultures, are unconscious of this interdependence between speech and silence.

Some Pragmatic Comparisons

In intercultural communication, while the basic *form* of silence *may be* universal, its functions and interpretations vary among cultures. For a newcomer to a foreign culture, a general knowledge of when and where to keep silent may be a basic social requirement, just as a little knowledge of verbal communication is. That is, in intercultural communication contexts a deep understanding comes from being sensitive and open-minded to cultural differences in communicative silences. According to

Wayne (1974), the U.S. interpretations of silence are: (1) sorrow, (2) critique, (3) obligation, (4) regret, and (5) embarrassment. Australian interpretations proved to be similar to the U.S. ones. Wayne goes on to conclude, "In every case the fact that the percentage of neutral or uncommitted responses was much higher for the Japanese and thus could be interpreted as a cultural difference" (pp. 127–130).

From the perspective of an ethnography of communication, the notion and significance of silent communication competence should be positively introduced and researched along with verbal communication competence. Humans become communicatively competent by acquiring not only the structure and use of language but also a set of values and patterns of silent interaction. Anthropologically, the relative quantities and values of the silence of children in communicative settings can be said to be related to socialization and child-rearing practices. According to Caudill and Weinstein (1969), for example, Japanese mothers make more efforts than do U.S. mothers to soothe their children with physical, rather than verbal, contact. This effort apparently suggests that Japanese mothers value silence and its association with self-restraint in Japanese society. In contrast to the Western significance of eloquence and self-assertion, the general attitude of Japanese people toward language and verbalization is that fewer words, supported by the *aesthetics of vagueness*, are better than more words.

Socio-cultural impact plays an important role in the characterization of communication patterns. It may be safely said that Japanese culture nurtures silence, reserve, and formality, whereas Western cultures place more value on speech, self-assertion, and informality. Ishii and Klopf (1976) ascertained from their cross-cultural survey results that the average person in the United States devotes about twice the time to conversation (6 hours, 43 minutes) than do the Japanese (3 hours, 31 minutes).

Further evidence to support the idea that the Japanese have negative attitudes toward speaking is in order. Values regarding appropriate communicative behavior are often most clearly reflected in traditional proverbs. Katayama (1982) analyzed 504 Japanese proverbs on the values of language and found: 124 (25 percent) of them had positive values; 320 (63 percent) had negative values; and 59 (12 percent) were neutral. Inagaki (1985) also investigated 3,600 Japanese people's attitudes toward speaking and obtained data indicating that 82 percent of them agreed with the saying, *"Kuchi wa wazawai no moto,"* or, in English, "Out of the mouth comes all evil" (p. 6). This finding is not surprising given the many Japanese proverbs expressing negativity toward speech. Ishikawa's (1970) survey results on businessmen and businesswomen in Tokyo revealed that (1) men should or need to be silent to be successful in life and (2) 65 percent of the businesswomen would choose silent males to marry (p. 5).

All these survey results show a contrast between Japanese and U.S. values of speech and silence. Rader and Wunsch (1980) obtained the following results from their survey on oral communication in U.S. businesses: (1) 95 percent responded that the ability to communicate orally and in writing was considered to be important in their jobs and (2) graduates in business were spending the greatest portion of time in speaking, followed by listening, writing, and reading. Woodstock (1979), who analyzed oral and written communication problems of managerial trainees, secretaries, and immediate supervisors, concluded that oral communication is an area that should be given more emphasis in the business communication classroom.

Not only in business but in everyday social life, people in the United States like to ask questions and force others to talk to fill interpersonal silences. Because silence is not valued and therefore not tolerated socially in U.S. society (and in many European societies), one function of speech is to avoid silence, generally, as well as to fill silences during the transference of messages. Contrary to the U.S. practice, in Japanese society silence and silences are generally considered to be positively meaningful; they are socio-culturally accepted to a much higher degree.

The point here is that the quantity of silences versus the quantity of speech is interpreted and val-

ued differently across cultures. Different norms of appropriate communicative behavior exist, and a variety of intercultural misunderstanding can occur if one does not know when, where, and how to remain silent. To promote natural and effective interaction, especially with Japanese, people in the United States need to learn to feel more comfortable in situations where silence and vagueness prevail. Learning the general rules for silence plays a more important part than generally thought for all people attempting to communicate successfully across cultures.

Japanese Enryo-Sasshi Versus U.S. Exaggeration-Reduction

Anthropologists, psychologists, sociologists, and communication scholars have often pointed out that Japanese people are oriented to nonconfrontational and nondialectical interpersonal relations. This orientation of the Japanese is unquestionably based on their nonverbal, intuitive communication practices, whereas Americans want to emphasize individualism and self-assertion supported by verbal communication. Barnlund (1975), who compared Japan-U.S. verbal and nonverbal self-disclosure, concluded: "The communicative consequences of cultural emphasis upon 'talkativeness' and 'self assertion' among Americans may cultivate a highly self-oriented person, one who prizes and expresses every inner response no manner how trivial or fleeting." As to Japanese self-disclosure, he goes on to say, "The communicative consequences of cultural encouragement of 'reserve' and 'caution' among Japanese may produce an other-oriented person, who is highly sensitive and receptive to meanings in others" (p. 160). Barnlund's observations are evidentially supported by Ishii, Klopf, and Cambra's (1979, 1984) PVB[1] findings on Japanese and U.S. students' verbal predispositions: The Japanese students were significantly different from the U.S. students, being less dominant, less inclined to initiate and maintain conversations, less apt to speak frequently and long, less inclined to talk, and less fluent than U.S. students (1984). How, then, can these

Japan-U.S. communication style differences be explained psychologically in terms of encoding and decoding messages?

In the high-context Japanese culture, most information tends to be in the physical context and internalized into the person. People, therefore, need not participate actively in verbal interaction. Ishii's (1984) study of *enryo-sasshi* communication in such a high-context culture was among the first attempts to analyze and clarify the general process of Japanese interpersonal empathic communication. The speaker, unconsciously depending on the other person and the communicative situation, simplifies and economizes messages rather than elaborating on them. His or her psychological "exit," through which the encoded messages are sent out under the impact of *enryo* (reserve or restraint), is considered to be much smaller than his or her own message-receiving "entrance," called *sasshi*. The sense of *enryo-sasshi* is of utmost importance in high-context Japanese interpersonal relations.

Intrapersonally, the person of good *enryo* considers the active, exaggerated expression of ideas and feelings to be degrading and foreign. Ideas and feelings that might hurt the other person or damage the general atmosphere when expressed are carefully sent back for re-examination in an internal self-feedback process. Only those ideas judged safe and vague are allowed to be sent out through the small exit that functions as a screening filter. This message-screening process in consideration of the other person and the context is *"enryo"*; it makes the Japanese appear silent, vague, and awkward in communicating with superiors, strangers, and people from different cultures. This observation apparently serves to explain the psychological backdrop of Japanese people's communication apprehension: Thirty-five percent of the Japanese considered themselves to be highly apprehensive in communication situations as compared to 20 percent of the Americans.

To make communicative interaction possible in the high-context situation, the Japanese listener is expected to possess good sensitivity and to receive the message through his or her wide entrance. In this message-receiving stage, the restricted and vague information is appropriately "developed" according to the listener's guess competence called *"sasshi."* In Japanese interpersonal relations, a person of good *sasshi*, who is good at mind-reading or perceiving intuitively people's ideas and feelings, is highly appreciated. This process of interaction is *enryo-sasshi* communication, one of the keys to understanding Japanese interpersonal relations.

In the U.S. multi-ethnic low-context culture, a communication process that is in contrast to the Japanese process seems to function. In low-context communication people depend on the active exchange of overt, verbal messages. The speaker is socialized and expected to send out his or her messages through the large exit, in an exaggerated way, rather than simplifying and economizing them. The psychological mechanism of American message-screening and internal self-feedback can be said to be rougher than that of Japanese *enryo-sasshi*. This fact is evidently based upon a *counter-Japanese value* of interpersonal communication that the more speaking, the better—at home, at school, and in business.

The U.S. listener, in receiving and decoding the exaggerated message, subconsciously attempts to reduce the information. The message-receiving entrance seems to be smaller than that of the Japanese; that is, the listener is not expected to guess and develop the message. Clarity and exactitude in decoding are not the norm. This whole process of sending and receiving messages can be called U.S. *exaggeration-reduction communication*.

CONCLUSION

Whereas verbal communication plays a very important role in promoting intercultural as well as interpersonal understanding, we should recognize that the ultimate goal-stage of communication—interpersonally or interculturally—may be communication through silence. Silence lends substance to speech and gives it tensive direction—being supports becoming. Baker (1955), who constructed a communication model of silence on the basis of "reciprocal identification," claims that silence *is the aim of human communication.* We do not dispute this claim, and although we have been forced here to use words to point to the muted world, we are hopeful that we have shared some of our interior silence and silences with those of the reader.

NOTE

1. PVB (Predispositions toward Verbal Behavior) is an instrument to measure a person's general feelings of his or her verbal behavior (see Mortensen et al., 1977). For details of the Japan-U.S. cross-cultural surveys, see Ishii et al., 1984.

REFERENCES

Baker, S. J. (1955). "The Theory of Silence." *Journal of General Psychology, 53,* 145–167.

Barnlund, D. C. (1975). *Public and Private Self in Japan and the United States.* Tokyo: Simul Press.

Bruneau, T. J. (1973). "Communicative Silences: Forms and Functions." *Journal of Communication, 23,* 1, 17–46.

Bruneau, T. J. (1982). "Communicative Silences in Cross-Cultural Perspective." *Media Development* (London), *29* (4), 6–8.

Bruneau, T. J. (1985). "Silencing and Stilling Process: The Creative and Temporal Bases of Signs." *Semiotica, 56* (3/4), 279–290.

Caudill, W., and Weinstein, H. (1969). "Maternal Care and Infant Behavior in Japan and America." *Psychiatry, 32,* 12–43.

Hammarskjold, D. (1971). *Markings* (Transl. L. Sjoberg and W. H. Auden). New York: Alfred A. Knopf.

Inagaki, Y. (1985). *Jiko Hyogen No Gijutsu* ("Skills in Self-Expression"). Tokyo: PHP Institute.

Ishii, S. (1984). *"Enryo-sasshi* Communication: A Key to Understanding Japanese Interpersonal Relations." *Cross Currents, 11* (1), 49–58.

Ishii, S., and Klopf, D. W. (1976). "A Comparison of Communication Activities of Japanese and American Adults." *Eigo Tembo (ELEC Bulletin), 53,* 22–26.

Ishii, S., Klopf, D. W., and Cambra, R. E. (1979). "Oral Communication Apprehension Among Students in Japan, Korea and the United States." *Jijiei-gogaku Kenkyu (Current English Studies), 18,* 12–26.

Ishii, S., Klopf, D. W., and Cambra, R. E. (1984). "The Typical Japanese Student as an Oral Communicator: A Preliminary Profile." *Otsuma Review, 17,* 39–63.

Ishikawa, H. (1970). "Chinmoku-gata Wa Shusse Suru" ("The Silent Type Succeeds"). *Mainichi Shimbun.*

Jensen, V. J. (1973). "Communicative Functions of Silence." *ETC: A Review of General Semantics, 30,* 259–263.

Katayama, H. (1982). "Kotowaza Ni Hanei Sareta Nipponjin No Gengokan" ("Japanese Views of Language as Reflected in Proverbs"). *Kyoiku Kiyo 8-go (Eighth General Education Annual).* Matsudo, Chiba-ken: Matsudo Dental School, Nihon University, 1–11.

Mortensen, C. D., et al. (1977). "Measurement of Verbal Predispositions: Scale Development and Application." *Human Communication Research, 3,* 146–158.

Rader, M., and Wunsch, A. (1980). "A Survey of Communication Practices of Business School Graduates by Job Category and Undergraduate Major." *Journal of Business Communication, 17,* 33–41.

Samovar, L. A., Porter, R. E., and Jain, N. C. (1981). *Understanding Intercultural Communication.* Belmont, Calif.: Wadsworth.

Tsu, Lao (1972). *Tao Te Ching* (Transl. Gia-Fu-Feng and J. English). New York: Alfred A. Knopf.

Wayne, M. S. (1974). "The Meaning of Silence in Conversations in Three Cultures." In *Patterns of Communication In and Out of Japan* (International Christian University Communication Student Group, ed.). Tokyo: ICU Communication Department, 127–130.

Woodstock, B. (1979). "Characteristic Oral and Written Business Communication Problems of Selected Managerial Trainees." *Journal of Business Communication, 16,* 43–48.

Variables in the Use of Personal Space in Intercultural Transactions

CAROL ZINNER DOLPHIN

I. BACKGROUND

The concept of personal space has been the subject of numerous analogies. David Katz compared it to the shell of a snail. Stern developed the concept of a personal world. Von Uexkull used the graphic analogy of people "surrounded by soap bubble worlds" (Sommer, 1959). Hayduk (1983), on the other hand, suggests that the bubble is not a good analogy since it does not characterize the gradual acceptance of space intrusion under varying circumstances and prefers Sundstrom's (1976) alternate analogy, which compares personal space to an electrical field which is three dimensional, possesses force which decreases with distance, and has positive/negative signs to account for attraction and repulsion of certain bodies.

Forston (1968) defined *proxemics* as "the study of how man communicates through structuring microspace—the distance that man consciously maintains between himself and another person while relating physically to others with whom he is interacting" (p. 109). *Personal space* may be viewed as "the way in which individuals expect the immediate space around them to be used," translating the "more general interpersonal goals into spatial and behavioral terms . . ." (Liebman, 1970, p. 211). Personal space differs from *territory*, "an area con-

trolled by an individual, family or other face-to-face collectivity," principally by virtue of its mobility (Sommer, 1966, p. 59). Whereas territory tends to remain stable with somewhat definable boundaries, personal space is carried with the individual. "Personal space has the body as its center; territory does not" (Sommer, 1959, p. 247). Hall (1966) adds another dimension to the concept of proxemics by terming it "the interrelated observations and theories of man's use of space as a specialized elaboration of culture" (p. 1).

Edward Hall (1966) maintains that "it is in the nature of animals including man to exhibit behavior which we call territoriality. In doing so, they use the senses to distinguish between one space or distance and another" (p. 128). The anthropologist's formal observations of interpersonal transactions led him to propose a system of classifying the use of personal space. Subjects in Hall's United States sample (middle class adults, mainly natives of the northeastern seaboard) exhibited four distance zones, marked particularly by shifts in vocal volume. The intimate zone (contact to eighteen inches) usually is reserved for spouses, lovers and close friends, people engaged in lovemaking, comforting, nursing and conversations of a private nature. The personal zone (eighteen inches to four feet) includes activities such as chatting, gossiping, playing cards and casual interactions and is the territory of friends and acquaintances. Those whom one does not know well are often kept in the social zone (four to twelve feet), the domain of interviews, business transactions and professional exchanges. The public zone (beyond twelve feet) makes interpersonal communication nearly impossible and often denotes a status difference between the speaker and listener. "Spatial changes," writes Hall (1959, p. 204), "give a tone to a communication, accent it, and at times can even override the spoken word. The flow and shift of distance between people as they interact with each other is part and parcel of the communication process."

Emphasizing the impact of culture on communication behaviors, Hall specifies that the above distances are relevant only for those who fit into his sample category and notes that, in the United States

From *The Howard Journal of Communications*, Volume 1 (Spring 1988), 23–38. Reprinted by permission of the publisher. Professor Dolphin teaches at the University of Wisconsin Center, Waukesha County.

and Northern Europe, individuals are guided in their use of space according to their concept of a partner as a stranger or as a familiar. Other cultures demonstrate other patterns such as the family/non-family distinction in Portugal and Spain or the caste/outcaste system of India (Hall, 1966, p. 128).

It is in this vein that Hall (1963), based upon Heidiger's division of animals into contact and non-contact species, expands his theories in the use of personal space to identify differences between contact and noncontact cultures. It is hypothesized that people from contact cultures, i.e. Arabs, Southern Europeans and Latin Americans, will use closer distances, maintain more direct axes and eye contact, touch each other more frequently, and speak more loudly than those from noncontact cultures, i.e. Northern Europeans, Asians, Americans and Indians.

According to Hall, then, culture inevitably plays *the* definitive role in determining how different individuals use personal space. People from different cultures are seen as not only speaking different languages, but inhabiting different sensory worlds. "Selective screening of sensory data admits some things while filtering out others, so that experience as it is perceived through one set of culturally patterned sensory screens is quite different from experience perceived through another" (Hall, 1966, p. 2). Moreover, cultural conditioning is seen as difficult if not impossible to overcome. "Cultural irrationality," writes Hall in *Beyond Culture* (1976, p. 192), "is deeply entrenched in the lives of us, and because of culturally imposed blinders, our view of the world does not normally transcend the limits imposed by culture. We are, in effect, stuck with the program culture imposes." Giving support to Hall's earlier theories were experiments by Baltus (1974) which led him to characterize proxemic behavior as "culturally conditioned and entirely arbitrary . . . binding on all concerned" (p. 7).

Early support for Hall's hypotheses was provided in experiments conducted by Watson and Graves in 1966 and by Watson in 1970. The 1966 study, which observed proxemic distances in dyads of male Arab students (from a contact culture) and male American students (from a noncontact culture), concluded that Arab subjects sat closer to one another,

faced each other more directly, maintained higher degrees of eye contact, touched each other more frequently, and were generally more involved with one another during interaction than the American students. Watson expanded his work in his 1970 study which included a greater number of students from a wider range of locations. Added to the original sample of only sixteen individuals were an additional one hundred and ten male students, all of whom were involved in pairs speaking their own native languages and were observed through a one-way glass. Contact cultures were represented primarily by subjects from Saudi Arabia, Latin America and Southern Europe, while those from Northern Europe, East Asia and India/Pakistan represented natives of noncontact cultures. Again, Hall's hypotheses were generally supported with there being no overlap in mean scores between contact and noncontact groups in the areas of directness of axis, frequency of touch, and maintenance of direct eye contact. A slight variance was noted in the use of proxemic distances where Indians/Pakistanis maintained a closer mean distance than all other groups except Arabs.

Other researchers, however, have not been as supportive of Hall's theories. Forston (1968) observed eight dyads of male Latin American students and eight dyads of male North American (United States) students, all of whom had been asked to work together to solve a problem. Contrary to Forston's expectations, the North Americans (noncontact culture) sat closer to one another than the Latin Americans (contact culture); no touch interaction occurred whatsoever except that of a single handshake between two North Americans. Similarly, studies conducted by Shuter (1977), Mazur (1977), and Sanders (1985), all cited later in this paper, produced results which raise serious questions about Hall's contact/noncontact theory and his view of culture as the primary factor in behavior, "the backdrop against which all other events are judged" (Hall, 1966, p. x).

In 1972, Madeline Schmitt proposed a theoretical network which identified culture as but one of five variables to predict social distance: (1) Social Identity (the identity of a particular individual and/or his/

her social role), (2) Status, (3) Cultural Distance (difference in values influenced by cultural variations), (4) Physical Distance (actual proximity and/or ecological position), and (5) Personal Distance (emotional differences and/or interpersonal closeness). Bochner (1982) believes that the determination of the "correct" distance in a relationship depends upon two things: the type of activity and the relationship of the individuals involved (p. 14). He proposes nine variables in the use of personal space, specifically considering cross-cultural contacts: (1) On whose territory the interaction occurs, (2) Time span of the contact, (3) Purpose of the meeting, (4) Type of involvement, (5) Frequency of contact, (6) Degree of intimacy, (7) Relative status and power, (8) Numerical balance, and (9) Visible distinguishing characteristics (such as race and sex). Significantly, Bochner suggests that a major difference may exist if the exchange is between two individuals from the same culture or if the individuals come from different cultures.

Finally, Canter (1975) cautions that the amount of space necessary in order for an individual to perform a certain task must be distinguished from the use of space by individuals in their daily transactions. It is the failure to separate these two concepts, he maintains, which have led some (notably Hall) to conclude that generalizations can be made about humans' spacial requirements across a sweeping cross-section of cultures (p. 132).

Hall, an anthropologist, has gone to some pains to point out the differences in the use of space between cultures. He rather confuses the argument by detailed categorizations of the spatial zones whilst still insisting that there are large cultural and, presumably, sub-cultural variations. Large individual differences combined with large sub-cultural variations could easily find two people using similar spatial distances in quite different ways. This makes the notion of tying distances to zones of space (or "proxemic behavior," as Hall calls it) quite inappropriate (p. 142).

The purpose of the remainder of this paper is not to disprove or to devalue the theories of Edward Hall, but rather to substantiate the claim that vari-

ables other than the broad scale categorization of a country into contact- or noncontact-oriented may play equally important roles in determining inhabitants' use of space. Furthermore, evidence will be offered which suggests that some of these variables do not rely to any extent whatsoever upon cultural conditioning but might be proposed as culture-general principles.

II. AGE AND SEX

Certainly the most obvious of these additional variables are those of the age and sex of the individuals involved in an interact. Of the two areas, age appears to be the more culture-general characteristic. Studies by both Baxter (1970) and Aiello and Jones (1971) indicate that the need for personal space increases with age. Both experiments were conducted by unobtrusively observing subjects in natural settings, and both found that children interacted the most proximally, adolescents at an intermediary distance, and adults at the greatest distance. Furthermore, Dean (1976) found that adults tend to respond more favorably to their space being invaded by smaller children, with a reduction of tolerance as the age of the uninvited visitor increases.

Pegán and Aiello (1982) observed 284 Puerto Rican children (138 males and 146 females) in grades one, six, and eleven in both New York City and Puerto Rico. In each location, a confederate who appeared to be a young teacher invited dyads of children to discuss their favorite television shows; each twenty seconds, she recorded the pair's distance and axis (shoulder orientation to one another). In both samples, older pairs used more space, with first graders using a mean distance of seven inches, sixth graders twelve inches, and eleventh graders twenty-four inches, thus moving out of Hall's "intimate" range into the close range of "personal" distance. It is important that both groups, whether in the United States or Puerto Rico, showed similar results; however, it is impossible to ascertain whether this was due primarily to the children's ages or familiar cultural environment.

Of more cultural significance, then, are the results of two studies done by Richard Lerner (1975 and 1976), who asked similar groups of kindergarten through third grade children in the United States and in Japan to illustrate comfortable interaction distances by the placement of figures on a flannel board. Despite cultural differences, the two groups yielded identical findings with mean distances between subjects increasing as the ages of the children increased. Additionally, Lerner determined that, beginning in the first grade, both male and female children used greater distances between opposite sex dyads than same sex dyads, illustrating the early influences of sex upon proxemic conditioning. Finally, children with endomorphic body types were given more surrounding space than either ectomorphs or mesomorphs, with males giving more space to endomorphs than females.

The observations of Heshka and Nelson (1972) focused on the behavior of adult dyads in an outdoor environment in London, England. Following each observation, which was also unobtrusively photographed, each individual was asked to fill out a brief questionnaire revealing his/her age and relationship to the other person. While Heshka and Nelson confirmed the hypothesis that distances are closer with young people and tend to increase, they have proposed that distance may vary in a curvilinear pattern, with spatial needs beginning to decrease at about age forty and continuing to decrease into old age.

Although the use of space by persons of certain ages appears to have some culture-general applications, the same can surely not be said about the sex variable. Use of personal space as influenced by the sex(es) of interacting individuals tends to differ dramatically from one culture to another. Whereas one culture may expect physical contact between males, in another it may be a taboo. While one country may expect females to maintain distances, the same behavior may be interpreted as coldness or disinterest in another. The examples which follow confirm two hypotheses: (1) Behavioral expectations for male/male, female/female, and male/female dyads differ according to the sex of the participants, and (2) These expectations are culture-specific but do not necessarily correspond to the contact or noncontact categorization of a culture.

For example, Jeffrey Sanders (1985) and his colleagues examined personal space zones by measuring distances maintained between 32 male and 32 female Arab students (a contact culture) and 32 male and 32 female American students (a noncontact culture). In the dyads, he varied the degree of relationship between the two participants as well as using both same sex and opposite sex pairs. Although Hall's theories would lead one to expect closer interactions between the Arabs than the Americans, the experimenters found very little difference between Arab males and Americans in general (male or female). Arab females, on the other hand, showed dramatic differences from the other three groups. Male friends were kept at a much farther distance than were female friends. For these females, the primary variable appeared to be sex, as male friends were kept nearly as far away as male strangers.

Studies conducted by Julian and Nancy Edney (1974) in the United States and by H. Smith (1981) in France and Germany examined crowding patterns on the beaches in these countries. Although the personal space needs were less for the French (a contact culture) than for the Germans and Americans (noncontact cultures) and thus confirmed Hall's hypothesis, similar variations were noted in all three cultures according to sex. Larger groups, mixed sex groups, and females tended to claim less space per person than small groups and males. In general, lone females used less space than lone males; similarly they used less space within their groups, placing themselves closer to other female groups than to male groups. These results are consistent with Smith's suggestion that "cross national commonalities in territorial patterns are more important than within cultural variations" (Smith, p. 132).

Curt and Nine (1983) noted that in Puerto Rico (a contact culture), people of the same sex and age touch a great deal and stand quite close together; whereas, people of the opposite sex and age do not touch at all and tend to stand farther apart than Americans do. Upon closer observation, Curt and Nine realized that, in closer male/female relationships, women may touch the males; however the men do not reciprocate. On the other hand, females

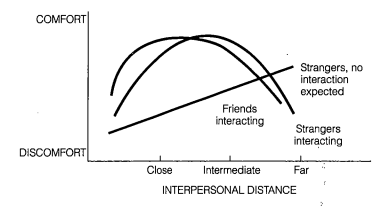

COMFORT

DISCOMFORT

Strangers, no
interaction
expected

Friends
interacting

Strangers
interacting

Close   Intermediate   Far

INTERPERSONAL DISTANCE

Figure 1 Sundstrom and Altman (1976, p. 61)

tend to avoid direct eye contact with males, with many Puerto Rican wives never looking directly at their husbands.

Latin Americans from three contact nations—Costa Rica, Panama and Colombia—were observed by Robert Shuter (1976) to note their proxemic angles toward one another, their proxemic distances, and their frequency of physical contact (touch). Shuter found that the mean axis score and the mean distance for Costa Ricans were significantly smaller than for those of Panamanians and Colombians; similarly, a greater number of Costa Ricans touched each other than did the two other cultures. Shuter's results indicate that the directness of interactions diminishes as one travels from Central to South America, despite the classification of all three as contact cultures. Across all three cultures, however, females tend to relate most directly, followed by male/female dyads, and, finally, by males. Accordingly, the mean distance score for females was considerably smaller than for male/female or male/male dyads—regardless of culture. Finally, in each of the three countries, female/female dyads were the most likely to make physical contact, followed by male/male and male/female in Costa Rica and Colombia (where 0% of the male/female pairs exhibited touch) and male/female, male/male in Panama.

Shuter (1977) conducted a similar study by observing interactions in Venice Mastre, Italy, Heidelberg, Germany, and Milwaukee, Wisconsin, to determine if sex and/or culture have an impact on distance, axis orientation and/or contact. Contrary to Hall's theories, Shuter's data suggest that a single culture may be both contact and noncontact oriented. For example, Italians, normally viewed as contact oriented, exhibited the greatest amount of tactility in male/male dyads; however, in male/female and female/female groupings, they did not differ significantly from the Germans (a noncontact culture). Furthermore, although male/male pairs exhibited a more active contact pattern, Italian males did not converse more closely nor more directly than the non-touching German male. Additionally, American females were as tactile as Italian women, while both were surpassed by the German female.

Based on this research, Shuter (1977) seriously questioned the validity of Hall's hypothesis:

Contrary to Hall's position, it appears that each of the cultures examined is so diverse that it cannot be classified as strictly contact or noncontact oriented. In fact, sex pairs within Germany, Italy and the United States displayed such a wide range of distance, axis, and tactile behaviors that gender-

free culture statements could not be advanced on any tested variable. Unsurprisingly, when sex pair behavior is compared across the three cultures, the limitation of Hall's categories is dramatically revealed (p. 304).

Upon an examination of even a limited number of contact and noncontact cultures, it is apparent that male/male, female/female, and male/female dyads most often respond differently within a single culture and that these patterns often vary from culture to culture. A recent experiment by Lombardo (1986) introduced yet another confounding factor, namely the influence of sex role (orientation toward androgyny) upon American males and females in their use of space. His results led Lombardo to propose that sex roles, as well as sex itself, may have an impact over how an individual uses space and his or her perception of space needs and space invasion. Clearly, it is impossible to make culture-general statements about "typical" behaviors when referring to the variable of sex.

III. RELATIONSHIPS AND ENVIRONMENT

Other than culture, age and sex, the interaction distance between two individuals can be affected by a host of other variables: relationship between the two, the environment of the transaction, attitudinal differences, occupation and/or status, the language used, etc. Of these, the first two, relationship and environment, will be considered in more detail.

In the presentation of his theory of the four distance zones, Hall (1966) notes that "how people are feeling toward each other at the time (of a meeting) is a decisive factor in the distance used" (p. 114). Yet, Hall effectively eliminates this consideration of relationships in his intercultural work. A theoretical model of personal space and interpersonal relationships, developed by Sundstrom and Altman (1976), follows three assumptions: that people seek an optimal distance for each interaction, that discomfort results from interaction outside of the optimal range (too close or too far) and that the optimal zone, as well as reactions to violations, will depend

upon the interpersonal situation. Their model (Figure 1) diagrams levels of comfort/discomfort in distances, based upon interactions with friends, strangers, and strangers where no interaction is anticipated, indicating that the highest degree of comfort at close distances occurs with friends interacting. The studies cited below support this model and suggest the basis for a culture-general hypothesis concerning the variable of relationship.

In 1968, Little studied social interaction distances by asking individuals from five countries (United States, Sweden, Scotland—noncontact cultures—and Greece and Southern Italy—contact cultures) to place figures of their own sex on a flannel board to represent various communication situations. Although Hall's contact/noncontact culture theory was supported, there was a general tendency across cultures for subjects to indicate closer proxemic distances as the indicated relationship became closer and the subjects more pleasant, leading Little to conclude that "the major single factor determining distances in dyadic schemata appears to be the relationship between the members, with the specific content or affective tone of the transaction as next important" (Little, p. 1). Identical results were noted by Watson (1970, also cited in Part I) who observed male college students from the noncontact cultures of North America, East Asia, India, Pakistan, and Northern Europe and the contact cultures of the Middle East, Latin America and Southern Europe. In Watson's expansive study, the rankings of cultural groups on interpersonal distance (far to near) was nearly identical to their rankings on average intensity of friendships within the pairs. That is, the more friendly the pairs representing a given culture, the closer their average interpersonal distance, regardless of culture. In a study cited earlier, Heshka and Nelson (1972) found that, in London, strangers, particularly females, stood farther apart than friends.

Lomranz (1976) tested three groups of sixteen to seventeen year old male sojourners (Argentineans, Iraqis, and Russians) who had lived in Israel for approximately one year. He found that proxemic distance in all three cultures varied along a continuum toward progressive greater distances as the level of friendship declined. Significantly, in dealing with a close friend, only a small variance was noted across these three very distinct cultures, a fact which did not hold true for meetings with strangers. A later study by Carolyn and E. Gregory Keating (1980) in yet another culture documented the behavioral pattern of dyads on park benches in Nairobi, Kenya. In this African culture also, the Keatings observed that those who appeared to be acquainted (spoke to each other, approached or left together) sat closer together than strangers.

Acceptable spatial distances may also vary according to the environment of a given interaction, as well as to people's (probably) cultural perception of crowding and privacy. Moreover, their use of space and tolerance for crowding may not be at all related to the concept of contact and noncontact cultures. Studies done by Robert Sommer as early as 1962 illustrate that the proxemic distances chosen by individuals may vary according to the placement of furniture, the specific setting (such as a living room or an office), and the size of the space. In the latter situation, Sommer (1962) determined that people feel more comfortable sitting at closer distances in a large room than in an intimate setting. Nasar and his colleagues (1984) further hypothesized that feelings of crowding may be affected by the amount of light available in a room. An experiment conducted by Mazur (1977), in which he observed the spacing of male strangers on park benches in the United States, Spain, and Morocco, led him to offer an alternate hypothesis to Hall's: "Under a given set of physical constraints (e.g. bench length, room dimensions, number of people per square yard, etc.), the spacing pattern of noninteracting strangers is similar across cultures" (p. 58).

On the other hand, culturally influenced privacy needs may complicate the establishment of such culture-general rules. "In the strictest sense," writes Canter (1975, p. 139), "privacy may be seen as the establishing of a physical and/or psychological barrier against the world." In Western societies, the need for privacy may take the form of territoriality and/or the setting up of physical barricades against others, thus creating the sense of aloneness. In East-

ern societies, however, the feeling of privacy may be reached even in a crowded room, as the individual simply retreats into him or herself. Neither the Arabs (a contact culture) nor the Japanese (a noncontact culture) have a word for "privacy" as we understand it in their languages. In public situations, both groups demonstrate a tolerance for crowding, pushing, and close proximity which is uncomfortable to the American. The homes of both peoples tend to be open and flexible, emphasizing a need to be with one another. (Arab homes are usually constructed without specific room dividers; whereas Japanese walls are flexible, and activity in the center of the space is emphasized.) In the use of personal interaction distance, on the other hand, the two cultures differ significantly with the Arab approaching close enough to smell the partner's breath, while maintaining direct eye contact, and the Japanese adopting a much more distant position with averted eyes.

Condon and Yousef (1975) offer a warning about careless attempts to categorize and predict nonverbal behaviors based on overly simplistic categorizations:

. . . one wonders, however, if it might be possible to anticipate relations between proxemic behavior and other cultural patterns of communication before completing detailed proxemic descriptions of many different societies. For example, are there likely to be some common value orientations among cultures which are characterized by frequent physical contact . . . ? Do relatively noncontact cultures reveal different value orientations? Or is there no more connection between values and the sound system of the language spoken in any given culture? . . . Perhaps the best we can do at this point is to warn of pushing analogies too far and point out that many codes of nonverbal interaction cannot be treated adequately by analogies to other forms of behavior (p. 141).

IV. ETHNICITY

The characteristics of age, sex, relationships, and environment can be seen as universal variables, possibly influenced by, but not dependent upon, a particular culture. The final aspect of this paper, on the other hand, focuses on an aspect of culture, namely ethnicity, which may supercede the categorization of a country or geographical area as a contact or noncontact culture. For example, will a group of Japanese Italian citizens living in a predominantly Japanese extended family group in Italy be more influenced by their ethnic background (the noncontact Japanese) than by the geographical area (the contact Italian) in which they live? This concept has particularly sweeping implications for countries such as the United States which, despite its "melting pot" composition, has been described as a noncontact culture by Hall.

In his description of the four spatial distances (public, social, personal, and intimate), Hall (1966) carefully explains the limitations of his sample:

It should be emphasized that these generalizations are not representative of human behavior in general—or even of American behavior in general— but only of the group included in the sample. Negroes and Spanish Americans as well as persons who come from southern European cultures have very different proxemic patterns (Hall, 1966, p. 116).

Interestingly, the anthropologist has had considerable experience in working with the Native Americans of United States Southwest, whom he often identifies as unique in their conceptualizations and use of time (1976, 1983). It is particularly ironic, then, that, in his writings about contact and noncontact cultures, Hall appears to adopt but two molds into which countries of the world must fit, apparently overlooking the multitude of co-cultures and subcultures which exist in most geographical areas.

Even more importantly, most researchers have been painstakingly cautious in separating contact culture and noncontact culture subjects. Studies and anecdotes abound which portray the classic behavioral patterns when two Arabs meet or when two Japanese converse. It is apparently assumed that, by studying such isolated examples, the individual from another culture can internalize and adapt to

the use of personal space in countries other than his/her own. What is sorely lacking in intercultural research are experiments and observations which survey the results of interactions between individuals from two different cultures or from two co-cultures within the same country. If age, sex, and a host of other variables can affect an interaction, it stands to reason that the presence of two cultures or co-cultures interacting side-by-side may carry an even greater impact. Studies of different ethnic groups within a single country, most notably blacks and whites in the United States, imply support of this hypothesis.

As early as 1970, Baxter noted differences for personal space needs in Hispanic-American, White-American, and Black-American children, with mixed race dyads exhibiting greater distances than any single-race pairs. In studies of black and white children, Severy (1979) determined that, by age seven, black children require less personal space than white children, with mixed sex dyads needing more space than same sex dyads. Somewhat paradoxically, through observations of fifth grade boys at play, Zimmerman (1975) noted that black boys talked to each other significantly less, faced each other less directly and interacted at greater distances than white boys. Racially-mixed dyads appeared to attempt to adjust to each other's needs and interacted at an intermediate distance.

Based on Hall's contact/noncontact culture theory, Aiello and Jones (1971) observed 210 same sex (male/male, female/female) first and second grade dyads from three diverse New York City subcultures: blacks, whites, and Puerto Ricans; they hypothesized that blacks and Puerto Ricans would interact at closer distances than the white children. In this study, in contrast to that of Zimmerman, the hypothesis was confirmed with whites maintaining distances nearly twice that of blacks and Puerto Ricans. An additional correlation was found, however, between distance and sex of the dyad. Both Puerto Rican and white female/female dyads stood closer than male/male dyads, with the opposite being true of blacks. Additionally, the axis orientation of white children was more direct than that of blacks or Puerto Ricans, with the latter being the least direct.

Across cultures, males tended to face their partners more directly than females. In a similar vein, Jones (1971) found that Chinese in New York City interacted at greater distances than either Puerto Ricans or Italians.

Perhaps related to their comfortability with closer proximities, there is also some indication that blacks will more readily invade the personal space of another black than will whites intrude upon the personal space of another individual of either race. When Bauer (1973) instructed blacks and whites to approach a same sex/same race confederate "as close as comfortable," white males chose the farthest distance, followed by white females, black males, and black females. An experiment by William Dick (1976) netted similar results. Four male confederates (two blacks, aged 20 and 30 years, and two whites, aged 20 and 30 years) were positioned individually on a university campus in front of a bubble gum machine so that subjects would need to invade their space in order to turn the knob to receive free gum. Significantly more black subjects invaded the space of the black confederates. Females tended to be more cautious than males, indicating that both race and sex influenced the subject's decision to "invade space."

Although conducted in the unlaboratory-like setting of the New York subway, the work of David Maines (1977) makes a unique contribution in his observation of mixed sex/mixed race dyads. In observing the elbow placement of individuals, either to the side or out to the front, Maines discovered that there was a general tendency for individuals to locate their elbows to their sides in noncrowded conditions and to the front in more crowded contexts. Movement to the front was particularly significant in mixed race and mixed sex dyads where individuals are apparently more reluctant to actually touch another person. A similar pattern was noticed in observing the physical contact patterns of the hands of passengers sharing a "balance strap." In these situations, there was an especially noticeable pattern of avoidance in the case of mixed race/same sex groupings. While Maines' observations did not include verbal interactions, his results are impor-

tant in suggesting further implications for mixed ethnic pairings. Unfortunately, studies of mixed race or mixed subculture groups in other cultures are difficult to locate.

A final significant contribution is that of Sussman and Rosenfeld (1982) who looked at the influence of culture and language on conversational distance. The researchers hypothesized that theories for contact/noncontact societies hold true primarily in same-culture interactions in which individuals speak in their native tongues and that, correspondingly, adopting the use of another language serves to create a distance which is evidenced through proxemics. Observations of Japanese, Venezuelan, and American student dyads substantiated their hypothesis, with all three groups maintaining further distances when speaking a foreign tongue than when using their native language. Although this study used dyads of individuals from the same culture, hypotheses might be suggested about the potential implications for interactions in mixed-culture pairs with differing native tongues.

V. CONCLUSIONS

The research in this paper holds suggestions for further study in the use of space in several different areas:

Can culture-general hypotheses for the following be substantiated?

• A curvilinear pattern of proxemic distances according to age

• A continuum of progressively smaller distances as relationships move from that of stranger to that of close friend

Can culture-specific theories for the following be generated?

• Interaction differences between male/male, female/female, and male/female dyads in different cultures

• The impact of environment and the perceptions of crowding and privacy in different cultures

Can (and should) Hall's theory of contact/noncontact cultures be redefined and refined?

More significantly, however, this research indicates a serious gap in the study of "intercultural" proxemics; indeed, there appears to be very little work with a truly intercultural focus being done. While anecdotal accounts are sometimes cited to explain the "East Meets West" phenomenon, I was unable to locate a single example of a study which used a scientific approach to examine interaction behaviors between individuals from different cultures. Only one (the Maines subway study) even touched upon United States patterns in racially mixed pairs. The experiments and hypotheses to date, then, have been based nearly totally on intracultural or, at best, cross-cultural studies. Some of the areas which might be probed are the following:

• Can any hypotheses be substantiated for intercultural interactions based upon contact/noncontact, noncontact/noncontact, contact/contact dyads?

• Can any hypotheses be substantiated in terms of the distance control factor for the host or the sojourner?

• Can any hypotheses be substantiated about the distance behaviors of two sojourners from different cultures interacting in a third culture?

• Can any hypotheses be substantiated about the impact of language choice in a transaction? Is there a correlation between use of the native tongue and the distance control factor?

• In any of the above cases, how might the sex, sex roles, age, relationship, status and ethnicity of the individuals influence the interaction patterns?

"Proxemics research" admits Edward Hall (1976, p. 86), "requires an inordinate amount of time." Because of the many variables present, he says, few studies have been done which examine its impact. In his first book, *The Silent Language* (1959), Hall offers this simplistic advice to the sojourner: "Watch

where people stand and don't back up." In this world of multinational companies and jet travel, however, we cannot afford to be so easily placated.

REFERENCES

Aiello, J. R. and S. E. Jones (1971). Field study of proxemic behavior of young school children in three subcultural groups. *Journal of Personality and Social Psychology*, **19**: 351–356.

Baltus, D. (1974). Proxemics. Conference paper.

Bauer, E. A. (1973). Personal space: A study of blacks and whites. *Sociometry*, **36**(3): 402–408.

Baxter, J. (1970). Interpersonal spacing in natural settings. *Sociometry*, **33**(4): 444–456.

Birdwhistell, R. (1970). *Kinesics and Context: Essays on Body Motion Communication*. Philadelphia: University of Pennsylvania Press.

Bochner, S. (1982). The social psychology of cross-cultural relations. In S. Bochner (Ed.) *Cultures in Contact*. New York: Pergamon Press: 5–44.

Canter, D., *et al.* (1975). *Environmental Interactions: Psychological Approaches to Our Physical Surroundings*. London: Surrey Press.

Condon, J. C. and F. Yousef (1975). *An Introduction to Intercultural Communication*. Indianapolis: Bobbs-Merrill.

Curt, C. and J. Nine (1983). Hispanic-anglo conflicts in nonverbal communication. In Isidora Albino (Ed.) *Perspectives Pedagogicas*. San Juan, Puerto Rico: Universidad de Puerto Rico.

Dean, L. M., F. N. Willis, and J. N. la Rocco (1976). Invasion of personal space as a function of age, sex and race. *Psychological Reports*, **38**(3)(pt.1): 959–965.

Dick, W. E. (1976). Invasion of personal space as function of age and race. *Psychological Reports*, **39**(1): 281–282.

Edney, J. and N. Jordon-Edney (1974). Territorial spacing on a bench. *Sociometry*, **37**(1): 92–104.

Edwards, D. J. (1980). Perception of crowding and tolerance of interpersonal proxemics and separation in South Africa. *Journal of Social Psychology*, **110**(1): 19–28.

Engebretson, D. and D. Fullmer (1970). Cross-cultural differences in territoriality. *Journal of Cross-Cultural Psychology*, **1**: 261–269.

Evans, G. W. (1978). Human spatial behavior: The arousal model. In Andrew Baum and Yakov M. Epstein (Eds.) *Human Response to Crowding*. N.J.: Erlbaum Associates.

Felipe, N. J. and R. Sommer (1966). Invasions of personal space. *Social Problems*, **14**: 206–214.

Forston, R. and C. Larson (1968). The dynamics of space. An experimental study in proxemic behavior among Latin Americans and North Americans. *Journal of Communication*, **18**: 109–116.

Goffman, E. (1971). *Relations in Public*. New York: Basic Books.

Hall, E. T. (1959). *The Silent Language*. New York: Doubleday.

Hall, E. T. (1960). The silent language in overseas business. *Harvard Business Review*, **38**(3): 87–96.

Hall, E. T. (1963). A system for the notation of proxemic behavior. *American Anthropologist*, **65**: 1003–1026.

Hall, E. T. (1964). Silent assumptions in social communication. *Disorders of Communication*, **42**: 41–55.

Hall, E. T. (1966). *The Hidden Dimension*. New York: Doubleday.

Hall, E. T. (1976). *Beyond Culture*. New York: Anchor Press.

Hall, E. T. (1983). *Dance of Life*. New York: Doubleday.

Hayduk, L. A. (1983). Personal space: Where we now stand. *Psychological Bulletin*, **94**: 293–335.

Heaton, J. (1978). Teaching culture as a second language. Private culture and kinesics. University of California, Los Angeles: Research Report.

Heshka, S. and Y. Nelson (1972). Interpersonal speaking distances as a function of age, sex, and relationship. *Sociometry*, **35**(4): 491–498.

Jensen, J. V. (1972). Perspectives on nonverbal intercultural communication. In Larry A. Samovar and Richard E. Porter (Eds.) *Intercultural Communication: A Reader*. Belmont, Calif.: Wadsworth.

Jones, S. E. (1971). A comparative proxemics analysis of dyadic interaction in selected subcultures of New York City. *Journal of Social Psychology*, **84**: 35–44.

Keating, C. E. and E. G. Keating (1980). Distance between pairs of acquaintances and strangers on public beaches in Nairobi, Kenya. *Journal on Social Psychology*, **110**(2): 285–286.

Kinloch, G. C. (1973). Race, socio-economic status and social distance in Hawaii. *Sociology and Social Research*, **57**(2): 156–167.

Lerner, R. M., *et al.* (1975). Effects of age and sex on the development of personal space schemata toward body build. *Journal of Genetic Psychology*, **127**: 91–101.

Lerner, R. M., *et al.* (1976). Development of personal space schemata among Japanese children. *Developmental Psychology*, **15**(5): 466–467.

Liebman, M. (1970). The effects of sex and race norms on personal space. *Environmental Behavior*, **2**: 208–246.

Little, K. B. (1968). Cultural variations in social schemata. *Journal of Personality and Social Psychology*, **10**(1): 1–7.

Lombardo, J. P. (1986). Interaction of sex and sex role in response to violations of preferred seating arrangements. *Sex Roles*, **15**: 173–183.

Lomranz, J. (1976). Cultural variations in personal space. *Journal of Social Psychology*, **99**(1): 21–27.

Maines, D. R. (1977). Tactile relationships in the subway as affected by racial, sexual and crowded seated situations. *Environmental Psychology and Nonverbal Behavior*, **2**(2): 100–108.

Mazur, A. (1977). Interpersonal spacing on public benches in contact vs. noncontact cultures. *Journal of Social Psychology*, **101**: 53–58.

Nasar, J. L., *et al.* (1984). Modifiers of perceived spaciousness and crowding among different cultural groups. Research report, November.

Noesjirwan, J. (1978). A laboratory study of proxemic patterns in Indonesians and Australians. *Journal of Social and Chemical Psychology*, **17**(4):333–334.

Pegán, G. and J. R. Aiello (1982). Development of personal space among Puerto Ricans. *Journal of Nonverbal Behavior*, **7**(2): 59–68.

Sanders, J., *et al.* (1985). Personal space amongst Arabs and Americans. *International Journal of Psychology*, **20**(1): 13–17.

Schmitt, M. H. (1972): Near and Far: A re-formulation of the social distance concept. *Sociology and Social Research*, **57**(1): 85–97.

Severy, L. J., *et al.* (1979). A multimethod assessment of personal space development in female and male, black and white children. *Journal of Nonverbal Behavior*, **4**(2): 68–86.

Shuter, R. (1976). Nonverbal communication: Proxemics and tactility in Latin America. *Journal of Communication*, **26**(3): 46–52.

Shuter, R. (1977). A field study of nonverbal communication in Germany, Italy and the United States. *Communication Monographs*, **44**(4): 298–305.

Singer, M. R. (1987). *Intercultural Communication: A Perceptual Approach*. N.J.: Prentice-Hall.

Six, B., *et al.* (1983). A cultural comparison of perceived crowding and discomfort: The United States and West Germany. *Journal of Psychology*, **114**(1): 63–67.

Smith, A. G. (Ed.) (1966). *Communication and Culture: Readings in the Codes of Human Interaction*. New York: Holt, Rinehart and Winston.

Smith, H. (1981). Territorial spacing on a beach revisited: A crossnational exploration. *Social Psychology Quarterly*, **44**: 132–137.

Sommer, R. (1959). Studies in personal space. *Sociometry*, **22**: 247–260.

Sommer, R. (1962). The distance for comfortable conversation: A further study. *Sociometry*, **25**: 111–125.

Sommer, R. (1966). Man's proximate environment. *Journal of Social Issues*, **22**(4): 59–70.

Sommer, R. (1969). *Personal Space*. N.J.: Prentice-Hall.

Sommer, R. and F. D. Becker, Territorial defense and the good neighbor. *Journal of Personality and Social Psychology*, **11**: 85–92.

Speelman, D. and C. D. Hoffman (1980). Personal space assessment of the development of racial attitudes in integrated and segregated schools. *Journal of Genetic Psychology*, **136**(2): 307–308.

Sundstrom, E. and I. Altman (1976). Interpersonal relationships and personal space: Research review and theoretical model. *Human Ecology*, **4**: 46–67.

Sussman, N. and H. M. Rosenfeld (1982). Influence of culture, language and sex on conversational distance. *Journal of Personality and Social Psychology*, **42**(1): 66–74.

Thayer, S. and L. Alban. A field experiment on the effect of political and cultural factors in the use of personal space. *Journal of Social Psychology*, **88**(2): 267–272.

Watson, O. M. (1970). *Proxemic Behavior: A Cross-Cultural Study*. The Hague: Mouton.

Watson, O. M. and T. D. Graves (1966). Quantitative research in proxemic behavior. *American Anthropologist*, **68**: 971–985.

Wysocki, B., Jr. (1986). Closed society: Despite global role, many Japanese try to avoid foreigners. *Wall Street Journal*, **68**(23): 1, 18.

Yousef, F. S. (1974). Cross-cultural communication aspects of contrastive social values between North Americans and Middle Easterners. *Human Organization*, **33**(4): 383–387.

Zimmerman, B. and G. H. Brody (1975). Race and modeling influence in the interpersonal play pattern for boys. *Journal of Educational Psychology*, **67**(5): 591–598.

Monochronic and Polychronic Time

EDWARD T. HALL

Lorenzo Hubbell, trader to the Navajo and the Hopi, was three quarters Spanish and one quarter New Englander, but culturally he was Spanish to the core. Seeing him for the first time on government business transactions relating to my work in the 1930s, I felt embarrassed and a little shy because he didn't have a regular office where people could talk in private. Instead, there was a large corner room—part of his house adjoining the trading post—in which business took place. Business covered everything from visits with officials and friends, conferences with Indians who had come to see him, who also most often needed to borrow money or make sheep deals, as well as a hundred or more routine transactions with store clerks and Indians who had not come to see Lorenzo specifically but only to trade. There were long-distance telephone calls to his warehouse in Winslow, Arizona, with cattle buyers, and his brother, Roman, at Ganado, Arizona—all this and more (some of it quite personal), carried on in public, in front of our small world for all to see and hear. If you wanted to learn about the life of an Indian trader or the ins and outs of running a small trading empire (Lorenzo had a dozen posts scattered throughout northern Arizona), all you had to do was to sit in Lorenzo's office for a month or so and take note of what was going on. Eventually all

the different parts of the pattern would unfold before your eyes, as eventually they did before mine, as I lived and worked on that reservation over a five-year period.

I was prepared for the fact that the Indians do things differently from AE cultures because I had spent part of my childhood on the Upper Rio Grande River with the Pueblo Indians as friends. Such differences were taken for granted. But this public, everything-at-once, mélange way of conducting business made an impression on me. There was no escaping it, here was another world, but in this instance, although both Spanish and Anglos had their roots firmly planted in European soil, each handled time in radically different ways.

It didn't take long for me to accustom myself to Lorenzo's business ambiance. There was so much going on that I could hardly tear myself away. My own work schedule won out, of course, but I did find that the Hubbell store had a pull like a strong magnet, and I never missed an opportunity to visit with Lorenzo. After driving through Oraibi, I would pull up next to his store, park my pickup, and go through the side door to the office. These visits were absolutely necessary because without news of what was going on life could become precarious. Lorenzo's desert "salon" was better than a newspaper, which, incidentally, we lacked.

Having been initiated to Lorenzo's way of doing business, I later began to notice similar mutual involvement in events among the New Mexico Spanish. I also observed the same patterns in Latin America, as well as in the Arab world. Watching my countrymen's reactions to this "many things at a time" system I noted how deeply it affected the channeling and flow of information, the shape and form of the networks connecting people, and a host of other important social and cultural features of the society. I realized that there was more to this culture pattern than one might at first suppose.

Years of exposure to other cultures demonstrated that complex societies organize time in at least two different ways: events scheduled as separate items—one thing at a time—as in North Europe, or following the Mediterranean model of involvement in several things at once. The two systems are logically and empirically quite distinct. Like oil and water, they don't mix. Each has its strengths as well as its weaknesses. I have termed doing many things at once: Polychronic, P-time. The North European system—doing one thing at a time—is Monochronic, M-time. P-time stresses involvement of people and completion of transactions rather than adherence to preset schedules. Appointments are not taken as seriously and, as a consequence, are frequently broken. P-time is treated as less tangible than M-time. For polychronic people, time is seldom experienced as "wasted," and is apt to be considered a point rather than a ribbon or a road, but that point is often sacred. An Arab will say, "I will see you before one hour," or "I will see you after two days." What he means in the first instance is that it will not be longer than an hour before he sees you, and at least two days in the second instance. These commitments are taken quite seriously as long as one remains in the P-time pattern.

Once, in the early '60s, when I was in Patras, Greece, which is in the middle of the P-time belt, my own time system was thrown in my face under rather ridiculous but still amusing circumstances. An impatient Greek hotel clerk, anxious to get me and my ménage settled in some quarters which were far from first-class, was pushing me to make a commitment so he could continue with his siesta. I couldn't decide whether to accept this rather forlorn "bird in the hand" or take a chance on another hotel that looked, if possible, even less inviting. Out of the blue, the clerk blurted, "Make up your mind. After all, time is money!" How would you reply to that at a time of day when literally nothing was happening? I couldn't help but laugh at the incongruity of it all. If there ever was a case of time not being money, it was in Patras during siesta in the summer.

Though M-time cultures tend to make a fetish out of management, there are points at which M-time doesn't make as much sense as it might. Life in general is at times unpredictable; and who can tell exactly how long a particular client, patient, or set of transactions will take. These are imponderables in the chemistry of human transactions. What can be

accomplished one day in ten minutes, may take twenty minutes on the next. Some days people will be rushed and can't finish; on others, there is time to spare, so they "waste" the remaining time.

In Latin America and the Middle East, North Americans can frequently be psychologically stressed. Immersed in a polychronic environment in the markets, stores, and souks of Mediterranean and Arab countries, one is surrounded by other customers all vying for the attention of a single clerk who is trying to wait on everyone at once. There is no recognized order as to who is to be served next, no queue or numbers to indicate who has been waiting the longest. To the North European or American, it appears that confusion and clamor abound. In a different context, the same patterns can be seen operating in the governmental bureaucracies of Mediterranean countries: a typical office layout for important officials frequently includes a large reception area (an ornate version of Lorenzo Hubbell's office), outside the private suite, where small groups of people can wait and be visited by the minister or his aides. These functionaries do most of their business outside in this semipublic setting, moving from group to group conferring with each in turn. The semiprivate transactions take less time, give others the feeling that they are in the presence of the minister as well as other important people with whom they may also want to confer. Once one is used to this pattern, it is clear that there are advantages which frequently outweigh the disadvantages of a series of private meetings in the inner office.

Particularly distressing to Americans is the way in which appointments are handled by polychronic people. Being on time simply doesn't mean the same thing as it does in the United States. Matters in a polychronic culture seem in a constant state of flux. Nothing is solid or firm, particularly plans for the future; even important plans may be changed right up to the minute of execution.

In contrast, people in the Western world find little in life exempt from the iron hand of M-time. Time is so thoroughly woven into the fabric of existence that we are hardly aware of the degree to which it determines and coordinates everything we do, including the molding of relations with others in many subtle ways. In fact, social and business life, even one's sex life, is commonly schedule-dominated. By scheduling, we compartmentalize; this makes it possible to concentrate on one thing at a time, but it also reduces the context. Since scheduling by its very nature selects what will and will not be perceived and attended, and permits only a limited number of events within a given period, what gets scheduled constitutes a system for setting priorities for both people and functions. Important things are taken up first and allotted the most time; unimportant things are left to last or omitted if time runs out.

M-time is also tangible; we speak of it as being saved, spent, wasted, lost, made up, crawling, killed, and running out. These metaphors must be taken seriously. M-time scheduling is used as a classification system that orders life. The rules apply to everything except birth and death. It should be mentioned, that without schedules or something similar to the M-time system, it is doubtful that our industrial civilization could have developed as it has. There are other consequences. Monochronic time seals off one or two people from the group and intensifies relationships with one other person or, at most, two or three people. M-time in this sense is like a room with a closed door ensuring privacy. The only problem is that you must vacate the "room" at the end of the allotted fifteen minutes or an hour, a day, or a week, depending on the schedule, and make way for the next person in line. Failure to make way by intruding on the time of the next person is not only a sign of extreme egocentrism and narcissism, but just plain bad manners.

Monochronic time is arbitrary and imposed, that is, learned. Because it is so thoroughly learned and so thoroughly integrated into our culture, it is treated as though it were the only natural and logical way of organizing life. Yet, it is *not* inherent in man's biological rhythms or his creative drives, nor is it existential in nature.

Schedules can and frequently do cut things short just when they are beginning to go well. For example, research funds run out just as the results are beginning to be achieved. How often has the reader had the experience of realizing that he is pleasurably immersed in some creative activity, totally unaware of time, solely conscious of the job at hand, only to be brought back to "reality" with the rude shock of realizing that other, frequently inconsequential previous commitments are bearing down on him?

Some Americans associate schedules with reality, but M-time can alienate us from ourselves and from others by reducing context. It subtly influences how we think and perceive the world in segmented compartments. This is convenient in linear operations but disastrous in its effect on nonlinear creative tasks. Latino peoples are an example of the opposite. In Latin America, the intelligentsia and the academicians frequently participate in several fields at once—fields which the average North American academician, business, or professional person thinks of as antithetical. Business, philosophy, medicine, and poetry, for example, are common, well-respected combinations.

Polychronic people, such as the Arabs and Turks, who are almost never alone, even in the home, make very different uses of "screening" than Europeans do. They interact with several people at once and are continually involved with each other. Tight scheduling is therefore difficult, if not impossible.

Theoretically, when considering social organization, P-time systems should demand a much greater centralization of control and be characterized by a rather shallow or simple structure. This is because the leader deals continually with many people, most of whom stay informed as to what is happening. The Arab fellah can always see his sheik. There are no intermediaries between man and sheik or between man and God. The flow of information as well as people's need to stay informed complement each other. Polychronic people are so deeply immersed in each other's business that they feel a compulsion to keep in touch. Any stray scrap of a story is gathered in and stored away. Their knowledge of each other is truly extraordinary. Their involvement in people is the very core of their existence. This has bureaucratic implications. For example, delegation of authority and a buildup in bureaucratic levels are not required to handle high volumes of business. The principal shortcoming of P-type bureaucracies is that as functions increase, there is a proliferation of small bureaucracies that really are not set up to handle the problems of outsiders. In fact, outsiders traveling or residing in Latin American or Mediterranean countries find the bureaucracies unusually cumbersome and unresponsive. In polychronic countries, one has to be an insider or have a "friend" who can make things happen. All bureaucracies are oriented inward, but P-type bureaucracies are especially so.

There are also interesting points to be made concerning the act of administration as it is conceived in these two settings. Administration and control of polychronic peoples in the Middle East and Latin America is a matter of job analysis. Administration consists of taking each subordinate's job and identifying the activities that go to make up the job. These are then labeled and frequently indicated on the elaborate charts with checks to make it possible for the administrator to be sure that each function has been performed. In this way, it is felt that absolute control is maintained over the individual. Yet, scheduling how and when each activity is actually performed is left up to the employee. For an employer to schedule a subordinate's work for him would be considered a tyrannical violation of his individuality—an invasion of the self.

In contrast, M-time people schedule the activity and leave the analysis of the activities of the job to the individual. A P-type analysis, even though technical by its very nature, keeps reminding the subordinate that his job is not only a system but also part of a larger system. M-type people, on the other hand, by virtue of compartmentalization, are less likely to see their activities in context as part of the larger whole. This does not mean that they are unaware of the "organization"—far from it—only that the job itself or even the goals of the organization are seldom seen as a whole.

Giving the organization a higher priority than the functions it performs is common in our culture. This is epitomized in television, where we allow the TV commercials, the "special message," to break the continuity of even the most important communica-

tion. There is a message all right, and the message is that art gives way to commerce—polychronic advertising agencies impose their values on a monochronic population. In monochronic North European countries, where patterns are more homogeneous, commercial interruptions of this sort are not tolerated. There is a strict limit as to the number as well as the times when commercials can be shown. The average American TV program has been allotted one or two hours, for which people have set aside time, and is conceived, written, directed, acted, and played as a unity. Interjecting commercials throughout the body of the program breaks that continuity and flies in the face of one of the core systems of the culture. The polychronic Spanish treat the main feature as a close friend or relative who should not be disturbed and let the commercials mill around in the antechamber outside. My point is not that one system is superior to another, it's just that the two don't mix. The effect is disruptive, and reminiscent of what the English are going through today, now that the old monochronic queuing patterns have broken down as a consequence of a large infusion of polychronic peoples from the colonies.

Both M-time and P-time systems have strengths as well as weaknesses. There is a limit to the speed with which jobs can be analyzed, although once analyzed, proper reporting can enable a P-time administrator to handle a surprising number of subordinates. Nevertheless, organizations run on the polychronic model are limited in size, they depend on having gifted people at the top, and are slow and cumbersome when dealing with anything that is new or different. Without gifted people, a P-type bureaucracy can be a disaster. M-type organizations go in the opposite direction. They can and do grow much larger than the P-type. However, they combine bureaucracies instead of proliferating them, e.g., with consolidated schools, the business conglomerate, and the new superdepartments we are developing in government.

The blindness of the monochronic organization is to the humanity of its members. The weakness of the polychronic type lies in its extreme dependence on the leader to handle contingencies and stay on top of things. M-type bureaucracies, as they grow larger, turn inward; oblivious to their own structure, they grow rigid and are apt to lose sight of their original purpose. Prime examples are the Army Corps of Engineers and the Bureau of Reclamation, which wreak havoc on our environment in their dedicated efforts to stay in business by building dams or aiding the flow of rivers to the sea.

At the beginning of this chapter, I stated that "American time is monochronic." On the surface, this is true, but in a deeper sense, American (AE) time is both polychronic and monochronic. M-time dominates the official worlds of business, government, the professions, entertainment, and sports. However, in the home—particularly the more traditional home in which women are the core around which everything revolves—one finds that P-time takes over. How else can one raise several children at once, run a household, hold a job, be a wife, mother, nurse, tutor, chauffeur, and general fixer-upper? Nevertheless, most of us automatically equate P-time with informal activities and with the multiple tasks and responsibilities and ties of women to networks of people. At the preconscious level, M-time is male time and P-time is female time, and the ramifications of this difference are considerable.

In the conclusion of an important book, *Unfinished Business*, Maggie Scarf vividly illustrates this point. Scarf addresses herself to the question of why it is that depression (the hidden illness of our age) is three to six times more prevalent in women than it is in men. How does time equate with depression in women? It so happens that the time system of the dominant culture adds another source of trauma and alienation to the already overburdened psyches of many American women. According to Scarf, depression comes about in part as a consequence of breaking significant ties that make up most women's worlds. In our culture, men as a group tend to be more task-oriented, while women's lives center on networks of people and their relations with people. Traditionally, a woman's world is a world of human emotions, of love, attachment, envy, anxiety, and hate. This is a little difficult for late-twentieth-century people to accept because it implies basic differences between men and women that are not fashionable at the moment. Nevertheless, for most cultures around the world, the feminine mystique is intimately identified with the development of the human relations side of the personality rather than the technical, cortical left-brain occupational side. In the United States, AE women live in a world of peoples and relationships and their egos become spread out among those who are closest to them by a process we call identification. When the relationships are threatened or broken or something happens to those to whom one is close, there are worries and anxieties, and depression is a natural result.

Polychronic cultures are by their very nature oriented to people. Any human being who is naturally drawn to other human beings and who lives in a world dominated by human relationships will be either pushed or pulled toward the polychronic end of the time spectrum. If you value people, you must hear them out and cannot cut them off simply because of a schedule.

M-time, on the other hand, is oriented to tasks, schedules, and procedures. As anyone who has had experience with our bureaucracies knows, schedules and procedures take on a life all their own without reference to either logic or human needs. And it is this set of written and unwritten rules—and the consequences of these rules—that is at least partially responsible for the reputation of American business being cut off from human beings and unwilling to recognize the importance of employee morale. Morale may well be the deciding factor in whether a given company makes a profit or not. Admittedly, American management is slowly, very slowly, getting the message. The problem is that modern management has accentuated the monochronic side at the expense of the less manageable, and less predictable, polychronic side. Virtually everything in our culture works for and rewards a monochronic view of the world. But the antihuman aspect of M-time is alienating, especially to women. Unfortunately, too many women have "bought" the M-time world, not realizing that unconscious sexism is part of it. The pattern of an entire system of time is too large, too diffuse, and too ubiquitous for most to identify its patterns. Women sense there is something alien about the way in which modern organizations handle time, beginning with how the workday, the week, and the year are set up. Such changes as flextime do not alter the fact that as soon as one enters the door of the office, one becomes immediately locked into a monochronic, monolithic structure that is virtually impossible to change.

There are other sources of tension between people who have internalized these two systems. Keep in mind that polychronic individuals are oriented toward people, human relationships, and the family, which is the core of their existence. Family takes precedence over everything else. Close friends come next. In the absence of schedules, when there is a crisis the family always comes first. If a monochronic woman has a polychronic hairdresser, there will inevitably be problems, even if she has a regular appointment and is scheduled at the same time each week. In circumstances like these, the hairdresser (following his or her own pattern) will inevitably feel compelled to "squeeze people in." As a consequence, the regular customer, who has scheduled her time very carefully (which is why she has a standing appointment in the first place), is kept waiting and feels put down, angry, and frustrated. The hairdresser is also in a bind because if he does not accommodate his relative or friend regardless of the schedule, the result is endless repercussions within his family circle. Not only must he give preferential treatment to relatives, but the degree of accommodation and who is pushed aside or what is pushed aside is itself a communication!

The more important the customer or business that is disrupted, the more reassured the hairdresser's polychronic Aunt Nell will feel. The way to ensure the message that one is accepted or loved is to call up at the last minute and expect everyone to rearrange everything. If they don't, it can be taken as a clear signal that they don't care enough. The M-time individual caught in this P-time pattern has the feeling either that he is being pressured or that he simply doesn't count. There are many instances where culture patterns are on a collision course and there can be no resolution until the point of conflict is identified. One side or the other literally gives up. In the instance cited above, it is the hairdresser who

usually loses a good customer. Patterns of this variety are what maintain ethnicity. Neither pattern is right, only different, and it is important to remember that they do not mix.

Not all M-times and P-times are the same. There are tight and loose versions of each. The Japanese, for example, in the official business side of their lives where people do not meet on a highly personalized basis, provide us an excellent example of tight M-time. When an American professor, business person, technical expert, or consultant visits Japan, he may find that his time is like a carefully packed trunk—so tightly packed, in fact, that it is impossible to squeeze one more thing into the container. On a recent trip to Japan, I was contacted by a well-known colleague who had translated one of my earlier books. He wanted to see me and asked if he could pick me up at my hotel at twelve-fifteen so we could have lunch together. I had situated myself in the lobby a few minutes early, as the Japanese are almost always prompt. At twelve-seventeen, I could see his tense figure darting through the crowd of arriving business people and politicians who had collected near the door. Following greetings, he ushered me outside to the ubiquitous black limousine with chauffeur, with white doilies covering the arms and headrests. The door of the car had hardly closed when he started outlining our schedule for the lunch period by saying that he had an appointment at three o'clock to do a TV broadcast. That set the time limit and established the basic parameters in which everyone knew where he would be at any given part of the agenda. He stated these limits—a little over two hours—taking travel time into account.

My colleague next explained that not only were we to have lunch, but he wanted to tape an interview for a magazine. That meant lunch and an interview which would last thirty to forty minutes. What else? Ah, yes. He hoped I wouldn't mind spending time with Mr. X, who had published one of my earlier books in Japanese, because Mr. X was very anxious to pin down a commitment on my part to allow him to publish my next book. He was particularly eager to see me because he missed out on publishing the last two books, even though he had written me in the United States. Yes, I did remember that he had written, but his letter arrived after the decision on the Japanese publisher had been made by my agent. That, incidentally, was the very reason why he wanted to see me personally. Three down and how many more to go? Oh, yes, there would be some photographers there and he hoped I wouldn't mind if pictures were taken? The pictures were to be both formal group shots, which were posed, and informal, candid shots during the interview, as well as pictures taken with Mr. X. As it turned out, there were at least two sets of photographers as well as a sound man, and while it wasn't "60 Minutes," there was quite a lot of confusion (the two sets of photographers each required precious seconds to straighten things out). I had to hand it to everyone—they were not only extraordinarily skilled and well organized, but also polite and considerate. Then, he hoped I wouldn't mind but there was a young man who was studying communication who had scored over 600 on an examination, which I was told put him 200 points above the average. This young man would be joining us for lunch. I didn't see how we were going to eat anything, much less discuss issues of mutual interest. In situations such as these, one soon learns to sit back, relax, and let the individual in charge orchestrate everything. The lunch was excellent, as I knew it would be—hardly leisurely, but still very good.

All the interviews and the conversation with the student went off as scheduled. The difficulties came when I had to explain to the Japanese publisher that I had no control over my own book—that once I had written a book and handed it in to my publisher, the book was marketed by either my publisher or my agent. Simply being first in line did not guarantee anything. I had to try to make it clear that I was tied into an already existing set of relationships with attached obligations and that there were other people who made these decisions. This required some explaining, and I then spent considerable time trying to work out a method for the publisher to get a hearing with my agent. This is sometimes virtually impossible because each publisher and each agent in the United States has its own representative in Japan. Thus an author is in their hands, too.

We did finish on time—pretty much to everyone's satisfaction, I believe. My friend departed on schedule as the cameramen were putting away their equipment and the sound man was rolling up his wires and disconnecting his microphones. The student drove me back to my hotel on schedule, a little after 3 P.M.

The pattern is not too different from schedules for authors in the United States. The difference is that in Japan the tightly scheduled monochronic pattern is applied to foreigners who are not well enough integrated into the Japanese system to be able to do things in a more leisurely manner, and where emphasis is on developing a good working relationship. . .

All cultures with high technologies seem to incorporate both polychronic as well as monochronic functions. The point is that each does it in its own way. The Japanese are polychronic when looking and working inward, toward themselves. When dealing with the outside world, they have adopted the dominant time system which characterizes that world. That is, they shift to the monochronic mode and, characteristically, since these are technical matters, they outshine us. . . . . .

CONCEPTS AND QUESTIONS
FOR CHAPTER 6

1. From your personal experiences can you think of additional ways that people in various cultures greet, kiss, show contempt, or beckon?

2. Are cultural differences that are based on linguistic problems harder or easier to overcome than the problems related to nonverbal actions?

3. In what ways do nonverbal behaviors reflect the values, history, and social organization of a culture?

4. What are some of the dangers of overgeneralizing from nonverbal communication?

5. Have you ever experienced situations where the nonverbal behavior of someone did not meet your expectations? How did you react? Could this have been a cultural problem?

6. How can we develop a theory of nonverbal behavior if we go beyond the anecdotal narration of bizarre behaviors?

7. Can you think of any cultural examples that would tend to support the notion that a culture's history influences its use of nonverbal communication?

8. What are the relationships between verbal and nonverbal forms of communication?

9. How might cultural differences in time conceptualization lead to intercultural communication problems?

10. What examples can you think of that illustrate differences between the sexes in nonverbal behavior?

11. How would you prevent the occurrence of intercultural communication problems that are brought about by the unconscious and unintentional performance of nonverbal behavior and that deeply offend members of another culture?

12. Why is it important to look at both intentional and unintentional forms of nonverbal communication? Can you give an example of each?

13. Is it easier to overcome problems related to nonverbal actions or verbal languages? Why?

14. Which one of the various types of nonverbal behaviors discussed in this chapter do you think is most important to the student of intercultural communication? Why?

15. What does Andersen mean when he writes, "Culture is an enduring phenomenon whereas the situation is a transient one with an observable beginning and end?"

16. Can you think of instances where your personal space was "invaded" by someone from another culture?

17. Dolphin notes that "Other than culture, age and sex, the interaction distance between two individuals can be affected by a host of other variables: relationship between the two, the environment of the transaction, attitudinal differences, occupation and/or status, the language used, etc." Can you think of any other variables not mentioned by Dolphin?

18. How have you seen Hall's concept of monochronic time reflected in your culture?

PART FOUR

Intercultural Communication: Seeking Improvement

Happy are they that hear their detractions and can put them to mending.

—Shakespeare

In a sense, this entire volume has been concerned with the practice of intercultural communication. We have looked at a variety of cultures and a host of communication variables that operate when people from different cultures attempt to interact. However, our analysis thus far has been somewhat theoretical. Previous selections have concentrated primarily on the issue of understanding intercultural communication. We have not, at least up to this point, treated the act of practicing intercultural communication.

We have already pointed out many of the problems that cultural differences can introduce into the communication process. And we have shown how an awareness of not only other cultures but also of one's own culture can help mediate some of the problems. But intercultural communication is not exclusively a single party activity. Like other forms of interpersonal communication, it requires for its highest and most successful practice the complementary participation of all parties to the communication event.

When elevated to its highest level of human activity, intercultural communication becomes what David Berlo described as "Interaction: The Goal of Human Communication": the communicative act in which "two individuals make inferences about their own roles and the role of the other at the same time."* Berlo calls this reciprocal role taking: In order for people to achieve the highest level of communication there must be a mutual reciprocity in achieving an understanding of each other. In

---

*David K. Berlo, *The Process of Communication.* New York: Holt, Rinehart & Winston, 1960, p. 130.

intercultural communication, this means that you must not only know about your culture and the culture of the one with whom you are communicating, but that that person must also know about his or her own culture and about your culture as well. Unless there is mutual acknowledgment of each other's cultures and a willingness to accept those cultures as a reality governing communicative interactions, intercultural communication cannot rise to its highest possible level of human interaction.

In this final section we have slightly modified our orientation so that we can include a discussion based on the activity of communication. For although the readings in this portion of the book will increase your understanding, their main purpose is to improve your behavior *during* intercultural communication.

The motivation for this particular section grows out of an important precept found in the study of human communication. It suggests that human interaction is a behavioral act in which people engage for the purpose of changing their environment. Inherent in this notion is the idea that communication is something people *do*—it involves action. Regardless of how much you understand intercultural communication, when you are communicating with someone from another culture you are part of a behavioral situation. You, and your communication counterpart, are doing things to each other. This final part of the book deals with that "doing." In addition, it is intended to help your communication become as effective as possible.

As you might well imagine, personal contact and experience are the most desirable methods for improvement. Knowledge and practice seem to work in tandem. The problem, however, is that we cannot write or select readings that substitute for this personal experience. Therefore, our contribution by necessity must focus on the observations of those who have practiced intercultural communication with some degree of success.

7

Communicating Interculturally: Becoming Competent

The primary purpose of this book is to help you become more effective intercultural communicators. To this end, the articles in this chapter offer advice and counsel aimed at improving the way you communicate when you find yourself in intercultural encounters. To help you achieve this goal, most of the essays discuss problems as well as solutions. Being alert to potential problems is the first step toward understanding. Once problems have been identified it is easier to seek means of improvement.

The first essay looks at both problems and solutions. In "Stumbling Blocks in Intercultural Communication," LaRay M. Barna deals with some specific reasons why intercultural communication often fails to bring about mutual understanding. She has selected six important causes for communication breakdown across cultural boundaries: assuming similarity instead of difference, language problems, nonverbal misunderstanding, the presence of preconceptions and stereotypes, the tendency to evaluate, and the high anxiety that often exists in intercultural encounters.

Our second essay moves us from potential problems to possible solutions. In his article "Intercultural Communication Competence" Brian H. Spitzberg offers a profile of the effective intercultural communicator. More specifically, he suggests a course of action that is likely to enhance our competence when we are in an intercultural situation. These suggestions take the form of propositions that can be used to guide our actions. We are told that intercultural competence is increased if we (1) are motivated, (2) are knowledgeable, (3) possess interpersonal skills, (4) are credible, (5) meet the expectations of our communication partner, (6) can strike a balance between autonomy needs and intimacy needs, (7) reflect similarities, (8) manifest trust, (9) offer social support, and (10) have access to multiple relationships.

In "Prejudice in Intercultural Communication" Richard W. Brislin examines this problem while looking at the functions and forms of prejudice. He warns of six different forms of prejudice: red-neck racism, symbolic racism, tokenism, arms-length prejudice, real likes and dislikes, and the familiar and unfamiliar. Each of these forms must be understood and controlled to achieve successful intercultural communication.

In recent years the concepts of "individualism" and "collectivism" have become important topics for anyone interested in intercultural communication. In the context of culture, these two words refer to the manner in which members of a culture perceive the individual and the group. In general, cultures that stress individualism are characterized by the subordination of a group's goals to a person's own goals, while collectivist cultures are marked by individuals subordinating their personal desires to the goals of collectives. As you would suspect, a number of specific communication behaviors grow out of each of these views, for example, differences in how each perceives personal accomplishments, short-term and long-term relationships, and status. These and other differences are explored in our final essay by Harry C. Triandis, Richard W. Brislin, and C. Harry Hui, "Cross-Cultural Training Across the Individualism-Collectivism Divide." After explaining some of the forms of these two outlooks, the authors offer some specific advice on how members from either group can adapt to the behaviors of their counterparts. They give twenty-three suggestions for use when collectivist and individualist cultures come together. As in all the selections in this chapter, the advice offered by these authors can assist us in our desire to become more effective communicators.

The final article deals with cross-cultural adaptation, a unique and often overlooked aspect of intercultural communication. Young Yun Kim examines this subject in her essay "Communication and Cross-Cultural Adaptation." Because over a million immigrants are coming to the United States each year, she is concerned that many of their communicative modes, internalized from early childhood, may prove dysfunctional in their new communication environment. She therefore presents a discussion of both the problems and solutions of cross-cultural adaptation. Her thesis is that one learns to communicate by communicating and that much of that communication takes place between immigrants and the dominant culture. By understanding the adaptation process, we can help these immigrants with the difficult transition facing all new arrivals.

Stumbling Blocks in Intercultural Communication

LARAY M. BARNA

Why is it that contact with persons from other cultures so often is frustrating and fraught with misunderstanding? Good intentions, a friendly approach, and even the possibility of mutual benefits don't seem to be sufficient—to many people's surprise. It's appropriate at this time of major changes in the international scene to take a hard look at the reasons for this. New proximity and new types of relationships are presenting communication challenges that everyone needs to be ready to meet.

One answer to the question of why misunderstanding occurs is that some people naively assume there are sufficient similarities among peoples of the world to make communication easy. They expect that since all people procreate, feel hunger and pain, need shelter and security, and group into families and/or societies, the forms of adaptation to these biological and social needs (and the values and attitudes surrounding them) will also be similar. It also reduces the uncomfortable feeling of strangeness to believe that "people are people" and "deep down we're all alike."

A search for proof of this, however, shows that the universal similarities are mainly biological. Eibl-Eibesfeldt lists the "sucking response, the breast-seeking automatism, smiling, crying, and a number of reflexes" as universals.[1] There is also Pavlov's "orienting reaction"—the instantaneous bodily changes that occur when threat is perceived. These include the pouring of extra adrenaline and noradrenaline into the system, increased muscle tension, cessation of digestive processes, and other changes that prepare the human animal to "fight or flee."[2] The universal needs mentioned above (for food, shelter, and so on) have cultural variations as to the type and amount required and do differ in this regard.

Unfortunately these common characteristics are not much help for purposes of communication where we need to exchange complex information and/or feelings, solve problems of mutual concern, cement business relationships, or just make the kind of impression we wish to make.

A little more promising are the cross-cultural studies seeking to support Darwin's theory that facial expressions are universal.[3] Ekman found that "the particular visible pattern on the face, the combination of muscles contracted for anger, fear, surprise, sadness, disgust, happiness (and probably also for interest) is the same for all members of our species."[4] This seems helpful until it is realized that a person's cultural upbringing determines whether or not the emotion will be displayed or suppressed, as well as on which occasions and to what degree.[5] The situations that bring about the emotional feeling also differ from culture to culture; for example, the death of a loved one may be a cause for joy, sorrow, or some other emotion, depending upon the accepted cultural belief.

Since there seem to be no universals or "human nature" that can be used as a basis for automatic understanding, we must treat each encounter as an individual case, searching for whatever perceptions and communication means are held in common and proceed from there. This is summarized by Vinh The Do. "If we realize that we are all culture bound and culturally modified, we will accept the fact that, being unlike, we do not really know what someone else 'is.' This is another way to view the 'people are people' idea. We now have to find a way to sort out the cultural modifiers in each separate encounter to find similarity."[6]

Persons from the United States seem to hold this assumption of similarity more strongly than some other cultures. The Japanese, for example, have the reverse belief that they are distinctively different from the rest of the world.[7] This notion brings intercultural communication problems of its own. Expecting no similarities, they work hard to figure out the foreign stranger but do not expect foreigners to be able to understand them. This results in exclusionary attitudes and only passive efforts toward mutual understanding.[8]

As Western trappings permeate more and more of the world, the aura of similarity increases. A look-alike facade deceives representatives from contrasting cultures when each wears Western dress, speaks English, and uses similar greeting rituals. It is like assuming that New York, Tokyo, and Tehran are all alike because each has the appearance of a modern city. But without being alert to possible underlying differences and the need to learn new rules for functioning, persons going from one city to the other will be in immediate trouble, even when acting simple roles such as pedestrian or driver. Also, unless a foreigner expects subtle differences it will take a long time of noninsulated living in a new culture (not in an enclave of his or her own kind) before he or she can be jarred into new perceptual and nonevaluative thinking.

The confidence that goes with the myth of similarity is much stronger than with the assumption of differences, the latter requiring tentative assumptions and behaviors and a willingness to accept the anxiety of "not knowing." Only with the assumption of differences, however, can reactions and interpretations be adjusted to fit "what's happening." Without it someone is likely to misread signs and symbols and judge the scene ethnocentrically.

The stumbling block of assumed similarity is a "troublem," as one English learner expressed it, not only for the foreigner but for the people in the host country (United States or any other) with whom the international visitor comes into contact. The native inhabitants are likely to be lulled into the expectation that, since the foreign person is dressed appropriately and speaks some of the language, he or she will also have similar nonverbal codes, thoughts, and feelings. In the United States nodding, smiling, and affirmative comments from a foreigner will probably be confidently interpreted by straightforward, friendly Americans as meaning that they have informed, helped, and pleased the newcomer. It is likely, however, that the foreigner actually understood very little of the verbal and nonverbal content and was merely indicating polite interest or trying not to embarrass himself or herself or the host with verbalized questions. The conversation may even have confirmed a stereotype that Americans are insensitive and ethnocentric.

In instances like the above, parties seldom compare impressions and correct misinterpretations. One place where opportunities for achieving insights do occur is in an intercultural communication classroom. Here, for example, U.S. students often complain that international student members of a discussion or project group seem uncooperative or uninterested. One person who had been thus judged offered the following explanation:

I was surrounded by Americans with whom I couldn't follow their tempo of discussion half of the time. I have difficulty to listen and speak, but also with the way they handle the group. I felt uncomfortable because sometimes they believe their opinion strongly. I had been very serious about the whole subject but I was afraid I would say something wrong. I had the idea but not the words.[9]

The classroom is also a good place to test whether one common nonverbal behavior, the smile, is actually the universal sign people assume it to be. The following enlightening comments came from international students newly arrived in the United States.[10]

Japanese student: *On my way to and from school I have received a smile by non-acquaintance American girls several times. I have finally learned they have no interest for me; it means only a kind of greeting to a foreigner. If someone smiles at a stranger in Japan, especially a girl, she can as-*

sume he is either a sexual maniac or an impolite person.

Korean student: *An American visited me in my country for one week. His inference was that people in Korea are not very friendly because they didn't smile or want to talk with foreign people. Most Korean people take time to get to be friendly with people. We never talk or smile at strangers.*

Arabian student: *When I walked around the campus my first day many people smiled at me. I was very embarrassed and rushed to the men's room to see if I had made a mistake with my clothes. But I could find nothing for them to smile at. Now I am used to all the smiles.*

Vietnamese student: *The reason why certain foreigners may think that Americans are superficial—and they are, some Americans even recognize this—is that they talk and smile too much. For people who come from placid cultures where nonverbal language is more used, and where a silence, a smile, a glance have their own meaning, it is true that Americans speak a lot. The superficiality of Americans can also be detected in their relations with others. Their friendships are, most of the time, so ephemeral compared to the friendships we have at home. Americans make friends very easily and leave their friends almost as quickly, while in my country it takes a long time to find out a possible friend and then she becomes your friend—with a very strong sense of the term.*

Statements from two U.S. students follow.[11] The first comes from someone who has learned to look for differing perceptions and the second, unfortunately, reflects the stumbling block of assumed similarity.

U.S. student: *I was waiting for my husband on a downtown corner when a man with a baby and two young children approached. Judging by small quirks of fashion he had not been in the U.S. long. I have a baby about the same age and in appre-*

ciation *of his family and obvious involvement as a father I smiled at him. Immediately I realized I did the wrong thing as he stopped, looked me over from head to toe and said, "Are you waiting for me? You meet me later?" Apparently I had acted as a prostitute would in his country.*

U.S. student: *In general it seems to me that foreign people are not necessarily snobs but are very unfriendly. Some class members have told me that you shouldn't smile at others while passing them by on the street in their country. To me I can't stop smiling. It's just natural to be smiling and friendly. I can see now why so many foreign people stick together. They are impossible to get to know. It's like the Americans are big bad wolves. How do Americans break this barrier? I want friends from all over the world but how do you start to be friends without offending them or scaring them off—like sheep?*

The discussion thus far threatens the popular expectation that increased contact with representatives of diverse cultures through travel, student exchange programs, joint business ventures, and so on will automatically result in better understanding and friendship. Indeed, tests of that assumption have been disappointing.[12] Research, for example, found that Vietnamese immigrants who speak English well and have the best jobs are suffering the most from psychosomatic complaints and mental problems and are less optimistic about the future than their counterparts who remain in ethnic enclaves without attempts to adjust to their new homeland. One explanation given is that these persons, unlike the less acculturated immigrants, "spend considerable time in the mainstream of society, regularly facing the challenges and stresses of dealing with American attitudes."[13]

After twenty-four years of listening to conversations between international and U.S. students and professors and seeing the frustrations of both groups as they try to understand each other, this author, for one, is inclined to agree with Charles Frankel, who says, "Tensions exist within nations and between nations that never would have existed were these nations not in such intensive cultural communication with one another."[14]

It doesn't have to be that way. Just as more opportunities now exist for cross-cultural contact, so does more information about how to meet this challenge. There are more orientation and training programs around the country, more courses in intercultural communication in educational institutions, and more published material.[15] Until persons can squarely face the likelihood of difference and misunderstanding, however, they will not be motivated to take advantage of these resources.

Many potential travelers who do try to prepare for sojourns gather information about the customs of the other country and a smattering of the language. Behaviors and attitudes of its people are sometimes researched, but almost always from a secondhand source, like a friend who has "been there." Experts realize that information gained in this fashion is general, seldom sufficient, and may or may not be applicable to the specific situation and area that the traveler visits. Also, knowing "what to expect" often blinds the observer to all but what confirms his or her image. Any contradictory evidence that does filter through the screens of preconception is likely to be treated as an exception and thus discounted.

A better approach is to begin by studying the history, political structure, art, literature, and language of the country if time permits. This provides a framework for on-site observations. Even more important is to develop an investigative, nonjudgmental posture and a high tolerance for ambiguity—all of which require lowered defenses. Margaret Mead suggests sensitizing persons to the kinds of things that need to be taken into account instead of developing behavior and attitude stereotypes. She reasons that there are individual differences in each encounter and that changes occur regularly in cultural patterns which makes researched information obsolete.[16]

Edward Stewart also warns against providing lists of "do's and don'ts" for travelers, for several reasons, the main one being that behavior is ambiguous. Another reason is that the same action can have different meanings in different situations and no one can be armed with prescriptions for every contingency. Instead Stewart encourages persons to understand the assumptions and values on which their own behavior rests. This can then be compared with what is found in the other culture, and a "third culture" can be adopted based on expanded cross-cultural understanding.[17]

The remainder of this article will examine some of the variables of the intercultural communication process itself and point out danger zones therein. The first stumbling block has already been discussed at length, the hazard of *assuming similarity instead of difference*. A second danger will surprise no one: *language difference*. Vocabulary, syntax, idioms, slang, dialects, and so on, all cause difficulty, but the person struggling with a different language is at least aware of being in trouble.

A worse language problem is the tenacity with which someone will cling to just one meaning of a word or phrase in the new language, regardless of connotation or context. The infinite variations possible, especially if inflection and tonal qualities are present, are so difficult to cope with that they are often waved aside. This complacency will stop a search for understanding. The nationwide misinterpretation of Khrushchev's sentence "We'll bury you" is a classic example. Even "yes" and "no" cause trouble. When a Japanese hears, "Won't you have some tea?" he or she listens to the literal meaning of the sentence and answers, "No," meaning that he or she wants some. The U.S. hostess, on the other hand, ignores the double negative because of common usage, and the guest gets no tea. Also, in some cultures, it is polite to refuse the first or second offer of refreshment. Many foreign guests have gone hungry because they never got a third offer. This is another case of where "no" means "yes."

Learning the language, which most visitors to foreign countries consider their only barrier to understanding, is actually only the beginning. As Frankel says, "To enter into a culture is to be able to hear, in Lionel Trilling's phrase, its special 'hum and buzz of implication.'"[18] This suggests the third stumbling block, *nonverbal misinterpretations*. People from different cultures inhabit different sensory realities. They see, hear, feel, and smell only that which fits into their personal world of recognition and then interpret it through the frame of reference of their own culture. An example follows.

An Oregon girl in an intercultural communication class asked a young man from Saudi Arabia how he would nonverbally signal that he liked her. His response was to smooth back his hair, which to her was just a common nervous gesture signifying nothing. She repeated her question three times. He smoothed his hair three times. Then, realizing that she was not recognizing this movement as his reply to her question, he automatically ducked his head and stuck out his tongue slightly in embarrassment. This behavior *was* noticed by the girl and she expressed astonishment that he would show liking for someone by sticking out his tongue.

The lack of comprehension of nonverbal signs and symbols that are easy to observe—such as gestures, postures, and other body movements—is a definite communication barrier. But it is possible to learn the meanings of these messages, usually in informal rather than formal ways. It is more difficult to note correctly the unspoken codes of the other culture that are further from awareness, such as the handling of time and spatial relationships and subtle signs of respect or formality.[19]

The fourth stumbling block is the presence of *preconceptions and stereotypes*. If the label "inscrutable" has preceded the Japanese guest, few try to understand his "strange" behavior, including the constant and seemingly inappropriate smile. The stereotype that Arabs are "inflammable" may cause U.S. students to keep their distance or even alert authorities when an animated and noisy group from the Middle East gathers. A professor who expects everyone from Indonesia, Mexico, and many other countries to "bargain" may unfairly interpret a hesitation or request from an international student as a move to manipulate preferential treatment.

Stereotypes help do what Ernest Becker says the anxiety-prone human race must do—reduce the threat of the unknown by making the world predictable.[20] Indeed, this is one of the basic functions of culture: to lay out a predictable world in which the individual is firmly oriented. Stereotypes are over-

generalized, second-hand beliefs that provide conceptual bases from which we "make sense" out of what goes on around us, whether or not they are accurate or fit the circumstance. In a foreign land their use increases our feeling of security and is psychologically necessary to the degree that we cannot tolerate ambiguity or the sense of helplessness resulting from inability to understand and deal with people and situations beyond our comprehension.

Stereotypes are stumbling blocks for communicators because they interfere with objective viewing of stimuli—the sensitive search for cues to guide the imagination toward the other person's reality. They are not easy to overcome in ourselves or to correct in others, even with the presentation of evidence. Stereotypes persist because they are firmly established as myths or truisms by one's own national culture and because they sometimes rationalize prejudices. They are also sustained and fed by the tendency to perceive selectively only those pieces of new information that correspond to the image held. For example, the Asian or African visitor who is accustomed to privation and the values of self-denial and self-help cannot fail to experience American culture as materialistic and wasteful. The stereotype for the visitor becomes a reality.

The fifth stumbling block and another deterrent to understanding between persons of differing cultures or ethnic groups is the *tendency to evaluate*, to approve or disapprove, the statements and actions of the other person or group. Each person's own culture or way of life always seems right, proper, and natural. This bias prevents the open-minded attention needed to look at the attitudes and behavior patterns from the other's point of view. A mid-day siesta changes from a "lazy habit" to a "pretty good idea" when someone listens long enough to realize the mid-day temperature in that country is 115°F.

The author, fresh from a conference in Tokyo where Japanese professors had emphasized the preference of the people of Japan for simple natural settings of rocks, moss, and water and of muted greens and misty ethereal landscapes, visited the Katsura Imperial Gardens in Kyoto. At the appointed time of the tour a young Japanese guide approached the group of twenty waiting U.S. Americans and remarked how fortunate it was that the day was cloudy. This brought hesitant smiles to the group who were less than pleased at the prospect of a shower. The guide's next statement was that the timing of the summer visit was particularly appropriate in that the azalea and rhododendron blossoms were gone and the trees had not yet turned to their brilliant fall colors. The group laughed loudly, now convinced that the young man had a fine sense of humor. I winced at his bewildered expression, realizing that had I come before attending the conference I would have shared the group's inference that he could not be serious.

The communication cutoff caused by immediate evaluation is heightened when feelings and emotions are deeply involved; yet this is just the time when listening with understanding is most needed. As stated by Sherif, Sherif, and Nebergall, "A person's commitment to his religion, politics, values of his family, and his stand on the virtue of his way of life are ingredients in his self-picture—intimately felt and cherished."[21] It takes both awareness of the tendency to close our minds and courage to risk change in our own perceptions and values to dare to comprehend why someone thinks and acts differently from us. Religious wars and negotiation deadlocks everywhere are examples of this.

On an interpersonal level there are innumerable illustrations of the tendency to evaluate which result in a breach in intercultural relationships. Two follow:[22]

U.S. student: *A Persian friend got offended because when we got in an argument with a third party, I didn't take his side. He says back home you are supposed to take a friend's or family's side even when they are wrong. When you get home then you can attack the "wrongdoer" but you are never supposed to go against a relative or a friend to a stranger. This I found strange because even if it is my mother and I think she is wrong, I say so.*

Korean student: *When I call on my American friend he said through window, "I am sorry. I have no time because of my study." Then he shut the window. I couldn't understand through my cultural background. House owner should have welcome visitor whether he likes or not and whether he is busy or not. Also the owner never speaks without opening his door.*

The admonition to resist the tendency to immediately evaluate does not intend to suggest that one should not develop one's own sense of right and wrong. The goal is only to look and listen empathically rather than through a thick screen of value judgments that would cause one to fail to achieve a fair understanding. Once comprehension of the other's view and circumstance is complete, it can be determined whether or not there is a clash of values or ideology. If so, some form of conflict resolution can be put into place.

The sixth stumbling block is the condition of *high anxiety*. The presence of some degree of anxiety/tension is common in cross-cultural experiences due to the number of uncertainties present and the personal involvement and risk. Whether or not the reaction will be debilitating depends on the level of activation (arousal) and whether the feeling is classified as being pleasant (thought of as excitement or anticipation) or unpleasant (anxiety). Moderate arousal and positive attitudes prepare one to meet challenges with energy. A state of too-high arousal caused by a buildup of *continued* moderate or high stress depletes the body's energy reserve quickly and some form of defense must be used whether or not the person wills it. These include skewing of perceptions, withdrawal, and hostility. If the stay in a foreign country is prolonged and the newcomer cannot let down his or her high level of stress, the "culture shock" phenomenon occurs. Illness may result, the body forcing needed rest and recuperation.[23]

This stumbling block of high anxiety (which always includes muscle tension) is separately mentioned for the purpose of emphasis. Unlike the other five (assumption of similarity, language, nonverbal misinterpretations, preconceptions and stereotypes, and the practice of immediate evaluation), it is not distinct but underlies and compounds the others. Different language and nonverbal patterns are difficult to use or interpret under the best of conditions. The distraction of feeling too much stress (sometimes called "internal noise") makes mistakes even more likely. As stated by Jack Gibb:

Defense arousal prevents the listener from concentrating upon the message. Not only do defensive communicators send off multiple value, motive, and affect cues, but also defensive recipients distort what they receive. As a person becomes more and more defensive, he becomes less and less able to perceive accurately the motives, the values, and the emotions of the sender.[24]

The stumbling blocks of using stereotypes and evaluations are defense mechanisms in themselves, as previously explained, and as such would obviously increase under stress.

Anxious feelings usually permeate both parties in a dialogue. The host national is uncomfortable when talking with a foreigner because he or she cannot maintain the normal flow of verbal and non-verbal interaction. There are language and perception barriers; silences are too long or too short; proxemic and other norms may be violated. He or she is also threatened by the other's unknown knowledge, experience, and evaluation—the visitor's potential for scrutiny and rejection of the person and/or country. The inevitable question, "How do you like it here?" which the foreigner abhors, is a quest for reassurance, or at least a "feeler" that reduces the unknown. The reply is usually more polite than honest but this is seldom realized.

The foreign members of dyads are even more threatened. They feel strange and vulnerable, helpless to cope with messages that swamp them. Their own "normal" reactions are inappropriate. Their self-esteem is often intolerably undermined unless they employ such defenses as withdrawal into their own reference group or into themselves, screening out or misperceiving stimuli, rationalization, overcompensation, "going native," or becoming aggressive or hostile. None of these defenses leads to effective communication.

Fatigue is a natural result of such a continued state of alertness, but, too often, instead of allowing needed rest, the body tenses even more to keep up its guard in the potentially threatening environment. To relax is to be vulnerable. An international student says it well:

During those several months after my arrival in the U.S.A., every day I came back from school exhausted so that I had to take a rest for a while, stretching myself on the bed. For, all the time, I strained every nerve in order to understand what the people were saying and make myself understood in my broken English. When I don't understand what American people are talking about and why they are laughing, I sometimes have to pretend to understand by smiling, even though I feel alienated, uneasy and tense.

In addition to this, the difference in culture or customs, the way of thinking between two countries, produces more tension because we don't know how we should react to totally foreign customs or attitudes, and sometimes we can't guess how the people from another country react to my saying or behavior. We always have a fear somewhere in the bottom of our hearts that there are much more chances of breakdown in intercultural communication than in communication with our own fellow countrymen.[25]

Knowing that the aforementioned stumbling blocks are present is certainly an aid in avoiding them, but these particular ones cannot be easily circumvented. For most people it takes insight, training, and sometimes an alteration of long-standing habits or cherished beliefs before progress can be made. The increasing need for global understanding and cooperation, however, makes the effort worthwhile. A few general suggestions follow.

We can study other languages and learn to expect differences in nonverbal forms and other cultural aspects. We can train ourselves to meet intercultural encounters with more attention to situational details, using an investigative approach rather than preconceptions and stereotypes. We can gradually expose ourselves to differences so that they become less threatening. By practicing conscious relaxation techniques we can even learn to lower our tension level when needed to avoid triggering defensive reactions. In a relaxed state it is also easier to allow the temporary suspension of our own world view, a necessary step to experience empathy.

Roger Harrison summarizes the goal when he says:

> . . . the communicator cannot stop at knowing that the people he is working with have different customs, goals, and thought patterns from his own. He must be able to feel his way into intimate contact with these alien values, attitudes, and feelings. He must be able to work with them and within them, neither losing his own values in the confrontation nor protecting himself behind a wall of intellectual detachment.[26]

NOTES

1. Eibl-Eibesfeldt, Irenaus, "Experimental Criteria for Distinguishing Innate from Culturally Conditioned Behavior," in *Cross-Cultural Understanding: Epistemology in Anthropology*, ed. F. S. C. Northrop and Helen H. Livingston (New York: Harper & Row, 1964), p. 304.

2. Furst, Charles, "Automating Attention," *Psychology Today* (August 1979), p. 112.

3. See Darwin, Charles, *The Expression of Emotions in Man and Animals* (New York: Appleton, 1872); Eibl-Eibesfeldt, Irenaus, *Ethology: The Biology of Behavior* (New York: Holt, Rinehart & Winston, 1970); Ekman, Paul, and Wallace V. Friesen, "Constants Across Cultures in the Face and Emotion," *Journal of Personality and Social Psychology* 17 (1971), pp. 124–129.

4. Ekman, Paul, "Movements with Precise Meanings," *Journal of Communication* 26 (Summer 1976), pp. 19–20.

5. Ekman, Paul, and Wallace Friesen, "The Repertoire of Nonverbal Behavior—Categories, Origins, Usage and Coding," *Semiotica* 1, p. 1.

6. Personal correspondence. Mr. Do is Multicultural Specialist, Portland Public Schools, Portland, Oregon.

7. Tai, Eiko, "Modification of the Western Approach to Intercultural Communication for the Japanese Context," unpublished Master's thesis, Portland State University, Portland, Oregon, 1986, p. 45.

8. Ibid, p. 47.

9. Taken from student papers on a course in intercultural communication taught by the author.

10. Ibid.

11. Ibid.

12. See for example: Wedge, Bryant, *Visitors to the United States and How They See Us* (New York: D. Van Nostrand Company, 1965); and Miller, Milton, et al., "The Cross-Cultural Student: Lessons in Human Nature," *Bulletin of Menninger Clinic* (March 1971).

13. Horn, Jack D., "Vietnamese Immigrants: Doing Poorly by Doing Well," *Psychology Today* (June 1980), pp. 103–104.

14. Frankel, Charles, *The Neglected Aspect of Foreign Affairs* (Washington, D.C.: Brookings Institution, 1965), p. 1.

15. One good source is the Intercultural Press, Inc., P.O. Box 768, Yarmouth, Maine 04096.

16. Mead, Margaret, "The Cultural Perspective," in *Communication or Conflict*, ed. Mary Capes (Association Press, 1960).

17. Stewart, Edward C., *American Cultural Patterns: A Cross-Cultural Perspective* (Yarmouth, Me.: Intercultural Press, Inc., 1972), p. 20.

18. Frankel, *The Neglected Aspect of Foreign Affairs*, p. 103.

19. For an overview, see Ramsey, Sheila J., "Nonverbal Behavior: An Intercultural Perspective," in *Handbook of Intercultural Communication*, eds. Molefi K. Asante, Eileen Newmark, and Cecil A. Blake (Newbury Park, Calif./London: Sage Publications, 1979), pp. 105–143.

20. Becker, Ernest, *The Birth and Death of Meaning* (New York: Free Press, 1962), pp. 84–89.

21. Sherif, Carolyn W., Musafer Sherif, and Roger Nebergall, *Attitude and Attitude Change* (Philadelphia: W. B. Saunders Co., 1965), p. vi.

22. Taken from student papers in a course in intercultural communication taught by the author.

23. Barna, LaRay M., "The Stress Factor in Intercultural Relations," in *Handbook of Intercultural Training, Vol II*, ed. Dan Landis and Richard W. Brislin (New York: Pergamon Press, 1983).

24. Gibb, Jack R., "Defensive Communication," *Journal of Communication* 2 (September 1961), pp. 141–148.

25. Taken from student papers in a course in intercultural communication taught by the author.

26. Harrison, Roger, "The Design of Cross-Cultural Training: An Alternative to the University Model," in *Explorations in Human Relations Training and Research* (Bethesda, Md.: National Training Laboratories, 1966), NEA No. 2, p. 4.

Intercultural Communication Competence

BRIAN H. SPITZBERG

The world we live in is shrinking. Travel that once took months now takes hours. Business dealings that were once confined primarily to local economies and occasional inroads into foreign markets have given way to an extensively integrated world economy. Information that once traveled through error-prone and time-consuming methods of personal transmittal now appears in the blink of an eye across a wide range of media technology. People in virtually all locations of the globe are more mobile than ever before and more likely to travel into cultures different from their own. Though we may not have fully become a "global village," there is no denying that the various cultures of the world are far more accessible than ever before, and that there are numerous forces bringing these cultures into contact at a rapid and increasing rate of interaction.

What transpires when people from different cultures come into contact has interested numerous scholarly disciplines. Anthropology, sociology, linguistics, communication, and clinical, social, and cognitive psychology are among the disciplines that have plowed the fields of intercultural interaction. The international nature of current economies makes the successful transaction of intercultural interaction a multibillion dollar concern. Furthermore, the successful establishment and maintenance of peaceful relations among governments requires at least occasional interaction to establish the nature of cooperation. Both government and business therefore have clear motives for better comprehending the processes and pitfalls of intercultural contact.

The sheer enormity and complexity of the parties to· these interactions may make such matters seem beyond the reach of interpersonal communication theory. However, the relationships among cultures ultimately are comprised of interpersonal encounters. Whether in the negotiation of an arms treaty, the settlement of a business contract, or merely an incident in which a sojourner gets directions from a native, cultures do not interact, people do. Given the economic, governmental, and societal implications of our increasingly intercultural environment, a thorough understanding of the nature of competent intercultural communication should have enormous practical advantages. Yet to date there is a general lack of specific or practical sources of advice and an obvious deficit of reasonable models for explaining intercultural competence.

The purpose of this chapter is to review concepts from several different disciplines concerning competent interaction and to apply these concepts to the intercultural context. For the purposes of this article, intercultural communication competence is considered very broadly as an impression that message behavior is appropriate and effective in a given context. Effectiveness is the successful accomplishment of valued goals, objectives, or rewards relative to costs. Appropriateness means that the valued rules, norms, and expectancies of the relationship are not violated significantly. With these dual standards, therefore, communication will be competent to an intercultural context when it accomplishes the objectives of an actor in a manner that is appropriate to the interpersonal context and relationship.

These two standards obviously bear on the concept of quality, since communication that is *in*appropriate and *in*effective is clearly of low quality. Further, communication that is *in*appropriate and effective would include such behaviors as lying, cheating, stealing, bludgeoning, and so forth, which are messages that ethically should not be conceptualized as competent. Finally, communication that

is appropriate but *in*effective suggests a social chameleon who does nothing objectionable but also accomplishes no personal objectives through interaction. Only the interactant who is simultaneously both appropriate and effective seems to meet the requirements of an ideal interpersonal communicator. The remainder of this article examines issues surrounding appropriateness and effectiveness in intercultural interaction.

A MODEL OF INTERCULTURAL COMPETENCE

Most existing models of intercultural competence have been fairly fragmented. Typically, the literature is reviewed and a list of skills, abilities, and attitudes is formulated to summarize the literature. Such lists appear to reflect useful guidelines for competent interaction and adaptation. For example, Spitzberg's (1989) review of studies (with two recent studies added: Chen, 1989; Martin and Hammer, 1989), conducted to discover the essential features of intercultural competence, produces the list in Table 1. While each study portrays a reasonable list of abilities or attitudes, there is no sense of integration or coherence across lists. It is impossible to tell which skills are most important in which situations, or even how such skills relate to each other.

A more productive approach would be to develop an integrative model of intercultural competence that is consistent with the theoretical and research literature and also provides specific predictions of competent behavior. The remainder of this article attempts to provide such a model. The model is displayed in its most simplistic form in Figure 1 and is elaborated by means of a series of propositions below. The propositions are broken down into three levels of analysis: the individual system, the episodic system, and the relational system. The individual system includes those characteristics an individual may possess that facilitate competent interaction in a social normative sense. The episodic system includes those features of a particular Actor that facilitate còmpetence impressions on the part of a specific Coactor in a specific episode of interac-

Table 1 Empirically Derived Factors of Intercultural Competence

Ability to adjust to different cultures	Frankness
Ability to deal with different societal systems	General competence as teacher (task)
Ability to deal with psychological stress	Incompetence
Ability to establish interpersonal relationships	Intellectualizing future orientation
Ability to facilitate communication	Interaction involvement
Ability to understand others	Interpersonal flexibility
Adaptiveness	Interpersonal harmony
Agency (internal locus and efficacy/optimism)	Interpersonal interest
Awareness of self and culture	Interpersonally sensitive maturity
Awareness of implications of cultural differences	Nonethnocentrism
Cautiousness	Nonverbal behaviors
Charisma	Personal/Family adjustment
Communication apprehension	Opinion leadership
Communication competence (ability to communicate)	Rigidity (task persistence)
Communication efficacy	Task accomplishment
Communicative functions	Transfer of "software"
Controlling responsibility	Self-actualizing search for identity
Conversational management behaviors	Self-confidence/Initiative
Cooperation	Self-consciousness
Cultural interaction	Self-disclosure
Demand (long-term goal orientation)	Self-reliant conventionality
Dependent anxiety	Social adjustment
Differentiation	Spouse/Family communication
Empathy/Efficacy	Strength of personality
Familiarity in interpersonal relations	Verbal behaviors

tion. The relational system includes those components that assist a person's competence across the life span of a particular relationship rather than in just a given episode of interaction. Each successive system level subsumes the logic and predictions of the former. The propositions serve both as an outline of a theory of interpersonal competence in intercultural contexts and as sources of practical advice. To the extent that a person can analyze intercultural situations sufficiently to understand initial conditions, each proposition suggests a course of action that is likely to enhance this person's competence in the situation encountered.

Individual System

1. *As communicator motivation increases, communicative competence increases.* Very simply, the more a person wants to make a good impression and communicate effectively, the more likely it is that this person will view self, and be viewed by others, as competent. The question then becomes: What constitutes or leads to high levels of motivation? The following propositions address this question.

1a. *As communicator confidence increases, communicator motivation increases.* Confidence results from several individual experiences and tendencies. A person who is anxious meeting strangers, for example, is likely to be less confident when encountering a new person from a different culture. Further, the more unfamiliar a person is with a given type of situation, the less confident that person is regarding what to do and how to do it. Finally, some situations carry more significant implications and are more difficult to manage than others (for example, getting directions to a major urban landmark is likely to permit greater confidence than negotiating a multimillion dollar contract for your company).

1b. *As valued efficacy beliefs increase, communicator motivation increases.* Efficacy beliefs are self-perceptions of ability to perform a given set of behaviors. Basically, the more a person believes that he or she is able to engage in a set of valued or positive actions, the more prone that person is to do so. A professional arbitrator is likely to have much higher efficacy beliefs in negotiating treaties or contracts than the average person, but this arbitrator might not have any greater confidence than the average person in developing friendships among others in a different culture. Efficacy beliefs are therefore usually task specific.

1c. *As task salience increases, communicator motivation increases.* Something that is salient is obvious or highly apparent. Thus, the more a situation provides a clear indication of what is to be done, or what can be done, and what the goals are, the more motivated a person is likely to be in pursuing the task and goals. The reverse of this proposition is that highly ambiguous situations usually diminish a person's motivation, since it is unclear what is likely to result from various courses of action, or what courses of action should even be taken.

1d. *As the relative cost/benefit ratio of a situation increases, communicator motivation increases.* Very simply, every situation can be viewed as having certain potential costs and benefits. Even in no-win situations, the behavior that leads to the least costly or painful outcomes is considered the most preferable or beneficial. Likewise, in a win-win situation the least desirable outcomes are also the most "costly." Thus, the more the perception of potential benefits increases relative to the potential punishments or costs of a course of action, the more motivated a person is to pursue that particular course of action. Obviously, the weighing of costs and benefits must always be done relative to alternatives. Asking directions from someone who does not speak your language may be considered too effortful, but only relative to the alternatives of consulting a map, trial-and-error exploration, or seeking someone who speaks your language who might be familiar with the locale.

1e. *As communicator approach dispositions increase, communicator motivation increases.* Approach dispositions refer to personality characteristics that prompt someone to value communicative activity. People who are higher in self-esteem, who generally believe they have high levels of control over their environment, who are low in social anxiety, and who are generally well adjusted psychologically are likely to seek out communication encounters and find them positively reinforcing.

2. *As communicative knowledge increases, communicative competence increases.* For an actor to give a good performance, it is important that stage fright is not debilitating and that there is a desire to perform well. It is also important, however, that the actor know the lines of the script. So it is with social interaction as well. The more an interactant knows about how to communicate well, the more competent that person is likely to be. Several predictions help specify the relevance of knowledge to competent interaction.

2a. *As contextual familiarity increases, communicator knowledge increases.* Obviously, the more familiar a person is with a given type of situation or relationship or encounter, the more knowledgeable this person is likely to be. Familiarity can result from numerous factors, including the variety of situations and relations within a culture, the duration of exposure to a culture, the frequency of contact with a culture, and even the exposure to similar encounters across different cultures.

2b. *As task-relevant procedural knowledge increases, communicator knowledge increases.* While exposure to a culture increases a person's store of familiarity with relevant subject matters, topics, language, and so on, it does not guarantee comprehension of the procedural features of interaction. Procedural knowledge concerns the "how" of social interaction rather than the "what." For example, knowing the actual content of a joke would be considered the substantive knowledge of the joke. Knowing how to tell it, with all the inflections, the timing, and the actual mannerisms, are all matters of the procedural knowledge of the joke. This knowledge is typically more "mindless" than other forms of knowledge. For example, many skill routines are overlearned to the point that the procedures are virtually forgotten. It is in this sense that you can drive

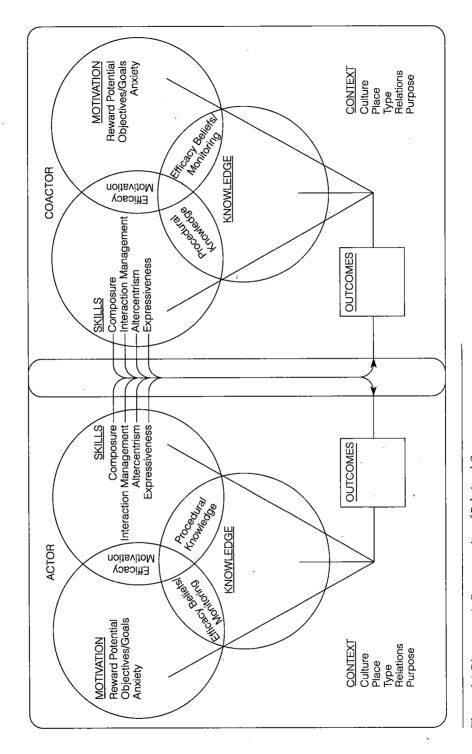

Figure 1 A Diagrammatic Representation of Relational Competence

a familiar route home and not remember anything about the drive upon arrival—you know how to drive, but you can do so with minimal conscious attention to the process. Thus, the more a person knows how to actually perform the mannerisms and behavioral routines of a cultural milieu, the more knowledgeable this person is likely to be in communicating generally with others in this culture.

2c. *As mastery of knowledge acquisition strategies increases, communicator knowledge increases.* A person who does not already know how to behave is not necessarily consigned to incompetence. People have evolved a multitude of subtle means of finding out what to do, and how to do it, in unfamiliar contexts. The metaphor of international espionage illustrates some of the strategies by which people acquire information about others, including interrogation (ask questions), surveillance (observe others), information exchange (disclose information to elicit disclosure from others), posturing (violate some local custom and observe reactions to assess value of various actions), bluffing (act as if we know what we are doing and let the unfolding action inform us and define our role), or acting as a double agent (use the services of a native or mutual friend as informant). The more of these types of strategies a person understands, the more able he or she is in obtaining the knowledge needed to interact competently in the culture.

2d. *As identity and role diversity increase, communicator knowledge increases.* In general, the more diverse a person's exposure to distinct types of people, roles, and self-images, the more this person is able to comprehend various roles and role behaviors characteristic of a given cultural encounter. In other words, a person who has a highly complex self-image, and who has interacted with a diversity of different types of other persons, is more able to understand the types of actions encountered in another culture.

2e. *As knowledge dispositions increase, communicator knowledge increases.* Many personality characteristics are related to optimal information processing. Specifically, persons high in intelligence, cognitive complexity, self-monitoring, listening skills, empathy, role-taking ability, nonverbal

sensitivity, perceptual accuracy, problem-solving ability, and so on, are more likely to know how to behave in any given encounter. In short, it is not just possession of information that is important—a person needs to know what to do with the information.

3. *As communicator skills increase, communicator competence increases.* Skills are any repeatable, goal-oriented actions or action sequences. An actor who is motivated to perform well and knows the script well may still not possess the acting skills required to give a good performance. All of us have probably encountered instances in which we knew what we wanted to say but just could not seem to say it correctly. Such issues concern the skills of acting on our motivation and knowledge. Research indicates that there are four specific types or clusters of interpersonal skills, as well as one more general type of skill.

3a. *As conversational altercentrism increases, communicator skill increases.* Altercentrism ("alter" meaning other, "centrism" meaning to center or focus upon) involves those behaviors that reveal interest in, concern for, and attention to another person. Behaviors such as eye contact, asking questions, maintenance of topics introduced by other, appropriate body lean and posture, and active listening all indicate a responsiveness to the other person.

3b. *As conversational coordination increases, communicator skill increases.* Conversational coordination involves all those behaviors that assist in the smooth flow of an encounter. Minimizing response latencies, providing for smooth initiation and conclusion of conversational episodes, avoiding disruptive interruptions, providing transitions between themes or activities, providing informative feedback cues, and so on, all assist in managing the interaction and maintaining appropriate pacing and punctuation of a conversation.

3c. *As conversational composure increases, communicator skill increases.* To be composed in a conversation is to reflect calmness and confidence in demeanor. Thus, composure consists of avoiding anxiety cues (such as nervous twitches, adaptors, avoidance of eye contact, and breaking vocal pitch) and displaying such behaviors as a steady volume and pitch, relaxed posture, and well-formulated verbal statements. A composed communicator comes across as assertive, self-assured, and in control.

3d. *As conversational expressiveness increases, communicator skill increases.* Expressiveness concerns those skills that provide vivacity, animation, intensity, and variability in communicative behavior. Specifically, expressiveness is revealed by such behaviors as vocal variety, facial affect, opinion expression, extensive vocabulary usage, and gestures. Expressive communication is closely associated with the ability to display appropriate affect and energy level through speech and gesture.

3e. *As conversational adaptation increases, communicator skill increases.* Adaptation is a commonly noted attribute of the competent intercultural communicator, but little is known about it. Presumably, however, it implies several characteristics. First, adaptation does not imply chameleon-like change but, instead, appropriate variation of self's behavior to the behavioral style of others. Second, it implies certain homeostatic, or consistency-maintaining, regulatory processes. That is, verbal actions are kept relatively consistent with nonverbal actions. Similarly, the amount of personal altercentrism, coordination, composure, and expressiveness are kept relatively consistent with personal style tendencies. Third, it suggests adaptation to the actions of the other person, as well as to one's own goal(s) in the encounter. Adaptation does not imply being completely altercentric or egocentric in orientation, but rather altering self's goals and intentions and balancing them with those of the other person. Thus, the skill of adaptation involves such behaviors as shifts of vocal style, posture, animation, and topic development, as the behaviors of the other person vary and as changes in self's goals occur over the course of a conversation.

The propositions in this section examined three basic components of interculturally competent communication. In general, the more motivated, knowledgeable, and skilled a person is, the more competent this person is likely to be. It is possible that a person can be viewed as highly competent if high in only one or two of these components. For example, a person who is very motivated may compensate for lack of knowledge and skill through perseverance and effort alone. Likewise, someone who is extremely familiar with success in a given type of encounter may be able to "drift" through certain encounters (for example, "I've written up so many contracts in my life that I can negotiate one in my sleep") with minimal motivation and little conscious awareness of the exact procedures involved. Nevertheless, across most encounters, the more of each of these components a person possesses or demonstrates, the more competent this person is likely to view himself or herself.

Episodic System

The first three primary propositions entailed factors that increase the likelihood that a person will produce behaviors that are normatively considered competent, so that the person producing them, and others generally, will tend to believe that he or she has behaved competently. However, competent behavior in certain situations is no guarantee that a person will be viewed as competent by a particular conversational partner in a particular relational encounter. The propositions in this section address this latter issue. These propositions are episodic in the sense that characteristics of an Actor influence the impressions of the Coactor in a specific episode of interaction. The statements concern those characteristics of Actor that predict Coactor's impression of Actor's competence.

4. *As Actor's communicative status increases, Coactor's impression of Actor's competence increases.* Communicative status is meant here to represent all those factors that enhance this person's positive evaluation. Competence is, after all, an evaluation. Generally, as a person's status goes, so goes his or her competence. There are obvious exceptions, but it is instructive to consider those status characteristics particularly relevant to communicative competence.

4a. *As Actor's motivation, knowledge, and skills increase, Coactor's impression of Actor's competence increases.* The logic of the individual system also applies to the episodic system. That is, the factors that lead a person to behave competently in a normative sense will usually lead to a competent relational performance as well (Imahori and Lanigan, 1989; Spitzberg and Cupach, 1984). This is true in two slightly different senses. In one sense, since norms are made up of the majority of people's views and behaviors, a person who is normatively competent will usually be viewed as competent in a given encounter. In a sense more relevant to episodic systems, an Actor who is motivated to interact competently with a particular Coactor, knowledgeable about this particular Coactor, and skilled in interacting with this particular Coactor is also more likely to communicate better and be viewed as competent by this Coactor in a given encounter.

Factors that facilitate motivation, knowledge, and skill in a particular episodic system are likely to be logical extensions of the individual system components. For example, motivation is likely to increase as attraction to Coactor increases and as positive reinforcement history with Coactor increases. Knowledge of Coactor is likely to increase with the duration of relationship and as depth and breadth of self-disclosure between Actor and Coactor increase. Skill in interacting with Coactor is likely to increase as adaptation and refinement increase over the lifetime of the relationship.

4b. *As contextual obstruction of Actor's performance increases, Coactor's impression of Actor's competence increases.* At first, this statement may seem counterintuitive, but it derives from a rather straightforward logic. When forming an impression of an Actor, a Coactor is left to determine the extent to which the Actor's behaviors and outcomes are due to the Actor's own abilities and effort, rather than the context or other factors. For example, a physically unattractive Actor who consistently makes friends and has dates is likely to be viewed as more communicatively competent than a person who is physically attractive. The reasoning is that the social context is weighted against the unattractive Actor and in favor of the attractive Actor. Thus, the attractive Actor would achieve the same outcomes due to attractiveness rather than his or her competence, whereas the unattractive Actor must overcome the contextual barriers through competent action. In essence, an Actor's competence is "dis-

counted" if there are obvious alternative explanations for the Actor's good fortune. Similarly, an Actor's incompetence is "forgiven" if there are many apparent alternative reasons for his or her failure.

4c. *As Actor's receipt of valued outcomes increases, Coactor's impression of Actor's competence increases.* While the discounting effect discussed above influences impressions of competence, it is not likely to outweigh other factors entirely. Thus, if an Actor is perceived as consistently achieving positive outcomes, a Coactor is likely to assume that the Actor has something to do with this success. The corporate salesperson who consistently outsells the others in the department is likely to be viewed as more communicatively competent simply as a result of the tangible outcomes, almost regardless of extenuating circumstances.

4d. *As Actor's extant status increases, Coactor's impression of Actor status increases.* An actor who comes into an encounter or situation with an established high level of status in a given Coactor's eyes is more likely to be viewed as competent in subsequent interactions. The reverse is also likely. An Actor who has established a satisfying relationship with a Coactor has, in effect, established a reserve of competence in the Coactor's views. Furthermore, certain cultures develop higher regard for other cultures generally. Shortly after Bush's invasion of Panama, for example, native views of Americans were characterized in the press as unusually high, whereas opinions elsewhere in Latin America were depicted as unusually low. Any given American then attempting to establish a competent relationship with Panamanian natives would be likely to receive better responses than those seeking contact in other Latin American cultural milieus. In essence, therefore, the impression we initially have of an Actor is likely to determine our later impressions until such time that significant events interfere with these impressions.

4e. *As Actor's and Coactor's collective relational satisfaction increases, Coactor's impression of Actor's competence increases.* There is an obvious but intentional circularity about this statement. To the extent that Actor and Coactor interact competently, they are also likely to be relatively satisfied with their relationship. Likewise, to the extent that people feel satisfied with their relationship, they are also likely to assume that part of the cause of this satisfaction is the other person's interpersonal competence. Conceptually, satisfaction occurs when a person has accomplished valued outcomes, and valued outcomes are more likely to result from relationally appropriate communication. Satisfaction is thus a common indicator that communication has been relatively competent (Spitzberg and Hecht, 1984).

5. *Coactor's impression of Actor's competence is a function of Actor's fulfillment of Coactor's expectancies.* Over time, interactants develop expectations regarding how interpersonal interaction is likely to, and should, occur in particular contexts. Not surprisingly, therefore, a person's competence in a given relationship is due in part to the extent to which expectancies are fulfilled or violated. Research indicates that expectancies generally develop along three fundamental dimensions: *evaluation, potency*, and *activity* (commonly referred to as the E-P-A dimensions, respectively; see Osgood, May, and Miron, 1975; Spitzberg, 1989). That is, most contexts are viewed in terms of their valence (good versus bad, pleasurable versus unpleasurable), power (strong versus weak, dominant versus passive), and activity (fast versus slow, noisy versus quiet) characteristics. A typical, noncharismatic church service is expected to be "good," with the audience passive and relatively quiet. A typical party, in contrast, is expected to be good, strong, fast, and noisy. Upon being fired, one's exit interview is expected to be unpleasurable, weak, and relatively passive. The point is that experience with interpersonal encounters produces expectancies and evaluations regarding both anticipated and appropriate behavior. The propositions below elaborate the influence of these cognitions on impressions of competence.

5a. *As Actor's fulfillment of positive Coactor expectancies increases, Coactor's impression of Actor's competence increases.* To the extent that Coactor expects an encounter with Actor to be positive, then Actor is likely to be viewed as competent to the extent that he or she fulfills these expectancies. Since the expectancies typically form a consistent system

in a Coactor's mind, an Actor needs to fulfill each of the E-P-A dimensions. If an interviewer expects interviews to be good (E), his or her own role to be powerful, and the role of the interviewee to be powerless (P), and for the encounter to be generally quiet but quick (A), the Actor is well advised to behave according to these expectancies. Since the interviewer has developed these expectancies along all three dimensions, they tend to be "set" in relationship to each other. Thus, part of what makes the interview "good" in the interviewer's opinion is that his or her role is typically powerful and the interviews tend to go quietly and quickly.

5b. *As Actor's normative violation of Coactor's negative expectancies increases, Coactor's impression of Actor's competence increases.* The logic of the former proposition reverses itself when a Coactor expects an encounter to be negative. To twist the same example from the other side of the desk, consider the interview from the interviewee's perspective. An interviewee may find interviews highly anxiety-producing, threatening, and difficult. As such, the interview context is expected to be unpleasurable, the interviewee's role to be submissive, and the encounter to be generally slow and inactive. If the interviewer wants to make a good impression, therefore, he or she needs to violate the interviewee's expectations. Such an interviewer might change the setting to a less formal lunchroom context, dress more casually, tell some stories and initially discuss topics unrelated to the position, and generally spend some time putting the interviewee in a good mood. Such an encounter violates the interviewee's expectancies but does so in a way that is normatively acceptable and positive.

5c. *As Actor's fulfillment of Coactor's competence prototype expectancies increases, Coactor's impression of Actor's competence increases* (Pavitt, 1989). A prototype is basically a cognitive outline of concepts. The prototype of a competent person, for example, might consist of several levels of concepts varying in their abstraction. A simplified and hypothetical example of a prototype for a "competent communicator" is displayed in Figure 2.

At the highest level is the category label that determines what types of inferences are relevant to a

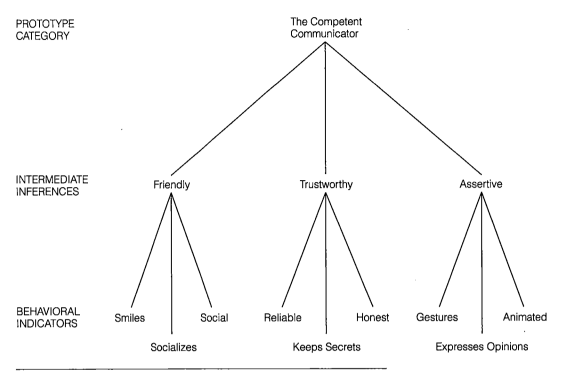

Figure 2 A Simple Cognitive Prototype of a Competent Communicator

given set of observed behavior. For example, observing someone changing the oil in a car is not relevant to the category of "competent communicator." At the next level are types of inferences or impressions that collectively make up the label of competent communicator. In this hypothetical example, a competent communicator is someone who is believed to be friendly, trustworthy, and assertive. Each of these inferences, in turn, is based upon certain types of behavior. To the extent that these behaviors are observed, the inferences follow. Assuming that the encounter is relevant to the category, then the behaviors observed are matched or compared to those that over time have come to occupy the position of indicators. If there is a good match, then the inferences and evaluations that constitute the label of competent communicator (in this case, friendly, trustworthy, assertive) are attributed to the interactant observed. If only some of the behaviors match,

then the inference of competence is diminished proportionately.

5d. *As Actor's normative reciprocity of positive affect increases, Coactor's impression of Actor's competence increases.* Research indicates that across most types of relationships and encounters, interactants are generally considered more competent when they reciprocate positive affect (Andersen, 1989; Spitzberg, 1989). Reciprocity implies a matching or similarity of response. Thus, to the extent that Coactor displays positive affect, the Actor's response in kind is likely to produce more positive impressions. Specifically, Coactor immediacy, in the form of smiling, eye contact, proximity, and so on, should be responded to with the same behaviors by Actor.

5e. *As Actor's normative compensation of negative affect increases, Coactor's impression of Actor's competence increases.* The same research that supports reciprocity of positive affect generally suggests that the opposite tack should be taken in response to negative affect. That is, if Coactor displays negative affect in the form of anger, attack, or exclusion, an Actor is generally considered more competent if he or she compensates for these affects with positive, patient, and accepting orientations. Of course, there are obvious exceptions, as when the exclusion communicated is the expression of a sincere desire to simply end the encounter or relationship. In general, however, positive affect is typically more competent than negative affect.

5f. *As Actor's normative compensation of power relations increases, the Coactor's impression of Actor's competence increases.* Across most types of interpersonal relationships, including organizational, social, and intimate relations, complementary power relationships tend to produce higher impressions of competence. This is a sweeping statement, and obviously it is an overstatement in many ways. Nevertheless, it suggests a useful principle in most relations.

Specifically, dominance is more competently met with passivity, and passivity is more competently met with dominance. The validity of this proposition is best illustrated by consideration of its alternative. Imagine, for example, what work relationships would be like if every time a superior gave a subordinate orders, they were met with counterorders or refusal. Imagine married couples in which neither person ever offers to actually make a decision. In other words, relationships and encounters tend to work more smoothly and comfortably when dominant moves are responded to with complementary passive moves, and passive moves are met with more directive moves. This does not imply that people should adopt a role of passivity or dominance, but that on a statement-by-statement basis, most interaction will be viewed as competent to the extent that its power balance is complementary rather than reciprocal.

This section has examined the episodic system of intercultural competence. Specifically, the propositions have involved those characteristics of an Actor that increase the likelihood that Coactor views Actor as competent in a given episode of interaction. The following section is an abbreviated excursion into the relational system, in which characteristics that facilitate competence across the lifespan of a relationship are considered.

Relational System

Relationships are not simply sums of episodes over time. Certainly there is likely to be a strong relationship, such that the more competent the average episode of interaction is, the more relationally stable and satisfying the relationship is likely to be as well. Thus, the logic of the individual system and episodic system are also likely to extend to the relational system. However, there are other factors at work, and this section examines some of these factors. In this discussion, the phrase "relational competence" refers to the level of communicative quality in an established relationship. It is an index of the mutual adaptation and satisfaction achieved by a relationship.

6. *As mutual fulfillment of autonomy and intimacy needs increases, relational competence increases.* Autonomy and intimacy are two fundamental human needs. Typically, they exist in a form of dialectical tension, in that each struggles for dominance over the other at any given time, but both are ever present to some degree. The need for intimacy involves the desire for human contact, camaraderie, communal activity, and nurturance. The need for autonomy, in contrast, is a need for self-control, independence, privacy, and solitude. Individuals seem to fluctuate between these two needs over time. It follows that if a relationship is competent over the course of its lifespan, the members need to fulfill each other's needs as they fluctuate. This implies a challenging but vital balancing act of skills, in which each person ascertains the need levels of the partner, and of self, and seeks to negotiate an optimal balance. Obviously, the ideal relationship seems to be the one in which both members have high intimacy needs or high autonomy needs. Relationships are likely to be more problematic when one person needs intimacy and the other needs au-

tonomy. However, even these problematic relationships are manageable if the partners seek creative solutions, as when the person needing high intimacy spends more time with friends or family rather than the relational partner.

7. *As mutual attraction increases, relational competence increases.* This highly intuitive proposition simply indicates that the more partners grow attracted to each other, the more this is likely to reflect, and result in, mutually competent interaction over time. This proposition gains support from the consistent finding that attraction is closely associated, at least initially, with interpersonal similarity—highly similar persons provide a world view of similar values and orientations, which in turn are reflected in a reinforcing and self-confirming manner of symbolic expression. In general, we enjoy interacting with those who are similar because "they speak our language." In intercultural contexts, it seems likely that those who are culturally dissimilar are also likely to be less initially attractive as well. One implication is that initial interactions with culturally dissimilar others should focus on or discover areas of similarity that can support sufficient motivation and reinforcement for continued interaction. This is not to imply that differences are always negatively reinforcing; however, they tend to make the *process* of communication more effortful and difficult, and thereby generally less rewarding.

8. *As mutual trust increases, relational competence increases.* Similar to the above proposition, the more partners trust one another, the more competent interaction is likely to be, and the more competent the relationship is likely to be. Trust provides a context in which interaction can be more honest, spontaneous, direct, and open. Over time, such a trusting climate is likely to be mutually reinforcing and lead to a productive and satisfying communicative relationship.

9. *As access to social support increases, relational competence increases.* Social support is anything that assists a person in coping with problematic or stressful situations. Since stresses stimulate personal and often relational crises, anything that diminishes the effects of these stresses is likely to enhance the person's ability to manage the relationship itself. That is, personal crises detract from that person's ability to manage the day-to-day problems of a given relationship. For example, if a car breaks down and a person needs to get to work, if a loved one dies and the person needs full-time emotional support, or if a person's schedule becomes overloaded and certain tasks simply cannot be performed, others can often provide services or resources to buffer the stress from such problems. This buffer then helps prevent the individual problem from becoming a relational problem. One of the common problems of sojourner couples or families is that the stresses of being in a new culture often cannot be resolved by the social support of a friendship network, since the friendship network has yet to be established in the new culture.

10. *As relational network integration increases, relational competence increases.* When discussing relationships, it is ironically easy to forget that individuals are always simultaneously members of multiple relationships. When two people come together and form a relationship, part of what determines the competence of this relationship is the extent to which each member's personal network integrates with the other person's network of social relationships. Increasingly, as businesses become multinational and move entire management teams to work with labor in other countries, the problems of social network integration will become substantial. The development of common activities and goals that require cooperation or interaction across social networks are likely to facilitate this aspect of intercultural competence.

CONCLUSIONS

Before attempting to summarize the implications of this article, an important qualification needs to be considered. Specifically, most of the propositions have what can be considered upper limits. In other words, too much of a good thing can be bad. To examine a very straightforward example, someone can be *too* motivated, *too* knowledgeable, use *too* much expressiveness, be *too* composed, and so on. Virtually any piece of advice, when carried to extremes, tends to lose its functional value.

Sir Karl Popper, an eminent philosopher of science, has warned us that a theory is only useful if it is in danger of failing. Theories that tell us what we already know must be true tell us nothing. The implication is that theories are only useful to the extent that they make risky predictions that may be untrue. It is in this sense that this article must be viewed with caution.

The predictions offered in this article represent statements that in the daily interplay of lives are often in danger of being false. None of the predictions should be taken to be absolutely true, or as an infallible guide to the complex canvas of intercultural relations. Nevertheless, progress in the development of knowledge results from such risky propositions, and this article has attempted to chart a path to progress. In doing so, I have painted with very broad brush strokes the outline of a theory of intercultural competence. The lines of this theory are strained by their abstraction to the point of no longer resembling the vibrant landscape they are meant to represent. Thus, like any theory or work of abstract art, the key is that the beneficiary will find some significant personal meaning in it, and be ever mindful that the symbol is not the thing to which it refers.

REFERENCES

Andersen, P. A. (1989, May). "A Cognitive Valence Theory of Intimate Communication." Paper presented at the Iowa Network on Personal Relationships Conference, Iowa City, Iowa.

Chen, G. M. (1989, November). "A Model of the Dimensions of Intercultural Communication Competence." Paper presented at the Speech Communication Association Conference, San Francisco, Calif.

Imahori, T. T., and Lanigan, M. L. (1989). "Relational Model of Intercultural Communication Competence." *International Journal of Intercultural Relations, 13*, 269–286.

Martin, J. N., and Hammer, M. R. (1989). "Behavioral Categories of Intercultural Communication Competence: Everyday Communicators' Perceptions." *International Journal of Intercultural Relations, 13*, 303–332.

Osgood, C. E., May, W. H., and Miron, S. (1975). *Cross-Cultural Universals of Affective Meaning.* Urbana: University of Illinois Press.

Pavitt, C. (1989). "Accounting for the Process of Communicative Competence Evaluation: A Comparison of Predictive Models." *Communication Research, 16*, 405–433.

Spitzberg, B. H. (1989). "Issues in the Development of a Theory of Interpersonal Competence in the Intercultural Context." *International Journal of Intercultural Relations, 13*, 241–268.

Spitzberg, B. H., and Cupach, W. R. (1984). *Interpersonal Communication Competence.* Newbury Park, Calif.: Sage.

Spitzberg, B. H., and Hecht, M. L. (1984). "A Component Model of Relational Competence." *Human Communication Research, 10*, 575–599.

Prejudice in Intercultural Communication

RICHARD W. BRISLIN

THE FUNCTIONS OF PREJUDICE

When people react negatively to others on an emotional basis, with an absence of direct contact or factual material about the others, the people are said to behave according to prejudice. The concept of prejudice has been subjected to first-rate research investigations by psychologists and sociologists. One of the conclusions of this research is that "prejudice" is a far more complex concept than would be judged from the way the word is used in ordinary, everyday usage. This complexity has to be understood if the problems of prejudice are to be addressed effectively. -

An understanding of prejudice can begin if its functions are analyzed. Katz[1] has written the clearest presentation of the functions of various attitudes which people hold, and these can be applied to the more specific case of prejudicial attitudes. In addition, the functions can be applied to the sorts of intercultural contact under scrutiny at this conference. In the past, the majority of research has dealt with interpersonal contact within countries, especially Black-White relations. The four functions that attitudes serve for people are:

1. *The utilitarian or adjustment function.* People hold certain prejudices because such attitudes lead to rewards, and lead to the avoidance of punishment, in their culture. For instance, people want to be well liked by others in their culture. If such esteem is dependent upon rejecting members of a certain group, then it is likely that the people will indeed reject members of the outgroup. Or, if jobs are scarce and if people from a certain group want those jobs, it is adjustive to believe that members of a certain group have no responsibility in work settings. Thus there will be less competition for the desired employment.

2. *The ego-defensive function.* People hold certain prejudices because they do not want to admit certain things about themselves. Holding the prejudice protects the people from a harsh reality. For instance, if a person is unsuccessful in the business world, (s)he may believe that members of a certain successful group are a scheming bunch of cheaters. This belief protects the individual from the self-admission that (s)he has inadequacies. Another example involves experiences that most people have during childhood, no matter what their culture. People believe, as part of their basic feelings of self-esteem, that they have grown up in a society where proper behavior is practiced. These people may look down upon members of other cultures (or social classes within a culture) who do not behave "correctly." This prejudicial attitude, then, serves the function of protecting people's self-esteem.

3. *The value-expressive function.* People hold certain prejudices because they want to express the aspects of life which they highly prize. Such aspects include basic values of people concerning religion, government, society, aesthetics, and so forth. Katz[2] emphasizes that this function is related to an individual's "notion of the sort of person he sees himself to be." For example, people who discriminate against members of a certain religious group may do so because they see themselves as standing up for the one true God (as defined by their own religion). As a more intense example, people have engaged in atrocities toward outgroup members so as to retain the supposed values of a pure racial stock (again, their own).

From *Intercultural Theory and Practice: Perspectives on Education, Training, and Research*, December 1979, pp. 28–36. Used with permission of the author. Footnotes have been renumbered. Richard W. Brislin is associated with the Culture Learning Institute, East-West Center, Honolulu, Hawaii.

4. *The knowledge function.* People hold certain prejudices because such attitudes allow individuals to organize and structure their world in a way that makes sense to them. People have a need to know about various aspects of their culture so that they can interact effectively in it. But the various aspects are so numerous that various discrete stimuli must be categorized together for efficient organization. People then behave according to the category they have organized, not according to the discrete stimuli.[3] Often these categories are stereotypes that do not allow for variation within a category. For instance, if people believe that members of a certain cultural group are childlike and cannot be given any responsibility, they may employ that stereotype upon meeting a member of that group. Given a set of stereotypes, people do not have to think about each individual they meet. They can then spend time on the many other matters that compete for their attention during an average day. The prejudicial stereotypes thus provide knowledge about the world. The problem, of course, is that the stereotypes are sometimes wrong and always overdrawn.[4]

Certain prejudices can serve several functions, particularly so when an individual's entire life span is considered. Young children develop a prejudice to please their parents (adjustment), continue to hold it because of what they learn in school (knowledge), and behave according to the prejudice since they wish to express their view of themselves (value). Programs to change prejudice often fail because the most important function, or functions, are not recognized. Most change-oriented programs are concerned with presenting well-established facts about the targets of prejudice. But such a program will only change people's attitudes which serve the knowledge function. Much more work has to be done on finding ways to change prejudices that serve the other three functions. This is a research area that should yield very important payoffs to careful investigators.

THE FORMS OF PREJUDICE

In addition to an understanding of the functions of prejudice, it is also important to consider various forms that prejudice takes in its expression. The range of such expression is large.

1. *Red-neck racism.* Certain people believe that members of a given cultural group are inferior according to some imagined standard and that the group members are not worthy of decent treatment. The term "red-neck" comes from the Southern United States where world attention was focused on the White majority's treatment of Blacks during political demonstrations prior to the Civil Rights Act of 1964. The type of prejudice summarized by the term "red-neck," however, is found all over the world. This extreme form of prejudice has most often been assessed by asking people to agree or disagree with statements like this:[5] "The many faults, and the general inability to get along, of (*insert name of group*), who have recently flooded our community, prove that we ought to send them back where they came from as soon as conditions permit." "(*Insert name of group*) can never advance to the standard of living and civilization of our country due mainly to their innate dirtiness, laziness, and general backwardness."

All of us cringe at the thought of such tasteless, abhorrent sentiments. But we all know that such prejudices exist, and all of us can give many examples from the countries in which we have lived. Formal education has had a tremendous influence on lowering the incidences of red-neck racism. Research has shown that as the number of years of formal education increases, the incidence of racism decreases. However, I do feel that we need accurate figures on the current levels of such prejudice, and only large scale surveys can give us this information. It is possible that attendees at a conference such as this one underestimate the current levels of red-neck racism since they do not normally interact with people who hold such views.

2. *Symbolic racism.* Certain people have negative feelings about a given group because they feel that the group is interfering with aspects of their culture with which they have become familiar. The people do not dislike the group per se, and they do not hold sentiments that are indicative of red-neck racism. Symbolic racism[6] is expressed in terms of

threats to people's basic values and to the status quo. When directly questioned, people will assert that members of a certain group are "moving too fast" and are making illegitimate demands in their quest for a place in society. Symbolic racism is expressed by responses to questions like these (the answer indicative of symbolic racism is noted in parentheses):

"Over the past few years, *(insert name of group)* have gotten more economically than they deserve." (agree)

"People in this country should support _____ in their struggle against discrimination and segregation." (disagree)

"_____ are getting too demanding in their push for equal rights." (agree)

Sentiments like these are probably more widespread than red-neck feelings among members of the affluent middle class in various countries. Again, however, exact figures are unavailable, and this lack hampers intelligent planning for programs to deal with this form of prejudice. It is important to understand the differences between red-neck and symbolic racism. People who hold symbolic sentiments do not view themselves as red-necks, and so programs aimed at changing extreme racist views (such programs are presently most common) are doomed to failure. McConahay and Hough[7] are accurate when they state that current change programs seem incomprehensible to holders of symbolic views "and they do not understand what all the fuss is about. This enables racism to be considered 'somebody else's' problem while holders of symbolic views concentrate upon their own private lives."

3. *Tokenism.* Certain people harbor negative feelings about a given group but do not want to admit this fact to themselves. Such people definitely do not view themselves as prejudiced and they do not perceive themselves as discriminatory in their behavior. One way that they reinforce this view of themselves is to engage in unimportant, but positive, intergroup behaviors. By engaging in such important behaviors people can persuade themselves that they are unprejudiced, and thus they can refuse to perform more important intergroup behaviors. For instance, Dutton[8] found that if people gave a small amount of money to an outgroup, they were less willing to later donate a large amount of their time to a "Brotherhood Week" campaign emphasizing intergroup relations and goodwill. Other people in the Dutton study donated time to the Brotherhood Week if they had previously not been asked to give the small sum of money. The small amount of money, then, was a token that allowed some people to persuade themselves that they are unprejudiced and so don't have to prove themselves again by engaging in the more important, time-consuming behavior.

4. *Arms-length prejudice.* Certain people engage in friendly, positive behavior toward outgroup members in certain situations but hold those same outgroup members at an "arm's length" in other situations. The difference across situations seems to be along a dimension of perceived intimacy of behaviors.[9] For semi-formal behaviors such as (1) casual friendships at a place of employment, (2) interactions between speaker and audience at a lecture, or (3) interactions at a catered dinner party, people who harbor an arms-length prejudice will act in a friendly, positive manner. But for more intimate behaviors such as (1) dating, (2) interactions during an informal dinner held at someone's home, or (3) relations between neighbors, people will act in a tense, sometimes hostile manner. Frankly, I have observed this sort of arm's-length prejudice at places where such behavior would ideally not be expected, as at the East-West Center. I have observed a Caucasian social psychologist (who has long lectured on prejudice), during a visit to my home, become non-communicative and ultimately rude when my Chinese-American neighbor unexpectedly dropped in for a visit. This form of prejudice is hard to detect since people who engage in it seem so tolerant of outgroup members much of the time.

5. *Real likes and dislikes.* Certain people harbor negative feelings about a given group because members of the group engage in behaviors that people dislike. This fifth category is derived from more common sense than scholarly literature, and

it represents an expression of my feelings that not all prejudice should be looked upon as an indication of some sickness or flaw. People *do* have real likes and dislikes. No one person is so saintly as to be tolerant and forgiving toward all who engage in behaviors (s)he dislikes. For instance, littering really bothers me, and there are certain groups more likely to leave their trash on the ground after a picnic. Sometimes they are from cultures where servants or laborers are expected to do such cleanup. But my realization of the group's background does not lessen my dislike of litter. Seeing members of a certain group engage in such disliked behaviors, I am less likely to interact pleasantly with other members of the group in the future. My recommendation is to give more attention to this common, but heretofore neglected, type of everyday prejudice.

6. *The familiar and unfamiliar.* People who are socialized into one culture are likely to become familiar and thus comfortable with various aspects of that culture. These people, when interacting with members of another culture, are likely to experience behaviors or ideas that are unfamiliar and hence they are likely to feel uncomfortable. Consequently, the people are likely to prefer to interact with members of their own cultural group. What might seem like prejudice and discrimination to an onlooker, then, may be simply a reflection of people's preference for what is comfortable and nonstressful. In a study of interaction among members of nine ethnic groups on Guam,[10] I found that informants were able to verbalize this reason for people's choices of friends. An informant from the Marshall Islands wrote:

Culture makes these groups stick together. Somebody might not get along with one from another country. He likes to find some friends who have the same beliefs he has, and he could only find these characteristics with the people from his own country.

And a resident of Truk wrote about the type of strained conversation that can arise when members of different groups interact:

A Trukese who has never experienced the cold winter of the U.S. could not comprehend and intelligently appreciate a Statesider telling him the terrible winter they had in Albany anymore than a person from Albuquerque who has never seen an atoll could visualize the smallness of the islets that make up such an atoll. (Truk, of course, is an atoll.)

I believe that this sort of mild prejudice based on what is familiar and unfamiliar is the sort of phenomenon recently referred to by the United States Ambassador to the United Nations, Andrew Young.[11] In mid-1977, Young labeled a number of people as "racists,"[12] but in explaining his use of the term he clearly was referring to a lack of understanding and an insensitivity regarding other cultural groups. When questioned by the press, Young had to admit that the insensitivity and misunderstanding stem from unfamiliarity. As with the type of prejudice described under "real likes and dislikes," this everyday type of behavior deserves more attention from behavioral scientists and educators than it has heretofore received.

NOTES

1. D. Katz, "The functional approach to the study of attitudes," *Public Opinion Quarterly*, 1960, 24, pp. 164–204.

2. Katz, 1960, p. 173.

3. H. Triandis, "Culture training, cognitive complexity and interpersonal attitudes." In R. Brislin, S. Bochner, and W. Lonner (eds). *Cross-Cultural Perspectives on Learning* (New York: Wiley/Halsted Division, 1976), pp. 39–77.

4. The fact that I use the term "prejudicial stereotypes" does not mean that stereotypes and prejudices are isomorphic. *Some* stereotypes stem from prejudicial attitudes, and only these are discussed in this paragraph. More generally, stereotypes refer to any categorization of individual elements that mask differences among those elements. Stereotypes are absolutely necessary for thinking and communicating since people cannot respond individually to the millions of isolated elements they perceive every day. They must group elements together into categories, and then respond to

the categories. Stereotypes are a form of generalization that involves names of some group of people and
statements about that group. Thus when we speak of
"conservatives" or "academics" or "educators," we are
using stereotypical categories that mask individual differences within those categories. Stereotypes will always be a factor in any sort of communication, a fact
that must be realized in any analysis of communication
between individuals from different backgrounds. I
mention this because, recently, I have found difficulty
in encouraging multicultural groups to discuss stereotypes since the link between prejudice and stereotypes
has become so strong. Stereotypes have acquired a distasteful status. Refusal to deal with them, however,
means a refusal to deal with one of the most basic aspects of thinking and communication.

5. These statements are adapted from the analysis of
such questionnaire items by R. Ashmore, "The problem of intergroup prejudice," in B. Collins, *Social Psychology* (Reading, Mass.: Addison-Wesley, 1970), pp.
245–296.

6. J. McConahay and J. Hough, "Symbolic racism,"
Journal of Social Issues, 1976, 32(2), pp. 23–45.

7. McConahay and Hough, 1976, p. 44.

8. D. Dutton, "Tokenism, reverse discrimination, and
egalitarianism in interracial behavior," *Journal of Social Issues*, 1976, 32(2), pp. 93–107.

9. H. Triandis and E. Davis, "Race and belief as determinants of behavioral intentions," *Journal of Personality and Social Psychology*, 1965, 2, pp. 715–725.

10. R. Brislin, "Interaction among members of nine
ethnic groups and the belief-similarity hypothesis,"
Journal of Social Psychology, 1971, 85, pp. 171–179.

11. *Playboy,* July 1977; also analyzed in *Newsweek,* June
20, 1977, p. 34.

12. An "unfortunate" use of the term, Ambassador
Young eventually admitted.

Cross-Cultural Training Across the Individualism-Collectivism Divide

HARRY C. TRIANDIS
RICHARD BRISLIN
C. HARRY HUI

A major dimension of cultural variation is individualism-collectivism. It has been identified as central
to an understanding of cultural values (e.g., Kluckhohn & Strodtbeck, 1961), of work values (Hofstede,
1980), of social systems (e.g., Parsons & Shils, 1951),
as well as in studies of morality (Schweder, 1982),
religion (Bakan, 1966), cognitive differentiation
(Witkin & Berry, 1975), economic development (Adelman & Morris, 1967), modernity (Inkeles & Smith,
1974), the structure of constitutions (Massimini &
Calegari, 1979), and cultural patterns (Hsu, 1981).
Individualism is assumed to be a relatively stable
and important attribute of U.S. samples (Bellah,
Madsen, Sullivan, Swindler, & Tipton, 1985; Inkeles,
1983) which contrast them sharply with the collectivism of samples from Africa, Asia, and Latin America. Most European cultures, particularly those in
the northwestern regions of Europe have been
found to be individualist.

There is a good deal of current research on the
construct (e.g., Hui, 1988; Hui & Triandis, 1986; Triandis et al., 1986; Triandis, Bontempo, Villareal, Asai,
& Lucca, 1988). Triandis (1984) argued that there are
a score of major dimensions of cultural variation

From *The International Journal of Intercultural Relations*,
Volume 12 (1988), 269–298. Reprinted by permission of the
publisher. Professor Harry Triandis teaches at the University
of Illinois. Professor Richard Brislin teaches at the Institute of
Culture and Communication, East-West Center, in Hawaii. Professor C. Harry Hui teaches at the University of Hong Kong.

that need to be investigated intensively. As research on each dimension becomes available it can be summarized for cross-cultural trainers. This will place cross-cultural training on a firm scientific basis. The present paper is the first that does offer trainers a summary of research on one major dimension of cultural variation.

This paper will begin with a summary of what is known about individualism and collectivism which appears relevant to the needs of trainers. We will be making firm generalizations, though we are aware of complexities, and the need for qualifications in particular instances, because we feel that constant qualifications will hinder the exposition of ideas. Then we will present recommendations for the training of collectivists to interact effectively with individualists, and in the last section recommendations for the training of individualists to interact effectively with collectivists.

This paper, then, can be considered as an example of the future of cross-cultural training. As more and more research on dimensions of cultural variation and their relevance for social behavior becomes available, the research will be summarized specifically for cross-cultural trainers. As research progresses on other dimensions (e.g., tightness vs. looseness of the culture; internal vs. external control of motivation), there should be reports on such dimensions and their implications for cross-cultural training.

DESCRIPTION OF INDIVIDUALISM-COLLECTIVISM

Individualism is a cultural pattern found in most northern and western regions of Europe and in North America. Collectivism is common in Asia, Africa, South America, and the Pacific. Recent research (Hui, 1988; Triandis et al., 1988) suggests that there are many kinds of collectivisms (differential emphasis on extended family, work group, tribe, caste, country, etc.) and individualisms (e.g., emphasis on nuclear family, narcissistic). In moving across cultural boundaries, people should know ex-

actly which (if any) groups are important to the others with whom they must interact extensively.

There are also individual differences within cultures. That is, in both collectivist and individualist cultures one can find individuals who are *allocentric* (pay primary attention to the needs of a group) or *idiocentric* (pay more attention to their own needs than to the needs of others). Allocentric people want to help serve the needs of their group because it gives them personal satisfaction. Idiocentric people are more interested in serving their own needs and, if members of a collectivist culture, they give attention to the needs of others out of a sense of obligation. Trainers should emphasize in their programs that it is not enough to know the culture of the other person. It is also necessary to know something about demographic and biographic information, because individuals from urban, industrialized, mobile, migrating, affluent environments with much exposure to the mass media, are likely to be idiocentric even if they come from collectivist cultures. One reason is these modernizing influences have exposed them to more idiocentric than collective possibilites since the influences most often emanate from individualist cultures.

Collectivism is characterized by individuals subordinating their personal goals to the goals of some collectives. Individualism is characterized by individuals subordinating the goals of collectives to their personal goals. A key belief of people in collectivist cultures is that the smallest unit of survival is the collective. A key belief of people in individualistic cultures is that the smallest unit of survival is the individual. In many situations people in collectivist cultures have internalized the norms of their collectives so completely that there is no such thing as a distinction between ingroup goals and personal goals (Bontempo, Lobel, & Triandis, 1988).

Social behavior tends to follow ingroup goals in collectivist cultures, and this is particularly true for allocentrics in such cultures. Even idiocentrics appear to follow ingroup norms, though they may be aware that *their* feelings are incompatible with these norms. Idiocentrics in individualist cultures, however, act out their feelings. That is, unless the sanctions for not following ingroup norms are severe, they do what they find enjoyable rather than what is their duty. Allocentrics in individualistic cultures are more likely to internalize ingroup norms so that there is less conflict for them between ingroup norms and their personal goals.

Though there are many kinds of collectivist patterns and many kinds of individualists, there are some common elements across these patterns which will be discussed below. In presenting these comments we will not be able to support each point with empirical research. Much of the research is in progress. While we do have several studies (e.g., Hui & Villareal, 1987; Triandis et al., 1985, 1988) which establish the major points, we have to supplement them with observations and impressions. All of us have had considerable experience dealing with people from both individualist and collectivist cultures and in observing their interactions. For instance, Hui was raised in a collectivist culture but studied in an individualist culture for several years.

DIFFERENCES BETWEEN COLLECTIVISM AND INDIVIDUALISM

The Self

The ideal in collectivist cultures is that the self be totally absorbed in the collective. Such an ideal is usually not attained, but there are many unstated assumptions and values that are consistent with it. The self is thus defined as part of a group (e.g., family, tribe, nation) in much the same way as the body parts are part of a body. Just as it is difficult to discuss "Jim's hand" independently of Jim, so it is unwise to discuss "Yasumasa" independently of "Yasumasa's ingroups." Jim may have beliefs, attitudes and values that are not related or in agreement with the beliefs, attitudes, and values of his group; this is less likely to be the case with Yasumasa. While in the United States we emphasize that stereotypes do not have predictive validity (and the empirical research supports that), in collectivist cultures people assume very definitely that they do have predictive validity. If I know Yasumasa's family, work group, or country

it is assumed that I already know a good deal about Yasumasa. Whether that is "valid" is not the point. A social fact has consequences regardless of the validity of the fact.

There is some research that suggests that the use of such stereotypes among collectivists may be more justified than is the use of stereotypes among individualists. When asked to give 20 descriptions of themselves by completing 20 sentences that start with "I am . . . " people from collectivist cultures used 35–45% group-related attributes (e.g., I am the third son of my family) while people in individualist cultures used such attributes only 15% of the time. When a person uses a family-related attribute that person is more likely to be aware of family roles, and to act according to norms that characterize the family. To put it differently, in collectivist cultures people represent their groups and in many cases the person and the group are not distinguishable. Thus the person's behavior is much more likely to be under the influence of group-defined norms and roles than is the case in individualist cultures.

An interesting example of the importance of the group comes from the way people are named. In Bali a personal name is a nonsense syllable that is almost never used. The name that is used is related to the family (e.g., second born of family X; mother of Y; grandfather of Z). Note also that in individualistic cultures we put the person's name first (e.g., *Harry* Triandis); in many collectivist cultures the family name comes first (e.g., *Hui* Chi-chiu). It is only in the "modern" Hong Kong that it switches to C. Harry (Anglo name needed since English speakers have trouble with the Chinese names) Hui.

In individualist cultures the self is autonomous and separate from groups. While one can be a member of many groups, no one group defines one's identity in its entirety and determines one's behavior, except under very unusual circumstances, such as in war. In collectivist cultures people are attached to fewer groups, but the attachment is highly defining of one's identity. In collectivist cultures the attachment is very strong; in individualist cultures it is mild. For example, a father in an individualist culture can discuss the shortcomings of a son with equanimity. The individualist father can separate

himself from his son. Such a discussion is surprising to people from collectivist cultures who would be totally crushed by the very same failures. Collectivists feel a far closer common identity in considering a father and his son.

To repeat, in the case of the collectivists, behavior is largely a function of norms and roles that are determined through tradition or interactions among ingroup members. A change in ingroups can produce major changes in attitudes and behavior, because the collectivist identity is so group-dependent. This is also true for changes in leadership. The leader (e.g., Mao) often defines the group norms. A change in leader results in an entirely new situation. Furthermore, when a large portion of a group, or body politic, changes attitude the rest of the group also changes attitude, so that decision by consensus is a prominent feature of group decision in collectivist cultures.

In the case of individualist cultures there are very many types of groups to which the person may be attached—neighborhood, work group, friendship circle, religious, political, athletic, social, education, residential, artistic, and so on. The University of Illinois has 915 accredited clubs that students can join for extracurricular activities! In theory a student could be a member of most of these clubs. Naturally the attachment to any one of them and the commitment to the goals of each group has restrictions since people have limited resources, energy, and desire to participate. Ways to resolve inconsistencies among norms when so many different groups are involved are to either ignore the norms (use internal standards for behavior, principles, or a philosophy of life that tells one what to do in each instance); segment one's commitments (e.g., get drunk with one's buddies on Saturday and go to church the following morning); or drop membership in a given group. While the unique combination of the groups that a person belongs to may tell us something about the person, the essential attributes of the person are the person's own beliefs, attitudes, principles, or points of view, rather than the group memberships. The availability of many groups also means that one assesses costs and benefits in determining whether or not to join and to continue

membership in the group. Over time, groups are dropped and new ones are joined and formed, in a constant flux of "joining" and "leaving" groups. This contrasts sharply with the stability of relationships in collectivist cultures.

In other words, if we want to know "who the other is" the best approach is to investigate the beliefs, attitudes, and values of individualists; and the attributes of the groups of collectivists. Among individualists one is what one does; among collectivists one is what one's group does.

Activities

In collectivist cultures people identify very strongly with their ingroups. They care a great deal about events that take place in them. As a minimum they feel obliged to care about these events. Minor celebrations involving these groups are attended even with great financial sacrifices.

Further, allocentric collectivists value highly their participation in the ceremonies and would feel gravely insulted if they were not invited. By contrast, in individualist cultures people are somewhat detached from their ingroups. Even major celebrations, for example, the wedding of one's brother, may not be attended especially if the event conflicts significantly with another activity highly relevant to personal goal attainment.

One can identify collectivist and individualist patients in hospitals, in part, by the number of visitors. Collectivists have a constant stream of visitors, while individualists have fewer. What is more important is that collectivists often actually enjoy visiting (Bontempo, Lobel, & Triandis, 1988) while individualists do it out of duty, but would rather not do it.

Attitudes

In collectivist cultures people tend to have positive attitudes toward their extended families. Similarly they feel very positively about their ingroups, and derive much of their identity from them. In individualist cultures these attitudes toward ingroups and extended families vary greatly and there are many instances when they are negative. For example, interaction with cousins and other more distant relatives is less common in individualist cultures, even when such interaction is convenient (e.g., they live in the same city). In collectivist cultures it occurs even when it is inconvenient.

In general, collectivists have the most positive attitudes toward vertical relationships (e.g., in China, father–son; in India, mother–son; in Africa, older brother to younger brother) while individualists have the most positive attitudes toward horizontal relationships (e.g., friend–friend; spouse–spouse).

People in collectivist cultures accept differences in power. A boss can get away with abuse of subordinates in a way that is rare in individualist cultures. People are comfortable in vertical relationships and have some trouble dealing with horizontal ones. Conversely, in individualist cultures people are more comfortable in horizontal relationships and are quite ambivalent about people in authority or vertical relationships. Many individualists like to have bosses whom they can call by first names. This is not as important in collectivist cultures.

Collectivists see competition as occurring among groups and dislike interpersonal competition within their group. While in some relatively collectivist cultures such as Japan there is interpersonal competition for entry into prestigious schools, once a Japanese has joined a corporation, as "salary man," cooperation is the most important attribute of his relationships with co-workers. While cooperation is the defining attribute of within-ingroup relationships in collectivist cultures, competition is the defining attribute of *intergroup* relationships. For instance, it is difficult to get groups of professionals belonging to different universities in collectivist cultures to cooperate, because they define intergroup relationships in confrontational terms. By contrast, individualists can cooperate or compete according to what maximizes benefits relative to costs. In individualist cultures competition is acceptable at all levels, though in many situations competition with co-workers is masked.

Cooperation is easy and strongly encouraged within the ingroup in collectivist cultures. However, when the situation requires cooperation with outsiders, other groups, outgroups and the like, the collectivists are unable to do what is required. In short, collectivists are poor "joiners" of new groups, and do very badly when they meet people for the first time. In such cases, they are most likely to act in a formal, stiff, and cold manner. However, once they get to know the other person, and particularly if they define the other as an ingroup member (e.g., because the other is a "guest"), they become extremely effective in their interactions. Conversely, individualists are superb "joiners" and start conversations with strangers very easily. They carry on the early stages of a relationship with great ease and effectiveness. However, they do not get into intimate relationships. So, the enthusiasm of the early stages of the relationship is replaced with stiff formality as soon as intimate regions of the self are about to be invaded.

Characteristic of collectivists is a very positive attitude toward ingroup harmony. Confrontation is taboo, and face-saving is of great value. In individualist cultures, on the other hand, confrontation is acceptable in order to "clear the air." In fact, people are encouraged to communicate in order to improve their relationships, even when they have rather different attitudes. Collectivists, on the other hand, tend to avoid such confrontations so as to preserve harmony. Disagreements do exist, of course, but the tendency is to circumvent them. When the extent and intensity of disagreements increases to a limit that cannot be ignored or suppressed, mutual face-saving breaks down. A bitter fight may follow. The subsequent relationship between two collectivists will be worse than what it would have been after a disagreement between two individualists. One reason is that collectivists have not had as much experience in patching up ill feelings due to quarrels. Common friends and other ingroup members will often mediate among conflicting parties if the conflict is threatening the cohesion and integration of the ingroup.

Both types of cultures have positive attitudes toward self-reliance. However, the meaning of self-reliance is different. In collectivist cultures self-reliance aims at not burdening the ingroup, even though ingroup members are usually ready (though sometimes reluctantly) to help other ingroup members. In individualist cultures self-reliance is associated with independence and the opportunity to do one's own thing. Pleasure is associated with it, as is competition. In other words, people see themselves as successful in their competition because of their self-reliant traits, and this results in pleasure.

Collectivists have only mildly positive attitudes toward short-term relationships. They much prefer long-term relationships. By contrast, individualists value meeting many new people, in a short period of time (the cocktail party was invented by them), forming short-term relationships, and often feel that long-lasting relationships are too demanding. A frequent complaint of collectivists, after a short-term relationship with an individualist, is that they expected the relationship to go a long way, to become close, and to be long lasting. Instead, the relationship remained superficial and was short-lived.

Values

The top collectivist values are: Harmony, Face-saving, Filial piety (duty toward parents), Modesty, Moderation, Thrift, Equality in the distribution of rewards among peers, and Fulfillment of other's needs. The top individualist values are: Freedom, Honesty, Social recognition, Comfort, Hedonism, and Equity (to each according to his/her contributions to group performance). Note the equality vs. equity distinction between collectivist and individualist values. Assume that there are four people in a work group and that an objective outsider concludes that the people contributed to the group's success in the following ratio: person A, 20%; B, 30%; C, 15%; and D, 35%. Equality means that any rewards are distributed evenly across the four people: 25% to each. Such a distribution recognizes the value placed on group membership in contrast to individual rewards. Equity means that the rewards are distributed according to contributions: 20%, 30%, 15%, and 35% for A, B, C, and D, respectively. Such a distribution recognizes the value placed on individual contributions in contrast to the overall group effort. Professors in individualist cultures complain how hard it is to form work groups and to give one grade for the completed project. One student will inevitably complain, "But what if I end up doing more than half the work and the others just slack off?"

Overt cost/benefit analyses are popular among individualists and are frowned upon by collectivists. Contracts are more important than good social relationships for individualists, while collectivists depend for their transactions on trust established in long-term relationships. There are probably not as many practicing lawyers in collective societies.

In collectivist cultures status is defined by ascription—age, sex, family, name, etc., are crucial determinants. The person's place of birth and place of residence have unusual importance in determining status. In individualist cultures status is defined by achievement. In such cultures, ascribed attributes are given relatively little weight, and place of birth is given very little, if any, weight as a determinant of status.

Behaviors

Within the ingroup in collectivist cultures one finds much social behavior that is associative (giving help, support). But when outgroups are involved there is often considerable distrust and even hostility. Since most people in a society are strangers, and hence outgroup members, distrust is widespread in collectivist cultures. That is, collectivists are more associative within their ingroups, and more dissociative towards their outgroups than are individualists. For example, collectivists arriving at an international airport are more likely to be met by a flock of ingroup members than are individualists. Help from friends, relatives, and even business partners is expected and frequent. On the other hand, outsiders (e.g., taxi drivers) are suspected as ready to take advantage of collectivists. Individualists, on the other hand, trust strangers and outsiders to a greater extent. So, they do not need to be met at the airport, since information booths and taxi drivers can be relied upon to act honestly. In other words, individualists do not need the "protection" of ingroup members to get their transactions carried out. Extreme cases of ingroup behavior of Japanese tourists include travelling as a group, and touring as a group. It is rare to see a Japanese wander around a strange town by himself (but such generalizations are not always valid: Triandis saw a Japanese *female*, alone, at a restaurant in Würzberg, Germany!—Exceptions prove the rule!).

Similar relationships between ingroup and outgroup can be found on other attributes of social behavior. In general, individualists show more subordination to ingroup than to outgroup authorities, but the difference is small; collectivists exaggerate that difference, showing much more subordination to ingroup than to outgroup authorities, which they often find ways to circumvent or ignore. Similarly, individualists are generally more relaxed and intimate with ingroup than with outgroup members; collectivists again exaggerate the relationship: they are much more intimate with ingroup members and much more formal with outgroup members than are individualists. Individualists, tired of competition in a capitalist system, who travel to a collective society expecting to meet cooperative and helpful people, are often rebuffed in their efforts to develop friendships. After all, these individualists are outgroup members in the collective society and so are held at a considerable psychological distance.

Family attachment tends to be high in traditional, collectivist cultures. Family obligations are felt deeply by collectivists (e.g., migrating to other lands under most unfavorable conditions to send money back home). Work-attachment and viewing the work group as the most important ingroup is more common among the individualists (with the exception of the Japanese, whose collectivism is work-centered). The stunning economic success of modern Japan may well be due to the successful transition from family to work-collectivism.

Social distance from outgroups tends to be strong in collectivist cultures, while it is attenuated in individualist cultures. However, the latter may have one group (e.g., blacks among U.S. whites) towards which there is substantial social distance. Outgroups tend to be perceived as extremely different by collectivists and as just a little different by individualists. Group norms appear to be part of the "natural world order" by collectivists, while individ-

ualists are more likely to recognize the cultural relativism of norms.

In collectivist cultures social behavior tends to be long-term involuntary (doing what the ingroup wants often requires one to perform behaviors that are not enjoyable), intensive, and occurs mostly within a very few ingroups. In individualist cultures there are many ingroups, and social behavior tends to be short-term, voluntary, less intensive, and involves little commitment to any particular ingroup.

In collectivist cultures there are many, frequent consultations with others about important matters, particularly in vertical relationships (e.g., parent–child, boss–subordinate). In individualist cultures there are fewer consultations, and those that do exist tend to be among equals in status. Individuals have stronger needs for autonomy while collectivists have stronger needs for affiliation, nurturance, abasement, and succorance (Hui & Villareal, 1987).

TRAINING COLLECTIVISTS TO INTERACT WITH INDIVIDUALISTS

When training individuals from collectivist cultures to interact with individuals from individualist cultures there are several points that should be kept in mind. They are presented here in the form of recommendations by the trainer to the trainee. "Other" refers to a person from a different cultural background. These points constitute suggested content for training. Later, recommendations for training methods will be made.

1. Pay less attention to the groups to which the Other belongs, when the Other comes from individualist cultures, than when the Other comes from your culture. You will not be able to predict the Other's behavior from your knowledge of the Other's group memberships, as you are used to in your own culture. Instead, pay attention to the Other's beliefs, attitudes, and principles. Try to discover the specific demands made by the Other's ingroups, but do not expect these groups to impose norms that control much behavior. Rather, they will

control very specific, short-lived voluntary behaviors. Once a person is outside the group or without the supervision of a boss, internal factors (such as beliefs) are the best predictors of behavior in both your own culture and other cultures. In any case, do not expect compliance with norms to be as high in the individualistic culture as it is in your culture.

2. The Other will be proud of accomplishments, past, present, and planned. Compliment the Other for the effort more than you are used to in your culture. The Other is going to value being "distinguished" and will have high self-esteem, will talk about personal accomplishments, and generally say more negative things about people than will happen in your culture.

3. Expect the Other to be more emotionally detached from events that occur in her ingroup than is likely in your culture. Do not attribute this behavior to some sort of personality defect. It is mandated by the culture.

4. Expect the Other to be more involved in horizontal and less involved in vertical relationships than happens in your culture. The Other's influential people will be peers and spouse; they are the ones likely to be consulted.

5. Do not feel threatened if the Other acts competitively. That is also mandated by the culture. The chances are that there will be more situations in which competition rather than cooperation will occur. Learn to expect them.

6. The Other will define status in terms of individual accomplishments, rather than on the basis of ascribed attributes (sex, age, family name, etc.), much more than is the case in your culture.

7. If you try to change the Other's opinions, do not expect that you will be as persuasive as you are in your own culture when you use arguments that stress cooperation, harmony, or avoidance of confrontation. Similarly, the Other may sound somewhat calculating to you when she uses arguments emphasizing personal costs and benefits.

8. Expect the Other to be less strongly attached to the extended family than is the case in your culture. Obligations to the extended family are less likely to be accepted by the Other as an excuse for failing to do your assignment. Remember the Other does not know much about your many obligations to your family and your other groups. Your duties are time consuming, but the Other does not know much about them. So, tell the Other that you have to do this or that, and explain why in your culture these activities are important.

9. Expect relationships with the Other to be superficial, short-termed, but good natured. Do not interpret initial friendliness as a cue that the relationship will be especially intimate.

10. You can do business with the Other very soon after you meet. You need not spend very much time on preliminaries. Time is money in the Other's culture and so the Other is likely to be impatient with preliminaries and ceremonies. "Getting to the point" and "Getting down to business" are important.

11. Expect relationships to last only so long as the Other gets more from them than it costs to maintain the relationship. This is likely to be a short time period, and you can expect the relationship to be resumed if circumstances (e.g., rewards over costs) favor that in the future.

12. Pay attention to contracts, to signatures, to the written word. All of these have much more significance in the Other's culture than in your culture. Informal agreements that are not covered by at least a letter mean much less in the Other's culture than in yours.

13. The Other will be more comfortable with equal social relationships than people in your culture. You will be uncomfortable with relationships that disregard status differences, but individualists enjoy equal or close-status relationships. Learn to expect and cope with this difference.

14. When resources have to be distributed the Other will expect that this will be done according to the principle of equity (to each according to her contributions). In many situations where you will think that it is best to distribute rewards equally or according to the needs of the participants, the Other will emphasize equity.

15. Do not expect to receive respect simply because of your position, age, sex, or family name. You must demonstrate accomplishments or achieve-

ments to get status. Do not expect that your place of birth, if it is prestigious in your eyes (e.g., Paris, France), will lead to receiving more respect from the Other. The Other is quite unlikely to be impressed even by the most prestigious place of birth.

16. It is all right to talk about your accomplishments. You do not have to be modest. Don't boast, but make sure people know your achievements. You are the best person to present yourself to Others in a positive light. The Other may not interpret your modest behavior in a positive light, but may regard it as suggestive of your lack of forthrightness or lack of ability and motivation. It is not uncommon, in an individualist society, for a professor to advise a student, "If you don't blow your own horn, nobody else will."

17. The chances are that you see your outgroups as very different from you. The Other views outgroups as less different than you view them. Try to match the Other's view.

18. Avoid behaviors that are extremely superordinate (bossy) or subordinate (submissive and servile). They make a bad impression on the Other.

19. Expect the Other to suspect authority figures of all kinds. In the United States, the founding fathers wrote the American constitution with an explicit distrust of powerful figures as a major guiding concept.

20. Expect to see more horizontal than vertical good relationships in the Other's culture. For example, boss–subordinate relationships may become friend–friend relationships.

21. Expect the Other to be upset by illicit behavior. If you have to act that way you better give a full justification to the Other. "Illicit behavior" means actions which favor the ingroup but put an outgroup at a disadvantage. If a person does not pay taxes, this illicit behavior favors the ingroup because there is more money to share with other members. Given that one's ingroup is both physically and psychologically close, the "nation" is too distant a group to benefit through one's taxes and is disregarded. Certain individualist countries (e.g., the U.S.A., Canada) are the envy of the world with respect to percentage of taxes due which are collected in these nations. Individualists are much less

tolerant of illicit behavior since it goes against their feelings of right and wrong concerning their entire society or nation. They are more likely to use negative words like "bribery" and "nepotism" when faced with requests to engage in illicit behavior.

22. Do not expect to be accompanied or assisted all the time. The Others have other commitments and may not have time for you. Besides that, by letting you do things on your own they show their confidence in you. They are not likely to believe you need as much help as you feel you have a "right" to expect.

23. The Other will find it more difficult than you to join work groups in which individual effort may go unrecognized. As with many behaviors, the Other will not know about your preferences and obligations to groups. So, tell the Other that you have to do this or that, and explain why in your culture these activities are important. Also, in general, try to see the causes of the Other's behavior the same way the Other sees the causes of his/her own behavior. This maximizes the chances that you will communicate well with the Other (Triandis, 1975).

TRAINING INDIVIDUALISTS TO INTERACT WITH COLLECTIVISTS

1. Learn to pay attention to group memberships. The Other's behavior depends on the norms of the ingroups that are important in the Other's life. In fact, you can predict the Other's behavior by knowing about the norms of the Other's groups, as well as by knowing how roles are defined, obligations and duties are specified, and the like, to a much greater extent than is possible in your culture.

2. Keep a close eye on the attitudes of the Other's ingroup authorities. It is likely that the Other's attitudes and behaviors will reflect them.

3. When the Other's group membership changes there is a high probability that the Other's opinions, attitudes, and even "personality" will change to reflect the different group.

4. Spend some time finding out about the Other's ingroups. What events occur in them? What

duties are specified? The Other is more likely to do what these norms specify than you are used to seeing in your culture.

5. Do not use yourself as a yardstick of involvement in activities that involve ingroups. The Other is likely to be much more involved with groups than you are used to seeing in your culture.

6. The Other is more comfortable in vertical than in horizontal relationships. In one case two collectivists had just met and sat next to each other at a dinner party. A major portion of their initial conversation was exchanges of "demographic" information. These two gentlemen were cautious in interacting until at some point one discovered that he knew the other's father. From then on the first gentleman acted like an "elder" while the other behaved in a much more respectful manner towards his "uncle."

7. If you want the Other to do something, try to see if the Other's superiors can give a signal that they approve of such behavior.

8. If you want the Other to do something, show how such behavior will promote the Other's ingroups.

9. The Other will be uncomfortable in competitive situations.

10. Emphasize harmony and cooperation, help the Other save face, and avoid confrontation. If criticism is absolutely necessary, it is better done in private than in public. A collectivist prefers that you talk "in his back" and save his face, than to be criticized in public (Smith, 1987).

11. If you have to criticize, do so very carefully. Keep in mind that you cannot criticize the Other's ideas without criticizing the person. In the Other's culture people generally do not say "No" or criticize. They indicate disapproval in very subtle ways. (In one case, a boy wanted to marry a girl. The girl's mother signaled that the relationship did not have her approval by serving tea and bananas to the boy's mother who came to visit her. Since the particular combination is considered "unsuitable" it told the boy's mother that the match was considered unsuitable. Nothing was said. Face was saved.) If you absolutely have to criticize, do so after making a large number of positive statements.

12. Cultivate long-term relationships. Be patient. Spend a great deal of time chatting with people. The Other values dealing with "old friends." The Other does not like doing business in the early phases of a relationship. Get to know the Other first. Be prepared for this to take much longer than you think it should.

13. If the Other comes from east Asia, expect extraordinary and unjustified modesty. A frequent beginning phrase of collectivists is "This presentation is inadequate, based on limited data. . . . Please forgive this unworthy effort. . . ." Individualist women who marry collectivist men are often unhappy when the men introduce their wives' cooking in this way. If you give presentations, consider beginning in a more modest manner than you would in your own country.

14. If resources are to be distributed among peers, expect the Other to use equity in the early phases of a relationship and equality or need in the later stages of the relationship. In fact, you can use as a clue to whether you are perceived as ingroup or outgroup whether the Other's distribution follows the equity (you are still an outgroup member) or the equality (you made it into the ingroup!) principles.

15. The Other is likely to be comfortable in unequal status relationships. Status in the Other's culture is likely to be based on age, sex, family name, place of birth and the like. In other words, it depends on who the Other is rather than what the Other has accomplished. While the Other will pay attention to accomplishments, the importance attached to accomplishments will not be as great in the Other's culture as it is in yours. Your social position in your own culture, insignia, and symbols of status count more in the Other's culture than in your own. Do not be shy about displaying them. Your position in your own society should be mentioned, so the Other knows how to relate to you. Furthermore, age is an important attribute of status in the Other's culture. It is likely that even small differences in age (e.g., one day older) will result in more respect for the older person. Collectivists will try to convert all horizontal relationships into vertical relationships. They are more comfortable with vertical relation-

ships and have more skills in dealing with such relationships. You will have to learn appropriate superordinate and subordinate behaviors, and these will be difficult for you.

Furthermore, people in authority in the Other's culture have more power and are less accountable than people in your culture. For example, a visitor from Korea expected an American administrator to assign to him half the research budget of a research institute, simply with the stroke of the pen. The visitor did not have any idea about the checks and balances that operate in U.S. administrative structures, limiting the power of administrators.

16. When you meet the Other for the first time expect the social behavior to be more formal than you are used to in your country. The behavior will be polite, correct, but not especially friendly. You may have to be introduced to people by someone you know who is also respected by the Other. You have to establish yourself as an ingroup member, by showing proper concern for the ingroup, before the behavior becomes friendly. For example, visiting ingroup members in the hospital, spending free time with ingroup members, giving gifts, and making sacrifices for the group can help establish you as an ingroup member. Then behavior becomes more genuinely friendly.

17. Gift giving is important. One must be generous and not expect immediate repayment. Gifts put you into the ingroup, if you play your role correctly. If you are helpful the Other is likely to repay much more than you expect. Generally, Others do not accept money for services. For example, if you give a gallon of gas to help the Other who has run out of fuel, it is unlikely you will get paid in cash. But you are quite likely to be given a gift, at a later time, that will be worth much more than the price of the gas.

18. Let the Other guide you toward intimacy. Be willing to disclose personal information, when asked for, but avoid giving information that makes you too different from the Other. Expect the Other to ask about your age, income, and to even show admiration if you earn a lot. In general, there are topics that people in collectivist cultures ask that are

embarrassing in individualist cultures (and vice-versa), but no one is necessarily trying to cause discomfort with their questions. However, avoid discussions about sexuality, or any topic that might dishonor the ingroup. Collectivists tend to present themselves in the best possible light and give socially desirable answers much more than do individualists (Hui, 1988).

19. Do not jump to conclusions when the Other makes what appears to be a strange suggestion. Try to "play along" until you get more information. In one case a Scottish visitor to Japan got along with his Japanese host extremely well. After a couple of weeks of close friendship, the host said: "I would like to sleep with you." The Scot, being sophisticated in intercultural matters, did not dismiss the suggestion. As it turned out the Japanese host had paid him the very highest compliment, since it indicated total trust, because one can kill a person in his sleep and he may not be able to defend himself.

20. Learn to understand illicit behavior. Remember that societies differ in the extent they force people to act or not act in illicit ways. The Other's culture is more likely to tolerate such behavior than is yours. For instance, you may consider that paying a government official to approve a visa extension is wrong. The official may consider such expected payment as part of his salary. The official may be supporting 15 people in his extended family.

21. Remember that the Other has many obligations and duties that you do not know about. So, it is not correct to expect the same devotion to work that you have. Also, if there is a conflict between work and social relationships, the Other is more likely to value the social relationship over the work. That is culturally mandated, and is not an indication of the Other's weakness of character. Learn to tolerate the Other's participation in ingroup ceremonies, and related activities, since if you object you will create hard feelings. Individualists who marry collectivists are often annoyed with the time, energy, and resources which the collectivist puts into the extended ingroup.

22. Expect the relationship with the Other to shift abruptly as you move from outgroup to in-

group membership. There will also be costs. You will be asked to contribute to ingroup goals, to sacrifice for the ingroup, and possibly to engage in illicit behavior. Once you are an ingroup member you will feel much rejection if you switch to outgroup status again. This is a difficult balancing act. Ideally, you want to be a member of the ingroup, but have enough flexibility to avoid acting in ways that are incompatible with your principles. Learn to avoid such actions by invoking your own ingroup culture's norms and the requirements set by your ingroup's authorities.

23. The Other may feel that only by spending time with you (e.g., accompanying you to the doctor's office, talking with you all night while one is staying at the other's place, unwilling to end a conversation) that she can establish or maintain a long-term relationship with you. You may feel that your privacy and right to be alone are infringed upon. But remember that a collectivist may find it unimaginable and painful to be without company.

CONCLUSION

Individualist cultures differ among themselves, and so do collectivist cultures. Moreover, there can be wide individual differences among people within a culture. It should, therefore, be remembered that the above suggestions are intended only as general guidelines but not as hard-and-fast rules for dealing with a specific person from a specific culture. Nevertheless, we still hold that the differences between individualist and collectivist cultures are important and can be bridged with proper training. The aforementioned points made in the case of each kind of training can be used as the basis of group discussions, behavior modification and other cross-cultural training techniques (Landis & Brislin, 1983). For instance, the points can be used in training based on the materials prepared by Brislin, Cushner, Cherrie, & Yong (1986). In that collection of 100 critical incidents, eleven deal with individualism and collectivism under the theme, "The importance of the group and the importance of the individual" (specifically, item numbers 1, 2, 6, 7, 11, 20,

36, 62, 78, 97, 100). After trainees become sensitized to individualism and collectivism through discussion of these critical incidents, they can move into coverage of the 23 points for each type of move, individualist to collectivist and vice-versa. Another way to use the points is to take advantage of the fact that in most training programs, some trainees have already had cross-cultural experiences or have interacted with members of different ethnic groups within their own country. The points can be read by the trainer one-by-one, and the question can be asked, "Does this point remind anyone of an incident in their own lives?" Another possibility is that the content of one or more points can form the basic script for role plays. For instance, one of the points (number 15) for the individualist to collectivist move indicates that people from the former type of culture value their personal accomplishments while people from the latter type want to know people's social position. Trainees could role play encounters in another culture during which individualists try to establish their credentials through a recitation of their accomplishments while the collectivist searches for indications of the person's position within the hierarchy of his or her company. As the role play continues, it becomes clear that the people involved are emphasizing very different aspects of their personal and collective identities. Such role plays can add a great deal of impact to coverage of the 23 points.

The points can form the basis for other activities of professionals in intercultural interaction. They can assist trainers during reorientation programs since one potential problem is that sojourners have learned the other culture's norms so well that they will have a difficult time readjusting to the individualism or collectivism of their *own* cultures. In addition to their uses in training, the points can form the basis of units within college and university courses concerned with intercultural communication. Finally, they can provide the basis for more in-depth cross-cultural research in which specific predictions about similarities and differences can be made given a knowledge of people's position with respect to the individualism-collectivism divide.

REFERENCES

Adelman, I., and Morris, C. T. (1967). *Society, politics and economic development: A quantitative approach*. Baltimore: Johns Hopkins Press.

Bakan, D. (1966). *The duality of human existence*. Chicago: Rand McNally.

Bellah, R. N., Madsen, R., Sullivan, W. M., Swindler, A., and Tipton, S. M. (1985). *Habits of the heart: Individualism and commitment in American life*. Berkeley: University of California Press.

Bontempo, R., Lobel, S., and Triandis, H. C. (1988). *Compliance and value internalization among Brazilian and U.S. students*. Manuscript submitted for publication.

Brislin, R., Cushner, C., Cherrie, C., and Yong, M. (1986). *Intercultural interactions; a practical guide*. Beverly Hills, CA: Sage.

Hofstede, G. (1980). *Culture's consequences*. Beverly Hills, CA: Sage.

Hsu, F. L. K. (1981). *American and Chinese: Passage to differences* (3rd ed.). Honolulu: University of Hawaii Press.

Hui, C. H. (1988). Measurement of individualism-collectivism. *Journal of Research in Personality*, pp. 17–36.

Hui, C. H., and Triandis, H. C. (1986). Individualism—collectivism: A study of cross-cultural researchers. *Journal of Cross-Cultural Psychology*, **17**, 225–248.

Hui, C. H., and Villareal, M. (1987). Individualism-collectivism and psychological needs: Their relationships in two cultures. Submitted for publication.

Inkeles, A. (1983, November–December). The American character. *The Center Magazine*, pp. 25–39.

Inkeles, A., and Smith, D. H. (1974). *Becoming modern*. Cambridge, MA: Harvard Press.

Kluckhohn, F., and Strodtbeck, F. (1961). *Variations in value orientations*. Evanston, IL: Row, Peterson.

Landis, D., and Brislin, R. (Eds.). (1983). *Handbook of intercultural training*. (3 vols.) Elmsford, NY: Pergamon.

Massimini, F., and Calegari, P. (1979). *Il contesto normativo sociale*. Milano: Angeli.

Parsons, R., and Shils, E. A. (1951). *Toward a general theory of action*. Cambridge, MA: Harvard Press.

Shweder, R. A. (1982). Beyond self-constructed knowledge: The study of culture and morality. *Merrill-Palmer Quarterly*, **28**, 41–69.

Smith, P. (1987, June). Organizational psychology. [Lecture given at Nag's Head Conference Center.]

Triandis, H. C. (1975). Culture training, cognitive complexity, and interpersonal attitudes. In R. Brislin, S. Bochner, and W. Lonner (Eds.), *Cross-cultural perspectives on learning* (pp. 39–77). Beverly Hills, CA: Sage.

Triandis, H. C. (1984). A theoretical framework for the more efficient construction of culture assimilators. *International Journal of Intercultural Relations*, **8**, 301–330.

Triandis, H. C., Leung, K., Villareal, M., and Clack, F. L. (1985). Allocentric vs idiocentric tendencies: Convergent and discriminant validation. *Journal of Research in Personality*, **19**, 395–415.

Triandis, H. C., Bontempo, R., Betancourt, H., Bond, M., Leung, K., Brenes, A., Georgas, J., Hui, C. H., Marin, G., Setiadi, B., Sinha, J. B. P., Verma, J., Spangenberg, J., Touzard, H., and De Montmollin, G. (1986). The measurement of the etic aspects of individualism and collectivism across cultures. *Australian Journal of Psychology*, **38**, 257–267.

Triandis, H. C., Bontempo, R., Villareal, M., Asai, M., and Lucca, N. (1988). Individualism-collectivism: Cross-cultural perspectives on self-ingroup relationships. *Journal of Personality and Social Psychology*, **54**, 323–338.

Witkin, H. A., and Berry, J. W. (1975). Psychological differentiation in cross-cultural perspective. *Journal of Cross-Cultural Psychology*, **6**, 4–87.

Communication and Cross-Cultural Adaptation

YOUNG YUN KIM

CROSS-CULTURAL ADAPTATION

Human beings are socio-cultural animals who acquire their social behaviors through learning. What we learn is defined largely by social and cultural forces. Of all aspects of human learning, communication is most central and fundamental. A great deal of our learning consists of communication responses to stimuli from the environment. We must code and decode messages in such a fashion that the messages will be recognized, accepted, and responded to by the individuals with whom we interact. Once acquired, communication activities function as an instrumental, interpretative, and expressive means of coming to terms with our physical and social environment. Communication is our primary means of utilizing the resources of the environment in the service of humanity. Through communication we adapt to and relate to our environment, and acquire membership and a sense of belonging in the various social groups upon which we depend.

Ultimately, it is not only the immigrant but also the host sociocultural system that undergoes changes as a result of the prolonged intercultural contact. The impact of immigrant cultures on the mainstream host culture, however, is relatively in-significant compared to the substantial influence of the host culture on the individual immigrant. Clearly, a reason for the essentially unidirectional change in the immigrant is the difference between the number of individuals in the new environment sharing the immigrant's original culture and the size of the host society. Also, the dominant power of the host society in controlling its resources produces more impact on cultural continuity and change in immigrants. The immigrant's need for adaptation to the host socio-cultural system, therefore, will be far greater than that of the host society to include elements of an immigrant culture.

Underlying an immigrant's adaptation process is the communication process. Adaptation occurs through the identification and the internalization of the significant symbols of the host society. Just as the natives acquire their cultural patterns through communication, so does an immigrant acquire the host cultural patterns through communication. An immigrant comes to organize himself or herself and to know and be known in relationship within the new culture through communication. The process of trial and error can often be frustrating and painful. In many instances, an immigrant's native language is extremely different from that of the host society. Other communication problems fall broadly into a nonverbal category such as differences in the use and organization of space, interpersonal distance, facial expression, eye behavior, other body movement, and in the perceived importance of nonverbal behavior relative to verbal behavior.

Even when an immigrant has acquired a satisfactory blend of using the verbal and nonverbal communication patterns, he or she may still experience a more subtle and profound difficulty in recognizing and responding appropriately to the culturally sanctioned communication rules. The immigrant is rarely aware of the hidden dimensions of the host culture that influence what and how to perceive, how to interpret the observed messages, and how to express thoughts and feelings appropriately in different relational and circumstantial contexts. Cross-cultural differences in these basic aspects of communication are difficult to identify and infrequently

This original essay appeared in print for the first time in the third edition. All rights reserved. Permission to reprint must be obtained from the publisher and the author. Professor Young Yun Kim teaches at the University of Oklahoma, Norman, Oklahoma.

discussed in public. They often seriously impede understanding between immigrants and members of the host society.

If we view adaptation as the process of developing communication competence in the host socio-cultural system, it is important to emphasize the fact that such communication competence is acquired through communication experiences. *One learns to communicate by communicating*. Through prolonged and varied communication experiences, an immigrant gradually acquires the communication mechanisms necessary for coping with the environment. The acquired host communication competence of an immigrant has a direct bearing upon his or her overall adaptation. The immediate effect lies in the control that the immigrant is able to exercise over his or her own behavior and over the host environment. The immigrant's communication competence will function as a set of adjustive tools assisting the immigrant to satisfy basic needs such as the need for physical survival and the need for a sense of "belonging" and "esteem" (Maslow, 1970, p. 47). Recent surveys of Korean and Indochinese immigrants in the United States clearly demonstrate the pivotal role that communication plays in the immigrants' psychological, social, and economic adaptation (Kim, 1976, 1980, 1989, 1990).

The adaptation process, therefore, is an interactive and continuous process that evolves in and through the communication of an immigrant with the new socio-cultural environment. The acquired communication competence, in turn, reflects the degree of that immigrant's adaptation. The degree to which an immigrant is adapted is not only reflected in, but also facilitated by, the degree of consonance between his or her communication patterns and the sanctioned communication patterns of the host society. This does not mean that every detail of an immigrant's communication behavior can be observed in understanding his or her adaptation, nor that all aspects of the adaptation can be understood through his or her communication patterns. However, by focusing on a few key communication variables that are of crucial importance in the adaptation process, we can approximate, with a rea-

sonable degree of accuracy, the reality of adaptation at a point in time, as well as predict the future development of adaptation.

COMMUNICATION VARIABLES IN ADAPTATION

One of the most comprehensive and useful conceptual frameworks in analyzing an immigrant's adaptation from the communication perspective is provided by the systems perspective elaborated by Ruben (1975). In the systems perspective, the basic element of a human communication system is viewed as the person who is actively being, seeking, and desiring communication with the environment. As an open communication system, a person interacts with the environment through two interrelated processes—personal communication and social communication. (See Kim, 1988, for a detailed presentation of the following discussion.)

Personal Communication

Personal (or intrapersonal) communication refers to the mental processes by which one organizes oneself in and with one's socio-cultural milieu, developing ways of seeing, hearing, understanding, and responding to the environment. "Personal communication can be thought of as sensing, making-sense-of, and acting toward the objects and people in one's milieu. It is the process by which the individual informationally fits himself into (adapts to and adopts) his environment" (Ruben, 1975, pp. 168–169). In the context of adaptation, an immigrant's personal communication can be viewed as the organization of adaptation experiences into a number of identifiable cognitive and affective response patterns that are consistent with the host culture.

One of the most important variables of personal communication is the complexity of an immigrant's *cognitive structure* in perceiving the host environment. During initial phases of adaptation, an immigrant's perception of the host culture is relatively simple; gross stereotypes are salient in the perception of the unfamiliar environment. As the immigrant learns more about the host culture, however, perception becomes more defined and complex, enabling the immigrant to detect variations in the host environment.

Closely related to the cognitive complexity is an immigrant's *knowledge* in patterns and rules of the host communication system. Sufficient empirical evidence supports the critical function of such knowledge (especially knowledge of the host language) in facilitating other aspects of adaptation. The adaptation function of the knowledge in the host communication system has been observed to be particularly important in increasing an immigrant's participation in interpersonal and mass communication networks of the host society (Breton, 1964; Chance, 1965; Richmond, 1967; Kim, 1977, 1980).

Another variable of personal communication in adaptation is an immigrant's *self-image* in relation to the immigrant's images of others. The relative position of the immigrant's self-image in relation to his or her images of the host society and the original culture, for example, provides valuable information about the immigrant's subjective reality of adaptation. Feelings of alienation, low self-esteem, and other similar psychological "problems" of immigrants tend to be associated with the greater perceptual distance between self and members of the host society (Kim, 1980).

Also, an immigrant's *motivation* has been observed to be functional in facilitating the adaptation process. Adaptation motivation refers to an immigrant's willingness to learn about, participate in, and be oriented toward the host socio-cultural system. Such positive orientation of an immigrant toward the new environment generally promotes participation in communication networks of the host society (Kim, 1977, 1980).

Social Communication

Personal communication is linked to social communication when two or more individuals interact, knowingly or not. "Social communication is the

process underlying intersubjectivization, a phenomenon which occurs as a consequence of public symbolization and symbol utilization and diffusion" (Ruben, 1975, p. 171). Through social communication, individuals regulate feelings, thoughts, and actions of one another. Social communication can be classified further into interpersonal communication and mass communication. Interpersonal communication occurs through interpersonal relationships, which in turn represent the purpose, function, and product of an individual's interpersonal communication. Mass communication, however, is a more generalized process of social communication, in which individuals interact with their socio-cultural environment without involvement in interpersonal relations with specific individuals. An individual's communication experiences through such media as radio, television, newspaper, magazine, movie, theater, and other similar public forms of communication, can be included in this category.

An immigrant's *interpersonal communication* can be observed through the degree of his or her participation in interpersonal relationships with members of the host society. More specifically, we can infer and predict an immigrant's adaptation from the nature of his or her interpersonal networks. An immigrant with a predominantly ethnic interpersonal network can be considered less adapted and less competent in the host communication system than an immigrant whose associates are primarily members of the host society. In addition, the degree of intimacy in the relationships an immigrant has developed with members of the host society is an important indicator of his or her acquired host communication competence. We may further elaborate on an immigrant's interpersonal communication by observing his or her specific verbal and nonverbal communication patterns in interacting with members of the host society.

The adaptation function of *mass communication* is limited in relation to that of interpersonal communication (Kim, 1979a). The immigrant's interpersonal communication experiences have intense and detailed influence over the immigrant's adaptation. Communication involving an interpersonal relationship provides the immigrant with simultaneous feedback, directly controlling and regulating the immigrant's communication behaviors. Though limited in its relative impact on an immigrant's adaptation, mass communication plays an important role in expanding the immigrant's experiences in the host society beyond the immediate environment. Through mass communication, an immigrant learns about the broader ranges of the various elements of the host socio-cultural system. In transmitting messages that reflect the aspirations, myths, work and play, and specific issues and events of the host society, the media explicitly and implicitly convey societal values, norms of behavior, and traditional perspectives for interpreting the environment. Of the immigrant's various mass communication experiences, exposure to the content of information-oriented media such as newspapers, magazines, television news, and other informational programs has been observed to be particularly functional for adaptation when compared to other media that are primarily entertainment oriented (Kim, 1977).

The adaptation function of mass communication should be particularly significant during the initial phase of resettlement. During this phase, the immigrant has not yet developed a sufficient competence to develop satisfactory interpersonal relationships with members of the host society. The communication experiences in direct interpersonal contact with members of the host society can often be frustrating. The immigrant may feel awkward and out of place in relating to others: The direct negative feedback from the other person can be too overwhelming for the immigrant to experience pleasure in the interaction with members of the host society. The immigrant naturally tends to withdraw from such direct interaction and, instead, resorts to mass media as an alternative, pressure-free channel through which elements of the host environment can be absorbed (Ryu, 1978).

Communication Environment

[Immigrants'] personal and social communication and their adaptation function cannot be fully understood in isolation from the communication environment of the host society. Whether the immigrant has resettled in a small rural town or a large metropolitan area, lives in a ghetto area or an affluent suburb, is employed as a factory worker or as an executive—all are environmental conditions that may significantly influence the socio-cultural development the immigrant is likely to achieve.

An environmental condition particularly influential in an immigrant's communication and adaptation is the availability of his or her native ethnic community in the local area. The degree to which the ethnic community can influence the immigrant's behavior depends largely upon the degree of "institutional completeness" of the community and its power to maintain the distinctive home culture for its members (Taylor, 1979). Available ethnic institutions can ameliorate the stresses of intercultural situations and provide context for acculturation under relatively permissive conditions. In the long run, however, an extensive involvement of an immigrant in the ethnic community without sufficient communication with members of the host society may retard the intensity and rate of adaptation (Broom and Kitsuse, 1976).

It is ultimately the host society that permits the degree of freedom, or "plasticity" (Kim, 1979b), for minority immigrants to deviate from the dominant cultural patterns of the host society and to develop ethnic institutions. Such permissiveness in the communication environment may vary even within the same country. In a relatively open and pluralistic society such as the contemporary United States, an immigrant may find a difference in the degree of receptivity and openness of the host environment between a large metropolitan area and a small town in a rural area.

ADAPTATION POTENTIAL

Individuals respond to the new change in terms of their prior experience, accepting what promises to be rewarding and rejecting what seems unworkable or disadvantageous. Adaptation patterns are not uniform among all individuals but vary depending upon their adaptation *potential* as determined by their preimmigration characteristics. Some are more predisposed toward the host culture than others. Among the multitude of background characteristics, the following are considered important in contributing to greater adaptation potential:

The *similarity* of the original culture to the host culture is perhaps one of the most important factors of acculturation potential. An immigrant from Canada to the United States, for example, will have a greater adaptation potential than a Vietnamese immigrant from Southeast Asia. Even two immigrants from the same culture may have different subcultural backgrounds. An immigrant from a more cosmopolitan urban center is likely to have a greater adaptation potential than a farmer from a rural area. To the extent that we can understand the similarities and discrepancies between an immigrant's original cultural background and the host culture, we can better understand the immigrant's acculturation potential.

Among demographic characteristics, *age* at the time of immigration and *educational background* have been found to be significantly related to acculturation potential. Older immigrants generally experience greater difficulty in adjusting to the new culture and are slower in acquiring new cultural patterns (Kim, 1976). Educational background of an immigrant prior to immigration facilitates acculturation (Kim, 1976, 1980). Education, regardless of its cultural context, appears to expand a person's capacity for new learning and the challenges of life. In some cases, an immigrant's educational process in the home country includes training in the language of the host society, which gives the individual a basis for building communication competence after immigration.

On the psychological level, an immigrant's *personality factors*, such as gregariousness, tolerance for ambiguity, risk-taking, cognitive flexibility, openmindedness, and other related characteristics, are likely to increase acculturation potential. These personality characteristics are likely to help restructure the immigrant's perception, feelings, and behaviors, facilitating adaptation in a new cultural environment.

Similarly, *familiarity* with the host culture prior to immigration through previous travel, interpersonal contacts, and through mass media may also increase the immigrant's adaptation potential.

FACILITATING ADAPTATION THROUGH COMMUNICATION

So far, immigrant adaptation has been defined and explained from a communication viewpoint. Just as any native-born person undergoes the enculturation process through communication, so an immigrant is adapted into the host culture through communication. Much of the adaptation process is to adapt to predominant patterns and rules of communication of the host culture. The acquired host communication competence, in turn, facilitates all other aspects of adjustment in the host society. Communication, therefore, is viewed as the major underlying process as well as an outcome of the adaptation process.

In order to understand an immigrant's adaptation, we must understand his or her communication patterns. Information about the immigrant's communication enables us to predict the degree and pattern of adaptation. As a conceptual framework to analyze the immigrant's communication patterns, the communication systems perspective has been presented. To summarize, the systems perspective recognizes the dynamic interaction processes of personal communication, social communication, and communication environment. Personal communication can be analyzed in terms of cognitive complexity, knowledge of the host communication patterns and rules, self-image, and motivation. Social communication is conceptualized in interpersonal communication and mass communication. Interpersonal communication is reflected in the nature and pattern of an immigrant's interpersonal networks and specific verbal and nonverbal communication behaviors. Patterns of use and participation in the host mass communication system, particularly the information-oriented contents of the mass media, are also useful adaptation indicators. The socio-cultural characteristics of the communication environment in which an immigrant carries out day-to-day activities influence the nature of the external communication stimuli that the immigrant is exposed to. Availability and strength of the ethnic community, as well as the plasticity of the host society, slow the adaptation process of an immigrant.

The adaptation potential of an immigrant prior to immigration may contribute to his or her subsequent adaptation in the host society. As discussed previously, adaptation potential is determined by such factors as: (1) similarity between the original culture and the host culture, (2) age at the time of immigration, (3) educational background, (4) some of the personality characteristics such as gregariousness and tolerance for ambiguity, and (5) familiarity with the host culture before immigration.

Once an immigrant enters the host society, the adaptation process is set in motion. The adaptation process will continue as long as the immigrant stays in direct contact with the host socio-cultural system. All of the adaptive forces—personal and social communication, communication environment, and pre-immigration adaptation potential—interactively influence the course of change in the immigrant's adaptation process. The adaptation process may not be a smooth linear process, but a forward-moving progression toward an ultimate assimilation, the hypothetical state of complete adaptation.

The extensive debate between "assimilationists" (who adhere to the "melting-pot" view) and "cultural pluralists" (proponents of conservation of ethnicity) loses its scientific relevance when we closely examine the inevitable adaptation of humans to their socio-cultural environment. No immigrant, as long as livelihood or other needs are functionally dependent upon the host society, can escape adaptation completely. Adaptation, in this sense, is a "natural" phenomenon. A prolonged, direct contact by the immigrant with a new socio-cultural environment leads to adaptive change. It is too simplistic to decree that one must be "either A or B," forced to accept or reject one of the two positions. In reality, ethnicity and assimilation can be considered to be two sides of the same coin; they are interrelated and inseparable phenomena. What is important is that both the assimilationist and the pluralist perspectives acknowledge some changes in immigrants

over time. When the changes are not complete, it is only natural that there remains a certain degree of ethnicity. Incomplete adaptation, depending on one's point of view, can be interpreted as evidence of (some) assimilation or (some) ethnicity.

Thus, the real issue between the two opposing views—assimilation vs. ethnicity—is not a scientific one, that is to say, whether or not there *is* such a phenomenon as adaptation. Rather, it is an ideological disagreement on the degree to which an individual immigrant *should* maintain (or lose) his or her original culture. Such ideological polarization along a continuum of adaptation among social scientists and social philosophers, however, does not interfere with the natural process of adaptive change. Nor should the philosophical disagreement interfere with the ultimate right of an individual immigrant to determine how far to acculturate beyond the minimum, functional level. In reality, most immigrants tend to follow the folk wisdom, "When in Rome, do as the Romans do." They recognize and accept the fact that it is they who are joining an existing socio-cultural system, and that the degree of success in building their new lives depends largely on their ability to adapt in the host society.

Should an immigrant choose to increase his or her adaptive capacity and consciously try to facilitate the adaptation process, then the immigrant must realize the importance of communication as the fundamental mechanism by which such goals may be achieved. To facilitate communication competence in the host culture, the immigrant must develop cognitive, affective, and behavioral competence in dealing with the host environment. By developing a strong motivation, the immigrant becomes positively oriented to the host society and accepts the norms and rules of the host culture. Through learning the host communication patterns and rules and by being open-minded, the immigrant becomes tolerant of the differences and uncertainties of the intercultural situations. Also, the immigrant must attempt, whenever possible, to maximize participation in the host interpersonal and mass communication systems. Through active participation in the host communication systems, the immigrant will develop a more realistic understanding of, and a more positive outlook on, a new way of life.

The immigrant, however, cannot accomplish his or her adaptive goals alone. The process of adaptation is an interactive process of "push and pull" between an immigrant and the host environment. But members of the host society can facilitate an immigrant's adaptation by accepting the original cultural conditioning of the immigrant, by providing the immigrant with supportive communication situations, and by making themselves patiently available through the often strenuous intercultural encounters. The host society can more actively encourage immigrant acculturation through communication training programs. Such training programs should facilitate the immigrant's acquisition of the host communication competence.

Although prolonged involvement in an ethnic community may ultimately delay the adaptation process, the ethnic community can play a significant adaptation function for the new immigrants in their early stages of resettlement. Ethnic communities can provide support systems to assist new arrivals in coping with the stresses and initial uncertainties and can guide them toward effective adaptation. Studies are beginning to investigate the coping, ego strength, and adaptation mechanisms that are built by natural support systems—family, neighborhood, ethnic associations, and self-help groups (Giordano and Giordano, 1977).

All in all, the adaptation process can be facilitated by cooperative effort among the immigrants themselves, the members of the host society, and the ethnic community. At the heart of interactive adaptation lies the communication process linking the individual immigrants to their socio-cultural milieu. The importance of communication to acculturation cannot be overemphasized. Acquisition of communication competence by the immigrant is not only instrumental to all other aspects of his or her life activities, but also vital for the host society if it is to effectively accommodate diverse elements and maintain the necessary societal unity and strength. As long as common channels of communication remain strong, consensus and patterns of concerted action will persist in the host society. As Mendelsohn (1964) describes it, communication makes it possible to merge the minority groups into one democratic social organization of commonly shared ideas and values.

REFERENCES

Breton, R. (1964). "Institutional Completeness of Ethnic Communities and the Personal Relations of Immigrants," *American Journal of Sociology, 70*, 193–205.

Broom, L., and Kitsuse, J. (1976). "The Validation of Acculturation: A Condition to Ethnic Assimilation." In D. E. Weinberg (ed.), *Ethnicity: A Conceptual Approach*. Cleveland: Cleveland Ethnic Heritage Studies, Cleveland State University.

Chance, N. A. (1965). "Acculturation, Self-Identification, and Personality Adjustment," *American Anthropologist, 67*, 373–393.

Giordano, J., and Giordano, G. (1977). *The Ethno-Cultural Factor in Mental Health: A Literature Review and Bibliography*. New York: Institute on Pluralism and Group Identity of the American Jewish Committee.

Kim, Y. Y. (1976). "Communication Patterns of Foreign Immigrants in the Process of Acculturation: A Survey Among the Korean Population in Chicago." Ph.D. Dissertation, Northwestern University.

Kim, Y. Y. (1977). "Communication Patterns of Foreign Immigrants in the Process of Acculturation." *Human Communication Research, 4*, 1, 66–77.

Kim, Y. Y. (1979a, May). "Mass Media and Acculturation: Toward Development of an Interactive Theory." Paper presented at the annual conference of the Eastern Communication Association, Philadelphia, Pennsylvania.

Kim, Y. Y. (1979b). "Toward an Interactive Theory of Communication-Acculturation." In D. Nimmo (ed.), *Communication Yearbook 3*. New Brunswick, N.J.: Transaction Books.

Kim, Y. Y. (1980). *Indochinese Refugees in the State of Illinois. Volume IV. Psychological, Social and Cultural Adjustment of Indochinese Refugees.*

Chicago: Travelers Aid Society of Metropolitan Chicago.

Kim, Y. Y. (1988). *Communication and Cross-Cultural Adaptation: An Integrative Theory*. Clevedon, England: Multilingual Matters.

Kim, Y. Y. (1989). "Personal, Social, and Economic Adaptation: 1975–1979 Arrivals." In D. Haines (ed.), *Refugees as Immigrants: Cambodians, Laotians, and Vietnamese in America*. Totowa, N.J.: Rowman & Littlefield.

Kim, Y. Y. (1990). "Communication and Adaptation: The Case of Asian Pacific Refugees in the United States." *Journal of Asian Pacific Communication, 1* (1), 1–17.

Maslow, A. H. (1970). *Motivation and Personality*, 2nd ed. New York: Harper & Row.

Mendelsohn, H. (1964). "Sociological Perspectives on the Study of Mass Communication." In L. A. Dexter and D. M. White (eds.), *People, Society and Mass Communication*. New York: Free Press of Glencoe.

Richmond, A. H. (1967). *Post-War Immigrants in Canada*. Toronto: University of Toronto Press.

Ruben, B. D. (1975). "Intrapersonal, Interpersonal, and Mass Communication Process in Individual and Multi-Person Systems." In B. D. Ruben and J. Y. Kim (eds.), *General Systems Theory and Human Communication*. Rochelle Park, N.J.: Hayden.

Ryu, J. S. (1978, May). "Mass Media's Role in the Assimilation Process: A Study of Korean Immigrants in the Los Angeles Area." Paper presented to the annual meeting of the International Communication Association, Chicago.

Taylor, B. K. (1979). "Culture: Whence, Whither and Why?" In A. E. Alcock, B. K. Taylor, and J. M. Welton (eds.), *The Future of Cultural Minorities*. New York: St. Martin's.

CONCEPTS AND QUESTIONS FOR CHAPTER 7

1. If you were going to travel abroad, what preparations would you make to ensure the best possible opportunity for effective intercultural communication?

2. What specific suggestions can you make that could improve your ability to interact with other ethnic or racial groups in your community? How would you go about gaining the necessary knowledge and experience?

3. What are the six stumbling blocks in intercultural communication discussed by LaRay Barna? How can you learn to avoid them?

4. Can you think of instances when you have been guilty of assuming similarity instead of difference?

5. Can you think of any mannerisms, behaviors, or styles that the U.S. businessperson reflects that are apt to stifle intercultural communication?

6. Why is it important to try to locate similarities between cultures as well as differences?

7. What current television programs and commercials encourage false media stereotyping?

8. Can you think of examples for each of the forms of prejudice discussed by Brislin?

9. What specific behaviors can you engage in that will help the immigrant in the adaptation process?

10. Can you generate a list of communication problems that were *not* included in this chapter?

11. From your own experiences, can you think of some ways intercultural communication can be improved?

12. What does Barna mean when she says, "The situations that bring about the emotional feelings differ from culture to culture"?

13. Can you think of specific examples for what Spitzberg calls "appropriate and effective" message behavior? How might appropriateness and effectiveness differ from culture to culture?

14. Can you think of intercultural examples for what Spitzberg refers to as "individual, episodic, and relational" systems?

15. Are there collectivist and/or individualist co-cultures in the United States?

16. Why is it important for people involved with training to have information about individualist and collectivist cultures?

17. Do you believe it is possible for someone to improve the manner in which he or she interacts with people from different cultures? Why?

8

Ethical Considerations: Prospects for the Future

The goal of this book is to help you understand intercultural communication and to assist you in appreciating the issues and problems inherent in interactions involving people from foreign and alien cultures. To this end we have examined a series of diverse essays that presented a variety of variables operable during intercultural encounters. But what we have looked at up to now is what is already known about intercultural communication. We now shift our emphasis and focus on two issues that are much harder to pin down. These are the ethical considerations that must be inherent in intercultural interactions and the future prospects of this developing field of study. In short, this chapter examines some of the following questions: What do we need to accomplish, what may we expect to accomplish, what philosophical issues must we deal with, and what kinds of personalities must we develop if we are to improve the art and science of intercultural communication during the remainder of this century?

To set the tone for this final chapter, we begin with an essay that deals with the ethical questions centering around how we go about judging the actions of people from different cultures. As you would suspect, this issue is indeed a difficult and complex one. In "The Evaluation of Culture," Elvin Hatch tackles this question with a rather optimistic premise. He maintains that "it is possible to arrive at a general principle for evaluating institutions without assuming that ours is a superior way of life." Admittedly, such an idealistic stance is not easy to put into operation. Yet Hatch does offer a framework that can be used to evaluate cultures. His philosophy is predicated on three generalizations: first, that humanistic values seem to be widespread among most human beings; second, that humanistic values are better than ethnocentrism—even though it too is universal; and third, that much of what we evaluate with regard to other cultures falls out of the scope of humanistic philosophy, and therefore we need a way to judge and evaluate such things as sexual mores, kinship relations, styles of leadership, and the like. Hatch offers some guidelines to help us make these ethical decisions.

Our next essay, by Young Yun Kim, is based on one of the basic themes of this book—that today's interconnected and fast-changing world demands that we all change our assumptions about culture and our individual places within that culture. Recognizing these changes, Kim advances a philosophical orientation that she calls *intercultural personhood*. For Kim, intercultural personhood combines the key attributes of Eastern and Western cultural traditions, and she presents a model using these attributes. This model takes into account basic modes of consciousness, cognitive patterns, personal and social values, and communication behavior. The notion of intercultural personhood also leads us into the concept of the multicultural person as set forth in the next article.

The next selection in this chapter is by Rosita D. Albert and Harry C. Triandis. It calls our attention to a topic that is bound to generate a great deal of discussion in the next few years. It is the issue of multicultural education. The concept behind multicultural education is rather simple to state but very complex and controversial to implement. Advocates of multicultural education maintain that pupils who are culturally different from the majority need multicultural education so that they can learn to function effectively in their own culture as well as in the majority culture. Some educators believe that students of the dominant culture can also benefit from education that asks them to learn about the patterns of perception, values, and behaviors of culturally different classmates. Because this philosophy is not without its critics, Albert and Triandis discuss some of the objections to multicultural education. They also point out three different approaches to teaching multicultural education and some advantages and disadvantages of each. Regardless of your personal feeling about multicultural education, it is a topic that is going to be debated by all people who are interested in the large influx of new minorities seeking an education in the United States educational system.

Our final selection, while touching on some of the same issues discussed by Hatch in the first essay

of this chapter, extends the importance of ethical judgments beyond those suggested by him. David W. Kale not only grants the significance of developing an ethical orientation toward other cultures, but he offers a number of specific challenges for the future. It is the future that is made real by Kale as he presents us with current examples, ranging from our role in the rain forests of Brazil to events taking place in the Soviet Union.

Kale begins by acknowledging that most people feel uncomfortable addressing cultural beliefs about what is right and wrong. He reminds us that most of these beliefs are at the very foundation of our lives and our culture. Yet even with this uneasiness, increased contact with diverse cultures, combined with the problems that can occur when cultures clash, demand that we must examine the issues associated with questions of right and wrong. To assist us in that examination, Kale asks that we begin by looking at five interrelated issues directly associated with any evaluation of intercultural ethics: (1) a definition of communication ethics, (2) cultural relativity versus universal ethics, (3) the concept of spirit as a basis for intercultural ethics, (4) peace as the fundamental value in intercultural ethics, and (5) a universal code of ethics in intercultural communication. Kale amplifies the fifth issue by advancing a specific code, which he urges us to follow, predicated on four principles that should guide the actions of *ethical communicators*: (a) Address people of other cultures with the same respect that they would like to receive themselves, (b) seek to describe the world as they perceive it as accurately as possible, (c) encourage people of other cultures to express themselves in their uniqueness, and (d) strive for identification with people of other cultures.

It might be well to view Kale's exploration, and all the other selections in this chapter, as only a sampling of the many issues that confront those involved in intercultural communication. The field is relatively new and the challenges are so varied that it is impossible to accurately predict future directions. Our intent in this chapter, therefore, is simply to introduce you to a few of the concepts that await further discussion in the 1990s.

One final note: Much of what we offer in this chapter is subjective, and, to some, might even appear naive. Neither we nor the authors of the articles apologize for maintaining that in intercultural contacts each person should aim for the ideal. What we introduce here are some suggestions for developing new ways of perceiving oneself and others. In so doing we can all help make this complex and shrinking planet a more habitable and peaceful place for its nearly five and one-half billion residents.

The Evaluation of Culture

ELVIN HATCH

If relativism is in such difficulty as a moral philosophy, is there any role at all left for it to play in our thinking? I believe so, and one of my purposes . . . is to indicate what that is. There is another purpose: Given that much of ethical relativism has been nudged aside by recent events, I want to advance a set of principles that will cover much of the ground that relativism has relinquished. These principals constitute a framework that we can use in evaluating cultures, including our own.

The first principle is that there is merit to the criticism that relativism has been accompanied by a conservative bias. What is at issue here is the relativist claim that all cultures or institutions are equally valid or fitting: Anthropologists tended to assume that the mere presence of a cultural trait warrants our valuing it. Elizabeth Colson has put the case quite simply; she wrote, "Ethnographers have usually presented each social group they study as a success story. We have no reason to believe that this is true" (1976, p. 264). A people may get by with inadequate solutions to their problems even judging by their own standards. For example, if the people are genuinely interested in ensuring the productivity of their gardens, they will find innovations like crop rotation and fertilization more effective than human sacrifice—although they will not have the statistical evidence to realize this (cf. Bagish 1981, pp. 12–20).

Second, a general principle is at hand for judging the adequacy of institutions. It may be called the hu-

From Elvin Hatch, *Culture and Morality: The Relativity of Values in Anthropology* (New York: Columbia University Press, 1983), 133–144. Copyright © 1983 Columbia University Press. Reprinted by permission of the publisher and author.

manistic principle or standard, by which I mean that the well-being of people ought to be respected. The notion of well-being is a critical aspect of the humanistic principle, and three points can be made with respect to it. For one, I assume that human well-being is not a culture-bound idea. Starvation and violence, for example, are hardly products of Western thought or a function of Western thinking, although they may be conceived in a peculiarly Western idiom. Starvation and violence are phenomena that are recognized as such in the most diverse cultural traditions. Another is that the notion of human well-being is inherently value-laden, and concepts of harm and beneficence are inseparable from it: it seems impossible to imagine the idea of human well-being divorced from moral judgments of approval and disapproval. Whereas such notions as sky or earth may conceivably be held in purely neutral terms in a given culture, such ideas as hunger and torture cannot be. It is even reasonable to argue that the *point* of morality, as a philosophical if not a sociological issue, is to promote the well-being of others (Warnock 1971, esp. pp. 12–26). Finally, the notion of human well-being, when used as the central point of morality, serves to root moral questions in the physical, emotional, and intellectual constitution of people. It may be that any rigorous attempt to work out the content of morality will have to include an analysis of such notions as human wants, needs, interests, and happiness.

    The humanistic principle can be divided into two parts. First is Redfield's point about humaneness, that it is good to treat people well, or that we should not do one another harm. We can judge that human sacrifice, torture, and political repression are wrong, whether they occur in our society or some other. Similarly, it is wrong for a person, whatever society he or she may belong to, to be indifferent toward the suffering of others. The matter of coercion, discussed earlier, fits here, in that we may judge it to be wrong when some members of a society deliberately and forcefully interfere in the affairs of other people. Coercion works against the well-being of those toward whom it is directed. Second is the notion that people ought to enjoy a reasonable level of material existence: we may judge that poverty, mal-

nutrition, material discomfort, human suffering, and the like are bad. These two ideas may be brought together to form one standard since both concern the physical well-being of the members of society, and the difference between them is that the former refers to the quality of interpersonal relations, and the latter to the material conditions under which people live.

    The humanistic principle may be impossible to define very tightly; it may even be that the best we can do to give it shape is to illustrate it with examples as I have done here. And surely it is difficult to apply in actual situations. Yet these are not good reasons to avoid making judgments about the relative merit of institutions or about the desirability of change. Although we may do harm by expressing judgments across cultural boundaries, we may do as much or more harm by failing to do so.

    The orthodox relativist would perhaps argue that there is no humanistic moral principle that we can use for this purpose, in that notions like harm and discomfort are quite variable from one culture to the next. Pain and personal injury may even be highly valued by some people. For example, the Plains Indian willingly engaged in a form of self-torture that a middle-class American could hardly tolerate. The Indians chopped off finger joints and had arrows skewered through their flesh; tied to the arrows were cords, by which the sufferer dragged buffalo skulls around the village. Some American Indians were also reported to have placed a very high value on bravery, and the captive who withstood torture without showing pain was highly regarded by the enemies who tormented him.

    Yet cases like these do not make the point that notions of pain and suffering are widely variable. Following this same logic one could say that middle-class Americans value pain since they willingly consent to surgery, and the man or woman who bears up well is complimented for his or her strength of character. The Indian who was tortured to death would surely have preferred a long and respectable life among his people to the honorable death that came to him. The Plains Indian who engaged in self-torture was trying to induce a vision (in our idiom, a hallucination) for the power and advantages it was believed such an experience would bring. The pain was a means to an end, and surely was not seen as a pleasurable indulgence to look forward to. The difference between middle-class Americans and Plains Indians on this point could be a difference in judgments of reality and not a difference in values—the American would not believe that the vision has the significance attributed to it by the Indian, so he or she would not submit to the pain. Similarly, the plains warrior might not believe in the efficacy of surgery and might refuse to suffer the scalpel.

The widespread trend among non-Western peoples to want such material benefits as steel knives and other labor-saving devices is a clear indication that all is not relative when it comes to hard work, hunger, discomfort, and the like. Cultural values may be widely different in many ways, but in this sphere at least, human beings do seem to have certain preferences in common.

The Yanomamö are an instructive case, for here is a people who do not seem to share the humanistic value I am suggesting. The level of violence and treachery in this society suggests that their regard for pain and suffering is demonstrably different from what I am arguing is the norm among human beings. Yet this is not clearly the case either: Individuals in Yanomamö society are more willing than middle-class Americans to inflict injury on others, yet they want to avoid injury to themselves. Why else would the wife flee in terror when her husband comes at her with a machete, and why else would a village seek refuge from enemies when it is outnumbered and weak? The Yanomamö seem rather to be a case in which we are warranted in making a value judgment across cultural boundaries: They do not exhibit as much regard for the well-being of other persons as they have for themselves, and this can be judged a moral error.

Does this point about the generality of the humanistic principle among human beings not make the same mistake that Herskovits, Benedict, and other relativists were accused of making, which is to derive an "ought" from an "is"? My argument is not quite that simple, for it has two parts. First is the

generalization that the humanistic value seems to be widespread among human beings. Second, I am making the moral judgment (quite separately from the empirical generalization) that this is an estimable value to hold, or that it warrants acceptance—in contrast, say, to another widespread value, ethnocentrism, which is not meritorious even if it is universal.

A third principle in the scheme that I propose is that a considerable portion of the cultural inventory of a people falls outside the scope of the humanistic standard mentioned above. In other words, once we have considered those cultural features that we can reasonably judge by this standard, a large portion remains, and it consists of those items which have little if anything to do with the strictly practical affairs of life and which then cannot be appraised by practical considerations. Included are sexual mores, marriage patterns, kinship relations, styles of leadership, forms of etiquette, attitudes toward work and personal advancement, dietary preferences, clothing styles, conceptions of deity, and others. Some of these nonappraisable features are closely linked to others that are, in that there are always nonessential cultural accouterments or trappings associated with institutions that are important on practical grounds. Western medicine provides a surfeit of examples. Health care clearly falls within the orbit of the humanistic principle, yet much of the medical system in the United States is hardly necessary for health's sake, including the rigid social hierarchy among doctors and nurses and the traditional division of labor between them. Successful health care systems can assume different forms from the one exhibited in this country. It is essential (but difficult) to keep in mind this division between what is essential and what is not in such matters as medicine, for otherwise civilization will tend to pack a good deal of unnecessary cultural baggage along with the genuinely useful features when it sets out to share its advantages with others.

Relativism prevails in relation to the institutions that fall outside the orbit of the humanistic principle, for here a genuine diversity of values is found and there are no suitable cross-cultural standards for evaluating them. The finest reasoning that we or anyone else can achieve will not point decisively to the superiority of Western marriage patterns, eating habits, legal institutions, and the like. We ought to show tolerance with respect to these institutions in other societies on the grounds that people ought to be free to live as they choose.

This leads to the fourth principle: Is it possible to identify any areas of culture in which we may speak of improvement? Are there any criteria that will produce a hierarchical ordering of societies that we may say represents a pattern of advance? Or is the distinction between primitive and civilized societies but an expression of our cultural bias?

The first criterion that comes to mind is Redfield's and Kroeber's, according to which civilization has brought a more humane existence, a higher level of morality to mankind, inasmuch as people treat one another better in complex societies. This judgment is very difficult to accept today, however. Recent events have left most of us with considerable ambivalence about Western democracy, to cite one instance. Politicians seem too often to be both incompetent and dishonest, and to be willing to allow private economic interests to influence programs and policies at all levels. Similarly, there is a very strong distrust of the power and intentions of big business, which seems to set its policies chiefly by looking at its margin of profit. The risk of producing a dangerous product is calculated by assessing how much the company is liable to lose in lawsuits relative to its profits, and not by considering the real dangers to human life. Much of the difficulty of assessing moral advance is that this is a highly impressionistic matter. The ledger sheets on which we tote up the pluses and minuses for each culture are so complex that summary calculations of overall moral standing are nearly meaningless. Perhaps the most one can say about whether or not there has been moral advance is that it is impossible to tell—but that it is not very likely.

It is important to distinguish between this conclusion and Herskovits'. According to him, we cannot speak of progress in this sphere because any humanistic principle we might use will necessarily

be culture-bound; we have no yardstick to measure with. My point is that we do have a suitable yardstick, but that there are so many measures to take in each culture that the sum total is too complicated to assess.

Another criterion for gauging improvement is the material well-being of people: disregarding whether or not the members of society behave well or ill toward one another, can we say that the material conditions of life have gotten better with civilization? In pursuing this question I need to digress somewhat. The issue of material improvement places the focus on economics and technology, and also on such technical knowledge as that which is provided by medical and agricultural research. So we need first to ask if it is possible to arrive at an objective and meaningful hierarchy of societies based on these features. Herskovits questioned that we can. To him, an ordering of societies according to our criteria of economic production and technological complexity will merely reflect our cultural perspective and not some fundamental principle of general significance to all peoples.

Herskovits' argument is off the mark. On one hand, the criteria of economic complexity and technological sophistication are objective in the sense that they are definable by reference to empirical features that are independent of our culture. For example, the intensity and scale of economic transactions have a physical aspect which is identifiable from other cultural perspectives than ours, and the same is true of such measures as the amount of food produced per farm worker.[1] What is more, the social hierarchy that results from the use of these criteria has historical significance: One would be astonished, say, to discover evidence of complex forms of agricultural production in the Paleolithic. But on the other hand, and even more important, this is a meaningful hierarchy, in that the point of this ordering of societies would not be lost on people from other cultures; it would be meaningful to them because they see the value of increasing agricultural productivity, the use of bicycles (and automobiles), the availability of running water, and the like. It is surely the case that non-Western peoples all over the world are more interested in the products of Western industrial production than they are in the intricacies of Australian kinship, and are more likely to incorporate such Western innovations as fertilizers and matches into their cultures than they are the particulars of the Australian system of marriage and descent. This is an important message we get from the post-World War II drive for economic development among the newly independent nations.

There is a danger in using people's perceptions of the relative superiority of economic and technological systems as a test for the meaningfulness of this social hierarchy, because not all of the world's populations agree about what it is that is good about development and modernization. For example, Burma and Iran are highly selective in the changes they will accept, and at least some very simple societies (like the Andaman Islanders) want little if any change.

There is another way to establish the hierarchy without relying completely and directly on people's opinions. However another society may feel about what they do or do not want with regard to development, the economic and technological relationship between them and Western societies is asymmetrical. It is true that the fully developed nations rely on the less developed ones for natural resources like oil, but processed goods, and both economic and technological innovations, flow chiefly to and not away from the societies that are lower on the scale. To take an extreme case, there is little in the sphere of technology and economics that the Australian aborigines or Andaman Islanders can offer to the developed nations, whereas the reverse is not true. For example, some of the most isolated Andaman Islanders occasionally find empty gasoline drums washed upon their shore. They cut these in half and use them as enormous cooking pots (Cipriani 1966, p. 52). It is unthinkable that this relationship could be reversed—that we would find some technological item from their cultural inventory to be especially useful in our everyday lives. It is true that we may value their pottery or other artifacts as examples of primitive art, but the use we have for such items is esthetic, not practical, and consequently

such items are of a different order from the gasoline drums that the Andamanese find so useful.

In noting this asymmetry I do not mean that cultures which are lower in the hierarchy do not have a very sophisticated technical knowledge of their own (they must in order to survive), and in this sense "they have something to teach us," as Brokensha and Riley remark concerning the Mbeere of Kenya. "In fact," these writers continue, "Mbeere and other folk-belief systems contain much that is based on extremely accurate, detailed and thoughtful observations, made over many generations" (1980, p. 115). It is easy to depreciate or ignore the cultural practices and ideas of another society, say, when assisting them in the process of development. In particular, it is tempting to want to replace their traditional practices with "modern" ones in wholesale fashion, instead of building on or incorporating the indigenous knowledge in helping to bring about change. Nevertheless, the presence of such useful knowledge in indigenous systems of thought does not negate the fundamental asymmetry that exists among societies or the hierarchy which the asymmetry suggests.

The pluralistic notion of development . . . has bearing on the way we should conceive this hierarchy. The idea that Third World countries should become more and more like Western industrial societies is subject to criticism, and it may be preferable to define development differently for each society according to the interests of the people concerned and the nature of their economic and ecological conditions. A people may have achieved as much development as they need and want without embarking on a trajectory of industrial "growth" in the Western sense. In other words, the hierarchy I am suggesting does not represent a set of stages through which all societies will necessarily want to pass. It is simply a ranking of cultural systems according to degrees of economic complexity, technological sophistication, and the like.

Yet this begs a crucial question. Is it not true that to suggest this hierarchy is to imply that the societies higher on the scale are preferable? Does the existence of the hierarchy not mean that the societies that fall below would be better off if only they could manage to come up to a higher level of economic complexity and technological sophistication?

The discussion now comes back to the issue that prompted this digression. Can we say that the social hierarchy we have arrived at represents improvement or advance? The response unfortunately is as indecisive as the one concerning moral progress, and for the same reason. On one hand, civilization has brought a lower infant mortality rate due to better diet, hygiene, and medical care; less vulnerability to infectious disease for the same reasons; greater economic security due to increased economic diversification; less danger from local famine due to improved systems of transportation and economic organization; greater material comfort due to improved housing, and the like. But on the other hand, we have pollution, the horrors of modern warfare, and the boredom and alienation of factory work, to name a few. On one hand we have labor-saving devices like automatic dishwashers, but on the other hand we have to spend our lives on a treadmill to pay for them. The tally sheet is simply too complicated to make an overall judgment. It is not at all clear that other people should want to become like Western civilization.

What we can say about the hierarchy is that the nations that fall toward the upper end of the scale have greater resources than the others. They have better technical knowledge from which the entire world may benefit—knowledge about hygiene, diet, crop rotation, soils, and the like. They also have the physical capacity to undertake programs of assistance when other societies are interested. Yet the higher civilizations also have the capacity to do far greater harm. The industrial system has exploited the powerless, ravaged the environment, meddled in the affairs of other countries, and conducted war in ways that the simpler societies never dreamed of. Even when we set out altruistically to help others we often mismanage the effort or misunderstand what it is we should do. Just as it is not at all clear that industrial civilization provides a happier or more fulfilling life for its members, so it is not clear whether its overall influence on those below it in

the hierarchy has been to their detriment or benefit. This is a pessimistic age, and at this point it is difficult to suppress a strong sense of despair on this score.

The place of Western civilization in the hierarchy of human societies is very different from what it was thought to be by Victorian anthropologists, who saw the differences among societies at bottom as a matter of intelligence: Civilization is more thoughtful and shows greater sense than the lower societies, and it provides a happier and more benign mode of living; savages would embrace our way of life if they had the intelligence to understand it, for their institutions are but imperfect specimens of our own. Clearly this is inadequate. Many areas of life cannot be judged by standards that apply across cultural boundaries, for in many respects cultures are oriented in widely different directions. Still, all people desire material comfort and security, and in this sense Western civilization is distinguished from other cultures. The relationship among societies in this respect is one of asymmetry. Just as we may do far more harm to others than they can do to us, so we may do them more good, and we have the obligation to share the material advantages our civilization has to offer. Yet this asymmetry should not be confused with superiority. As a total way of life ours may not be preferable to others, and we need not try to turn them into copies of Western civilization.

An important implication follows from these conclusions: It is possible to arrive at a general principle for evaluating institutions without assuming that ours is a superior way of life. Herskovits for one seems to have believed that this could not be done, and that any general moral principle we might advance would express our own cultural bias and would tacitly make us appear to occupy a position superior to the rest. But this is not so. The matter of arriving at general moral principles and of how we measure up to these principles are two very separate issues.

The idea of ethical relativism in anthropology has had a complicated history. Through the 1930s the discipline expressed an overwhelming confidence in the notion, a confidence that was fortified by the empirical findings about the variability of moral values from culture to culture. And relativism was thought to be an idea of signal importance, for it could be used in world affairs and would contribute to peace and human understanding. But suddenly and with firm conviction, relativism was swept aside. It had all been a mistake.

Was relativism completely mistaken? After we have excised what is unacceptable, is there something left, a residuum of some kind, that still warrants approval? Certainly the relativists' call for tolerance contained an element that is hard to fault. This is the value of freedom: People ought to be free to live as they choose, to be free from the coercion of others more powerful than they. Equally fundamental, perhaps, is the message that relativism contained about the place of Western civilization among human societies. Rejected was the smug belief in Western superiority that dominated anthropological thinking during the 1800s. Just as the universe has not looked the same since the Copernican revolution, so the world and our place in it has not looked the same since ethical relativism appeared at about the turn of the century.

NOTE

1. The World Bank and other organizations commonly use a number of objective measures in assessing such matters as poverty, physical quality of life, and economic and social development. For example, see Lizer 1977, and World Bank 1979, pp. 117–188.

REFERENCES

Bagish, H. (1981). *Confessions of a Former Cultural Relativist*. (Second Annual Faculty Lecture, Santa Barbara City College) Santa Barbara: Santa Barbara City College Publications.

Benedict, R. (1934). *Patterns of Culture*. Boston: Houghton Mifflin.

Benedict, R. (1934). "Anthropology and the Abnormal." *Journal of General Psychology, 10*, 59–82.

Brokensha, D. and Riley, D. (1980). "Mbeere Knowledge of Their Vegetation, and Its Relevance for Development (Kenya)" in D. Brokensha, D. Warren, and O. Werner, eds., *Indigenous Knowledge Systems and Development*. Lanham, Md.: University Press of America.

Cipriani, L. (1966). *The Andaman Islanders*, edited and translated by D. Cox. New York: Praeger.

Colson, E. (1976). "Culture and Progress," *American Anthropologist, 78*, 261–271.

Herskovits, M. (1947). *Man and His Works*. New York: Knopf.

Herskovits, M. (1973). *Cultural Relativism: Perspectives in Cultural Pluralism*. New York: Vintage Books.

Kroeber, A. (1917). "The Superorganic," *American Anthropologist, 19*, 163–213.

Kroeber, A. (1948). *Anthropology*, rev. ed. New York: Harcourt Brace.

Kroeber, A. (1952). *The Nature of Culture*. Chicago: University of Chicago Press.

Redfield, R. (1953). *The Primitive World and Its Transformations*. Ithaca: Cornell University Press, 1957 ed.

Redfield, R. (1957). "The Universally Human and Cultural Variable," *Journal of General Education, 10*, 150–160.

Intercultural Personhood: An Integration of Eastern and Western Perspectives

YOUNG YUN KIM

Today we live in a world of global community. Rigid adherence to the culture of our youth is neither feasible nor desirable. The tightly knit communication web has brought cultures of the world together closer than ever before. Strong cultural identity is more a nostalgic conception than a realistic assessment of our attributes. Indeed, we live in an exciting time in which we are challenged to examine ourselves critically. As Toffler (1980) states in *The Third Wave*, "Humanity faces a quantum leap forward. It faces the deepest social upheaval and creative restructuring of all time. Without clearly recognizing it, we are engaged in building a remarkable new civilization from the ground up" (p. 10).

Reflecting the interactive realities of our time, a number of attempts have been made to explore ideologies that are larger than national and cultural interests and that embrace all humanity. As early as 1946, Northrop, in *The Meeting of the East and the West*, proposed an "international cultural ideal" to provide intellectual and emotional foundations for what he envisioned as "partial world sovereignty." Among contemporary critics of culture, Thompson (1973) explored the concept of "planetary culture" in which Eastern mysticism was integrated with Western science and rationalism. Similarly, Elgin (1981) proposed "voluntary simplicity" as an emerging global "common sense" and a practical

life style to reconcile the willful, rational approach to life of the West and the holistic, spiritual orientation of the East.

In this frame of ideas, the present writer has presented the concept "intercultural person" as an image of future human development (Kim, 1982; Gudykunst & Kim, 1984; Kim and Ruben, 1988). The intercultural person represents a type of person whose cognitive, affective, and behavioral characteristics are not limited but are open to growth beyond the psychological parameters of his or her own culture. Other similar terms such as "international" (Lutzker, 1960), "universal" (Walsh, 1973), and "multicultural" (Adler, 1982) person have also been used to project an essentially similar image of personhood with varying degrees of descriptive and explanatory utility.

To envision how we may renew ourselves and grow beyond our own cultural conditioning in this intercultural world, we need to comprehend and to seek meaning and order in the complexity of the fundamental human condition. Our task is to look at both Eastern and Western cultures in their "original form" rather than in their contemporary cultural patterns. The linking back to the origin not only enables us to see the respective foundation of the two cultures clearly, but also creates the possibility of recognizing and bringing into play new lines of development. In this essay, we will examine the basic cultural *a priori* or world view of East and West, concepts deeply rooted in the religious and philosophical traditions of the two cultural groups. Once we rediscover the cultural roots of Eastern and Western worlds, we will then be able to develop a broad perspective on the ground-level human conditions without being restricted by our own cultural "blind spots." Such a pan-human understanding will enable us to construct an image of intercultural personhood—a way of life that is called for by the increasingly intercultural realities of our world.

EASTERN AND WESTERN WORLD VIEWS

Traditional cultures throughout Asian countries including India, Tibet, Japan, China, Korea, and Southeast Asia have been profoundly influenced by such religious and philosophical systems as Buddhism, Hinduism, Taoism, and Zen. On the other hand, the Western European nations have historically followed the Greek and the Judaeo-Christian traditions. Of course, any attempt to present the cultural *a priori* of these two broadly categorized civilizations inevitably sacrifices specific details and the uniqueness of variations within each group. No two individuals or groups are identical in their beliefs and behaviors, and whatever we characterize about one culture or cultural group must be thought of as variable rather than as rigidly structured. Nevertheless, there are several key factors in the two perspectives that distinguish each group clearly from the other. To examine these factors is to indicate the equally evident interconnectedness that ties different nations together to constitute the Eastern or Western cultural group.

The characterization of Eastern and Western world views in this section and throughout this article is based on the observations of many authors. Of the existing comparative cultural analyses, Northrop's *The Meeting of the East and the West* (1946/1966), Gulick's *The East and the West* (1963), Nakamura's *Ways of Thought of Eastern Peoples* (1964), Oliver's *Communication and Culture in Ancient India and China* (1971), Capra's *The Tao of Physics* (1975), and Elgin's *Voluntary Simplicity* (1981) have provided a particular influence.

Universe and Nature

One of the most fundamental ways culture conditions our existence is through explicit and implicit teachings about our relationship to the nature of the universe and to the non-human natural world. Traditional Eastern and Western perspectives diverge significantly in this basic premise. As Needham (1951) observed in his article, "Human laws and the laws of nature in China and the West," people in the West have been dominated by the view that the universe was initially created, and has since been externally controlled, by a divine power.

In this sense, the Western view of the universe is characteristically dualistic, materialistic, and lifeless. The Judaeo-Christian tradition sets God apart from this reality; having created it and set it into motion, God could then be viewed as apart from His creation. The fundamental material of the universe is thought to be elementary particles of matter that interact with one another in a predictable fashion. Furthermore, since the foundation of the universe is seen as consisting of matter, it is viewed as essentially non-living. It is seen as an inanimate machine in which humankind occupies a unique and elevated position among the sparse life-forms that exist. Assuming a relatively barren universe, it seems only rational that humans exploit the lifeless material universe (and the lesser life-forms of nature) on behalf of those who live most intensely—humankind itself.

On the other hand, the Eastern view is profoundly holistic, dynamic, and spiritual. From the Eastern perspective, the entirety of the universe is a vast, multidimensional, living organism consisting of many interrelated parts and forces. The universe is conscious and engaged in a continuous dance of creation: the cosmic pattern is viewed as self-contained and self-organizing. It unfolds itself because of its own inner necessity and not because it is "ordered" to by any external volitional power.

What exists in the universe is a manifestation of a divine life force. Beneath the surface appearance of things, an ultimate reality is continuously creating, sustaining, and infusing our worldly experience. The all-sustaining life force that instant by instant creates our manifest universe is not apart from ourselves or our worldly existence. Rather, it is continuously creating and intimately infusing every aspect of the cosmos—from its most minute details to its most grand scale features.

Thus, the Eastern view reveres the common source out of which all things arise, and at the same time recognizes that everything in this dynamic world is fluid, ever-changing, and impermanent. In Hinduism, all static forms are *maya*, that is, they exist only as illusory concepts. This idea of the impermanence of all forms is the starting point of Buddhism. The Buddha taught that "all compounded things are impermanent," and that all suffering in the world arises from our trying to cling to fixed forms—objects, people, or ideas—instead of accepting the world as it moves. This notion of the impermanence of all forms and the appreciation of the aliveness of the universe in the Eastern world view is strongly contrasted with the Western emphasis on the visible forms of physical reality and their improvement through social and material/technological progress.

Knowledge

Since the East and West have different cosmic patterns, we can expect a different approach to knowledge. In the East, because the universe is a harmonious organism, there is a lack of any dualism in the cosmic pattern as well as in epistemological patterns. The Eastern view places an emphasis on perceiving and knowing things and events holistically and synthetically, rather than analytically. Furthermore, the ultimate purpose of knowledge is to transcend the apparent contrasts and to "see" the interrelatedness and underlying unity of all things.

When the Eastern mystics tell us they experience all things and events as manifestations of a basic oneness, this does not mean they consider all things equal. They recognize the individuality of things but at the same time are aware that all differences and contrasts are relative within an all-embracing unity. The awareness that all opposites are polar, and thus a unity, is seen as one of the highest aims of knowledge. Suzuki (1968) writes, "The fundamental idea of Buddhism is to pass beyond the world of opposites, a world built up by intellectual distinctions and emotional defilements, and to realize the spiritual world of non-distinction, which involves achieving an absolute point of view" (p. 18).

Since all opposites are interdependent, their conflict can never result in the total victory of one side, but will always be a manifestation of the interplay between the two sides. In the East, therefore, a virtuous person is not one who undertakes the im-

possible task of striving for the "good" and eliminating the "bad," but rather one who is able to maintain a dynamic balance between the two. Transcending the opposites, one becomes aware of the relativity and polar relationship of all opposites. One realizes that good and bad, pleasure and pain, life and death, winning and losing, light and dark, are not absolute experiences belonging to different categories, but are merely two sides of the same reality—extreme aspects of a single whole. This point has been emphasized most extensively by the Chinese sages in their symbolism of the archetypal poles, yin and yang. And the opposites cease to be opposites in the very essence of Tao. To know the Tao—the illustrious way of the universe—is the ultimate purpose of human learning.

This holistic approach to knowledge in the East emphasizes understanding concepts and the aesthetic components of things by intuition. A concept by intuition is one of complete meaning and is something immediately experienced, apprehended, and contemplated. Northrop (1946/1966) described it more accurately as the "differentiated aesthetic continuum." Within the total differentiated aesthetic continuum, there is no distinction between subjective and objective. The aesthetic continuum is a single all-embracing continuity. The aesthetic part of the self is also an essential part of the aesthetic object, whether it is a person or a flower. With respect to the immediately apprehended aesthetic nature, the person is identical with the aesthetic object; only with respect to his differentiation is the self other than the aesthetic object.

In this orientation, Taoism pursues the all-embracing, immediately experienced, emotionally moving aesthetic continuum with respect to its manifestations in the differentiated, sensed aesthetic qualities of nature. Confucianism pursues the all-embracing aesthetic continuum with respect to its manifestations in human nature and its moral implications for human society. The Taoist claim is that only by seeing the aesthetic continuity in its all-embracing-ness as ultimate and irreducible will we properly understand the meaning of the universe and nature. The Confucian claim, similarly, is that only if one takes the same standpoint, that of recognizing the all-embracing aesthetic whole to be an ultimate and irreducible part of human nature, will we have a compassionate feeling for human beings other than ourselves.

The ultimate, irreducible, and undifferentiated aesthetic continuum is the Eastern philosopher's conception of the constituted world. The differentiations within it, such as particular scenes, events, or persons, are not the irreducible atomic identities, but merely arise out of the ultimate undifferentiated reality of the aesthetic continuum. Sooner or later, they fade back into it again and thus are transitory and impermanent. When Eastern sages insist that one must become self-less, they mean that the self consists of two components: one, a differentiated, unique element, distinguishing one person from any other person; and the other, the all-embracing, aesthetically immediate, emotionally moving, compassionate, undifferentiated component. The former is temporary and transitory, and the cherishing of it, the desire for its immortality, is the source of suffering and selfishness. The part of the self that is not transitory but rather immortal is the aesthetic component, and it is identical not merely in all persons, but in all aesthetic objects throughout the universe.

While the East has concentrated its mental processes on the all-embracing, holistic, intuitive, aesthetic continuum, the Western pursuit of knowledge has been based on the doctrine of a dualistic world view. Since in the West the world and its various components came into existence through the individual creative acts of a God, the fundamental question is, how can I reach out to the external inanimate world or to people? In this question, there is a basic dichotomy between the knower and the things to be known.

Along with this epistemological dualism, the West has emphasized rationality in the pursuit of knowledge. Since the Greek philosopher Plato "discovered" reason, virtually all subsequent Western thought—the themes, the questions, and the terms—exists in essence in the writing of Plato (Wei, 1980). Even Aristotle, the great hero of all anti-Platonists, was not an exception. Although Aristotle

did not have, as Plato did, a realm of eternal essences that were "really real" and that guaranteed the primacy of reason, he was by no means inclined to deny this realm.

Thus, while the East has tended to emphasize the direct experience of oneness via intuitive concepts and contemplation, the West has viewed the faculty of the intellect as the primary instrument of worldly mastery. While thinking in the East tends to conclude in more or less vague, imprecise statements with existential flexibility, Western thinking emphasizes clear and distinct ideas by means of categorization and the linear, analytic logic of syllogism. While the Eastern view expresses its drive for growth in spiritual attainment of oneness with the universe, the Western view expresses its drive for growth in material progress and social change.

Time

Closely parallel to the differing perception of the nature of knowledge, the perception and experience of time differs significantly between Eastern and Western traditions.

Along with the immediate, undifferentiated experiencing of here and now, Eastern time orientation can be portrayed as a placid, silent pool within which ripples come and go. Historically the East has tended to view material existence as cyclical and has often characterized worldly existence with the metaphor of a wheel. The "wheel of existence" is continually turning but is not seen as going in any predetermined direction. Although individuals in the world may experience a rise or fall in their personal fortunes, the lot of the whole is felt to be fundamentally unchanging. As Northrop (1946/1966) illustrated, "the aesthetic continuum is the great mother of creation, giving birth to the ineffable beauty of the golden yellows on the mountain landscape as the sun drops low in the late afternoon, only a moment later to receive that differentiation back into itself and to put another in its place without any effort" (p. 343).

Because worldly time is not experienced as going anywhere and because in spiritual time there is nowhere to go but to eternity within the now, the

future is expected to be virtually the same as the past. Recurrence in both cosmic and psychological realms is very much a part of Eastern thought. Thus, the individual's aim is not to escape from the circular movement into linear and profane time, but to become a part of the eternal through the aesthetic experience of here and now and the conscious evolution of spirituality in knowing the all-embracing, undifferentiated wholeness.

Whereas the East traditionally has perceived time as a dynamic wheel with circular movements and the "now" as a reflection of the eternal, the West has represented time either as an arrow or as a moving river that comes out of a distant place and past (not here and now) and goes into an equally distant place and future (also not here and now). In this linear view of time, history is goal-directed and gradually progressing in a certain direction, such as toward universal salvation and the second coming of Christ or, in a secular form, toward an ideal state such as boundless freedom or a classless society.

Closely corresponding to the above comparison of Eastern and Western time orientations is the recent work of anthropologist Edward Hall in his *Beyond Culture* (1976) and *The Dance of Life: The Other Dimension of Time* (1983). Hall considers Asian cultures "polychronic" and Western cultures "monochronic." The polychronic system is less inclined to adhere rigidly to time as a tangible, discrete, and linear entity; it emphasizes completion of transactions here and now, often carrying out more than one activity simultaneously. On the other hand, the monochronic system emphasizes schedules, segmentation, promptness, and standardization of human activities. The traditional Eastern orientation to time depends on the synchronization of human behavior with the rhythms of nature. The Western orientation to time depends on the synchronization of human behavior with the rhythms of clocks or machines.

Communication

The historical ideologies examined so far have made the empirical content of the East and West what they are. Eastern and Western perspectives on the universe, nature, knowledge, and time are reflected in many specific activities of individuals as they relate themselves to fellow human beings—how individuals view "self" and the group and how they use verbal and nonverbal symbols in communication.

First, the view of self and identity cultivated in the Eastern view of reality is embedded within an immutable social order. People tend to acquire their sense of identity from an affiliation with, and participation in, a virtually unchanging social order. The sense of "self" that emerges from this social context is not the strongly differentiated "existential ego" of the West, but a more weakly distinct and unchanging "social ego" as pointed out in many contemporary anthropological studies. Thus, individual members of the family tend to be more willing to submit their own self-interest to that of the family. Individuals and families are often expected to submit their views to those of the community or the state.

Also, the Eastern view accepts hierarchy in social order. In a hierarchical structure, individuals are seen as differing in status although all are equally necessary for the total system and its process. A natural result of this orientation is the emphasis on authority—the authority of the parents over the children, of the grandparents over their descendants, and of the official head of the community, the clan, and the state over all its members. Authoritarianism is a distinct feature of Eastern life, not only in government, business, and family, but also in education and beliefs. The more ancient a tradition, the greater its authority.

Furthermore, the Eastern view asserts that who we are is not limited to our physical existence. Consciousness is seen as the bridge between the finite and differentiated (our sense of uniqueness) and the infinite and undifferentiated (the experience of wholeness and eternity). With sufficient training, each person can discover that who we are is correlated with nature and the divine. All are one and the same in the sense that the divine, undifferentiated, aesthetic continuum of the universe is manifested in us in nature. Through this aesthetic connection, we and nature are no other than the Tao, Ultimate Reality, the divine life force, nirvana, God.

On the other hand, the Western view—in which God, nature, and humans are distinctly differentiated—fosters the development of autonomous individuals with strong ego identification. The dualistic world view is manifested in an individual's view of his or her relationship to other persons and nature. Interpersonal relationships, therefore, are essentially egalitarian—cooperative arrangements between two equal "partners" in which the personal needs and interests of each party are more or less equally respected, negotiated, or "compromised." While the East emphasizes submission (or conformity) of the individual to the group, the West encourages individuality and individual needs to override the group. If the group no longer serves the individual's needs, it—not the individual—must be changed. Thus, the meaning of an interpersonal relationship is decided primarily by what functions each party performs to satisfy the needs of the other. A relationship is considered healthy to the extent that it serves the expected function for all parties involved. As anthropologist Frances Hsu (1981) notes, individualism is a central theme of the Western personality, which distinguishes the Western world from the non-Western.

This functional, pragmatic interpersonal orientation of the West is contrasted with the Eastern tradition—where group membership is a "given" that goes unchallenged—in which individuals must conform to the group in the case of conflicting interest. Members of the group are encouraged to maintain harmony and to minimize competition. Individuality is discouraged while moderation, modesty, and "bending" of one's ego are praised. In some cases, individual and group achievement (in a material sense) must be forsaken to maintain group harmony.

In this social milieu, the primary source of interpersonal understanding is the unwritten and often unspoken norms, values, and ritualized mannerisms relevant to a particular interpersonal context. Rather than relying heavily on verbalized, logical expressions, the Eastern communicator "grasps" the aesthetic "essence" of the communication dynamics by observing the various nonverbal and circumstan-

tial cues. Intuition rather than logical reasoning plays a central role in the Eastern interpersonal understanding of how one talks, how one addresses the other and why, under what circumstances, on what topics, in what varied styles, with what intent, and with what effect. Verbal articulation is less important than nonverbal, contextual sensitivity and appropriateness. Eastern cultures favor verbal hesitance and ambiguity to avoid disturbing or offending others (Doi, 1976; Cathcart & Cathcart, 1976). Silence is often preferred to eloquent verbalization even in expressing strong compliments or affection. Sometimes individuals are suspicious of the genuineness of excessive verbal praise or compliments since, to the Eastern view, true feelings are intuitively apparent and therefore do not need to be, nor can be, articulated. In this sense, the burden of communicating effectively is shared equally between all parties involved.

While interpersonal meaning in the Eastern perspective resides primarily in the subtle, implicit, nonverbal, contextual realm and is understood aesthetically and intuitively, the Western communicative mode is primarily a direct, explicit, verbal realm, relying heavily on logical and rational perception, thinking, and articulation. Communicators are seen as distinct individuals, expressing their individuality through verbal articulation and assertiveness. Feelings inside are not to be intuitively "grasped" and understood, but to be clearly verbalized and discussed. In this sense, the burden of communicating effectively lies primarily in the speaker.

The above characterization of communication patterns in the Eastern and the Western traditions parallels the notion of "high-context" and "low-context" communication proposed by Hall (1976). Hall's conceptualization is based on empirical studies of many cultures, and it focuses on the degree to which information is either embedded in physical context or internalized in the person communicating. In this scheme, a low-context communication—more prevalent in the West than in the East—is when most of the interpersonal information is carried in the explicit, verbalized codes.

A SYNTHESIS

So far, a number of basic dimensions of cultural *a priori* in the Eastern and the Western traditions have been examined. To recapitulate, the many differences between the two civilizations stem fundamentally from their respective premises on the reality of the universe, nature, time, and communication. Based on an organic, holistic, and cyclic perspective, the East has developed an epistemology that emphasizes direct, immediate, and aesthetic components in human nature's experience of the world. The ultimate aim of human learning is to transcend the immediate, differentiated self and to develop an integrative perception of the undifferentiated universe; that is, to be spiritually one with the universe and to find the eternal within the present moment. In this view, the present moment is a reflection of the eternal, and the eternal resides in the present moment.

On the other hand, the West, founded on the cosmology of dualism, determinism, and materialism, encourages an outlook that is rational, analytic, and indirect. History is viewed as a linear progression from the past into the future. The acquisition of knowledge is not so much for spiritual enhancement as for utilization to improve the human condition.

These different world views, in turn, have been reflected in the individual conception of the self, of others, and of the group. While the East has stressed the primacy of the group over the individual, the West has stressed the primacy of the individual over the group. Interpersonally, the Eastern concept of self is less differentiated and more deeply merged in "group ego," while the West encourages distinct and autonomous individuality. Explicit, clear, and logical verbalization has been the most salient feature in the Western communication tradition, compared to the implicit, intuitive, nonverbal messages in the East.

Thus, the mechanistic Western world view has helped to systematically describe and explain the physical phenomena we encounter daily. It has proved extremely successful in technological and scientific development. The West has also learned, however, that the mechanistic world view and the corresponding communication patterns are often inadequate for the subtle, complex phenomena of human relationship—causing alienation from self and others. The West has also learned that its dualistic distinction between humanity and nature has brought about alienation from nature. The analytical mind of the West has led to modern science and technology, but it has also resulted in knowledge that is departmentalized, specialized, fragmented, and detached from the fuller totality of reality.

The East has not experienced the alienation the West has been experiencing in recent centuries. But, at the same time, the East has not developed as much science and technology since its view of the world does not promote material and social development. It does not encourage worldly activism or promote the empowerment of individuals to fundamentally change the social and material circumstances of life. Furthermore, instead of building greater ego strength and the capacity for more self-determining behavior, the Eastern view tends to work toward ego extinction (transcendence). It also tends to encourage ego dependency and passivity since people feel locked into an unchanging social order.

It should be stressed at this point that the Western emphasis on logical, theoretical, dualistic, and analytic thinking does not suggest that it has been devoid of an intuitive, direct, purely empirical, aesthetic element. Similarly, emphasizing the Western contributions (of worldly dynamism and socio-material development) does not suggest that the East has been devoid of learning in these areas. The differences are not in diametric opposition: rather they are differences in emphasis. As a result, the range of sophistication of Western contributions to the sociomaterial process far exceeds the historical learning of the East. Conversely, the aesthetic and holistic view and self-mastery of the East offers a greater depth and range of human experience vis-à-vis other humans, the natural world, and the universe, than the West.

Thus, East and West are not competing views of reality, but are, instead, intensely complementary. It needs to be emphasized that the values, behaviors, and institutions of the West should not be substituted for their Eastern counterparts, and vice versa. The West should no more adopt the world views of the East than the East should adopt the world views of the West. Our task is not to trade one view for another—thereby repeating the excesses of the other—but to integrate. Our task is to find our human unity and simultaneously to express diversity. The purpose of evolution is not to create a homogeneous mass, but to continuously unfold a diverse yet organic whole.

COMPLEMENTARITY

To explore the possibilities of integrating the two cultural traditions in a limited space, we need to take a one-sided perspective by focusing on significant limitations in either of the two and then projecting the complementary aspects from the other. In the following discussion, then, we will look critically at possible limitations of the Western cultural orientation, and attempt to integrate the complementary Eastern cultural insights.

A growing realization of limitations in the Western world view is expressed by many writers. Using the term "extension transference," Hall (1976) points out the danger of the common intellectual maneuver in which the extensional systems—including language, logic, technology, institutions, and scheduling—are confused with or take the place of the process extended. For instance, the tendency in the West is to assume that the remedy for problems with technology should not be the attempt to minimize our reliance on technology, but the development of even more technology. Burke (1974) calls this tendency of extension transference "technologism":

There lie the developments whereby "technologism" confronts its inner contradictions, a whole new realm in which the heights of human rationality, as expressed in industrialism, readily become "solutions" that are but the source of new and aggravated problems (p. 148).

Criticisms have also been directed at the rigid scientific dogmatism that insists on the discovery of "truth" based on mechanistic, linear causality and "objectivity." In this regard, Thayer (1983) comments:

What the scientific mentality attempts to emulate, mainly, is the presumed method of laboratory science. But laboratory science predicts nothing that it does not control or that is not otherwise fully determined. . . . One cannot successfully study relatively open systems with methods that are appropriate only for closed systems. Is it possible that this is the kind of mentality that precludes its own success? (p. 88)

Similarly, Hall (1976) points out that the Western emphasis on logic as synonymous with "truth" denies that part of the human self that integrates. Hall sees logical thinking as only a small fraction of our mental capabilities, and he suggests that there are many different and legitimate ways of thinking that have tended to be less emphasized in Western cultures (p. 9).

The criticisms raised by these and other critics of Western epistemology do not deny the value of rational, inferential knowledge. Instead, they relate to the error in traditional Western philosophy and science, of regarding concepts that do not fit into its mode as not equally valid. It refers to the arrogance or over-confidence of believing that scientific knowledge is the only way to discover "truth," when, in reality, the very process of doing science requires immediate, aesthetic experience of the phenomenon under investigation. Without the immediately apprehended component, the theoretical hypotheses proposed could not be tested empirically with respect to their truth or falsity and, therefore, would lack relevance to the corresponding reality. As Einstein once stated:

Science is the attempt to make the chaotic diversity of our sense-experience correspond to a logically uniform system of thought. In this system single experiences must be correlated with the theoretic structure in such a way that the resulting coordination is complete and convincing (Northrop, 1946/1966, p. 443).

In this description of science, Einstein is careful to indicate that the relation between the theoretically postulated component and the immediately experienced aesthetic component is one of correspondence.

In fact, the wide spectrum of our everyday life activities demands both scientific and aesthetic modes of apprehension: from critical analysis to perception of wholes; from doubt and skepticism to unconditional appreciation; from abstraction to concreteness; from the general and regular to the individual and unique; from the literalism of technological terms to the power and richness of poetic language, silence, and art; from casual acquaintances to intimate personal engagement. If we limit ourselves to the traditional Western scientific mode of apprehension, and if we do not value and practice the Eastern aesthetic mode, we are limiting the essential human to only a part of the full span of life activities.

One potential benefit of incorporating the Eastern aesthetic orientation into Western life is a heightened sense of freedom. As discussed earlier, the aesthetic component of human nature is in part indeterminate, and it is this aesthetic component in us that is the basis of our freedom. We would also transcend the clock-bound worldly time to the Eternal Now, the timeless moment embedded in the center of each moment. By withdrawing into the indeterminate aesthetic component of our nature, away from the determinate, transitory circumstances, we may in part overcome the pressures of everyday events and creatively integrate them as a basis for the renewal of our life spirit. The traditional Eastern practice of meditation is designed primarily for the purpose of moving one's consciousness from the determinate to the indeterminate, freer state.

Second, the Eastern view would bring the West to a heightened awareness of the aliveness of the universe. The universe is engaged in a continuous dance of creation at each instant. Everything is intensely alive—brimming with a silent, clear energy that creates, sustains, and infuses all that exists. With the expanded perspective on time, we would increase our sensitivity to rhythms of nature such as the seasons and the cycles of birth and decay.

Third, the holistic, aesthetic component, in human nature and in the nature of all things, is a factor that pacifies us. Because of its all-embracing oneness and unity, the indeterminate aesthetic continuum also tends to make us compassionate and flexible human beings with intuitive sensitivity—not only for other humans but for all of nature's creatures. In this regard, Maslow (1971) refers to Taoistic receptivity or "let-be" as an important attribute of "self-actualizing" persons:

We may speak of this respectful attention to the matter-in-paradigm as a kind of courtesy or deference (without intrusion of the controlling will) which is akin to "taking it seriously." This amounts to treating it as an end, something per se, with its own right to be, rather than as a means to some end other than itself; i.e., as a tool for some extrinsic purpose (p. 68).

Such aesthetic perception is an instrument of intimate human meeting, a way to bridge the gap between individuals and groups. In dealing with each other aesthetically, we do not subject ourselves to a rigid scheme but do our best in each new situation, listening to the silences as well as to the words of the other, and experiencing the other person or group as a whole living entity without being biased by our own egocentric and ethnocentric demands. A similar attitude can be developed toward the physical world around us, to strengthen our determination to achieve maximum ecological and environmental integrity.

TOWARD INTERCULTURAL PERSONHOOD

The movement from a cultural to an intercultural perspective in our individual and collective consciousness presents one of the most significant and exciting challenges of our time. As Toffler (1980) convincingly documented and articulated in *The Third Wave*, there are numerous indications today that point clearly to the need for us to actively pursue a new personhood and a culture that integrates Eastern and Western world views. Toffler notes:

This new culture—oriented to change and growing diversity—attempts to integrate the new view of nature, of evolution and progress, the new, richer conceptions of time and space, and the fusion of reductionism and wholism with a new causality (p. 309).

Similarly, Gebser's "integral consciousness" (Mickunas, 1973; Feuerstein, 1987) projects an emerging mode of experiencing reality in which "rational," "mythological," and other modes of consciousness are integrated.

If we are to actively participate in this evolutionary process, the dualism inherent in our thinking process, which puts materialism against spiritualism, West against East, must be transcended. The traditional Western emphasis on the intellect and on material progress need not be viewed as "wrong" or "bad." Rather, the Western orientation is a necessary part of an evolutionary stage, out of which yet another birth of higher consciousness—an integration of East and West—might subsequently evolve. We need to acknowledge that both rational and intuitive modes of experiencing life should be cultivated fully. When we realize that both types of concepts are real, ultimate, and meaningful, we also realize that Eastern and Western cultures have given expression to something in part true. The two seemingly incompatible perspectives can be related and reconciled without contradictions in a new, higher-level, intercultural perspective—one that more closely approximates the expression of the whole truth of life.

As Jantsch (1980) observes, "Life, and especially human life, now appears as a process of self-realization" (p. 307). With an openness toward change, a willingness to revise our own cultural premises, and the enthusiasm to work it through, we are on the way to cultivating our fullest human potentialities and to contributing our share in this enormous process of civilizational change. Together, the East and the West are showing each other the way.

REFERENCES

Adler, P. (1982). "Beyond Cultural Identity: Reflections on Cultural and Multicultural Man." In L. Samovar and R. Porter (Eds.), *Intercultural Communication: A Reader*, 3rd ed. Belmont, Calif.: Wadsworth.

Burke, K. (1974). "Communication and the Human Condition." *Communication, 1*, 135–152.

Capra, F. (1975). *The Tao of Physics*. Boulder, Colo.: Shambhala.

Cathcart, D., and Cathcart, R. (1976). "Japanese Social Experience and Concept of Groups." In L. Samovar and R. Porter (Eds.), *Intercultural Communication: A Reader*, 2nd ed. Belmont, Calif.: Wadsworth.

Doi, T. (1976). "The Japanese Patterns of Communication and the Concept of Amae." In L. Samovar and R. Porter (Eds.), *Intercultural Communication: A Reader*, 2nd ed. Belmont, Calif.: Wadsworth.

Elgin, D. (1981). *Voluntary Simplicity*. New York: Bantam Books.

Feuerstein, G. (1987). *Structures of Consciousness: The Genius of Jean Gebser—An Introduction and Critique*. Lower Lake, Calif.: Integral Publishing.

Gudykunst, W., and Kim, Y. (1984). *Communicating with Strangers: An Approach to Intercultural Communication*. Reading, Mass.: Addison-Wesley.

Gulick, S. (1963). *The East and the West*. Rutland, Vt.: Charles E. Tuttle.

Hall, E. (1976). *Beyond Culture*. Garden City, N.Y.: Anchor Press.

Hall, E. (1983). *The Dance of Life: The Other Dimension of Time*. Garden City, N.Y.: Anchor Press.

Hsu, F. (1981). *The Challenges of the American Dream*. Belmont, Calif.: Wadsworth.

Jantsch, E. (1980). *The Self-Organizing Universe*. New York: Pergamon.

Kim, Y. (1982, May). "Becoming Intercultural and Human Development." Paper presented at the annual conference of the International Communication Association, Boston, Mass.

Kim, Y., and Ruben, B. (1988). "Intercultural Transformation: A Systems Theory." In Y. Kim and

W. Gudykunst (Eds.), *Theories in Intercultural Communication*. Newbury Park, Calif.: Sage.

Lutzker, D. (1960). "Internationalism as a Predictor of Cooperative Behavior." *Journal of Conflict Resolution, 4*, 426–430.

Maslow, A. (1971). *The Farther Reaches of Human Nature*. New York: Viking.

Mickunas, A. (1973). "Civilizations as Structures of Consciousness." *Main Currents, 29* (5), 179–185.

Nakamura, H. (1964). *Ways of Thought of Eastern Peoples*. Honolulu: University of Hawaii Press.

Needham, J. (1951). "Human Laws and Laws of Nature in China and the West." *Journal of the History of Ideas*, XII.

Northrop, F. [(1946) 1966]. *The Meeting of the East and the West*. New York: Collier Books.

Oliver, R. (1971). *Communication and Culture in Ancient India and China*. New York: Syracuse University Press.

Suzuki, D. (1968). *The Essence of Buddhism*. Kyoto, Japan: Hozokan.

Thayer, L. (1983). "On 'Doing' Research and 'Explaining' Things." *Journal of Communication, 33* (3), 80–91.

Thompson, W. (1973). *Passages About Earth: An Exploration of the New Planetary Culture*. New York: Harper & Row.

Toffler, A. (1980). *The Third Wave*. New York: Bantam Books.

Walsh, J. (1973). *Intercultural Education in the Community of Man*. Honolulu: University of Hawaii Press.

Wei, A. (1980, March). "Cultural Variations in Perception." Paper presented at the Sixth Annual Third World Conference, Chicago, Ill.

Intercultural Education for Multicultural Societies: Critical Issues

ROSITA D. ALBERT
HARRY C. TRIANDIS

This article focuses on the need for intercultural education in multicultural societies. In the first section, we begin by presenting evidence for the notion that individuals from a given cultural group develop behavior patterns and subjective cultures (Triandis 1972) that are functional for their particular environment. We then indicate that when, due to such factors as immigration, colonization, etc., such individuals are forced to function in a different cultural environment, they are likely to experience stress, alienation, and other negative consequences.

In the second section, we propose that an important objective of education should be to prepare such individuals to function effectively in *both* their culture of origin and in their new culture. We further suggest that all children in a multicultural society should have the benefit of intercultural education. We propose that teachers, as well as pupils, should be made aware of cultural differences and should learn something about the patterns of behavior, values, and expectations of persons from other cultures. We present evidence from our own research, as well as that of other researchers, which illustrates the need for this kind of knowledge on the part of teachers.

From the *International Journal of Intercultural Relations* 9 (1985), 391–397. Reprinted by permission of the publisher and the author. Professor Albert teaches at the University of Minnesota and Professor Triandis teaches at the University of Illinois.

In the third part of the article, we present a number of objections which have been raised to intercultural education and propose some refutations based on current work.

In the fourth section, we present three approaches for teaching culture and discuss the advantages and disadvantages of each. The attributional approach (a cognitive approach) is presented in some detail because it is especially suited for use in educational settings. We cite evidence of its effectiveness from evaluation studies done by ourselves and others.

We conclude with a section on the implications of intercultural education.

ETHNICITY, BEHAVIOR, AND SUBJECTIVE CULTURE

In many countries, the population is polyethnic. This is the case in the United States, where a number of distinct groups (i.e. blacks, Native Americans, Latin Americans, to mention just a few) enjoy cultural traditions that are different from the traditions of the white, Anglo-Saxon or melting-pot-produced majority. A characteristic of any cultural group is that it has a particular way of viewing the social environment, that is, a unique subjective culture (Triandis 1972). Such subjective cultures lead members of a cultural or ethnic group[1] to behave in characteristic ways and to perceive their own behavior and the behaviors of others in a particular manner.

Personality refers to a behavior pattern characteristic of a particular individual. To the extent that ethnic groups have characteristic ways of behaving, they exhibit somewhat different distributions of behavior configurations. Thus, for example, it is widely acknowledged that Latin American individuals tend to be more (overtly) expressive than Anglo-Saxons. An ethnic group, then, may consist of individuals having characteristic behavior patterns and subjective cultures. Behavior patterns comprise patterns of abilities, habits, and predispositions to behave which emerge when individuals interact with their social environments. Subjective cultures can be viewed as consisting of norms, roles, values, and attitudes characteristic of persons in a particular

social environment. An important aspect of subjective culture is the language used by an ethnic group, since language is intimately connected with the way in which experience is interpreted and with the cognitive and affective categories which are used to conceptualize the world (Triandis 1964, 1972).

Most of the elements comprising the behavior patterns and subjective cultures of an ethnic group can be shown to be functional for the particular environment in which that cultural group has existed for a long time. For example, in the Arctic, survival requires the development of skills in hunting. Such hunting is usually done most effectively on an individual basis. Studies (e.g., Barry, Child, and Bacon 1959) of peoples who subsist through hunting and fishing (e.g., Berry 1966) have shown that members of these groups develop a highly differentiated perceptual and cognitive style (see Witkin and Berry 1975, for a review), and a personality that is characterized by independence, self-reliance, little affect, and poor interpersonal skills. On the other hand, agricultural societies such as the Temne (Berry 1966) require group action for survival. Tests administered to such groups indicate that their members develop less differentiated perceptual and cognitive styles, and their personality is characterized by much affect, interdependence, reliance on others, and good interpersonal skills. Persons with a less differentiated, or field-dependent, cognitive style are generally more skillful in interpersonally demanding occupations such as selling or entertaining, whereas persons with a highly differentiated, or field-dependent, cognitive style tend to perform well in such tasks as flying airplanes, taking aerial photographs, and doing mechanical work. Thus the ecology determines subsistence patterns, which in turn contribute to distinctive behavioral patterns.

The fact that many cultural elements are functional implies that individuals who have appropriate behavior patterns and personalities for a particular environment will fare well and will receive positive outcomes in that environment. When individuals from one culture are forced to adopt a very different cultural pattern, however, they are likely to experience high levels of stress, a reduction in positive outcomes, lower self-esteem, anomie, and general demoralization. The high rates of alcohol consumption found among Native American (Jessor, Graves, Hanson, and Jessor 1968), and the high incidence of "eco-system distrust" (distrust of people, things, and institutions in one's environment) experienced by the black ghetto unemployed (Triandis 1976) are examples of behavioral and experiential disorientation which can occur when a group is forced to exist in situations for which its culture is not appropriate.

THE NEED FOR INTERCULTURAL EDUCATION

One of the main purposes of education is to prepare an individual to function effectively in his or her environment. Viewed in this manner, education should provide skills, perspectives, and information, and should help develop attitudes which would enable pupils to obtain more positive outcomes than they would have received otherwise. Individuals who belong to an ethnic group which differs from the majority must often be able to function effectively in *two* different social environments. The degree to which such individuals will be part of each environment will, of course, vary, and will be a function of the interaction of a host of complex factors. It would seem, however, that the education of such children should ideally foster the development of skills, perspectives, and attitudes which would enable them to be effective members of both environments. A good model of how this can be done is that of a fully bilingual person. Such a person is able to switch with ease and without interference from one language to the other (Lambert 1967). His or her linguistic skills are suitable not only for one environment, but also for the other. Thus he or she is able to function linguistically in an effective manner in both environments. In a similar manner, a bicultural person should be able to interact effectively with persons from *both* cultures.

In order to enable children who differ in ethnic background from the majority to do this, it is important that educators and teachers take into account the skills, perspectives, and orientations that these children bring with them to school. Ideally, of course, this should be done for *all* children, and not just for those from a different cultural background. Thus, for example, a child who arrives in school with a field-independent orientation ideally should not be given the same curriculum as a child who arrives with a field-dependent, or field-sensitive, orientation, since for reasons discussed above, a curriculum which emphasizes exposure to many graphic materials would tend to be most helpful to the first child, but not to the second. The latter may well profit more from a curriculum which emphasizes good interpersonal relationships between teachers and students, or group learning as used by Johnson and Johnson (1983).

Ramírez and Castañeda (1974) have argued that our educational system has relied almost exclusively on the use of methods which are appropriate for persons whose cognitive and perceptual style is field-independent. Yet despite intracultural variations, many children from certain cultures (i.e., Mexican-American children) have been found to have a field-dependent or field-sensitive cognitive style. They suggest that to optimize the learning environment of these Mexican-American children, culture-matching teaching strategies, which in this case are field-sensitive strategies, should be utilized as well. Among the strategies that teachers can use, Ramírez and Castañeda mention the following: displaying expressions of approval and warmth, using personalized rewards, expressing confidence in the child's ability to succeed, giving guidance, encouraging cooperation, stressing achievement for the family, eliciting expressions of feelings from the students, emphasizing global aspects of concepts, and encouraging modeling of behaviors. Hale (1982) makes similar suggestions concerning the teaching of black children.

Schools and teachers, then, need to develop diagnostic skills which will lead to different emphases for different pupils. In addition, schools need to utilize culture-sensitization methods to make both teachers and pupils aware of cultural differences to a greater extent than they have so far. Our own research with Latin American or Hispanic pupils and Anglo-American teachers in U.S. schools (Albert 1983b, 1984a, 1984b; Albert and Adamopoulos 1976;

Albert and Triandis 1979) can be used to illustrate the importance of this.

Our objective was to find out if there were significant differences in how Latin American pupils and their Anglo teachers interpreted a wide range of common, naturally occurring school situations and behaviors. Very briefly, the procedure used was the following (see Albert 1983b for a more detailed description): Interviews with samples of teachers ($N = 70$) and pupils ($N = 150$) and detailed observations of classroom interactions were conducted to generate "critical incidents" depicting interactions between a Latin American or Hispanic[2] pupil and an American teacher.

The following is an example of a critical incident or story used in the research:

Mr. Jones was talking with a group of his students about different kinds of food. Some of the Spanish-speaking students started telling him about a dish from their native country, and Mr. Jones mentioned that he had never tasted it. The next day one of those students brought in a plate of the food they had been talking about for Mr. Jones (Albert 1984a, p. 70).

These incidents, or stories, were then presented to new samples of teachers and pupils from each ethnic group. We asked these persons to provide an interpretation of the behaviors and feelings of pupils and teachers in each of the stories. These interpretations, which were given in the respondents' own words and language, were carefully synthesized by a panel of bicultural judges into four alternative interpretations for each story.

The interpretations provided for the above incident were:
Mr. Jones thought that:

1. The student was very nice.

2. The student wanted him to know more about his country.

3. It would be interesting to try it.

4. The student should not have brought the food (Albert 1984a, p. 70).

These alternative interpretations were paired with each other for each story, and samples of Latin American teachers and pupils, and Anglo teachers and pupils, were asked to choose for each pair of interpretations the one that they preferred. These patterns of preference were then analyzed for significant differences between groups of respondents.

It was found (Albert 1983b) that there were significant differences between groups of respondents in 1,158 out of 5,922 comparisons made. This is four times the number of significant differences which could be expected by chance alone. Furthermore, there were one or more significant differences in preferences between groups of respondents in 141 out of 176 stories presented to the respondents. As expected, the greatest number of significant differences occurred between American teachers and Hispanic pupils. Some of the differences found between the two groups can be briefly summarized as follows: Latin American pupils tended to favor more personalized, individualized treatment; tended to place greater emphasis on interpersonal aspects of the situation; tended to blame the Hispanic children in the stories, rather than the teacher, for problems; expressed the view that children in several stories felt ashamed and fearful; and tended to feel that reliance on the family was extremely important. American teachers, on the other hand, tended to emphasize fairness and equality, focused more on task-related aspects rather than on interpersonal aspects of the situation, expressed the feeling that the teachers in the stories were uncomfortable with close interpersonal distances and touching, and tended to favor greater independence for the pupils. These are just some of the differences suggested by the data. There are, of course, many others, but we cannot adequately cover them here. (See Albert 1983b, 1984a, and 1984b for a detailed account of the differences found.)

A few examples may illustrate the relevance of these differences to the education of children of Latin American origin (see Albert and Triandis 1979).

The first example concerns the culturally based expectation on the part of many Hispanic children that their teachers will be as physically expressive and affectionate towards them as adults tend to be in their culture. Young Hispanic children, for example, like to cluster around the teacher's desk and touch her and kiss her goodbye. Many American teachers, being used to a different cultural pattern, are not aware of this need for touching; even if they are, they may not feel comfortable with this degree of physical closeness and may avoid these behaviors. The children, in turn, may experience the teacher's behavior as a rejection and may even come to think of their teacher as cold and distant. The Latin American teachers we have observed often reward a child who gives a correct answer with a hug or by touching him gently and with affection. (These teachers, incidentally, have reported that many Anglo kids like this, too.) Clearly here we are dealing with a cultural difference in paralinguistic behavior that has been described as well by Hall (1959) and documented by Sussman and Rosenfeld (1982).

During the interviews we conducted in the preliminary phase of the research (Albert and Triandis 1979), we were told about an instance in which a Hispanic child who did not speak much English was given a workbook and told by the teacher to work on her English lessons for a while, while the rest of the class worked in groups on a different task. The child felt not only isolated, but rejected by the teacher as well. In this particular case the teacher probably intended to help her learn English in the most effective way, but due to both a greater need for personal attention and the more communal nature of her culture, the child experienced the situation in a very negative way.

It is interesting to note that in a number of these situations the teacher is actually doing something which he or she feels is most efficient for teaching purposes (such as, for example, dealing with the class as a whole rather than with each child individually). Because of culturally based differences in expectations and interpretation of behavior, however, some of these actions turn out to have a negative impact on Hispanic children. In fact, in many situations Hispanic children do come to feel that their teacher dislikes them personally, or at least dislikes

Hispanic children. This feeling obviously has a detrimental effect on the child's motivation and is counter-productive for the teachers.

Teachers can help avoid this vicious circle by being aware of the children's culturally based expectations and by providing them, whenever possible, with the kind of personal attention that they need, or by finding other ways of dealing effectively with the problem. At the same time, of course, Hispanic children can be taught that their teachers behave as they do because they have different ways of doing things and not because they do not like them. These students can also be made aware that the teachers do not always have the time to provide individualized attention. (See Albert 1984a and 1984b for examples of one approach to sensitizing Anglo teachers to the perspectives of their Hispanic pupils and vice versa.)

Yet another perspective is provided by a situation in which white middle-class teachers interact with black ghetto children whose parents are unemployed. The parents of such children are likely to view the world with great distrust (Triandis 1976). The establishment, in particular, is distrusted and is often seen as exploitative. Consequently, persons who have "succeeded," such as teachers, are seen as exploitative agents of that establishment. Under these conditions it is not particularly surprising if the children of such parents view the teacher's behavior with considerable skepticism, if not with outright hostility.

Almost any behavior, no matter how positive, can be misinterpreted if the perceiver is strongly inclined to make hostile attributions. For example, if the teacher offers help, this could be viewed as the result of orders received from above and not really as a result of the teacher's good will. Alternatively, the teacher's behavior could be interpreted as ingratiation, the aim of which is to extract valuable information from the students. In short, given a negative perceptual framework on the part of the children, almost any action of the teacher could be seen as a hostile or, at best, a neutral behavior. Conversely, a teacher who is racially prejudiced could interpret any positive behavior of a pupil in a really negative manner. These conditions are obviously ripe for hostility and conflict, no matter how positive the behavior of the actors. In order to extricate teachers and pupils from such a vicious circle, it is necessary to break the perceiver's habit of automatically giving negative interpretations to the behavior of the other person.

The above examples suggest that intercultural education is necessary not only for students from diverse ethnic groups, but also for their teachers. In the course of interviewing teachers for our research, we found that many of these teachers failed to realize that cultural differences do exist and that they probably exert a powerful influence on their own, as well as on their pupils', behaviors. Some teachers, for example, would proffer the view that all children are alike. Others would attribute most, if not all, of the behavior patterns found among Hispanic children to their low socioeconomic status (SES). There is no question that low SES does contribute in important ways to certain behavior patterns. Yet it is also clear from our own research (where the socioeconomic status of the Hispanic pupils in our sample was the same as that of Anglo pupils), as well as from research conducted by other investigators (e.g., Díaz-Guerrero 1975), that cultural factors beyond socioeconomic status affect behavior patterns of members of a group in very important ways.

Albert (1979) has noted, in a different context, that this failure to perceive, or at any rate, to acknowledge, cultural differences has important historical, psychological, and cultural bases. She has identified a number of factors which may contribute to the relative lack of concern with cultural variables on the part of American investigators. These may well apply, perhaps in modified form, to American educators. They are the following: lack of direct experience with other cultures; a psychological need to simplify events, and hence to assume cross-cultural similarities; the realization that differences in test performance can be, and have been, used to discriminate against minority groups; an egalitarian ideology that postulates that teachers should treat every child in the same general manner; the fear of

creating stereotypes; the historical experience of forging a nation out of a multitude of ethnic groups; the dominant economic and political position of the United States in the world; and ethnocentric tendencies which lead us to assume that our patterns of behavior are universal.

Teachers, then, need to develop skills which will enable them to attend to ethnic group *and* individual differences in their students, so that they can understand, and effectively reach, these students. This requires not only a variety of skills, but also flexibility and sensitivity to the cultural background of the students.

Pupils from other ethnic backgrounds need to learn a variety of skills, ideas, and principles which would enable them to function more effectively in both their own and the dominant culture. Thus an understanding of their own culture as well as of the dominant culture would seem to be vitally important for these students.

OBJECTIONS FREQUENTLY RAISED TO INTERCULTURAL EDUCATION

Having argued for the need for intercultural education, we can reasonably ask whether such education should be provided by our schools, or whether it should be left to other institutions.

For a variety of reasons, the school seems to be the most appropriate setting for intercultural education efforts. A school is often the first institution of the dominant culture which children from a minority group encounter. Their experiences in this setting are, therefore, critical to their subsequent attitudes and feelings about the dominant society. Similarly, it is often in this setting that children from the dominant culture have their first exposure to members of other ethnic and cultural groups. Schools are charged with the function of "educating" students, of teaching them about the physical and social world, as well as giving them some basic skills for functioning as members of society. Thus, while an understanding of different cultural patterns would seem critical for the minority child, it would also seem important and valuable for majority children in a multiethnic society.

A number of objections to the ideas presented here can be anticipated. Some will argue that with limited resources we cannot afford the luxury of multicultural education. The issue of cost is a complicated one, for no one knows how much money various kinds of intercultural education programs would require. Yet there is evidence that minorities drop out from school at higher rates than majority students. To cite but one example, Lucas (1971) found a 70 percent drop-out rate among Puerto Ricans in Chicago. It is well known that dropping out of school lowers a person's earning potential and may be related to higher rates of unemployment and, possibly, to higher rates of welfare payments. Thus the loss of income which results to the minority person who drops out of school, as well as society's loss of well qualified employees, and of the taxes which such employees could contribute—not to mention the human costs—should be entered into the cost equation.

In any case, there is clearly a need for making teachers aware of cultural differences through teacher in-service and pre-service training and by other means as well. Also, many of our schools already have pupils from many cultures and could utilize them as sources of information about other cultures without spending very much money. Either approach would require educational innovations and some effort on the part of teachers and administrators. It seems to us that in a society that spends over $100 billion a year on armaments that become obsolete every few years, there must be mechanisms to accomplish other kinds of goals as well. The crucial question, then, is whether we are willing to spend time, money, and above all, effort, to improve the quality of education in our society.

Another objection is centered around the argument that mainstream culture is "obviously best." This is an ethnocentric argument. As we have discussed previously, a culture produces a particular pattern of assumptions about the way the world is structured. That pattern often appears to be correct to the members of that culture, and the less informa-

tion they have available concerning other patterns, the more totally correct that pattern will appear to be. Ethnocentrism (see LeVine and Campbell 1972) tends to be characteristic of persons who have been exposed to little diverse information and to child-rearing practices which did not allow them to learn about value systems which differ from those of their parents. An ethnocentric person usually considers his or her culture completely correct, better in all respects than other cultures, and obviously suitable for adoption by all others. Yet, as we have previously discussed, there is evidence that forcing members of an ethnic group to adopt the dominant cultural pattern may *not* be the best for these individuals.

Still others may see providing intercultural education as "coddling" some minorities, since in the past other ethnic groups "adjusted" without such help. The implication which underlies this argument is that such "coddling" may be unhealthy and/or unnecessary. But the discussion presented earlier suggests that for the minority child this may not be the case. In fact, the minority child needs to develop multiple skills in order to function effectively in his or her own environment and also in the environment of the majority.

The case can be made that majority children will also profit from the broad perspectives and the greater cognitive flexibility that are likely to come from intercultural education (Triandis 1976). There is already evidence that multilingual individuals are more creative than their monolingual counterparts (Segalowitz 1981). It is quite likely that *multicultural* individuals will be even more creative. Intercultural education would also probably help children develop a greater appreciation for diversity. In addition, this country is deficient in language skills (United States President's Commission on Foreign Language and International Studies 1979) and mainstream children exposed to other cultures may develop an interest in learning foreign languages.

Finally, some will argue that this is not compatible with American values. This argument is based on historical and cultural assumptions which have been alluded to above. Yet, if there is something unique about this society it is that it permits enough freedom for individuals to actualize their potential in unique ways. The imposition of a particular, limited, ethnocentric perspective limits these freedoms. Hence, it is fundamentally compatible with the American way to move toward multiculturalism and, therefore, toward intercultural education.

METHODS FOR TEACHING CULTURE IN INTERCULTURAL EDUCATION PROGRAMS

Supposing we wish to provide intercultural education in our schools, the question which arises next is how to do it. We will discuss several ways in which culture has been taught and will point out some of the advantages and disadvantages of each. A broad review of procedures which have been developed for intercultural training can be found in Brislin and Pederson (1976), Landis and Brislin (1983), and Seelye (1975). The three procedures we present below seem to be the most promising. The theoretical underpinnings of these three procedures rest on analyses of social behavior (Triandis 1975, 1977).

The first method is *experiential*. At its best it would entail having the student live in a particular culture for many years. This, however, is not a feasible way to teach a large number of students. Thus, experiential exposure to other cultures utilizing "controlled" or laboratory situations (e.g., setting up a village where trainees interact with their language teachers from the other culture over a period of months) . . . [is] used by some culture-trainers (Trifonovitch 1973). Other experiential activities which can more easily be employed by schools involve tasting foods from different countries, going to ethnic neighborhoods, and participating in relevant parades and festivals.

A second method for teaching culture is *behavioral* (David 1972). This method would entail reinforcing the individual for producing behavioral patterns which are commonly found in another culture, and discouraging behaviors which are inappropriate to that other culture. This approach would probably be most effective when what is desired is a modification of behaviors which are

primarily determined by habits. This method is time-consuming, however, since it requires that each behavior be reinforced. Furthermore, it may be contended that in settings such as schools, where persons from several cultural backgrounds interact, the aim should not be to change behaviors per se, but rather to teach individuals *about* another culture. Since the focus of this approach is changing specific behaviors (e.g., always shaking hands when meeting a person from the other culture), it does not necessarily result in increased knowledge or understanding of diverse aspects of the other culture.

A third method of teaching culture emphasizes *informational* aspects of learning. One way to provide information about another culture is to assign readings about other peoples' customs or history. This alone, however, does not usually teach a person to "see the world" from the perspective of members of the other culture. A special technique designed to do this has been recently derived from social psychological theorizing (Fiedler, Mitchell, and Triandis 1971; Heider 1958; Triandis 1975). This technique, called *attribution training*, aims to teach members of one culture to make attributions commonly made by members of another culture (Triandis 1975). Attributions are *interpretations* of behavior; that is, they are inferences about the cause of a given behavior. Thus teachers commonly make attributions about the causes of their pupils' behaviors. For example, when a pupil performs poorly on a test the teacher will tend to make attributions about the child's performance. The teacher may attribute the poor performance to the pupil's lack of ability, to lack of preparation, to his or her "laziness," to lack of time on the test, or to a myriad of other factors. Pupils similarly make attributions about the actions of their teachers. Attributions are dependent on the norms, role, affects, and consequences of actions seen to be operating in a given situation (Triandis 1975). For this reason, persons from different cultures may make different attributions to the *same* behavior.

When teachers and students come from different cultural backgrounds, they are likely to have some different expectations about what behaviors are appropriate in a given situation and, at least some of the time, they are likely to make different attributions about the same behavior. Misunderstandings can then occur which impede effective interaction between the teacher and the students. It must be noted that people are often not aware of the cause for their difficulty. Thus, for example, a Hispanic student may be doing something "perfectly normal" from his perspective when he spends some time after recess helping a friend look for his lost braces. Consequently, he may be genuinely surprised when his American teacher reacts with anger when he arrives in class ten minutes late.

Attribution training is a technique designed to teach persons from one culture to interpret events as persons from another culture do. It consists of a programmed learning approach in which a person is exposed to an instrument known in the literature as the "intercultural sensitizer" (ICS) or "culture assimilator" (Albert 1983a; Albert and Adamopoulos 1976). The assimilator is an instrument for culture learning which consists of several dozen short episodes depicting a problematic interaction between persons from one culture and persons from another culture. Each episode is followed by several alternative attributions to the behavior of one of the characters in the episode. Some of the attributions provided are those which are typically made by persons from the individual's own culture, while others are attributions commonly made by persons from the other culture. The aim of the training is to teach the individual to choose the attribution typically made by members of the other culture, and thus to expand the trainee's conception of possible attributions in that situation.

At first, the individual will have difficulty doing this, and will select attributions which are made by members of his own culture. With the aid of the feedback which is provided after each choice, the individual gradually learns to select the attributions which tend to be more typical of the members of the other culture. When the individual does this, he is given additional information about the differences between the two cultures. (See Albert 1983a for details about the process of constructing "intercultural sensitizers.")

SOME IMPLICATIONS OF INTERCULTURAL EDUCATION

Providing intercultural education is one way that schools can add flexibility and richness to each child's experience, and can teach the child that there are many ways of behaving and of perceiving the world. Such an approach could help teachers develop a new appreciation for students from diverse backgrounds, seeing their differences as resources to be explored rather than as sources of difficulty to overcome. As a result of a greater awareness of their students' backgrounds, teachers may develop new modes of teaching which may enhance their effectiveness with particular pupils.

Intercultural education could help children who belong to different ethnic groups to explore and to deal more explicitly with the difficult issue of identity, since such children would learn about their culture of origin as well as about the dominant culture of the society in which they live.

From their inception, the mission of many systems of education has been not only to provide skills and impart information, but also to provide understanding of the society in which the pupils live. Intercultural education would naturally enhance this broader mission.

NOTES

1. We will use the terms interchangeably following Glazer and Moynihan. Glazer, N., and D. P. Moynihan, (1975) "Introduction." In N. Glazer and D. P. Moynihan (eds.), *Ethnicity: Theory and Experience*. Cambridge, MA: Harvard University Press.

2. We use the terms *Latin American* and *Hispanic* interchangeably, as our samples consisted of immigrant children from Mexico, Puerto Rico, Cuba, and a number of other Latin American countries.

REFERENCES

Albert, R. D. (September 1979). "The Place of Culture in Modern Social Psychology." Paper presented at the meeting of the American Psychological Association, New York City.

Albert, R. D. (1983). "Mexican American Children in Educational Settings: Research on Children's and Teachers' Perceptions and Interpretations of Behavior." In E. E. García (ed.), *The Mexican American Child: Language, Cognition, and Social Development* (pp. 183–194). Tempe, AZ: Arizona State University.

Albert, R. D. and J. Adamopoulos. (1976). "An Attributional Approach to Culture Learning: The Culture Assimilator." *Topics in Culture Learning* 4, 53–60.

Albert, R. D. and H. C. Triandis. (1979). "Cross-Cultural Learning: A Theoretical Framework and Some Observations." In H. Trueba and C. Barnett-Mizrahi (eds.), *Bilingual Multicultural Education and the Professional: From Theory to Practice* (pp. 181–194). Rowley, MA: Newbury House.

Barry, H., I. Child, and M. Bacon. (1959). "Relation of Child Training to Sustenance Economy." *American Anthropologist* 61, 51–63.

Berry, J. W. (1966). "Temne and Eskimo Perceptual Skills." *International Journal of Psychology* 1, 207–229.

David, K. H. (1972). *Intercultural Adjustment and Application of Reinforcement Theory to Problems of Culture Shock*. Hilo, HI: Center for Cross-Cultural Training.

Díaz-Guerrero, R. (1975). *The Psychology of the Mexican*. Austin: University of Texas Press.

Hale, J. E. (1982). *Black Children: Their Roots, Culture, and Learning Styles*. Provo, UT: Brigham Young University Press.

Hall, E. T. (1959). *The Silent Language*. New York: Doubleday.

Heider, F. (1958). *The Psychology of Interpersonal Behavior*. New York: Wiley.

Jessor, R., T. D. Graves, R. G. Hanson, and S. L. Jessor. (1968). *Society, Personality, and Deviant Behavior*. New York: Holt, Rinehart & Winston.

Johnson, D. W. and R. T. Johnson. (1983). "The Socialization and Achievement Crises: Are Cooperative Learning Experiences the Solution?" In L. Bickman (ed.), *Applied Social Psychology Annual* 4 (pp. 119–164). Newbury Park, Calif.: Sage Publications.

Lambert, W. E. (1967). "The Social Psychology of Bilingualism." *Journal of Social Issues* 23, 91–109.

Landis, D. and R. Brislin. (1983). *Handbook of Intercultural Training*. New York: Pergamon Press.

LeVine, R. A. and D. T. Campbell. (1972). *Ethnocentrism: Theories of Conflict, Ethnic Attitudes, and Group Behavior*. New York: Wiley.

Lucas, I. (1971). *Puerto Rican Dropouts in Chicago: Numbers and Motivation*. Chicago: Council on Urban Education.

Ramírez, M. and A. Castañeda. (1974). *Cultural Democracy, Bicognitive Development, and Education*. New York: Academic Press.

Seelye, H. N. (1975). *Teaching Culture*. Skokie, IL: National Textbook Company, in conjunction with the American Council on the Teaching of Foreign Languages.

Segalowitz, N. (1981). "Issues in the Cross-Cultural Study of Bilingual Development." In H. C. Triandis and A. Hernon (eds.), *Handbook of Cross-Cultural Psychology* (Vol. 4) (pp. 55–92). Boston: Allyn and Bacon.

Sussman, N. M. and H. M. Rosenfeld. (1982). "Influence of Culture, Language, and Sex on Conversational Distance." *Journal of Personality and Social Psychology* 42, 66–74.

Triandis, H. C. (1964). "Cultural Influences upon Cognitive Processes." In L. Berkowitz (ed.), *Advances in Experimental Social Psychology* (pp. 1–48). New York: Academic Press.

Triandis, H. C. (1972). *The Analysis of Subjective Culture*. New York: Wiley.

Triandis, H. C. (1975). "Training, Cognitive Complexity, and Interpersonal Attitudes." In R. W. Brislin, S. Bochner, and W. Lonner (eds.), *Cross-Cultural Perspectives on Learning* (pp. 39–77). New York: Halsted/Wiley/Sage.

Triandis, H. C. (1976). *Variations of Black and White Perceptions of the Social Environment*. Champaign, IL: University of Illinois Press.

Triandis, H. C. (1977). *Interpersonal Behavior*. Monterey, CA: Brooks/Cole.

Trifonovitch, G. (1973). "On Cross-Cultural Orientation Techniques." *Topics in Culture Learning* 1, 38–47.

United States President's Commission on Language and International Studies. (1979). *Strength through Wisdom: A Critique of U.S. Capability.* Washington, DC: U.S. Government Printing Office.

Witkin, H. A. and J. W. Berry. (1975). "Psychological Differentiation in Cross-Cultural Perspectives." *Journal of Cross-Cultural Psychology* 6, 4–87.

Ethics in Intercultural Communication

DAVID W. KALE

A Ford Foundation executive with over twenty years experience in overseas travel has been quoted as saying that "most problems in cross-cultural projects come from different ideas about right and wrong" (Howell, 1981, p. 3). This executive's statement refers to two problem areas involving diversity in cultural values, areas which have caused a great deal of difficulty in intercultural communication.

The first type of problem arises when people do something that is completely acceptable in their own country but unknowingly offends the people of the culture they are visiting. As an example, this problem arose when a group of students visited Guyana in South America. In that warm climate, the students wore the same shorts they would have worn at home, but the Guyanese were offended by what they perceived to be skimpy clothing, particularly when worn by women.

The second problem that often arises in intercultural situations is due to ethnocentric cultural value differences and occurs when we attempt to influence the rest of the world to live according to our culture's ideas about what is right and wrong. We become rather upset when people from another culture tell *us* how to behave. We like to believe that

The author wishes to thank Angela Latham-Jones for her critical comments of an earlier version of this paper. This essay was prepared especially for this volume. All rights reserved. Permission to reprint must be obtained from the publisher and the author. David W. Kale teaches at Olivet Nazarene University, Kankakee, Illinois.

the way our culture chooses to do things is the right way, and we do not appreciate people of other cultures telling us we are wrong.

Both of the above problems have a bearing on the topic of ethics in intercultural communication. Discussing this topic causes stress to people of all cultures. Bonhoeffer (1965) suggests this is so because we get the feeling that the basic issues of life are being addressed, and when that happens some of our most cherished beliefs may be challenged. When our cultural beliefs about right and wrong are threatened, the very foundation of our lives may be under attack. Although such a discussion may be threatening, it must be undertaken nonetheless. With contact among people of various cultures rapidly on the rise, an increase in the number of conflicts over matters of right and wrong is inevitable.

This article will address the ethics of intercultural communication by (1) developing a definition of communication ethics, (2) discussing cultural relativity versus universal ethics, (3) developing and discussing the concept of spirit as a basis for intercultural ethics, (4) developing and discussing peace as the fundamental value in intercultural ethics, and (5) posing four principles as a code of ethics for intercultural communication.

DEFINING COMMUNICATION ETHICS

Johannesen (1978) has said that we are dealing with an ethical issue in human communication when "people voluntarily choose a communication strategy; the communication strategy is based on a value judgment; the value judgment is about right and wrong in human conduct, and the strategy chosen could positively or negatively affect someone else" (pp. 11–12). It is important to note that in this definition values are the basis for communication ethics. For example, we place a value on truth and, therefore, it is unethical to lie to another person. Without a basis in values, there can be no ethical system whatsoever.

Our society faces a major problem because many people think they can decide right and wrong for themselves with no regard for what others think.

Such a mind-set shows that these people really do not understand ethics. If they did, they would realize that ethics are based on values and values are culturally determined. Thus, there cannot be such a thing as an entirely individual system of ethics. Such an approach would eventually result in the total destruction of human society (Weaver, 1971; Hauerwas, 1983).

Within a culture there is a continual dialogue about those things that are the most meaningful and important to the people of that culture. As a result, cultures are continually in a state of change, and when a culture changes, so does that culture's values. We must acknowledge that there is not a fixed order of values that exist within a given culture (Brummett, 1981, p. 293). This does not mean, however, that we are free to determine right and wrong for ourselves. It is much more accurate to say that we are shaped by the values of our culture than to say that we shape the values of our culture (Hauerwas, 1983, p. 3).

CULTURAL RELATIVITY VERSUS UNIVERSAL ETHICS

The fact that values on which our ethics are built are generated by dialogue within our culture begs the question: Should a person of one culture question the conduct of a person in another culture? The concept of cultural relativity suggests that the answer to this question is generally "No."

Cultural relativity suggests that a culture will develop the values it deems best for the people of that culture. These values are dependent on the context in which the people of that culture work, raise their children, and run their societies. People from different contexts will develop different sets of cultural values and, therefore, have no basis on which to judge the conduct of people in any culture other than their own.

There are few who would be willing to follow strictly the concept of cultural relativity. To do so would suggest that it was proper for Hitler to murder six million innocent people since the German people did nothing to stop it (Jaska and Pritchard, 1988). At the same time, however, few are willing to support the idea that people of all cultures must abide by the same code of ethics. We know that cultures develop different value systems and, thus, must have different ethical codes.

Both Brummett (1981) and Hauerwas (1983) have argued that since values are derived through dialogue, there is nothing wrong with attempting to persuade people of other cultures to accept our values. Before we do that, however, we must be convinced that our values are worthy and not based on limited self-interest. We must also be willing to work for genuine dialogue since so often these discussions tend to become monologues. We are generally far more willing to present the case for our own value system than we are to consider carefully the arguments for those of other cultures.

Currently, people of many cultures are attempting to get the people of Brazil to stop cutting down their rain forests. As long as these persuasive efforts are based on a genuine concern for the negative effect cutting these trees may have on the global climate, there is nothing unethical about them. As a reciprocal act, however, we also must be willing to understand what is motivating the Brazilian behavior and accept some responsibility for helping them solve the serious economic problems their country is facing.

SPIRIT AS THE BASIS FOR ETHICAL UNIVERSALS

If we are truly concerned about how we are to make ethical decisions in intercultural communication, we need a concept upon which we can base a universal code of ethics. This concept is that of the human spirit (Eubanks, 1980), and it is well spelled out by Vivas (1963):

The person deserves unqualified respect because he (or she) is not merely psyche but also spirit, and spirit is, as far as we know, the highest form of being. It is through the human spirit that the world is able to achieve cognizance of its status as creature, to perceive its character as valuable, and through human efforts to fulfill a destiny which it freely accepts (p. 235).

It is this human spirit, which people of all cultures have in common, that serves as a basis for the statement that there are some universal values on which we can build a universal code of ethics in intercultural communication.

We have watched dramatic changes take place in the world as people in Eastern Europe, Panama, and the Philippines have attempted to improve the quality of life for themselves and their offspring. We can identify with their efforts because we have a human spirit that is the same regardless of cultural background.

It is this spirit that makes the person a valuing being in the first place. It is from this spirit that the human derives the ability to make decisions about right and wrong, to decide what makes life worth living, and then to make life the best it can possibly be. The guiding principle of any universal code of intercultural communication, therefore, should be to protect the worth and dignity of the human spirit.

PEACE AS THE FUNDAMENTAL HUMAN VALUE

There is a strong temptation for those of us in Western democracies to identify freedom of choice as *the* fundamental human value. Hauerwas (1983) has convincingly argued that freedom of choice is not an achievable goal for human endeavor. A goal that is possible to achieve, however, is the direction of our efforts toward creating a world where people of all cultures live at peace with one another.

The Soviet republics of Armenia and Azerbaijan are currently locked in a bitter ethnic conflict over a territory within the Republic of Azerbaijan that is populated mostly by Armenians. Since the territory is in their republic, the people of Azerbaijan say they should control it. Since the territory is populated largely by Armenians, the Armenians say they should have control over it. Both groups cannot have freedom of choice in this situation, but they may live in peace if they are willing to submit to reasonable dialogue on their differences.

The concept of peace applies not only to relations between cultures and countries but also to the right of all people to live at peace with themselves and their surroundings. As such, it is unethical to communicate with people in a way that does violence to their concept of themselves or to the dignity and worth of their human spirit.

A UNIVERSAL CODE OF ETHICS IN INTERCULTURAL COMMUNICATION

Before presenting the ethical code itself, a preamble is in order. This is based on Howell's (1982) suggestion that the first step to being ethical in any culture is the intent to do what one knows is right. All societies set out rules of ethical conduct for people to follow based on cultural values. The foundation of ethical behavior is that people intend to do what they know is right. To choose to do otherwise is unethical in any culture.

The code of ethics for intercultural communication is presented in the form of four principles. These principles and a discussion of each is set forth below.

Principle Number One

Ethical communicators address people of other cultures with the same respect that they would like to receive themselves. It is from this principle that ethnic jokes are unethical. Some people may argue that ethnic jokes are harmless in that they are "just in fun," but no one wants to be on the receiving end of a joke in which their own culture is demeaned by people of another culture (LaFave and Mannell, 1978).

The unethical violence found here is, of course, not physical in nature. Verbal and psychological abuse, however, can damage the human spirit in the same way that physical abuse damages the body. Verbal and psychological violence against another person, or that person's culture, is therefore just as unacceptable as physical violence. People of all cultures are entitled to live at peace with themselves and the cultural heritage that has had a part in shaping them. It is, therefore, unethical to use our verbal and/or nonverbal communication to demean or belittle the cultural identity of others.

Principle Number Two

Ethical communicators seek to describe the world as they perceive it as accurately as possible. While in our culture we might call this telling the truth, what is perceived to be the truth can vary greatly from one culture to another. We know that reality is not objectively the same for people of all cultures. Reality is socially constructed for us by our culture; we live in different perceptual worlds (Kale, 1983).

The point here is that ethical communicators do not deliberately set out to deceive or mislead, especially since deception is very damaging to the ability of people from various cultures to trust one another. It is only when people of the world are able to trust one another that they will be able to live in peace. That trust is only possible when the communication occurring between those cultures is devoid of deliberate attempts to mislead and to deceive (Hauerwas, 1983; Bok, 1978).

Principle Number Three

Ethical communicators encourage people of other cultures to express themselves in their uniqueness. This principle is reflected in Article 19 of the Universal Declaration of Human Rights as adopted by the United Nations. It states:

Everyone has the right to freedom of opinion and expression; this right includes the freedom to hold opinions without interferences and to seek, receive, and impart information and ideas through any media and regardless of frontiers (Babbili, 1983, p. 9).

In his book, *I and Thou*, Buber (1965) cogently discusses the need to allow the uniqueness of the other to emerge if genuine dialogue is to take place. Frequently, we place demands on people of other cultures to adopt our beliefs or values before we accept the others as full partners in our dialogue.

Ethical communicators place a high value on the right of cultures to be full partners in the international dialogue, regardless of how popular or unpopular their political ideas may be. It is both unethical and the height of ethnocentrism to accord people of another culture equal status in the international arena only if they choose to express themselves in the same way we do.

In Central Europe, we celebrate the fact that people of several countries are finally being allowed to express themselves by throwing off the hold of communist ideology that has been imposed on them by forces outside their culture. Yet is it the right of the United States government to demand that Nicaragua elect a noncommunist government before that country is granted full partnership in the intercultural dialogue of this hemisphere? It is certainly possible that the people of that country might elect a communist government, and if they do, they are still entitled to equal status with the other governments of Central America.

Principle Number Four

Ethical communicators strive for identification with people of other cultures. Identification has been achieved when people share some principles in common, which they can do while still retaining the uniqueness of their cultural identities (Burke, 1969). This principle suggests that ethical communicators encourage people of all cultures to understand each other, striving for unity of spirit, by emphasizing the commonalities among cultural beliefs and values, rather than their differences.

At the present time, we are, unfortunately, seeing an increasing number of racial incidents occurring on our college and university campuses. Many times these take the form of racist slogans appearing on the walls of campus buildings. The purpose of these actions is often to stir up racial animosity, creating wider division among the ethnic and racial groups. Such behavior is unethical according to this principle in that it is far more likely to lead to conflict than it is to peace.

SUMMARY

It has been the purpose of this article to argue for the existence of a set of principles that form the groundwork for the making of ethical judgments across cultures. This is based upon the position that the recent arguments by Brummett (1981) that allow for the retention of ethical relativism while at the same time making ethical judgments across cultural boundaries are in fact arguments that can be used for the defense of ethical universalism rather than ethical relativism. The article then offered four principles to make our communicative efforts aspire to the protection of the human spirit.

REFERENCES

Babbili, Anantha S. (1983). "The Problem of International Discourse: Search for Cultural, Moral and Ethical Imperatives." Paper presented at the convention of the Association for Education in Journalism and Mass Communication, Corvallis, Oregon.

Bok, Sissela (1978). *Lying: Moral Choice in Public and Private Life*. New York: Random House.

Bonhoeffer, Dietrich (1965). *Ethics*. New York: Macmillan.

Brummett, Barry (1981). "A Defense of Ethical Relativism as Rhetorically Grounded," *Western Journal of Speech Communication, 45*, 286–298.

Buber, Martin (1965). *I and Thou*. New York: Peter Smith.

Burke, Kenneth (1969). *A Rhetoric of Motives*. Berkeley: University of California Press.

Eubanks, Ralph (1980). "Reflections on the Moral Dimension of Communication," *Southern Speech Communication Journal, 45*, 240–248.

Hauerwas, Stanley (1983). *The Peaceable Kingdom*. South Bend, Ind.: University of Notre Dame Press.

Howell, William (1981). "Ethics of Intercultural Communication." Paper presented at the 67th convention of the Speech Communication Association, Anaheim, California.

Howell, William (1982). "Carrying Ethical Concepts Across Cultural Boundaries." Paper presented at the 68th convention of the Speech Communication Association, Louisville, Kentucky.

Jaska, James and Pritchard, Michael (1988). *Communication Ethics: Methods of Analysis*. Belmont, Calif.: Wadsworth.

Johannesen, Richard (1978). *Ethics in Human Communication*. Wayne, N.J.: Avery.

Kale, David (1983). "In Defense of Two Ethical Universals in Intercultural Communication," *Religious Communication Today, 6*, 28–33.

LaFave, Lawrence and Mannell, Roger (1978). "Does Ethnic Humor Serve Prejudice?" *Journal of Communication*, Summer, 116–124.

Vivas, Eliseo (1963). *The Moral Life and the Ethical Life*. Chicago: Henry Regnery.

Weaver, Richard (1971). *Ideas Have Consequences*. Chicago: University of Chicago Press.

CONCEPTS AND QUESTIONS FOR CHAPTER 8

1. What do you see as most necessary for the improvement of intercultural communication during the next decade?

2. How can intercultural communication be improved domestically? Internationally? Is one form more important than the other? Why?

3. Given all the complexities associated with intercultural communication, do you think there is really any hope for the future?

4. From Hatch's article on the evaluation of culture, what have you discovered that will permit you to evaluate your own culture?

5. What does Hatch mean when he differentiates between ethnocentric and humanistic values? Which are best in your opinion? Why?

6. What are the important ethical questions that communicators must ask themselves as they engage in intercultural communication?

7. What does Kim mean when she refers to a holistic approach to knowledge in the East and how does this approach differ from Western tradition?

8. Explain how Kim views Eastern and Western views of reality as complementary rather than competitive.

9. How do you believe the educational needs of a multicultural society can best be met?

10. What do Albert and Triandis suggest as the best way to achieve intercultural education?

11. Do you see a future where people of different cultures come closer together or one where they become increasingly isolated from each other? Why?

12. Why does Kale believe that ethnocentric behavior is such a serious problem in intercultural communication?

13. How can we persuade people to accept our values because they are not based on self-interest? Can there even be persuasion without self-interest?

14. Can you offer an ethical position that goes beyond the ones offered in this chapter? What is it?

15. Is it possible in this age of international contact to have a philosophy based on "live and let live"?

Epilogue

We introduced the topic of intercultural communication by pointing out both its boundaries and its territory. By looking at what intercultural communication is and is not, we were able to establish some guidelines for our investigation. In general terms, we suggested that intercultural communication occurs whenever a message sender is a member of one culture and a message receiver is of another culture. Once this broad definition was presented we were able to survey some specific refinements. We noted that culture is the sum total of the learned behaviors of a particular group and that these behaviors (attitudes, values, language, and so forth) are transmitted from generation to generation. Differences among international, interracial, and cross-cultural communication also were examined.

Following our general introduction to intercultural communication, we focused on one of the conceptual threads woven through this book. This concept suggests that to understand intercultural communication one must realize the impact and influence of past experience. Anyone who has observed human interaction will have little trouble accepting the notion that where people come from—their cultural histories—is crucial to communication. Your prior experiences, structured by your culture, help to determine what you value, what you see, and how you behave. In short, what your culture has taught you, in both conscious and unconscious ways, will be manifest during intercultural communication. For example, Navajo Indians believe that the universe is full of dangers and that illness is a price to be paid for disorder and disharmony. These particular views are bound to be reflected in Navajo intercultural interactions. In another example, people from some cultures deem men more important than women. These people's behavior toward each sex will be influenced by this orientation. Even one's background colors what is perceived. Judgment of beauty is an example. In the United States, the slim, statuesque female represents the cultural stereotype of beauty. Yet in

427

many Eastern European countries, a heavier, stockier body reflects the ideal. These examples—and there are countless others—point out that your culture gives the framework for your experiences and values. They, in turn, define your view of the world and dictate how you interact within that world.

Because people share cultural experiences in a symbolic manner, we explored the two most common symbol systems—verbal and nonverbal. Representing ideas and feelings by symbols is a complex and complicated procedure at best. When the dimension of culture is added to the encoding and decoding process, however, the act of sharing internal states becomes even more intricate. To help you understand this act, we sought to demonstrate the relationship between three closely related axioms: (1) language helps shape thoughts and perceptions (Whorf's linguistic relativity hypothesis), (2) diverse cultures have *different* words with *similar* meanings (foreign languages), and (3) cultures can have the *same* words with vastly *different* meanings (subcultural use of vernacular and argot). We noted that the problems of coding systems plague actions as well as words. Even a simple hand motion can convey a host of unrelated meanings and interpretations. The hand gesture used by a hitchhiker in the United States is apt to produce a punch in the nose in Ghana. In short, the symbols used to share cultural experiences may often be subject to confusion and ambiguity.

In the next section of the book we examined ideas and techniques that contribute to successful intercultural communication. We proceeded on the assumption that intercultural communication is, by its very definition and nature, an action and an overt activity. Intercultural communication is, in short, something people do to and with each other. Because of advances in technology, such as improved air travel and communication satellites, all people seem to be engaging in more and more of this activity. In addition to increased communication among foreign cultures, the late 1960s and 1970s revealed that there were a number of subcommunities within the boundaries of the United States. Subcultures such as the blacks, the urban

poor, women, gays, the elderly, youth, Chicanos, and Asians wanted and demanded contact and dialogue with the main culture. Consequently, all Americans are engaging in intercultural communication at an accelerating rate. If this interaction is to be significant, and if intercultural communication is to foster increased understanding and cooperation, then potential problems must be avoided.

Finally, we extended our analysis toward the future. This is due, in part, to the fact that most intercultural interactions and meetings lie in the future. The success of your communication experiences may well depend on your philosophy and attitude toward intercultural communication. The way you behave around others is often a reflection of your philosophy toward life and toward yourself. Yet each person is capable of change from day to day and from situation to situation. Individual alterations represent a gift that accompanies personal liberty. As Plutarch noted over two thousand years ago, "All things are daily changing." If intercultural exchanges are to be considered worthy of time and energy, each person must begin to realize that such change is possible.

But change, as everyone knows, is not simple. Many attitudes and behaviors are deeply ingrained. And many of them are subject to ethnocentric influences. By this we mean that as each person learns a cultural pattern of behavior that person is, in both obvious and subtle ways, acquiring a corresponding subjective and normative value judgment associated with that behavior. Many people are guilty of assuming that their cultural group, whatever it may be, is superior to all other groups. Everyone therefore judges other cultures by his or her own standards. How often do people say, "Our way is the right way"? Or they may foolishly assume that their ideas and solutions to problems are the only correct ones. This attitude is often manifest in such ideas as are expressed by the statement, "If you are not part of the solution, you are part of the problem." This shortsighted notion fails to recognize that most social problems are complex and must be solved by many ideas and many approaches. The danger of such a philosophy should be self-evident. It is indeed difficult to achieve mutual understanding if one's culture is placed in a central position of priority or worth. How foolish to assume that because one culture prays on Saturday while another worships on Sunday, one is superior to the other. Or take, for example, the cultural values of competition and winning. Because they are important values to North Americans, many assume that all cultures ought to strive to win and to be first. There are numerous cultures, however, where competition and winning are unimportant. On the contrary, cooperation and sharing are valued highly. To be guilty of ethnocentrism is to doom intercultural communication to failure.

The new mode of communicative behavior should not only be void of ethnocentrism, but it also ought to reflect an attitude of mutual respect and trust. We emphasize that intercultural communication will not be successful if, by actions or words, the communicators appear to be condescending. Every individual and every culture wants to believe it is as worthy as any other. Actions that manifest the opposite will diminish the worth and tend to stifle meaningful interaction.

The changes required are not easy. They require that we all possess a willingness to communicate, have empathy toward foreign and alien cultures, be tolerant of views that differ from our own, and develop a universalistic, relativistic approach to the universe. If we have the resolve to adopt these behaviors and attitudes and the desire to overcome ethnocentrism and feelings of superiority, we can begin to know the feelings of exhilaration that come when we have made contact with someone far removed from our own sphere of experiences. Intercultural communication offers the arena for this interpersonal contact. Our ability to change, to make adjustments in our communication habits, gives us the potential tools to make that contact successful.

Index

Motivation, achievement, 40
Mounin, Georges, 252, 263
Movement of Maasai, 94
M-time, 333–338
Muller, Max, 78
Muntu, 278

Nakamura, H., 66, 236, 239
Nasar, J. L., 326
Native American languages, 230,
    244–250. *See also* Hopi language;
    Navajo language
Native Americans
    exclusion from U.S. culture, 107
    growth in percentage of, 117–118
    problem solving among, 229, 230
    view on time, 211
Naturalistic medical systems, 200–203
Nature, 91–92, 402–403
Navajo Indians, 249, 250
Navajo language, 245, 246, 250
Need to be liked, 175–176
Negotiation styles, cultural variations
    in, 185–191
Neighborhoods, gay, 161–162
Neko system, 171–172
Nelson, Y., 323
Nepotism, 37
Neubert, Albrecht, 258
News reports, 5
Nida, Eugene, 252, 254, 258, 260
Nine, J., 323–324
Nommo, 278–279
Nondominance, 123–126
Nonverbal communication, 18
    in classroom environments, 211–212
    codes of, 287–288
    in deaf individuals, 145
    in Eastern cultures, 406
    explanation of, 17–19, 284–285
    intercultural differences in, 35–36,
        286–294
    interpreting and, 269
    of Maasai, 94–95
    misunderstandings in, 24–25,
        348–349
    sex differences in, 297–313. *See also*
        Sex differences
    status and, 312–313
Normative values, 15–16
North Americans. *See also* Americans
    communication of truth by, 110
    communication patterns in, 67,
        71–75
    comparison with East Asians, 66–75
    individualism of, 108–109
    interpersonal communication
        between Mexicans and, 106–111
    interpersonal relationship patterns
        of, 69–71
    meaning of time to, 111
Northrop, F., 401
Numbers, interpreting, 268
Nyrop, R. F., 176

Oculesics, 287. *See also* Eye messages
Olfactics, 287–288
Ong, Walter J., 105*n*

Oral societies
    background of, 270
    high-residual versus low-residual,
        275–276
    learning in, 272
    of Maasai, 89
    memory in, 272–273
    study of Hmong, 270–276
    stylistic patterns of, 273
Organizational structure, negotiations
    and, 191
Ouchi, William, 170, 173
Outcome-oriented communication,
    71–72
Out-group members, 70–71

Palestine, 105*n*
Palmore, Erdman, 132
Panamanians, 324
Pants, significance of, 308
Paralanguage, 94–95, 287
Particularistic relationships, 69
Patterns of thought, 17
Peace, 423–424
Peace Corps training methods, 42, 43
Pearson, Judy C., 114, 115, 150
Pedersen, Anne, 169, 193
Pedersen, Paul, 169, 193
Peet, Elizabeth, 147
Pegán, G., 322
Perceptions
    color, 50
    explanation of, 14
    similarity in, 26–27
    social, 14–17
Perceptual orientation, 28
Personal communication, 384–385
Personal experiences, intercultural
    communication and, 63–64
Personalistic medical systems, 200, 201
Personality, 412
Personal space. *See* Space
Persuasion, Arab and American
    orientations toward, 96–97
Persuasive language, Arab view of,
    97–98
Philosophy
    Chinese, 239–242
    Japanese, 239–242
Physical appearance, 287, 306–309
Physical surroundings, 10
Plath, David, 133
Poets in Arab society, 97
Polanyi, Michael, 47
Politeness in classroom, 212
Polychronic time, 333–338
Pomos, 229, 230
Popovič, Anton, 261, 263
Popper, Karl, 365
Porter, Richard E., 5, 124
Posture
    of Maasai, 94
    as nonverbal communication,
        303–305
Powell, Robert, 208, 213
Power in use of silence, 315
Power distance, 292–293
Power elite, 122
Preconceptions. *See* Stereotyping

Prejudice
    forms of, 367–369
    functions of, 366–367
    in media, 59
Prenegotiation, 191. *See also*
    Negotiation styles
Pride in Maasai culture, 91
Privilege, assignment of, 123
Problem solving, 180
    cultural variations in, 190–191
    ethnocognitivism and, 229–233
    of Kpelle, Fiji, Pomo, and Trobriand,
        229–230
    in mainstream cultures, 230–231
Process-oriented communication,
    71–72
Programmed contexting, 51
Protestant ethic, 41
Proverbs
    of black Americans, 280–281
    of Maasai, 93–94
Proxemics, 19, 52, 287, 320. *See also*
    Space
P-time, 333–338
Public housing, 51
Public speaking in China and Japan,
    234–235. *See also* China; Japan
Puerto Ricans, 323–324, 327–328, 416
Pulakos, John, 105*n*
PVB measurement, 317, 319*n*

Quality, 118, 119
Questions, 269
Quran, 97–98

Racism, 367–368
Ramírez, M., 413
Ramos, Samuel, 108
Rappin', 279–280
Reagan, Ronald, 127*n*
Reality in Hinduism, 80–81
Receiver, sender versus, 75
Reciprocity, 68
    asymmetrical versus symmetrical,
        69–70
    in relationships, 71
Recoding, 252–257
Redefinition of disability, 138–141
Redfield, R., 395, 397
Red-neck racism, 367
Reincarnation, 81–82
Reischauer, Edwin, 23
Relationships. *See also* Interpersonal
    relationships; Social relationships
    personal space and, 325–326
    public versus personal, 71
Relativism, 394–396, 399–400
Religion. *See also* specific religions
    connection between inspired
        language and, 97–98
    in Maasai culture, 92
    rules regarding, 38
Respect, 109
Responder, 9
Response, 9
Rewards, 57–58
Rewording, 252
Rhetorical strategies in advocacy
    advertisements, 99–105